Contents

P9-BZZ-182

TABLE OF WALKS   4

TABLE OF MAPS   8

THE AUTHORS   9

WALK DESCRIPTIONS   13

FOREWORD   16

INTRODUCTION   17

FACTS ABOUT FRANCE   19

History 19
Geography 22
Watching Wildlife..............23
Geology 32
Climate 32
Conservation &
Environment........................ 34
National Parks & Reserves 35
Population & People 37
Society & Conduct 37

FACTS FOR THE WALKER   38

Suggested Itineraries............ 38
When to Walk 39
What Kind of Walk? 40
Organised Walks.................. 40
Responsible Walking............ 41
Accommodation 42
Food................................... 44
Drinks 45
Women Walkers 47
Walking with Children 47
Maps.................................. 48
Useful Organisations 48
Digital Resources 49
Books................................. 49
Magazines 49
Weather Information 49
Photography 50

CLOTHING & EQUIPMENT   51

Clothing 51
Equipment........................... 52
Navigation Equipment.........54

HEALTH & SAFETY   56

Predeparture Planning 56
Staying Healthy 57
Medical Problems &
Treatment........................... 58
Safety on the Walk 61

PARIS REGION   63

Paris Parklands &
Landmarks 66
Paris Ancient & Modern........ 70
Medieval Provins 72
Forêt de Fontainebleau 75
Other Walks......................79

BRITTANY & NORMANDY   80

Brittany 80
Côte de Granit Rose 80
Presqu'île de Crozon 88
Normandy 94
Giverny 94
Côte d'Albâtre 97
Mont St-Michel.................... 101
Other Walks 105

AUVERGNE & MASSIF CENTRAL   107

Monts Dômes..................110
Puy de Dôme 110
Monts Dore.....................113
Puy de Sancy 115
Col de Guéry....................... 118
Monts du Cantal 119
Puy Mary & Jordanne
Valley 120
Plomb du Cantal.................. 124
Les Cévennes...................126
Mixing with Menhirs 127
Walking Through Chaos 129
In Stevenson's Steps............ 131
Other Walks.....................133

CHEMIN DE ST-JACQUES HIGHLIGHT 134

PYRENEES 157

Vallée d'Aspe 160
Lac de Lhurs....................... 162
Around Ansabère 164
Les Orgues de Camplong.... 165
Chemin de la Mâture.......... 167
Pic de Labigouer 168

Vallée de Cauterets 171
In Vignemale's Shadow 173
Pic du Cabaliros 180
Vallée de Lutour................. 181
**Around Bagnères de
Luchon 182**

Slipping into Spain 183
Passes & Lakes.................... 185
Refuge d'Espingo 188
Other Walks.....................190

CORSICA 192

The GR20............................ 198

Other Walks.....................217

PROVENCE 219

Les Baux & Chaîne des
Alpilles 221
Les Calanques 223
Gorges du Verdon 226

The Luberon 230
Grand Luberon & Mourre
Nègre 231
Provence's Colorado............ 233

Other Walks.....................236

SOUTHERN ALPS 237

Cirque d'Archiane 240
In the Shadow of La Meije ... 248
The Wild Heart of the
Queyras 256

**Parc National du
Mercantour 264**
Col de Cerise....................... 267
Lac de Trécolpas 268

La Madone de Fenestre...... 268
Vallon de Prals Lakes
& Peaks............................... 270
Other Walks.....................271

NORTHERN ALPS 273

Chamonix Valley 275
Lac Blanc............................. 277
Grand Balcon Nord 279

Montagne de la Côte.......... 282
**Parc National de la
Vanoise...........................284**

Tour of the Vanoise
Glaciers 285
Other Walks.....................291

TOUR DU MONT BLANC 293

WINE & MOUNTAINS 320

Massif des Vosges............320
Crête des Vosges 320
Burgundy 331

Avallon & Vézelay 331
The Jura..........................335
Above the Valserine Valley ... 335

Other Walks.....................339

TRAVEL FACTS 340

Tourist Offices 340
Visas & Documents............. 340
Embassies............................ 341
Customs............................... 341
Money 341
Post & Communications 342
Time..................................... 343
Electricity 343

Business Hours 343
Public Holidays.................... 343
Getting There & Away 344
Air.. 344
Land..................................... 345
Sea....................................... 346
Getting Around...............346
Air.. 346

Bus....................................... 347
Train..................................... 347
Car & Motorcycle 348
Bicycle................................. 349
Hitching 349
Local Transport 349

Walking in
FRANCE

Sandra Bardwell
Miles Roddis
Gareth McCormack
Helen Fairbairn

LONELY PLANET PUBLICATIONS
Melbourne • Oakland • London • Paris

FRANCE

WINE & MOUNTAINS
Magnificent views from the long, crest of the Massif des Vosges, with vineyards and fairytale villages below

PARIS REGION
Grand boulevards and secret corners in Paris, stately forests and historic towns far from the capital's tumult

NORTHERN ALPS
Mont Blanc and the TMB, with glaciers, soaring peaks, ibex and paths showcasing the highest mountain in the Alps

BRITTANY & NORMANDY
Coastal cliffs and quiet coves, fascinating historic sites, extraordinary rock architecture and coast walking par excellence

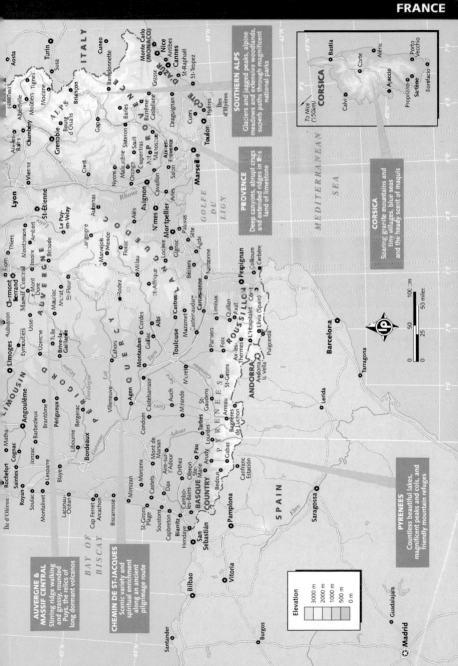

FRANCE

CORSICA

Bastia
Calvi
Corte
Aléria
Porto Vecchio
Ajaccio
Propriano
Sartène
Bonifacio

To Nice
(~150km)

MEDITERRANEAN SEA

SOUTHERN ALPS
Glaciers and jagged peaks, alpine meadows and extensive woodlands, superb paths through magnificent national parks

PROVENCE
Deep canyons, abrupt crags and extended ridges in a land of limestone

CORSICA
Soaring granite mountains and tiny villages, blue seas and the heady scent of maquis

PYRENEES
Countless beautiful lakes, magnificent peaks and cols, and friendly mountain refuges

CHEMIN DE ST-JACQUES
Scenic variety and spiritual enrichment along an ancient pilgrimage route

AUVERGNE & MASSIF CENTRAL
Stirring ridge walking and grassy, rounded Puys, the relics of long dormant volcanos

ITALY
Aosta
Turin
Cuneo
Susa
Monte Carlo (MONACO)
Nice
Antibes
Cannes
St-Raphaël
St-Tropez

Alléville
Mocûne
Tignes
Modtiers
Albertville
Chambéry
Aiguebelle
Bars
Bardonnette
Briançon
ALPS
Bourg d'Oisans
Grenoble
Gap
Barles
Barrème
Castellane
Grasse
Îles d'Hyères
Toulon
Hyères

Vienne
Lyon
St-Étienne
Crest
Nyons
Sisteron
Sault
Carpentras
A-1o-P
Manosque
Orange
Cavaillon
Salon Provence
Aix-en-Provence
Marseille

Thiers
Clermont-Ferrand
Massif Central
Le Mont Dore
St-Flour
Le Puy-en-Velay
Aubenas
Albenas
Florac
Mende
Locève
Nîmes
Montpellier
Palavas
Sète
Agde

GOLFE DU LION

Béziers
Narbonne
Perpignan
Collioure
Cerbère

Limoges
Eymoutiers
Uzerche
Tulle
Brive-la-Gaillarde
Aubusson
Ussel
Mauriac
Murat
Rodez
Millau
Marvejols
St-Affrique
Castres
Mazamet
Carcassonne
Quillan
Axat
L'Hospitalet
Cérot

LIMOUSIN
Périgueux
Brantôme
Bergerac
Villeneuve
Cahors
Montauban
Gaillac
Albi
Toulouse
Muret
Mirande
Auch
St-Girons
Foix
Ax-les-Thermes
ANDORRA
Andorra la Vella
Puigcerdà
Llívia (Spain)

QUERCY
PÉRIGORD

Angoulême
Cognac
Matha
Jonzac
Barbezieux
Libourne
Blaye
Bordeaux
Ste-Foy
Condom
Castelsarrasin
Agen

Rochefort
Saintes
Royan
Soulac
Montalivet
Lacanau Océan
Cap Ferret
Arcachon
Biscarrosse
Mimizan

Île d'Oléron

BAY OF BISCAY

Morcenx
Castets
Mont de Marsan
Dax
Aire-sur-l'Adour
Tarbes
St-Gaudens
Arreau
Bagnères-de-Luchon

St-Girons-Plage
Soustons
Capbreton
Biarritz
Hendaye
Cambo-les-Bains
Orthez
Oloron-Ste-Marie
Pau
Arudy
Lourdes
Gabas
Bedous
Canfranc Estación

BASQUE COUNTRY
San Sebastián
PYRENEES
PAYS

Bilbao
Vitoria
Pamplona
Lérida
Barcelona
Tarragona

SPAIN

Santander
Burgos
Saragossa
Guadalajara
Madrid

ROUSSILLON
LANGUEDOC
AUVERGNE

Elevation

| 3000 m |
| 2000 m |
| 1000 m |
| 500 m |
| 0 m |

0   25   50 miles
0   50   100 km

Walking in France
2nd edition – April 2004
First published – July 2000

Published by
Lonely Planet Publications Pty Ltd ABN 36 005 607 983
90 Maribyrnong St, Footscray, Victoria 3011, Australia

Lonely Planet offices
Australia Locked Bag 1, Footscray, Victoria 3011
USA 150 Linden St, Oakland, CA 94607
UK 72-82 Rosebery Ave, London, EC1R 4RW
France 1 rue du Dahomey, 75011 Paris

Photographs
Many of the images in this guide are available for licensing from
Lonely Planet Images.
W www.lonelyplanetimages.com

Main front cover photograph
Mer de Glace and Grandes Jorasses (right background), seen from the
Grand Balcon Nord, northern Alps (Glenn van der Knijff)

Small front cover photograph
Walking through the wildflowers at Vallorcine, Chamonix Valley
(Gareth McCormack)

ISBN 1 74059 243 3

LANGUAGE   350

GLOSSARY   358

INDEX   361
Text..................................... 361   Boxed Text........................... 368

METRIC CONVERSION   inside back cover

The Walks	Duration	Difficulty	Best Time
Paris Region			
Paris Parklands & Landmarks	4–4¼ hours	easy	All year
Paris Ancient & Modern	4–4¼ hours	easy	All year
Medieval Provins	3–3¼ hours	easy	Apr–Oct
Forêt de Fontainebleau	6½–7 hours	moderate	Apr–Oct
Brittany & Normandy			
Côte de Granit Rose	3 days	moderate	May–Sep
Presqu'île de Crozon	2 days	moderate	May–Sep
Giverny	2¾–3 hours	easy–moderate	Apr–Oct
Côte d'Albâtre	4–4½ hours	moderate	May–Sep
Mont St-Michel	7¼–7½ hours	moderate	May–Sep
Auvergne & Massif Central			
Puy de Dôme	2 days	moderate	Jun–Sep
Puy de Sancy	6–6¾ hours	moderate–demanding	Jun–Sep
Col de Guéry	5–5½ hours	easy–moderate	Jun–Sep
Puy Mary & Jordanne Valley	2 days	moderate	Jun–Sep
Plomb du Cantal	3¾–4¼	moderate	Jun–Sep
Mixing with Menhirs	8–8½ hours	moderate–demanding	Oct–May
Walking Through Chaos	3¾–4 hours	easy–moderate	Oct–May
In Stevenson's Steps	4–4¼ hours	easy	Oct–May
Chemin de St-Jacques (Way of St James)			
Chemin de St-Jacques Highlight	6 days	moderate	May–Jun; Sep
Pyrenees			
Lac de Lhurs	5–5½ hours	moderate	Jun–Sep
Around Ansabère	6½–7½ hours	demanding	Jun–Sep
Les Orgues de Camplong	6¼–6¾ hours	moderate–demanding	Jun–Sep
Chemin de la Mâture	3¾–4 hours	moderate	Jun–Sep
Pic de Labigouer	2 days	demanding	Jun–Sep
In Vignemale's Shadow	3 days	moderate–demanding	Jun–Sep
Pic du Cabaliros	6¼–6¾ hours	demanding	Jun–Sep

Transport	Summary	Page
train	Quiet streets and parklands, past many Paris landmarks and into some hidden byways	66
train	Something different around every corner – canals, a miniature mountain and infinitely varied streetscapes	70
train	Through woods, fields and Provins' timeless hamlets; superbly preserved medieval buildings	72
train	Labyrinthine paths among mazes of sandstone boulders and through beautiful forests; visit Château de Fontainebleau	75
train, bus	Superb paths, fantastic clusters of pink granite boulders, sandy beaches, rocky headlands	80
bus	Marvellous clifftop and beach walking through fragrant pine woods, past historic defences	88
train, bus	Landscapes that inspired Impressionist painter Claude Monet and a wander through his house and gardens	94
train, bus	Breathtaking paths above sheer limestone cliffs, extraordinary natural arches and slender pinnacles	97
train, bus	Entrancing views of the renowned Mont St-Michel from the shoreline of Baie du Mont St-Michel	101
bus	Puy de Dôme, highest of the northern volcanic craters	110
bus, train, taxi	Roller-coaster ridge walk with glorious views from Puy de Sancy	115
train	Superb views from the Col de Guéry and surrounding peaks	118
train	Magnificent ridge walking and two of the massif's finest peaks	120
train	Stupendous views from Plomb du Cantal, highest peak in the Cantal range	124
bus, taxi	Mixed wood, open grassland, and megalithic-shaped stones	127
private	Fantastic dolomite shapes and an optional loop into Causse Méjan's wilder interior	129
private	Forest walking along the Robert Louis Stevenson trail, home via an abandoned railway line	131
train	Great variety and satisfaction, a flexible route linking two historic towns	135
taxi	Isolated small lake, almost surrounded by towering mountains	162
taxi	Outstandingly scenic walk to view an awesome trio of peaks	164
taxi	Golden eagles, vast cliffs and a traditional mountain cheese-maker	165
bus	Historic path cut into vertical cliffs; superb views of the Vallée d'Aspe	167
bus	Scenic and challenging ridge walk off the beaten track	168
bus, taxi	Superb Hautes Pyrénées circuit near the French Pyrenees' highest peak	173
bus	Vast panorama from an exceptional mountain summit	180

The Walks	Duration	Difficulty	Best Time
Pyrenees (continued)			
Vallée de Lutour	5¾–6¼ hours	easy–moderate	Jun–Sep
Slipping into Spain	5½–6 hours	moderate–demanding	Jun–Sep
Passes & Lakes	2 days	moderate–demanding	Jun–Sep
Refuge d'Espingo	2 days	moderate	Jun–Sep
Corsica			
GR20	15 days	demanding	May–Oct
Provence			
Les Baux & Chaîne des Alpilles	5–6 hours	moderate	Oct–May
Les Calanques	5½–6½ hours	demanding	Oct–May
Gorges du Verdon	2 days	moderate–demanding	May & Sep
Grand Luberon & Mourre Nègre	5–5½ hours	moderate	Oct–May
Provence's Colorado	5¾–6¼ hours	moderate	Oct–May
Southern Alps			
Cirque d'Archiane	3 days	moderate–demanding	May–Sep
In the Shadow of La Meije	3 days	moderate–demanding	Jun–Sep
The Wild Heart of the Queyras	4 days	moderate	Jun–Sep
Col de Cerise	4–4¼ hours	moderate	Jun–Sep
Lac de Trécolpas	5¼–5½ hours	moderate	Jun–Sep
La Madone de Fenestre	2 days	moderate	Jun–Sep
Vallon de Prals Lakes & Peaks	5¼–5½ hours	moderate	Jun–Sep
Northern Alps			
Lac Blanc	4 hours	easy–moderate	Jun–Sep
Grand Balcon Nord	6–7 hours	moderate–demanding	Jun–Sep
Montagne de la Côte	5–6 hours	moderate–demanding	Jun–Sep
Tour of the Vanoise Glaciers	5 days	moderate–demanding	Jun–Sep
Tour du Mont Blanc			
Tour du Mont Blanc	11 days,	moderate–demanding	Jun–Sep
Wine & Mountains			
Crête des Vosges	4 days	moderate	Jun–Sep
Avallon & Vézelay	2 days	easy–moderate	Jun–Sep
Above the Valserine Valley	2 days	moderate	Jun–Sep

Transport	Summary	Page
bus, taxi	Magnificent valley walk to a *refuge* on peaceful Lac d'Estom's shores	181
taxi	Port de Vénasque, with stunning views of Pic d'Aneto, the Pyrenees' highest point	183
taxi	Gentle Chemin de l'Impératrice, Col de Pineta and three mountain tarns	185
bus, train	Out-and-back route, magnificent ridge walking along the Chemin des Crêtes	188
bus	Legendary walk across Corsica's rugged mountain interior	198
bus, taxi	Fine ridge-walking to the limestone jumble of Les Baux	221
train, bus	Walking and scrambling in and out of a series of steep coastal inlets	223
bus, taxi	Spectacular walking above and down into Europe's largest canyon	226
bus, taxi	Wraparound views from the Luberon's highest point	231
taxi	Ochre quarries and ancient packhorse trails	233
train, bus	Magnificent Cirque d'Archiane, delightful Jardin du Roi and expansive Glandasse meadows	240
bus	Scenic traverse of Écrins valleys, passes and wildflower-carpeted meadows	248
bus	Panoramic views, beautiful remote lakes and traditional hamlets and villages	256
taxi	Larch woodland, a rocky valley guarded by dramatic peaks and an inviting lake	267
taxi	Tranquil lake overlooked by towering crags, remote *refuge* in the Boréon Valley	268
taxi	High pass, along an ancient Roman route and a historic place of sanctuary	268
private	Serene lakes and spectacular views of the Mercantour's highest peak	270
train, bus	Classic view of Mont Blanc from a beautiful Alpine lake	277
train, bus	Wonderful *balcon* path and views of the Mer de Glace	279
train, bus, chairlift	Europe's largest icefall and Balmat and Paccard's route up Mont Blanc	282
bus	Memorable circuit in a national park created to protect the ibex	285
bus, train	World-famous route round the highest mountain in the Alps	294
bus, train	Ridge striding through woods and high pasture	320
bus	Walk between two of Burgundy's most historically rich small towns	331
bus	Forest trails and bare ridges, views across Lake Geneva	335

Map Index

Paris Region	p64
Paris Parklands & Landmarks	p68
Paris Ancient & Modern	p71
Medieval Provins	p74
Forêt de Fontainebleau	p77

Brittany & Normandy	p82
Côte de Granit Rose	p86
Presqu'Île de Crozon	p91
Giverny	p96
Côte d'Albatre	p98
Mont St-Michel	p104

Auvergne & Massif Central	p108
Puy de Dôme	p111
Puy de Sancy & Col de Guéry	p116
Puy Mary & Jordanne Valley	p122
Plomb du Cantal	p125
Mixing with Menhirs	p128
Walking through Chaos	p130
In Stevenson's Steps	p132

Chemin de St-Jacques	p137
Pilgrimage Paths	p134
Chemin de St-Jacques (Days 1 & 2)	p142
Chemin de St-Jacques (Days 3 & 4)	p146
Chemin de St-Jacques (Days 5 & 6)	p152

Pyrenees	p158
Lescun	p163
Vallée d'Aspe	p170
Around Cauterets	p178
Slipping into Spain	p184
Passes & Lakes	p186
Refuge d'Espingo	p189

Corsica	p193
GR20 (North)	p202
GR20 (South)	p203

Provence	p220
Les Baux & Chaîne des Alpilles	p222
Les Calanques	p224
Gorges du Verdon	p229
Grand Luberon & Mourre Nègre	p232
Provence's Colorado	p235

Southern Alps	p238
Cirque d'Archiane	p246
In the Shadow of La Meije	p252
The Wild Heart of the Queyras	p260
Parc National du Mercantour	p265

Northern Alps	p274
Lac Blanc	p278
Grand Balcon Nord	p280
Montagne de la Côte	p284
Tour of the Vanoise Glaciers	p288

Tour du Mont Blanc	p294
Tour du Mont Blanc	p302

Wine & Mountains	p321
Crête des Vosges (Day 1)	p323
Crête des Vosges (Day 2)	p326
Crête des Vosges (Day 3)	p327
Crête des Vosges (Day 4)	p329
Avallon & Vézelay	p332
Above the Valserine Valley	p337

The Authors

Sandra Bardwell

Reluctantly entering the real world after eight years at university in Sydney and Melbourne, Sandra worked as an archivist and then as historian for the National Parks Service. She has been a dedicated walker since joining a bushwalking club eons ago and became well known through a Melbourne newspaper column and as the author of several guidebooks on the subject. Since 1989 Sandra and her husband Hal have lived in the highlands of Scotland, in a village near Loch Ness where they feed Nessie regularly. For several years she worked as a monument warden for Historic Scotland until Lonely Planet took over her life, opening new horizons in Italy, Ireland, France, Scotland and even in Australia.

Miles Roddis

Over 25 years, Miles has lived, worked and walked in eight countries, including Laos, Iran, Egypt, Jordan, Sudan and France. Nowadays based across the Pyrenees in Valencia, Spain, he and his wife, Ingrid, like to hop back over the mountains on the least pretext, the updating of this book being one of the most satisfying. He celebrated his new life by cycling nearly 20,000km around the rim of the USA and has walked, among other trails, the Zagros mountains in Iran, Britain's Pennine Way and the Pyrenees from the Atlantic to the Mediterranean. Miles has contributed to over 20 Lonely Planet titles including *France*, *Spain*, *Walking in Britain* and *Walking in Spain*.

Helen Fairbairn

Helen is a writer specialising in adventure travel. Born in Suffolk, England, she now resides in Northern Ireland. Several years spent abroad, an MA in International Development, and her current work all feed an ongoing interest in the wider impact of travel. A dedicated outdoor enthusiast, Helen is most at home in wild, mountainous places. This is her sixth walking guide for Lonely Planet.

Gareth McCormack

Gareth is a writer and photographer based in Ireland, and a contributor to several outdoor and adventure-travel magazines. He has travelled and climbed extensively in Asia, Australia, New Zealand and North America. Other titles he has co-authored for Lonely Planet include *Walking in Ireland*, *Walking in France*, *Walking in Scotland*, *Walking in Australia* and *Hiking in the Rocky Mountains*.

Contributing Authors

Laurence Billiet After five years at the French office Laurence immigrated to Melbourne's head office to set up Lonely Planet Television. While she never misses an opportunity to travel to build her collection of airline spoons, she still enjoys going home to eat much missed Roquefort, drink Champagne and occasionally walk.

Jean-Bernard Carillet A diving instructor and incorrigible traveller, Jean-Bernard will decamp at the slightest opportunity to travel, photograph, walk and dive around the world. He is the co-author of numerous Lonely Planet guidebooks, including diving & snorkelling guides. When not travelling, Jean-Bernard has a weird passion for industrial architecture.

Olivier Cirendeni After studying English and journalism and visiting London, Olivier opted for a job in newspapers. There he learned to take an interest in subjects as varied as frozen French fries and flights in space. Olivier has contributed to Lonely Planet's *Jordanie et Syrie, Madagascar, Réunion & Maurice* and *Corse*.

Arno Lebonnais Arno joined the Lonely Planet team in the Paris office in 1995. Originally from Brittany, he has a passion for sailing and clocks up nautical miles whenever possible. His many stops (not always planned!) have allowed him to keep his sense of adventure alive. He contributed to Lonely Planet's *Corse*.

Tony Wheeler The very first Lonely Planet guidebook back in 1973 was the result of Tony Wheeler's Asian overland trip with his wife, Maureen, in the early seventies. He has been travelling, writing and publishing ever since and manages to fit in at least one long walk every year.

FROM THE AUTHORS

Sandra Bardwell Staff at several tourist offices provided advice with all the usual professional aplomb: Avranches, Pontorson, Châtillon-en-Diois, St-Vc, Abriès and St-Martin-Vésubie. The life of an author is usually a solitary one, but several pilgrims soon became congenial companions, especially Eileen and Chris, and Elisabeth who politely suffered my antiquated French. Fritz and Bev's warm, welcoming hospitality made Paris a real home away from home, and their extensive knowledge and love of France was inspirational. One couldn't ask for better colleagues than Miles, the unquenchably enthusiastic *montagnarde*, and supremely practical and down to earth Gareth and Helen. In the Melbourne office, Marg's eminently reasonable and good-humoured approach has been greatly appreciated, along with Yvonne's and Helen's patience in managing the editorial and cartographic phases while I was having a lovely time wandering about northern Australia. Hal's unfailing support from go to whoa helped immeasurably to make the assignment even more enjoyable.

Miles Roddis Miles' chapters are all for Eben. May he come to love the Pyrenees as much as his Yo Yo does. Huge thanks to Ingrid without whose logistical and every other kind of support, I'd still be out there walking.

Special thanks go to Christiane Rabasse, Bureau des Guide de Luchon, *refuge* wardens Elodie and Tristan Badie (Wallon/Marcadau) and Karine Depeyre (Oulètes de Gaube), Mireille Claverie (Maison du Parc National des Pyrenees, Etsaut) plus Christine Buisan and Alexandra Mercier (Cauterets). Also to Elena Valero and colleagues for patiently photocopying with such precision strategic sections of billowing, unwieldy maps.

As always, tourist office staff answered my queries patiently and cheerfully. Thank you, Françoise Lafforgue (St-Rémy de Provence), Claude Knoll (La Palud-sur-Verdon), Christine Francia (Cassis), Martine di Cicco (Apt), Natalie (Luchon), Mathilde (Cauterets) and Julie Grob (St-Amarin).

It was a pleasure to be working again with both Sandra, as wise and companionable as ever, and cheery, so sensible Marg Toohey.

Helen Fairbairn & Gareth McCormack Thanks to Lindsay Brown and Andrew Bain at Lonely Planet for their help in the planning stages for this book, and to Marg Toohey for her help with the nitty gritty during research and writing up. Special thanks to Cait who braved the heatwave to walk with us in the Vanoise and Chamonix Valley – the daily swims were a treat.

This Book

The 1st edition of *Walking in France* was written by Sandra Bardwell, Miles Roddis, Gareth McCormack, Jean-Bernard Carillet, Laurence Billiet, Tony Wheeler, Caroline Guilleminot, Sophie Haudrechy and Bénédicte Houdré.

Sandra again took on the task of coordinating this 2nd edition. She also compiled the introductory chapters and wrote Watching Wildlife, Paris Region, Brittany & Normandy, Chemin St-Jacques Highlight and Southern Alps. Miles Roddis contributed Auvergne & Massif Central, Pyrenees, Provence and Wine & Mountains. Helen Fairbairn and Gareth McCormack wrote Northern Alps and Tour du Mont Blanc.

The Corsica chapter was updated by Adrienne Costanzo using material written by Olivier Cirendini and Arno Lebonnois from the 3rd edition of *Corse*.

FROM THE PUBLISHER

This edition of *Walking in France* was conceived and commissioned at Lonely Planet's Melbourne base by Andrew Bain, Lindsay Brown and Marg Toohey. The coordinating editor was Yvonne Byron and the coordinating cartographer was Helen Rowley. Editorial assistance was provided by Dan Caleo, Simon Sellars, Angie Phelan, Nick Tapp and Meg Worby. Marion Byass, Andrew Smith, Chris Thomas and Natasha Velleley assisted with mapping. Thanks to Jennifer Garrett for advice on everything from captions to indexing. The book was laid out by Michael Ruff, with assistance from Vicki Beale and the cover was designed by Wendy Wright. The language chapter was produced by Quentin Frayne and Pepi Bluck organised the illustrations. The project was managed through production by Glenn van der Knijff.

Thanks

Many thanks to travellers Paul and Marion Beadle, Bob Carlson, Yaron Degani, Jim Fox and Timo Keil, who used the last edition and took the time to write to us with helpful hints, advice and interesting anecdotes.

GR and PR are trademarks of the FRRP (Fédération Française de la Randonée Pédestre).

Walk Descriptions

This book contains 50 walk descriptions ranging from day trips to the 15-day GR20 across Corsica, plus suggestions for side trips and alternative routes. Each walk description has a brief introduction outlining the natural and cultural features you may encounter, plus information to help you plan your walk – transport options, level of difficulty, time frame and any permits required.

Day walks are often circular and are located in areas of uncommon beauty. Multiday walks include information on camp sites, refuges (mountain huts), hostels or other accommodation and where you can obtain water and supplies.

Times & Distances

These are provided only as a guide. Times are based on actual walking time and do not include stops for snacks, taking photographs, rests or side trips. Be sure to factor these in when planning your walk. Distances are provided but should be read in conjunction with altitudes. Significant elevation changes can make a greater difference to your walking time than lateral distance

In most cases, the daily stages are flexible and can be varied. It is important to recognise that short stages are sometimes recommended in order to acclimatise in mountain areas or because there are interesting features to explore en route.

Level of Difficulty

Grading systems are always arbitrary. However, having an indication of the grade may help you choose between walks. Our authors use the following grading guidelines:

Easy – a walk on flat terrain or with minor elevation changes usually over short distances on well-travelled routes with no navigational difficulties.

Moderate – a walk with challenging terrain, often involving longer distances and steep climbs.

Demanding – a walk with long daily distances and difficult terrain with significant elevation changes; may involve challenging route-finding and high-altitude or glacier travel.

True Left & True Right

The terms 'true left' and 'true right', used to describe the bank of a stream or river, sometimes throw readers. The 'true left bank' simply means the left bank as you look downstream.

Maps

Our maps are based on the best available references, often combined with GPS data collected in the field. They are intended to show the general route of the walk and should be used in conjunction with maps suggested in the walk description.

Maps may contain ridge lines in addition to major watercourses depending on the available information. These features build a three-dimensional picture of the terrain, allowing you to determine when the trail climbs and descends. Altitudes of major peaks and passes complete the picture by providing the actual extent of the elevation changes.

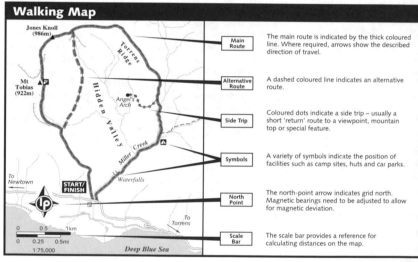

Walking Map

The main route is indicated by the thick coloured line. Where required, arrows show the described direction of travel.

A dashed coloured line indicates an alternative route.

Coloured dots indicate a side trip – usually a short 'return' route to a viewpoint, mountain top or special feature.

A variety of symbols indicate the position of facilities such as camp sites, huts and car parks.

The north-point arrow indicates grid north. Magnetic bearings need to be adjusted to allow for magnetic deviation.

The scale bar provides a reference for calculating distances on the map.

Walk Profiles

Graphing the elevation against the hours of walking offers an idea of a walk's steepness and how long it climbs or descends. The scale is consistent throughout the book so you can compare different routes.

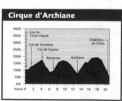

Route Finding

While accurate, our maps are not perfect. Inaccuracies in altitudes are commonly caused by air-temperature anomalies. Natural features such as river confluences and mountain peaks are in their true position, but sometimes the location of villages and trails is not always so. This may be because a village is spread over a hillside, or the size of the map does not allow for detail of the trail's twists and turns. However, by using several basic route-finding techniques, you will have few problems following our descriptions:

14

1. Always be aware of whether the trail should be climbing or descending.
2. Check the north-point arrow on the map and determine the general direction of the trail.
3. Calculate your progress over a known distance and work out the speed at which you travel in the given terrain. You can then determine with reasonable accuracy how far you have travelled.
4. Watch the path – look for boot prints and other signs of previous passage.

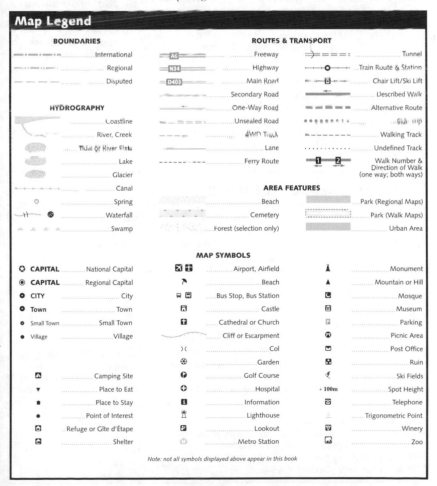

Map Legend

BOUNDARIES

- International
- Regional
- Disputed

HYDROGRAPHY

- Coastline
- River, Creek
- Tidal or River Flats
- Lake
- Glacier
- Canal
- Spring
- Waterfall
- Swamp

ROUTES & TRANSPORT

- **AG** Freeway
- **N34** Highway
- **D403** Main Road
- Secondary Road
- One-Way Road
- Unsealed Road
- 4WD Track
- Lane
- Ferry Route
- Tunnel
- Train Route & Station
- Chair Lift/Ski Lift
- Described Walk
- Alternative Route
- Side Trip
- Walking Track
- Undefined Track
- **1** **2** Walk Number & Direction of Walk (one way; both ways)

AREA FEATURES

- Beach
- Cemetery
- Forest (selection only)
- Park (Regional Maps)
- Park (Walk Maps)
- Urban Area

MAP SYMBOLS

- ⊙ **CAPITAL** National Capital
- ◉ **CAPITAL** Regional Capital
- ● **CITY** City
- ● **Town** Town
- ● Small Town Small Town
- ● Village Village

- Camping Site
- ▼ Place to Eat
- ■ Place to Stay
- ● Point of Interest
- Refuge or Gîte d'Étape
- Shelter

- Airport, Airfield
- Beach
- Bus Stop, Bus Station
- Castle
- Cathedral or Church
- Cliff or Escarpment
-)(Col
- Garden
- Golf Course
- Hospital
- Information
- Lighthouse
- Lookout
- Metro Station

- Monument
- ▲ Mountain or Hill
- Mosque
- Museum
- Parking
- Picnic Area
- Post Office
- Ruin
- Ski Fields
- + 100m Spot Height
- Telephone
- Trigonometric Point
- Winery
- Zoo

Note: not all symbols displayed above appear in this book

Foreword

ABOUT LONELY PLANET GUIDEBOOKS

The story begins with a classic travel adventure: Tony and Maureen Wheeler's 1972 journey across Europe and Asia to Australia. There was no useful information about the overland trail then, so Tony and Maureen published the first Lonely Planet guidebook to meet a growing need.

From a kitchen table, Lonely Planet has grown to become the largest independent travel publisher in the world, with offices in Melbourne (Australia), Oakland (USA), London (UK) and Paris (France).

Today Lonely Planet guidebooks cover the globe. There is an ever-growing list of books and information in a variety of media. Some things haven't changed. The main aim is still to make it possible for adventurous travellers to get out there – to explore and better understand the world.

At Lonely Planet we believe travellers can make a positive contribution to the countries they visit – if they respect their host communities and spend their money wisely. Since 1986 a percentage of the income from each book has been donated to aid projects and human rights campaigns, and, more recently, to wildlife conservation.

Although inclusion in a guidebook usually implies a recommendation we cannot list every good place. Exclusion does not necessarily imply criticism. In fact there are a number of reasons why we might exclude a place – sometimes it is simply inappropriate to encourage an influx of travellers.

UPDATES & READER FEEDBACK

Things change – prices go up, schedules change, good places go bad and bad places go bankrupt. Nothing stays the same. So, if you find things better or worse, recently opened or long-since closed, please tell us and help make the next edition even more accurate and useful.

Lonely Planet thoroughly updates each guidebook as often as possible – usually every two years, although for some destinations the gap can be longer. Between editions, up-to-date information is available in our free, monthly email bulletin *Comet* (www.lonelyplanet.com/newsletters). You can also check out the *Thorn Tree* bulletin board and *Postcards* section of our website which carry unverified, but fascinating, reports from travellers.

Tell us about it! We genuinely value your feedback. A well-travelled team at Lonely Planet reads and acknowledges every email and letter we receive and ensures that every morsel of information finds its way to the relevant authors, editors and cartographers.

Everyone who writes to us will find their name listed in the next edition of the appropriate guidebook. The very best contributions will be rewarded with a free guidebook.

We may edit, reproduce and incorporate your comments in Lonely Planet products such as guidebooks, websites and digital products, so let us know if you don't want your comments reproduced or your name acknowledged.

How to contact Lonely Planet:
Online: talk2us@lonelyplanet.com.au, www.lonelyplanet.com
Australia: Locked Bag 1, Footscray, Victoria 3011
UK: 72-82 Rosebery Ave, London, EC1R 4RW
USA: 150 Linden St, Oakland, CA 94607

Introduction

From the Atlantic to the Mediterranean, from Paris to the Pyrenees, walking in France is more an experience of walking in several countries than in just one.

Through the byways of Paris, the massed ranks of vineyards in Burgundy and Alsace, the unspoiled beaches of western Brittany and the Cévennes woodlands, the walking is easy. Further south, the deep Gorges du Verdon, extraordinary volcanic formations of the Massif Central and the colourful Mediterranean coast of Les Calanques offer adventurous walks in widely contrasting settings. There's much more to France's mountainous areas than the famous names of the Alps. You can explore from the narrow spines of the Vosges to the rolling meadows of the Jura, the glaciers of the Northern Alps, high plateaus, deep valleys and lakes of the Southern Alps, the vast chain of the

France

Pyrenees and precipitous paths through the rugged Corsican mountains.

France is blessed with an incomparable network of walking routes. These famous *grandes randonnées* and many other way-marked routes offer a tantalising array of choices, from half-day strolls to months-long odysseys across the country, the supreme example being the renowned Chemin de St-Jacques pilgrimage route. Many routes follow age-old paths and make it possible to explore the settled countryside on foot; greater freedom can be savoured in sparsely populated mountainous areas.

France's national parks may be few in number, but in a country with a widely dispersed population, they are invaluable islands of relative wildness and superlative beauty. The many regional natural parks are quite different, with living, working communities, scenic landscapes and no shortage of outstanding natural attributes.

Providing information about the heritage of these areas is taken very seriously in France. You could spend weeks visiting national park information centres and top-class museums devoted to wildlife and cultural themes. Superb Topo-Guides for walkers, and guides for flora and fauna, geology and history fill dozens of metres of bookshelves. All important maps for walkers are second to none for accuracy.

France has posted many positive achievements in wildlife protection – the reintroduction of ibex, bearded vultures and other species previously persecuted almost to extinction. Indeed, wildlife can be a highlight of walks almost anywhere in France:

golden eagles, vultures, chamois, izards and marmots in the Alps and Pyrenees; sea birds in Brittany; wildflowers in the Alps, Pyrenees and Massif Central; heavily scented maquis in Corsica and Provence; the oak woodlands of Quercy; and larch, beech and pine woodlands of the high country.

French walkers may take to their pastime with serious enthusiasm, but along the *grandes randonnées* cheerful *'Bon jours'* are invariably exchanged with the passing walkers. Staying at *gîtes* (walkers' hostels) and *refuges* (mountain huts) provides many memorable experiences, especially for the camaraderie among walkers from France and further afield, when language differences are irrelevant.

Gastronomic delights can enhance a walking holiday in France as most, if not all, chapters demonstrate. Great pride is taken in the preparation and presentation of good food; sampling regional specialities at small village restaurants, or preparing al fresco feasts from the huge variety of fresh produce, are fitting conclusions to a day's walking.

You can leave a car behind and use public transport in many areas covered in this book. Fast, reliable train services link the cities and many towns; bus services bring quite remote small towns and villages within reach.

Walking is the unrivalled means of bringing together the best of France's richly diverse natural and cultural heritage in an absorbing, rewarding experience. It can clearly reveal the wisdom of the famous statement that every person belongs to two countries: their own and France.

Facts about France

HISTORY

From the time of the earliest human settlement in Western Europe, France's history was long dominated by battles and alliances to consolidate and expand the power of successive dynasties. At the same time, religious conflict waxed and waned, great architectural and engineering works were wrought, and France became a focal point for libertarian philosophers. There are many dark corners in the country's more recent history and bringing them to light has been painful. To this day the French are a proud people. Their past lives on but without suffocating the present.

25,000 BC – cave-dwelling Cro-Magnon people living in Périgord

15,000 BC – hunting communities established

5500 BC – farming began to develop in the south, much later in the north

1200 BC – Celtic tribes moved into Alsace, Lorraine and Burgundy

600 BC – Massalia (Marseilles) established as a Greek colony; grapevines introduced

52 BC – Regime change by Roman legions throughout area of modern-day France

AD 313 – Christianity officially accepted

476 – Western Roman Empire collapsed

507 – Paris made capital of Frankish (Germanic) territory

590 – St Columba introduced Irish brand of Christianity

800 – Charlemagne crowned Holy Roman Emperor

843 – Boundaries of Carolingian (Holy Roman) empire, roughly equivalent to modern France and Germany

1066 – William the Conqueror (Duke of Normandy) invaded England

1096 – first French crusade to the Holy Land

1152 – Aristocratic liaison brought one-third of France under English control

c 1215 – University of Paris founded

1259 – Skilful French manoeuvres regained Normandy, Maine, Anjou and Poitou from England

1337 – Hundred Years' War between England and France erupted

1348 – Great Plague arrived, eventually killing about one-third of France's population

1416 – Henry V of England became King of France

1429 – Jeanne d'Arc (Joan of Arc) led French forces to victory against the English

1453 – English driven from French territory, apart from toehold in Calais

1532 – Brittany united with France

1539 – French made the official state language

1562 – Protestant Huguenots at war with Catholics

1572 – mass slaughter of Huguenots in Paris on St Bartholomew's Day

1598 – Henri IV granted civil rights to Huguenots

1631 – *La Gazette*, France's first newspaper, hit the streets

1643 – Juvenile Louis XIV (Sun King) crowned; later created first centralised French state

1685 – Protestantism banned; about 300,000 Huguenots fled the country

1720s – Atlantic coast towns prospered from trade with Caribbean and American colonies

1760s – France took up radical ideas of American Revolution

1768 – Corsica purchased from Genoa by Louis XV

1774 – Louis XVI became king; dire economic woes

1789 – Storming of Bastille in Paris ignited French Revolution

1791 – constitution adopted – parliamentary government with hereditary monarch

1792 – Jacobins ousted moderates and established First Republic

1799 – Napoleon Bonaparte assumed power as First Consul; introduced legal, educational and financial reforms; France became Europe's most populous country

1812 – Napoleon exiled to Elba

1815 – Louis XVIII planted on French throne; Napoleon escaped, was defeated at Battle of Waterloo and exiled to St-Helena

1830 – Charles X overthrown during July Revolution; replaced by Louis-Philippe, chosen by parliament

1848 – Second Republic supplanted Louis-Phillippe; Louis Napoleon Bonaparte elected president

1852 – Louis led coup d'état and crowned Emperor Napoleon III

1853 – Baron Haussmann began modernising Paris

1870 – France declared war on Prussia but was soon defeated and lost Alsace and Lorraine

1875 – Republican constitution approved by National Assembly

1895 – trade union movement unified; first Peugeot car took to the road

1905 – church and state legally separated

1914 – start of WWI during which 2.3 million French killed or maimed, much of northeastern France devastated, industry almost ruined

1919 – Treaty of Versailles signed after end of WWI

1936 – left-wing Front Populaire won national elections but lasted only a few months

1939 – Britain and France declared war on Germany

1940 – France occupied by German forces; General Charles de Gaulle installed French government-in-exile in London

1944 – Paris liberated in August

1945 – end of WWII

1946 – Fourth Republic established with new constitution

1949 – Council of Europe set up, precursor to European Economic Community (EEC)

1954 – government decided to develop nuclear weapons

1957 – French initiative inspired creation of EEC with five partner countries

1958 – Fifth Republic founded with de Gaulle as president

1963 – first nuclear power station built

1968 – civil unrest culminated in student uprising in Paris, national strike in May; de Gaulle introduced reforms and restored peace

1969 – Georges Pompidou succeeded de Gaulle

1971 – Ministry of the Environment established

1974 – right-wing Valéry Giscard d'Estaing elected president

1981 – first TGV *(train à grand vitesse)* into service; socialists in power with president and majority in National Assembly

1984 – Les Verts (Greens) political party formed

1986 – right-wing parties under Jacques Chirac as prime minister took over National Assembly

1989 – ecologists won 5% to 21% of votes in municipal elections

1992 – European integration (Maastricht Treaty) adopted by narrow majority vote

1994 – Channel tunnel opened for rail freight traffic and passengers

1995 – Chirac elected president; decision to resume nuclear weapons testing in the Pacific caused outrage; public-sector strike paralysed the country

1997 – Socialist-Communist-Green coalition victorious at parliamentary elections; negotiations about European Monetary Union (EMU)

1998 – Premier Lionel Jospin took France into EMU; national celebrations when France won football's World Cup

1999 – disastrous fire in Mont Blanc tunnel

2002 – franc replaced by euro; astonishing success of far-right candidate in first round of presidential elections; resulting backlash returned Chirac with huge majority

2003 – France led international opposition to invasion of Iraq; catastrophic summer heatwave and drought.

History of Walking

Two distinct strands make up France's enviable walking heritage: a vast, ancient network of paths – *chemins* and *sentiers* – with many different practical origins, and the growth of walking for pleasure rather than sheer necessity.

The origins of France's extraordinary path network go back to Gallic and Roman times when defined routes developed between isolated communities. Other, strictly utilitarian paths emerged: shepherds' paths for taking stock to summer pastures; ways followed by itinerant tradespeople, worshippers and pilgrims; tracks used by foresters and farmers to their more remote holdings; routes used by customs officers chasing smugglers along the coast. Some were state-owned, some were owned by the local *commune* (the basic local government unit), others were private, while some accumulated a long tradition of uncontested use. It was estimated that in 1945 there were one million kilometres of *sentiers* and *chemins* throughout France.

By the mid-20th century, many of these old routes had declined into disuse or disappeared as the rural populations dwindled, small farms were amalgamated, and as the road network spread its tentacles ever wider. In face of declining use of local tracks there was little incentive to maintain them and many were merged into adjacent private properties.

During the 18th and 19th centuries, travel for pleasure and for discovery became a popular pastime among wealthy people. The more hardy adventurers spurned coaches and horses and went on foot. From the late 18th century, the challenges held out by unclimbed

Alpine peaks spurred the growth of climbing/ mountaineering. Local people became mountain guides and the Club Alpin Français (CAF; French Alpine Club) was founded in 1874, two years after the Club Vosgien set about methodically marking routes through the Massif des Vosges.

Cyclists set up Le Touring-Club de France (TCF) in 1890 and in 1904 it sprouted a special walkers section. The growth of scouting, with its emphasis on camping, and later the youth hostelling movement, helped to stimulate popular interest in the outdoors. The revolutionary granting of paid holidays to French workers in 1936 also helped to stimulate the growth of recreational walking after WWII.

In 1947 the TCF, the CAF, the Camping Club of France and the Club Vosgien, inspired by the visionary Jean Loiseau, founded the Comité National des Sentiers de Grande Randonnée (CNSGR) to promote recreational walking. Affiliated clubs mushroomed and members set about surveying, clearing and waymarking about 20,000km of walking routes, following recognised *chemins* and *sentiers*, to create continuous longer-distance routes and so coining a new term – *grande randonnée* or GR, by which the routes are now known. The GR1 around Paris, the GR2 along the Seine and the GR3 beside the Loire River were the pioneers.

In the late 1950s the CNSGR decided to publish guidebooks to promote the GRs. The first, for the Mont Blanc area, appeared in 1957 but lacked any maps. Later, the Institut Géographique National (IGN) allowed extracts from its 1:50,000 topographical maps to be used in the guides, immeasurably improving their usefulness. Now called Topo-Guides, there are at least 200 of these superb guides in print, in three series: *Promenades et Randonnées* for easy-to-moderate circular walks; *À Pied en Famille* for family walks; and *Grandes Randonnées* for the long-distance routes.

In the 1970s the CNSGR realised that it wasn't enough to just identify and waymark routes and to publish guidebooks. It had succeeded in prising money out of the government to extend the route network but many *sentiers* where still disappearing as urbanisation flourished and new roads were built. During that decade, public meetings highlighted the lack of permanent legal protection for these paths. A 1977 decree gave legal right of passage along the coast exclusively to walkers; since then more than 1300km of paths have been cleared and opened, thanks to substantial government funds. Nevertheless, paths elsewhere remain at risk.

The immensely valuable economic benefits of walking for local communities and tourism generally prompted the development of *gîtes d'étape*, providing hostel-style accommodation specifically designed to cater for GR walkers. They were pioneered in 1971 along an Alpine section of the GR5 (Belgium to Nice) and others soon followed in the Pyrenees. Nowadays there are *gîtes* to welcome walkers at the end of the day along the great majority of GRs (and other similar routes).

In 1978 the CNSGR renamed itself Fédération Française de la Randonnée Pédestre (FFRP) as a more appropriate title for an organisation consisting of many local groups. Its tireless efforts to secure permanent legal protection for France's *sentiers* and *chemins* scored some success with the passing of a law in 1983 which gave *départements* – another local government unit – the responsibility for protecting and maintaining rural paths.

Ever since, the FFRP and local groups have been cooperating to keep alive and even improve the path heritage. As part of this effort, 2003 was declared L'Année des Chemins to celebrate this achievement, encourage even better cooperation between all concerned, and promote the association's work, not the least to the government. At that time, 'rando' (walking) was on the cusp of a boom in France: a 2001 survey by l'AFIT, an agency of the French Ministry of Tourism, found that 15 million people go walking at least two or three times each month on an outing averaging almost three hours. Interestingly, 60% of walkers are women. The FFRP is going from strength to strength with 2600 member groups and it has waymarked a mind-boggling 60,000km of GRs and at least 120,000km of Promenade et Randonnée routes (short, circular routes). For contact details see Useful Organisations, p48.

The CAF has grown to embrace over 193 member clubs in 2003, with 90,000 members; it also manages 142 mountain *refuges*. Among its goals are promotion of awareness of the mountains, and preservation of the mountain environment. To help achieve these aims, it has set up the Commission National de Protection de la Montagne (CNPM; see Conservation Organisations p35) based on a commitment to do nothing to harm and everything to protect the natural environment and heritage of the mountains, always recognising that the mountains are home to many small communities. For contact details for CAF, see Useful Organisations (p48).

GEOGRAPHY

With an area of nearly 551,000 sq km, and extending for around 1000km from north to south and from east to west, France is the third-largest European country. Known to the French as the 'divinely moulded hexagon', it borders Belgium, Luxembourg, Germany, Switzerland, Italy and Spain. The borders generally correspond with distinctive natural features. The Atlantic Ocean and English Channel wash the western and northwestern shores and the Mediterranean the south. In the east, the Rhine River separates France from Germany. On the Swiss frontier, Lake Geneva (Lac Léman) is cradled between the Jura Mountains (rising to 1700m) and the rugged French Alps, which reach south to the edge of the Côte d'Azur. The Alps are crowned by Mont Blanc (4807m), the highest mountain in Western Europe. The Pyrenees stretch along the greater part of the 450km Spanish border, Vignemale (3298m) being the highest summit.

France has three other upland areas. The Massif Central, west of the Alps and across the Rhône Valley, is dominated by extinct volcanoes (to 1465m high); deep gorges slice through its limestone plateau. The wooded Massif des Vosges in the northeast is cut by steep, ice-carved, U-shaped valleys in the north; to the south

wide glacial valleys sweep through higher, rockier ground (up to 1424m). The more subdued Massif Armoricain is the spine of Normandy and Brittany, the highest point being in the Monts d'Arrée (348m).

A small corner of the Ardennes Plateau is cut by the Belgian and Luxembourg borders. Corsica, the third-largest island in the Mediterranean, is mainly mountainous, the highest peak touching 2719m; it is also graced by deep gorges, sea cliffs and sandy beaches.

Even so, the greater part of France is gently undulating lowland, scarcely exceeding 200m elevation. The most fertile part of the country, it is dominated by the Seine, Loire and Garonne Rivers.

The Atlantic receives the outflow of three of France's five major river systems. The longest, the Loire (1020km), rises in the Massif Central and flows out at Nantes near the southern edge of Brittany; the Garonne (combining the Dordogne, Lot and Tar) debouches near Bordeaux; and the Seine (775km) flows northwest from Burgundy, through Paris, to the English Channel at Le Havre. The Paris basin, formed by the Seine, comprises about 20% of the country. Draining the southern end of the Vosges, the Jura Mountains and the Alps, the Rhône system (including the Durance, Isère and Saône Rivers) has the greatest outflow. The Rhine gathers in the rivers north and east of Paris and flows into the North Sea.

The country's 3120km-long coastline is very diverse. The English Channel is fringed by high chalk cliffs separating bays and estuaries. The northwest peninsula, with France's most westerly mainland point at Pointe du Raz, is riven by deep inlets and lined by low cliffs pounded by the Atlantic. Most of France's beaches (including Europe's longest at 228km), and the highest sand dunes on the continent, are found along the unwavering Atlantic seaboard of the Bay of Biscay. In the extreme south of the Atlantic coast, the sands are pure white. The western half of the Mediterranean coast is mainly sandy, but east of the Rhône delta and the Camargue wetlands sand gives way to pebbles and rocks.

WATCHING WILDLIFE

France has a remarkably rich and diverse natural heritage, despite land clearing and drainage, road and railway building, urbanisation and hunting. National parks, regional natural parks and the many smaller nature reserves, several of which are featured in this guide, are the places to visit to observe and learn more about the natural world (see National Parks & Reserves, p35). In the following pages, we present a guide to species that walkers are most likely to see throughout France. For spot-on identification you can't do without a field guide; a selection of books is given on p48. To find out more about organisations working for the protection of wildlife see Conservation Organisations, p35.

ANIMALS

Birds

France is a great place for bird-watching – 502 species spend at least part of the year here, from magnificent raptors in the mountains to hardy, ocean-going sea birds. Of these, 266 species nest in France. The following selection of species is divided into four very broad habitat types.

France's Endangered Species

About 40 species of flora disappeared from France during the 20th century. Scores are rare or threatened with extinction by both natural and human agencies, the latter being the far more serious threat: reckless collection, especially of orchids and medicinal species; habitat destruction, especially wetlands drainage; changing agricultural practices; and road and building construction. Four hundred species now enjoy full protection nationwide; 36 species are partially protected, and the collection of many more (such as lily of the valley) is limited at specific sites.

Many mammal species have a precarious hold on survival in the face of human intrusion into habitats and illegal hunting, trapping and poisoning. The wolf did disappear from France but has made a controversial return in the Southern Alps, as has the brown bear in the Pyrenees (see the boxed texts on p271 and p159). Other species, notably the ibex, have been reintroduced locally to areas where they were once hunted mercilessly, including the Queyras in the Southern Alps. All bats, the wild cat, hedgehog, beaver, red squirrel, most reptiles, all raptors and several other bird species have full legal protection. Hunting of game species (wild boar, goats and roe deer) is regulated season by season (late September to late February), area by area; for detailed information, contact the **Office National de la Chasse et de la Faune Sauvage** (☎ 01 44 15 17 17; www.oncfs.gouv.fr).

According to the IUCN's *Red List of Threatened Species* for 2003, 12 animal species were endangered and 92 animal and plant species were vulnerable. For annually updated information about endangered species, go to www.redlist.org.

LISA BORG

Brown Bear

Sea Birds Corsica and the rocky shores and nearby islands of the Brittany and Normandy coasts are the best places for sea-bird watching.

Difficult to distinguish from a shag, the **cormorant** *(le grand cormoran)* is larger, has some white on its otherwise black face and a bronze sheen on its dark back. It stands nonchalantly on rocks or mooring posts, wings outstretched though slightly bent, in drying mode.

Easy to spot by its stiff-winged flight as it glides close to the cliffs, the **fulmar** *(le pétrel fulmar)* has a white body and lightish-grey wings.

A spectacular diver, the **gannet** *(le fou de Bassan)* plummets arrow-like into the sea from as high as 30m. A largish, mainly white bird, it has a distinctive yellow head; the wings appear black when folded for diving. Be on the watch for them out to sea all around the French coast.

Black of back and head and white of chest, the **guillemot** *(le guillemot de Troïl)* spends most of its time at sea. The tail is short and stubby so that in flight its feet are clearly visible trailing behind. It nests on north-coast cliffs during late winter and spring.

The **herring gull** *(le goéland argenté)*, perhaps the commonest of the gulls, is relatively small and predominantly white, with grey, black-tipped wings, and pink legs. It's noisy and a skilful and aggressive scavenger, often seen inland from its coastal haunts wherever there's easily snatched food.

Frequenting shingle and sand beaches in Normandy and Brittany, the sociable **oystercatcher** *(le huitrier pie)* usually congregates in flocks. It's readily identifiable by the straight red bill, black head, back and outer wing, red legs and loud, high-pitched 'pik, pik' call.

The **puffin** *(le macareux moine)* – there's no mistaking this comical character with its squat, black-and-white body, large grey-white face patch, upright stance and large bill – has a brightly multicoloured bill during the summer (June to August) breeding season. Watch out for puffins along the Brittany coast.

Looking much like the cormorant but smaller and sleeker, the **shag** *(le cormoran huppé)* sports all black plumage and extends its wings fully for drying. Shags live around the Corsica, Brittany and Normandy coasts.

Water Birds Along rural waterways, in the coastal estuaries of Brittany, Normandy and the Mediterranean, scores of species are residents or long-term visitors. Apart from numerous ducks, geese and mute swans, these are the species you're most likely to see.

The diminutive **dipper** *(le cincle plongeur)* is inseparable from fast-flowing streams and pools in central and eastern France. Its small dark-brown and black body sets off a white bib, colouring that blends with the rocks and turbulent water of its favourite haunts, where it dives to the bottom to forage for larvae and snails.

The beautiful **greater flamingo** *(le flamant)* congregates in vast flocks on saline marshes in and around the Rhône estuary on the Mediterranean coast. Its beautiful pinkish plumage and legs are acquired gradually – juveniles have dark brown backs and become white before turning pink at three or four years; adults reach a height of 145cm. Flamingos feed in large flocks, steadily advancing in search of food.

The **grey heron** *(le héron cendré)*, a near-certain sighting along rocky, indented northern coasts and along northern inland waterways, stands quietly, motionless in the shallows. It's generally mid-grey with a black V pattern down the white chest, and long orange bill. The grey heron looks ungainly in flight, with the head tucked right in and legs trailing in the breeze.

Birds of the Countryside Here we have a select sample of the species who prefer more open ground and the spaces above it, and those who like the shelter and food sources of the extensive woodlands most notably (in this book) along the Chemin de St-Jacques, in the Cévennes and the rural Paris Region walks.

Widespread throughout France the **buzzard** *(la buse variable)* is mainly dark brown with some lighter patterning on the chest. This raptor habitually glides and soars with wings V-shaped, often giving out a high-pitched whistle; it is also often seen perched on fence posts.

With its monotonously unforgettable call the **cuckoo** *(le coucou)* is much more readily heard than seen. It has a dark brown, lightly patterned back and a white, brown striped chest. Living almost anywhere in France, it prefers open ground with scattered trees and bushes.

True to its name, the **golden oriole** *(le loriot)* has a brilliant yellow head, back and chest, and black wings. A small bird (about 24cm long) it doesn't make itself obvious but can be detected by its clear, quick, whistling call. It prefers tall deciduous woodlands throughout the country.

Commonly seen in both lowland and upland areas with some tree cover, the **sparrowhawk** *(l'épervier)* has a grey-blue back and white, rust-striped chest.

It's easy to be startled by the loud clatter of the **woodpigeon**'s *(la palombe)* wings as it takes off or lands. It is distinguished by white wing markings and collar, and has a grey-brown back and pink-and-grey chest. At home in woodlands throughout the country, it feeds on buds, seeds and nuts.

Birds of the Mountains These habitats embrace forested uplands, sub-Alpine meadows and woods, and Alpine grasslands, heaths and rocky ground, reaching well above 2500m in the Northern and Southern Alps, Pyrenees, Jura and Massif Central.

Frequenting mountain slopes and alpine meadows in the Alps and the Pyrenees during summer, the small **alpine accentor** *(l'accenteur alpin)* descends to less harsh environments for the winter. Its plumage remains unchanged all year – grey head, black-and-brown-barred wings and speckled throat.

The **alpine chough** *(le grand corbeau)* confines itself to ravines and the higher mountains up to 4000m, and is usually seen in flocks, both in the wild and around villages and tourist resorts. Black all over with a yellow bill, it has a long tail and rather slender wings. A skilled acrobat, it is a past master of the art of soaring. The most common call is a shrill whistle.

The largest and most powerful of all eagles, the **golden eagle** *(l'aigle royale)* has a wingspan exceeding 2m, held in a V shape during its awesome gliding and soaring displays; it dives with wings folded to catch small rodents or carrion. Plumage is generally dark brown with white wing patches when seen from below. Golden eagles are largely confined to the far southeast of the country wherever there are cliffs or tall trees for nesting.

Happy on rocky ground up to 3500m in the Maritime Alps and the eastern Pyrenees, the **ptarmigan** *(le lagopède)* blends with its surroundings by changing colours at least three times during the year, from spotted grey in summer to pure white in winter. To protect its legs against the cold, the bird has its own thermal long johns – a layer of insulating feathers. The ptarmigan lets out a rather rasping, croaking call as it moves about.

The diminutive **snow finch** *(la niverolle d'Europe)* adapts to its changing surroundings as the brown back and black throat become paler to blend with the whitish head and chest during colder months. It lives in large flocks on stony ground, and sometimes around villages, between 2000m and 3000m, in the Pyrenees and the Alps where in summer it may be seen around the highest summits.

Mammals

Here we have a very diverse assembly, from the grey seal to forest dwellers to the denizens of high and rocky mountains; 93 mammal species have been recorded in France. In the safe havens of the large national parks the spectacle of herds of chamois and families of marmots at play and, in some areas, small herds of peacefully grazing ibex, are almost guaranteed.

Belying its somewhat lugubrious appearance, the **alpine ibex** *(le bouquetin)* can perform incredibly acrobatic feats on cliff faces. With unmistakeable large, tapering, ridged horns (shorter in the female), they are usually seen in small groups on sunny slopes between 800m and 3500m. The ibex is very tame, a propensity that has made it easy prey for illegal hunting.

The name of the **brown hare** *(le lièvre commun)* accurately describes its appearance – it has long, black-tipped ears. Although it prefers farmland and nearby grassland during summer, this animal is also seen in open woodland and on mountain slopes.

Chamois
(Rupicapra rupicapra)

One of the most endearing alpine dwellers, the **chamois** *(le chamois)* stands about 80cm tall at the shoulder and has a white head with broad black strips across the eyes, and shortish, slightly hooked horns. It exchanges its yellow-brown summer coat for thick dark brown or black winter fur. The chamois is amazingly agile on the steepest cliffs, fearlessly balancing on its flexible hooves; if disturbed it can climb 1000m in barely 15 minutes. Although it can

REITA WILSON-WRIGHT

range as high as 4000m in summer, usually in large groups of females and young (born in May to June), it is most likely to be seen up to 2500m. Chamois head for cover at much lower levels during winter.

Despite its name, the bull **grey seal** *(le phoque gris)* can be brown or silver, even black and varying shades of grey with dark blotches, whereas the cow (female) is lighter coloured. It spends plenty of time basking on sandbanks and smooth rocks and is most likely to be seen off the Brittany coast.

A close relation of the chamois, the **izard** *(l'isard)* is similar in appearance and equally agile, though slightly smaller, and largely confined to the Pyrenees.

Marmot
(Marmota
marmota)

KATE NOLAN

The shrill whistle of the **marmot** *(la marmotte)* is a characteristic sound of the high valleys and mountain slopes up to 2700m. Not unlike a large, dark, chunky squirrel, it has grey-brown fur, lighter on the undersides; the rounded head has a characteristically flat forehead. Marmots live in small colonies and build extensive burrow systems; as soon as the lookout sounds the alarm the slopes suddenly become alive as other marmots scurry into a burrow entrance. After a long winter hibernation in their sealed-off burrows, they emerge slim and agile, but as summer progresses they put on weight and slow down, so are easily spotted.

A resident of Corsica since prehistoric times, the **mouflon** *(le mouflon)* has declined drastically during the last hundred years; it was introduced to mainland Alpine France during the later 20th century. About the size of a small sheep, it is mainly reddish brown. The males have a white saddle patch and sport a fine pair of backward-curving, nearly circular horns. The Corsican female's short pointed horns are generally absent in her mainland counterpart.

A very adaptable species, the **mountain hare** *(le lièvre variable)* changes from pale grey-brown in summer to pure white in winter. Although mainly nocturnal, large groups may be seen during the day on scree slopes up to 3000m and in open birch or pine woodland.

Measuring as much as 120cm, of which half is the tail, the **otter** *(le loutre)* has a sinuous body clothed with mid-brown fur; the head is rather flat with long whiskers. With luck you might just spot an otter or two along river banks well away from any habitation. Otters are most active soon after dawn or at dusk and their presence is betrayed by a worn path over the edge of the bank from where they plop into the water; their tracks show five-clawed digits on each webbed foot.

The largest wild animal in France, the **red deer** *(le cerf élaphe)* stands up to 150cm at the shoulder. In summer the red deer has a generally reddish brown to beige appearance; the winter coat has more of a grey look. The male's antlers, which can grow as many as 16 points from the central spine, are usually shed in March or April. Red deer commonly congregate in large herds, stags and hinds keeping their distance except during the breeding season (October to November).

Though naturally preferring woodland, red deer may also be seen in Mediterranean lowlands and in the mountains up to 2500m.

The **red fox** *(le renard)* may be seen almost anywhere, though it prefers open ground, and is instantly recognisable by its red-brown coat, long bushy tail and canine profile. It may be seen during the day, though is mainly nocturnal in its habits.

The **red squirrel** *(l'écureuil roux)* divides its time between foraging on the ground for berries, fruit and seeds, especially from conifer cones, and scampering through the branches. With a dark bushy tail as long as its dark chestnut furred body (24cm), it is readily identifiable. Its nest of twigs and forest litter is firmly wedged into a tree fork.

Europe's smallest indigenous deer, the **roe deer** *(le chevreuil)* reaches just 80cm at the shoulder. Its summer dress is reddish brown with a distinctive white patch on the rump. The stag's three-spined mini-antlers are no more than 30cm long. Roe deer are usually seen singly in woodlands or around cultivated ground.

Reptiles

You're much more likely to read about these creatures than see them, so don't panic – snake bite is *not* a hazard of walking in France!

Ranging very widely, the **adder** *(la vipère)* prefers undisturbed ground and can be found as high as 2750m. The males are usually yellowish, pale grey or silvery with black markings and a characteristic inverted V at the back of the head. Up to 65cm in length, they are usually active during the cool of the day, spending the rest of the time sun baking. They rarely bite and fatalities are extremely unusual.

Despite its name, the **grass snake** *(la couleuvre à collier)* is commonly found in wet areas, and on dry ground up to 2300m. It is generally olive or bluish-grey in colour, with a yellow or orange collar and a pair of black crescents behind the head. Up to 150cm long, the grass snake spends much of the day coiled up in the sun; it also enjoys basking afloat, and retreats to the water if threatened. Its bite is not harmful.

The **green lizard** *(le lézard vert)* grows to 40cm; the male is bright green or yellow-green with an attractive black stipple pattern on the back and an obvious blue patch on the throat. It's most likely to be seen in sunny spots in the mornings and evenings throughout the country.

PLANTS

Nearly 5000 species of flowering plants and ferns are found in France in a huge array of habitats, from coastal marshes to deciduous woodlands to the limits of plant growth high in the mountains.

Shrubs & Flowers

Wildflowers are one of the outstanding attractions of mountain walks between late May and August; indeed, there are colourful and often aromatic floral displays to be enjoyed almost wherever you wander in France.

Medicinal Trees & Plants

Did you know that:

• **Pine** leaves can be added to the bath water to allay feelings of tiredness and insomnia.

• An **elder flower** infusion is believed to help cure flu, and the berry juice is thought to ward off colds.

• To help improve your blood circulation, drink an infusion made from **rosemary leaves**.

• Roots of the **yellow gentian**, mashed or as an infusion, can improve digestion.

Maquis & Garrigue

Farming and tree-felling have transformed the lower mountain slopes of the Mediterranean from thick forest.

Maquis grows in dense thickets of often thorny, leathery-leaved plants. The perfume of some maquis species – myrtles, thyme, laurels, rosemary and mints – wafts far and wide.

Garrigue is a less-diverse collection of plants that survive on sparse limestone soils, including gorse, lavender and small oaks.

Alpenrose
(*Rhododendron ferriguneum*)

Found in grasslands, heaths and rocky ground above 2500m and as high as 3200m, **alpenrose** *(le rhododendron sauvage)* grows in dense colourful thickets up to 1m high, interspersed among grasses and rocky outcrops. Small clusters of bell-shaped, deep pinkish red flowers last through summer.

Alpine pasqueflower *(l'anémone des Alpes)* is a prominent species in meadows up to 2700m. It has relatively large white flowers with pointed tips, appearing between May and July.

Growing in low mats on damp or stony ground up to 3000m, the small **alpine snowbell** *(la soldanelle des alpes)* has deep-green, round-ish leaves. The violet or violet-blue, bell-shaped and fringed flowers appear between April and August.

Bell heather *(la bruyère cendrée)* is particularly common in coastal heaths, but is also found in moorland up to 1500m This twiggy, small-leaved plant produces masses of small, purple bell-shaped flowers between May and September.

One of the earliest spring flowers in the woodlands, **bluebell** *(le jacinthe des bois)* has beautiful sky-blue, slender, bell-shaped flowers on fine stems which carpet the forest floor from April to June.

Broom *(le genêt)* is found all over the place, especially along the coast and on disturbed ground. A tall, rather graceful bush, it has long branchlets with trefoil leaves; the yellow blossoms make a colourful display in June and July.

A dense, evergreen bush, **common juniper** *(le genévrier)* grows over a wide range, from Mediterranean forest to moorland as high as 1500m. The small spiny leaves are greyish in colour, and the berries, used to make gin, ripen to black after the May to June flowering season.

The large, rounded, yellow heads of the **globeflower** *(la boule d'or)* are very distinctive, precariously supported by long stems above notched, palm-shaped leaves. The flowering seasons lasts from May to August in woodlands and on damp ground.

Widespread along the coast and nearby inland areas in grasslands and heaths, dense thickets of **gorse** *(l'ajonc)* often colonise disturbed ground. The yellow flowers have a strong almond perfume and the abundant leaves are tipped with spines.

Growing in small clumps, the popular **lily of the valley** *(le muguet)* has fragrant, delicate, white, globular blossoms which appear between April and June. It favours dry ground on lime-rich soil up to 2300m.

The **mountain pansy** *(la pensée jaune)* is fairly common in mountains on grassy and rocky ground as high as 2000m. Its yellow, violet or bicoloured blooms appear between May and July.

Prominent in the maquis (see the boxed text above) and on dry rocky ground in southern areas, **rockrose** *(la ciste)* – both pink and white – blossoms abundantly during April and May.

Rosemary *(le romarin)* is common in maquis, thriving in the sunny Mediterranean climate, where dense bushes sprout masses of aromatic, lilac-coloured flowers from March onwards. The short spiky leaves are highly prized for the wonderfully earthy flavour that they impart to meat dishes.

Sea campion (le silène maritime) is easily identified in coastal areas where it grows in large clumps on rocky ground and on sand dunes. The white flowers emerge from enlarged pinkish tubes of the calyx (leaves surrounding the petals) during June to August; it has small fleshy leaves.

Spring gentian (la grande gentiane) is a small plant found on damp ground as high as 3000m, with bright green leaves forming a rosette at the base of the stem. On top is a single, five-petalled pale- to deep-blue flower, usually appearing between March and August.

Also called sea pink, **thrift** (l'armérie maritime) grows in rock crevices on the coast. Masses of striking deep- to pale-pink flowers make a showing in April and can last for a few months. **Mountain thrift** (le gazon d'Olympe), a subspecies, grows on rocky ground up to 3100m; it too produces pink blooms, during July and August.

Trumpet gentian (le gentiane de Koch) is among the largest of the gentians; its deep-blue flowers, 40mm to 70mm long, bloom between May and August. It is found on rocky or boggy ground as high as 3000m in the Pyrenees, Southern Alps and the Jura.

Wood anemone (l'anémone) has a single white flower on each stem, set off by slender dark-green lobed leaflets. Preferring woodlands up to 1800m, it blooms from March to May.

Yellow anemone (l'anémone fausse renoncule) is widespread in woodlands to 1500m. It has notched leaves and buttercup-like flowers, which appear between March and May.

Common in freshwater ponds and marshes throughout the country and as high as 1200m, the **yellow iris** (l'iris faux-acore) has rather long sword-shaped leaves and small clusters of yellow flowers in the characteristic iris shape – three outer petals and three erect inner ones.

Trees

France is one of the most wooded countries in Europe, with 44% of its area under forests or scattered woodlands. These are highlighted on several walks this book: near Paris, in the lower and middle reaches of the Pyrenees, Southern Alps, Cévennes and the Vosges.

Aleppo pine (le pin d'Alep) is found in Mediterranean forests; it has distinctive shiny, bright green leaves and colourful deep purple-brown, orange-streaked bark.

A plentiful waterside tree, **common alder** (l'aulne) is readily identifiable by its spoon-shaped dark green leaves. The catkins (flowers), appearing during March and April, are dark yellow (male) and dark red (female).

Forests of **common beech** (le hêtre) are characteristic of limestone uplands. Trees can reach 25m in height with a huge crown; the bark is smooth and silvery grey. During May the forest floor is carpeted with the cast-off pale yellow male flowers. In October the bright-green foliage turns from pale yellow to rich orange-brown then reddish brown.

Friend & Foe

Le muguet (lily of the valley) decorates many a lapel on May Day, not only those of marchers in the traditional trade-union parades. Many people give a sprig to friends for good luck. The normal strict protection of the plant is relaxed on this day only and anyone can sell wild muguet.

Although it can be used for the treatment of heart conditions, it is undoubtedly toxic.

Usually growing as a tall bush in most parts of the country, **common hazel** *(le noisetier)* has rather hairy leaves, deep green on top and whitish beneath. The tasty brown nuts are protected by papery bracts (modified leaves).

Prominent in Provence's woodlands, the **cork oak** *(la chêne liège)* reaches 20m in height and has characteristic low, twisted branches. The spongy, fissured bark is removed every eight to 10 years and is traditionally, though decreasingly, used to make corks.

Found at higher elevations in Corsica, the tall slender, grey-green foliaged **Corsican pine** *(le pin larico)* can live to a considerable age.

Elder *(le sureau)*, a small shrub or tree up to 10m tall, is covered in massed dense clusters of tiny white flowers in April and May. The edible black fruit can make a powerful wine.

The widespread **English oak** *(la chêne pédoncule)* grows to a great size with a trunk several metres across, and usually lives for several hundred years. The largish dark-green leaves are lobed and slightly tapered; the acorns emerge in pairs on a long stalk

Branch section of the European larch *(Larix decidua)*

The **European larch** *(le mélèze)* grows up to 2500m, the usual limit of tree growth, though hardy specimens are found at 2800m. Readily distinguished as the only deciduous conifer, it glows gold in late autumn. Conical in shape, with the lowest branches often bending abruptly skywards about 2m out from the trunk, it can reach massive proportions. Specimens up to 500 years old are not uncommon.

Prominent on limestone in Mediterranean regions, the **holm oak** *(la chêne verte)* has a dense grey-black crown, deep-hued bark and dark evergreen, spine-tipped leaves, oval in shape.

An evergreen of the maquis (see the boxed text on p29), **kermes oak** *(la chêne kermes)* has spiny leaves and a prickly, scaly acorn cup.

The **Lombardy poplar** *(le peuplier)* is often seen beside rivers and roads and is readily recognisable by the familiar tall, slender tapering profile; it has bright dark-green leaves.

Found in limestone country, **sweet chestnut** *(le châtaignier)* is widely cultivated for its timber. The longish dark green leaves are prominently veined and the fruit husk, protecting two nuts, is covered with tiny hairs.

Found in Mediterranean forests, usually on limestone soil, **white** or **downy oak** *(la chêne blanche)* is of medium height and takes its name from its hairy shoots and leaves.

Most likely seen in Mediterranean forests, the **wild olive** *(l'olivier)* is smaller than the commercial variety. It has diminutive oval leaves, clusters of tiny white flowers and small black fruit, usually ripening during September and October.

GEOLOGY

About 300 million years ago, upheavals in the earth's crust throughout northwestern Europe, where the land mass of France had long been submerged, pushed up three major mountainous areas. The Massif Central, the Massif des Vosges and the Massif Armoricain (in Brittany) arose, composed of granites, gneiss, mica-schist, sandstones and some volcanic rock. These ancient mountain ranges were worn down over vast periods of time to relatively modest levels. The Corsican uplands were also formed during this mountain-building era but were subjected to more violent convulsions, resulting in a very rugged, dissected mountainscape.

The Alps, the Pyrenees and the Jura emerged after several phases of mountain-building. They originally took shape about 100 million years ago, were then intensively folded, thrust up again and eroded. It is in these mountain ranges, and in the Vosges, that the impact of the advance and retreat of vast ice sheets during the succession of ice ages of the past two million years is most striking: deep valleys (starkly U-shaped in the Vosges); narrow ridges, cirques (glacier-head valleys); and low ridges of moraine (debris left behind by retreating glaciers). Glaciers are still active in the Northern Alps (see the boxed text opposite) and to a lesser extent in parts of the Southern Alps and central Pyrenees, though many have retreated dramatically in recent decades.

At the end of the last ice age, sea levels rose sharply and flooded coastal valleys, notably in Brittany, creating a deeply in-dented coastline, and former hills became the offshore islands.

The large sedimentary basins of the major river systems, the Alsace plain and the Rhône delta began to take shape about 250 million years ago when sediments were deposited in shallow seas; these sediments turned into the sandstones and limestones of the Paris, Aquitaine and Saône-Rhône basins. The limestones are youngest – a mere 65 million years old.

The Rhine rift valley was created by massive blocks in the earth's crust shifting along fault lines during one of the mountain-building eras. Later upheavals pushed the river away from its westward and southerly course and out into the North Sea.

Volcanic activity was largely confined to the Massif Central, its landscape still dominated by extinct volcanoes. They were active between 20 million and three million years ago; lava flowed as recently as 8000 to 10,000 years ago. Erosion has reduced the volcanoes to their conical basalt cores *(puys)* and the attendant lava flows; some of the volcanic craters contain lakes. The Massif Central also has an extensive lime-stone plateau, raised by as much as 1000m by crustal movements during the last 10 million years.

CLIMATE

Three major influences, somewhat modified by topography, define France's climate.

The Atlantic Ocean is responsible for the maritime climate of the northwest coast and hinterland. A procession of low-pressure systems and associated fronts bring change-able, mild, cloudy and wet weather. Rain is likely on 200 days annually, the heaviest falls being between November and January. Hours of summer sunshine are the lowest in France – averaging seven to eight daily – and summer maximum temperatures don't often exceed 30°C.

This maritime regime extends south to the Loire estuary and inland to the western fringes of the Vosges, Massif Central and the Pyrenees, though modified inland by continental influences. Rainfall is more con-centrated in summer storms, making spring and autumn relatively dry. The far southwest is warmer and sunnier than the northwest; winter is mild but summer is rather damp, especially in the far south where short, sharp showers are plentiful.

The inland areas' continental climate, influenced mainly by high-pressure systems travelling from the north and east, is typified by snowy winters and hot, thundery summers. In areas sheltered from maritime clouds, an-nual rainfall can be as low as 600mm or as high as 2000mm in mountainous areas. Frost and snow are common in winter, especially in the east. Summer is warmest in the south of

Signs of a Glacial Past

Many of the world's finest walks are through landscapes that have been – or are being – substantially shaped by glaciers. As a glacier flows downhill its weight of ice and snow creates a distinctive collection of landforms, many of which are preserved once the ice has retreated (as is happening in most of the world's ranges today) or vanished.

The most obvious is the *U-shaped valley* (1), gouged out by the glacier as it moves downhill, often with one or more bowl-shaped *cirques* (2) at its head. Cirques are found along high mountain ridges or at mountain passes or *cols* (3). Where an alpine glacier – which flows off the upper slopes and ridges of a mountain range – has joined a deeper, more substantial valley glacier, a dramatic *hanging valley* (4) is often the result. Hanging valleys and cirques commonly shelter hidden alpine lakes or *tarns* (5). The thin ridge that separates adjacent glacial valleys is known as an *arête* (6).

As a glacier grinds its way forward it usually leaves long, *lateral moraine* (7) ridges along its course – mounds of debris either deposited along the flanks of the glacier or left by sub-ice streams within its heart (the latter, strictly, an *esker*). At the end – or *snout* – of a glacier is the *terminal moraine* (8), the point where the giant conveyor belt of ice drops its load of rocks and grit. Both high up in the hanging valleys and in the surrounding valleys and plains, *moraine lakes* (9) may form behind a dam of glacial rubble.

The plains that surround a glaciated range may feature a confusing variety of moraine ridges, mounds and outwash fans – material left by rivers flowing from the glaciers. Perched here and there may be an *erratic* (10), a rock carried far from its origin by the moving ice and left stranded when it melted.

View of area before glacier's retreat

Climate

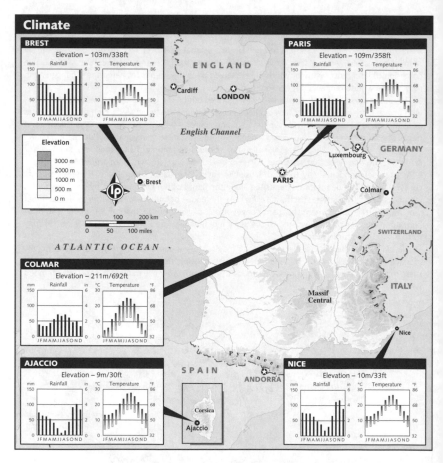

the region and sunshine can average around nine hours daily.

The timing of the wettest season in the mountains varies. In the Pyrenees, it's during autumn and winter, while in the Vosges, Jura and the Northern Alps, summer and autumn are the wettest times. Summer in the Southern Alps, the Pyrenees and parts of the Massif Central is relatively fine and fairly warm, though cloud, heavy showers and afternoon thunderstorms are not uncommon.

The Languedoc, the Provence coast, Corsica, the Maritime Alps, the Rhône Valley and the southern Massif Central all enjoy a Mediterranean climate. Winters are mild and not too damp (though heavy snow on the Corsican mountains can often last well into spring) and summers are hot and dry with up to 12 hours of sunshine daily; any rain is heavy and often thundery.

CONSERVATION & ENVIRONMENT

The Ministry of Ecology & Sustainable Development is the principal government conservation agency. Its five central policy directorates include Nature et Paysages (Nature and Landscapes), responsible for protection of reserves, species and landscape. Among a clutch of associated agencies are the national parks, the National Forestry Office and the Conservatoire du Littoral, which looks after the coast.

Various nationwide issues galvanise the environmental groups, especially pollution of the coast by oil spills. However, local issues such as the drainage of wetlands and the disappearance of rural paths and byways (either through disuse or under the relentless extension of bitumen surfaces) have a more direct impact on the walking environment. Despite dire warnings of the relatively rapid retreat of glaciers and climate change, continuing development of skiing facilities in fragile Alpine areas causes consternation. The disastrous fire in the Mont Blanc tunnel in 1999 put a harsh spotlight on the damage wrought by juggernaut road transports thundering through Alpine valleys. However, some lobby groups are stronger than others: the Vallée d'Aspe in the Pyrenees now reverberates to a huge volume of road freight traffic and the Mont Blanc tunnel has reopened for business.

For visiting walkers the most striking aspect of environmental conservation is the existence of legally protected reserves: national parks, regional natural parks and a host of smaller, specialised sites. Management of the regional parks directly involves local people, giving them a stake in their future, and helping in no small measure to ensure their wellbeing.

The FFRP undoubtedly figures most prominently in protecting and promoting walkers' interests and trying to safeguard the areas through which its vast network of waymarked paths passes. It rightly sees France's path heritage as indispensable to protecting the natural heritage, promoting tourism and creating jobs. It appears to have enjoyed some success, if the ever-growing number of paths in lowland areas near towns and villages is anything to go by.

Conservation Organisations

Here are the contact details for some of France's major environmental organisations, including government agencies. Each has publications available online. For the FFRP and CAF see Useful Organisations (p48).

Association for the Protection of Wild Animals (☎ 04 75 25 10 00; www.aspas-nature.org; ASPAS-BP 505, 26401 Crest) campaigns on a wide front for the protection of wolves and migratory birds, and to put an end to hunting during the period from the end of January to late September It manages its own hunting-free reserves.

Commission National de Protection de la Montagne (CNPM; www.clubalpin.com/fr/prescnpm .html), established by the CAF, is committed to protection of undeveloped landscapes and protected species of flora and fauna, imposing controls on motorised recreation, limited skiing developments and creating national reserves (such as national parks).

Fédération des Parcs Naturels Régionaux de France (FPNRF; ☎ 01 44 90 86 20; www.parcs -naturels-regionaux.tm fr; 4 rue de Stockholm, 75008 Paris) promotes the regional parks and organises guided walks. Publications include Catalogue des Gîtes Panda, a guide to quality accommodation in the parks.

La Ligue Française pour la Protection des Oiseaux (☎ 05 46 82 12 34; www.lpo.fr; La Corderie Royale, BP 263, 17305 Rochefort) was founded in 1912; its aims are the protection of birds and the ecosystems on which they depend. It has 33,000 members, manages eight reserves and has a mobile scheme to help 'birds in distress'.

Ministère de l'Ecologie et du Developpement Durable – Direction de la Nature et Paysages (☎ 01 42 19 20 21; www.environnement.gouv .fr; 20 av de Ségur, 75302 Paris) oversees the network of protected areas, preserves protected species of wild flora and fauna, landscapes and biological diversity. It also supervises hunting and plays a major role in the conservation of migratory birds.

Office National des Forêts (ONF; ☎ 01 40 19 58 00; www.onf.fr; 2 av de Sainte Mandé, 75570 Paris) manages state and communally owned forests for timber production, environment protection and public recreation.

NATIONAL PARKS & RESERVES

France was a latecomer to the international community of national parks, even though a reserve was established at Fontainebleau in 1861. To make up for lost time, a burst of creative activity began in 1960 making possible the declaration of a national park where the natural environment is specially important and where its legal protection is deemed necessary. Two parks were set up in 1963: Parc National de la Vanoise (in the Alps, east of Grenoble) and tiny Parc National de Port Cros, a Mediterranean islet off the Côte d'Azur. The other four in mainland France followed during the decade from 1967: Parcs Nationals des Pyrénées, des Cévennes (the largest, in Languedoc), des Écrins and du Mercantour. Their total area of 1257 sq km amounts to about 2% of the land area of France.

The parks are areas of outstanding cultural, ecological and landscape value where biological diversity and landscapes are protected. This may involve supporting traditional activities which have helped shape today's landscape; only the Pyrenees, Port Cros and Cévennes have small permanent populations in their heartlands. Each park is run by a public agency bringing together representatives of local organisations, tourism interests and natural scientists.

Development in national parks is not totally prohibited; activities which promote local development, in particular 'green' tourism projects, are permissible. Park regulations are, however, pretty strict in banning anything that would alter the park's character (see the boxed text on p42).

Programmes to reintroduce flora and fauna species to various parks have been particularly successful; ibex, long absent from the mountains, now live in all the alpine parks. The numerous *maisons du parc* run education programmes and activities to teach people more about the parks.

France is serious about its cross-border, cooperative management of parks and reserves. It is a major player in the European Natural Sites Twinning Programme set up in 1987 for cooperation in research and protection work. At least 14 French reserves are twinned with reserves in other countries, mainly those popular with migratory birds and where habitat management is vital. Of the national parks, Mercantour and Vanoise cooperate with neighbouring Italian parks in all kinds of natural conservation and recreation activities.

Regional Natural Parks

There are 40 *parcs naturels regionaux* protecting more than 10% of the country's land area.

Unlike national parks, which are concentrated in the mountainous periphery, regional natural parks are scattered from one end of France to the other, including Corsica. They protect a very wide range of features, from the gentle mountains of the Queyras and Jura, to the rugged volcanic peaks in the Auvergne, the Camargue wetlands, heathlands in western Brittany, the limestone *causses* (plateaus) in Quercy, and numerous forests. The largest is Volcans d'Auvergne (395 sq km), followed by Corse (Corsica; 375 sq km). The big difference between them and national parks are that the regional natural parks are home to relatively large numbers of people (eg, about 105,000 in Livradois-Forez) and that regional, rather than central, government provides the money to look after them.

Their managers aim to balance the preservation of natural and cultural heritage features with sustainable social and economic development based on tourism, environmental education and traditional rural activities. Low-key facilities such as paths for walkers and trails for horse riders and cyclists are provided. The strict regulations applying in national parks don't relate to regional parks, although managers take a strong line on responsible walking and other activities (see Conservation Organisations, p35).

Other Reserves

There are more than 150 *réserves naturelles*, many of which are within national and regional parks (eg, the Écrins and Vercors). Most are small areas (less than 300 ha) of particular importance as habitats, notably for migratory species, or with remarkable geological, geomorphological or speleological features. Some are privately owned, though many are readily accessible.

Sites of outstanding natural beauty or of artistic, historical, scientific or traditional importance can be protected as *sites naturels classés*. They range from individual trees to high mountains.

Public Forests

France is the third-most-forested country in Europe (after Sweden and Finland), with 14,000 sq km of wooded land. However, 70% is privately owned and more than likely closed to public access. Of the rest, state-owned forests are known as *forêts domaniales*; about 1500 of them cover 1750 sq km. Other public forests, owned by local collectives or public agencies, cover 2700 sq km. *Forêts domaniales* are managed by the Office National des Forêts (see Conservation Organisations, p35) to protect their natural values, for production of timber, for public enjoyment and in partnership with other national and international bodies responsible for the natural environment.

POPULATION & PEOPLE

Nearly 61 million people live in France, 20% of whom are packed into the greater metropolitan area of Paris. The overall number of people living in mountain areas has been declining since the 1950s, though some rural areas have managed to reverse this trend.

During the last 200 years, France has accepted more immigrants than any other European nation. Until the mid-20th century most came from other parts of Europe; the economic boom after WWII attracted millions of mainly unskilled workers and their families from French-speaking North and sub-Saharan Africa and Indochina. Millions of non-French-speaking people from the same areas were also welcomed as much needed workers during a prolonged period of rapid economic growth.

Since the early 1970s, successive changes to immigration laws have been directed at stemming the inflow, making it more difficult for people to obtain citizenship and easier for the government to repatriate others. This has been against the background of a backlash against non-white immigrant groups, especially North African Muslims – Muslims comprise France's second-largest religious group.

About 80% of French people identify themselves as being Roman Catholics; although most have been baptised, few attend church.

SOCIETY & CONDUCT

From afar, the French have something of a reputation for arrogance and rudeness. At first hand, you'll find this is a piece of foreign folklore bearing scant resemblance to real life, especially beyond Paris.

Generally, the French (and especially older generations) are rather formal and polite in their behaviour, especially when meeting people. Wherever you are – in a shop (particularly small ones), in the post office, climbing into a bus, arriving at a hotel or camping ground – always say *'Bonjour, monsieur/madame/mademoiselle'*, and when you leave, *'Merci monsieur/madame/ mademoiselle'*. Forget or avoid this and you'll find it much more difficult to make genuine contacts. Any attempt to speak French, however halting and stilted, will be appreciated – the French are extremely proud of their language. Especially in rural areas, expect that most people will *not* speak English; even if they do, it will be a while before they feel confident enough to try. In conversation, the subject of money is definitely off the agenda; not surprisingly the French don't share the British obsession with the weather. You can't go wrong by practising a few set pieces about where you come from (especially if it's beyond European shores), and by being able to say how much you enjoy their food, their wine, their food ...

Facts for the Walker

Coastal Walks

Watch constantly changing patterns of sea and rock along Côte de Granit Rose (p80). Scramble in and out of the steep inlets of the Calanques (p224). Face bracing westerly winds along the rugged Finistère cliffs, buffeted by the restless sea (p88).

Glacier Scenery

Gaze awestruck at vistas of glistening white glaciers dominated by La Meije (p251). Walk beside Europe's largest icefall on Montagne de la Côte (p282). Look out over the Mer de Glace, which is Europe's second-longest glacier, from the Grand Balcon Nord (p279). Revel in the stunning views of the Maladeta glacier from Port de Vénasque (p183).

Historical Tours

Explore Paris off the beaten track with its canals, churches and magnificent mansions (p66). Follow in the footsteps of thousands of pilgrims who have walked the centuries-old Chemin de St-Jacques (p134). Join the famous Scottish writer Robert Louis Stevenson in the beautiful Cévennes forests (p131). Visit the fine walled town of Avallon, and Vézelay with its magnificent basilica (p334).

Natural Wonders

Marvel at stupendous vertical cliffs of the Cirque d'Archiane (p246). Explore the most spectacular range of mountains in Europe on the Tour du Mont Blanc (p293). Walk the Gorges du Verdon (p226), Europe's longest canyon. Discover a French volcano on the Puy de Dôme walk (p110). See old ochre quarries and cross the mountainMediterranean vegetation divide (p234).

Authors' Favourites

Varied, challenging walking with Vignemale, the highest peak in the French Pyrenees – a near-constant visual companion (p173). A mirror-like dawn reflection of Mont Blanc in the waters of Lac Blanc (p278). Seeing herds of wild chamois and ibex on the Tour du Mont Blanc above Chamonix (p276). Striding the spring turf of the Crête des Vosges under a clear sky (p321). Delighting in the feeling of remoteness and isolation in the Vercors' beautiful Jardin du Roi (p248). Romping down the wonderfully scenic valley from Col Vieux past glorious Alpine lakes (p263).

SUGGESTED ITINERARIES

If time is short, we suggest that you concentrate on just one area, or perhaps parts of two that are side by side. With a more expansive itinerary, make the most of France's extensive public transport system, though make sure the final link in your connections operates a relatively frequent timetable. If you have a month or more, then the potential is bewildering. We hope the following ideas will help to guide you through the maze of France's superlative walking venues.

One Week

With just a week to spare, base yourself in Paris, first wandering across the capital from west to east or from north to south. Then head out into the countryside to explore the wonderful maze of rocky outcrops around Fontainebleau, and don't miss the magnificent chateau. For cultural variety, you could also work in a day at Giverny, famous for its association with painter Claude Monet. If you feel the need for a blast of sea air, then it's possible to do the Côte d'Albâtre walk, spread over two days from Paris.

With careful planning, you could spend the whole time on the coast (easily accessible from Britain), combining the Mont St-Michel and Côte de Granit Rose walks. If your week can stretch to 10 days, then set your sights on the Chemin de St-Jacques (Way of St James). There would be ample time to absorb the ambience of the historic towns en route.

Two Weeks

For something completely different combine the soul-stirring Crête des Vosges in Alsace with more gentle walking through Burgundy's vineyards, then head east to the lovely forests and ridges of the Jura Mountains above the Valserine Valley. The delights of the Auvergne, Massif Central and the Cévennes could easily eat up a fortnight. Set out from Clermont Ferrand and work your way southwards to enjoy walks in the volcanic Monts Dômes and the fascinating Monts du Cantal; in the neighbouring Cévennes, follow in the footsteps of author Robert Louis Stevenson through the Cévennes forest.

The island of Corsica deserves a fortnight all to itself, so you can mix mountains and low-level walking along the coast and through beautiful villages. Combine an expedition through Provence's spectacular Gorges du Verdon and a stroll over the Grand Luberon with some fine mountain walking through magnificent valleys and past scenic lakes in the Parc National du Mercantour.

One Month

Immerse yourself in the wonders of the mountains, lakes and high passes of the Pyrenees, then for a complete contrast follow the Chemin de St-Jacques. Combine the Northern Alps, including the iconic Tour de Mont Blanc, and the gentler Jura Mountains, or the gastronomic delights of Burgundy. All four areas featured in the Southern Alps, each with its own distinctive character, fit neatly into a month; alternatively, concentrate on two – ideally the Vercors and the Queyras – then have a look at the Massif Central and the Auvergne for a very different type of mountain landscape.

WHEN TO WALK

If you're free to choose your dates, avoid the second half of July and August. At this time the pressure on accommodation can be intense, most of Europe seems to be on the move and prices increase with the volume of visitors. It's virtually essential to secure a place to stay at least 24 hours in advance.

In the Alps and the Pyrenees, the window for walking is fairly small. Snow drifts can

Surviving Summer

Thoughts of warm sunny days striding along high ridges, or strolling through historic villages somewhere – anywhere – in France, sustain many walkers (the present authors included) through long winters. However, none of us could have imagined the record heat wave of the 2003 European summer.

The way the climate's going this may not have been a once-in-a-lifetime event, so our experiences and survival techniques may become standard practice during future summers. Indeed, summer could become a time *not* to go walking in France – or almost anywhere in Europe, except perhaps the far north.

As the white limestone paths shimmered blindingly, a hat with a deep brim and sunglasses were *de rigueur*, though many ambled along hatless and even bare-chested. Every scrap of shade was savoured for as long as possible; lucky were those who found the deepest, coolest havens for long lunches or a true siesta.

We shamelessly lounged by swimming pools or mountain tarns during the hottest hours, and lingered at bars or cafés with shady terraces. We drank copiously and frequently, especially with breakfast.

Starting time became earlier and earlier, with due reward – several hours of walking in cool, crisp mornings along shaded paths, though none of us ever felt so desperate as to start at 4am as did one pair at a Mercantour *refuge*. After a break, we'd put in a couple more hours in the late afternoon and arrive at the destination still feeling relatively human, and fit for another day.

Sandra Bardwell

linger into late June, even mid-July. Until then, you're likely to be following beaten tracks across softish or crusty snow when crossing cols above 2500m. Summers are normally brief at this altitude and the earliest snows may fall during the first half of September. Most *refuges* (mountain chalets) are open from mid-June until late September; some have a self-contained wing with limited services that's open during winter and early spring for walkers, mountaineers and skiers. From mid-July until the end of August, many *refuges* are stretched to the limit and unpleasantly overcrowded. If you're camping you can just blithely ignore this problem.

In the Massif Central, Jura and the Massif des Vosges the walking season is longer – generally from early May until mid-October in the Massif Central, and well into November in the Jura and Vosges. Even at the height of summer, it's rarely too hot to prevent pleasant walking. Corsica is at its best from late May to late June, and from September to October, when temperatures are comfortable and paths not overcrowded.

May and September are the best months for Brittany and Normandy while further south, in Quercy (Chemin de St-Jacques) and Burgundy, the potential walking season extends from mid-April through to mid-October.

During July and August, it's far too hot for enjoyable walking in Provence and many paths are closed because of the risk of forest fire. However, the area is ideal for a winter walking holiday, though many hotels and camping grounds close outside summer.

WHAT KIND OF WALK?

The range of walks in France is limitless – from tranquil riverside and coastal strolls to demanding mountain treks. Although much of the French countryside is occupied by farms large and small, there are still substantial wild areas in the Pyrenees and the Alps.

France has a huge network of waymarked paths allowing for easy navigation through a fascinating variety of rural landscapes. At almost every turn there's something to stimulate the senses: small villages, chateaus, historic towns with soaring cathedrals, archaeological sites and endless gastronomic delights.

You can enjoy a selection of one-day outings or plan longer walks of a fortnight's duration – or even more. There's no shortage of accommodation, especially along the waymarked paths, from camping grounds (often complete with pool), *gîtes d'étape* providing hostel-style accommodation, and B&Bs in private homes, to hotels ranging from simple to luxurious.

None of the walks described in this book depend on the services of a professional guide. If you'd prefer to leave the organising to someone else, there are lots of companies that run walking holidays in the major walking areas – see the following section.

ORGANISED WALKS

An organised walking holiday can provide a relaxing change of pace during a longer visit, or perhaps an introduction to France before you embark on an independent trip. Numerous companies, large and small, operate walking holidays in all France's major walking regions and in several less well-known areas. Two types of holidays may be offered: fully guided, with the services of a guide from start to finish; and self guided, where the company organises all accommodation, possibly luggage transfer between bases, and provides maps and detailed notes for the walks. All companies are run by people with detailed local knowledge, experience and, commonly, with appropriate professional qualifications. Specialist walking magazines in your home country are a good source of contacts, in addition to those following.

When making enquiries, check the coverage of insurance included in the price of the holiday and whether the tariff includes transport to and from the place(s) where the walks are based, and whether the leaders have formal mountain leadership qualifications. Following is a small selection of companies, both in France and abroad, offering organised walks in France.

Organised Walks within France

Au Vieux Campeur Voyages (☎ 01 53 10 09 02; *www.avc-voyages.com; 15 rue du Cardinal*

Lemoine, 75005 Paris) is an offshoot of the ubiquitous outdoor-equipment establishment. It organises both accompanied and independent walks, mostly seven days, in Provence, the Pyrenees and northern Alps.

Chamina Sylva (☎ 04 66 69 00 44; www.chamina-sylva.com; Naussac BP 5, 48300 Langogne) offers a vast range of week-long tours including Brittany's coast and islands, several areas in Provence and the Auvergne.

Terres d'Aventure (☎ 01 53 73 77 73; www.terdav.com; 6 rue St-Victor, 75005 Paris) runs a huge and varied programme that includes week-long walking adventures in the Cévennes, coastal Brittany, central Pyrenees and the Queyras.

Trekking in the Alps (☎ 04 50 54 62 09; www.trekkinginthealps.com; chemin des Biolles, Vallorcine 74660) is run by an English trekker and mountaineer who will lead you through the Pyrenees, along Corsica's GR20 and several routes in the northern and southern Alps (mainly six days' duration).

Walk Operators Abroad
The UK
ATG Oxford (☎ 01865-315 678; www.atg-oxford.co.uk; 69–71 Banbury Rd, Oxford OX2 6PJ) operates escorted and independent variants, including eight-day tours in the Jura, Cévennes and Dordogne.

Sherpa Expeditions (☎ 020-8577 2717; www.sherpaexpeditions 131A Heston Rd, Hounslow TW5 0RF) operates a programme of independent Inn to Inn walks in several areas including Provence and Corsica, of seven to 12 days' duration.

Walks Worldwide (☎ 01524-262 255; www.walksworldwide.com; 15 Main St, High Bentham, Lancaster LA2 7LG) will take you to the Pyrenees, Corsica, the Auvergne and around the Tour of Mont Blanc, on trips ranging from eight to 14 days.

The USA
Backroads (☎ 510-527-1555; fax 510-527-1444; www.backroads.com; 801 Cedar St, Berkeley, CA 94710-1800) programmes walks mostly lasting six days, with variants in Provence, the Dordogne and the Northern Alps

Cross Country International (☎ 800-828 8768; www.walkingvacations.com; PO Box 1170, Millbrook, NY 12545) operates seven-day trips to Provence, Burgundy, the Lot Valley and the Mont Blanc area.

Wilderness Travel (☎ 1-800-368 2794; www.wildernesstravel.com; 1102 Ninth St, Berkeley, CA 94710-1800) has 13-day hikes on the Haute Route and Tour du Mont Blanc, and shorter walks in Provence and Dordogne.

Australia
Ecotrek: Bogong Jack Adventures (☎ 08 8383 7198; www.ecotrek.com.au; PO Box 4, Kangarilla 5157) goes walking for 11 days along the Loire and in the Dordogne.

Peregrine Adventures (☎ 03 9663 8611; fax 9663 8618; www.peregrine.net.au) has an inventory of independent and guided eight-day walks to Provence, the Dordogne, Haute Pyrenees and Burgundy.

RESPONSIBLE WALKING

The popularity of walking in France, particularly in its wild regions, puts a great deal of pressure on the natural environment. Keep in mind the following guidelines and the national park regulations when you're out walking and play a small part in helping to preserve the ecology of the French countryside.

Rubbish
• If you've carried it in, you can carry it back out. Everything, including empty packaging, citrus peel and cigarette butts, can be stowed in a dedicated rubbish bag. Make an effort to pick up rubbish left by others.

• Sanitary napkins, tampons and condoms don't burn or decompose readily, so carry them out, whatever the inconvenience.

• Burying rubbish disturbs soil and ground cover and encourages erosion and weed growth. Buried rubbish takes years to decompose and will probably be dug up by wild animals who may be injured or poisoned by it.

• Before you go on your walk, remove all surplus food packaging and put small-portion packages in a single container to minimise waste.

Human Waste Disposal
• If a toilet is provided at a campsite, please use it.
• Where there isn't one, bury your waste. Dig a small hole 15cm deep and at least 30m from any stream, 50m from paths and 200m from any buildings. Take a lightweight trowel or a large

tent peg for the purpose. Cover the waste with a good layer of soil. Toilet paper should be burnt, although this is not recommended in a forest, above the tree line or in dry grassland; otherwise, carry it out – burying is a last resort. Ideally, use biodegradable paper.

• Contamination of water sources by human faeces can lead to the transmission of giardia, a human bacterial parasite.

Camping

• If camping near a farm or house, seek permission first.

• In remote areas, use a recognised site rather than create a new one. Keep at least 30m from watercourses and paths. Move on after a night or two.

• Pitch your tent away from hollows where water is likely to accumulate so that it won't be necessary to dig damaging trenches if it rains heavily.

• Leave your site as you found it – with minimal or no trace of your use.

Washing

• Don't use detergents or toothpaste in or near streams or lakes; even if they are biodegradable they can harm fish and wildlife.

• To wash yourself, use biodegradable soap and a water container at least 50m from the water-

---

National Park Regulations

The following rules and regulations are designed to protect the fragile environment in France's six national parks. Be caught flouting any of these and you may incur a fine.

• No camping, although you can *faire le bivouac* – pitch your tent at dusk (say, 7pm) and strike camp in the early morning and move on before 9am – provided you're more than an hour's walk from a park entrance.

• No motor vehicles.

• No dogs, even on a lead.

• No collection of flowers, insects or rock samples.

• No open fires, although use of gas stoves is permitted.

• No leaving rubbish. Everything, even cigarette butts and fruit peel, should be packed out.

• No mountain bikes.

• No hunting.

• No hang-gliding or parapenting below 1000m.

---

course. Disperse the waste water widely so it filters through the soil before returning to the stream.

• Wash cooking utensils 50m from watercourses using a scourer or gritty sand instead of using detergent.

Fires

• Use a safe existing fireplace rather than make a new one. Don't surround it with rocks – they're just another visual scar – but clear away all flammable material for at least 2m. Keep the fire small (under 1 sq m) and use a minimum of dead, fallen wood.

• Be absolutely certain the fire is extinguished. Spread the embers and drown them with water. Turn the embers over to check the fire is extinguished throughout. Scatter the charcoal and cover the fire site with soil and leaves.

Access

• Many of the walks in this book, along recognised routes, pass through private property (although it may not be obvious at the time) where access is freely permitted. If there seems to be some doubt about this, ask someone nearby if it's OK to walk through.

ACCOMMODATION
Camping

France has in excess of 12,000 *campings* (camping grounds – the term we use). They are each awarded between one and four stars by the Fédération Française de Camping et de Caravanning (FFCC; see Useful Organisations, p48), reflecting the services and facilities available rather than price or friendliness. Some charge by the *emplacement* (pitch or tent site), which covers any sized tent and a car, adding a charge per person.

The cheapest are the *camping municipals* run by the local *commune*; prices are surprisingly low – rarely more than €6 for two people and a tent – and the facilities (showers, hot water) compare favourably with what's provided at privately run grounds. Some places, especially along the coast, are open year-round, others only from around Easter to October, others again for shorter periods. The FFCC's *Le Guide Officiel Camping Caravaning* is a hefty tome but invaluable if you're planning to camp most of the time you're in France; it's widely available in bookshops and Maisons de la Presse. Another useful organisation (see p48), Gîtes de France, publishes a guide to *Camping à la Ferme*, covering fairly basic camping grounds on working farms.

Camping is generally permitted only at designated camping grounds. On long walks in remote areas such as the Pyrenees camping wild – known as *camping sauvage* – is tolerated if you have a lightweight tent and follow the camping code (see Responsible Walking, p41). If you need to pitch your tent on private land within sight of a house, then do the right thing and ask first.

Refuges & Gîtes d'Étape

Refuges are run by private individuals or by organisations, mainly the CAF and Club Vosgien. Most are staffed and usually open from mid-June until mid-September, though the more accessible ones may be open throughout the year. During July and August, in popular areas such as the Pyrenees and the Alps, *refuges* can be booked solid, so reservations well ahead are essential.

Tariffs range from €11 (near a road) to €17 in the high mountains for a bed/mattress and €11 to €14 for a four-course evening meal. Some larger *refuges* have an area for cooking, but it may lack equipment. Meals are communal – they are quite often very lively events with people from all round the world; the three- or four-course menu is set (stew or stew) but it's very satisfying. Drinks are extra; a litre of *vin ordinaire* will set you back €6. Breakfast is spartan – usually thick chunks of bread, jam and butter, and hot milky coffee. Don't expect to find a shower, and running hot water is a luxury. Mattresses are laid out on long platforms in the dormitories; newer *refuges* have bunks in smaller rooms. Blankets are provided but you must bring your own sheet, known in French for some strange reason as a *sac à viande* – meat sack. Lights out at 10pm is the norm in the CAF *refuges* and you may be mercilessly roused at 7am. Especially during the height of summer, you'll have to move on after three nights.

Gîtes d'étape are usually found in villages and small towns, especially along the routes of the *grandes randonnées* (long-distance paths). Most are privately owned and offer greater comfort and privacy than *refuges* – showers are the rule. Basic overnight tariffs range from €12 to €18; some have well-equipped kitchens for guest use. Others provide breakfast and a decent evening meal, for which a per-person *demi-pension* (half board) tariff is charged covering dinner, bed and breakfast (€30 to €40). *Gîtes d'Étape et de Séjour*, published by Gîtes de France (see Useful Organisations, p48), is a useful source of information, though remember that *gîtes de séjour* are popular with school and similar groups. At least as useful is a privately run website, www.gites-refuges.com, which provides free basic information, like name, telephone number and link to website; for full details you have to download a simple programme. Gîtes Panda are excellent, environmentally-friendly establishments in regional natural parks (see p35).

Hostels

The great majority of *auberges de jeunesse* (youth hostels) belong to the Fédération Unie des Auberges de Jeunesse (FUAJ) or the smaller Ligue Français pour les Auberges de Jeunesse (see Useful Organisations, p48); both are affiliated to Hostelling International (HI). In university towns, you may also find *foyers*, student dormitories made available for travellers during the summer vacation.

A bunk in a single-sex dormitory costs from €7.35 to €12.70. You'll need a sheet sleeping bag which can be hired at the hostel for €2.75 per stay. Most *auberges de jeunesse* have kitchens for guest use. If you don't have a HI membership card, or one from the affiliated association in your home country, you can pick up a guest card and buy a Welcome Stamp (€2.90) each night you stay at a hostel; accumulate six stamps and you're a member.

There are also plenty of privately owned hostels, especially in the cities and large towns, which don't have membership requirements, and may be more free and easy, though standards vary hugely – dirty, badly run dives certainly aren't unknown

Chambres d'Hôtes

There are at least 15,000 *chambres d'hôtes* scattered about France, offering bed and breakfast in a room in a private home. Prices vary enormously, from €20 to €65 (or more) for the last word in luxury and pampering. *Chambres d'hôtes* can be a wonderful means to meeting real French people (rather than other travellers) and learning about their country. Gîtes de France (see Useful Organisations, p48) publishes more than 100 guides to accommodation provided by its list of local *chambres d'hôtes*: they are usually available from TICs.

Hotels

Hotel ratings are usually displayed beside the main entrance as a number of stars on a one to four scale. Ratings are based on strictly objective criteria (eg, the size of the entry hall) so a one-star place may turn out more pleasant than two- or three-star establishments. Many tourist offices will help you make hotel reservations, usually for a small fee (€2). Staff often have information about vacancies but it's unlikely you'll persuade them to make recommendations. If you're making your own reservations, many places will ask for your credit-card number by way of confirmation.

Most offer a *petit déjeuner*, a continental or buffet breakfast, for €4.50 to €8 – slightly up on café prices. Some include the cost of breakfast in the tariff, which is quoted by the room, *not* per person. Others may insist on charging for *demi-pension* (half board – dinner, bed and breakfast) during the peak season.

One- and perhaps two-star hotels generally give excellent value for money, especially for couples, and may not be far ahead of the cost of two beds in a hostel. Most rooms have a washbasin but not private shower or toilet. Using the shower in the hall is usually free. More expensive rooms or hotels will almost always have shower, toilet and other amenities. Double rooms, which are marginally more expensive than singles, have double beds (rather than separate twin beds).

At least two hotel chains offer incredibly cheap, no-frills rooms, though they're usually located on town and city fringes – fine if you're travelling by car, but potentially impracticable otherwise. Expect to pay as little as €24 for a basic double and up to €40 for a double room with bathroom. Check **Formule 1** (☎ 08 92 68 56 85; www.hotelformule1.com) or **Etap** (☎ 08 92 68 89 00; www.etaphotel.com).

FOOD

The French have got it right. Eating well is still extremely important and many spend an immense amount of time thinking about food, consuming it and recovering from overindulgence.

French cuisine owes a lot to the variety and freshness of its ingredients. Just about every region in France has its own tempting array of local specialities, thanks to the great diversity of climate and terrain. The infinitely varied regional styles range from those strong on olive oil, garlic and tomatoes in the south, to generous use of butter, cream and apples in the north. In between you can find anything from *truffes* (truffles) in Quercy to *choucroute* in the Vosges, freshwater fish from lakes and rivers, and abundant seafood and saltwater fish along the coast. And then there are 350 varieties of cheese to sample.

Vegetarians are still regarded with curiosity and some bemusement in most parts of France, though the number of restaurants offering at least one specifically vegetarian dish is steadily growing. Especially in *gîtes d'étape* and *refuges* you may have to accept an omelette rather than face bread and salad while everyone else is enjoying a hearty meal. If you're a committed vegan, then self-catering is the only safe option.

For a list of food and menu terms, consult the Language chapter at the end of this book. For a more extensive vocabulary to help you navigate a detailed restaurant menu or go beyond the basics on shopping expeditions, carry Lonely Planet's *French Phrasebook*, or better still, Lonely Planet's

Word Food France for a really informative guide.

Restaurants usually open just for lunch and dinner; brasseries stay open throughout the day. Cafés also keep long hours and most can rustle up at the very least a sandwich, baguette or pastry. Restaurants are obliged by law to display their menus. Most offer at least one fixed-price set menu, which is called simply the *menu* or *menu du jour*, offering either a very limited or no choice for two, three or four courses. Many places also have a *plat du jour* (dish of the day). Opening hours vary from place to place; it's often difficult to find anything other than take-away places open before 7pm.

Even the tiniest village usually has a café or bar serving sandwiches and snacks. Many have a restaurant where the quality of the cooking belies its unassuming appearance. Wherever you are, you'll find restaurants serving good simple food at affordable prices and featuring regional specialities.

On the Walk

On every walk described in this book, you can count on finding at least one place that serves meals at the end of the day. In towns and villages there's usually a choice, even if limited. *Refuges* and most *gîtes d'étape* serve breakfast and evening meals; many *refuges* stay open during the day for snacks and offer a substantial lunch menu.

Buying Food For fresh bread, cakes and pastries, drop into a *boulangerie* (bakery); France has a great array of specialist breads, from light, crusty flutes to solid, doorstopper rye-based breads such as *pain au levain*. To replenish your supplies visit an *alimentation* or *épicerie*, general grocery shops that often sell fruit and vegetables too. Go to a *boucherie* (butcher shop) for meat, a *fromagerie* for cheese. *Charcuteries*, roughly the equivalent of delicatessens, sell cold meats, pâtés and salads.

Nothing can equal an open-air market as a food shopping experience: stalls groaning under piles of locally made cheeses, hams and sausages, olives, pâtés, really fresh fruit

and vegetables – just remember you have to carry it all! Of course you could ignore all this advice and just head for a *supermarché* (supermarket), but it's not as much fun.

There's usually at least one shop at the beginning and end of each walk in this book. For multiday walks, we also indicate places to pick up supplies en route – though don't always expect to find such places, especially when in the Alps and the Pyrenees. For wild camping most major equipment shops (see Buying Locally, p52) sell dehydrated foods. Alternatively, you shouldn't have trouble finding suitable high-energy, lightweight food in even a small one-shop village.

Cooking Most of the *refuges* and some *gîtes d'étape* have a self-caterers' kitchen. If you are camping wild and eat one meal each day in a *refuge*, you could reasonably dispense with a stove and fuel – but at the cost of a steaming mug of tea or coffee first thing in the morning.

DRINKS
Nonalcoholic Drinks

Tap water everywhere is safe to drink, so you don't have to buy plastic bottles of expensive *eau de source*, which comes *plate* (plain) or *gazeuse* (fizzy).

Particularly refreshing on a hot day are a *citron pressé*, a glass of iced water with freshly squeezed lemon juice and sugar, and a *panaché*, a beer and lemonade shandy.

Espresso coffee is invariably excellent. For a small, strong black coffee, ask for *un café noir* or simply *un café*. *Un petit café crème* or *une noisette* is an espresso with a dash of steamed milk or cream. *Un café au lait* is lots of hot milk with a little coffee served in a large cup or bowl, usually ordered only at breakfast.

The French are not great tea drinkers so they don't understand the importance of boiling water in making a decent cuppa. However, if you're still game, ask for an *un infusion* or *une tisane* – herbal tea.

The price of a drink in a café varies – in ascending order – according to whether you're sitting at the bar, at a table or on a terrace outside.

Wines of France

Of the dozens of wine-producing regions throughout France, the eight principal regions are Alsace, the Loire Valley, Bordeaux, Burgundy, Champagne, Beaujolais, Languedoc-Roussillon and the Rhône. Wines in France are named after the area in which they're grown, rather than the grape variety, except in Alsace. Under French law, wines are divided into four categories.

Appellation d'origine contrôlée (AOC) These wines have met stringent government regulations governing where, how and under what conditions they are grown, fermented and bottled. Covering a region, *commune* or village, they are almost always good and may even be superb.

Vin délimité de Qualité Superieure (VDQS) These are good wines from a specific place or region that follows rigorous tests, though stricter criteria for production and tasting apply to AOC wines.

Vin de Pays (Country Wine) Wines with this label are of reasonable quality and are generally drinkable because they do have to meet certain standards. You can recognise them from the word **pays** on the label in front of the region or *département* name (such as Vin de Pays d'Oc).

Vin de Table (Table Wine) Also known as **vin ordinaire**, only two rules govern its production: only real, authorised grapes can be used and the alcoholic content must be between 8.5% and 15%. You can buy litre bottles in supermarkets but don't get carried away and forget that spending an extra euro or three can often make a big difference in quality, drinkability and the severity of your hangover.

Alcoholic Drinks

Wine remains one of France's great glories and walks in this book take in three of its foremost wine-producing regions: Burgundy, Languedoc-Roussillon and Alsace, and some smaller ones – Corsica, Cahors and Moissac on the Chemin de St-Jacques. You can purchase *vin ordinaire* for as little

as €3 or a bottle of something very acceptable for €10 to €15. Whenever you're shopping or in restaurants, don't miss the local vintages.

In bars and cafés beer is served by the *demi* (about 330mL). It's usually cheaper *à pression* (draught) than by the *bouteille* (bottle), which is what you'll be given if you simply as for *une bière*. Expect to pay up to €3 for a *demi* at a modest sort of place.

Mass-produced beers dominate the market, but small independent brewers are producing a wide variety of distinctive brews. Brittany, where the history of brewing goes back a long way, is probably the beer aficionado's paradise. About 15 breweries, all committed to the highest standards, produce a great variety of styles. Names to look out for are Lancelot, Coreff, Britt, Dremwell (whose blonde is the only international prize-winner in France) and Les Diaouligs.

Cidre (cider) is popular in Brittany and in Normandy where it is treated with all the reverence bestowed on wine elsewhere in France. It can be either *doux* (sweet) or *brut* (dry) and, like champagne, comes in corked bottles. Look for *sec* (at least a year old), *pur jus* (no water added), *mousseaux* (naturally carbonated), or *bouché* (fermented in the bottle).

Aperitifs are many and varied. *Pastis* is a refreshing, anise-flavoured drink which turns cloudy when added to water. It's a particular favourite in southern France; well-known brand names are Pernod and Richard. *Kir*, chilled white wine with cassis (sweet blackcurrant syrup), is popular and highly recommended.

On the Walk

Water is by far the best and most readily available thirst-quencher when you are walking. In mountain regions away from areas where livestock graze, it should be safe to drink from flowing springs. Village *fontaines* (fountains) usually have a sign indicating whether the *eau* (water) is *potable* (safe to drink) or *non potable* (not safe). For advice about water purification see p57.

Strikes

France is the only European country in which public workers enjoy an unlimited right to strike and they avail themselves of it with enthusiasm. During 2001, 2002 and again during 2003, *les grèves* (major public transport strikes) paralysed the country; other public sector workers downed tools, lorry drivers stopped driving from time to time, and many ordinary French people despaired of the chaos, confusion and frustration caused. Miraculously, however (in 2003 at least), the strikes stopped as soon as the summer school holidays began – as many cynically predicted they would. The moral: try to leave a couple of days floating in your itinerary, just in case.

WOMEN WALKERS

You'll be extremely unlucky if you strike a problem related specifically to gender when you're out walking; solo women walkers may notice the occasional expression of bemusement but nothing more. Indeed, women are very often in the majority among French groups.

In *refuges*, toilets, washrooms and dormitories are unisex; in the older *refuges* with mattresses on long sleeping platforms, male and female, young and old sleep side by side.

Hitching alone is risky at best and we do not advise it (see Hitching, p349).

WALKING WITH CHILDREN

It's true that walking with your kids is very different from walking as you knew it before they came along. If you can adjust happily to living with children, you'll probably enjoy walking with them.

'Kids – they slow you down', you'll often hear, and that's never truer than when you set out on a walk. There's an age when children go at exactly your pace because you're carrying them all the way (a good backpack built for the purpose is worth its weight in chocolate), but their increasing weight, and a growing determination to get down and do everything for themselves, mean that phase soon passes. Once your first child is too big or too independent for the backpack, you simply have to scale down your expectations of distance and speed.

This is when the fun really starts. No longer another item to be carried – at least, not all the time – a walking child must be factored into your planning at the most basic level. Rather than get partway into a walk and ask yourself in desperation, 'Why are we doing this?', make that the first question you ask. While any walking that is driven by statistics – kilometres covered, peaks bagged – isn't likely to work with kids, other important goals can surface: fun and a sense of something accomplished together, joy in the wonders of the natural world.

Easy and small is a good way to start – you can always try something more difficult next time. Too hard, and what should be fun can become an ordeal for all – especially the child.

Don't overlook time for play. A game of hide and seek during lunch might well be the highlight of your child's day on the track. A few simple toys or a favourite book brought along can make a huge difference. Play can also transform the walking itself: a simple stroll in the bush becomes a bear hunt in an enchanted forest.

For the sake of sanity, or at least increased satisfaction, you may need to plan for some walking *without* children. This is harder to arrange away from home and the regular network of family, friends, babysitters, etc.

Child-minding services are often accessible to travellers, though some parents will feel uncomfortable leaving kids with unfamiliar carers.

There's another alternative: if you're desperate to stretch the legs and enjoy some terrain that's simply beyond you as a family, split up for a few hours. Find a short but suitably challenging walk – maybe a peak close to a town or road, or a side trip – and take turns. Consider whether you could take your walking holiday with another young family. This enlarges the pool of both walkers and carers, and gives the kids company their own age.

Here is a selection of walks in this book most suitable for children:

Paris Region Shortened versions of both walks in Paris and of the Fontainebleau walk
Brittany & Normandy Part or all of both Brittany walks; Côte d'Albâtre walk from Yport
Auvergne & Massif Central First and last parts of Walking Through Chaos
Pyrenees Core section of Les Orgues de Camplong from Refuge de Labérouat to Cabanes du Cap de la Baitch and back; central part of Vallée de Lutour walk to Lac d'Estom and back
Southern Alps Parc National du Mercantour – Lac de Trécolpas

MAPS

France's largest mapping organisation, the Institut Géographique National (IGN) covers the country with numerous excellent maps at various scales. Contact details are given under Buying Maps (right). Most, if not all its maps have French-English keys; for additional help consult the Glossary (p358) and Language (p350) sections in this book.

Small-Scale Maps

A particularly useful, and tantalising, map for walkers is the IGN's 1,000,000 *France Grandes Randonnées* No IM903 (€4.90), which covers the whole country. It's useful for general trip planning and shows all the *sentiers de grande randonnée* (GRs; long-distance routes). On the reverse side a basic map of France shows the coverage of all 1:25,000 maps (see Large-Scale Maps below).

IGN's 1:250,000 Regional series maps the country in 18 sheets (€4.90).

The Top 100 series comprises 74 maps at 1:100,000 (€4.90) with touring information and depicting GR routes. While too small for serious route-finding, they are useful for finding your way about an area by car.

Large-Scale Maps

At 1:25,000 and with a 10m contour interval, two IGN series map the whole of France. The Top 25 maps (€8.99) cover the major tourist areas, the older Série Bleue (Blue Series; €7) everywhere else. Maps in both series provide an impressive amount of information useful

to walkers. With each sheet covering about 22km east to west and 20km north to south, they're fine for day walks (unless of course you start in the corner of one and finish on another), though you will of course need a bundle of them for multiday expeditions.

Both map series have the same four-digit numbering system. Each number has an Est (East) and a Ouest (West) map, which is indicated by the E and O suffixes on Série Bleue maps and ET and OT on Top 25s (eg, 2616O, 3328ET).

Rando Éditions (☎ 05 62 90 09 90; *4 rue Maye Lane, 65421 Ibos*) spans the whole of the French side of the Pyrenees in 11 maps at 1:50,000 with 20m contour interval. The maps contain much useful information, but paths are sometimes more evident on the map than on the ground.

Didier Richard (☎ 04 76 99 20 20; *www .didierrichard.fr; 2 allée de l'Atrium, 38640 Claix*) publishes nearly 30 maps at 1:50,000 for walking areas in the southeastern quarter of the country. They show all the GR routes and are generally reliable.

Buying Maps

In Paris, **Espace IGN** (☎ 01 43 98 80 00; *www .ign.fr; 107 rue de la Boétie; metro George V, line 1; open Mon-Sat*), the IGN's retail outlet, is a mecca for cartophiles. You can also order IGN maps online, though be warned that postal charges for small orders from outside France can exceed the cost of the maps.

In many towns the most likely source for maps, particularly the two 1:25,000 series, is Maison de la Presse, a nationwide chain of newsagents and stationers. The local tourist office, *librairie* (bookshop), small newsagents and even souvenir shops usually also stock maps, though probably only of the surrounding area.

In the UK, **Stanfords** (☎ 020 7836 1321; *www.stanfords.co.uk; 12-14 Long Acre, London WC2E 9LP*) carries a wide range of IGN maps and is able to handle online orders very efficiently.

USEFUL ORGANISATIONS

See also Conservation Organisations (p35) and Organised Walks (p40).

Fédération des Clubs Alpins Français (CAF; ☎ 01 53 72 87 00; www.clubalpin.com; 24 av de Laumière, 75019 Paris)

Fédération Française de Camping et de Caravanning (☎ 01 42 72 84 08; www.campingfrance.com; 78 rue de Rivoli, 75004 Paris)

Fédération Française de la Randonnée Pédestre (FFRP; ☎ 01 44 89 93 93; www.ffrp.asso.fr; Centre d'Information, 14 rue Riquet, 75019 Paris) Open Mon-Sat

Fédération Nationale des Logis de France (☎ 01 45 84 70 00; www.logis-de-france.fr; 83 av d'Italie, 75013 Paris)

Fédération Unie des Auberges de Jeunesse (FUAJ; ☎ 01 48 04 70 30; www.fuaj.org; 9 rue Brantôme, 75003 Paris) Open Tue-Sat

Gîtes de France (☎ 01 49 70 75 75; www.gites-de-france.fr; 59 rue Saint-Lazare, 75009 Paris) Shop open Mon-Sat

Ligue Française pour les Auberges de la Jeunesse (LFAJ; ☎ 01 44 16 78 78, www.auberges-de-jeunesse.com; 67 rue Vergniaud 75013 Paris) Open Mon-Fri

DIGITAL RESOURCES

You can check up-to-date travel advice, obtain some basic background information and chat with other travellers via the Thorn Tree on Lonely Planet's own website at www.lonelyplanet.com.au.

The websites of both the FFRP (www.ffr.asso.fr) and the CAF (www.clubalpin.org) have dozens of links to other sources for useful information.

BOOKS
Lonely Planet

Lonely Planet has France covered, with countrywide *France*, and its invaluable companions *French Phrasebook* and the richly informative *World Food France*. If you'd like to vary your means of exploring the country, *Cycling France* has loads of ideas. The capital is covered by the full-scale *Paris* and *Best of Paris*. The several regional guides are noted in the relevant walks chapters.

Natural History

The French coast, and to a lesser extent the Pyrenees and Southern Alps, are good for bird-watching. *A Field Guide to the Birds of Britain and Europe*, by Roger Peterson and others, and the superbly illustrated *Birds of Europe* by Lars Jonsson are worth their weight.

Flowers of South-West Europe: A Field Guide by Oleg Polunin & BE Smythies is an excellent guide. Compendious and reliable, *Mediterranean Wild Flowers* and *Alpine Flowers of Britain & Europe*, both by Marjorie Blamey and Christopher Grey Wilson, are excellent references though a bit weighty for field use.

In French, *Les Animaux de Nos Forêts* (Animals of our Forests) published by the Organisation National des Forêts (ONF) is a good general – if rather didactic – introduction to the fauna of the forest. Other useful ONF publications include *Les Arbres de Nos Forêts* (Trees of our Forests) and *La Vie de la Forêt* (Life in the Forest) that explore the forest ecosystem. If you're comfortable with French, the conveniently pocket-sized *Nature-Poche* series, including *Fleurs Sauvages* (Wildflowers), *Arbres* (Trees) and *Plantes Médicinales* (Medicinal Plants), are worth hunting for.

Buying Books

Every self-respecting town and most larger villages in France have at least one good bookshop. Branches of Maison de la Presse, the nationwide chain of newsagents, usually carry a wide range of natural and general history titles.

MAGAZINES

Few French outdoor magazines are easy to find on the newsagents' shelves. *Alpinisme et Randonnée* contains lots of route descriptions and natural history articles, but little on conservation issues affecting walkers. *Montagnes* focuses, of course, on the mountains. The journals published by the CAF and FFRP for their members can usually be found among the stacks of magazines in *refuges* and *gîtes*, and make very interesting reading.

WEATHER INFORMATION

Meteo France provides a host of useful forecasting and information services. From

Taking Photos Outdoors

For walkers, photography can be a vexed issue – all that magnificent scenery but such weight and space restrictions on what photographic equipment you can carry. With a little care and planning it is possible to maximise your chance of taking great photos on the trail.

Light & Filters In fine weather, the best light is early and late in the day. In strong sunlight and in mountain and coastal areas where the light is intense, a polarising filter will improve colour saturation and reduce haze. On overcast days the soft light can be great for shooting wildflowers and running water and an 81A warming filter can be useful. If you use slide film, a graduated filter will help balance unevenly lit landscapes.

Equipment If you need to travel light carry a zoom in the 28mm to 70mm range, and if your sole purpose is to photograph landscapes consider carrying just a single wide-angle lens (24mm). A tripod is essential to capture really good images and there are some excellent lightweight models available. Otherwise a trekking pole, pack or even a pile of rocks can be used to improvise.

Camera Care Keep your gear dry – a few zip-lock freezer bags can be used to double wrap camera gear and silica-gel sachets (a drying agent) can be used to suck moisture out of equipment. Sturdy cameras will normally work fine in freezing conditions. Take care when bringing a camera from one temperature extreme to another; if moisture condenses on the camera parts make sure it dries thoroughly before going back into the cold, or mechanisms can freeze up. Standard camera batteries fail very quickly in the cold. Remove them from the camera when it's not in use and keep them under your clothing.

For a thorough grounding on photography on the road, read Lonely Planet's *Travel Photography*, by Richard I'Anson, a full-colour guide for happy-snappers and professional photographers alike. Also highly recommended is the outdoor photography classic *Mountain Light*, by Galen Rowell.

Gareth McCormack

its website www.meteo.fr you can check the forecast for the next three days *département* by *département*; you can find out what conditions are like in the mountains – snow depth, temperature, hazards – at a few stations in the Alps. Alternatively you can call ☎ 32 50 and select *Choix 4* – choice No 4 – for mountain forecasts (updated three times daily) up to a week ahead, followed by the *département* number; leave out the 4 if you're in the lowlands. Calls cost €0.34 per minute.

On your mobile, dial ☎ 711 (Orange, cost included in billing arrangements), ☎ 866 (Bouygues – €0.30 per minute) or ☎ METE (SFR) to check on the weather forecast.

PHOTOGRAPHY

Costs of film and of processing vary between cities and towns and between individual shops. For ISO 100 print film expect the cost to be about €7 (36 exposures) and €13 for developing, and for ISO 100 slide film (36 exposures) €16 plus €5 for processing.

Clothing & Equipment

CLOTHING
Layering

A secret of comfortable walking is to wear several layers of light clothing, which you can easily take off or put on as you warm up or cool down. Most walkers use three main layers: a base layer next to the skin; an insulating layer; and an outer, shell layer for protection from wind, rain and snow.

For the upper body, the base layer is typically a shirt of synthetic material such as polypropylene, with its ability to wick moisture away from the body and reduce chilling. The insulating layer retains heat next to your body, and is often a windproof synthetic fleece or down jacket. The outer shell consists of a waterproof jacket that also protects against cold wind.

For the lower body, the layers generally consist of either shorts or loose-fitting trousers, polypropylene 'long-john' underwear and waterproof overtrousers.

Footwear

Runners (training shoes) are quite adequate for the walks described in this book graded easy and easy–moderate. You'll appreciate, if not need, the support and protection provided by boots for the more challenging walks.

Head Protection

The importance of wearing a hat with a wide, all-round brim on sunny days can't be overemphasised. It will help to stop you overheating and will guard against painful sunburn – especially if your hair isn't as thick on top as it once was!

EQUIPMENT
Inner Sheet

A sleeping bag inner sheet (usually called a *sac à viande* – meat sack, in French) is mandatory in *refuges* and almost always required in *gîtes d'étape* and hostels; the latter places often have sheets for hire at a nominal charge. Silk is the ideal, if rather expensive, material – a one-person sheet compresses to the size of a tennis ball and weighs no more than 200g.

Walking Poles

Poles can help to ease the jarring during descents, provide stability when crossing flooded streams and traversing the snow-covered slopes. However, they are *not* a substitute for an ice axe and, perhaps, crampons if the snow is hard, let alone icy.

Fuel

By far the easiest type of fuel to use is butane gas in disposable canisters – not the most environmentally friendly, true, but it's much easier to come by than liquid fuels. *Campingaz* (in blue containers) and Coleman gas are two of the most widely available brands, from sports & outdoor shops and those selling fishing and hunting gear. Expect to pay about €5 for a 500mL container.

Liquid fuel includes methylated spirits *(alcool à brûler* or *alcool dénature),* kerosene *(kerosène)* and white spirit or Shellite *(essence blanche).* For supplies, try hardware shops *(droguerie)* or ironmongers *(quincaillerie)* or a do-it-yourself (DIY) place – *bricolage.*

Airlines, and possibly also the Eurostar authorities (the London–Paris train), absolutely prohibit the carriage of gas canisters and may well reject empty liquid fuel bottles or even the stoves themselves.

Buying Locally

In Paris, **Au Vieux Campeur** (☎ 01 53 10 48 48; www.au-vieux-campeur.fr - French only) is a sprawling collection of 20 specialist shops between rue des Écoles and blvd St-Germain (metro Maubert Mutualité or Cluny-La Sorbonne, line 10) where you'll find every conceivable item of clothing and equipment. In general they open from 10am or 11am and close at 7.30pm or 9pm. This retailing marvel has a few provincial branches:

Lyon *(Cours de la Liberté - four shops • 3 rue Mortier - one)*
Sallanches *(☎ 04 50 91 26 62; 893 & 925 route du Fayet)* About 20km west of Chamonix
Toulouse *(☎ 05 62 88 27 27; Parc Commercial, rue de Sienne, route la Pyrénéenne)*

For a more personal and probably better informed service in Paris, try **La Haute Route** *(☎ 01 42 72 38 43; 33 blvd Henri IV; metro Bastille, lines 1, 8,10).*

Décathlon *(☎ 08 10 08 08 08; www .decathlon.com)* is a nationwide chain of shops that sells sports and outdoor equipment, including footwear, packs, sleeping bags and mats, and gas canisters. Its stuff will generally make a smaller hole in your wallet than shopping in Au Vieux Campeur, for example, with little compromise on quality or durability. Of the five branches in Paris, the most central is at 17 blvd Madeleine

Buying Tips

Backpack
For day walks, a day-pack (30L to 40L) will usually suffice, but for multiday walks you will need a backpack of between 45L and 90L capacity. A good backpack should be made of strong fabric such as canvas or Cordura, with a lightweight internal or external frame and an adjustable, well-padded harness that evenly distributes weight. Even if the manufacturer claims your pack is waterproof, use heavy-duty liners.

Footwear
Runners or walking shoes are fine over easy terrain but, for more difficult trails and across rocks and scree, the ankle support offered by boots is invaluable. Nonslip soles (such as Vibram) provide the best grip.

Buy boots in warm conditions or go for a walk before trying them on, so that your feet can expand slightly, as they would on a walk.

Most walkers carry a pair of sandals or thongs (flip flops) to wear at night or rest stops. Sandals are also useful when fording waterways.

Gaiters
If you will be walking through snow, deep mud or scratchy vegetation, gaiters will protect your legs and help keep your socks dry. The best are made of strong fabric, with a robust zip protected by a flap, and secure easily around the foot.

Overtrousers
Choose a model with slits for pocket access and long leg zips so that you can pull them on and off over your boots.

Sleeping Bag & Mat
Down fillings are warmer than synthetic for the same weight and bulk but, unlike synthetic fillings, do not retain warmth when wet. Mummy bags are the best shape for weight and warmth. The given figure (-5°C, for instance) is the coldest temperature at which a person should feel comfortable in the bag (although the ratings are notoriously unreliable)

An inner sheet helps keep your sleeping bag clean, as well as adding an insulating layer. Silk 'inners' are lightest, but they also come in cotton or polypropylene.

Self-inflating sleeping mats work like a thin air cushion between you and the ground; they also insulate from the cold. Foam mats are a low-cost, but less comfortable, alternative.

Socks
Walking socks should be free of ridged seams in the toes and heels.

Stoves
Fuel stoves fall roughly into three categories: multifuel, methylated spirits (ethyl alcohol) and butane gas. Multifuel stoves are small, efficient and ideal for places where a reliable fuel supply is difficult to find. However, they tend to be sooty and require frequent maintenance. Stoves running on methylated spirits are slower and less efficient, but are safe, clean and easy to use. Butane gas stoves are clean and reliable, but can be slow, and the gas canisters can be awkward to carry and a potential litter problem.

Tent
A three-season tent will fulfil the requirements of most walkers. The floor and the outer shell, or fly, should have taped or sealed seams and covered zips to stop leaks. Most walkers find tents of around 2kg to 3kg a comfortable carrying weight. Dome- and tunnel-shaped tents handle windy conditions better than flat-sided tents.

Waterproof Jacket
The ideal specifications are a breathable, waterproof fabric, a hood that is roomy enough to cover headwear but still allows peripheral vision, capacious map pocket, and a heavy-gauge zip protected by a storm flap.

(metro Madeleine, lines 8, 12 and 14) – complete with café. Among the dozens of provincial branches are those in Arles, Avranches, Brest, Grenoble, Lannion, Nice, Quimper and Toulouse. Details of other individual outlets are given where available in the Nearest Towns sections of the walks chapters.

NAVIGATION EQUIPMENT
Maps & Compass

You should always carry a good map of the area you are walking in (see p48), and know how to read it. Before setting off on your trek, ensure that you understand the contours and the map symbols, plus the main ridge and river systems in the area. Also familiarise yourself with the true north–south directions and the general direction in which you are heading. On the trail, try to identify major landforms, such as mountain ranges and gorges, and locate them on your map. This will give you a better understanding of the region's geography.

Buy a compass and learn how to use it. The attraction of magnetic north varies in different parts of the world, so compasses need to be balanced accordingly. Compass manufacturers have divided the world into five zones. Make sure your compass is balanced for your destination zone. There are also 'universal' compasses on the market that can be used anywhere in the world.

How to Use a Compass

This is a very basic introduction to using a compass and will only be of assistance if you are proficient in map reading. For simplicity, it doesn't take magnetic variation into account. Before using a compass we recommend you obtain further instruction.

1. Reading a Compass

Hold the compass flat in the palm of your hand. Rotate the **bezel** so the **red end** of the **needle** points to the **N** on the bezel. The bearing is read from the **dash** under the bezel.

2. Orientating the Map

To orientate the map so that it aligns with the ground, place the compass flat on the map. Rotate the map until the **needle** is parallel with the map's north/south grid lines and the red end is pointing to north on the map. You can now identify features around you by aligning them with labelled features on the map.

1	Base plate
2	Direction of travel arrow
3	Dash
4	Bezel
5	Meridian lines
6	Needle
7	Red end
8	N (north point)

3. Taking a Bearing from the Map

Draw a line on the map between your starting point and your destination. Place the edge of the compass on this line with the **direction of travel arrow** pointing towards your destination. Rotate the **bezel** until the **meridian lines** are parallel with the north/south grid lines on the map and the N points to north on the map. Read the bearing from the dash.

4. Following a Bearing

Rotate the **bezel** so that the intended bearing is in line with the **dash**. Place the compass flat in the palm of your hand and rotate the **base plate** until the **red end** points to N on the bezel. The **direction of travel arrow** will now point in the direction you need to walk.

5. Determining Your Bearing

Rotate the **bezel** so the **red end** points to the **N**. Place the compass flat in the palm of your hand and rotate the **base plate** until the **direction of**

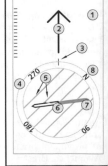

travel arrow points in the direction in which you have been walking. Read your bearing from the **dash**.

GPS

Originally developed by the US Department of Defense, the Global Positioning System (GPS) is a network of more than 20 earth-orbiting satellites that continually beam encoded signals back to earth. Small, computer-driven devices (GPS receivers) can decode these signals to give users an extremely accurate reading of their location – to within 30m, anywhere on the planet, at any time of day, in almost any weather. The cheapest hand-held GPS receivers now cost less than US$100 (although these may not have a built-in averaging system that minimises signal errors). Other important factors to consider when buying a GPS receiver are its weight and battery life.

Remember that a GPS receiver is of little use to walkers unless used with an accurate topographical map. The receiver simply gives your position, which you must then locate on the local map. GPS receivers will only work properly in the open. The signals from a crucial satellite may be blocked (or bounce off rock or water) directly below high cliffs, near large bodies of water or in dense tree cover and give inaccurate readings. GPS receivers are more vulnerable to breakdowns (including dead batteries) than the humble magnetic compass – a low-tech device that has served navigators faithfully for centuries – so don't rely on them entirely.

Altimeter

Altimeters determine altitude by measuring air pressure. Because pressure is affected by temperature, altimeters are calibrated to take lower temperatures at higher altitudes into account. However, discrepancies can still occur, especially in unsettled weather, so it's wise to take a few precautions when using your altimeter.

1. Reset your altimeter regularly at known elevations such as spot heights and passes. Do not take spot heights from villages where there may be a large difference in elevation from one end of the settlement to another.

2. Use your altimeter in conjunction with other navigation techniques to fix your position. For instance, taking a back bearing to a known peak or river confluence, determining the general direction of the track and obtaining your elevation will usually give you a pretty good fix on your position.

Altimeters are also barometers and are useful for indicating changing weather conditions. If the altimeter shows increasing elevation while you are not climbing, it means the air pressure is dropping and a low-pressure weather system may be approaching.

Health & Safety

Keeping healthy on the trail depends on predeparture preparations, daily health care while travelling and how you handle any medical problems that develop. While the potential problems can seem quite frightening, in reality few travellers experience anything more than an upset stomach. The sections that follow aren't intended to alarm, but they are worth reading before you go.

PREDEPARTURE PLANNING
Medical Cover

Citizens of European Union countries are covered for emergency medical care upon presentation of an E111 form, which you need to get before you travel. In Britain, you can pick forms up free at a post office. In other EU countries, obtain information from your doctor or local health service.

Although the form will entitle you to free treatment in government clinics and hospitals, you will have to pay for dental treatment, any medicines bought from pharmacies, even if a doctor has prescribed them, and also possibly for tests. Once home, you may be able to recover some or all of these costs from your national health service.

Health Insurance

Make sure you have adequate health insurance. See Travel Insurance (p340).

Physical Preparation

Some of the walks in this book are physically demanding and most require a reasonable level of fitness. Even if you're tackling the easy or easy–moderate walks, it pays to be relatively fit. If you're aiming for the demanding walks, fitness is essential.

Unless you're a regular walker, start your get-fit campaign at least a month before your visit. Take a vigorous walk of about an hour, two or three times per week, and gradually extend the duration of your outings as the departure date nears. If you plan to carry a full backpack on any walk, carry a loaded pack on some of your training jaunts.

First-Aid Check List

Following is a list of items you should consider including in your first-aid kit – consult your pharmacist for brands available in your country.

Essentials
- [ ] **adhesive tape**
- [ ] **bandages** and **safety pins**
- [ ] **elasticated support bandage** – for knees, ankles etc
- [ ] **scissors** (small)
- [ ] **sticking plasters** (Band-Aids, blister plasters)
- [ ] **tweezers**

Medications
- [ ] **antidiarrhoea drugs**
- [ ] **antifungal cream** or **powder** – for fungal skin infections and thrush
- [ ] **antihistamines** – for allergies, eg, hay fever; to ease the itch from insect bites or stings; and to prevent motion sickness
- [ ] **antinausea drugs**
- [ ] **antiseptic** (such as povidone-iodine) – for cuts and grazes
- [ ] **cold and flu tablets**, **throat lozenges** and **nasal decongestant**
- [ ] **painkillers**, eg, aspirin or paracetamol (acetaminophen in the USA) – for pain and fever

Miscellaneous
- [ ] **calamine lotion**, **sting-relief spray** or **aloe vera** – to ease irritation from sun burn and insect bites or stings.
- [ ] **eye drops** – for washing out dust
- [ ] **multivitamins** – consider for long trips, when dietary vitamin intake may be inadequate
- [ ] **rehydration mixture** – to prevent dehydration, eg, due to severe diarrhoea; particularly important when travelling with children

Immunisations

No immunisations are required for France, but before any trip it's a good idea to make sure you are up to date with routine vaccinations such as diphtheria, polio and tetanus.

First Aid

Although detailed first-aid instruction is outside the scope of this guidebook, some basic points are listed under Traumatic Injuries (p60). Prevention of accidents and illness is as important – read Safety on the Walk (p61) for more advice. You should also know how to summon help should a major accident or illness befall you or someone with you – see Rescue & Evacuation (p62).

Other Preparations

If you have any known medical problems or are concerned about your health in any way, it's a good idea to have a full check-up before you go. It's better to have any problems recognised and treated at home than to find out about them halfway up a mountain. It's also sensible to have had a recent dental check-up since toothache on the trail, with solace a couple of days away, can be a miserable experience. If you wear glasses, take a spare pair and your prescription.

If you need a particular medicine, take enough with you to last the trip. Take part of the packaging showing the generic name, rather than the brand, as this will make getting replacements easier. It's also a good idea to have a legible prescription or letter from your doctor to prove that you legally use the medication to avoid problems at customs.

Travel Health Guides

Specialised travel health guides aren't necessary for walking in France, but *Travel with Children* from Lonely Planet does include advice on travel health for younger children.

Digital Resources

There are some excellent travel health sites on the Internet. The health page of the Lonely Planet website at www.lonelyplanet.com /health has extensive travel health information, with links to many other useful sites.

STAYING HEALTHY
Hygiene

To reduce the chances of contracting an illness, you should wash your hands frequently, particularly before handling or eating food.

Water

Tap water in France is generally safe to drink, as is the water from village fountains, indicated by a sign *'eau potable'* (drinkable water), although you may find some with a notice indicating quite the opposite: *'eau non potable'*.

Always beware of natural water sources. A mountain stream may be crystal clear, but if it's in an area where animals graze, resist the temptation unless you're at the source or can see it bubbling from a spring.

Water Purification The simplest way of purifying water is to boil it thoroughly. If you cannot boil water you can use a chemical agent to purify water. Chlorine and iodine are usually used, in powder, tablet or liquid form, available from outdoor equipment suppliers and pharmacies. Follow the recommended dosages and allow the water to stand for the correct length of time. Chlorine tablets will kill many pathogens, but not some parasites like giardia and amoebic cysts. Iodine is more effective in purifying water. Follow the directions carefully and remember that too much iodine can be harmful.

Food

The stringent food hygiene regulations imposed by the EU are in force in France, so you can be confident that the food you eat in restaurants is safe.

Common Ailments

Blisters This problem can be avoided. Be sure your walking boots or shoes are well worn in before your visit. At the very least, wear them on a few short walks before tackling longer outings. Your boots should fit comfortably with enough room to move your toes; boots that are too big or too small will cause blisters. Similarly for socks – be sure they fit properly and are specifically made for walkers; even then, check that there are no seams across the widest part of your foot. Wet and muddy socks can also cause blisters, so even on a day walk, pack a spare pair. Keep toenails clipped but not too short. If you do feel a blister coming on, treat it sooner rather then later. Apply a simple sticking plaster, or preferably one of the special blister plasters that act as a second skin.

Fatigue A simple statistic: more injuries happen towards the end of the day than earlier, when you're fresher. Although tiredness can simply be a nuisance on an easy walk, it can be life-threatening on narrow exposed ridges or in bad weather. You should never set out on a walk that is beyond your capabilities on the day. If you feel below par, have a day off or take a bus. To reduce the risk, don't push yourself too hard – take a rest every hour or so and build in at least a half-hour's lunch break. Towards the end of the day, take down the pace and increase your concentration. You should also eat properly throughout the day, to replace the energy used up. Nuts, dried fruit and chocolate are good energy-giving snack foods.

Knee Strain Many walkers feel the judder on long steep descents. While you can't eliminate all strain on the knee joints when dropping steeply. Reduce it by taking shorter steps, which leaves your legs slightly bent, and ensure your heel hits the ground before the rest of your foot. Some walkers find tubular bandages help, while others use hi-tech, strap-on supports. Walking poles are effective in taking some of the weight.

Warning

Self-diagnosis and treatment can be risky, so you should always seek medical help. The tourist office can usually recommend a local doctor or clinic. Although we do give drug advice in this section, it is for emergency use only. Correct diagnosis is vital.

Note that we have used generic rather than brand names for drugs throughout this section – check with a pharmacist for locally available brands.

MEDICAL PROBLEMS & TREATMENT
Environmental Hazards

Altitude Lack of oxygen at high altitudes (over 2500m) affects most people to some extent. The effect may be mild or severe and occurs because the air pressure is reduced, and the heart and lungs must work harder to oxygenate the body. Although the likelihood of suffering any significant effects on walks described in this book is very slight, it's still worth taking a couple of days to accustom yourself to altitudes above 2500m if planning to cross the higher passes in the Alps or the Pyrenees.

Sun Protection against the sun should be taken seriously. Particularly in the rarefied air and deceptive coolness of the mountains, sunburn occurs rapidly. Slap on the sunscreen and a barrier cream for your nose and lips, wear a broad-brimmed hat and protect your eyes with good-quality sunglasses with UV lenses, particularly when walking near water, sand or snow. If, despite these precautions, you get yourself burnt, calamine lotion, aloe vera or other commercial sunburn-relief preparations will soothe.

Heat Take time to acclimatise to high temperatures, drink sufficient liquids and do not do anything too physically demanding until you are acclimatised.

Dehydration & Heat Exhaustion Dehydration is a potentially dangerous and generally preventable condition caused by excessive fluid loss. Sweating, combined with inadequate fluid intake, is one of the commonest causes of dehydration in walkers, but other important causes are diarrhoea, vomiting, and high fever – see Diarrhoea (opposite) for more details about appropriate treatment in these circumstances.

The first symptoms are weakness, thirst and passing small amounts of very concentrated urine. This may progress to drowsiness, dizziness or fainting on standing up and, finally, coma.

It's easy to forget how much fluid you are losing via perspiration while you are

Everyday Health

Normal body temperature is up to 37°C (98.6°F); more than 2°C (4°F) higher indicates a high fever. The normal adult pulse rate is 60 to 100 per minute (children 80 to 100, babies 100 to 140). As a general rule the pulse increases about 20 beats per minute for each 1°C (2°F) rise in fever.

Respiration (breathing) rate is also an indicator of illness. Count the number of breaths per minute: between 12 and 20 is normal for adults and older children (up to 30 for younger children, 40 for babies). People with a high fever or serious respiratory illness breathe more quickly than normal. More than 40 shallow breaths a minute may indicate pneumonia.

walking, particularly if a strong breeze is drying your skin quickly. You should always maintain a good fluid intake – a minimum of 3L a day is recommended.

Dehydration and salt deficiency can cause heat exhaustion. Salt deficiency is characterised by fatigue, lethargy, headaches, giddiness and muscle cramps. Salt tablets are overkill; just adding extra salt to your food is probably sufficient.

Cold Too much cold can be just as dangerous as too much heat.

Hypothermia This occurs when the body loses heat faster than it can produce it and the core temperature of the body falls.

It is frighteningly easy to progress from very cold to dangerously cold due to a combination of wind, wet clothing, fatigue and hunger, even if the air temperature is above freezing. If the weather deteriorates, put on extra layers of warm clothing: a wind and/or waterproof jacket plus wool or fleece hat and gloves are all essential. Have something energy-giving to eat and ensure that everyone in your group is fit, feeling well and alert.

Symptoms of hypothermia are exhaustion, numb skin (particularly toes and fingers), shivering, slurred speech, irrational or violent behaviour, lethargy, stumbling, dizzy

spells, muscle cramps and violent bursts of energy. Irrationality may take the form of sufferers claiming they are warm and trying to take off their clothes.

To treat mild hypothermia, first get the person out of the wind and/or rain, remove their clothing if it's wet and replace it with dry, warm clothing. Give them hot liquids – not alcohol – and some high-energy, easily digestible food. Do not rub victims; instead, allow them to slowly warm themselves.

Infectious Diseases

Diarrhoea Simple things like a change of water, food or climate can all cause a mild bout of diarrhoea, but a few rushed toilet trips with no other symptoms are not indicative of a major problem. Paying particular attention to personal hygiene, drinking purified water and taking care of what you eat should avoid getting diarrhoea.

Dehydration is the main danger, so *fluid replacement* (at least equal to the volume being lost) is the most important thing to remember. Weak black tea with a little sugar, soda water, or soft drinks allowed to go flat and diluted 50% with clean water are all good. With severe diarrhoea, oral rehydration salts (ORS) are very useful. In an emergency you can make up a solution of six teaspoons of sugar and half a teaspoon of salt to a litre of boiled or bottled water. Urine is the best guide to the adequacy of replacement – if you have small amounts of concentrated urine, you need to drink more. Keep drinking small amounts often. Stick to a bland diet as you recover.

Gut-paralysing drugs such as diphenoxylate or loperamide can be used to bring relief from the symptoms, although they don't cure the problem. Only use these drugs if you do not have access to toilets, eg, if you *must* travel. These drugs are not recommended for children under 12 years, or if you have a high fever or are severely dehydrated.

Seek medical advice if you pass blood or mucus, are feverish, or suffer persistent or severe diarrhoea.

Fungal Infections Sweating liberally, probably washing less frequently than usual and going longer without a change of clothes mean that long-distance walkers risk picking up a fungal infection, which, while an unpleasant irritant, presents no danger.

Fungal infections are encouraged by moisture, so wear loose and comfortable clothes, wash when you can and dry yourself thoroughly. Try to expose the infected area to air or sunlight as much as possible and apply an antifungal cream or powder like tolnaftate.

Insect-Borne Diseases

Lyme Disease This is a tick-transmitted infection (see Ticks, opposite). The illness begins with a spreading rash at the site of the tick bite and is accompanied by fever, headache, extreme fatigue, aching joints and muscles and mild neck stiffness. If untreated, symptoms usually resolve over several weeks but over subsequent weeks or months disorders of the nervous system, heart and joints may develop. Treatment works best early in the illness. Medical help should be sought.

Traumatic Injuries

Sprains Ankle and knee sprains are common injuries among hikers, particularly when crossing rugged terrain. To help prevent ankle sprains, wear boots that have adequate ankle support. If you do suffer a sprain, immobilise the joint with a firm bandage, and, if feasible, immerse the foot in cold water. Distribute the contents of your pack among your companions. Once you reach shelter, relieve pain and swelling by keeping the joint elevated for the first 24 hours and, where possible, by putting ice on the swollen joint. Take simple painkillers to ease the discomfort. If the sprain is mild, you may be able to continue your walk after a couple of days. For more severe sprains, seek medical attention.

Major Accidents Falling or having something fall on you, resulting in head injuries or fractures, is always possible when walking, especially if you are crossing steep slopes or unstable terrain. Following is some basic advice on what to do in the event of a major accident. If a person suffers a major fall:

1. make sure you and other people with you are not in danger
2. assess the injured person's condition
3. stabilise any injuries, such as bleeding wounds or broken bones
4. seek medical attention – see Emergency Communications (p62) for details

If the person is unconscious, immediately check whether they are breathing – clear their airway if it is blocked – and check whether they have a pulse – feel the side of the neck rather than the wrist. If they are not breathing but have a pulse, you should start mouth-to-mouth resuscitation immediately. In these circumstances it is best to move the person as little as possible in case their neck or back is broken.

Check for wounds and broken bones – ask the person where they have pain if they are conscious, otherwise gently inspect them all over (including their back and the back of the head), moving them as little as possible. Control any bleeding by applying firm pressure to the wound. Bleeding from the nose or ear may indicate a fractured skull. Don't give the person anything by mouth, especially if they are unconscious.

You'll have to manage the person for shock. Raise their legs above heart level (unless their legs are fractured); dress any wounds and immobilise any fractures; loosen tight clothing; keep the person warm by covering them with a blanket or other dry clothing; insulate them from the ground if possible, but don't heat them. Some general points to bear in mind are:

• Simple fractures take several weeks to heal, so they don't need fixing straight away, but should be immobilised to protect them from further injury. Compound fractures need urgent treatment.
• If you do have to splint a broken bone, check regularly that the splint is not cutting off the circulation to the hand or foot.
• Most cases of brief unconsciousness are not associated with any serious internal injury to the brain, but as a general rule of thumb in these circumstances, any person who has been knocked unconscious should be watched for deterioration. If they do deteriorate, seek medical attention straight away.

Cuts & Scratches
Even small cuts and grazes should be washed well and treated with an antiseptic such as povidone-iodine. Dry wounds heal more quickly, so where possible avoid bandages and Band-Aids, which can keep wounds wet. Infection in a wound is indicated by the skin margins becoming red, painful and swollen. More serious infection can cause swelling of the whole limb and of the lymph glands. The patient may develop a fever, and will need medical attention.

Burns
Immerse the burnt area in cold water as soon as possible, then cover it with a clean, dry, sterile dressing. Keep this in place with plasters for a day or so in the case of a small mild burn, longer for more extensive injuries. Seek medical help for severe and extensive burns.

Bites & Stings
Bees & Wasps These are usually painful rather than dangerous. However, in people who are allergic to them severe breathing difficulties may occur and urgent medical care is required. Calamine lotion or a commercial sting relief spray will ease discomfort and ice packs will reduce the pain and swelling.

Snakes You are unlikely to encounter a snake during the walks described in this book. However, to minimise your chances of being bitten always wear boots, socks and long trousers when walking through undergrowth where snakes may be present. Don't put your hands into holes and crevices. If bitten, immediately wrap the bitten limb tightly, as you would for a sprained ankle, and then attach a splint to immobilise it. Keep the victim still and seek medical help; it will help if you can describe the offending reptile. Tourniquets and sucking out the poison are now discredited.

Ticks Always check all over your body if you have been walking through a potentially tick-infested area as ticks can cause skin infections and more serious diseases (see Lyme Disease, opposite). Ticks are most active from spring to autumn, and especially where there are plenty of sheep or deer. They usually lurk in overhanging vegetation, so avoid pushing through tall bushes if possible.

If a tick attached to the skin, press down around its head with tweezers, grab the head and gently pull upwards. Avoid pulling the rear of the body as this may squeeze the tick's gut contents through its mouth into your skin, increasing the risk of infection and disease. Smearing chemicals on the tick will not make it let go and is not recommended.

Hay Fever
If you suffer from hay fever, and will be walking in lowland areas during June or July, bring your usual treatment.

SAFETY ON THE WALK
You can significantly reduce the chance of getting into difficulties by taking a few simple precautions. These are listed in the boxed text on p62.

Crossing Rivers
Sudden downpours are common in the mountains and can speedily turn a gentle stream into a raging torrent. If you're in any doubt about the safety of a crossing, look for a safer passage upstream or wait. If the rain is short-lived, it should subside quickly.

If you decide it's essential to cross (late in the day, for example), look for a wide, relatively shallow stretch of the stream rather than a bend. Take off your trousers and socks, but keep your boots on to prevent injury. Put dry, warm clothes and a towel in a plastic bag near the top of your pack. Before leaving the bank, unclip your chest strap and belt buckle. This makes it easier to slip out of your backpack and swim to safety if you lose your balance and are swept downstream. Use a walking pole, grasped in both hands, on the upstream side as a third leg, or go arm in arm with a companion, clasping at the wrist, and cross side-on to the flow, taking short steps.

Dogs
Any dog you meet is a potential attacker. Be prepared to take evasive action; even

Walk Safety – Basic Rules

- Allow plenty of time to finish a walk before dark, particularly when daylight hours are short.
- Study the route carefully before setting out, noting possible escape routes and the point of no return (where it's quicker to continue than to turn back). Monitor your progress during the day against the time estimated for the walk, and keep an eye on the weather.
- It's wise not to walk alone. Always give the details of your intended route, number of people in your group, and expected return time to someone responsible before you set off; let that person know when you return.
- Before setting off, make sure you have a relevant map, compass and whistle, and that you know the weather forecast for the area for the next 24 hours.

just crossing the road can take you out of its territory and to safety. A walking pole may be useful, though use it as a last resort.

Lightning

If a storm brews, avoid exposed areas. Lightning has a penchant for crests, lone trees, small depressions, gullies, caves and cabin entrances, as well as wet ground. If you are caught out in the open, try to curl up as tightly as possible with your feet together and keep a layer of insulation between you and the ground. Place metal objects such as metal-frame backpacks and walking poles away from you.

Rescue & Evacuation

If someone in your group is injured or falls ill and can't move, leave somebody with them while another one or more goes for help. They should take clear written details of the location and condition of the victim, and of helicopter landing conditions. If there are only two of you, leave the injured person with as much warm clothing, food and water as it's sensible to spare, plus the whistle and torch. Mark the position with something

conspicuous – an orange bivvy bag, or perhaps a large stone cross on the ground.

Emergency Communications Call ☎ 112 (toll free) from anywhere in France for any of the emergency services. In some areas it is possible to contact the local service direct; appropriate numbers are given in individual walks sections.

Be ready to give information on where an accident occurred, how many people are injured and injuries sustained. If a helicopter needs to come in, what are the terrain and weather conditions at the accident site?

Telephone Outside the Alps and the Pyrenees, mobile-phone reception is virtually guaranteed throughout France. Within the mountains, reception is patchy at best and often nonexistent.

Distress Signals If you need to call for help, use these internationally recognised emergency signals. Give six short signals, such as a whistle, a yell or the flash of a light, at 10-second intervals, followed by a minute of rest. Repeat the sequence until you get a response. If the responder knows the signals, this will be three signals at 20-second intervals, followed by a minute's pause and a repetition of the sequence.

Helicopter Rescue & Evacuation If a helicopter arrives on the scene, there are a couple of conventions you should be familiar with. Standing face on to the chopper:

Arms up in the shape of a letter 'V' means 'I/We need help'
Arms in a straight diagonal line (like one line of a letter X) means 'All OK'

For the helicopter to land, there must be a cleared space of 25m x 25m, with a flat landing pad area of 6m x 6m. The helicopter will fly into the wind when landing. In cases of extreme emergency, where no landing area is available, a person or harness might be lowered. Take extreme care to avoid the rotors when approaching a landed helicopter.

Paris Region

Although Paris and its hinterland are extensively built up and densely populated, it's an area of considerable natural beauty. Amazing as it may seem, it is still possible to walk through almost unspoiled countryside only 60km from Paris.

Paris itself is best explored on foot – the ideal way to experience its extraordinarily varied streetscapes, the subtly different ambience of each *arondissement* (district) and to immerse yourself in its long history. Two walks through Paris, from west to east and north to south, are described in this chapter. Away from the city, another two walks visit towns of great historical importance, Provins and Fontainebleau, and explore the very different countryside surrounding each – richly fertile agricultural land, and beautiful old forests.

INFORMATION
Maps & Books
If you're planning to spend any time in Paris, you'll need a map of the city centre. Lonely Planet's *Paris City Map* is indexed, easy to use and includes a metro guide.

The IGN 1:250,000 map No R12 *Île de France* provides excellent coverage of that area. The maps covering individual walks are noted in their respective Planning sections.

Useful English-language walking guides include *Walking Paris* by Gilles Desmond, describing 30 mostly short walks, and the *Time Out Book of Paris Walks*, edited by Andrew White, featuring 23 themed walks from 1km to 11km long.

Lonely Planet publishes two guides to the capital: *Paris*, a complete guide, and the pocket-sized *Best of Paris*. Both books contain detailed information on accommodation and the world-class gastronomic experience that Paris offers.

The **Espace IGN** (☎ 01 43 98 80 00; www.ign.fr - French only; 107 rue de la Boétie; metro George V, line 1; open Mon-Sat) is a real trap for map-lovers. It's the best place to go for all IGN's publications, and many

Highlights

- Savouring the tranquillity and cool shade of Paris' many beautiful parks and gardens (p66)
- Strolling along canals, climbing a butte and discovering St-Paul, a village-within-a-city (p73)
- Journeying back to the 13th century in the medieval town of Provins (p73)
- Exploring the intricate mazes of sandstone boulders in the historic Forêt de Fontainebleau (p76)

others, including the FFRP's Topo-Guides. Alternatively **Au Vieux Campeur** (☎ 01 53 10 48 48; 2 rue de Latran; metro Maubert-Mutualité; open Mon-Sat) has a branch dedicated to maps and books.

PARIS
Information
Paris' main **tourist office** (☎ 08 92 68 31 12; www.paris-touristoffice.com; 127 av des Champs-Élysées; metro George V, line 1; open daily) is near the Arc de Triomphe. Among much else it handles hotel bookings. Internet access is available with a France Télécom *télécarte*.

Supplies & Equipment
Shopping for food and drink is one of the great delights of staying in Paris, at small *boulangeries*, fruit and veg shops, specialist cheese shops and wine cellars. Among dozens, rue Ste-Antoine (not far from the Marais) is a colourful and diverse shopping street. Of the supermarket chains, **Monoprix** is better than most; its numerous branches include 62 av des Champs-Élysées, corner of rue Ste-Antoine and rue St-Martin, and rue de Rivoli near Châtelet metro.

For your walking equipment, the several branches of **Au Vieux Campeur** (☎ 01 53 10 48 48; www.au-vieux-campeur.fr - French only; metro Maubert-Mutualité, line 10), clustered between rue des Écoles and blvd St-Germain, stock anything that you're likely to need.

Places to Stay & Eat

Here is a tiny sample of the vast range of accommodation and dining venues available in Paris. For more information, consult the Paris tourist office and Lonely Planet's *Paris* guide.

Camping du Bois de Boulogne (☎ 01 45 24 30 00; www.mobilhome-paris.com; 2 allée du Bord de l'Eau; camping for 2 people with/ without car €24/15, 4-bed mobile home €66, first time booking fee €10) is fairly crowded with campervans and mobile homes, but quiet enough, close to the Seine. There are a **bar-restaurant** and small **shop** on-site. A private shuttle bus plies between Porte Maillot metro (line 1) near av de la Grande Armée and the camping ground (€1.60, 10 minutes, half-hourly from 8.30am to 1pm and 6pm to midnight daily).

La Maison Hostel (☎ 01 42 73 10 10; www.mamaison.fr; 67 bis rue Dutot; metro Volontaires, line 12; B&B in dorm/private room €21/24) is not in a particularly colourful

Paris Region

Paris Region – Maps	
1 Paris Parklands & Landmarks	p68
2 Paris Ancient & Modern	p71
3 Medieval Provins	p74
4 Forêt de Fontainebleau	p77

area but is well served locally by bars and brasseries. The hostel is closed between 11am and 4pm.

Hôtel Castex (☎ 01 42 72 31 52; www .castexhotel.com; 5 rue Castex; metro Bastille, lines 1, 5, 8; singles/doubles with bathroom €95/120; breakfast €8) has an unprepossessing exterior but the interior has been beautifully restored in 17th-century style. It's in a fairly quiet street within the lively Marais district.

Aquarius (☎ 01 48 87 48 71; 54 rue Ste-Croix de la Bretonnerie; metro Rambuteau, line 11; menus €12.60-15.40, mains €3.65-10.60; open Mon-Sat), on the western side of the Marais, is a haven for vegetarians. Salads are large and varied, the vegetable pie very filling. Wine, beer and delectable fresh juices are available.

Chartier (☎ 01 47 70 86 29; www.bouillon -chartier.com; 7 rue du Faubourg Montmartre; metro Grands Boulevards, lines 8 & 9, mains €7.05-18.10; open daily), opened in 1896, is a Parisian institution and a classified historical monument; a meal here is definitely an experience. Be prepared to queue for a table. Menus, based on traditional French dishes, change daily; you'll search in vain for a vegetarian dish, but the faintly arrogant waiters will deign to oblige.

Partie de Campagne (☎ 01 43 40 44 00; Bercy Village; mains €9.50-13.50; open daily) is ideally placed at the end of the Paris Parklands & Landmarks walk (p66). Eat inside or out, starting with a pool-sized bowl of soup (€5.80) and moving on to a tartin, pain au levain, traditional, chewy bread topped with a mountainous, savoury concoction, then exercise no self-control at all and go for a tarte or crêpe to finish.

Getting There & Away

Air For information about travel to and from Paris and overseas see the Getting There & Away section of the Travel Facts chapter (p344).

Details of air transport within France are covered in the Getting Around (p346) section of the Travel Facts chapter

Of the public transport links from Orly airport to central Paris, **Jetbus** (☎ 01 69 01 00 09) is relatively cheap (€4.80, 15 minutes, every 15 minutes). It links the terminal with the Villejuif Louis Aragon metro station at the southern end of line 7. **Air France** (☎ 01 41 56 89 00) operates its No 1 bus service to/from the eastern side of Gare Montparnasse (€7.50, 45 minutes, every 12 minutes). **Orlyval** (☎ 08 92 68 77 14) is an automated shuttle train linking the airport with the Antony RER train station (€8.75, 34 minutes, frequent); from there take RER line B into the city. To reach Antony from the city take line B4 towards St-Rémy-les-Chevreuse.

The best public-transport link between the city and Roissy Charles de Gaulle airport is the RER line B3 (€7.70, 40 minutes, every 15 minutes).

Bus Most inter-regional bus services operate between regional centres rather than to and from the capital. Details of these appear under the relevant Getting There & Away sections of the walks chapters.

Train France's major train lines radiate from Paris to reach almost all parts of the country.

Services to destinations found in this guide operate from the following five of the six main line stations:

Gare d'Austerlitz Loire Valley, Languedoc, Pyrenees, Roussillon, southwestern France
Gare de l'Est Champagne, Alsace
Gare de Lyon Burgundy, Provence, Mediterranean coast, the Alps
Gare Montparnasse Brittany, southern Normandy
Gare St-Lazare Northern Normandy

For more information see the Getting There & Away sections of the walks chapters and the Getting Around section of the Travel Facts chapter (p346).

Getting Around

Paris' underground network consists of two separate but linked systems: the Métropolitain, known as the metro, which has 14 lines and more than 300 stations, and the RER, a network of five suburban lines (A to E) that pass through the city centre.

They're operated by the Régie Autonome des Transports Parisiens (RATP).

Metro maps are available free at metro ticket windows. For detailed information on the metro, RER and the bus system, call the RATP's 24-hour inquiries number ☎ 08 92 68 77 14 (French) or ☎ 08 92 68 41 14 (English).

RATP tickets are valid on the metro, RER (within the city limits) and buses, and on the two tram lines (T1 in the northeastern fringes, and T2 just west of the Seine). They cost €1.30 individually or €9.60 for a carnet of 10.

Paris Parklands & Landmarks

Duration	4–4¼ hours
Distance	12km
Difficulty	easy
Start	Bir-Hakeim metro station
Finish	Cour St-Émilion metro station
Transport	train

Summary Weave your way along quiet streets and through parklands, past Paris landmarks and into some hidden byways.

From the banks of the Seine beside the Eiffel Tower, this walk crosses the city from west to east, for most of the way on the left bank. It takes in some famous sites including the Eiffel Tower and Hôtel des Invalides and some lesser-known places. You'll sense the diverse ambience of the various *quartiers*, and discern their differing architectural styles in subtle changes from the well-heeled 16th *arrondissement* to the more plebeian 12th in the east, via the ancient heart of Paris and some fine parks and gardens. The walk follows part of the FFRP's GRP2 route and is marked intermittently by red-and-yellow waymarkers, though it would be difficult to follow relying solely on these discreet signs.

PLANNING

This is a walk for any time of the year; the only deciding factor is the weather. You're never far from all kinds of refuelling stops from beginning to end.

Maps

Lonely Planet's *Paris* map includes a useful 1:16,000 Central Paris map. Alternatively, the IGN 1:16,000 map *Paris Poche* is a good buy. The FFRP's Topo-Guide No 75 *Paris à pied* describes two trans-Paris routes and others in the Bois de Boulogne and Bois de Vincennes.

GETTING TO/FROM THE WALK

The walk starts from metro station Bir-Hakeim on line 6 and finishes at metro station Cour St-Émilion on the fully automatic (driverless) line 14.

THE WALK (see map pp68-9)

From Bir-Hakeim metro station walk northwest along blvd de Grenelle; at the start of Pont de Bir-Hakeim cross busy quai Branly to the path between the Seine and gardens fringing the quay. Follow the path to Pont d'Iéna and cross the quay to the **Eiffel Tower** *(steps to 2nd level of south pillar €3.30; lift to top €10.20; open daily)*. Make your way across Parc du Champ de Mars, keeping on the left (northeastern) side to anticipate the next section of the walk. This huge park was used as a parade ground in the 18th century. At the far end, facing the imposing École Militaire (completed in 1773), go left to place de l'École Militaire. Cross three streets to av de Tourville; it's not far along the avenue to the **Hôtel des Invalides** (45 minutes from the start). Dating from the 17th century, it was used as a hospital for wounded soldiers. Towering over it is the opulent **Église du Dôme** *(admission including Musée Militaire €7; open daily)*, its gilded dome glinting in the sunlight; it houses Emperor Napoléon I's tomb. There are toilets located beside the church.

Negotiate place Vauban in front of the church to reach wide av de Breteuil leading away from the place. Tree-lined and with a grassed central strip, it's one of the grandest avenues in Paris. Take the first left (rue d'Estrées) to place André

Tardieu, where there's a good view of the dark, columnar Tour Montparnasse (210m high, built in 1974) to the right. Stay on the northern side of the place, cross blvd des Invalides and keep going along rue de Babylone, then right into rue Monsieur. At rue Oudinot it's left, then first right along rue Rousselet which comes out on rue de Sèvres, a very busy shopping street. You'll find a cluster of enticing *boulangeries*, bars and brasseries around here, in the unobtrusively affluent 6th *arrondissement*.

A few hundred metres further on, bear right into rue St-Romain, then left for rue Cherche-Midi, a very old thoroughfare. It's lined with antique shops and late-18th-century **mansions**, notably Nos 85, 87 and 89. Walk right along this street to rue du Regard and its dignified mansions; Nos 1, 5, 7, 13 and 15 have particularly fine carved timber doors. Cross rue de Rennes, passing St-Placide metro, line 4, and continue straight on, down rue Notre Dame des Champs, which crosses blvd Raspail 300m further on. Keep going for another 200m then turn left into rue Vavin which takes you to **Jardins du Luxembourg** (about an hour from Église du Dôme). As an open space, this oasis dates from the 13th century, settling at its present extent (25 hectares) in the mid-19th century. Forget about collapsing on the lawn under one of the many spreading chestnut trees – the grass is strictly off limits.

To continue the walk from the entrance, follow the path to the left, past an apiary (established in 1856), children's play area, tennis courts, pitches for *pétanque* (a type of bowls), chess and card tables. At the end of the path, go right beside the **Orangerie** to the **Palais du Luxembourg**. Built at the beginning of the 17th century, it's now the seat of the French Senate (the upper house of parliament). From here, contemplate a fine example of one of Paris' most impressive features – the long vista or prospect, extending hundreds of metres southwards. From the far corner of the palace wander across to the left to **La Fontaine des Médicis** then go up nearby steps and through the gate

to place Edmond Rostand. Cross rue de Médicis and blvd St-Michel and turn left to rue Soufflot. Along here you have a choice. Whichever route you choose, don't miss the great vista to the left as you cross rue St-Jacques – the buildings of the Sorbonne, Paris' oldest university.

One option takes the first street on the right (rue le Goff) then first left, cobbled rue Lebranche which crosses rue St-Jacques, one of the oldest thoroughfares in Paris, established in the 2nd or 3rd century AD. Continue along rue Fossés St-Jacques to secluded place de l'Estrapade.

Alternatively, you can go right up rue Soufflot to the massive **Panthéon** (*admission €7; open daily*), the mausoleum for several great Frenchmen (no women!). To rejoin the main route, walk along short rue Clotaire from the southern side of place du Panthéon to place de l'Estrapade.

From the place, follow the rue of the same name to the left, which soon becomes rue Blainville, to picturesque place de la Contrescarpe, lined on three sides by cafés with outdoor tables. Walk around the place and take the second on the left, rue du Cardinal Lemoine, then the cobbled rue Rollin on the right. It leads, via a flight of steps, down to rue Monge near Place Monge metro. Cross it and walk left to No 49. Go through the archway to **Arènes de Lutèce**, originally an amphitheatre used by the Gallo-Romans and probably built at the end of the 1st century AD. It wasn't discovered until 1858; the stonework is still in good condition and the area is used, in the best tradition, by football-loving kids. Go through the alley on the right to a gate leading on to rue de Navarre; follow this to rue Lacépède. Turn left and go on, across rue Geoffroy St-Hilaire, to the entrance to the **Jardin des Plantes** (*botanical garden; admission free; closes 8pm midsummer, 5.30pm midwinter*), an hour from Palais du Luxembourg. It was founded as a medicinal herb garden for Louis XIII in 1626. There's plenty to see if you wander through the grounds: the rather formal gardens; the Serres Tropicales – greenhouses filled with tropical plants; the

Paris Parklands & Landmarks

Musée National d'Histoire Naturelle; and the Grande Galerie d'Évolution, a massive, pale sandstone building that serves as a useful landmark. Handy map boards are scattered about; eventually, reach the southwestern exit.

Opposite here is the white **Mosquée de Paris**, built in 1926, with its striking 26m-high minaret. Turn left along rue Geoffroy St-Hilaire and take the second street on the left, rue Poliveau, which leads to blvd de l'Hôpital. Gare d'Austerlitz metro, lines 5 & 10, is 300m to the left. Cross the boulevard, go under the railway viaduct, past a

small stone building and into the grounds of **Hôpital La Pitié-Salpêtrière**. One of the biggest hospitals in Europe, its buildings date back to the 17th century. Head towards the large chapel, then turn right to go through the Porche Lassay. Continue straight ahead for about 400m to the southern gate, on to rue Bruant which leads on to blvd Vincent Auriol.

This takes you on to the Seine and the meeting of quai d'Austerlitz on the left and quai de la Gare on the right. Cross **Pont de Bercy**. From the southeastern side of the bridge there's a good view of Bibliothèque

Paris Parklands & Landmarks

National de France François Mitterand, a few hundred metres downstream: four right-angled buildings representing four open books, set on the corners of a square, and housing over 12 million volumes.

Across the bridge, turn right in front of Palais Omnisports de Paris-Bercy, notable for its sloping turfed walls and used for sports and concerts. Follow the entrance road then continue for about 100m around the palais until parkland opens up on the right. Head off through Le Parc de Bercy, developed in the 1990s on the site of former wine depots, originally established outside

Paris' walls to avoid taxes. Wander through Jardin Yitzhak Rabin (a memorial to the Israeli prime minister who was assassinated in 1995), cross rue Joseph Kessel to the southeastern section of the park.

The walk finishes at Cour St-Émilion metro station in the far left southeastern corner of the park (about an hour from Jardin des Plantes). A few steps to the right is **Bercy Village** with shops, bars and restaurants occupying late-19th-century former wine vaults. Partie de Campagne (see Paris Places to Stay & Eat, p65) is a good choice for some end-of-walk nourishment.

Paris Ancient & Modern

Duration	4–4¼ hours
Distance	10.4km
Difficulty	easy
Start	Corentin Carriou metro
Finish	Cité or St-Michel metro
Transport	train

Summary Something different and unexpected around every corner: a science park, canals, a miniature mountain, superb late-Renaissance buildings, infinitely varied streetscapes.

The landmarks at the start and finish of this walk could scarcely be further removed from each other – a late-20th-century science park and the Notre Dame cathedral, finished in the 15th century and a Paris icon. From the down-to-earth 19th *arrondissement* to the discreetly affluent 4th, the route passes some well-known places and many perhaps less so. It follows parts of the FFRP's GRP *Traversée de Paris 2*, indicated intermittently by red-and-yellow waymarkers. The locations of key intermediate metro stations are noted – this walk could well be split between two days to allow time for all the visits en route.

PLANNING
This is a year-round walk, limited only by the weather on the day. From beginning to near the end, cafés, bars and restaurants are thick on the ground.

Maps
See the Paris Parklands & Landmarks walk (p66).

GETTING TO/FROM THE WALK
The walk starts at metro station Corentin Carriou on line 7 and finishes near either Cité or St-Michel (both line 4).

THE WALK
From the metro station walk east, across the canal and on into Parc de la Vilette, home of the moated **Cité des Sciences** (*admission from €3*), housing several permanent and temporary exhibitions. It's worth going in-

side just to look at the interior design – all the ducts and conduits are exposed full frontal. Continue south, past the extraordinary silver ball of the Geode on the left, to a canal. Cross a footbridge and go right down stairs; have a look round the tent-like **Zenith** building then make your way across lawns, dotted with contemporary artworks, to a canal junction. Follow the cobbled quai de la Marne southwest beside Canal de l'Ourcq. About 600m along come to a lifting bridge; cross the road and turn left then right, skirting a restored warehouse, to follow quai de la Loire beside Bassin de la Villette. Soon you pass a small flight of canal locks (still in use) and arrive at place de la Bataille de Stalingrad.

Cross av Jean Jaurès to rue Armand Carrel, slightly to the left and follow it to place Armand Carrel with the magnificent early-19th-century *mairie* (town hall) of the 19th *arrondissement* on one side. Negotiate the place to the entrance of **Parc des Buttes Chaumont** (1¼ hours from the start). One of Paris' largest parks and a truly green, open space, it was created in 1867 with an exceptional collection of indigenous and exotic trees. Inside the park, bear right along av Michal to a footbridge across the lake. A short distance from the far end go under an arch, along a path, through a tunnel beneath rock pinnacles and up to the summit of **Butte Chaumont** (a butte is a small, isolated, steep-sided hill). From this 99m-high lookout the remarkably varied panorama includes the white dome of Sacré Coeur. Go down a path on the left, across a bridge and straight on; bear sharp right at a junction along a roadside path. Cross an intersection, go through a large gate and left along rue Manin.

Just past the end of the brick Rothschild building on the right, cross to a steep flight of steps, up to the built-over summit of another butte. Bear right along rue Phillippe Hecht then left at a junction to an excellent lookout. Keep right, via rue Georges Lardennois to steps on the right; descend and cross av Simon Bolivar. Bear slightly right to allée Louise Labé, between plain and not-so-plain 20th-century apartments.

Paris Ancient & Modern

Continue down to rue Rébeval and turn right. Cross rue de l'Atlas to **Aux Bons Amis** bar and turn left to blvd de la Villette, a Chinese-Vietnamese-Thai quarter (Belleville metro, lines 2 & 11, is 250m left). Turn right, then shortly cross to rue de Sambre et Meuse, marked by a prominent post office. A little way along turn left along rue Ste-Marthe, through an area which has clearly fallen on hard times, to rue St-Maur and turn left. Then take the first right (rue Arthur Groussier) to av Parmentier; cross, turn right then left down much more prosperous rue Alibert. Go on

to **Canal St-Martin** and quai de Jemmapes (dating from 1822; about an hour from place Carrel).

Walk south along the quay to a canal tunnel; cross rue du Faubourg du Temple and bear slightly right to enter a garden parallel to blvd Jules Ferry. Exit right just past a fountain; a short distance further on cross av de la République then go right to rue Lampon, well endowed with restaurants. It leads to blvd Voltaire, with a good view of the place de la République to the right; Oberkampf metro (lines 5 & 9) is nearby to the left. Cross to rue Amelot and turn left.

Take the first right along rue Timbaud to cross blvd du Temple to rue de Saintonge; follow it to rue de Normandie and turn left, briefly. Go right along rue Debelleyme; follow it, across rue de Bretagne into the colourful **Marais** district, with dozens of bars and bistros.

Continue around to rue de Thorigny and turn right, soon reaching **Musée National Picasso** (admission €5.50; open Wed-Mon) at No 5. This 17th-century building is the largest of the Marais' *hôtels particuliers* (private mansions). Follow rue de Thorigny to rue de la Perle, bear left across place Thorigny and left along rue du Parc Royal (a clutch of cafés and three fine hotels here) to rue de Sévigné and turn right. Along here is the excellent **Musée Carnavalet** (admission entry free; open Tue-Sun) devoted to the history of Paris.

From rue de Sévigné turn left along rue des Francs Bourgeois to the superb **place des Vosges**. Either walk through the central formal park or along the 17th-century arcades lined with expensive galleries and restaurants. In the southwestern corner go through an archway, across a courtyard, through another archway and courtyard to rue St-Antoine. Cross and turn right, then first left along rue St-Paul and into the village of the same name with its many galleries and craft and antique shops. A few steps along, passage de St-Paul leads right to 17th-century **Église St-Louis-St-Paul** (open daily). Return to rue St-Paul and take next right (rue Charlemagne) then turn left along rue des Jardins de St-Paul. Bear right along rue de l'Ave Maria; at the end cross rue du Figuier and turn right beside **Hôtel de Sens**, the oldest in the Marais (1475). This brings you back to rue Charlemagne. Turn left to rue des Nonnains d'Hyères, leading to the Seine, Pont Marie and Pont Marie metro (line 7; 1¼ hours from Canal St-Martin).

Cross the bridge, continue along rue des Deux Ponts on **Île St-Louis** then turn right along rue St-Louis en l'Île, soon passing an excellent *gelateria* on the left. The street leads to Pont St-Louis; cross it and quai aux Fleurs to square Jean XXIII beside **Notre Dame**. Cross the park and go on, between the Seine and Notre Dame to rue d'Arcole with Pont au Double on the left. The nearest metros (both line 4) are Cité (250m north via the front of Notre Dame and rue de la Cité) or St-Michel (across the bridge, 300m right along quai Montebello).

Medieval Provins

Duration	3–3¼ hours
Distance	12km
Difficulty	easy
Start	Longueville
Finish	Provins
Nearest Towns	Paris (p63), Provins (right)
Transport	train

Summary Pleasant walking through woods, fields and the timeless hamlet of Chalautre-la-Petite to Provins, with its superbly preserved medieval buildings.

Merely 80km southeast of Paris, Provins' ancient buildings dominate the Brie plains, the premier wheat-growing area in the Île de France. The imposing Tour César and the Église Saint-Quiriace are prominent landmarks in a town that was declared a World Heritage Site in 2001. This walk takes you through fertile, intensively cultivated countryside and the gently undulating plains above the valley of the Voulzie River. The route follows part of the FFRP's GR11 and is waymarked to Provins. An outline of a walk around the old town follows the main walk description.

HISTORY

Provins' heyday was during the 12th and 13th centuries, as the principal seat of the counts of Champagne. It became famous for its annual fairs attended by merchants from as far afield as Flanders and Lombardy. However, from the early 14th century, new trade routes bypassed Provins and the town subsided into obscurity, but its ancient decline has turned to modern fame as a remarkably well-preserved medieval fair town. The Unesco citation for World Heritage status highlights the preservation of its 'original urban fabric' and its authenticity. Even so, Provins does not depend utterly on its past and suffers typical modern ills – traffic jams, incongruous advertising signs and dilapidated roads.

PLANNING
Provins is thronged between April and September, and at the height of the season many festivals are staged in the town. By catching the early train (around 7.40am) or even the midday train, it's possible to do the walk and explore the town in a day from Paris, returning mid-evening.

There are no shops or cafés along the walk.

Map
The IGN 1:25,000 map No 2626O *Provins* covers the walk.

NEAREST TOWNS
See Paris (p63).

Provins
The **tourist office** (☎ *01 64 60 26 26; www .provins.net; chemin de Villecran; open daily)* has a wealth of information about the town.

Places to Stay & Eat About 30 minutes' walk from the train station, **Hôtel Ibis** (☎ *01 60 67 66 67, fax 01 60 67 86 67; 77 av Général de Gaulle, Giratoire N19, Upper Town; doubles with bathroom €49; breakfast €6; meals €9- 15)* is southwest of the town centre on the N19 road. It has a **restaurant**.

Au Vieux Remparts (☎ *01 64 08 94 00; www.auxvieuxremparts.com; 3 rue Couverte, Upper Town; singles/doubles with bathroom from €55/60, half board from €80; breakfast €10)* is the only conveniently located hotel, not far from Tour César.

In rue du Val in the lower town you'll find several enticing *boulangeries*, and an assortment of bars.

There's also a **Monoprix supermarket** on place du Général Leclerc. Head for the upper, older part of town for a good choice of restaurants.

Bar Brasserie Chez Denis (☎ *01 64 08 97 34; rue Couverte; menus €12-16)* a totally unpretentious place, all dark beams and quiet corners. The menu includes a variety of meat and poultry dishes and salads for vegetarians. An international range of beers is on offer.

Auberge de la Grange (☎ *01 64 08 96 77; rue St-Jean; menus €16.50-27.50; closed Tue & Wed)* offers local specialities in slightly more formal surroundings.

Getting There & Away Trains operated by **SNCF** (☎ *08 92 35 35 35)* run from the Île de France platforms of Paris' Gare de l'Est to Provins (€10.20, one hour 25 minutes, three daily).

GETTING TO/FROM THE WALK
The train between Paris and Provins (see above) passes through Longueville (€9.45, 63 minutes, three daily). The walk finishes in Provins.

THE WALK
From Longueville station exit walk down the road to the right (north) to a junction and turn right along rue André Taton. At the junction with rue l'Armourée, join the waymarked route and turn right under the railway and bear right along rue Adrée. This minor road bends right and ducks under another railway bridge to an intersection. Go straight ahead on a gravel track for 50m then right up a grassy track. Soon, look back for a fine view of the railway viaduct. The track leads up to a water tower from where Église St-Quiriace in Provins dominates the northeastern skyline, beyond the Voulzie Valley.

Continue along the track to the edge of the village of **Septveilles-le-Haut** and turn left along chemin du Moulin. Where the bitumen bends right keep to a grassed track for 150m then turn right at an intersection. Soon, continue along rue Jean Jaurès to a crossroads and take rue Honoré de Balzac (straight ahead), lined with old houses surrounded by luxuriant gardens. The road bends left and descends; leave it at the next left bend to follow a grassed track. Woods and fields alternate for the next kilometre or so; at a prominent intersection, bear right then left with a sign '*Sur les coteaux de la*

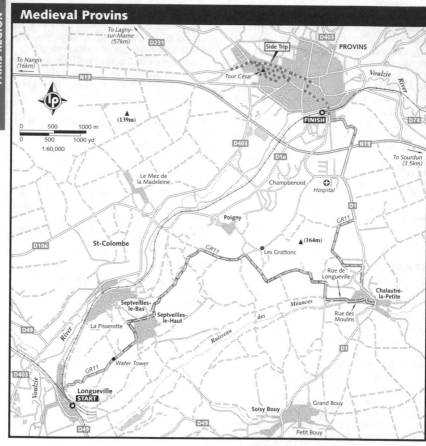

Medieval Provins

Voulzie'. It's right at the next intersection, through woods typical of the area with oak, ash and hazel in dense profusion, and on to lovely views over undulating fields and groves of trees. On the edge of Les Grattons, turn right at an intersection (1¼ hours from the start).

The track leads left through woods and fields for 500m then into the open above a wide green valley; bear right at a fork and descend. Take rue de Longueville left into the quiet village of **Chalautre-la-Petite**. Turn left at the next junction along rue des Moulins, then go right and on through the older part of the village. Several of the centuries-old stone-and-timber buildings have been superbly restored. The road changes identity to rue de la Fontaine d'Orson; shortly go right along ruelle des Bretons, across the mill race and left between old buildings. Turn right in front of a large church and follow rue Claude Chappe to the main road (D1; 45 minutes from Les Grattons).

Turn left and follow the road for 400m; bear right along quieter rue de Provins to bypass a bend on the D1. Rejoin it briefly to the right; turn left along a track, past an old quarry, across fields and back to the D1. The verge is just wide enough for safe walking, northwards for about 700m to an intersection. Follow the Paris–Troyes road to the right along a wide verge. As you near a major intersection, cross to the eastern side, then negotiate the N19's dual carriageway. Go up the bank just to the right of a small poplar tree to meet a track; it leads northeast then northwest across fields with an excellent view of Église de St-Quiriace. Turn right at a road; soon, quiet ruelle des Vignes brings you into outer suburban **Provins**. Turn right at a junction along route de Chalautre; cross it and 200m further on reach the train station (one hour from Chalautre-la-Petite).

Side Trip: Tour of Old Provins
1 hour, 2–3km
From the far (western) end of the train station cross the road and follow signs 'Piétons' and 'Cité Médiévale'. Cross over a small bridge then follow rue Hegesippe Moreau; at a fork bear left into rue des Marais, then soon after right along rue du Commandant Genneau. At a junction it's right into rue Hugues le Grand, then shortly left along rue Edmond Nocard which soon lands you in place St-Ayoul.

On the right is the venerable **Église St-Ayoul**, Provins' oldest church, probably dating from the 11th century. Nearby and just north of the place are the slight 14th-century remains of **Nôtre Dame du Val**. From place St-Ayoul, walk west along rue de la Cordonnerie, across place du Général Leclerc and along rue du Val. Second on the right is rue Ste-Croix, a few metres along which is the huge **Église Ste-Croix** probably dating from the 12th century. Back on rue du Val, continue west and walk up steep, cobbled rue St-Thibaud.

On the left is the **Hôtel-Dieu** under which are the souterrains, a multi-level labyrinth of chambers and passages. At place du Châtel turn sharp left along rue du Palais. To reach the massive **Tour César** (admission €3.70; guided tours daily) follow a path opposite the École Maternelle up a bank and walk around the perimeter to the entrance on the

southwestern side. The tower was the 12th-century seat of the counts of Champagne. Return to rue du Palais; next comes the **Musée de Provins** (admission €3.40; open afternoons daily) in 11th-century Maison Romane. Continue along the street to place St-Quiriace and the awesome 12th-century church. Go back to place du Châtel; from the western corner rue Couverte leads to a junction with rue St-Jean on the left. A short step along is **Grange aux Dîmes** (admission €3.40; open daily), a 12th-century tithe barn where Provins fairs were once held and which now houses a permanent exhibition about the fairs.

Forêt de Fontainebleau

Duration	6½–7 hours
Distance	18km
Difficulty	moderate
Start/Finish	Fontainebleau (p76)
Transport	train
Summary	Labyrinthine paths among mazes of sandstone boulders, and more direct paths through beautiful forests; don't miss the magnificent Château de Fontainebleau.

The 20-sq-km Forêt de Fontainebleau, only 50km southeast of Paris, is crisscrossed by a dense web of waymarked footpaths, about 365km in all and including the FFRP's GRs 1 and 11. Shaded by tall conifers and broadleaves are several extraordinary outcrops of sandstone boulders – rock climbers' delights and great fun to walk through, though even the most acute sense of direction could be confused by the twists and turns of the interweaving paths.

Used as a royal hunting domain from the 16th century, it was marked out as a forest by Louis XIV when only 13% of the area was wooded. Replanting with oak, beech and birch began in 1716; the first Scots pines were planted in 1786. The railway reached Fontainebleau in 1849 and soon visitors began arriving en masse and the path network, initiated a decade earlier, was soon extended. Management of the forest

Château de Fontainebleau

Any list of chateaus to visit in France should have Fontainebleau near, if not at, the top. Used by kings of France from the 12th century, its walls and ceilings are lavishly adorned with wood panelling, gilded carvings, frescoes, tapestries and paintings. Fireplaces are ornately decorated and many items of furniture are from the early 16th century.

The greater part of the chateau dates from the same period, a blend of Italian and French Renaissance styles. It was enlarged later in the same century when the surrounding, mostly formal gardens were laid out. Fontainebleau survived the Revolution intact and was partly restored by Napoléon I. From the end of WWII it was used as the Allied then NATO headquarters until 1965. The chateau and the gardens were designated a World Heritage Site in 1981.

The **Grands Appartements** (state apartments; admission €5.50; open Wed-Mon) are entered from place Général de Gaulle on their western side. The **Petits Appartements** and **Musée Napoléonien d'Art et d'Histoire Militaire** keep the same hours; admission costs €3. Access to the **gardens** (open daily) is free. For more information contact ☎ 01 60 71 50 70 or check www.musee-chateau -fontainebleau.fr – French only.

now emphasises protection of biological reserves and catering for the large numbers of visitors enjoying the boulders, paths and picnic areas.

The walk described here goes through a good cross-section of the forest's landscapes – rocky ridges, forests and sandy plains. With the recommended map, it would be possible to shorten the outing to 12.5km by ignoring the northern section via La Butte St-Louis. Turn south at the junction of paths Nos 14 and 15 and pick up the route described east of Le Cabaret Masson.

PLANNING

The forest is at its best during early May and late October. There are no refreshment

facilities along the walk described. Given the walk's duration, you could stay in Fontainebleau to enjoy a leisurely visit to the chateau and gardens. However, it is possible to do the gardens between finishing the walk and a mid-evening train back to Paris. It's worth noting that very few restaurants open before 7pm.

The IGN 1:25,000 map No 2417OT *Forêt de Fontainebleau* covers the walk area. The Office National des Forêts booklet *La Forêt de Fontainebleau* (in French) is recommended for the wealth of background information that it contains. It's available from the local tourist office and from the IGN shop in Paris (see p63).

NEAREST TOWN
Fontainebleau

The **tourist office** (☎ 01 60 74 99 99; www .fontainebleau-tourisme.com; 4 rue Royale; open daily) has a useful brochure with a town map and accommodation contacts; it also sells maps and books related to the walk.

Places to Stay & Eat Just off the southern side of place Napoléon Bonaparte, **Hôtel de la Chancellerie** (☎ 01 64 22 21 70; 1 rue de la Chancellerie; doubles with bathroom €46) is beside the chateau.

Hôtel Victoria (☎ 01 60 74 90 00; www .hotelvictoria.com; 112 rue de France; singles/ doubles with bathroom €58/64; breakfast €7) is a shortish distance north of rue Grande. The uncluttered rooms are tastefully furnished in period style.

Ty-Koz (☎ 01 64 22 00 55; meals €17; open daily) is down a side street from 18 rue de la Cloche and is ideal if you're heading back to Paris mid-evening. It offers many and varied Breton savoury and sweet *crêpes* in homely surroundings; beer, cider and wine are available.

La Taverne (☎ 01 64 22 20 85; 23 rue Grande; menus €12-20, mains €7-14; open daily) is one of several bistros along the main street and is one of the less frenetic; sip one of the excellent *bières à la pression* before tucking into one of the steaks or pizzas.

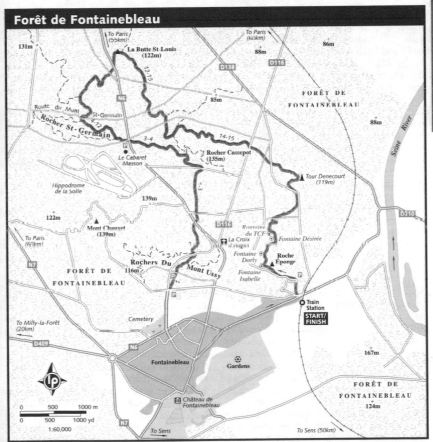

Forêt de Fontainebleau

To Paris (55km)
To Paris (60km)

131m

La Butte St-Louis (122m)

86m

88m

D138

D116

Route du Mont St-Germain

N6

85m

FORÊT DE FONTAINEBLEAU

88m

Rocher St-Germain

12-13

14-15

3-4

Rocher Cassepot (135m)

Le Cabaret Masson

Tour Denecourt (119m)

Hippodrome de la Solle

2-3

139m

122m

D116

Fontaine du TCF

Fontaine Désirée

Seine River

D210

Mont Chauvet (139m)

La Croix d'Augas

To Paris (60km)

N7

FORÊT DE FONTAINEBLEAU

Rochers Du

116m

Mont Ussy

Fontaine Dorly

Fontaine Isabelle

Roche Éponge

Train Station
START/ FINISH

To Milly-la-Forêt (20km)

Cemetery

D409

N6

Fontainebleau

Gardens

167m

0   500   1000 m
0   500   1000 yd
1:60,000

Château de Fontainebleau

FORÊT DE FONTAINEBLEAU

124m

N7

To Sens

To Sens (50km)

Getting There & Away From Paris' Gare de Lyon main line platforms, **SNCF** (☎ 08 92 35 35 35) trains run to Fontainebleau (€7.30, 38 minutes, at least eight daily). Destinations of suitable services include Montargis, Montreu and Laroche-Migennes.

THE WALK

In front of the station is a small park where you'll find information boards about the forest. From the northern end of the station, go diagonally left up steps. Cross the road to Maison Forestière and turn left to follow a waymarked route to Roche Éponge. About

250m along the minor road, turn right into the forest on path No 2, which leads steeply up to a parking area. Turn left then right, past boulders bearing **plaques** commemorating people formerly associated with the forest. Swing left along a path clinging to a steep slope; soon, head north across a relatively open area towards a stone wall, past another memorial plaque on the left above a small cave. Flights of steps lead to **Roche Éponge**, a sponge-like sandstone boulder. Continue with it on the right, shortly passing Fontaine Isabelle on the left; go up steps and turn right at a junction. Soon, on the left you pass Fontaine Dorly and a few hundred metres further on, two more *fontaines*. The route zigzags, crosses a forest track and leads northeast, with high ground to the left. Several hundred metres further on at a road junction, cross a forest track and a road to continue northwest along a waymarked path. Next, bear right at a fork and follow a sinuous route through large boulders to the crest of a small ridge. Make your way eastwards; the devious route soon sneaks through a boulder tunnel then comes to a road and informal parking area beside **Tour Denecourt** (1½ hours from the start). Although orientation tables on top point out lots of features, trees have grown since they were installed in 1984 and the view is mostly of – well, trees.

From the northern side of the parking area follow a path signposted 'Sentiers Samosiens No 14'. It descends, wiggles about, crosses a narrow road and leads into flat country to cross the D116 road. Soon you're back in rocky ground, the path wandering through clumps of boulders to gain a small rocky ridge where you need to keep an eagle eye on the path. Continue over a relatively high tor, across another flattish ridge where the route makes particularly cunning twists and turns. Bear left at a junction about 250m further on. Take this to Sentier No 15 southwest through tall beeches and conifers. A few hundred metres further on, turn right along a wide track. Then, at a signposted junction, turn left towards Butte St-Louis along Sentiers Nos 12–15. The route weaves a generally northwesterly course through flat sandy plains. Cross a small fenced area via gateways and after a few more hundred metres, ascend to the wooded summit of **La Butte St-Louis** (122m; two hours from Tour Denecourt).

Continue west briefly then south, down to cross the busy N6 road diagonally left to a wide path. The direction is southwest up to an oblique track junction. A sharp bend takes you onto a flat crest to resume the southwestward course. After a few hundred metres, bear left towards Rocher St-Germain. The wide path leads on over broken ground,

across Route du Mont St-Germain. Then comes another devious bouldery section, from where you can see the Hippodrome de la Solle to the south. At a junction (an hour from La Butte St-Louis) bear left for Cabaret Masson. Keep cliffs on the left but work your way leftwards to a point near the end of the rocky outcrop, via a couple of short easy scrambles through **Rocher St-Germain**. This is the most labyrinthine and exciting section of the entire walk, impossible to describe in detail, but generally trend south then east through the boulders in an intricate chain of right and left turns.

Half an hour from the Cabaret Masson track junction, you reach an open sandy area. Cross its eastern (left) edge to a short white post with a '3' marker, indicating a narrow path through trees; bear left along a wider path, across a parking area then the N6 road, bearing slightly right. Continue on a narrow path with a sign 'Jonction 4/3 Rocher Cassepot'. Gain some height then you're back among big sandstone boulders; bear right in front of a large specimen marked 'G'. Up near the crest follow path '3' through rocky defiles and on to a junction. Turn right and descend, following red-and-white waymarkers briefly. No more than 200m further on, continue more or less straight ahead at the next junction, following blue waymarkers, through a short boulder tunnel and two narrow clefts. Contour a steep rocky slope, cross a road and press on along Sentier No 3, shortly bearing left towards Croix d'Augas. When you reach the N6 dual carriageway cross slightly left to join an obscure path (still No 3). Cross a minor track and a few steps further, fork right, soon passing a turn-off right for routes via Mont Ussy. Then cross a minor road, now following Sentier 1, through some fairly innocuous bouldery outcrops. With a parking area in sight, keep left of a large family of boulders and drop down to cross a wide track (1½ hours from the open sandy area).

Bear right at a fork and go on to an intersection; cross the east–west road, pass through a parking area, then cross to the western side of the north–south road. Walk along the verge, then a parallel path into the outskirts of **Fontainebleau**, past a walled cemetery, to an intersection with traffic lights. Cross and continue along rue Doc-teur Clément Matry, past a hospital on the left. From the second intersection beyond the hospital, rue des Bois leads southeast to rue Grande (about 30 minutes from the wide track). To reach the station (about 1.5km) follow rue Aristide Briande, second left opposite the rue des Bois junction. For the town centre and the chateau, bear right along rue Grande (about 1.5km).

Other Walks

Dampierre-en-Yvelines & the Vaux de Cernay

The Parc Naturel Régional de la Haute Vallée de Chevreuse protects the natural environment and historical heritage of a valley rich in picturesque villages, chateaus and wooded hills. Marked paths cross the park, through woodlands of oak, chestnut and Scots pine. Dampierre-en-Yvelines, which is a convenient base, is 36km southwest of Paris. The IGN 1:25,000 map No 2215OT *Forêt de Rambouil-let* covers the area. To reach Dampierre-en-Yvelines take the train on the RER line B to St-Remy-les-Chevreuse and then a bus from there.

For more information about the walk, contact the **park office** (☎ 01 30 52 09 09; *www.parc -naturel-chevreuse.org - French only*) and **Damp-ierre tourist office** (☎ 01 30 52 57 30).

Forêt d'Ermenonville

The small town of Ermenonville, 45km northeast of Paris, has become famous for its association with the Swiss philosopher Jean-Jacques Rous-seau, who inspired a local estate owner to design a beautiful park beside his chateau. It is also on the edge of the Forêt de Ermenonville, well endowed with paths and tracks. The IGN 1:25,000 map No 2412OT *Forêts de Chantilly* covers the walk.

The nearest train station is located 4km from Ermenonville at Nanteuil-le-Haudoin on the SNCF line direction Crépy-en-Valois from Paris' Gare du Nord; there's a relatively infrequent bus running to Ermenonville.

For more information about the walk contact **Ermenonville tourist office** (☎ 03 44 54 01 58; *www.ot-ermenonville.com*).

Brittany & Normandy

Two of the more evocatively named of France's *départements* speak of the sea, battles, cider – and the sea. To prove the point, this chapter describes four very different coastal walks and one inland gem on the Normandy–Île de France border.

Brittany

The farther west you venture in Brittany (Bretagne), the more you come to realise that its claim to be different from the rest of France is absolutely spot-on. The 1300km coastline is crumpled into innumerable bays, beaches and long estuaries separated by rocky headlands; many small islands defy the capricious English Channel and the turbulent western seas. Breton culture, especially music and language, is alive and well and the age-old maritime heritage is proudly protected. Most importantly for walkers, there are many accessible and memorable walks along the coastline. Two coastal walks are described in this section; outlines of other worthwhile coastal paths and inland routes are in the Other Walks section (p105).

Highlights

- Admiring fantastic red granite boulders on the Côte de Granit Rose (right) and its myriad offshore islets

- Traversing long sandy beaches, rocky headlands and pine woodlands along the Presqu'île de Crozon coast (p88)

- Wandering amid the beauty of Impressionist painter Claude Monet's gardens, and the charms of the countryside that inspired him, in and around Giverny (p94)

- Gazing across the extraordinary natural features of the Baie de Mont St-Michel to the awe-inspiring Mont itself (p101)

INFORMATION
Maps & Books
The IGN 1:100,000 map Nos 13 *Brest Quimper* and 14 *Saint-Brieux Morlaix* cover the areas described in this section and are useful for trip planning.

Lonely Planet's *Brittany & Normandy* and the French-language *Bretagne et ses îles* will be invaluable companions during your visit.

Information Sources
A good place to start gathering information is Brittany's **CRT** (☎ 02 99 28 44 30; www .brittanytourism.com; 1 rue Raoul Ponchon, 35069 Rennes).

Côte de Granit Rose

Duration	3 days
Distance	58km
Difficulty	moderate
Start	Trégastel (p82)
Finish	Tréguier (p84)
Transport	train, bus

Summary The best of Brittany's north coast: superb paths, fantastic clusters of pink granite boulders, sandy beaches and rocky headlands.

Of all the northern Brittany coast, the beautiful Côte de Granit Rose has the lowest density of seaside resorts and the longest unbroken shoreline paths. Although some of the towns and villages have sold their souls to the leisure industry and tourism and are blighted by some truly awful modern buildings, there are still plenty of farms, their cereal and vegetable fields blending easily with the scenic and endlessly fascinating coastline.

This walk follows coastal paths eastwards around shallow, reef-crowded bays to the head of the long Jaudy River estuary, its wooded slopes rising from rocky shores.

Brittany is Different

Ploumanac'h, Plouguiel and Veryarc'h (typical Breton place names), a distinct preference for cider and beer over wine, spirited Breton music and the distinctive black-and-white Breton flag are just some of the striking features that set Brittany apart from the rest of France. The nine black and white stripes of the flag, adopted in 1923, represent former bishoprics; the rectangle in the upper left corner displays ermines (stoats in winter garb), the region's traditional symbol.

Immense importance is attached to Brittany's Celtic heritage, which it shares with Cornwall, Ireland, the Isle of Man, Scotland, Wales, Galicia and Asturias (in northwestern Spain). The Breton language, spoken by around 500,000 people, is closely linked to Cornish and Welsh. Although taught in schools, it has been scorned by the central government, which legislated to entrench French as the country's official language in 1992. The letters BZH on car badges derive from the Breton word for the region, Breizh. Breton music and arts are thriving, and are celebrated at the Festival Interceltique (www.festival-interceltique.com), held annually during August at Lorient and attended by artists from the international Celtic community.

Breton separatism has waxed and waned; having recovered from the odium of Nazi associations during WWII, it now draws strength from close association with other Celtic nations.

Here low tide reveals shoals, part-time islets, seaweed, sand, shingle and carpets of salt-tolerant plants.

Although it's generally a flat walk (except along the estuary), the moderate grading recognises the rocky paths and shingle beaches you'll traverse – not the easiest of walking surfaces. It's impossible to avoid road walking, but overall the distance isn't great. Several of the paths were originally *sentiers des douaniers* (customs officers' paths), reminders of the days when smuggling was a popular pastime along this coast. The route follows that of the FFRP's GR34.

You could start the walk at Perros-Guirec; it's more lively – and also more expensive – than Trégastel and would make an easier first day (3¾ to four hours, 9.5km). Camping areas are conveniently spaced along the route, making a tent (or bungalow where available) the ideal accommodation. It's possible to do the walk by staying in hotels, though you'll have a rather long day from Port Blanc to Tréguier.

NATURAL HISTORY

There are four nature reserves *(sites naturels protégés)* along the coast. The much visited Landes et Rochers de Ploumanac'h site protects the extraordinary pink granite outcrops, some of which are strikingly similar to various animals, and the fringing heathland. Another reserve embraces the nearer islets and beaches between Port Blanc and Plougrescant; among the great mounds of shingle that form the islands, brackish marshes support unusual associations of flowering plants. Around Pointe du Château, the Castel Meur reserve features an unusual triple shingle bar formation, enclosing brackish ponds. The Jaudy estuary is a European bird conservation area.

PLANNING
When to Walk

During May and June, before the crowds arrive, there's a reasonably good chance of settled weather, although some camping grounds don't open until June. Good weather is also likely in September. At least two short sections of this walk are only accessible at low tide, although there are road-walking alternatives. Tide tables aren't much help without local knowledge of the critical height and time on any given day, so trust your own observation. Remember that the highest tides each month coincide with a full moon.

Maps & Books

You'll need IGN 1:25,000 map Nos 0714OT *Lannion Perros-Guirec* and 0814OT *Paimpol*. The FFRP French-language Topo-Guide

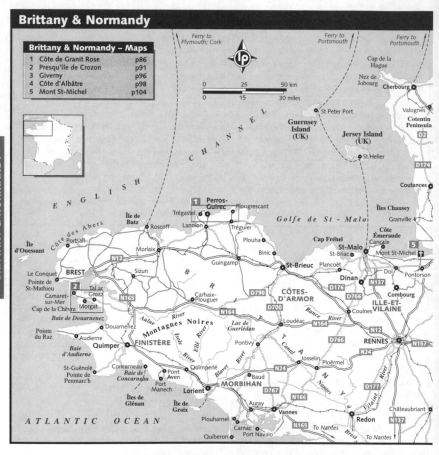

Ref 346 *Côte de Granit Rose* includes background information, a route description from St-Brieuc to Roscoff (in the opposite direction to the walk described here) and variants from the main route.

NEAREST TOWNS
Trégastel

Comparatively small and not overly commercialised, Trégastel is attractively spread out along the shore of Baie de Ste-Anne.

The **tourist office** (☎ 02 96 15 38 38; www .ville-tregastel.fr - French only; place Ste-Anne; open Mon-Sat year-round, Sun & holidays Jul & Aug only). Accommodation information is displayed on the front door.

There's an ATM opposite the tourist office. The nearby **Maison de la Presse** stocks local maps and numerous French-language books about Brittany.

Places to Stay & Eat Beside the walk route, **Camping Tourony** (☎ 02 96 23 86 61; www .camping-tourony.com; 105 rue Poul-Palud; camping 2 people & tent €14.70) is 2km east of Trégastel. Although catering mainly for campervans, it also has some nice shady tent sites.

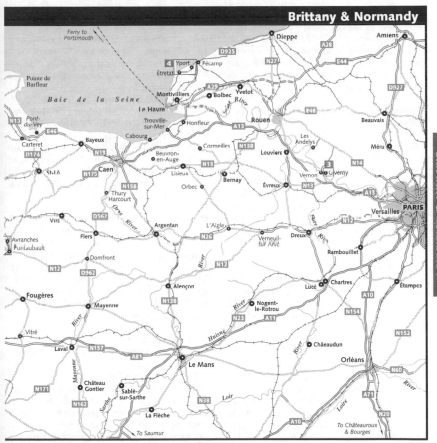

Brittany & Normandy

Ferry to Portsmouth

Pointe de Barfleur

Baie de la Seine

Dieppe

Amiens

Yport Fécamp

Étretat

Montivilliers Yvetot

Le Havre Bolbec

Trouville-sur-Mer Honfleur Rouen

Beauvais

Cabourg Cormeilles Les Andelys

Bayeux Méru

Carteret Beuvron-en-Auge Louviers

St-Lô Caen Lisieux Bernay Giverny

Thury Harcourt Orbec Évreux Vernon

Pont-du-Vey

Vire Argentan L'Aigle PARIS

Avranches Flers Dreux Versailles

Pontaubault Verneuil-sur-Avre

Domfront Rambouillet

Fougères Alençon Lucé Chartres Étampes

Mayenne Nogent-le-Rotrou

Vitré Châeaudun

Laval Orléans

Château Gontier Le Mans

Sablé-sur-Sarthe La Flèche

To Saumur To Châteauroux & Bourges

BRITTANY & NORMANDY

Hôtel des Bains (☎ 02 96 23 88 09; www
.hotellesbains.com; bvd du Coz Pors; doubles
with bathroom €35-55, half board €43-51.50;
breakfast €7) overlooks the bay and is good
value. Ask for a room in the annexe for the
best views.

Hôtel de la Corniche (☎ 02 96 23 88 15,
fax 02 96 23 47 89; 38 rue Charles le Goffic;
doubles with bathroom €45-55, half board
€41.50-54.50; breakfast €7) is 500m west of
the town centre, neatly located on a corner
so that all rooms have a wide outlook.

Hôtel Belle-Vue (☎ 02 96 23 88 18;
bellevue-tregastel@wanadoo.fr; 20 rue des

Calculots; singles/doubles with bathroom €58/
72, half board €59-65; breakfast €9, menus
€16-45) is very comfortable without being
opulent, in a quiet corner away from the
main road. Menus at the light and airy restaurant include locally caught fish.

For supplies there are **Shopi supermarket**
(place Ste-Anne; open Mon-Sat & Sun morning) and an excellent **boulangerie**, also on
place Ste-Anne.

Crêperie Ty Maï (☎ 02 96 23 41 95; 21 bis
place Ste-Anne; mains €15-18; closed Wed) is
an informal, one-woman place – watch out
for the huge black dog as you enter. The

galette fillings include seafood, and several of the *crêpes* are flambéed with calvados.

Les Papilles (☎ 02 96 23 46 43; 2 rue de la Grève Blanche; menus €16-28) has a pretty dining room in a stone cottage 500m west of the town centre. The house speciality is seafood-rich *bouillabaisse bretonne* (€19).

Getting There & Away From Lannion train station, there is a CAT (☎ 02 96 46 76 70; www.cotesdarmor.fr - French only) bus service (line 15) to Trégastel (€2.90, 47 minutes, four daily Monday to Saturday); alight at the Ste-Anne stop near the town centre.

SNCF (☎ 08 92 35 35 35) trains from Paris' Montparnasse to Brest stop at Plouaret (€55.70, 3¾ hours, at least one daily); change here for the branch-line service to Lannion (€21.40, 24 minutes, at least three daily).

Tréguier

A historic town dating back to the 6th century, Tréguier at first seems like a metropolis but its narrow winding streets and superbly preserved 17th- and 18th-century buildings are captivating.

The town's **tourist office** (☎ 02 96 92 22 33; 1 place du Général Leclerc; open Mon-Sat, daily Jul & Aug) is near the port. Out of hours a list of local accommodation places is available next door at the Cafàdu Port.

You'll find ATMs, several bars, *crêperies* and *boulangeries* around place Martray, about seven minutes' walk up from the port and riverside via rue St-André.

Places to Stay & Eat A small place with rather basic rooms, **Hôtel le Saint-Yves** (☎ 02 96 92 33 49; 4 rue Colvestre; singles shared facilities/doubles with bathroom €18/38; breakfast €4) has the best location in the old quarter near place Martray.

Hôtel de l'Estuaire (☎ 02 96 92 30 25, fax 02 96 92 94 80; 5 place du Général de Gaulle; singles/doubles with washbasin €22/30, doubles with bathroom €40; menus €13.50-32.50) occupies an old building close to the port and has rather plain, potentially noisy rooms. Its upstairs restaurant offers three seafood-oriented *menus*.

Hôtel des Roches Doures (☎ 02 96 92 27 27; 17 rue Marcellin Berthelot; singles €35, doubles with bathroom €41; breakfast €6) is a friendly hotel, well back from the main road, overlooking the southern end of the marina. The plain rooms are perfectly adequate and well maintained.

Restaurant St Bernard (☎ 02 96 92 20 77; 3 rue Marcellin Berthelot; menus €12.50-24) offers an escape from fish and seafood with a wide selection of grills.

Le Cantonier (☎ 02 96 92 41 70; 5 rue Ernest Renan; menus €9.50-24.50) is close to place Martray; you can dine inside or out and enjoy fish soup and swordfish, among much else.

Getting There & Away The line No 7 CAT (☎ 02 96 46 76 70; www.cotesdarmor.fr - French only) bus departs from the gated entrance to the port to Paimpol (€4.20, 30 minutes, at least five Monday to Saturday). There you connect with **SNCF** (☎ 08 92 35 35 35) trains to Guingamp (44 minutes) on the Brest–Paris' Montparnasse line (€52.60, three hours 10 minutes, at least four daily).

THE WALK (see map pp86-7)
Day 1: Trégastel to Port l'Epine
5¾–6 hours, 21km

Set out along quai de Ste-Anne beside the shore, then take to the beach. If the tide is in, detour along the main road (route Poul Palud) to an intersection (where route de Kervoennes leads right) and turn left to an informal parking area and the waymarked route. Follow the broad path around a headland, beside a small beach and on to Plage de Tourony. Turn right near its eastern end to a junction; bear left, soon following chaussée du Port to the shore. Continue on to a path beside the main road opposite the entrance to **Camping Tourony** (p82). Pass a stone building housing a tidal water mill, cross the bridge and walk along the beach. At the eastern end, cross a causeway and continue left beside quai Bellevue in Ploumanac'h. Beyond **Bistrot du Port** (a bar that serves snacks) you come to the start of the Sentier des Douaniers (1¼ hours from Trégastel). Follow a wide cobbled path to reach a small beach; bear right up steps then down, past a stone chapel, to Plage St-Guirec, where a small oratory sits on a tide-washed rock. The nearby **Hôtel de l'Europe** offers ice creams, drinks and meals.

From the end of the beach follow a path past houses; no more than 200m along, a view of the open sea and Les Sept Îles unfolds. Bear right past a chapel; a little further on, you can diverge left to a small stone lighthouse. The large **Maison du Littoral** (coastal visitor centre; ☎ 02 96 91 62 77) is open only on school holiday afternoons. Walk down the path, past a rocky cove and on to a path junction. Continue straight on; after a few hundred metres pass the customs officers' lookout on the right and a 17th-century, stone-built powder magazine on the left. Beyond Porz Roland and **Camping Le Ranolien** (☎ 02 96 91 43 58; camping 2 people & tent €27), the path continues above the rocky shore for 1.5km. Then follow minor roads to **Plage de Trestraou** (1½ hours from Ploumanac'h) with several crêperies and bars along the promenade. **La Marie Galante**, probably the least expensive, offers takeaway sandwiches or crêpes (to €5) and menus (€20 to €80).

From the Seven Islands Surf Club walk up roadside paths for 800m; go left along rue des Sept Îles, then follow the minor roads to chemin de la Messe (15 minutes from Trestraou beach). From here the Perros-Guirec town centre is only 200m away. Follow chemin de la Messe for a few hundred metres; leave it opposite a tall house (called 'Ker-an-Gwell') and go down a narrow path (the route thus differs from that shown on the recommended map). Swing right in front of the first group of boulders you come to, and continue up, then down and along the shore to a fork beside a hedge; go right up to a road. This takes you past the seriously expensive hotel **Le Manoir du Sphinx** (☎ 02 96 23 25 42; rooms from €93) and down to Plage de Trestrignel. Here you'll find **Le Trestrignel** (☎ 02 96 23 03 86; menus €14.50-27.50; closed Tue) bar-crêperie-restaurant.

Walk along the promenade, up blvd de Trestrignel and rue Maurice Denis, at the end of which bear right along a path, with Pointe du Château nearby on the left. Several

hundred metres along, descend to a junction and go right for about 250m, then turn off through a gap between two stone walls down steps to the shore. Walk across the rocks (except perhaps at high tide) for only 30m, then up a minor road and left along rue de Trestrignel; this leads to the D788 (1¼ hours from Trestraou). From here you can reach Perros-Guirec town centre in 10 to 12 minutes by crossing to rue de Coas an Abat, following it to rue Maréchal Joffre and on to the main road near the Hotel de Ville.

The largest town along this part of the Brittany coast, Perros-Guirec has a life of its own as well as all the usual facilities. **Hôtel de France** (☎ 02 96 23 20 27; 28 chemin de la Messe; doubles with bathroom €44/54; breakfast €6.50, menus €16-28) is right on the route. Its **restaurant** features fish-based dishes.

To continue, follow the path down beside blvd de la Mer; where the road bends right, continue across a large parking area. From a big roundabout walk along the wide road verge; about 250m past the entrance to **Camping Municipal Ernest Renan** (☎ 02 96 23 11 78; fax 02 96 49 04 47; camping 2 people & small tent €8.20; open Jun-Sep) turn left along the Chemin du Littoral (1¼ hours from the D788 near Perros-Guirec). Turn right in front of the last house to follow a path to a beach. Continue along a field-edge path (another variation from the route on the recommended map); a few hundred metres along there's a sign to Stella Maris Gîte (closed at the time of research). Near the hamlet of Nantouar follow the shore-side path, then continue above Poull ar Gouec to Plage de Porz-Garo. Descend steps to the left to a vehicle track, which leads to a road (1½ hours from Truzugal).

Nearby is the entrance to **Camping Port l'Epine** (☎ 02 96 23 71 94; www.camping-port-lepine.com; camping 2 people & tent €25, chalets for 2 or 3 people €40 Sep-Jun). Oriented towards families and campervans, it has a bar, restaurant and small shop.

It's another 200m to **Camping Municipal Le Palud** (☎ 02 96 91 73 11; mairie.trelevern@wanadoo.fr; camping 2 people & tent €15; meals to €10), which is better suited to small tent camping than the competition. It has a small shop, bar and restaurant, which serves snacks and more substantial fare, including steak, omelettes and scallops.

Day 2: Port l'Epine to Porz Hir
5–5¼ hours, 20km

Follow the road past Camping Le Palud to a path beside a beach. At the eastern end, bear right along a road; continue round an unobtrusive headland, past another beach, to Port le Goff and on to Plage de Trestel. Along here are **Le Trestel** bar and *crêperie*, where you can succumb to the *crêpes* (to €3) or mussels (to €12), and **Camping Le Mat** (☎ *02 96 23 71 52; camping 2 people & tent €9.50)*.

At the end of the promenade take to the beach for a few hundred metres then go up a ramp to the road. Follow roads and paths to Le Royo, then a road for a few hundred metres. Continue past Plage des Dunes and **Camping Municipal des Dunes** (☎ *02 96 92 63 42; camping per person & tent €7.78)*. Another 500m of path overlooking a vast expanse of tidal rock platform bring you to another beach-side road and the peaceful hamlet of **Port Blanc** (1¾ hours from Port l'Epine).

Le Grand Hôtel (☎ *02 96 92 66 52, fax 02 96 92 81 57; twins/doubles with bathroom €43/53; breakfast €5, daytime menu €8, evening meal €12, menus €15-32)* gazes straight out to the offshore islets. The bar stocks Drem Mwel, a superb Breton beer.

To continue, walk up the road, go left at a junction and around the port of Port Blanc. Leave the road along a path, soon diverging inland to a road, and continue via Pellinec to the causeway across Anse de Pellinec. If the tide is up, follow the field edge parallel to the shore to a stone wall, then bear left past a stone cottage. At very high tide, the next 20m or so across a stone causeway could be awash, though you can keep dry by ploughing through the fringing reeds; rejoin

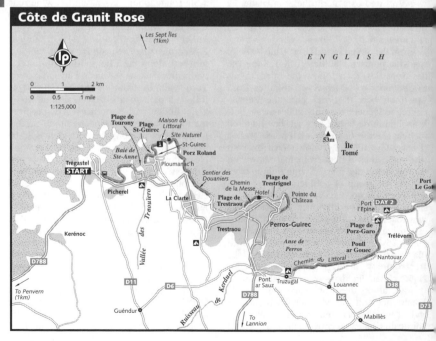

Côte de Granit Rose

the route at Placen Amic. Continue into the village of Buguélès and follow left and right turns to an intersection. Here you can either keep to the waymarked route or take a shortcut by heading towards signposted 'La Plage', then taking the first left turn along rue A Thomas, shortly to rejoin the route at venelle St-Thomas to the right. Go left at the next junction in front of Chapelle St-Nicolas.

If the causeway was impassable, you'll soon need to turn right along rue de l'Île Istan to bypass the shore route. From the end of this road, make your way around field edges to a small beach, then follow clearer paths beside fields and through woodland to rejoin the waymarked route.

Normally, you would continue north from the chapel, then east to Buguélès beach. When the walk was surveyed the author reached the shore to find a rock with a waymarker just poking out of the water. Eventually, fork left from the sandy shore

and go on to a road, then turn left to the shore of Anse de Gouermel (1½ hours from Port Blanc). About 700m along you come to **Le Gouermel** (☎ 02 96 92 55 26; dishes €3-9; closed Mon & Sun evening) for crêpes, salads, galettes and mussels.

Where the road bends right, take to the shore-side path; further on a road leads to **Porz Scaff** and a world of dull pink, columnar granite tors. Soon you're off the road along a wide path to a road near Castel Meur (an hour from Anse de Gouermel). Turn right, and 50m along keep straight ahead (differing from the mapped route), then bear right – you can see the unusual maison entre deux rochers (house between two rocks) not far to the left. Soon you come to the **Maison du Site** (visitor centre; open Mon-Wed & Fri afternoon). Next, swing left at a junction and follow wide paths beside the shingle. You can't come this far and not visit the northernmost point of the walk, **Pointe du Château**. From a stand of

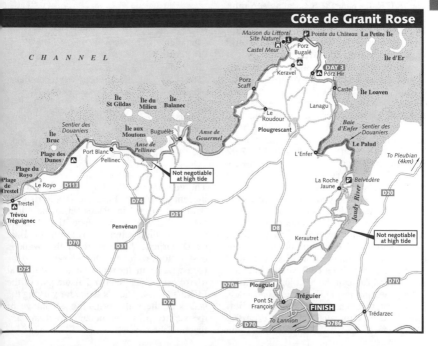

Côte de Granit Rose

conifers, it's only a short walk to the point, a wildly beautiful place, especially in spring when pink thrift (sea pink) sprouts from every available rock crevice. Back on the route, follow the path through the conifers to a road at Porz Bugalé. Continue via the road, a short path and more road to **Porz Hir** (45 minutes from Castel Meur), the point of departure for local accommodation.

Camping Le Varlen *(☎ 02 96 92 52 15, fax 02 96 92 50 34; camping per person & tent €12)* is a fairly small, sheltered camping ground. There's a **bar** that serves fast-food style meals from June to August. The nearest shops are in Plougrescant.

Day 3: Porz Hir to Tréguier
4¼–4½ hours, 17km
From the intersection at Porz Hir, turn east down a minor road to reach the shore. Head south, past a handful of houses at Castel, a turn-off at Lanagu to Plougrescant (2km) and on to a broad woodland path. This takes you to L'Enfer near the head of a deep inlet (an hour from Porz Hir). Go a little way along the road to a path on the left; several hundred metres further on, high tide could inundate the path for a few metres, but it should be safe to wade rather than make a detour. Around 1km takes you out of Baie d'Enfer to a road at Le Palud. Continue for another few hundred metres; cross a road end, and 250m further on, go right up to a road then left into the village of La Roche Jaune (45 minutes from l'Enfer). Here the excellent bistro **Chez Louise** *(☎ 02 96 92 02 82)* welcomes even wet, bedraggled walkers with *crêpes*, *galettes*, salads (€2 to €9) and daily specials (€9 to €12.50).

From the village you can diverge to the signposted **belvédère** (lookout) for a fine view of the estuary. Then either follow the contortions of the waymarked route (down to the shore and back up) or go straight on at a nearby intersection. Take the third on the left (rue St-Gueno), and rejoin the waymarked route at the next junction (after 250m), bearing right. This quiet road leads southwest through farmland via one left turn, to a junction marked by a crucifix. If the tide is up, you'll have to miss the

delights of the next and last shoreline path, and continue on southwestwards for about 1km to rejoin the route at Kerautret (see the 1:25,000 map).

Otherwise, turn left along a vehicle track and descend, via a series of turns, to a rough track on the edge of the shingle. After about 1.2km and just past a house in the trees above, turn right up a track to a road; follow it to a crossroads and turn left. This takes you southwestwards for about 1.5km; turn left, and left again to the D8 road in Plouguiel. Keep on in the same direction for 200m, then turn right down rue Jarl Priel. Further on a path to the right takes you to Pont St-François. A few steps beyond the bridge, bear left in front of houses to a riverbank path. Follow it through a broad arch and continue beside the river to the Jaudy River bridge in **Tréguier** (2½ hours from La Roche Jaune). Turn right along rue du Port to reach the bus stop and tourist office.

Presqu'île de Crozon

Duration	2 days
Distance	47.5km
Difficulty	moderate
Start	Camaret-sur-Mer (opposite)
Finish	Tal ar Groaz (p90)
Transport	bus
Summary	An outstandingly scenic clifftop and beach walk along good paths, through fragrant pine woods, across open heaths and past historic defences.

The coastline of the Presqu'île de Crozon in central-western Finistère is surprisingly wild and rugged in places, from the windlashed headlands that face the Atlantic Ocean to the sheltered coves on the Baie de Douarnenez. The route of this walk is easy to follow, it being both a *sentier côtier* (coast path) in the Parc Naturel Régional d'Armorique (PNRA) and also a part of the FFRP's GR34. There's scope for varying the stages of the walk by taking advantage of the variety of accommodation within easy reach of the coast.

NATURAL HISTORY

The main rock type on the peninsula is ancient Armorican quartz sandstone, extensively displayed at several of the points and at Cap de la Chèvre; schists are prominent at Anse de Pen-Hat and Porz Naye.

The greater part of the peninsula is within the PNRA, a large reserve (172 sq km) extending from the Monts d'Arrée to Pointe de Pen-Hir and seaward to Île d'Ouessant. Six sites on the peninsula are particularly important for nature conservation. Les Tas de Pois off Pointe de Pen-Hir make up a bird sanctuary where shags, gulls and kittiwakes nest; the point itself is distinguished by unusual geological formations. More than 100 species of birds have been recorded at L'Étang de Kerloc'h, which is also home to families of otters. At Cap de la Chèvre rare heathland includes bell heather, ling and summer gorse. Numerous bird species, including some migrants, congregate around the Aber estuary; the Falaises de Guern harbour several protected species. For more about the park contact ☎ 02 98 81 90 08 or visit www.parc-naturel-armorique.fr – French only.

PLANNING
When to Walk

May and June, when there's the best chance of settled weather and the heathland wild flowers are in bloom, are the ideal months for Finistère.

Maps & Books

IGN's 1:25,000 map No 0418ET *Camaret Presqu'île de Crozon* covers the area. The FFRP's Topo-Guide Ref 380 *Le Tour des Monts d'Arée et la Presqu'île de Crozon* includes other walks in the area. 'Fiches de Randonnées', plastic cards describing walks around Camaret-sur-Mer, are available locally.

NEAREST TOWNS
Camaret-sur-Mer

A small, distinctly maritime town, Camaret enjoys a superb setting, overlooked by rugged cliffs to the northeast and guarded by the massive Tour Vauban.

At the **tourist office** (☎ 02 98 27 93 60; www.camaret-sur-mer.com - French only; 15 quai Kleber; open Mon-Sat) a list of local accommodation is on display outside.

The ATM easiest to find is opposite the bus stop. Internet access is available using Cyberposte at the **post office** (rue de la Marne; open Mon-Fri & Sat morning). It costs €7 per hour, using a card on sale at the post office. Maps, books and walking guides are stocked by the **Maison de la Presse** in place St Thomas.

Places to Stay & Eat Approximately 500m west of the tourist office, **Camping Municipal du Lannic** (☎ 02 98 27 91 31; rue du Grouannoc'h; camping per person & tent €3.80, shower €1.50) is close to shops. The individual camp sites are sheltered and facilities are well maintained.

Mme le Mignon B&B (☎ 02 98 27 81 04; 2 rue Mers-Crez; doubles with washbasin €25; breakfast €4) is in a very quiet street with seawards outlook.

At **Hôtel Vauban** (☎ 02 98 27 91 36; 4 quai de Styvel; doubles with toilet/bathroom €28/34; breakfast €5.50) the friendly hosts welcome you to superbly decorated and cared-for rooms.

Hôtel le Styvel (☎ 02 98 27 92 74, fax 02 98 27 88 37; quai de Styvel; singles/doubles with bathroom €34/42, half board €42; breakfast €5, menus €13.50-30.50) has several comfortable rooms with a sea view. The **restaurant** offers four *menus*.

The **Huit à 8 supermarket** on quai Gustave Toudouze is open Monday to Saturday and Sunday morning. Along the quay you'll also find a *boulangerie*, several bars (including an Irish pub for Guinness-deprived visitors), pizzerias and *crêperies*.

L'Abri du Marin (☎ 02 98 27 99 55; rue Abri du Marin; mains €6-14; open daily), a bright, pleasant place, has some of the best views to go with a meal. Seafood and fish are to the fore; vegetarians can take refuge in better-than-average pizzas.

Getting There & Away There's a Brest (bus station) to Camaret service (€9.50, one hour 20 minutes, two Monday to Saturday, one on Sunday during school term only) with **Douguet Autocars** (☎ 02 98 90 88 89). From Brest there are **SNCF** (☎ 08 92 35 35 35) trains (mostly TGVs) to Paris' Montparnasse (€72.30, four hours 20 minutes, at least two daily).

You can also reach Camaret from Quimper by bus (€9.50, 1½ hours, two Monday to Saturday, one Sunday school term only) with **Effia Voyageurs** (☎ 02 98 90 88 89). SNCF TGVs run from Paris' Montparnasse to Quimper (€62.10, four hours 50 minutes, at least two daily).

Tal ar Groaz

A very small village, scattered around a major road junction, Tal ar Groaz is about 1.5km inland from Plage de l'Aber.

The nearest tourist offices are in Morgat and Crozon, and there's an ATM in Telgruc-sur-Mer (p93).

Places to Stay & Eat With an onsite bar, **Camping de l'Aber** (☎ 02 98 27 02 96; camping.aber.plage@presquile-crozon.com; camping per person & tent €5.60) has panoramic views of the coast from its grassy sites.

Hôtel de l'Aber (☎ 02 98 27 13 92; 5 route de Châteaulin; doubles/twins with washbasin €28/32; breakfast €5.80; meals €6-8) offers quite acceptable, older-style rooms, some with nice pastoral and sea views. The hotel has a bar and serves basic fare such as steak with chips and salad, or omelette.

There's a very good **boulangerie** (open daily) beside the roundabout.

At **Le Capri** (☎ 02 98 27 05 61; mains €7.50-16, pizzas €8-11.50) fish and seafood are grilled on a wood fire and mussels come in several different guises.

Crêperie Maeligwenn (☎ 02 98 26 18 02; route de Châteaulin; crêpes €1.80-6.10; closed Mon) is 200m east of the roundabout. With panoramic views from the upstairs dining room you can sample savoury and sweet crêpes from an extensive menu.

Getting There & Away The regular **Douguet and Effia Voyageurs** (☎ 02 98 90 88 89) bus services pass through Tal ar Groaz to Quimper (€8.20, one hour seven minutes, at least two Monday to Saturday, one Sunday) and Brest (€8.20, one hour 17 minutes, at least two Monday to Saturday, one Sunday).

THE WALK
Day 1: Camaret-sur-Mer to St-Hernot

6½-6¾ hours, 27.5km

From the northwestern end of quai Styvel, beyond the marina, go left around the corner for 150m to a path that leads through an informal picnic area. Just ahead, however, the cliff edge has collapsed so you need to detour inland. The deviation is clearly signposted; at the end bear right to rejoin the route. Soon you pass a large stone building, then Pointe de Grand Gouin. Descend to a road junction just above Porz Naye; turn right and 100m along leave the road to go steeply up to the cliff edge and a good view of Pointe du Toulinguet. Continue down; cross the entrance road to the firmly closed Semaphore du Toulinguet and bear left and steeply down. Part-way along, above Anse de Pen-Hat beach, swing left to a road near its end. Cross a nearby picnic area and continue through low dunes, then go up to the clifftop.

Soon you will come to the **International Memorial Museum to the Battle of the Atlantic** (admission €3), which is dedicated to the men of the merchant navy who died during WWII. From here bear diagonally left to a clifftop path; 1km further south pass an impressive memorial to the Breton people who died for France. Another few minutes bring you to Pointe de Pen-Hir (two hours from Camaret).

Pick up the path leading almost north down to Veryac'h Plage where **Bar-Crêperie du Veryac'h** (open Thu-Tue school holidays, Sat & Sun rest of year) serves crêpes and galettes (€2 to €9) and drinks.

Walk down the access road, then up a path above the crumpled cliff-lined coast to Pointe de la Tavelle. From here the route keeps fairly level, past Pointe de Portzen and into the confines of Anse de Dinan. Nearing a fairly busy road and opposite the first house you reach, turn right down to the

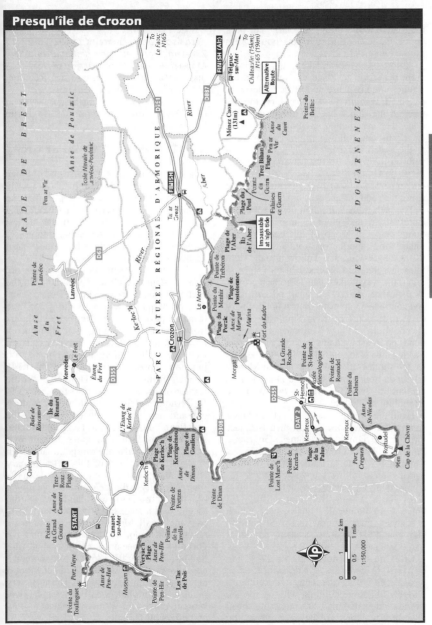

Presqu'île de Crozon

shore. Continue to a car park, then follow the road across a bridge to a large car park above Plage de Kerloc'h (1½ hours from Pointe de Pen-Hir).

At low tide you can take to the beach for more than 2km to Plage de Goulien at the southern end of Anse de Dinan. Otherwise, cross a low bluff to a path which threads through the dunes backing the long sandy Plage de Kerziguénou for about 2km. Cross a car park and follow a minor road parallel to the beach. At a left bend, leave it for a path on the right. To reach **Camping de la Plage de Goulien** (☎ 02 98 27 17 10; camping per person & tent €12.50) continue inland along the road for about 250m.

The path tunnels through dense scrub for about 100m and emerges into heathland. Soon, below a group of tall conifers, the route swings uphill away from a fragile cliff, to a wide grassed track. Follow it to the right for a few hundred metres then turn right to rejoin the waymarked path. The best part of 1km further on, cross a small parking area and continue on the path, almost unnervingly close to the cliff edge, to Pointe de Dinan (1½ hours from Plage Kerloc'h). The direction is now east for a few hundred metres to a parking area at the end of the D308. The next stretch southwards to Pointe de Lost Marc'h (about an hour from Pointe de Dinan) gives exhilarating walking, rarely far from the crumbling cliff edge.

From the Pointe descend directly; cross a small stream near the beach, then meander through the Dinan sand dunes. Go round Pointe de Kerdra and down to the dunes fringing Plage de la Palue. From a small parking area follow the vehicle track for about 200m, then diverge right to a path that takes you to a sign 'Bel Goul a Mor' (1½ hours from Pointe de Dinan), near which is a grassy track. Follow this to **St-Hernot**, 2km inland via Kerdreux, a sleepy hamlet of traditional stone cottages.

Gîtes de St-Hernot (☎ 02 98 27 15 00; beds/private rooms €9/16, half board €28/35; breakfast €4.50) is in the centre of the village – a lovely old stone building with up-to-date fittings and furnishings. You *must* ring ahead to ensure the *gîte* will be open when you

arrive. Drinks are available at the adjacent **Bar de l'Hermine**.

Maison des Mineraux (☎ 02 98 27 19 73; admission €4; open daily Jul–mid-Sep, Mon-Fri & Sun afternoon rest of year) has displays about the Parc Naturel Régional d'Armorique's intricate geology.

If the *gîte* is full in St-Hernot, Morgat (see Day 2) offers other options. Taxis run between the two centres.

Day 2: St-Hernot to Tal ar Groaz
6½–6¾ hours, 20km

Rejoin the route at the southern end of Plage de la Palue. The wide path heads generally south on a roller coaster ride past a string of small coves. At **Cap de la Chèvre** (1¼ hours from the start), at 96m the highest point on the coast so far, stand impressive memorials to the naval air force in western France during WWII.

The route turns north 1km further on, into the dense scrub and woodland on the sheltered slopes above Baie de Douarnenez. The route passes close to the D255 and leads on past Pointe du Dolmen (1¼ hours from the Cap), diverging well inland from Pointe de Rostudel. It then traverses a steep slope through conifers and heathland to a junction opposite Pointe de St-Hernot (45 minutes from Pointe du Dolmen). A little further on, pass a turn-off to the left up to St-Hernot. With little respite from the steep ups and downs, the path continues to the excellent vantage point of **La Grand Roche**. About 1.5km further on, pass through **Beg ar Gador Site Naturel Protégé**; a large sign explains the geology of this extraordinary coastline, its caves, underground shafts *(puits)* locally called *cheminées du diable* (devil's chimneys), and landslips. Soon, ascend past a large crucifix, then turn right, past the small Morgat lighthouse and the remains of Kador battery, then the massive **Fort du Kador**, one of four built around Anse de Morgat during the 1860s. From there, it's down to a road beside the marina at **Morgat** (1¾ hours from Pointe de St-Hernot), very much a traditional, small maritime town. Morgat makes an attractive place to stay and offers all facilities.

Morgat Ouest Découvertes (☎ 02 98 26 22 11; contacts@ouest-decouvertes.com; 2 bis rue Garn an Aod; singles/doubles with bathroom €27/34; with half board per person €44/35) is a superior gîte d'étape with a small kitchen for guest use.

Hôtel de la Baie (☎ 02 98 27 07 51; 46 bvd de la Plage; doubles with washbasin/bathroom €29/39) has modernised, good-value rooms, while **Hôtel de la Plage** (☎ 02 98 16 02 16; 42 bvd de la Plage; doubles with bathroom €42-53; breakfast €6) is very comfortable. You'll pay more for a view.

Walk along the promenade rising above the beach. Follow the D887 inland, across a hotel entrance, and turn right along a road that leads to Residence Cap Morgat. Follow minor roads and a track down to Plage du Porzic. Weave through a string of left and right turns along minor roads, then tracks, back to the clifftop path and on up to **Pointe du Menhir** with a circular orientation table. Nearby is the eponymous menhir, a tall standing stone. The way onward leads along the clifftop to a roadside path at Plage de Postolonnec (1¼ hours from Morgat). At the eastern end turn right in front of a small A-shaped building. Veer left to pass **Le Korrigan Crêperie** (☎ 02 98 27 14 37; crêpes €1.55-9.15; open daily Jun-Sep).

Continue on the clifftop path up to Pointe de Trébéron, then descend to a minor road at the northwestern end of Plage de l'Aber (30 minutes from Plage de Postolonnec). Turn left here with the waymarked route to reach **Tal ar Groaz**; leave the waymarkers where they point right at the second intersection (25 minutes from the beach).

Alternative Finish: Telgruc-sur-Mer
1½ hours, 6km

From Tal ar Groaz, return to the junction where you left the waymarkers on Day 2 and follow the waymarked route south along the road. Cross a causeway and, 200m further on, turn right along a shore-level track. If the tide is in, follow a small detour (see the 1:25,000 map). Continue for 120m beyond where the shore track fades, then go left up a narrow path to the low cliff edge. Soon

there's an opportunity for an interesting detour to Île de l'Aber, a proper island at high tide, and its massive fort built in 1862. Back on the clifftop, the path passes above two small beaches, then Plage de Poul. Near the end of the beach keep right at a fork and soon pass through the Falaises du Guern Biotype Reserve. Soon Pointe du Guern gives a superb panoramic **view** of Baie de Douarnenez. The route then leads through pines and down, around Trez Bihan Plage and the low headland Pen ar Vir, and on to the road at Anse du Caon. To reach the Telgruc-sur-Mer camping areas, walk north from here up a minor road signposted 'Circuit du Ménez-Caon'.

To return to Tal ar Groaz either retrace your steps or use the 1:25,000 map to devise an inland route along quiet roads, taking in Ménez Caon for the views.

Telgruc-sur-Mer
A small, rather plain village actually more than 2km from the sea, it has a seasonal **tourist office** (☎ 02 98 27 78 06; 6 rue Ménez-Hom; open mid-Jun–mid-Sep) next to the prominent mairie. There's an ATM almost opposite.

Camping Le Panoramic (☎ 02 98 27 78 41; www.camping-panoramic.com; camping per person €15) is 100m on the left along the main road from where you join it. Most of the sites on this terraced area have good views.

Camping Armorique (☎ 02 98 27 77 33; www.campingarmorique.com; camping per person/site €4.60/8.50) is a bit closer to Telgruc. It's a rather open area with a good outlook and a pool.

Camping Les Mimosas (☎ 02 98 27 76 06, fax 02 98 27 76 06; camping per person & tent €8.60) is closest to the village.

In the village centre are a **boulangerie**, **bar-newsagent** and a **Huit-à-8 supermarket** (open Tue-Sat & Sun morning); it sells local maps and you'll find an ATM inside.

Telgruc is located on the Camaret–Brest and Camaret–Quimper bus routes (€7.30, one hour to Quimper, 1 hour 10 minutes to Brest). See Getting There & Away on p90 for more bus details.

Normandy

A large and diverse *département*, Normandy is blessed with a wonderfully varied and intensely historic coastline; this section features superb day walks along two of the finest stretches. In the north the spectacular white chalk cliffs of the Côte d'Albâtre breast the English Channel. In the south, the coast is lower but crumpled and indented, most dramatically by the Baie du Mont St-Michel. For a complete contrast, explore a sample of the gently undulating hinterland on an easy day outing focussed on the village of Giverny, famously associated with Impressionist artists.

INFORMATION
Maps & Books
The IGN 1:100,000 map Nos 7 *Le Havre/Rouen* and 16 *Rennes/Granville* are useful for planning your visit, as is Lonely Planet's *Brittany & Normandy* guide.

Information Sources
A good source of information about Normandy is the **CRT de Normandie** (☎ 02 32 33 79 00; www.normandy-tourism.org; 14 rue Charles Corbeau, 27000 Evreux). Local sources are given in the following walks sections.

Giverny

Duration	2¾–3 hours
Distance	13km
Difficulty	easy–moderate
Start/Finish	Giverny (right)
Transport	train, bus
Summary	Discover the landscapes that inspired the Impressionist painter Claude Monet and wander through his house and garden.

The village of Giverny owes its fame to Claude Monet and other late-19th-century Impressionist painters, who were captivated by its rustic charm and peaceful atmosphere. Giverny has retained much of its allure even

as it struggles, at times, to absorb thousands of visitors making the pilgrimage to Monet's house and gardens every day. The surrounding countryside is equally attractive in its own pastoral way. Wooded hills rise steeply from the plains through which threads the Epte River, a small stream that was one of Monet's sources of inspiration, as was the more majestic Seine. The walk, initially following the FFRP's waymarked GR2, takes you across the flanks of these hills, through typical Normandy villages, woodlands and fields – before or after a visit to Monet's beautiful house and gardens.

PLANNING
Giverny is rarely quiet, though weekdays may be less crowded than weekends; each season has its own particular beauty.

Maps
The walk is covered by the IGN 1:25,000 map No 2113OT *Vernon*.

NEAREST TOWN
Giverny
Giverny means Monet of course but it also means fine Normandy produce, including apples and cheese.

The **Fondation Claude Monet** (☎ 02 32 51 28 21; www.fondation-monet.com; open Tue-Sun) serves as the local tourist office.

Places to Stay & Eat Occupying a cottage once owned by Monet, the **B&B Chauveau** (☎ 02 32 51 10 67; ameliphi@club-internet.fr; 127 rue Claude Monet; singles/doubles with bathroom €46/61) has beautiful, lavishly furnished rooms with garden views. Rates include breakfast.

Hôtel La Musardière (☎ 02 32 21 03 18; iraymonde@aol.com; 123 rue Claude Monet; doubles with bathroom €51; breakfast €5.50; menus €25-36), built in 1880 and a bit shabby externally, is nonetheless very comfortable, the generously appointed rooms harking back to the past. The attached **restaurant-crêperie** offers a large selection of *crêpes* (to €7.30), steaks and fish.

Although there are no food shops within the village, there are plenty of cafés and

Giverny, Monet & Impressionism

In 1874 Claude Monet exhibited his new work *Impression, Soleil Levant* (Impression, Sunrise), which became the progenitor of a new movement in painting – Impressionism. Benefiting by the invention of tubes in which to carry paint, he and other painters moved outdoors and strove to capture contrasts and shades of colour, shimmering reflections, and the ever-changing aspects of the natural world – light on a field, flowing rivers, the sky at dusk.

Monet established his studio in Maison du Pressolr at Giverny in 1883 and lived there until he died in 1926. Inspired by the landscapes, waterways and gardens that surrounded him, he embarked on an immense artistic and botanical project in the garden beside his house. Beds of iris, dahlias, clematis, orchids, roses, poppies and many other flowers produce beautifully colourful seasonal displays for weeks at a time throughout the whole year. The water garden is a dense pattern of channels lined with weeping willows and bamboo, with the lily pond the as its central feature. Here Monet painted his famous *Nymphaéas*, in which water and plants combine in a marvellous play of light and colour. He completed this series shortly before his death.

Monet had close ties with another area that is featured in this chapter – Normandy's Côte d'Albâtre (p97). During a fruitful period between 1880 and 1883, while based at Étretat, Fécamp and Pourville, he produced about 150 canvases, using new pictorial techniques to capture the ever-changing light falling on the white cliffs and the sea.

The house and gardens at Giverny were bequeathed to the Académie des Beaux-Arts in 1966 by the painter's son and, after extensive renovation that was guided by the Fondation Claude Monet, opened to the public in 1980. The **house** *(admission €5.50; open Tue-Sun)* is filled with furniture and paintings. An adjacent shop, astutely placed to waylay visitors en route to the house and gardens, is filled with souvenirs, ranging from prints to mouse pads and aprons.

Many American painters were attracted to Giverny in the late 19th and early 20th centuries, fascinated by Monet's approach, and briefly turning the village into an artists' colony. Some of their works are exhibited in the **Musée d'Art Americaine** *(99 rue Claude Monet; ☎ 02 32 51 94 65; www.maag.org; admission €5.50; open Tue-Sun)*.

---

restaurants along rue de Falaise and rue Claude Monet. Here is a selection.

La Terrasse Café-Bar *(☎ 02 32 51 36 09; 87 rue Claude Monet; menu €15)* is a small, intimate place specialising in Normandy produce. Try the delicious apple tart.

Ancien Hôtel Baudy *(☎ 02 32 21 10 03; 81 rue Claude Monet; mains €10-11, menu €18.50*, an artists' haunt since the late 19th century, offers salads and hot dishes.

Getting There & Away Trains operated by SNCF *(☎ 08 92 35 35 35)* travelling from Paris' Gare St-Lazare on the line to Rouen and Le Havre stop at Vernon (€10.60, 47 minutes, at least six daily). A shuttle bus from/to Giverny meets each train (€4 return, 10 minutes). From the bus stop, which is in a large parking area, access to Monet's house and gardens is very clearly

signposted via an underpass, roadside path and rue Claude Monet.

THE WALK (see map p96)

With your back to Monet's house, bear left along rue Claude Monet for about 200m then first right along chemin Blanche Hoschedé-Monet, but only for a few steps. Then veer right along rue Hélène Pillon; beyond a road diverging downhill to the right you pass elegant villas separated by steeply sloping fields. A grassed track leads onwards, gently uphill for about 250m. Leave the track to ascend a steep path with a hedge on its right. After about 250m swing right along a path through a gap in the hedge which takes you on a superb contouring route, mostly through woodland. After a few hundred metres, you come to a junction. Follow a track diagonally right, now in the heart

BRITTANY & NORMANDY

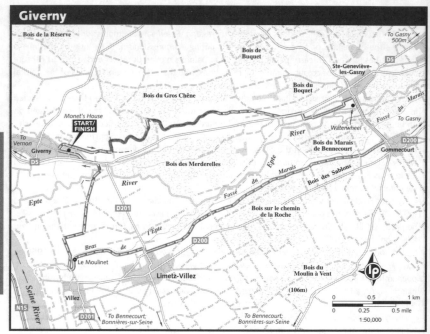

Giverny

of Bois du Gros Chêne (Big Oak Wood). Several hundred metres further on, the path dodges around a jumble of fallen trees, then soon leads out into the open, though fringed with a dense, high hedge. At the next cross-tracks swing right downhill.

Cross the D5; turn left along the verge for about 250m. Go down chemin du Moulin Brûlé (one hour from Giverny) then left along rue des Jacobins in the village of Ste-Geneviève-les-Gasny. At a fork 75m further on bear right along rue des Cascades to a junction. Turn right into rue des Jacobins, which takes you to a crossroads with an old church on the left; turn right along rue de l'Eau. Further on, crossing the Epte River, you'll see a decrepit wooden millwheel just downstream. The road leads into the quiet village of Gommecourt, where shortly it's right along narrow rue des Sablons. This leads almost unerringly eastwards for 2.7km, initially through **Bois des Sablons**, a *site naturel classeé* (classified natural site).

Cultivated fields signal the outskirts of the village of Limetz-Villez to the left. As you pass house gardens on the left, bear right at a fork and continue to the D201. Turn right for 50m, cross and follow a track leading west marked by two whitish pillars. About 1km further on, the track skirts the fenced grounds of a large house, jealously protected by guard dogs. Turn left at a road in the locality of Le Moulinet for 50m; beside an old communal laundry, bear right to cross a bridge over a branch of the Epte River (1½ hours from Ste-Geneviève).

Take the first track on the right, soon passing a clump of trees on the left, then go left at an intersection. About 400m further on, continue straight ahead; this minor road crosses the Epte River and brings you to the D5 road – turn left towards Giverny. Shortly, at another junction, either turn right into the village or left along chemin du Roy to the bus stop and car park (30 minutes from Le Moulinet).

Côte d'Albâtre

Duration	4–4½ hours
Distance	15.5km
Difficulty	moderate
Start	Fécamp (right)
Finish	Étretat (p99)
Transport	train, bus

Summary Quiet rural roads lead to breathtaking paths above sheer white limestone cliffs, extraordinary natural arches and slender wave-washed pinnacles.

It's as if the forces that shaped and carved rocks had acquired imaginative powers, so remarkable are the formations along Normandy's Côte d'Albâtre (Alabaster Coast). In Haute-Normandie, northeast of Le Havre, protruding fragments of the chalk cliffs, rising to 100m, have been sculpted into spires, arches and slender blades. The gently undulating countryside extending inland is riven by deep valleys, some wide, some narrow, where the largest towns have developed over the centuries.

The walk described here links two popular coastal towns and includes a breathtaking clifftop path past the finest examples of geological fantasy. The route follows part of the FFRP's GR21 (Le Tréport to Le Havre), making use of quiet roads, tracks and footpaths. A scenic side trip that takes you from Étretat to a prominent lighthouse offers some quieter paths, which were originally used by customs officers chasing smugglers. It's possible to shorten the journey and avoid most of the road walking by starting at the village of Yport, 5km southwest of Fécamp.

Les Autos Cars Gris (☎ 02 35 27 34 00) runs a bus service between Fécamp and Le Havre via Yport (15 minutes from Fécamp, one hour 20 minutes from Le Havre; at least six Monday to Saturday, three Sunday and holidays).

PLANNING

The area is hectically busy between June and the end of August, though some places may close through the cooler, quieter months.

Maps & Books

You'll need IGN 1:25,000 map Nos 1809OT *Fécamp* and 1710ET *Le Havre*. The FFRP's Topo-Guide Ref 202 *Le Pays de Caux. La Côte d'Albâtre* describes the route of the GR21 from Le Tréport to Le Havre.

NEAREST TOWNS
Fécamp

A centuries-old commercial centre and fishing port that has adapted to changing fortunes, Fécamp enjoys a superb setting in the steep-sided valley of the Valmont, with vertical cliffs guarding its grey shingle beach.

The **tourist office** (☎ 02 35 28 51 01; 113 rue Alexandre Le Grand; open daily) provides accommodation information and a useful town map. It sells the local IGN 1:25,000 map and books on local history.

The **Maison de la Presse** (rue Jacques Huet) also sells maps and books. There are ATMs at 6 av Gambetta and place Charles de Gaulle.

For camping gas try **Intersport** (place du Carreau), southeast of the train station. Internet access is available via Cyberposte at the **post office** (place Bellet).

Places to Stay & Eat In a wonderful location, **Camping Municipal de Renéville** (☎ 02 35 28 20 97, fax 02 35 29 57 68; chemin de Nesmond; camping 2 people & tent €6.10) is on grassed terraces above the southern end of the beach.

Hôtel Vent d'Ouest (☎ 02 35 28 04 04; www.hotelventdouest.tm.fr - French only; 3 av Gambetta; singles/doubles with bathroom €34/41; breakfast €5) overlooks the station and offers compact, pleasant rooms.

Hôtel d'Angleterre (☎ 02 35 28 01 60; www.hotelangleterre.com; 93 rue de la Plage; doubles/twins with bathroom €39/49; continental/buffet breakfast €4.60/6.10) is a friendly place, close to the beach, with fairly plain rooms, many looking seawards.

Hôtel le Commerce (☎ 02 35 28 19 28, fax 02 35 28 70 50; 26 place Pigot; doubles/twins with bathroom €49/55; breakfast €5.50, menus €13-28) near the station has tastefully furnished, largish rooms. The **restaurant** features local herring, beef and lamb.

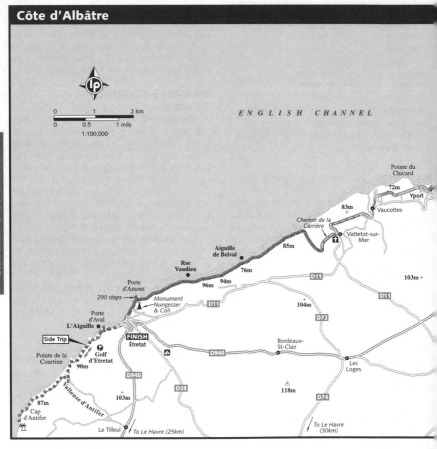

Côte d'Albâtre

ENGLISH CHANNEL

0   1   2 km
0   0.5   1 mile
1:100,000

BRITTANY & NORMANDY

Pointe du Chicard
72m
83m — Yport
Vaucottes
Chemin de la Carrière
Vattetot-sur-Mer
85m
103m +
Aiguille de Belval
76m
Roc Vaudieu
94m
96m
D11
D11
104m +
Porte d'Amont
290 steps
Monument Nungesser & Coli
D11
D72
Bordeaux-St-Clair
Porte d'Aval
L'Aiguille
FINISH
Étretat
D940
Les Loges
Side Trip
Golf d'Etretat
90m
Pointe de la Courtine
D940
103m +
D39
118m
D74
87m
Cap d'Antifer
Valleuse d'Antifer
Le Tilleul
To Le Havre (25km)
To Le Havre (30km)

There's a **Marché Plus supermarket** *(83 quai Bérigny)*; market day, on place Charles de Gaulle, is Saturday. Of several alluring *boulangeries*, **Les Carolines** *(44 rue Théagène Boufant)* is distinguished not only by its delicious breads and pastries but also by the murals on its outside wall. There's **Bio Horizon**, a health food shop on place Bellet.

Vegetarians searching for somewhere to dine will be basically limited to pizzerias and *crêperies* – this is a very carnivorous town!

La Galette d'Alex *(☎ 02 35 10 03 02; place Nicolas Selle; closed Tue & Wed; mains €2.80-12)* has outside tables. Apart from *galettes* and *crêpes*, there are also some more-filling *tartines au fromage* (cheese tarts) and fondues to choose from.

L'Escalier *(☎ 02 35 28 26 79; quai Bérigny; menus €11-23)* overlooks the marina. At this popular restaurant, fish is everything, served in generous quantities.

Getting There & Away Trains by SNCF *(☎ 08 92 35 35 35)* from Paris' St Lazare to Rouen stop at Breauté-Beuzeville, from where a small train shuttles back and forth to Fécamp (€23.80, two hours 10 minutes, at least four Monday to Saturday, two Sunday).

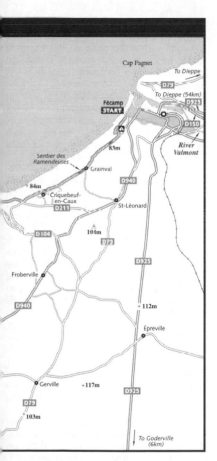

Les Autos Cars Gris (☎ 02 35 27 04 25; 8 av Gambetta) operates buses between Le Havre and Fécamp (€7.15, 45 minutes, at least four Monday to Saturday).

Étretat

Despite the hordes flocking to wander about on the cliffs, Étretat retains a great deal of the charm that has attracted artists (including Claude Monet) and visitors down the ages since the 1850s (see the boxed text on p95).

The **tourist office** (☎ 02 35 27 05 21; www.etretat.net; place Maurice Guillard) is useful for accommodation information and tide times.

Maps are available from the **Maison de la Presse** (13 rue Georges V). There's a bank with an ATM in blvd René Coty.

Places to Stay & Eat Fifteen to 20 minutes' walk east from the beach is the **Camping Municipal** (☎ 02 35 27 07 67; rue Guy de Maupassant; camping per person & tent €5). The grassed sites are well back from the main road.

Hôtel de la Poste (☎ 02 35 27 01 34, fax 02 35 27 76 28; 6 av George V; singles/doubles with bathroom €30/35; breakfast €5.50) represents good value locally; most of the small rooms overlook a busy street.

Hôtel La Residence (☎ 02 35 27 02 87; 4 blvd René Coty; singles/doubles with washbasin €26/29, with bathroom €42/45; menus €14-32) is easily the most picturesque place to stay – a magnificent 14th-century timber building complete with creaking floors and modern facilities. The attached **La Salamandre** restaurant, with tables outside under the massive timber eaves, serves organic produce and three vegetarian dishes.

For self-caterers, there is the **COOP supermarket** (40 rue Nôtre Dame; open Tue-Sat & Sun morning) and a weekly **market** in the timber building on place Flory. Don't miss **Guelin Patisserie** (19 av George V) for tempting pastries and breads.

La Belle Époque (☎ 02 35 28 83 74; blvd René Coty; mains €9-12) is a cheerful, rather crowded restaurant, which makes a feature of mountainous plates of mussels and chips. The pizzas rate above average.

Le Corsaire (☎ 02 35 10 38 90; Front de Mer; menus €14.50-24.50), in the hotel of the same name, has a beachside terrace; appropriately, the sea dominates the menus.

Getting There & Away There's a bus service to Le Havre (€6.10, 50 minutes, at least three daily) with **Les Autos Cars Gris** (☎ 02 35 27 04 25). Plenty of trains leave Le Havre for Paris via Rouen (€24.40, two hours, at least five daily). On Friday and weekends an early-evening bus service to Breauté-Beuzeville connects with a train to Paris' St-Lazare.

BRITTANY & NORMANDY

THE WALK (see map pp98-9)

Near the southern end of the promenade, bear left between Hôtel de la Mer and the casino to a road, turn left, then 50m along go sharp right towards the camping area. The way-markers start a few metres along here. After about 100m turn right at a junction; continue uphill, through the camping area, then bear right along a minor road in front of a magnificent three-storey house. Almost 1km from the junction, descend into the narrow valley sheltering the hamlet of Grainval (30 minutes from Fécamp). Close to a crossroads is **Auberge les Tonnelles** (☎ 02 35 28 77 18; *singles/doubles with bathroom €29/38, half board €32; breakfast €4.50, menus €14-23)*. Its restaurant offers two *menus*.

From the intersection, go across route de Grainval, then straight up Sentier des Ramendeuses and on along a minor, field-lined road to the hamlet of **Criquebeuf-en-Caux** (the name reflecting Norse influence and meaning 'village with the church'). Veer right at a junction, still on chemin des Ramendeuses, and continue to a junction with a crucifix on the left. Turn right to a fork where the road bends right. Then swing left along a track, which soon plummets towards the grey slate roofs of the village of **Yport**, packed into its small valley. Next, bear left at a junction as you descend to reach a road, where it's right for 30m to place Jean Paul Laurens (an hour from Grainval).

A fishing port from long ago, now geared modestly to tourism, Yport is a quiet and attractive alternative starting point, with all facilities. **Hôtel-Restaurant La Sirène** (☎ 02 35 27 31 87, fax 02 35 29 47 37; *7 blvd Alexandre Dumont; singles/doubles with bathroom €45/55; menus €17-25)*, a modernised old building, overlooks the beach. The restaurant's *menus* promote Normandy produce.

To continue, follow rue Emmanuel Foy to the beach. Turn left, then fork right; 100m beyond La Sirène, go up steps on the left to rue Jean Helie. Turn right and ascend extremely steeply to a minor road. Where it bends left, go straight on along a farm track to a road on the edge of the hamlet of Vaucottes. Cross and go left for 150m, then right along a grassy track, with the first view of

the awesome coastal cliffs. Soon, at a junction, keep going down along a shady track (diverging from the route on the 1:25,000 map), which leads to a road. Turn right towards Vaucottes for about 120m, then left up a track beside a large house. Continue along a road for about 150m then go right along chemin de Randonnée. This leads gently uphill for 400m; bear left to a junction in front of a church. If you go through the churchyard you'll find **Auberge Le Puits Fleuri** (☎ 02 35 91 31 02; *menus €12-32)*.

Turn right along chemin de la Carrière, down to a valley where you swing right to a parking area. Continue along the path towards the coast. A steep concrete road leads to the shore but the route goes left up a narrow, steep path to the clifftop (1½ hours from Yport). From here there's a marvellous view southwestwards of vertical cliffs, their stark whiteness softened by thin horizontal, grey-black bands. Aiguille de Belval and Roc Vaudieu lie offshore and the graceful arch of Porte d'Amont beckons in the distance. Just southwest of the Roc comes the first of several lookouts, safely affording spectacular views northwards. Past a few of these, a flight of steps leads down to the shore across the steep side of **Porte d'Amont**. It's well worth taking 20 to 30 minutes to descend (and climb back up) the 290 steps for a seagull's-eye view of the cliffs and the base of the arch.

Continue along the path. Now you have the chance to answer a question that's probably been nagging for a while: 'What on earth is that tall, graceful white arrowhead?' Beside the monument is a small **museum** (*admission €0.95; open Sat, Sun & public holidays)* commemorating the ill-fated flight of Charles Nungesser and François Coli on 8 May 1927. They took off from Étretat aiming to complete a trans-Atlantic flight, but disappeared without trace. The monument, *L'Oiseau Blanc* (White Bird, the name of their plane), replaces one destroyed by the German army in 1942. From the nearby church, follow steps down to the promenade in Étretat (1½ hours direct from the start of the clifftop path). To orient yourself, go along to steps just past a *boules* pitch on the left; there's a town map down beside the parking area.

Side Trip: Phare d'Antifer
2 hours return, 8km

Take the steps at the far end of the promenade in Étretat, then follow the path beside the golf course and the much-traversed clifftop paths to Porte de Courtine; here the waymarked route turns left. Descend into Valleuse d'Antifer along a wide path; cross a road and follow a path to the right leading back to the coast. Above the cliffs, bear left uphill. Generally keep close to the cliff edge, across another two valleys, to a fence enclosing the lighthouse grounds. The towering **Phare d'Antifer** lighthouse (closed to the public) overlooks dozens of remnant WWII defences and vertical cliffs crowded with sea birds. The huge breakwater to the south provides docking for small oil tankers. Retrace your steps; approaching Étretat, break off to the paths and bridges above Porte d'Aval for awesome views.

Mont St-Michel

Duration	7¼–7½ hours
Distance	30km
Difficulty	moderate
Start	Avranches
Finish	Mont St-Michel (landward) (p105)
Nearest Towns	Avranches (right), Pontorson (p102)
Transport	train, bus

Summary The renowned Mont beckons all the way on an unusual route along the shores of Baie du Mont St-Michel, past vast grazing meadows and historic towns.

Mont St-Michel is the second-most-visited site in France, but it's likely that relatively few of the 3.5 million visitors annually realise that the surrounding bay, as well as the incomparable Gothic and Romanesque buildings on the Mont, is a World Heritage Site. The bay is also a *site classée* (protected

site) and is home to large numbers of waders and sea birds whose numbers swell to at least 150,000 during winter, before the waders migrate to summer breeding grounds. Another distinctive feature of the bay is the vast area of grazing meadows, subject to occasional flooding, but usually grazed by large flocks of sheep.

This walk follows the shore of the estuary of the Sée and Sélune Rivers in the eastern corner of the bay, making use of quiet roads and paths on the edge of the grassland, part of the FFRP's waymarked GR22. The bay is remarkably peaceful, the perfect background for the constantly changing vistas of sky, land and water, and of the distinctive silhouette of the Mont, becoming ever clearer as you walk west.

PLANNING
The Mont is rarely not busy; try to avoid peak holiday periods; early morning and evening are the least crowded times. The walk described should be negotiable except possibly at monthly peak tide times (when the moon is new or full) and during high seas (see the boxed text on p102).

It is possible to start the walk at Pontaubault, thereby saving 12km and three hours, although this necessitates an overnight stay if you arrive on the early evening bus from Avranches.

Maps & Books
IGN 1:25,000 map Nos 1215ET *Avranches-Granville* and 1215OT *Le Mont-St-Michel* cover the walk.

The FFRP's Topo-Guide Ref 200 *Tour du Cotentin* is highly informative.

NEAREST TOWNS
Avranches
A fine old town, dating back to the Romans, Avranches is impressively sited on a ridge overlooking Baie du Mont St-Michel.

The **tourist office** (☎ *02 33 58 00 22; www.ville-avranches.fr; 2 rue du Général de Gaulle; open Mon-Sat year-round*) is well organised. It you arrive after hours, there's a town map and list of hotel phone numbers outside.

Tide Watch

Baie du Mont St-Michel experiences the greatest difference between low and high tides anywhere in Europe, an incredible 15m. The tide advances across the sands at about 10km per hour and the bay can fill in 4½ hours.

High and low tides are a daily event in the bay but the water must reach a level of at least 12m for them to be perceptible at the Mont, which happens on 15 or 16 days per month. Peak tides occur twice during any month 36 to 48 hours after the full or new moon. The big 15m tides are only twice-yearly events, at the equinoxes in spring (around 21 March) and autumn (around 23 September).

Ideally visit the Mont during full moon at the spring equinox or new moon at the autumn equinox. Next best is to come during the full-moon period between January and June or the new-moon period through to December. As a last resort, arrive during full or new moon at any time of the year.

The most convenient ATM is opposite the tourist office.

Maps and guides are available from **Maison de la Presse** (place Littré). Internet access is available via Cyberposte at the **post office** (42 rue St-Gervais).

Places to Stay & Eat The rooms are fresh and comfortable at **Hôtel La Renaissance** (☎ 02 33 58 03 71, fax 02 33 60 86 12; rue des Fossés; singles/doubles €23/33; breakfast €5) – despite creaking floorboards and old-style atmosphere.

Hôtel Normandie (☎ 02 33 58 01 33; 2 blvd Jozeau Marigné; doubles with toilet/bathroom €25/39; menus €13-18) is a tall, ivy-encrusted building beside a busy intersection. It benefits by being on the route of the walk, 250m northwest of the tourist office. In the timber-panelled dining room you can select from two *menus*, which offer staples such as oysters, homemade terrine and *sole meunière*.

Le Jardin des Plantes (☎ 02 33 58 03 68; www.le-jardin-des-plantes.fr; 10 place Carnot; doubles with bathroom €52-79) is the

best place to stay on all counts, for comfort and understated luxury.

There's a **Champion supermarket** (open Mon-Sat & Sun morning) near to the tourist office. **Market** days are Tuesday, Friday and Saturday.

Le Montépéggo (☎ 02 33 48 65 74; 20 rue des Chapeliers; closed Wed evening and Sun; menus €14-18.50) is brightly decorated with well-spaced tables. The eclectic offerings include kangaroo with pepper sauce.

Le Bistrot de Pierre (☎ 02 33 58 07 66; 5 rue du Général de Gaulle; menus €12.30-14.80; closed Sun) creates a relaxed atmosphere in which to enjoy such delights as whelks and sea bream with red peppers.

Getting There & Away Take one of the **SNCF** (☎ 08 92 35 35 35) trains from Paris' Montparnasse to Rennes and change for Caen to reach Avranches (€36.70, 3¼ hours, two daily Caen–Avranches). The easiest way to reach the town centre from the train station (€4) is by **taxi** (☎ 02 33 68 32 70).

Les Courriers Bretons (☎ 02 99 19 70 70) operates a late-afternoon bus service to Pontaubault and Pontorson (about €2.50, 10 minutes, Monday to Friday school term, Tuesday and Thursday in school holidays).

Pontorson

A down-to-earth place 9km south of the causeway and an amenable and popular alternative to places closer in.

The **tourist office** (☎ 02 33 60 20 65; www.mont-saint-michel-baie.com - French only; place de la Mairie; open Mon-Sat) is very helpful. It handles bookings for the walk across the bay from Mont St-Michel to Rocher de Tombelaine; this costs €5 for the 3½-hour expedition in small groups with an experienced guide. Internet access is available at the office (€4.50 per 30 minutes).

There's at ATM at 19 rue Couesnon (the main street).

Places to Stay & Eat Beside the Couesnon River, **Camping Haliotis** (☎/fax 02 33 68 11 59; chemin des Soupirs; camping per person & tent €7.70; cabins for 2 €55) has sheltered sites to pitch your tent.

Auberge de Jeunesse (☎ 02 33 60 18 65; rue Général Patton; beds €8; breakfast €3.50) is a large rambling building with basic dorms and a self-catering kitchen.

Hôtel La Tour Brette (☎ 02 33 60 10 69; 8 rue Couesnon; singles/doubles with bathroom €30/35, half board €36; breakfast €6, menus €10-25) on a busy corner in the town centre has comfortable, modern rooms. There is an attached informal **restaurant** (closed Wednesday), which features seafood.

There's a **Champion supermarket** (open Mon-Sat) on route du Mont St-Michel at the edge of town and a **Huit à 8 supermarket** at 3 rue Couesnon (open Mon-Sat & Sun morning). Market day is Wednesday (morning).

La Squadra (☎ 02 33 68 37 17, 102 rue Couesnon; mains €4.60-10.50) is a popular, colourful place; the menu focuses on pasta, salads and pizza. It serves an excellent local beer, in *brun* (dark) and *blonde* (light) styles.

Getting There & Away Between Pontorson and Mont St-Michel there are **Les Courriers**

Mont St-Michel & the Future

Mont St-Michel is a tidal island, surrounded by water for only a couple of hours at high water during the highest tides, for 36 to 48 hours after the new and full moon each month. At low tide the sea retreats by as much as 12km; the tidal variation is a huge 15m, the greatest in Europe.

Since the 1.9km causeway was built in 1879 and the Couesnon River canalised around the same time, enormous quantities of silt have accumulated in the surrounding area, threatening the Mont's island status.

An ambitious project has been launched to alter the tidal flow around the island to reduce or even reverse silt deposition. The causeway and car parks beside the Mont will be replaced by a low bridge with footpaths, under which tidal currents will flow. A shuttle service will link a huge car park on the mainland with the Mont; work is to be completed by 2007.

The website www.projetmontsaintmichel.fr has more information about the project.

Bretons (☎ 02 33 60 11 43) buses (€1.70, 13 minutes, at least eight daily). The company also operates a service to Rennes train station (€11, one hour 15 minutes, four Monday to Saturday, three Sunday). From Rennes, **SNCF** (☎ 08 92 35 35 35) TGVs run to Paris' Montparnasse (€56.10, two hours 10 minutes, four Monday to Saturday, three Sunday).

GETTING TO/FROM THE WALK

Start the walk at Avranches (p101). There's a **Les Courriers Bretons** (☎ 02 99 19 70 70) bus service between Pontorson and Mont St-Michel (landward), stopping in the village (€1.40, eight minutes, at least eight daily).

THE WALK (see map p104)

Follow rue du Général de Gaulle northwest from the tourist office in Avranches to a roundabout; walk down Tertre de la Gare (beside Hôtel Normandie) and cross the bridge spanning the busy N175. Turn left along a gravel path that leads to a minor road. Follow it south for 250m; turn right along a minor road, which shortly crosses the railway, and continue around to the left, past a timber mill. About 300m further on you come to Les Herbus and, beyond, the vast expanses of the bay, with Mont St-Michel visible above a low ridge to the southwest. About 200m beyond the end of the bitumen go through a gate. Continue southwest along this exhilaratingly open grassland to a small airfield; go through a gate to a road (1¼ hours from the start).

The road takes you into the long inlet of the Sélune River; about 1.2km along you pass a graphic sign illustrating the dire consequences of venturing onto the tidal flats around the bay. Beyond Le Gué de l'Epine and where the road bends left, look out for a striking view of the Mont, rising from, but clearly separate from, the headland to the west. At the hamlet of Flaget the road bends left; instead go straight on across the grass, through a gate, across a small bridge and back to the road, soon passing a veritable menagerie of a farm. A few hundred metres further on, bear right at a junction and shortly go through a gate to the grassland. Continue to the D43E at Pontaubault; turn right and

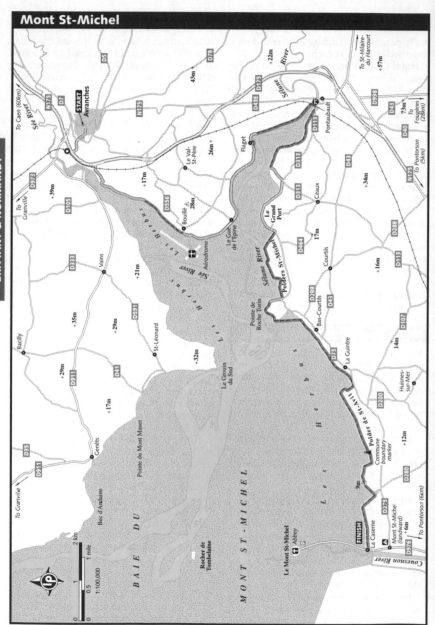

Mont St-Michel

cross the Sélune River bridge (1¾ hours from the airfield).

If you go straight ahead into the village from the bridge there's a small *boulangerie*-grocery, **Hotel-Restaurant Au Soleil Levant** *(☎/fax 02 33 60 47 39; 15 rue Patton; doubles with bathroom €26.50-30; breakfast €5.30, menus €13-27.50)*, and **Restaurant à la Grillade** *(☎ 02 33 60 47 28; 21 bis rue Patton; menus €13-24)*. If you've arrived here by bus simply head west to reach the river.

To continue the walk from the bridge, head northwest across a small park, right along a gravel road, and soon you're on grass. It's best to keep close to the fence, resisting the temptation to wander across Les Herbus, so as not to miss a gate, 2.2km from Pontaubault. Go through it and follow a road southwest for about 500m to an intersection and turn right. Soon, at a fork, follow an old road to the right for a few hundred metres, then continue northwest then west. At Le Grand Port, go through a gate on the right; several hundred metres further on, follow a narrow path between the shore and the dike, on the edge of the reclaimed marshland in Polders St-Michel. With another kilometre behind you and where the dike heads south, go through a gate onto the grassland for about 500m. Leave the fields by another gate and turn right along a road to Pointe de Roche Torin (1¾ hours from Pontaubault).

Although the open grasslands seem to offer easy walking, they're riven by surprisingly deep, soft-sided channels; you can spend an awful lot of time trying to find safe crossings. The designated route leads southwestwards, passing quite close to the hamlet of Bas-Courtils, to Le Guintre, then following the dike beside Polder de St-Avit. After about 700m, bear left onto the crest – the path may be rougher but the views are better – for a good 2km, past a commune boundary marker and a trig point. Cross two stiles fairly close together, then go along a path between fences, over another stile and right. Less than 2km more brings you to the D976 at La Caserne (2½ hours from Pointe de Roche Torin). It's another 2km to **Mont St-Michel** or scarcely 500m left to hotels, shops and the bus stop for Pontorson at Mont St-Michel (landward). See p103 for bus details.

The somewhat artificial village near the area of La Caserne calls itself Mont St-Michel, sometimes with 'landward' or the equivalent tacked on. It lacks the atmosphere of a lived-in town but is vastly less expensive than the Mont itself.

Camping du Mont St-Michel *(☎ 02 33 60 09 33; camping per person & tent €9.70, bed in bungalow €8)* is close to the main road. **La Jacotière** *(☎ 02 33 60 22 94; doubles with bathroom €38; breakfast €4)* is a friendly B&B in a restored and extended farmhouse, 400m along the D275 from the junction with the D976. **Hôtel Formule Verte** *(☎ 02 33 60 14 13, stmichel@le-mont-saint-michel.com; doubles with bathroom €45.60; breakfast €6.85)* is a modern establishment.

Other Walks

BRITTANY
Île d'Ouessant

The most westerly outpost of the country, Île d'Ouessant, is a small, low island (8km by 4km) that is bounded by 30km of magnificent coastline protecting a largely unspoiled hinterland. Following paths and quiet roads you can explore the island in three days' easy walking (around 50km). Ouessant's lighthouses are the theme of an ecomuseum; the island offers outstanding seabird watching.

You'll need IGN 1:25,000 map No 0317OT. Contact the **tourist office** *(☎ 02 98 48 85 83; www .ot-ouessant.fr - French only)* for more information; it issues detailed guides to local walks. **Penn ar Bed** *(☎ 02 98 80 80 80; www.pennarbed.fr; Port de Commerce, Brest)* runs a year-round, daily ferry service from Brest (€29.50, two hours) and Le Conquet (€25.50, one hour); ferries also operate from Camaret-sur-Mer (see p89; €26.40, about 1½ hours, one per week April to mid-July and early September, one Monday to Saturday mid-July to August).

NORMANDY
Cotentin Peninsula

The FFRP's GR223 closely follows the coastline of Manche *département* from Pont-du-Vey to Mont St-Michel, via Cherbourg, Coutances and

Avranches, 444km in all, providing at least three weeks' walking. The route embraces many and varied historical sites, some awesome coastal cliffs, including 126m-high Nez de Jobourg, beautiful beaches backed by sand dunes, and timeless villages. Part of the route, from Avranches to Mont St-Michel, is described in detail earlier in this chapter (p99).

A recommended five-day sample is the section west and south from Cherbourg to Carteret. The Topo-Guide is Ref 200 *Tour du Cotentin;* of the nine IGN 1:25,000 maps needed for the full route, Nos 1210ET, 1110ET and 1211OT cover the recommended section. For more information contact **Manche CDT** (*☎ 02 33 05 98 70; www.manchetourisme.com).*

Auvergne & Massif Central

The Massif Central is France's spine, its vertebrae the plugs and cones of extinct volcanoes, known as *puys*. In the relatively rich volcanic soil of its plains and valleys, maize, tobacco and vines all thrive. Its rumpled slopes are clad in either dense forest or sweet pasture where cattle and sheep graze, producing some of France's finest cheeses.

Two conflicting theories seek to explain the origin of the Massif. Was it a result of the clash of European and African tectonic plates at the beginning of the tertiary era, a recoiling of the colossal force that thrust the Alps skywards? Or could it be the consequence of a 'hot spot', a heat surge of indescribable intensity from the earth's mantle, bursting through its crust?

The three regions of the Massif, in ascending order of age, are the Monts Dômes, Monts

Highlights

- Crunching across volcanic cinders, tiny and light as rice cereal, on Puy de la Vache (p112)
- Gazing at the sudden vista of Puy de Sancy (p117) and its cirque from the Roc de Cuzeau's narrow plateau
- Marvelling at postcard-perfect views of the gentle valley between the pinnacles of Roche Tuilière and Roche Sanadoire (p118)
- Admiring the twisted dolomite shapes of Nîmes-le-Vieux (p129)

Dore and Monts du Cantal. Formed during very different periods of volcanic activity, each has its own character. Much of the area falls within the boundaries of Parc Naturel Régional des Volcans, France's largest regional nature park (3950 sq km). At the range's southern limit are the Cévennes, a wild region of limestone and granite, as akin to Languedoc and the Midi as to Auvergne.

CLIMATE

Unlike elsewhere in France, the Massif Central receives the major part of its rainfall in summer, frequently in the form of late afternoon storms. The Cévennes and Grands Causses mountains have a more Mediterranean, more constant climate. Winters are milder and summer – when midday temperatures can make walking uncomfortable – is the extreme season.

In the north of the range, it's wise to check the weather forecast before setting out each day; the mountains can be capricious in their sudden changes of mood.

INFORMATION
What to bring

Always set out with plenty of water. While almost every community at the base of the volcanic massifs boasts a flowing *fontaine* (fountain or spring, often the focal point of the village), rainfall percolates quickly through

Auvergnat Cheeses

For centuries, Auvergne has had a thriving cheese industry. From as early as the 1st century AD, the lush grasses of the volcanic soils have fed the cows that give the milk that farmers ferment into a range of excellent cheeses. The region has no less than five cheeses that are classified as Appellation d'Origine Contrôlée (the highest category of French cheese, with an officially controlled declaration of origin): Cantal, white and full flavoured; Salers, similar, from the same area but made only from the milk of cows that graze on high summer pastures; St-Nectaire, rich-scented, flat and round like a discus; Fourme d'Ambert, a mild, smooth blue cheese; and Bleu d'Auvergne, blue and stronger, with a creamier texture than its much-touted cousin, Rocquefort.

The story goes that Bleu d'Auvergne was first developed in the middle of the 19th century by an Auvergnat farmer dubiously experimenting with the effects of rye bread mould on his milk curd!

Take your pick; each in its distinct way makes a delightful sandwich filling.

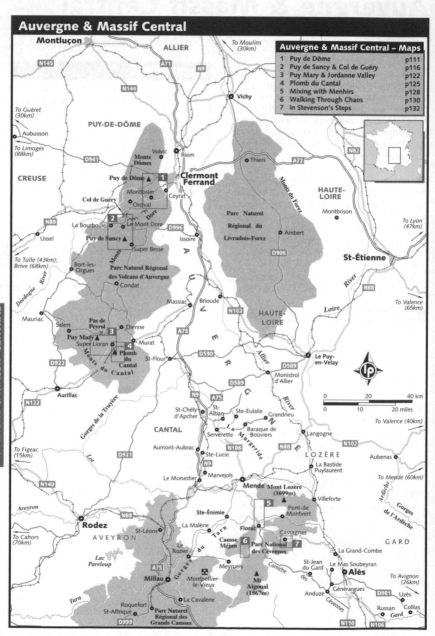

Auvergne & Massif Central

Auvergne & Massif Central – Maps

1 Puy de Dôme — p111
2 Puy de Sancy & Col de Guéry — p116
3 Puy Mary & Jordanne Valley — p122
4 Plomb du Cantal — p125
5 Mixing with Menhirs — p128
6 Walking Through Chaos — p130
7 In Stevenson's Steps — p132

Montluçon
ALLIER
To Moulins (30km)
N145
A71
N9
N144
Vichy
To Guéret (30km)
Aubusson
PUY-DE-DÔME
Thiers
A72
To Limoges (88km)
D941
Volvic
Riom
HAUTE-LOIRE
CREUSE
Monts Dômes
Puy de Dôme ▲ 1
Clermont Ferrand
To Lyon (47km)
Col de Guéry
Montlosier
Ceyrat
Montbrison
N89
Ordival
Le Mont Dore
D996
Parc Naturel Régional du Livradois-Forez
La Bourboule
2
Ambert
St-Étienne
Ussel
Puy de Sancy ▲
Issoire
D906
Super Besse
To Tulle (43km); Brive (68km)
Bort-les-Orgues
Parc Naturel Régional des Volcans d'Auvergne
Condat
River
To Valence (65km)
Dordogne River
Massiac
Brioude
N102
N88
Mauriac
Salers
Pas de Peyrol
Dienne
HAUTE-LOIRE
Loire
To Valence (65km)
3
Puy Mary ▲
Super Lioran
Murat
Le Puy-en-Velay
D922
4
Plomb du Cantal ▲
St-Flour
D590
Allier River
D589
Monistrol d'Allier
Aurillac
N122
Monts du Cantal
D589
0   20   40 km
0   10   20 miles
Gorges de la Truyère
St-Chély d'Apcher
St-Alban
Ste-Eulalie
Grandrieu
To Valence (40km)
To Figeac (15km)
CANTAL
Serverette
Baraque de Bouviers
Langogne
N102
Aubenas
N9
N106
LOZÈRE
N14U
D921
Aumont-Aubrac
Ste-Lucie
La Bastide Puylaurent
To Mende (60km)
Le Monastier
Marvejols
Mende
Mont Lozère (1699m)
Villefort
Aveyron
N88
Ste-Énimie
5
Pont-de-Montvert
Gorges de l'Ardèche
To Cahors (70km)
St-Léons
La Malène
Florac
Cassagnas
GARD
Rodez
AVEYRON
Le Rozier
Causse Méjean
6
Parc National des Cévennes
7
La Grand-Combe
Lac Pareloup
Meyrueis
St-Jean du Gard
Le Mas Soubeyran
Alès
Millau
A75
Montpellier-le-Vieux
Corniche
To Avignon (26km)
Mt Aigoual (1567m)
Anduze
Générargues
D981
Uzès
Roquefort
La Cavalerie
Collias
St-Affrique
Parc Naturel Régional des Grands Causses
Russan
Gard
D999
N110
N106

the limestone and thin soil and streams flow only briefly after heavy rainfall.

Maps
The walk region is covered by Michelin's 1:200,000 map No 239 *Auvergne-Limousin* and IGN's 1:250,000 map No 111 *Auvergne*.

Books
Alan Castle's excellent *Walks in Volcano Country* (Cicerone Press) describes a 15-day traverse of the high crests following, in the main, the GR4 and GR441, plus an eight-day circuit of the Velay region around Le Puy-en-Velay. For details of Castle's equally evocative *The Robert Louis Stevenson Trail* in the Cévennes, see Other Walks, p133.

Describing day walks, Maurice Turner in the Pathmaster Guides series adopts a different, equally thorough (but more stylistically plodding) approach in his *The Auvergne: 30 Circular Walks from Regional Centres*. If you read French, the best book for an overview of walking options is *Weekends Dans le Massif Central* published by Chamina.

To learn more about the flowers and animals of the region there are two excellent books in French, each supported by a wealth of photographs: *Fleurs Familières et Meconnues du Massif Central* by Noel Graveline and *Fauna d'Auvergne et du Limousin* by Christian Bovehardy.

Regulations
In certain fragile moorland areas, it's forbidden to leave the waymarked route. This restriction limits the amount of incidental damage caused by walkers to the vulnerable vegetation.

GATEWAY
Clermont Ferrand
Clermont Ferrand, largest town in the Massif Central, sits on a long-extinct volcano. Alive and animated, it makes a good base for exploring the Monts Dômes and the northern part of the Massif. Its main **tourist office** (☎ 04 73 98 65 00; www.ot-clermont-ferrand .fr; place de la Victoire) shares space with and observes similar hours to Espace Massif Central (see Information following).

Virtua Network (☎ 04 73 91 65 53; 5 blvd Trudaine; €4/hr) has Internet access.

Information The superlative organisation **Chamina** (☎ 04 73 92 81 44; www.chamina .com - French only; 5 rue Pierre-le-Venérable, BP 436, 63012 Clermont Ferrand) operates from its base at the heart of the Massif Central. It researches and waymarks trails, approves accommodation for walkers and produces its own fine series of walking guides, mainly, but not exclusively, of the Massif Central.

Espace Massif Central (☎ 04 73 42 60 00; place de la Victoire; open Mon-Sat), also in Clermont Ferrand, has a full range of Chamina guides and carries both IGN maps and Fédération Française de la Randonnée Pédestre (FFRP) Topo-Guides of the region.

Places to Stay & Eat Bus No 4 stops right outside **Camping Le Chanset** (☎/fax 04 73 61 30 73; camping.lechanset@wanadoo.fr; av Jean Baptiste, Ceyrat; camping per person/tent/ car €2.60/4/1.50; open year-round) in Ceyrat, virtually a suburb of Clermont Ferrand.

Auberge du Cheval Blanc (☎ 04 73 92 26 39, fax 04 73 92 99 96; dorm beds €8.40; open Apr-Oct), Clermont's HI-affiliated youth hostel, is 100m from the train station.

Hôtel Ravel (☎ 04 73 91 51 33; hotelravel 63@wanadoo.fr; 8 rue de Maringues; singles/ doubles with bathroom €33/39), also handy for the train station, has pleasant, old-fashioned rooms.

Hôtel Foch (☎ 04 73 93 48 40; regina.foch@ wanadoo.fr; 22 rue Maréchal Foch; singles/ doubles/triples/quads with bathroom from €36/40/50/52) is just off central place de Jaude. Rooms, some with aircon, are smallish but represent good value.

Rue St-Dominique and nearby rue St-Adjutor, two blocks north of place de Jaude, sprawl with reasonably priced **French and ethnic restaurants**.

Getting There & Away Clermont Ferrand's train station, on av de l'Union Soviétique, is the most important rail junction in the Massif Central. Major destinations include Paris' Gare de Lyon (€39, three hours, six to nine daily) and Lyon (€25.10, via St-Étienne, up to 12 daily).

For other areas in the Massif Central, three to five trains a day serve – for the Monts Dore – La Bourboule and Le Mont-Dore (€10.70, 1¼ hours) and – for the Monts du Cantal – Murat (€15.40, 1½ hours).

Car-rental companies include **Ada** (☎ 04 73 91 66 07; 79 av de l'Union Soviétique) and **Budget** (☎ 04 73 92 22 66; 106 av du Brezet).

For a taxi, call **Taxi 63** (☎ 04 73 31 53 15) or **Allo Taxi Radio** (☎ 04 73 19 53 53).

Monts Dômes

The Monts Dômes are the babies of the Massif Central, thrust up by the range's most recent volcanic activity in the late quaternary period. Their oldest rocks, formed about 100,000 years ago, are youngsters in geological terms. The most recent eruptions were probably only 7000 years ago, well after the first humans had arrived in Auvergne.

Puy de Dôme

Duration	2 days
Distance	36km
Difficulty	moderate
Start	Ceyrat Robinson car park
Finish	Royat
Nearest Town	Clermont Ferrand (p109)
Transport	bus

Summary A couple of minor volcanic peaks to whet the appetite, then a steep but brief ascent to the summit of Puy de Dôme, unofficial emblem of Auvergne.

In addition to the Puy de Dôme, Clermont Ferrand's round-shouldered sentinel, the walk takes in a couple of minor and more tranquil puys. Below their bare upper flanks, it passes through typical mixed woodland and a selection of small Auvergnat villages.

You can shorten Day 1 if you bypass the Puy de la Vache and Puy de Lassolas and continue along the GR4, which runs along their base. However, if you do so, you'll miss some spectacular scenery.

PLANNING
When to Walk
The walk is normally possible and pleasurable from April to November. However, cloud and rain can obscure the splendid summit views at any time of year.

Maps
The IGN 1:25,000 map No 2531ET *Chaîne des Puys* covers the whole walk.

GETTING TO/FROM THE WALK
Ceyrat Robinson, at the beginning of the walk, is at the end of No 4 bus line. Pick it up from Clermont Ferrand's train station, place de Jaude or the bus station on blvd Gergovia. Buses run every half hour and stop outside Camping Le Chanset.

Bus No 16 for Clermont Ferrand passes Royat's post office two or three times an hour on weekdays, the last one leaving at 9.30pm (8.50pm on Saturday; you're on your own on Sunday). No 41, which runs infrequently (last bus 6.40pm), passes by Camping Le Chanset.

THE WALK
Day 1: Ceyrat to Laschamp
4¼–4¾ hours, 18km

From the Ceyrat Robinson car park and bus terminus follow the sign, 'Gorges de l'Artière'. After five minutes, take a hairpin left at a stone bridge beside a recent landslide to bear away from the stream up a series of gentle zigzags.

A brief ascent, guided by yellow waymarkers, leads to a long, flat stroll through woodland, then open pasture.

After 35 to 40 minutes, go round a metal barrier and pass through the farm of Redon Haut. Just beyond, continue along a rough track then, at a four-way junction, leave the yellow blazes and go straight ahead up a cinder track. Bear right after 200m to join a narrow road that winds down to the heavily trafficked N89. Turn right to skirt the village of Theix and, after an unpleasant, traffic-heavy 500m, right again

Puy de Dôme

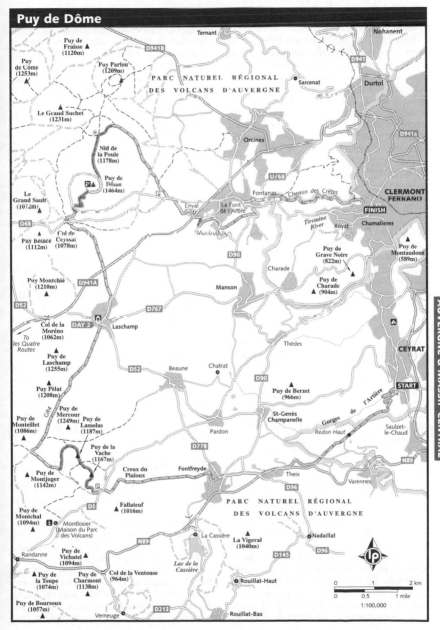

onto the altogether quieter D52, signed 'Fontfreyde'.

Bear left onto the D778 and follow it to the village of Fontfreyde, keeping straight where the main road turns sharp right. At place de la Fontaine (indeed with a flowing fountain), take rue de la Souche, the first exit on the right, and leave the village by a muddy cart track. You're now following intermittent green flashes, positioned very much in favour of walkers coming from the opposite direction.

Turn left beside a large barn and sustain a westerly bearing along a pleasant, shady lane as tracks join from right and left. Some five minutes beyond Creux du Pialoux, a cultivated patch on the right of the path, watch out for an unmarked, easily missed sharp left turn onto a footpath that heads southwest and go right at a T-junction, signed 'Laschamp'. If you overshoot the earlier turn, simply continue, then go left along the sunken path that runs parallel to the D5 to pick up the route again at a large parking area.

At this car park, reached about 45 minutes beyond Fontfreyde, take the GR4 in the direction of Laschamp. Less than five minutes later, you have a choice: to continue along the route we describe or to go straight ahead along the GR4 (saving 2km and about an hour's walking).

To stay with the main route, go right to mount a flight of log steps and walk round the rim of a small side crater. Where a fence bars progress, keep north and turn left at a T-junction after 50m – in defiance of the seductive green triangle pointing to the right – to begin the steep, rugged ascent, assisted by more log steps.

The ancient volcanic vents, chimneys and cones of the range of puys to the south and southwest reveal themselves, as does Puy de Dôme, topped by its radio and TV mast and looking for all the world like a giant thermometer.

Once at the highest point of **Puy de la Vache** (1167m), follow a bare, cinder path around the lip of its crater and drop northwest to a small pass. Here, where the main path heads away left, go straight (north) up a much narrower footpath to **Puy de**

Lassolas (1187m). The path threads its way along the rim of this second crater before descending steeply south to rejoin the GR trail beside a particularly fine beech tree, where you turn right.

At a T-junction around 10 minutes later, turn right and northeast, the direction this easy woodland track maintains all the way to **Laschamp**, reached around an hour later.

For a walker-welcoming, ecofriendly overnight stop, we warmly recommend pushing on a mere 400m into Day 2 along route de Clermont to **Archipel Volcans** (☎ 04 73 62 15 15; www.archipel-volcans.com - French only; dorm beds €13, with half board €28, doubles/triples/quads €48/57/76, half board from €35; open year-round), a recently opened, purpose-built gîte d'étape (modest walkers' accommodation). The owners can advise on a wealth of walks in the area – and even rent you a donkey, if you're so inclined.

In Laschamp village, there's a **gîte d'étape** (☎ 04 73 62 12 50; route de la Moreno; dorm beds €13) just before the church, with self-catering facilities. Renowned in its time for the warmth of its welcome and copious meals, it was administered by Espace Volcan when we last passed through, but its future is uncertain.

Espace Volcan (☎ 04 73 62 26 00; www .espacevolcan.fr - French only; singles/doubles €30.50/40, half board from €36; regional menu €15) is scarcely 100m away. It has gîte-type accommodation for €11. The other eating alternative in the village is the **Bar-Restaurant GR**.

Day 2: Laschamp to Royat
4–4½ hours, 18km

Turn left beyond Laschamp's church onto route de Clermont (D767A), staying with the GR4. At the second of two metal crosses, bear left onto a dirt track to pass beside serried ranks of Scots pine, grown for the woodcutter's chainsaw. Cross a main road and continue straight (northwest) beyond a metal barrier along a forest track, bordered by more phalanxes of pine. The several junctions with active or dormant logging tracks are all well waymarked except one; at the maverick, fork left to stay on a northwest bearing where a fresh loggers' track goes muddily right.

Col de Ceyssat (1078m), around 45 minutes out, is a popular parking spot for walkers attempting the Puy de Dôme. A couple of roadside auberges serve drinks, snacks and breakfasts. Cross the car park beside Auberge des Muletiers to join the footpath heading upwards and turn right after 100m onto the Sentier des Muletiers (Mule Drivers' Trail).

A series of regular bends and zigzags leads you up the precisely 368m of lung-expanding vertical ascent from the Col to the Puy de Dôme summit. As you gain height, the views, particularly of the chain of volcanic summits extending south, become increasingly splendid, the dark stains of implanted spruce and Scots pine contrasting with the lighter green foliage of endemic oak.

At the **summit** (1464m), reached about 45 minutes beyond the Col, don't expect quiet contemplation of nature. There's a big bus park, a huge **bar-restaurant**, souvenir shop, picnic room and a small but informative display about volcanoes, captioned in both French and English. Above is the severely ruined Gallo-Roman Temple of Mercury. Most windy days – which means most days – you'll see hang-gliders, *parapentistes*, overhead, enjoying a bird's-eye view of some 70 extinct volcanoes and the Clermont Ferrand conurbation to the east, the twin black spires of its Gothic cathedral prodding the air like a toasting fork.

Leave by the cinder track that runs beside the vehicle road. Less than 10 minutes from the top, go right beside a rocky spur and drop northwest along a grassy track. Shortly after the small side crater of **Nid de la Poule** (The Chicken's Nest; 1178m), turn right (northeast) at a water fountain in the form of a cairn as the GR4 heads away westwards.

From here on, yellow waymarkers lead all the way to Royat. The path soon becomes a wide cinder track, descending through a forest of beech, which gives way to hazel, ash and hawthorn. Around 15 minutes beyond the junction, go straight ahead into a leafy tunnel where the dominant path bends left. Ten minutes later, turn right at a T-junction, then almost immediately left (ignoring an unnecessary yellow cross) along a grassy path bordered by a fence. Be careful to keep to the west side of a field with a windsock, a favourite landing area for *parapentistes*. The path joins a wide, shaded track that heads straight and southeast to meet the junction of the Puy de Dôme access road and the D68 beside a car park.

Turn left and take a cinder lane to the right after 150m. Go left at a T-junction to follow a tarred road through the hamlet of Enval (passing a pair of fountains) and cross over a busy road to join rue de l'Étang, signed 'Montrodeix'.

After 150m, go right up a lane between two huge electricity pylons, then left along a cinder track as far as **Montrodeix**. Keeping the village fountain to your left, drop down a lane and cross a wider road to take chemin des Charrioux, beside the old village washing place. The narrow grassy path becomes a 4WD track, then a residential road (rue de Missole) which meets the D90.

Go left and, less than 10 minutes later, turn right onto the D768 to pass through the hamlet of Fontenas. Some 50m beyond the exit sign for Fontenas, bear right along a track. Where it divides, take the right fork, signed 'Royat par le chemin des Crêtes', to enjoy an easy, agreeable stroll along the western flank of the Tiretaine Valley as far as Royat, the pleasure marred only by the constant growl of traffic from far below.

On the outskirts of Royat, turn right where the track meets av du Paradis, then left into rue Docteur Petit. At its end, go down a flight of steps, turn right to cross the main road and drop by more steps into the park that runs along the valley bottom.

Head downstream and, just before it peters out at a car park, take a steep path to the right to emerge in front of Royat's post office and the No 16 bus stop for Clermont Ferrand.

Monts Dore

The Monts Dore, wedged centrally in the Massif Central, are also in the middle of the age band. Formed by successive eruptions between three million and 100,000 years ago, they're considerably older than the Monts Dômes to the north, yet defer to the more ancient Monts du Cantal found in the south.

PLANNING
When to Walk
In most years it's possible to walk the heights of the Monts Dore from mid-May, once most of the snows have melted, until late November. For the Col du Guéry, the walking season extends into December.

Maps
The excellent Chamina/IGN 1:30,000 map *Massif du Sancy* has clear contour markings. The IGN's 1:25,000 map No 2432ET *Massif du Sancy* also covers both walks. Neither represents the most recent diversions made to the Puy de Sancy route. Maison de la Presse, opposite the Établissement Thermal (Thermal Baths) in Le Mont-Dore, sells both maps.

ACCESS TOWNS
Le Mont-Dore and its neighbour, La Bourboule, 7km away, are both spa towns, small winter ski stations and popular summer resorts in the upper Dordogne Valley.

Le Mont-Dore
The **tourist office** (☎ 04 73 65 20 21; www .mont-dore.com; open Mon-Sat & Sun morning) is in a square off av de la Libération.

Places to Stay & Eat Le Mont-Dore has a couple of municipal camping grounds. **Camping Les Crouzets** (☎/fax 04 73 65 21 60; camping per person/site €2.60/2.35; open mid-Dec–mid-Oct), opposite the train station, has a grassy but often crowded area reserved for tents. **Camping L'Esquiladou** (☎ 04 73 65 23 74; camping.esquiladou@wanadoo.fr; camping per person/site €3/2.45; open May–mid-Oct), 1.5km north of town, beside the Puy de Sancy route, is more tranquil and roomy.

Below Station du Mont Dore and above the town, **Le Grand Volcan** (☎ 04 73 65 03 53; le-mont-dore@fuaj.org; dorm B&B €11.70; open Jan-mid-Nov & Dec) is an HI-affiliated youth hostel.

The CAF **Chalet du Sancy** (☎ 04 73 65 07 05; olivier.legrand@caramail.com; dorm beds €10, half board €27.50; menu €12.50), 300m down the road towards Le Mont-Dore, has a **restaurant**, open to all, with a filling menu.

Hôtel aux Champs d'Auvergne (☎ 04 73 65 00 37, fax 04 73 65 00 30; 18 rue Favart; basic singles/doubles €17.55/23.65, with bathroom €28.20/34.50, half board €29-38; menus €11 & 13) is welcoming and strong on regional cuisine, strictly for guests, plus a range of takeaway dishes (€5.35).

The **restaurants** of many of Le Mont-Dore's hotels offer moderately priced and sometimes quite imaginative cuisine.

Le Bougnat (☎ 04 73 65 28 19; 23 rue Clemenceau; menus €15-23) with its low-beamed wooden interior and attractive, flowery terrace is a splendid place to sample Auvergnat cooking.

Le Boeuf dans l'Assiette (Beef on Your Plate; ☎ 04 73 65 01 23; 9 av Michel Bertrand; mains €7-11.50, menus €10.40-14.50; open Tue-Sun) is, as its name suggests, for serious carnivores.

Getting There & Away There are up to seven trains or SNCF buses daily between Le Mont-Dore and La Bourboule (€1.30), the last leaving Le Mont-Dore at 5.30 pm (4.55 pm on Saturday) and La Bourboule at 8.50pm (7.30pm on Sunday). Four trains daily continue beyond La Bourboule to Clermont Ferrand (€10.70, 1¼ hours). For a taxi, call **Allo Claude Taxi** (☎ 04 73 65 01 05).

La Bourboule
The **tourist office** (☎ 04 73 65 57 71; www.bourboule.com; place de la République) is in the *mairie* (town hall).

Places to Stay & Eat La Bourboule has four camping grounds. The municipal **Camping Des Vernières** (☎ 04 73 81 15 28, fax 04 73 65 54 98; av Maréchal de Lattre de Tassigny; camping per person/site €2.80/2.35; open Easter-Sep) is large and shady.

Hôtel des Anglais (☎/fax 04 73 81 02 39; rooms without/with bathroom €23/31) is one of several budget hotels on av Gueneau de Mussy.

Hôtel-Restaurant Les Sources (☎ 04 73 81 01 48, fax 04 73 81 15 32; doubles/triples 17.50/26, with bathroom from €23.50/29; menus €8.50-14) is a simple, friendly, family hotel with a **restaurant**.

Getting There & Away For trains, see Getting There & Away under Le Mont-Dore, opposite. To call a taxi, ring **Allo Bourboule Taxi** (☎ 04 73 65 52 38).

GETTING TO/FROM THE WALKS

Between mid-May and the end of September, there is a shuttle bus that runs between Station du Mont Dore, Le Mont-Dore and La Bourboule, leaving Station du Mont Dore several times each afternoon. The last return bus leaves La Bourboule at around 5.30pm.

Puy de Sancy

Duration	6–6¾ hours
Distance	19.5km
Difficulty	moderate–demanding
Start	Le Mont-Dore (opposite)
Finish	Station du Mont-Dore
Transport	bus, train, taxi

Summary It's splendid views all day long on this rich roller coaster walk as you bag five peaks, including Puy de Sancy, Auvergne's highest.

The difficulty of this walk resides in both its length and overall height gain. However in the Alternative Routes (p117) you'll find two possible cut-out points. These enable you to shorten the route or make it a less rigorous two-day walk. If you have wheels, consider starting at Col de la Croix Morand, thus omitting the first 6.5km, saving 1½ hours and enjoying an entire day of vast, open vistas. Another possibility, in season, is to take the *téléférique* down from Puy de Sancy.

The route has been diverted in several places (notably, on either side of Col de la Croix St-Robert) to limit erosion and encourage new growth. Our walk map reflects such changes, which don't yet feature on the latest Chamina or IGN maps, but others may have been introduced since we last took the trail.

THE WALK (see map p116)

From Le Mont-Dore train station, turn left along av Guyot Dessaigne, then left again onto av de la Bourboule. At the far end of the hamlet of Le Queureuilh, take a right fork, signed 'Camping L'Esquiladou'.

Beyond **Camping L'Esquiladou** (see opposite), fork right on a narrow bitumen road. Where it dips and bends sharply left, go straight then veer left and pass the base of the Cascade du Queureuilh waterfall. The route heads northwest then turns sharply northeast to climb gently, parallel with a stream

Some 40 to 45 minutes after Camping L'Esquiladou, cross the D983 and go up a narrow tarred road. Where it veers to the left towards Ferme de la Tache, keep straight on a grassy track, then take a dogleg just beyond a stile.

The path, broad and springy, enters a maturing conifer wood then emerges on the D996, where it joins the GR4. After 250m of roadwork, curl right to bypass the bleak car park and trashed buildings at **Col de la Croix Morand** (1401m), reached after 1½ hours of walking. Here, the small **Bar Buron du Col** serves drinks and snacks (a *buron* is a small summertime shepherd's cabin).

Turn right to follow the well-defined path that zigzags up the steep flank. The vegetation is now strictly moorland: heather, bilberry and, in late spring, a positive brass band of miniature alpine daffodils nodding their trumpets. The trajectory differs from the straight line, tracing a long-abandoned ski lift, marked on the recommended IGN 1:25,000 map. As you ascend, Lac de Guéry comes into view, watched over by Roche Tuilière just beyond it. Also in view is the town of La Bourboule, well to its west, dominated by the escarpment of Puy Gros (a feature of the next walk, 'Col de Guéry').

A wooden post marks the top of **Puy de la Tache** (1629m). From here, the roller-coaster path broadly follows the ridge, ducking

Puy de Sancy & Col de Guéry

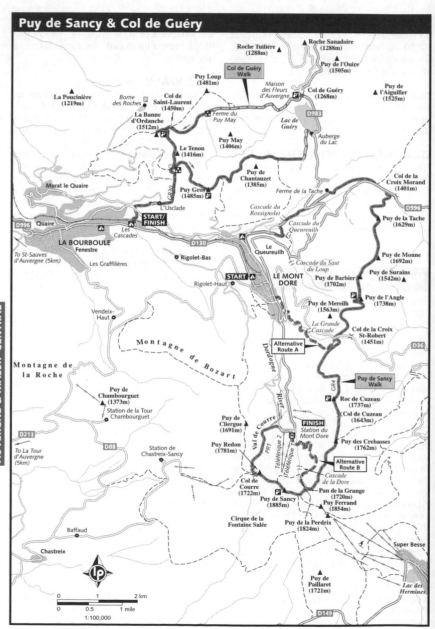

just below the summits of **Puy de Monne** (1692m) and **Puy de Barbier** (1702m). Then it follows an easy ascent to **Puy de l'Angle** (1738m), reached about 45 minutes beyond Col de la Croix Morand.

The path follows the ridge to a white cross then, in a new tracing, angles its way down to the small unnamed col at the foot of Puy de Mereilh and describes a short dogleg before meeting the D36 near Col de la Croix St-Robert (1451m). (From here, the waymarked descent to Le Mont-Dore via La Grande Cascade waterfalls – see Alternative Route A (right) – is pleasant in itself and is an opportunity to spread the walk over two days.)

To continue, take the short bitumen track heading in a southeasterly direction and bear right at a bend after 300m onto a narrow, grassy footpath. From here to flat-topped Roc de Cuzeau, the path, always signed, has been substantially re-routed to give much-pounded turf the chance to recover.

Follow it along fences – including a short unnecessary stretch where walkers, like sheep, are herded between a pair of them – and over stiles into open country some 20 minutes beyond the D36.

About 30 minutes later, the narrow plateau of **Roc de Cuzeau** (1737m) offers perhaps the most stunning and certainly the most sudden view of the day as the Puy de Sancy and the cirque below, snow still streaking its gullies until well into June, spread before you.

Descend to the **Col de Cuzeau**. From here, you can take the GR trail, which hugs the edge of the precipice. If it's windy, take the safer path – saving yourself a little climbing into the bargain – that follows the contour of the hill. Both rise to the top of twin ski lifts at the summit of **Puy des Crebasses** (1762m).

Another half-hour of easier walking brings you to Pan de la Grange (1720m). (From here a wide track descends to Station du Mont-Dore – see Alternative Route B, this page).

A further 20 to 30 minutes of hard, unremitting ascent brings you to the magnificent panorama and pair of orientation tables at the summit of **Puy de Sancy**. Also known as Pic de Sancy, at 1885m it's the highest peak in the Massif Central. You'll probably be in the company of crowds of huffing, puffing visitors who have walked 500m up the 850 wooden steps from the top of the **téléférique** *(one way/return €5/6.50; operates daily May-Sep)*, by which you can descend, cutting out the walk's final 45 minutes.

Take the steps, in summer as crowded as any Metro escalator. Where they veer right to the *téléférique*, go straight to stay with the GR30. Around 15 minutes later, leave the GR at Col de Courre (1722m) and follow yellow waymarkers down Val de Courre, where an initially rocky descent gives way to pleasant meadow.

Just before the scatter of buildings of Station du Mont-Dore, pause at a ruined *buron*. Despite appearances, it's far from being just another summer cowherd's cabin, left to subside into the mountain: on 27 April 1944, three resistance fighters were shot there by the Gestapo, who then torched the building. Its shell is preserved in their memory.

For buses to Le Mont-Dore and La Bourboule, see Getting to/from the Walks (p115). As you wait, **Bar-Restaurant Azur Sancy** can offer drinks, snacks or a full meal.

Alternative Route A: Descent to Le Mont-Dore
45 minutes, 3km

From Col de la Croix St-Robert, bear away southwest along the PR12, waymarked with green stripes. With a net height loss of 450m, it's a pleasant descent to Le Mont-Dore and the Dordogne Valley via the gushing waterfall of La Grande Cascade.

Alternative Route B: Shortcut to Station du Mont-Dore
35–45 minutes, 3km

From Pan de la Grange a well-trodden track leads down past a craggy wilderness, where several winter ski lifts meet, and down to Station du Mont-Dore. Resist the temptation to short-cut down a ski-season red run; the vegetation needs every second of convalescence it can get before next season's onslaught. The track may be bald and ugly, but fine views of the valley compensate for the roughness.

Col de Guéry

Duration	5–5½ hours
Distance	19km
Difficulty	easy–moderate
Start/Finish	La Bourboule (p114)
Transport	train

Summary Through woodland and pasture to a *bijou* lake then, above it, Col de Guéry and one of France's most photographed panoramas.

It's a varied day; meadow and woodland, a pair of peaks with fine panoramas, a lake, and the Col de Guéry, from where more film must have been shot than anywhere else in the whole of France, but for the Eiffel Tower.

THE WALK (see map p116)

As far as the Col de Guéry, you're on the red-and-white stripes of the GR30. From there to Col de St-Laurent, follow single orange flashes.

Set out from the roadside parking area of Les Cascades (895m), on the D130 1.25km east of Camping Des Vernières (see p114). Cross the Dordogne River, here no more than a beck (small mountain stream). Don't be misled by the sign 'Lac de Guéry 9km' that points straight upstream. Instead, bend left with the service road and walk up the left-hand side of a warehouse.

Cross the railway at a pair of metal gates and continue up a track to walk straight over the D996 and take the unmade road in front of you.

After 50m, turn sharp right onto a forest trail, in its early stages much churned up by loggers. Cobbled in patches, it narrows to a footpath that runs between a pair of fences. Once in open meadow, turn left (northeast) at a T-junction with a broad cart track, then right to pass through the semi-abandoned hamlet of L'Usclade with its pair of flowing water troughs, reached

a little under half an hour from the start of the walk.

Continue due east as the trail, now running between fields bright with wildflowers and beside a small brook, begins to steepen, elbowing north to enter the welcome shade of a beech wood, springy underfoot from the thick carpet of last year's leaves.

Emerging from the wood something under the hour mark, bear right (northeast) onto an ancient track bordered by crumbling walls. Turn right where it joins a wider track beside a concrete trough, just west of the remnants of an abandoned *buron*, on which a couple of tall trees now perch.

Around 250m from the turning, go right on a grassy footpath. Signed by low, wooden pegs, it climbs the northwest spur of **Puy Gros** (1485m), from where it's easy, scenic walking along a cliff edge. Below spreads La Bourboule and the rich valley of the upper Dordogne. To the northwest is the wedge-shaped summit of La Banne d'Ordanche, a goal for later in the day. And then, just to complete the picture, Le Mont-Dore reveals itself as you round a bend.

After a brief, steep descent to a junction, turn left to follow a sign for Lac de Guéry. About five minutes later, it's easy to miss a right turn downhill as you leave the main track and drop to where three fences meet. Climb over a stile to follow the path winding around the shoulder of Puy de Chantauzet.

Something under 30 minutes later, heave yourself over another stile, after which the trail, hemmed in between a pair of fences, descends beside a conifer plantation. Turn left at a T-junction along a broad logging track that leads to the shore of **Lac de Guéry** (1247m) and **Auberge du Lac** (☎ 04 73 65 02 76; menus from €10.50), a lovely spot for a lunch break.

From here, there's no alternative to a 1.25km slog up the D983 (no footpath runs along the lake's western bank). The noisy traffic's an intrusion but the verges are broad and there's more than adequate compensation at **Col de Guéry** (1268m), with its magnificent and much photographed picture-postcard vista northwards of the twin volcanic pinnacles of Roche Tuilière and Roche Sanadoire watching over the gentle valley between.

At the pass, build in time to visit **Maison des Fleurs d'Auvergne** (☎ 04 73 65 20 09; open Sat & Sun May–mid-Jun, daily mid-Jun–mid-Sep). Although information is only in French, the display is highly visual and in its *jardin écologique* (ecology garden) you'll find many examples of flowers and trees encountered on the walk. Ask for their multilingual explanatory folder.

To return to La Bourboule, take the tarred lane heading southwest. At a three-pronged fork, after less than five minutes, choose the left-hand cinder track. It's easy, whistle-while-you-walk striding all the way from here to the Col de St-Laurent. The track runs through rolling, open pasture – bobbing in season with wild daffodils – to the mournful, derelict house and outbuildings of **Ferme du Puy May** (1390m). (See the tempting Alternative Route at the end of this walk description for a way of bypassing the farm and fitting in an extra peak.) The track now becomes a grassy lane, leading after 20 minutes to **Col de St-Laurent** (1450m), a junction fussy with signs for walkers, cyclists and horse riders.

For **La Banne d'Ordanche**, which is a highly recommended and none too strenuous 20- to 30-minute round trip, turn left. There's an easier option to the tough path which heads straight up the hill's steep eastern slope. Follow the narrow trail that curls more gently around the western flank to meet a footpath coming up from the car park at Borne des Roches. Climb a series of wooden steps to the **summit** (1512m) with its superb views of the Chaîne des Puys, blocking the horizon to the northeast like a rippling sea monster, its central, largest hump topped by the TV mast of Puy de Dôme.

On the way down, turn right to take a footpath 200m before Col de St-Laurent. This meets a fence that drops southwards, then tacks southeast. Turn right to follow a series of wooden posts with yellow dots that guide you over the inconsequential crest of Le Tenon (1416m) and bring you to the water trough and ruined *buron* passed on the

outward leg. Retrace your steps back to Les Cascades, 40 to 50 minutes' walk away.

Alternative Route: Puy Loup
30–40 minutes, 2km
A detour from the farm track (about 600m before the ruins of Ferme du Puy May) up an easily distinguished path takes in the summit of Puy Loup (1406m), offering great views to the north, before rejoining the main route at Col de St-Laurent.

Monts du Cantal

The 2700 sq km Cantal caldera is Europe's largest volcanic massif by area. Peak volcanic activity occurred between nine and seven million years ago, when the whole central area of a giant volcano collapsed in on itself. As its magma chamber emptied, it created the huge caldera. Its rim, still discernible in many places today, includes the Col de Cabre, Puy Mary, Puy Chavaroche and Plomb du Cantal, all of which feature in the walks in this section.

PLANNING
Both walks are possible from the second half of June to early November. Since accommodation is limited in the Jordanne Valley, it's essential to reserve in July and August.

Maps
Both routes feature on the IGN 1:25,000 map No 2435OT *Monts du Cantal*, available from Maison de la Presse on rue St-Martin in Murat.

ACCESS TOWN
Murat
The friendly **tourist office** (☎ 04 71 20 09 47; www.ville-de-murat.com - French only; 2 rue Faubourg Notre Dame; open daily Jul-Aug, Mon-Sat Sep-Jun) is beside the town hall.

Places to Stay & Eat Next to the Alagnon River, **Camping Municipal Stalapos** (☎ 04 71 20 01 83; rue du Stade; camping per person/site €2/1.60; open May-Sep) is 750m south of the train station.

L'Auberge de Maître Paul (☎ 04 71 20 14 66, fax 04 71 20 22 20; 14 place du Panol; singles/doubles/triples €28/34/42; pizzas €7, menu €17) has spruce, charmingly decorated rooms. A cheerful place, it serves pizzas the size of flying saucers to eat in or takeaway and does an excellent regional *menu*.

Hôtel Les Messageries (☎ 04 71 20 04 04; www.hotel-les-messageries.com; 18 av du Dr Mallet; singles/doubles/triples/quads €35/41/ 50.50/58; menus €12-22), a Logis de France, has a sauna (€3.80), pool (free for guests) and **restaurant**.

Getting There & Away There are at least four trains a day between Clermont Ferrand (€15.40, 1½ hours) to the north and Aurillac (€7.50) to the southwest.

For a taxi, telephone ☎ 04 71 20 04 08 or ☎ 04 71 20 00 55.

Puy Mary & Jordanne Valley

Duration	2 days
Distance	31.5km
Difficulty	moderate
Start/Finish	Le Lioran (p124)
Nearest Town	Murat (p119)
Transport	train

Summary Magnificent ridge-striding, taking in two of Auvergne's finest peaks, with an overnight stay in the gentle Mandailles Valley.

This walk takes in two of the Massif's finest peaks and there is also the opportunity of side trips to bag another pair. Day 1 in particular offers some superb extended views to the north and east from the intervening ridges.

GETTING TO/FROM THE WALK

The 15-minute train journey between Murat and Le Lioran is €2.20. A train leaves Murat every morning in July and August (not Sunday, when the first train passes in late morning – during the rest of the year). To return, take the train from Le Lioran.

Should you want to leave the route at Mandailles, call **Mme Pechaud** (☎ 04 71 47 94 51), who runs the local taxi service.

If you've wheels you'll lose nothing and save yourself 1.25km each day by driving to the Font d'Alagnon car park. If you fancy an even easier start to Day 1 or a cosy end to Day 2, take the **Télésiège de Rombière** (chairlift; one way/return €4.50/6; open 9-11.45am & 1.30-5pm daily mid-Jul–Aug), which will lift you to or drop you from the ridge near Col de Rombière.

THE WALK (see map p122)
Day 1: Le Lioran to Mandailles
4¾–5¼ hours, 17km, 820m ascent

From Le Lioran train station, turn left onto the busy N122, then right after 300m onto the D67, signed 'Super Lioran'. Fork right after 600m beside a large parking area. Go right again, 75m beyond the Font d'Alagnon car park to take a track signed 'Combe Nègre'. Veer sharp left after 75m to follow a path southwards at the fringe of a firebreak. A couple of minutes later, turn right onto a broader trail then cross a tarred road where it makes a hairpin and keep climbing up an evident footpath (a ski run was being modified when we last passed so this short section may vary slightly from our description).

When you again meet the tarred road, go right to reach **Col de Font de Cère** (1289m) some 10 minutes beyond the Font d'Alagnon car park. Turn right (northwest) again beside **Auberge le Buron** to join the GR4 and a wide dirt track. Stay with it, ignoring a brief and unnecessary GR divergence to the right.

A little before the crest and about 30 minutes beyond Auberge le Buron, curl around the top of a chairlift to take a more northerly bearing that leads you just below **Col de Rombière** (1550m). The narrow path, where patches of snow are possible until early June, gives great views eastwards over the wooded bowl of the Alagnon Valley.

Once over an intervening hillock, the wider, more open basin of the upper Jordanne Valley suddenly reveals itself to the west, with a thin thread of path unravelling beneath the rim.

Beyond **Col de Cabre** (1528m), from where there's a fine plunging view northeastwards, the path continues along its level course, running beneath the crags of the unfortunately named (for anglophones) **Puy de**

Peyre Arse. About 25 minutes later, there's a second surprise vista as the valley to the north stretches before you with the village of Le Claux snug at its heart and, on the horizon, Puy de Sancy's sharp-sided cone.

All along this section, wooden steps have been laid here and there to combat erosion from the passage of so many boots. A short, steep descent to the **Brèche de Roland** and a clamber to regain height bring hands and feet into play. Around 10 minutes later, just before the final steep push to the summit of Puy Mary, never dangerous but fairly lung-bursting, there are two alternatives, each bypassing the steep climb. There's a diversion around the *puy*'s eastern flank to the D680, or the less evident but quite manageable westbound path that descends to the D17, thus bypassing Pas de Peyrol and shortening the route by 1.5km.

Once you've heaved your way to the top of **Puy Mary** (1783m), you'll be sharing the orientation table with those who have taken the easier way up: a flight of hideous concrete steps from the car park at Pas de Peyrol. At other visitor high spots in the Massif Central, such as the Puy de Sancy (p117)

and Plomb du Cantal (p125), relatively harmonious wooden steps protect the thin soil from human traffic. Why not here?

Pas de Peyrol at 1588m is the Massif Central's highest road pass. Here, you can rehydrate with a **drink** on the terrace of **Chalet du Puy Mary** or enjoy the cool, free waters of the roadside pipe.

Turn left to leave the milling crowds and follow the D17 as it snakes round the western flank of Puy Mary. Around 20 minutes from the pass, leave the road at a hairpin bend and strike out westwards up a grassy track. After 50m, bear left at a sign, 'Puy Chavaroche'.

At **Col de Redondet** (1640m), bear left (southwest), heading for **Puy Chavaroche** (1739m) with its flat top from which tall cairns poke. Twenty to 30 minutes of easy ascent brings you to its **summit** (1739m), where over-assiduous walkers have piled the loose stones into neat, tidy formations.

Continue southwest, following the ridge and intermittent GR400 flashes. In early summer, the moor is a riot of wildflowers breaking free from the clutches of winter snow: alpine daffodil, narcissus, small violet pansies, buttercups and white heather.

AUVERGNE & MASSIF CENTRAL

Walking a Little History

When the new season's grass starts to shoot on the Monts du Cézallier, it's time for the Transhumance: the driving of the cattle up to their summer pastures. Though nowadays transported by truck, every last weekend in May a small herd is driven through the village of Allanche towards the hills, followed by a slipstream of interested walkers.

We set out to a trumpet fanfare from the village band. The air is filled with the bass lowing of the cows, the hollow clonk of their bells and the stern call of the cowherds.

As cows and walkers start to pant in the mid-morning heat, the cortege pauses at the hamlet of Pradier to take on water. The bull pulls rank, drinking deep before his favourite concubines shove their way to the front, while the young heifers hold back in deference. Walkers sup robust Auvergnat red wine to sluice down the wedges of sugary cake baked by the women of the village.

The band compensates for the occasional bum note with their volume and enthusiasm. The snare drum player thumps his instrument so hard that its strap breaks and his instrument rolls away while the saxophonists, septuagenarians to a man, have trouble sustaining the beat.

The cows are finally released beside a ruined *buron* and fan out over the flanks of the Cézallier. For us too, the feeding begins: shots of Salers, a local gentian-based liqueur, more red wine, coarse country sausage, slices of ham thick as a cow's tongue and chunky pâté are passed around.

Then, as the sharpening breeze whips away the sound of the band, walkers, satiated and with navigating skills no longer too sharp, begin to drift back down to Allanche.

To join in next year's fun, ring Allanche's **tourist office** (☎ 04 71 20 48 43).

Miles Roddis

Puy Mary & Jordanne Valley

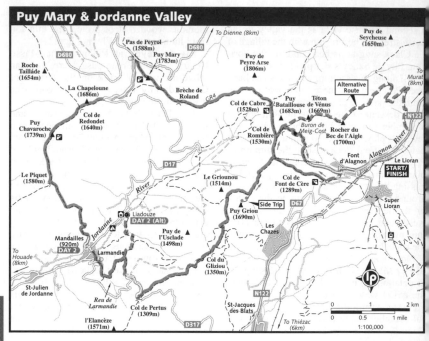

After 20 minutes, fork left (southeast) at Le Piquet pass to leave the GR400 and pick up the green blazes that guide you down to the Jordanne Valley. The path drops steeply via a couple of hairpins (take the first one, to the left, about seven minutes below the Col, ignoring the seductive, wider, cow-created variant that goes straight, only to peter out). The route then runs along the western fringe of a beech wood before diving into its shade. On emerging, it follows a spur where patches of eye-high broom alternate with lush grass.

Descend a rocky track, sunken in places, where in early summer dog roses may tear and nettles lie in wait. Go straight ahead down a bitumen lane beside a welcome, flowing trough to drop to the D17 and Mandailles village in the valley bottom, reached around 45 minutes beyond Le Piquet.

In **Mandailles** (920m), the overnighting opportunities are excellent but limited, so it's wise to reserve in advance. The village has a small **grocery**.

Auberge au Bout du Monde (☎ 04 71 47 92 47; www.auberge-auboutdumonde.com - French only; rooms for up to 4 with bathroom €33, up to 6 €42, half board for 1/2/3/4 people per person €49/36/33/30), run by the same family for five generations, is excellent value and full of character. Catering primarily for walkers, it does a great-value half board with copious meals.

Hôtel aux Genêts d'Or (☎ 04 71 47 96 45, fax 04 71 47 93 65; doubles/triples/quads €32.50/40.50/48.50, half-board €35; menus €10.80-21) is another family-run choice that also does meals.

Pleasant, riverside **Camping du Puy Mary** (in season ☎ 04 71 47 90 39, year-round ☎ 04 71 47 94 71; camping per person/site €2/2.40; open Jul-Aug) is 600m northeastwards up the valley along the GR400 or D17.

One kilometre beyond the camping ground is **Gîte d'Étape de Liadouze** (☎ 04 71 47 93 81; vert.azur@wanadoo.fr; dorm beds €8.50; open May-11 Nov), also bang beside the GR400.

Friendly and highly recommended, it has self-catering facilities and does a bargain packed lunch for €6 (see the walk map for an attractive alternative way of beginning Day 2 from here, following the GR and avoiding a return down the valley to Mandailles).

Day 2: Mandailles to Le Lioran

3¾–4¼ hours, 14.5km, 780m ascent

From Mandailles to the junction with the GR400, you're guided by single blue stripes. Thereafter, it's the familiar red-and-white flashes all the way home.

Cross Mandailles' road bridge to the east bank of the Jordanne. After 50m, turn left up a lane then, after a further 50m, right between two gateposts to take a narrow footpath, signed 'Col de Pertus'. At the hamlet of Larmandie, tack left onto a cobbled lane. Beside a gushing water pipe and troughs, turn briefly right then left at another sign for Col de Pertus. The path, a finely cobbled track now much deteriorated, climbs steadily with meadows to the right and mixed wood to the left. After rain or snowmelt, a positive stream dances towards you but it's nothing that a stout pair of boots can't repel.

Fifteen to 20 minutes from Mandailles, the path merges with a wide cart track that turns east to cross the Reu de Larmandie stream and wriggle its way up the valley's eastern flank. Just beyond a *buron* with a red-tiled roof, bear away northwards, ig-noring a wider track on the right. The path expands into a wide track that you soon leave to turn right up a narrow rocky gulley. Turn right at another *buron* with a corrugated iron roof. At a T-junction, the route intersects with the GR400, coming up from Liadouze and the Jordanne Valley.

Turn right to follow this broad grassy track to the D317 and an information panel, about 45 minutes from Mandailles, proclaiming 'Col de Pertus'. Not so, however — the pass is still a good 15 minutes' walk up the road.

From **Col de Pertus** (1309m) head north-east along a path signed 'Col du Gliziou' and 'Le Griou'. The route alternates between deep shaded beech wood (in early summer, look out for violets peeking through the leaf mould) and open meadow, bright with broom and wildflowers.

About 35 minutes from the Col, continue straight ahead where the main path descends to meet a wider 4WD track coming up from the valley. Col du Gliziou (1350m), without a halfway decent view in any direction, is one of the Massif Central's less dramatic passes. From it, continue northeast along a graded forest track signed 'Le Puy Griou'. At a fork after three minutes, bear left and uphill, again heading northeast onto what soon becomes narrow footpath.

At a small col (1400m), where the path joins an alternative route coming up from Col du Gliziou, go right along a forest track, then after 25m, right again and steeply upwards. About 30 minutes beyond Col du Gliziou, the path emerges from forest onto open ground at a pass slung between Le Griounou to the northwest and Puy Griou, its much bigger sibling. Veer right to curve round the western slopes of the latter as the trail ascends parallel to a barbed-wire fence.

Where the stony trail meets a broad, well-trodden dirt path, you can make a short, tax-ing but strongly recommended diversion to bag Puy Griou (see the Side Trip at the end of this walk description).

To continue, go left. About 15 minutes from the junction, go through a pair of spring gates and then left again, briefly retreading the Day 1 route. A little under 10 minutes later, turn right (northeast) to leave yesterday's

The Wolf Trap

Wolves have long been hunted and hounded from the Massif Central. But until the end of the 19th century, villagers of the upland villages of Cantal would dig wolf traps: deep pits camouflaged with twigs and leaves and baited with carrion. If a wolf that fell into the trap wasn't killed, it might be muzzled and paraded through the streets of Aurillac, the nearest town, to show it off and, no doubt, pick up a few centimes.

A 10- to 15-minute round trip from Col de Pertus, following the sign 'Piège au Loup', brings you to one such pit, recently cleaned out and restored.

trail at a sign, 'Col de Rombière', and reach the pass a couple of minutes later.

From the Col, descend gently northwards then fork right at a sign, 'Font d'Alagnon'. Here, if you want to stay up high and extend what is a relatively short walking day by an additional hour, take the alternative route to Rocher du Bec de l'Aigle (see the Alternative Route at the end of this walk description).

The trail drops steeply to the Buron de Meig-Cost (1450m) with its roof of grey slate. Follow the zigzagging track that leads generally southeastwards from the cabin into yet more beech wood, interspersed with Scots pine and ash, fighting the conifers for its share of the light.

At a T-junction with a dirt road, some 25 minutes below Col de Rombière, turn right. About 20 minutes later, you emerge onto the tarred road beside Font d'Alagnon car park. For Le Lioran, retrace your Day 1 steps.

Le Lioran and Super Lioran are fairly bleak places, any time. A small **supermarket** is open only in the skiing and summer high seasons and there's a **bar-restaurant** or two where you can at least get a cold beer. To overnight, **Residence le Bec de l'Aigle** (☎ 04 71 49 52 00; www.le-lioran.com - French only; apartments for 2/3/4 €34/46/57; open year-round) is a reasonably priced option.

Alternative Route: via Rocher du Bec de l'Aigle
1½-2 hours, 8km
At the junction before Buron de Meig-Cost, continue straight to pass Puy Bataillouse, Le Téton de Venus (Venus' Breast) and **Rocher du Bec de l'Aigle** (The Eagle's Beak). Take a pronounced path to the right at the 1493m spot height. Bend sharply southwest beside a ruined *buron* onto a track and descend to the N122 for an anticlimactic last kilometre back to Le Lioran along the busy highway.

Side Trip: Puy Griou
40–50 minutes, 1.25km return
To reach the summit of Puy Griou (1690m), it's a strenuous ascent over basalt, requiring a bit of clambering along an unsigned trail. The effort is well worthwhile, since you've had its rounded peak in your sights

for so long and because the views surpass those from either Puy Chavaroche or Puy Mary. You can retrace your route back to the main trail.

Plomb du Cantal

Duration	3¾–4¼ hours
Distance	15km
Difficulty	moderate
Start/Finish	Super Lioran
Nearest Town	Murat (p119)
Transport	train
Summary	Stride along and dodge between the winter ski trails up to Plomb de Cantal and build in time for a particularly enticing side trip.

From Plomb du Cantal (1855m), a giant hunk of basalt and the highest peak in the Cantal range, there's a magnificent panorama in every direction. If you want to retain the views longer, stay up high to undertake part or all of the spectacular ridgeback out-and-back Puy Gros side trip (p126).

You can bisect this circular route by catching the **téléférique** (single/return €5/6.50; open daily Jun-early Sep) between Super Lioran and its upper station, just below the summit of Plomb du Cantal.

The flanks of the mountain, particularly Pres Marty, have been heavily scarred by ski runs and installations. What they can't damage are the superlative 360° wraparound views that make this walk so worthwhile.

GETTING TO/FROM THE WALK
From Le Lioran train station, turn left onto the busy N122 then right after 300m to take the minor D67 as far as Super Lioran (1.25km).

THE WALK
From the rear of the *téléférique* station – beside which is a small **tourist office** (☎ 04 71 49 50 08, fax 04 71 49 51 01) that displays the weather forecast on its main door – take the GR4 up a path signed 'Plomb du Cantal'. This runs parallel to the easternmost of the ski lifts that radiate like spokes from

the valley and ascends steeply, straight as a die, without the least concession to self-propelling walkers.

After emerging from wood into open grassland just before the top of the drag lift, bear left (generally southeast) along a narrow, stony track that, for its part, has the good grace to zig and zag, then merge with a wider one. Pass beside a sheep fold and a severely ruined *buron* (1304m), then fork left (southeast) to join, after something over 30 minutes of ascent, a blue run, signed 'Les Alpins', and a well-defined 4WD track.

As you ascend, the puys to the northwest and west reveal themselves: Puy Griou and its smaller neighbours Le Griounou, Chavaroche, Mary, Peyre Arse and Bataillouse. Then suddenly, as you cross the **ridgeline** after one to 1¼ hours of walking, the green bowl of the Prés Marty meadows presents itself, with the cluster of buildings marking the Col de Prat de Bouc at its lower, open end.

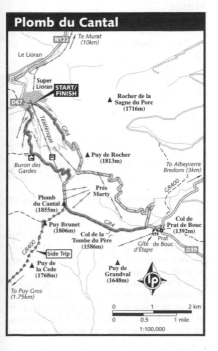

Postpone for now the ascent to the summit of Plomb du Cantal. To drop to Col de Prat de Bouc with maximum fun, simply yomp down the mountainside, aiming for the cluster of buildings below and slipping under a fence or two as you drop. If you like life a little more structured, begin by descending a path, occupied in season by a ski run signed 'Prat de Bouc', and follow the run's green lollipops all the way down through the meadows. To play really safe, follow the 4WD track (the tracing indicated on our map) down to Prat de Bouc.

At **Col de Prat de Bouc** (1392m), **Bar-Grill Prat de Bouc** does a range of tasty lunchtime dishes. There's also a **gîte d'étape** (☎ 04 71 20 20 92; bunk beds €9.50, half board €25).

To regain the ridge, follow the red and white bars of the GR4, which lead you initially up the valley's southern flank. After five minutes, just before a cattle pen, strike left through a swing gate to follow the manifest scar of this popular trail.

After passing below Col de la Tombe du Père, take a northwesterly course beside the stakes of an old fence and pass through a swing gate. Here at a col, seriously consider adding a little to the day's walk time and heading southwest, then generally westwards to enjoy a slice of magnificent ridge walking (see the Side Trip at the end of this walk).

To continue to the peak, veer almost due north from the Col for the last 25m of height gain, then turn left up a flight of wooden steps, laid to protect the summit from erosion. Reach the crest of **Plomb du Cantal** 60 to 75 minutes after leaving Col de Prat de Bouc.

Drop down to the *téléférique* station with its small **café**, open when the cable car is operating. From here, the route descends by a PR trail to Buron des Gardes. About 150m beyond a microwave station, aim for a sign indicating St-Jacques-de-Blat and Buron des Gardes. Turn left (initially southwest) to follow an unmaintained track, in its time a ski run, waymarked with single green flashes. Buron des Gardes, distinguishable by the small **reservoir** beside it, is clearly visible.

The trail narrows to a single-file footpath and passes well to the right of the *buron*. Aim for a broad track coming from the reservoir and turn right onto it. Just beyond the base of Téléski du Slalom, turn right (north) to head down a broad break between the trees, following the 'Le Buron' red run to its conclusion before the unharmonious architecture of Super Lioran, reached about an hour after leaving Plomb du Cantal.

Side Trip: Puy Gros
2 hours, 8km return
For great views and relatively flat walking, follow the GR400 southwest along the ridge for just as long as you like. **Puy Gros**, (1594m) reached after about an hour, makes a discernible goal.

Les Cévennes

The heart of the Cévennes was designated a national park in 1970 and is also recognised as a Unesco World Biosphere Reserve. In general drier and hotter than the Auvergne to its north, it has more in common with Mediterranean lands and, administratively, lies within the Languedoc-Roussillon region.

The Mont Lozère range, in its northern sector, is of tough, impenetrable granite from which the rainfall sluices in small streams. It's the source of the Tarn River, which flows in its early stages through the spectacular Gorges du Tarn (see Other Walks at the end of this chapter). Bright with broom in springtime, its grasslands, strewn with rock fields and hefty boulders, revealed by erosion, provide fodder for the sheep that graze the slopes in summer.

The Causse, by contrast, is all high, limestone plateau from which the least dribble of water percolates through the soft rock to emerge in the valleys at its feet. The arid south-facing slopes of the Vallées Cévenoles (Cévennes Valleys) are clad in holm oak and *garrigue*, or Mediterranean heathland. On other shadier, more gentle slopes flourish chestnuts (staple of the local diet until quite recently) indigenous beech woods and conifer plantations.

The three walks here give a flavour of each of these three distinct environments. The Mixing with Menhirs walk, at the southern limit of Mont Lozère, passes through southern France's most significant concentration of these prehistoric hewn blocks. The Walking through Chaos walk takes in a part of the plateau of Causse Méjan, while the In Stevenson's Steps walk explores the valleys and woodlands of the Park's eastern sector.

PLANNING
When to Walk
Between June and September, the heat can be quite fearsome and shade, except for the In Stevenson's Steps walk, is sparse. Winter walking, when the air is at its clearest, is exhilarating.

Maps & Books
The best overall map of the area is the IGN's 1:100,000 map *Parc National des Cévennes*. For larger scale maps, see each walk description.

ACCESS TOWN
Florac
Information Occupying the handsome 17th-century Château de Florac, the **Maison du Parc National des Cévennes** (☎ 04 66 49 53 01; www.cevennes-parcnational.fr - French only; open daily year-round) has a wealth of information, maps and books, including an English version of the guidebook *Parc National des Cévennes*.

Florac's **tourist office** (☎ 04 66 45 01 14; www.florac-tourisme.com; open daily Jul-Aug, Mon-Sat Sep-Jun) is on av Jean Monestier.

Places to Stay & Eat Florac has a pair of municipal riverside **camping** grounds, each 1.5km from town.

Camping le Pont du Tarn (☎ 04 66 45 18 26; camping per person/tent/car €2.70/ 2.70/2.10; open Apr–mid-Oct), with a pool, is north of town. To the south, the smaller **Camping La Tière** (☎ 04 66 45 00 53; camping per person/tent/car €2.40/2.30/1.50; open Jul-Aug) may well be less crowded.

Le Presbytère (☎ 04 66 45 24 54; lagrave .alain@wanadoo.fr; 18 rue du Pêcher; beds in doubles or quads €11; open Feb–mid-Nov) is an airy, walker-friendly *gîte*. Alternatively, try the town-run **gîte communal** (☎ 04 66

45 14 93; 1 rue du Four; dorm beds €8.40; open mid-Mar–Oct). Both places have self-catering facilities.

Le 21 (☎ 04 66 45 11 19; 21 l'Esplanade; basic doubles €25, with bathroom €42) is your cheapest hotel option.

Grand Hotel du Parc (☎ 04 66 45 03 05; www.grandhotelduparc.fr; 47 av Jean Monestier; doubles €41.50-53.50, half board €50.50-62.50; menus €15-29.50; open mid-Mar–Nov) has a pool, delightful gardens and a good restaurant.

L'Esplanade, a shady, pedestrianised allée, becomes one long dining area in summer. Here, you can eat well and economically at one of the restaurant terraces

Le Chapeau Rouge (☎ 04 66 45 23 40; 3 bis rue Roussel; menus €15-29), beside the tourist office, is run by a friendly young crew. You'll eat well beneath the vines that shade its pleasant terrace.

Getting There & Away It's not easy without your own transport. There's precisely one minibus, Monday to Saturday, to/from Alès (€12, 1½ hours), leaving from the old railway station early morning and departing from the bus station in Alès late morning. From Alès, you can plug into the rail network.

Ring **Autocars Reilhes** (☎ 04 66 45 00 18), who also operates a taxi service.

Mixing with Menhirs

Duration	8–8½ hours
Distance	34km
Difficulty	moderate–demanding
Start/Finish	Florac (opposite)
Transport	taxi, bus

Summary A mixed-woodland walk to Malbosc that joins up with the Tour du Mont Lozère GR trail. Some strange constructions to ponder at Les Combettes.

The core of this walk, at the limit of the Mont Lozère range, is over open grassland. You'll pass several of southern France's most significant concentrations of menhirs, erected between BC 2500–1800. Chiselled

from blocks of granite, some as tall as 5.5m, were they part of a religious, maybe solar cult? Phallic earth symbols? Or, then again, simply landmarks?

We grade the walk moderate to demanding simply because of its length; the walking itself holds no great challenges. With a vehicle, you can clip off 13km and about three hours of walking by driving to the small parking area below the hamlet of Malbosc and, at the end of the day, taking a 20 minute link route via Chavenet. Alternatively, with the same result, you can start and finish at the small car park beside the D35 at the route's northernmost tip.

An Autocars Reilhes taxi (see Getting There & Away under Florac, left) between Florac and Malbosc costs around €15.

PLANNING
Maps
All but the northernmost kilometre of the route features on the IGN 1:25,000 map Mont Lozère & Florac No 2739OT.

THE WALK
From Florac's tourist office, walk northwards along av Jean Monestier, cross the bridge onto the N106 and turn left. After 750mm, go right onto the D998. At the entry to the village of **Bédouès**, head left down a lane, enticingly signed 'Fromage 800m'. Cross the bridge over the Tarn River and turn right to stroll along its north bank for a pleasant 10 minutes.

At a junction beside Camping Chantemerle, go left. Just after an elongated S-bend some 10 minutes later, bear left at a fork to take a minor dirt track (look for a tell-tale yellow stripe on a nearby rock).

Five minutes later, continue straight at a second fork. You're now following a pleasant, shaded track, which soon becomes simple path, rising fairly gently for the most part through mixed wood of oak, beech and chestnut.

At the farm of **Chadenet**, about 1¼ hours beyond Bédouès, you pick up the first of the day's yellow Parc National waymarkers, indicating the Route des Menhirs. Turn right down a tarred lane, then left after 200m at a hairpin bend to enter chestnut wood. The path, banked and partly cobbled, runs up to **Malbosc**.

Just when you need the waymarkers most, they disappear as you negotiate this hamlet. No matter; head for the tiny cemetery at its highest point and continue northeast along a narrow, bitumen road that hairpins up between cereal and hay fields. Some 30 minutes beyond Malbosc, with the equally tiny settlements of Monteils and Les Bondons well in your sights below to the east, bear left onto a 4WD track and, less than five minutes later, right up a dirt track with Causse Méjan now clearly visible behind you to the southwest.

Les Puechs, the phallic menhirs lie ahead – it's easy to appreciate why ancient peoples regarded the area as one of especial fecundity. Local legend has it that they were clods of mud that Gargantua, Rabelais' larger-than-life hero, scraped from his boots. Where two fences meet at the northeast corner of the base of the right-hand hillock, it's well worth clambering under and climbing the evident path to its summit for superb wraparound views. Allow 15 minutes for the round trip – or else cut corners, yomp down the hill, slice between a pair of hayfields and rejoin the walk, now heading east–west, near a sign, 'Les Puechs'.

If you decided not to climb the eastern hillock, ascend the second one – at 1217m, you'll be all of 3m higher!

At a T-junction, bearing a sign 'Eschino d'Ase', turn right as you pick up the red-and-white stripes of the Tour du Mont Lozère GR trail. The stony track divides, then fuses again – just keep heading steadily downhill.

At a road, turn right, then almost immediately left to descend to the cluster of houses at **Les Combettes** and their most welcome trough with cool, flowing water about 20 minutes beyond the junction with the GR. Just beyond the houses, turn right (north) up a dusty path beside an electricity pole, with your first, rather weedy menhir just beyond it. You soon pass by several more impressive ones as the path climbs, passing briefly through a young pine wood that doesn't feature on the IGN map.

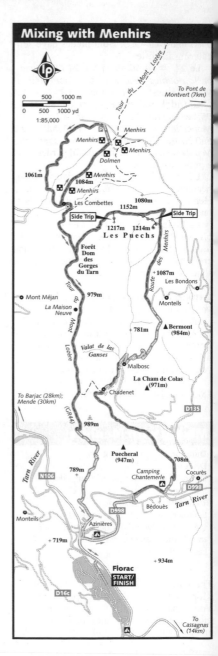

Salt pasture in front of the fortified abbey of Mont St-Michel, Normandy

Illuminated Gothic Notre Dame Cathedral at the end of the Paris Ancient & Modern walk

Near the summit of the Puy de Sancy, the highest peak in the Massif Central

Roche Sanadoire and the gentle valley beyond, seen from Col de Guéry, Auvergne

Chestnut: All-Purpose Tree

In much of the Cévennes, you'll find yourself walking through chestnut groves, nowadays untended and slowly being assimilated into natural woodland. Indigenous to the region, the chestnut tree was cultivated and tended across the centuries. Known as *l'arbre à pain*, the bread tree, it was the staple food of many Auvergnat families. The nuts were eaten raw, roasted and dried, or ground into flour. Once blended with milk or wine, chestnuts were the essence of *bajanat*, a nourishing soup. Part of the harvest would feed the pigs while the leaves of pruned twigs and branches provided fodder for sheep and goats.

Harvested at ground level with small forks – of chestnut wood, of course – the prickly husks (called *hérissons*, hedgehogs) were removed by being trampled upon in spiky boots. Nowadays, they're the favourite food of the Cévennes' wild boars and still feature in a number of local sauces and desserts.

Nothing was wasted. Sections of hollowed-out trunk would serve as beehives, smaller branches would be woven into baskets while larger ones were whittled into stakes for fencing or used to build trellises. The wood, hard and resistant to parasites, was used for rafters rakes and household furniture – everything from, quite literally, the cradle to the coffin.

The rounded shapes of Les Puechs are to the southeast. All the way up the hill, there are tiny rock constructions at ankle level. Far too neat and structured to be mere cairns, they emulate tumuli, menhir complexes and dolmens in miniature. Kids at work? Weirdos and neo-druids? It's all mildly spooky.

About 25 minutes above Les Combettes and just to the right of the track, there's a real dolmen but, victim of distant, insensitive excavation, it has little to reveal.

Once you reach a narrow, tarred lane, a little beyond a menhir with two deeply incised horizontal grooves and, nearby, a giant, reeking dunghill, turn left, then left again at a road junction and parking area (an alternative start to the walk for those

with a vehicle). The path runs parallel with the road for a while, veers broadly southwest then southwards as it joins a dirt track that takes you to Les Combettes.

At a four-way junction bounded by a trio of handsome menhirs, about 30 minutes from the car park, turn left (southeast) to reach Les Combettes some 15 minutes later.

From here, retrace your steps up the hillside to the point where you first joined the Tour du Mont Lozère and continue south, following the GR flashes. Around 20 minutes later, you pass La Maison Neuve (The New House), looking venerable despite its name, its ecofriendly credentials proclaimed by two enormous solar panels.

After 30 minutes, the Route des Menhirs – the path to take if you've left your vehicle at Malbosc – peels away, initially southeastwards. To continue, stick with the main track to descend to **Azinières**, reached about 45 minutes later. Pass through the village, rejoin the morning route at the junction of the D998 and N106 and retrace your steps to Florac.

Walking Through Chaos

Duration	3¾–4 hours
Distance	16km
Difficulty	easy–moderate
Start/Finish	Le Veygalier
Nearest Town	Florac (p126)
Transport	private
Summary	Wander through the weathered dolomite shapes of Le Chaos of Nîmes-le-Vieux. A northern circuit takes you into Causse Méjan's wilder interior.

You're treading the Causse Méjan, one of the Cévennes' four high, arid plateaus that make up the Grands Causses. Their bedrock is limestone, their steep, craggy edges dolomite. Of dolomite too, tougher and more resistant to erosion than softer limestone, are the contorted pillars, blocks and masses of Le Chaos de Nîmes-le-Vieux.

It's a modular, pick-and-choose day with two optional loops. Families might want to

AUVERGNE & MASSIF CENTRAL

choose an out-and-back ramble through Le Chaos de Nîmes-le-Vieux, with excellent scrambling opportunities for kids. The first bolted-on circuit gives you a sense of the gentler aspects of the Causse Méjan, where cereals still grow and the eye is engaged by distant forests. For a feel of its wild, windswept heart, tag on the second, which takes you where few walkers penetrate and crops grow only in the small, sheltered dips and bowls, known locally as *dolines*. The 'moderateness' of this walk resides simply in its length. This apart, it's an easy enough stroll.

PLANNING
The route features on the IGN 1:25,000 map No 2640O *Les Gorges du Tarn*.

GETTING TO/FROM THE WALK
You need wheels. From Florac, take the D907 south and fork right onto the D996 after 13km. At Col de Perjuret, 9km later, turn right and follow signs for Le Veygalier, 3.5km later. Park your vehicle beside the large sheep shed as you enter the hamlet.

THE WALK
Single yellow stripes and wooden posts bearing the yellow rectangular plaque of the Parc National guide you from Le Veygalier to Gally and along the loop as far as the turn for L'Hom at the 1080m spot height on the recommended IGN map.

Turn left along a grassy track beside the small **café** at the northeast end of the hamlet; ignore the sign 'Demandez vos Tickets. Depart Visite' ('Ask for your tickets. Visit starts here'). Access to Nîmes-le-Vieux is free and the 'Visite' is a €2 tour around the hamlet that few would want to make.

The track narrows to a path between hay and cereal fields and over a couple of stiles to the equally small settlement of L'Hom where there's a **gîte d'étape** (☎ *04 66 45 66 14; camping per person €5.50; dorm beds €10, singles/doubles €30/40, half board €26).*

Go through the village and turn right (west). Just after the first of several descriptive panels on the route is the old village *ferradou*, the wooden stall where oxen would be

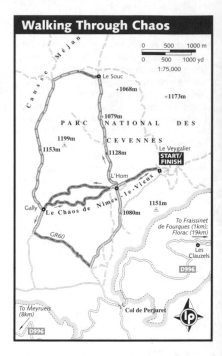

shod. Fork right after 150m to take the more northerly of the routes through the Chaos.

The route snakes its way through the contorted shapes of Le Chaos to the hamlet of **Gally**, 45 to 55 minutes from Le Veygalier. Here, there's a refreshing *buvette* (drinks stall), if you're lucky enough to find it open.

If you're undertaking only the short stroll, turn left just above Gally and head back through Nîmes-le-Vieux via the more southerly route (see the end of this walk description). Otherwise, head south on a tarred road and bear left onto a stony track after barely five minutes, then left again after 150m to pick up the GR60 with its red-and-white bars. Where this wide track meets a bitumen road, turn left, savouring the extensive views of the forested slopes to the east.

After 15 minutes, go left towards L'Hom, and straight through the hamlet, beyond which the road soon becomes dirt track. After 15 minutes, keep to the main track as a signed Parc National route breaks away left, then go straight when another track branches off left a couple of minutes later. You're now without waymarking but navigation is no problem. Head steadily north; bear left at a fork (not on the IGN map) after less than 10 minutes, then left again along the less dominant branch five minutes later.

Once at the abandoned farm buildings of **Le Souc**, just beyond a pair of impressive sink holes, you're off-*piste* for a minute or two; head west-northwest across open meadow, where grasshoppers by the hundred leap at your feet, aiming for a manifest gap in the fir trees on the horizon. After about five minutes – and well before the gap – turn left as you intersect with a cairned path and follow it west into pinewood. After 10 minutes, you emerge into a clearing, just beyond a wooden barrier. Turn left onto the dirt track that skirts the forest, then bears south over grassland. Continue straight where, when you're again parallel with the outer jumble of Le Chaos, a Parc National route comes in from the left.

At Gally (and perhaps checking if that *buvette* is open!) climb above it, go through a latch gate and turn right onto the lower, more southerly path back through Le Chaos. In autumn, there are hazelnuts for the picking. Thirty minutes later, pass through L'Hom for the third and last time and retrace your first steps of the day back to Le Veygalier.

In Stevenson's Steps

Duration	4–4¼ hours
Distance	16.5km
Difficulty	easy
Start/Finish	Relais Stevenson
Nearest Town	Florac (p126)
Transport	private

Summary Through forest on the Robert Louis Stevenson trail to meet the GR7. A walk through the Mimente Valley and along a railway line, long-abandoned.

If you're feeling a little overbaked after too much walking under the sun, this shady, undemanding forest walk through the Forêt Domanial de Fontmort is the ideal pick-

me-up. For the most part, it follows sandy tracks that are so wide that you never feel hemmed in.

It's a day of following the GRs that thread and rethread their way through the Cévennes. It begins with a section of the Robert Louis Stevenson Trail (the GR70), the route taken by the Scottish writer in 1878 and described in his *Travels with a Donkey in the Cévennes* (for more detail, see Other Walks at the end of the chapter). The route then picks up the GR7, tackles a section of the Parc National trail and heads home via the GR72.

PLANNING

The walk features on IGN 1:25,000 map No 2740ET *Corniche des Cévennes*.

NEAREST TOWN & FACILITIES

See Florac (p126).

Le Relais Stevenson

Consider staying or camping at friendly **Le Relais Stevenson** (☎ 04 66 45 20 34; *singles/doubles/triples with bathroom 32/41.60/49.70; half board €47.70; menu €14; open year-round*). Occupying the old Cassagnas railway station, it has a small Robert Louis Stevenson exhibition and its **restaurant** does a filling *menu*. Half board is compulsory in July and August. It also runs the adjacent **camping ground** (*camping 2 people & tent/car €9/2*).

GETTING TO/FROM THE WALK

From Florac, take the N106, signposted Alès, to follow the attractive valley of the Mimente River. After about 15km, and before the hamlet of Cassagnas, turn right at a sign for Relais Stevenson and park beside the *gîte*.

THE WALK

From Relais Stevenson, cross the bridge to the south bank of the Mimente River, following the D62. Just beyond the first bend, bear left onto a sandy track, staying with the GR70 as the GR72 heads away uphill. The track ascends, oh-so-gently, through silent fir forest and chirruping mixed wood.

In Stevenson's Steps

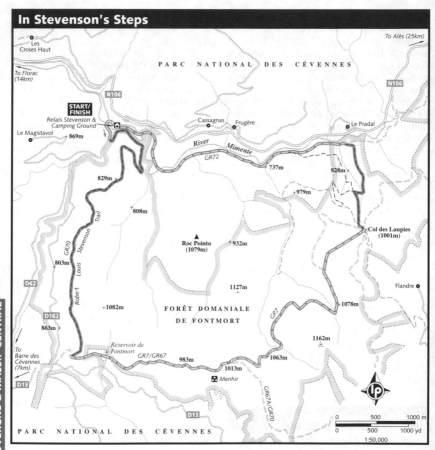

The occasional clods of donkey dung (if it's fretted, it's fir cone!) give solid evidence that more and more walkers these days are emulating Robert Louis Stevenson. Not every false fork is signed with the usual red-and-white GR cross; stick always to the main track where there's a choice.

At a T-junction, about 1¼ hours out, turn left (east) to stay with the Stevenson trail and join the GR7/GR67. Five minutes later, pause at a flowing wooden trough and solid bench, fashioned from the same tree trunk. Here, or just above at the Réservoir de Fontmort (reservoir's a grand name; it's a tiny cistern), you

can replenish your water bottles. 'Eau non analysée' (untested water) says a sign but it seems safe enough; the only animals around are the few humans and fewer donkeys that pass on the track beneath it.

As you head east, a panorama of rolling blue and grey forested hills, layer upon layer like some Japanese print, opens before you with Mont Aigoual (1567m) on the farthest horizon. About 25 minutes beyond the reservoir, a detour of no more than 50m to the right brings you to a stubby menhir and a tiny prehistoric burial pit. With its commanding view, it makes an excellent rest stop.

About 200m beyond this brief diversion, keep straight, following the GR7 and leaving the Robert Louis Stevenson trail as it drops away to the right. Dense fir now gives way to occasional tall, elegant pines, beneath which evergreens flourish.

From here until a large clearing with a solitary pine tree at its heart, reached some 45 minutes beyond the menhir, your boots kick up thick, silvery dust, rich in mica, as you walk the wide track. At the clearing, make a 90° right turn to descend northeastwards, still following the GR.

Ten minutes later, you arrive at **Col des Laupies** (1001m), an even broader forest clearing with a couple of handy picnic tables. Here, where seven tracks intersect, leave the GR to take the one that drops northwest, then due north, signed Cassagnas (note the menhir just beyond the sign).

After 500m, take a tight hairpin right onto a path as the main track continues straight. This signed variant – indicated 'Cassagnas' at junctions – curls around the head of a small valley. Overgrown in places, it winds downhill, broadening into a narrow track, banked in places and carpeted with beech leaves.

On meeting a wider track at a four-way junction, turn left at a sign (broken when we passed) for Relais Stevenson. The straight, near-level track follows the old **train line**, closed in 1968, that linked Florac and Alès; you can still see the wooden sleepers in places. Follow it back to Relais Stevenson, perhaps pausing just before the *gîte* at a lovely **pool**, backing up behind a small dam, the perfect spot to revitalise hot, pink feet.

Other Walks

MONT DÔME
Traverse of the High Auvergne
This 15-day, 293km linear route mainly follows the GR4 over the high peaks of the Massif Central from Volvic, just north of Clermont Ferrand, to Langogne, on the main railway line between Paris and Nîmes and accessible by bus from Le Puy-en-Velay. For a shorter walk, which still includes all the major summits of the Parc des Volcans, cut out at St-Flour, on the railway line between Paris and Béziers, at the end of Day 10. The route is described in detail in Alan Castle's *Walks in Volcano Country* (see Books, p109).

MONTS DU CHANTAL
Robert Louis Stevenson Trail
This trail, designated the GR70, follows the itinerary of Robert Louis Stevenson and his wayward donkey, Modestine, in the autumn of 1878 – but for minor variations to avoid tedious or overtrafficked sections. From Le Monastier-sur-Gazelle, southeast of Le Puy-en-Velay, it meanders for 232km as far as St-Jean du Gard, west of Alès.

Alan Castle, in his guide *The Robert Louis Stevenson Trail*, divides the walk into 13 stages – one more than the pioneering Stevenson, whose wry account of his own journey, *Travels with a Donkey in the Cévennes* you should also pack.

Trains link Le Puy-en-Velay with Lyon, Clermont Ferrand and Toulouse. At journey's end, a daily bus operates between St-Jean du Gard and Alès, from where there are several trains daily to Nîmes, on the TGV (*train à grande vitesse*; high speed train) line to Paris.

For more information, check the website www.chemin-stevenson.org or pick up the pamphlet *Sur le Chemin de Robert Louis Stevenson*, which is stocked by the region's tourist offices, with a comprehensive list of accommodation en route.

Gorges du Tarn
A linear 200km route stretches from the source of the Tarn River on the slopes of Mont Lozère to Albi, from where there's a frequent train service to Toulouse. Divided into 12 stages, it's described in Chamina's *Vallée et Gorges du Tarn* in French, together with seven other circular routes in and around the gorges, varying in duration from one to three days.

On weekdays, there's one bus daily between Alès and Florac (p126) a good jumping-off point for the start of the trail.

CHEMIN DE ST-JACQUES HIGHLIGHT

The Chemins de St-Jacques (Ways of St James) are a network of four routes followed by pilgrims through France, across the Pyrenees and on to Santiago de Compostela in Spain, the burial place of the apostle and martyr St-Jacques. The best-known route starts at Le Puy-en-Velay in the Auvergne and extends for 1500km via Figeac, Cahors, Moissac and Montréal to St-Jean Pied de Port at the foot of the pass through the Pyrenees into Spain. The distance is split between France (735km) and Spain (783km). (For the other routes, see Other Walks, p156.) The Le Puy route was pioneered in AD 951 and pilgrims have followed it ever since; between 1000 and 1500, Santiago rivalled Rome and Jerusalem as a destination for Christian pilgrims. Most made the arduous, often hazardous journey on foot, inspired by the desire to express their faith, seek penance for sins and ensure salvation in the afterlife. Hospices along the way provided simple shelter, and the route became an important conduit for religious, political and cultural ideas. The many churches and shrines built to fulfil pilgrims' spiritual needs founded an enduring architectural tradition.

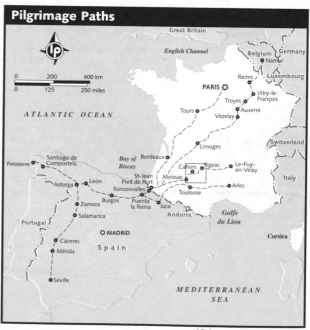

Pilgrimage Paths

Highlights

- Experiencing the camaraderie among pilgrims and walkers, young and old, from many different countries
- Exploring the architectural heritage of timeless towns and villages
- Soaking up landscape contrasts: the deep, cliff-lined Lot Valley (p143); the dry, wooded limestone Causses (p146); and the fertile ridges and valleys (p151) south of Cahors

During the 1990s the pilgrimage routes enjoyed a renaissance; the number of pilgrims reaching Santiago has grown from 2491 in 1986 to 68,952 in 2002, of whom more than 70% made the journey on foot. In 1998 the Chemins de St-Jacques were designated as a World Heritage Site by Unesco, thanks to the efforts of the FFRP and several kindred groups. The FFRP revived the route from Le Puy and labelled it the GR65. This chapter features a six-day highlight on the Le Puy route between the traditional pilgrimage towns of Figeac and Moissac.

Chemin de St-Jacques Highlight

Duration	6 days
Distance	159km
Difficulty	moderate
Start	Figeac (p137)
Finish	Moissac (p140)
Transport	train

Summary An immensely varied and enriching walk linking two of the most historic towns along the best-known of the Chemins de St-Jacques.

Not only can this walk offer an insight to the rewarding experience of pilgrimage, it also passes through a variety of landscapes of seductive, subtle beauty. The deep Célé and Lot Valleys give way to the undulating, wooded limestone plateau of the Causses between Limogne and Cahors. This flat, dry, subtly attractive area is in the region of Quercy, a pre-Revolutionary name still in use, especially in association with its distinctive cuisine. Further south the ridges are more sharply defined and the valleys more fertile. The sense, even feel, of history is ever-present in archaeological features, timeless villages and their beautiful churches. Several towns and villages have historic buildings, most well preserved and presented, so it's worth allowing time to visit at least some (see the boxed text on p148). The itinerary described allows little time for diversions but there are plenty of other places to stay en route; basic details of a selection are included, enabling you to plan shorter days. While the daily ascent averages only 380m, it comes in many short, surprisingly tiring bursts. The route is generally well waymarked with the FFRP's red-and-white stripes and occasional signposts, though experience shows that the times displayed are either impossibly fast or at a snail's pace.

Who was St-Jacques?

Jacques (James in English) was a Christian disciple who spent a couple of years in Spain attempting in vain to spread the gospel after Christ's death. Soon after returning to Jerusalem he was beheaded and became a martyr. It's said that his followers jumped aboard a *stone* boat and took his body to Spain where they landed on the Galician coast, only 20km from present-day Santiago de Compostela. The body was interred on a hillside and forgotten for 750 years.

A hermit's vision led to the opening of the tomb whereupon the local ruler, Alfonso II declared St-Jacques the patron saint of Spain. A church and monastery were built over the tomb in his honour and a town, Santiago de Compostela, developed there. It is believed that the saint's remains lie somewhere in the magnificent cathedral in Santiago.

PLANNING
When to Walk

Conditions can be too hot for comfortable walking during July and August, also the most popular time with pilgrims. September and October are ideal, especially for autumn colours.

You'll need a sheet sleeping bag and towel if you plan to stay in *gîtes d'étape*. A water carrier of at least 1.5L capacity is absolutely essential, especially during the warmest months.

Maps

Nine IGN 1:25,000 maps cover the walk described. Though not essential for route finding, they do enable you to pinpoint surrounding features. They are: Nos 2238O *Cajarc*, 2238E *Figeac*, 2139O *Cahors*, 2139E *Limogne-en-Quercy*, 2239O *Martiel*, 2039E *Cahors (Ouest)*, 2138O *Cahors Vallée du Lot,* 2039O *Montcuq* and 2040O *Moissac*. Local sources are given under individual towns later.

Books

For English speakers, at least one of two guides are indispensable. *Pilgrim Guides to the Roads Through France to Santiago de Compostela, 3. Le Puy to the Pyrenees* by Alison Raju, published by the Confraternity of Saint James (CSJ; see opposite) is a step-by-step guide with accommodation information and some historical detail, but no maps. By the same author, *The Way of St James: Le Puy to the Pyrenees* (published by Cicerone) is similar, but prettier and includes maps.

If you can read even some French another pair of guides are just as good. The FFRP's Topo-Guide Ref 652 *Sentier de Saint-Jacques-de-Compostelle. Le Chemin du Puy* covers the section of the GR65 (the Pilgrim Route) from Figeac to Moissac. It includes 1:50,000 maps and plenty of background information, but limited coverage of accommodation and transport. (Another two FFRP Topo-Guides, Refs 651 and 653, cover the sections from Le Puy to Figeac, and from Moissac to Roncevaux respectively.) The extraordinarily named *miam-miam-dodo*

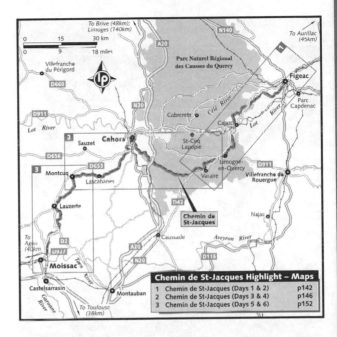

Chemin de St-Jacques Highlight – Maps		
1	Chemin de St-Jacques (Days 1 & 2)	p142
2	Chemin de St-Jacques (Days 3 & 4)	p146
3	Chemin de St-Jacques (Days 5 & 6)	p152

(published by Editions du Vieux Crayon) is an exhaustive compendium of information about everything, which few French walkers would be without; it's widely available locally or from the CSJ.

Information Sources

The **Confraternity of Saint James** (CSJ; ☎ 020 79 28 99 88; www.csj.org.uk; 27 Blackfriars Rd, London SE1 8NY, UK) was founded in 1983 to provide advice and information to pilgrims. It is an invaluable resource for English-speakers; members can obtain a pilgrim's passport (see the boxed text on p148). Several French organisations provide generally less-detailed coverage of the route.

NEAREST TOWNS
Figeac

Clustered around the Célé River, Figeac is a fascinating old town of narrow streets, hidden alleys and beautiful old buildings, some dating back to the 12th century.

The **tourist office** (☎ 05 65 34 06 25; www.quercy-tourisme.com/figeac; place Vival; open Mon-Sat & Sun morning) has numerous local-history publications. **Maison de la Presse** (2 rue Gambetta; open Mon-Sat & Sun morning) is a good source of books and maps.

You can check emails via Cyberposte at the **post office** (6 av Ferdinand Pezet; €7/hr; open Mon-Fri & Sat morning). There are several ATMs in

SALLY DILLON

Left: Half-timbered house with classic attic on blvd Gambetta, Figeac

the town. For the local weather forecast ring ☎ 3250; the local *département* number is 46.

Places to Stay & Eat Approximately 2km from the the town centre, **Camping les Rives du Célé** (☎ *05 65 34 59 00; www.domaianedesurgie .com; La Domaine du Surgié; camping 1 or 2 people & tent €15.50)* is beside a leisure park.

Gîte d'étape Mme Faivre-Pierret (☎ *05 65 50 01 83; 26 chemin de Bataillé; dorm beds €10.50; breakfast €4)* is a friendly place in a large old stone house, about 15 minutes' walk from the town centre; a kitchen is provided.

Le Champ des Étoiles (☎ *05 65 31 16 10; 5 place Louis-Lacombe; dorm beds €10)* is in the heart of town, just off place Carnot; there's a kitchen.

Hôtel le Foirail (☎ *05 65 34 11 36; place du Foirail; singles/doubles with washbasin €23/25; doubles with bathroom €38; breakfast €4.50)* has functional rooms above a busy place, and is 800m north of the river.

Hôtel Courte Paille (☎ *05 65 34 21 83; fax 05 65 14 01 87; 12 place Carnot; doubles with bathroom €35; breakfast €4.50)* overlooks the picturesque square in the town centre.

For food shopping there are **Petit Casino supermarket** (*28 place Carnot; open Tue-Sat & Sun morning)* and **Centre Leclerc Gambetta** (*34*

The Pilgrim's Passport

Since early times pilgrims have carried a passport, issued by their home church, the key to shelter and food at hospices along the route to Santiago. Stamps in the passport obtained at such places provided recognised evidence of the undertaking of the journey to the authorities at Compostela cathedral. They alone were (and are) entitled to issue the coveted certificate of pilgrimage, the sole proof of completion.

Nowadays, pilgrims carry a passport just as they once did, collecting stamps at each night's resting place on their journey. With few exceptions accommodation in France is universally available and not exclusively for pilgrims, though discounts are often available or preference may be given to genuine *pèlerins*. In Spain however the extensive network of pilgrim *albergues* is intended for their particular use. In Britain the Confraternity of Saint James (CSJ; see p137) also issues passports to its members.

Continuing a tradition dating from the 12th century, many pilgrims display the distinctive scallop shell, *coquille de St-Jacques*, on their packs. The origin of its association with the pilgrimage remains a mystery. According to the most colourful legend, the martyred James arrived on the Galician (Spanish) coast in his stone boat during a pagan wedding. It almost ended in tragedy when the bridegroom and his horse, seeing the strange sight, crashed into the sea. James saved them from the waves; when they arose, scallop shells covered their bodies.

rue Gambetta; open Tue-Sat). Keep in mind that very few shops open on Monday.

Le Crêp'Uscule *(☎ 05 65 34 28 53; 4 rue de la République; mains €5.35-15, menus €9-13; open daily)* is a *crêperie*-restaurant which has some outside tables.

La Puce à l'Oreille *(☎ 05 65 34 33 08; 5 rue St-Thomas; menus €13-33.50)* occupies a beautiful old stone building situated in a narrow alley. Menus feature unusual items such as local duck with a honey-chestnut-pepper sauce.

Restaurant à l'Escargot *(☎ 05 65 34 23 84; 2 av Jean Jaurès; menus €27.50; open daily)* offers much more than the eponymous snails, including many Quercy specialities (€9 to €17).

Getting There & Away From Paris' Gare d'Austerlitz, **SNCF trains** *(☎ 08 92 36 35 35)* to Rodez stop at Figeac (€50, 5¾ hours, at least four daily); it may be necessary to travel to Brive and change there. Figeac is also on the Clermont-Ferrand–Toulouse line (€24.70, 3½ hours from Clermont-Ferrand; €18.60, 2¼ hours from Toulouse; at least two daily from both places). SNCF runs a bus service from Cahors to Capendac via Figeac (€11, one hour 40 minutes, at least four daily).

Moissac

A place of great significance in pilgrimage history with its magnificent abbey, Moissac in the early 21st century is a curious mix of scruffy residential streets and magnificent architectural heritage (see the boxed text on p148).

The **tourist office** (☎ *05 63 04 01 85; www.frenchcom.com/moissac; 6 place Durand de Bredon; open daily*) has a good selection of walking and history guides. Tickets for the abbey and cloister (€5) are sold here.

There are ATMs on place des Récollets and in rue de la République. Internet access is available at the **post office** (*17 blvd Alsace Lorraine; €7/ hr; open Mon-Fri & Sat morning*) via Cyberposte. **Maison de la Presse** (*rue Ste-Catherine; open daily except Sun afternoon*) sells maps and guides.

Places to Stay & Eat On an islet in the Lot River, **Camping de l'Île de Bidounet** (☎ *05 63 32 52 52, fax 05 63 32 52 82; St-Benoît; camping per adult & tent €8.30; open Apr-Sep*) has shady sites; access is via Pont Napoléon.

Centre International d'Acceuil et de Séjour (☎ *05 63 04 62 21, fax 05 63 04 62 22; acceuil.cafmoissac@wanadoo.fr; 5 sentier du Calvaire; dorm beds €11; rooms with shower & toilet €16; breakfast €4, evening meal €11*) is uphill from the D4 road, north of the abbey in a former convent. It was rescued from dereliction by the local commune and opened in July 2000 as a centre for pilgrims and artists.

Hôtel des Récollets (☎*/fax 05 63 04 25 44; place des Récollets; singles/ doubles with washbasin €24/30; with bathroom €29/39; breakfast €5.50; menus €9-15.50*) has straightforward rooms, most overlooking the square. Its unpretentious bistro, with some outdoor tables, offers five *menus*.

Hôtel-Restaurant Le Luxembourg (☎ *05 63 04 00 27; www.hotel luxembourg82.com; av Pierre Chabrié; doubles/twins with bathroom €39/45; breakfast €5, menus €12-25; closed Sun evening*) is on a busy road, near the route of the walk and the train station.

Hôtel Le Chapon Fin (☎ *05 63 03 04 22, fax 05 63 04 58 44; place des Récollets; doubles with shower/bathroom €36/49*) has pleasantly furnished rooms overlooking the lively square; for peace and quiet ask for a back room.

For supplies there's **Ecomarché supermarket** (*place des Récollets; open Mon-Sat & Sun morning*). On Sunday place des Récollets is taken over by the irresistible weekly **market**.

Lou Grill (☎ *05 63 04 32 80; 3 rue du Marché; menus €9.50-14.50*) is an attractive, rustic little bistro, strong on lamb, beef and fish.

Le Verdi (☎ *05 63 04 48 90; 8 place Roger Delthil; menus €15-20; closed Mon*) is right in front of the massive abbey door. Entrees include delectable Quercy melon; pasta dishes are vegetarians' lifelines in a sea of snails, frogs' legs and salmon.

L'Auberge du Cloître (☎ *05 63 04 37 50; 1 place Roger Delthil; menus €20-23.50*) is opposite the side entrance to the abbey. Truffles are used in entrees and in mains focussing on meat and fish.

Getting There & Away Moissac is on the **SNCF** (☎ *08 92 36 35 35*) Carcassonne–Toulouse–Bordeaux St-Jean line (€21.70, one hour 40 minutes, at least three daily to Bordeaux). From Bordeaux TGVs operate to Paris' Montparnasse (€67.60, 3½ hours, several daily).

THE WALK
Day 1: Figeac to Cajarc (see map pp142-3)
6¾–7 hours, 31km

Cross the Célé River bridge, take av Jean Jaurès on the right and follow it for several hundred metres to a road on the left at Le Cingle Bas. Pass under a railway bridge and follow the twists and turns up the steep, wooded escarpment to a large war memorial and an excellent view of Figeac.

Bitumen roads then take you to an intersection and **L'Aiguille du Cingle**, a slender tapering column, its purpose a mystery, though the theory of boundary markers for the nearby Benedictine abbey carries some weight. Turn right at the main road for a short distance, then first right. The road leads across a plateau to La Cassagnolle (1¼ hours from Figeac). Here, in an idyllic setting, you'll find a *gîte d'étape* **Relais St Jacques** (☎ 05 65 34 03 08; *dorm beds €8.90; singles/doubles with breakfast €28/32*)

Continue southwest, soon passing the first of many *bories* you'll see on this journey – small circular or stone buildings, traditionally used for storage or shelter. The route follows minor roads generally southwestwards through several junctions. About 2km from La Cassagnolle, a church spire appears ahead and soon you reach the peaceful village of **Faycelles** (45 minutes from La Cassagnolle).

Right on the route is **M Besse Daynac's Chambre d'hôte** (☎ 05 65 34 07 66; *singles/doubles with bathroom €34/40; kitchen for guest use €7*) in a lovely old stone building. Nearby to the right is **La Forge** (☎ 05 65 34 65 09; *menus €11.50-15.50; open daily*), which offers daily specials (€8.50), pasta and omelettes (€9.50). Next door is a small shop; there's a public telephone near the large church. Faycelles is on the Cahors–Figeac bus route (see p140).

Once you've left the village, the route direction now changes to northwest, following the D21 road for 2km. At a junction where Lascamp is to the right, leave the road for a minor deviation, rejoining it at Mas de la Croix. From this intersection it's 800m downhill to the hamlet of Béduer; by turning left at the first junction you come to **La Taverne Bar-Restaurant** (☎ 05 65 11 23 42; *menus €9-15*), which also offers daily specials, drinks and snacks.

To continue from Mas de la Croix towards Cajarc, follow a minor road to the left then go left along a path opposite a small cross. About 25 minutes from Mas de la Croix, via a minor road and pleasant tracks, you come to a minor road junction. From this point **Camping Pech Ibert** (☎ 05 65 40 05 85; www.camping-pech-ibert.com; *camping per person €7.50, caravan €11, cabin €14; breakfast €4*) is 300m to the right in the grounds of a large stone house.

Bear left at the junction then continue through three junctions to the entrance to Combe Salgues farm and bear right. Soon, beyond another junction you cross the highest point on the walk, Pech Favard, at about 390m. About 1.2km further on, turn left along a road then go on via roads, a track and paths to a road at Le Puy-Clavel. Here it's right then left along a wide track. Gain some height to a minor east–west road

Chemin de St-Jacques (Days 1 & 2)

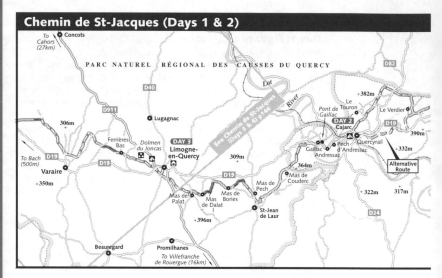

from where a series of turns brings you to the hamlet of **Gréalou** (two hours from near Pech Ibert). Follow the road around to a junction, near the village's ancient church, and turn right.

This minor road soon becomes a track and passes a cemetery then a well-preserved *borie* on the left. About 1.3km further on at a junction you'll find a lopsided **dolmen** (prehistoric tomb). The route now leads generally south for 2.2km without complications to a junction near Le Verdier (an hour from Gréalou), where a slightly shorter, non-GR65 route takes off for Cajarc. Turn right and follow a minor road for a good kilometre to a junction and turn left. Soon, heading southwest, leave the road and follow a track between fields, through woodland, across a minor road to a junction; turn left towards Cajarc.

A string of tracks and paths leads on through farmland; after about 1.6km the depths of the Lot River Valley take shape ahead. At a junction where Le Touron is to the right, turn left then bear right on a bend along a track with a great view of the valley. Descend beside limestone cliffs and past a large cave. Make a right turn along a narrow path to a road on the outskirts of **Cajarc**. Turn left at a junction and continue straight on (past rue du Cuzoul – the start of tomorrow's walk) to place du Foirail; the tourist office is on the left (1½ hours from Le Verdier).

Cajarc

Cajarc has been a popular staging place for pilgrims for centuries – a hospice was in business by the mid-13th century, and it enjoys a scenic setting overlooked by impressive limestone cliffs. This small town almost goes to sleep on Monday – very few shops or restaurants are open that day.

Chemin de St-Jacques (Days 1 & 2)

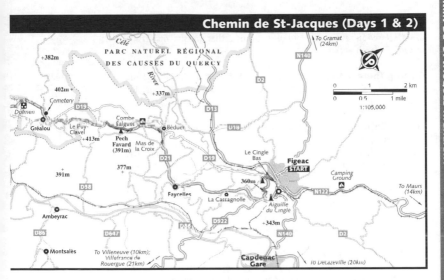

The **tourist office** (☎ 05 65 40 72 89; Mon-Sat & Sun morning) issues accreditation stamps; the local weather forecast is available here. There's an ATM on place du Foirail. Maps and guides are sold by **Maison de la Presse** (63 blvd de Tour-de-Ville; open daily except Sun afternoon).

Places to Stay & Eat Right beside the route, **Camping du Terriol** (☎ 05 65 40 72 74, fax 05 65 40 39 05; rue du Terriol; camping per person & tent €5.50) has plenty of quiet sheltered **camp sites**.

Gîte d'étape Communal (☎ 06 14 66 54 89; place du Foirail; dorm beds €6.10) has traditional bunk rooms and a small, basic kitchen. There are also beds in two large tents at the camping ground.

Gîte d'étape (☎ 05 65 440 65 31; 2 av Marius Couybya; bed €9) is a few metres from the route, in a former private house. It has double and twin rooms, a small dorm and two kitchens.

Auberge du Pont (☎ 05 65 40 67 84; av Coluche; doubles €31; breakfast €5, menus €13-29) is a small, homely inn close to the Lot River. In the restaurant you can choose from four menus.

Hôtel-Restaurant la Ségalière (☎ 05 65 40 65 35, fax 05 65 40 74 92; hotel.segaliere@wanadoo.fr; av François Mitterand; singles/doubles €45/56; with bathroom €55/66, half board €50-77; breakfast €8, menus €14-46) is in a world of its own about 400m east of the town centre. The **restaurant** features local produce.

For self-caterers there are **Ecomarché supermarket** (av Germain Cavet; open Mon-Sat), about 200m from place du Foirail on the D19 road, **Petit Casino supermarket** (place du Foirail; open Tue-Sat & Sun morning) and an excellent **boulangerie** nearby.

Restaurant La Promenade (☎ 05 65 40 61 21; 22 place du Foirail; menus €13-31; closed Sun evening & Mon) offers some rather unusual dishes such as Quercy lamb with saffron.

Getting There & Away Cajarc is on the **SNCF** (☎ 08 92 35 35 35) bus route linking Cahors and Capendac (€6.90, 55 minutes, at least four daily). Figeac is also on this route.

Day 2: Cajarc to Limogne-en-Quercy (see map pp142-3)
4–4¼ hours, 20km

Pick up rue du Cuzoul and follow it past the camping area, beside fields then the Quercyrail tourist rail line. Go through the second underpass then shortly later right to bypass a house and garden; go up to the road. Follow it left for 250m to a junction and turn left along chemin de la Route Vieille towards Pech d'Andressac. Continue down to the intensively cultivated river flats – asparagus and strawberries are staple crops. Merge with the D19 road, cross Pont de Gaillac over the Lot and go up a path on the left. Follow a minor road past Gaillac's few houses; continue on a track beside a stone wall. The route leads generally south through oak woodland, traversing several junctions. Bear right at a bitumen road in more open country with wide views, and pass the entrance to Mas de Couderc farm (1¾ hours from Cajarc). One kilometre further on, at a junction where there's a small stone cross on the left, go right down a track. Continue west then south through several junctions to a road and bear right into the hamlet of Mas de Bories (45 minutes from the Mas de Couderc entrance).

Follow the road for several hundred metres to a junction; go left up a woodland path and on to the hamlet of Mas de Dalat. From there a string of turns, through path and road junctions heading southwest, brings you to the handful of buildings that is Mas de Palat (45 minutes from Mas de Bories). Turn right at each of the next four junctions and go through a track intersection to reach a junction where the Limogne gîte d'étape is 1.1km to the right. If you decide to break off here, follow a wide track which becomes a road to the D911; follow it for a few hundred metres to the gîte on the right. Otherwise, turn left, cross the D911 road, then follow right and left bends in a road between farmhouses to a wider road; turn left and follow it to a junction. Go right for 60m then left up a track and on to a crossroads. Turn right towards **Limogne-en-Quercy** at a roundabout; the camping area is to the left. In the village, cross place Yves Ouvrieu and follow the D911 for about 200m to the gîte on the left (1¼ hours from Mas de Palat).

Limogne-en-Quercy

This is a compact town where life revolves around the sociable and occasionally busy place Yves Ouvrieu; it's about 1.1km from the route via either approach.

The **tourist office** (☎ 05 65 24 34 28; tourisme.lomogne@wanadoo.fr; place Yves Ouvrieu; open Mon-Sat & Sun morning) has plenty of useful local information. There's an ATM on route Cahors (the D911 road). The **Maison de la Presse** (*route de Langagnac*) sells maps and guides.

Places to Stay & Eat A short distance west of the route, **Camping Municipal Bel-Air** (☎ 05 65 31 51 27, fax 05 65 24 73 59; alainbach@ minitel.net; camping per person & tent €9) is a shady site right beside the local swimming pool.

Gîte d'étape de Limogne-en-Quercy (☎ 05 65 24 34 12; route Ville-franche; dorm beds €7) has small bunk rooms, a single and a double, and a compact kitchen in an old two-storey building.

Mme Gavens Chambre d'hôte (☎/fax 05 65 24 37 32; Bastide de Vinel, route de Cènevières; singles/doubles with bathroom & breakfast €37/41) is about 200m along the D24 road, in a stone farm building.

For catering supplies there's a **Petit Casino supermarket** (place Yves Ouvrieu, open Tue-Sat & Sun morning) and an excellent **boulangerie** (route Cahors).

Café-Bar Le Galopin (☎ 05 65 31 55 56; place Yves Ouvrieu; open Mon-Sat) is the social centre of Limogne and the outside tables are nearly always crowded. The choice of drinks is long, but not so of food – daily specials (€6.50 to €8) or steak and chips (€10).

Le Vieux Quercy (☎ 05 65 31 51 17; route de Laugagnac; open daily; menus €13.30-19) specialises in local cuisine, such as Quercy salad, which includes ham, bacon and duck breast.

Getting There & Away Between Cahors and Villefranche, **SARL Cars** (☎ 04 65 34 00 70) operates a service via Limogne (55 minutes, at least one daily, late afternoon, Monday to Friday).

Day 3: Limogne-en-Quercy to Cahors (see map pp146-7)
8–8½ hours, 39km

Back on the way at the southwestern edge of Limogne, go right (northwest) at an intersection (along the D24) for about 150m; turn left along a track and follow it southwest for 2.3km. Along the way is an opportunity for a short diversion, to **Dolmen du Joncas** on the right – a sizable prehistoric burial cairn. At a three-way junction distinguished by a small memorial cross at **Ferrières Bas** keep left; 200m further on at a bend, follow a path straight on. Then, another few hundred metres further, it's a right turn through a moveable fence. This path curves around, through another barrier, to a minor road – cross directly over. The route turns sharply left (south) 1.1km further west and continues in that direction for 1.9km to a junction (1½ hours from Limogne) where Varaire is about 1km straight on, though off the route.

To reach the village bear left at a junction further on to find **Rando-Étape de Varaire** (☎ 05 65 31 53 85; dorm beds €12, half board €26). **Les Marronniers** bar-restaurant (same telephone number) is next door and across the road is a small **shop**.

To continue along the route, follow a track across two roads then head west for 2.2km. A forbidding 'Keep Out' sign on a large gate

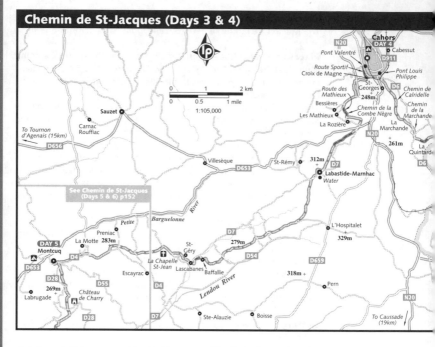

Chemin de St-Jacques (Days 3 & 4)

dictates a left turn; gravel tracks then a road lead southwest for 2km to the hamlet of Bach (an hour from the Varaire junction). Walk southwest along the D19 for about 500m then bear right along a track and at the next junction go right. The next few kilometres, following the ancient route *Cami Ferrat* are straightforward, generally westwards then northwest; this was originally a paved road, built by the Romans and feared by pilgrims for its isolation and lack of stopping places. En route cross the D42, the usually dry Ruisseau des Valses and a fairly open limestone plateau to the comparatively prosperous hamlet of Mas de Vers (1¾ hours from Bach). About 150m from the crossroads you come to the welcoming **Relais St-Jacques** set up by an enthusiastic local fellow to provide drinks and sandwiches for pilgrims and walkers – for whatever price you care to pay.

Continue northwestwards through more undulating country for 3.3km, across a minor road and the D10 road, down to a minor road where there's an old communal laundry. Bear left and follow the road into a valley; turn right and go on to the turn-off for Le Pech (an hour from Mas de Vers). It's a steep ascent to **Le Pech Gîte d'Étape** (*☎/fax 05 65 24 72 84; Labugade; dorm beds €10; breakfast €4, evening meal €10*).

The route continues left at three closely spaced junctions, up to the D6 road. Turn right, go through an underpass (beneath the A20 autoroute) and up the D6. At Le Gariat, follow the blue signs and you'll

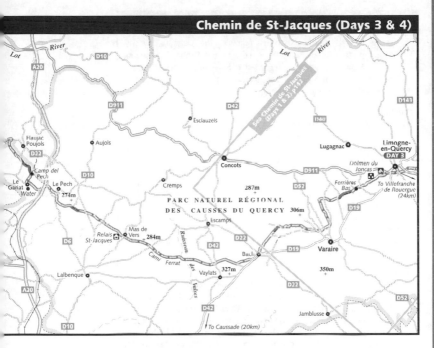

find drinking water from a tap specially provided for pilgrims beside the front gate of a private house. Just 50m further on, turn right along a track, then left at 'Camp del Pech' junction. Next come a couple of sharp ups and downs, in and out of small valleys, through the locality of La Quintarde to the D6. Turn right then shortly right again to La Marchande (1¾ hours from the Le Pech turnoff). Soon after, turn left along chemin de la Marchande. Cross the D6 to chemin de Calridelle leading northwest along a ridge. Eventually this joins a bitumen road and soon **Cahors** materialises below. The steep descent starts from the first communications mast you pass, down through tight bends to a road. Turn left, go under a railway bridge to a major junction opposite Pont Louis-Philippe, which takes you across the Lot and into town along blvd Gambetta (an hour from La Marchande).

Cahors

A large town with several different faces, from the narrow, canyon-like alleys and atmospheric bistros of the old town to the relatively anonymous modern quarter. After a tour of the historic buildings return to the here-and-now indulgently, at the open-air markets.

The **tourist office** (☎ 05 65 53 20 65; place François Mitterand; cahors@wanadoo.fr; open Mon-Sat & Sun morning Jul & Aug only) has a short list of hotel contact numbers on display outside. If the office

Cahors & Moissac

There's more to the Chemin than just following the route day by day. Spending time in five towns between Le Puy and Santiago, including Cahors and Moissac, is generally regarded as an essential part of the experience, to explore their historic associations with the pilgrim route and their architectural heritage. The highlights are:

Cahors

Pont Valentré A magnificent fortified medieval bridge, built in the 14th century as part of the town's defences. It has six arches and three tall towers, two equipped with projecting parapets with openings from which missiles could be dropped on attackers below.

Cathédrale St-Étienne A Romanesque-style cathedral consecrated in 1119, and crowned with two huge cupolas (obviously an Eastern import). The chapels along the nave are Gothic; certain wall paintings are early 14th-century originals. The cloister is in the Flamboyant Gothic style of the early 16th century.

Medieval Quarter East of blvd Gambetta, it's crowded with old four-storey houses along streets and the narrowest of alleyways. Visit the 16th-century Hôtel des Roaldès and the older Tour du Pape Jean XXII.

Moissac

Abbaye St-Pierre From the early 11th century, what was originally a Benedictine monastery became one of southern France's most influential monasteries, spiritually and artistically. That it's still standing is little short of a miracle; it has survived sieges, wars, defacement, the threat of demolition and now, the thundering passage of high-speed TGVs. Today's it's part of the World Heritage Site. The southern portal features a panorama of biblical stories in stone; over the door is an extraordinary sculpture depicting St John's Vision of the Apocalypse. The tranquil cloister is superb – 116 marble columns each topped with a different carving.

is open, ask about access across Pont Valentré – then you'll avoid an unlovely road walk tomorrow morning.

There are several ATMs along blvd Gambetta, the main thoroughfare leading into town from the bridge. Check emails via Cyberposte at the **post office** (257 rue Président Wilson; €7/hour; Mon-Fri & Sat morning).

Places to Stay & Eat On the eastern side of the river, **Camping Rivière de Cabessut** (☎ 05 65 30 06 30; www.cabessut.com; rue de la Rivière; camping per person & tent €10.50) is a shady site 1.5km from the town centre.

Auberge de Jeunesse (☎ 05 65 35 64 71, fax 05 65 35 95 92; 20 rue Frédéric Suisse; dorm beds €8.50; breakfast €3.20, evening meal €7.80) has rooms with two to 10 beds.

Foyer de Jeunes en Quercy (☎ 05 65 35 29 32, fax 05 65 53 69 68; 129 rue Fondue-Haute; dorm beds €8.80; breakfast €2.30, evening meal week-

days only €6.40) looks rather forbidding, in a narrow dark street, but walkers are warmly welcomed.

Hôtel-Restaurant Le Melchior *(☎ 05 65 35 03 38, fax 05 65 23 92 /5; place de la Gare; singles/doubles with shower & toilet €26.90/42.30; breakfast €5.50, menus €10-40-17.80)* is opposite the station; simply furnished, compact rooms are quite comfortable. Reception is closed on Sunday (except in July and August). The restaurant features grills, mussels, pasta and salads

Hôtel-Restaurant La Chartreuse *(☎ 05 65 35 17 37, fax 05 65 22 30 03; www.hotel-la-chartreuse.com; chemin de la Chartreuse; singles/doubles with shower & toilet €44/49; breakfast €6.50, menus €29-58)* is a modern establishment beside the river and right on the route. The restaurant fare shows a predilection for truffles with almost everything except ice cream.

For self-caterers, there are **Petit Casino supermarkets** *(224 rue National • 32 rue de la Préfecture)*, both in Old Cahors, east of blvd Gambetta. In the same area, around place des Halles, you'll find covered and open-air **markets** (Tuesday to Saturday and Sunday morning).

The choice of food ranges from takeaway pizzas and Turkish kebabs to gourmet dining in elegant restaurants.

La Pizzeria *(☎ 05 65 35 12 18; 58 blvd Gambetta; mains €5-12, menus €8.90-15; open daily)* is much more than a pizzeria and a haven for vegetarians with the word *végétarienne* appearing twice on the menu. Its varied offerings include grills, fish, pasta and of course pizzas – the Quercy version, with bacon and goats' cheese.

L'Auberge des Gabares *(☎ 05 65 53 91 47; place Champollion; open daily)* has a first floor terrace overlooking the river. You can make up your own €13 menu from the diverse *carte*.

Getting There & Away At least four **SNCF** *(08 92 35 35 35)* trains daily operate between Paris Gare d'Austerlitz and Cahors (€51, five hours).

JULIA WILKINSON

Right: Pont Valentré, Cahors

CHEMIN DE ST-JACQUES

Day 4: Cahors to Montcuq (see map pp146-7)

6–6½ hours, 31km

From the intersection on the southern side of the Lot River across Pont Louis-Philippe, go down a minor road, past Hôtel Chartreuse then beside the main road to a point almost opposite Pont Valentré. The way onwards is signposted as a *Route Sportif* (demanding) but in reality is just a very steep flight of steps through the cliffs; an alternative is waymarked to the right. Up on the plateau, the route leads southeast to a road. It's worth diverting 150m left here for a fine view of Cahors from **Croix de Magne**. Turn right at the road and go on to an intersection. From here a series of turns soon takes you past the N20 autoroute (not shown on the Topo-Guide map) to a small valley. At a fork turn left along route des Mathieux, then shortly continue on chemin de la Combe Nègre to a road. Turn left to pass the hamlet of La Rozière (1¼ hours from Cahors); at a sharp right bend, go straight on along a path (don't be misled by a wider track to the right), then

SALLY DILLON

Left: Cahors market, outside Cathédrale St-Étienne, Cahors

down to a road. The route dodges around the D653 and D7 roads to a vehicle track; a traditional path then leads steeply up to a wooded plateau. It's straightforward then for about 3km to **Labastide-Marnhac** (an hour from La Rozière), an attractive village of well-kept cream sandstone houses. Slake your thirst from a tap on the front wall of the prominent church.

Follow the main road past the *mairie* to a junction with the D7 and turn left for 75m, then diverge along a track southwards. The route then follows a minor road briefly, traverses a narrow valley, then rises past a stone house, to a lightly wooded plateau. Continue generally southwest for a good 5km along minor roads and tracks traversing a narrow ridge with lovely views of patchwork fields and stone-built mansions. At a crossroads turn right down into a wide, intensively cultivated valley and pass through the hamlet of Baffallie. Turn left along a path between fields; bear left beside a bridge and left again next to an old communal laundry. Continue up to Lascabanes, another lovely old village (2¼ hours from Labastide-Marnhac). Go right for 100m from opposite the *mairie* to reach the excellent **Gîte Rando Étape** (☎ 05 65 31 49 12; *half board €24*) in a former presbytery. Revive with a cold drink from a machine by the front door.

From the far side of the *gîte*, turn right along a road for a few hundred metres then left to leave the valley behind. A right then a left turn bring you to tranquil La Chapelle de St-Jean; continue through farmland, past a track on the left to Escayrac, across a road and on to another where you turn right for several hundred metres to a track on the left. Continue past a track right to Preniac and on to the D4 road – turn right. Follow it for 1.2km to a track on the right towards La Motte. About 1km further on there's a path down left to Le Souleillou Gîte (see Montcuq). To reach **Montcuq**, fork left near a large communications tower and descend to a road and place du Faubourg St-Privat (two hours from Lascabanes).

Montcuq

Clustered onto a small hill to one side of the wide, fertile valley of the Petite Barguelonne Rivière, this lovely old town is a far cry from the frenetic pace of Cahors.

The helpful staff at the **tourist office** (☎ 05 65 22 94 04; *8 La Promenade; open Mon-Sat*) can provide plenty of local information. Go to the **Maison de la Presse** (*4 La Promenade*) for maps and guides. There are ATMs at 6 La Promenade and in rue Faubourg St-Privat.

Camping Municipal St-Jean (☎ 05 65 22 93 73; *camping per person & tent €5; open mid-Jun–mid-Sep*) is a small site west of the town centre.

Le Souleillou Gîte d'étape (☎ 05 65 31 87 88; *22 rue du Souleillou; dorm beds €9.50, doubles per person €10.50; breakfast €3, evening meal €9.50*) is very close to the route on the outskirts of Montcuq. A kitchen is available.

Chambre d'hôte Borredon (☎ 05 65 31 82 92; *3 rue de Souleillou; dorm beds/doubles with breakfast €15/23*) is only 50m from the route in the town; a kitchen is available.

CHEMIN DE ST-JACQUES HIGHLIGHT

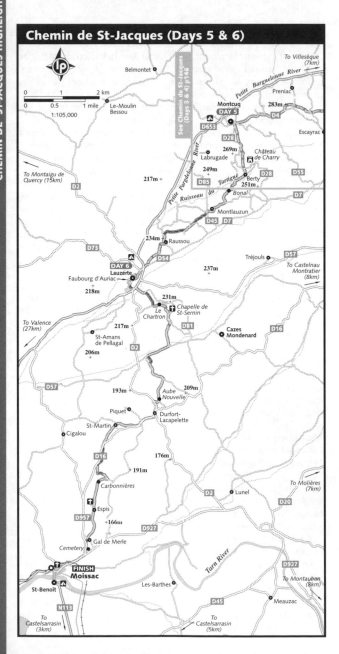

Chemin de St-Jacques (Days 5 & 6)

To Villesèque (7km)

Belmontet

Le-Moulin Bessou

Petite Barguelonne River

Preniac

283m

Montcuq

DAY 5

D4

Escayrac

D653

D28

269m

Château de Charry

249m

Labrugade

D28

D55

217m +

D85

Tartigné

Berty

251m

To Montaigu de Quercy (15km)

D2

Petite Barguelonne River

Ruisseau du

Bonal

D7

234m

D73

D54

D45

Montlauzun

D7

Raussou

Tréjouls

D57

237m

To Castelnau Montratier (8km)

DAY 6

Lauzérte

Faubourg d'Auriac

218m

231m

Chapelle de St-Sernin

Le Chartron

D81

Cazes Mondenard

D16

To Valence (27km)

St-Amans de Pellagal

217m

D2

206m

193m

209m

Aube Nouvelle

D57

Piquet

Durfort-Lacapelette

St-Martin

Cigalou

D16

176m

191m

D2

Lunel

To Molières (7km)

D20

Carbonnières

Espis

D957

166m

D927

Gal de Merle

Tarn River

Cemetery

FINISH
Moissac

D927

To Montauban (8km)

St-Benoît

Les-Barthes

N113

D45

Meauzac

To Castelsarrasin (3km)

To Castelsarrasin (5km)

0   1   2 km
0   0.5   1 mile
1:105,000

See Chemin de St-Jacques (Days 3 & 4) p146

Mas Labrugade (☎ 05 65 31 84 66; Labrugade; mas.labrugade@club
-internet.fr; singles/doubles with bathroom & breakfast €29/37; evening
meal €13) is 4km from Montcuq, but a pick-up and deliver service
is available by prior arrangement. The French-speaking hosts offer
beautifully decorated rooms in a large farmhouse; the magnificent
four-course dinner comes complete with homemade aperitifs and
Cahors wines.

For self-caterers there are **Petit Casino supermarket** (La Promenade,
open Tue-Sat & Sun morning) and a **boulangerie** in the same street. In
rue du Faubourg St-Privat you'll find a **greengrocer, patisserie** and takeaway **pizzeria**. Sunday morning is **market** day.

Restaurant-Café de France (☎ 05 65 22 90 29; 5 place de la République;
menus €12-22; open daily Jun & Aug, closed Mon & Wed rest of year) is highly
regarded; choose from a range of salads or imaginative daily specials
(up to €15).

Day 5: Montcuq to Lauzerte (see map p152)
3½–3¾ hours, 14km

Leave Montcuq's place du Faubourg St-Privat down rue du Pontet.
After 400m continue straight on from a bend, up a shady track to level
ground. Soon it's down to a sequence of right and left turns, then the
minor road to Charry for a short distance. Beyond a field edge and
woodland paths, cross the entrance road to Château de Charry soon
glimpsed fleetingly through trees. The route descends into the wide
valley of the Ruisseau du Tartuguié where you turn right along a minor
road at Berty. Continue for several hundred metres, past fields likely to
be growing delectable pale green Quercy melons. Cross a footbridge
and soon gain height quickly to a farm at **Bonal** (1¼ hours from
Montcuq) where you can buy locally grown walnuts, prunes, delicious
home-baked cakes and drinks.

Continue to a junction, then straight up above large fields via more
turns. Continue southwest, bypassing the hillock on which sits the
hamlet of Montlauzun, to the D45. Go left for 100m then follow a
path steeply up into woodland. The next 2.5km take you generally
southwest along a narrow ridge between two beautiful wide valleys
along pleasant paths and short stretches of road. As the path swings
left (south) there's a good view of Lauzerte on its hilltop. Descend to
a road at Raussou (1½ hours from Bonal).

Turn right and soon, opposite a large grey building, right again along
a track. On the far side of a farm veer right down a wide path to the
D7 road and turn right. A few hundred metres further, beside a major
junction, is an Ecomarché supermarket. At the junction (where it's right
for the camping ground), bear left for **Lauzerte** and a few hundred
metres further on, go right up a path. Next it's right, then left, still
uphill, to a minor road. Make another left turn then go up right at
an intersection. Pass a parking area to follow rue d'Eveillé for a short
distance to place des Cornières where you'll find the tourist office (an
hour from Raussou).

Lauzerte

A very well preserved *bastide* or walled village founded in the 12th century, it crowns a hill rising precipitously from the intensively cultivated Lendou River Valley.

The **tourist office** (*☎ 05 63 94 61 94; www.quercy-blanc.net - French only; place des Cornières; open Mon-Sat Sep-Jun, daily Jul & Aug*) provides, among much else, a useful map of the village, almost essential to making the most of your stay.

In the main street of **Faubourg d'Auriac,** a suburb of sorts below and south of the hilltop, you'll find an ATM, and a **Tabac-Presse** for maps and guides.

Places to Stay & Eat Beside Petite Barguelonne River, **Camping Melvin** (*☎/fax after 4pm 05 63 94 75 60, otherwise ☎ 06 72 17 76 54; Vignals; camping per person & tent €7*) is 2km from Lauzerte. Access is along a road at the bottom of the hill near the large supermarket.

Gîte d'étape (*☎ 05 63 94 61 94; rue du Millial; dorm beds €8*) is in a large old stone building near the town centre. Dorms are less cramped than you often find but the kitchen is shoe box-sized. Check in at the tourist office, usually closed between noon and 2pm and after 6pm.

Hôtel-Restaurant du Quercy (*☎ 05 63 94 66 36; Faubourg d'Auriac; doubles with shower & toilet €40; menus €9.50-23.50*) is below the village proper. The restaurant features many regional specialities.

The large **Ecomarché supermarket** (*open Mon-Sat, closed 12.30-3pm*) is beside the route, at the bottom of the final ascent. Alternatively, in Faubourg d'Auriac are **Petit Casino supermarket** (*open Tue-Sat & Sun morning*), a **boulangerie** and **health food shop**. Local market day is Saturday morning in place des Cornières.

Pizzeria L'Etna (*☎ 05 63 94 18 60; Faubourg d'Auriac; mains €6.50-9; closed Tue*) does a long list of pizzas including – with an eye to the market – *Pélérin* with *crème fraiche,* garlic and nuts.

Café du Commerce (*☎ 05 63 94 65 36; place des Cornières; open daily; daily menu €12*) serves a range of beers (including Fosters) and basic daily specials.

Le Puits de Jour (*☎ 05 63 94 70 59; place des Cornières; daily specials €10-12*) is a lively music café where you can have a *crêpe* or two (€2 to €8.50), salad or something more substantial (to €12); a free concert is staged on Sunday evening – expect anything from Reggae to Bach.

Getting There & Away From Lauzerte (Faubourg d'Auriac), **Bus Gerla** (*☎ 5-8pm only 05 63 04 55 50*) operates two services to Moissac on Wednesday and Saturday in the morning and early afternoon; a reservation the night before is essential.

Day 6: Lauzerte to Moissac (see map p152)

6¼–6½ hours, 24km

From place des Cornières head off along a short street to Grand Rue and follow it west. Bear left down steps in front of the Maison de Retraite;

cross a minor road to more steps. At the next road, veer diagonally left then right down a lane. Pass a cemetery then turn right for 50m; drop down a grassy track to the left. Then a minor road, the briefest stretch of main road (D593), minor roads, a track and a path take you generally southeast, across Lendou River and up to a crest (about an hour from Lauzerte). Shortly after you pass **Le Chartron** *(☎ 05 63 94 66 82; dorm beds €10; doubles with bathroom & breakfast €40; breakfast €3)* in a 13th-century priory, with a picturesque *pigonnier* (dovecot) in the grounds. Then a right turn starts a descent, past the secluded, tranquil **Chapelle de St-Sernin** – inside are photos of its remarkable restoration during the 1990s – into the wide Barguelonne Valley.

Follow minor roads through a farmyard and an intersection to the D57 road (30 mins from Le Chartron). Turn right and follow it for 1.3km to a field path on the left. The route now takes you over a spur, along tracks between fields and down to a lovely small valley. Then, it's along the valley for 0.7km to the next ascent, south through a vineyard and on to an auberge (1¼ hours from the D57) – **Aube Nouvelle** *(☎ 05 63 04 50 33, fax 05 63 04 57 55; www.chez.com/aubenouvelle - French only; singles/doubles half board with bathroom €54/85; menus €11-24)*; it has a **bar** and **restaurant**.

From there turn right at a junction and go up through cherry and plum orchards and on to the D16 road. Go right then left via a roundabout to **Durfort-Lacapelette** (15 minutes from Aube Nouvelle). A village of no great charm, perhaps because it lacks a church, it does have a **boulangerie** and **Le Relais St-Jacques**, a bar-shop. Then comes an unpleasant stretch of road walking beside the D16, second only to the walk out of Cahors in awfulness. After about 10 minutes, pass the turn to Piquet and the versatile **Besses** *(☎ 05 63 05 01 92; camping €5; beds in tent/dorm €7/9; singles/doubles with breakfast €19/30)*. Soon leave the D16, turning right towards St-Martin, and follow minor roads past orchards and the village of St-Martin, down to the D16. Turn right and shortly diverge left to follow a path parallel to the road. Swing left 1.4km further on along a minor road, then go right to continue on a track beside a field.

Right: Approaching the entrance of Abbaye St-Pierre, Moissac

INGRID ROODIS

The inevitable ascent starts 500m further on, through trees up to the ridge crest. Two right turns bring you to the distinctive brick farmhouse **Carbonnières** (two hours from Durfort-Lacapelette).

The minor road leads on along the ridge, past vineyards and orchards and the hamlet of Espis with a prominent church. After about 45 minutes the road descends to Gal de Merle. Go through a minor crossroads and across a footbridge; at the D957 road turn left. Negotiate the roundabout without changing direction; about 500m further on, at the far end of a cemetery, cross the road to follow chemin des Vignes to the right in outer suburban **Moissac** (p140). Back on the D927, go right for 300m; follow chemin de Ricard to the right, parallel to the railway, along which the abbey comes into view. Cross the railway, go down to the main road (opposite a Casino supermarket). Turn right for about 100m then left to follow *Itinéraire Cloîture* briefly; where it veers right, continue ahead along rue Guileran and on to the awesome south door of the abbey itself (1½ hours from Carbonnières).

OTHER WALKS

Of the other three Chemins de St-Jacques in France, one route links Paris, Tours and Bordeaux with St-Jean Pied de Port.

Another starts at Namur in Belgium and passes through Reims, Vézelay and Limoges to meet the Le Puy route between Le Romieu and Montréal. The Namur to Nevers section has been designated the GR654 for which you'd need Topo-Guide Ref 654. Vézelay features on a walk in the Wine & Mountains chapter (see p331). No 3 in the CSJ's *Pilgrim Guides to the Roads through France* covers the route from Vézelay to the Pyrenees.

The third Chemin takes off from Arles in Provence, visits Toulouse, crosses the Pyrenees via Col du Somport and meets the main route at Puente-la-Reina. This is now the FFRP's 900km-long GR653. The CSJ covers it in No 4 of its *Pilgrim Guides* series.

For a description of the *Camino Francés*, the most popular Camino de Santiago, from Roncesvalles to Santiago, you can't go wrong with Lonely Planet's *Walking in Spain*.

Pyrenees

For many, the Pyrenees offer France's finest walking. Less well known and much less developed than the higher and world-famous Alps, its towns and villages are smaller and fewer. For walkers, the overwhelming attractions of the Pyrenees are the continuity of its mountainous country – hundreds of virtually uninterrupted kilometres of peaks, ridges, cols and valleys – and the immense variety between and within three broad geographical sections.

The Pyrénées Atlantiques rise steadily through the lush forests of the Pays Basque to France's westernmost summits and valleys. The Hautes Pyrénées comprise a dense mosaic of steep peaks, rugged ridges and deep valleys, high cols and innumerable lakes, largely within the Parc National des Pyrénées. The Pyrénées Orientales, tapering down towards the Mediterranean, are distinctly warmer and drier. Particularly in the Hautes Pyrénées, there are plenty of *refuges* (refuges or mountain huts) and a variety of accommodation in valleys within easy reach of the mountains. But it's also possible to disappear into the mountains for several days at a time and have no contct at all with settlements.

We concentrate on three areas: the Vallée d'Aspe on the eastern fringes of the Pyrénées Atlantiques, Vallée de Cauterets in the heart of the Hautes Pyrénées and the area around Bagnères de Luchon, farther east. Within Other Walks (p190), we outline two end-to-end routes, right through the Pyrenees from the Atlantic Ocean to the Mediterranean.

NATURAL HISTORY

The Pyrenees form an almost unbroken barrier of hills and mountains 400km long, straddling the border between France and Spain, from Atlantic to Mediterranean. Geologically complex, the range consists essentially of granite and gneiss in the east, and limestone capped by granite in the west. A vast ice sheet once covered most of the area,

Highlights

- Looking from Port de Vénasque across to Pic d'Aneto, the Pyrenees' highest point, and the Maladeta glacier (p184)

- Walking Chemin de la Mâture, a path hacked into vertical rock walls (p167)

- Admiring Vignemale's sheer face and the wide flood plain at its feet in the early morning light (p173)

- Roaming high among lakes – large and small – waterfalls, alpine meadows and groves of hardy pines (p185)

leaving behind a myriad of glacial landscape features, although only very small glaciers (see the boxed text on p33). The largest of these on the French side is Glacier d'Ossoue on Vignemale in the Hautes Pyrénées; there are also miniature glaciers on Balaïtous, west of Vignemale, and a handful of other peaks. Here too are magnificent cirques, the headwalls of glaciated valleys, of which the Cirque de Gavarnie, over 400m high, and the nearby Cirque de Troumouse, around 5km across, are the finest. Lakes, both large and small and always colourful, number in the hundreds. Waterfalls are probably even more numerous, from the huge fall on Cirque de Gavarnie to tumbling cascades in mountain streams.

Rolling foothills rise steadily from the Atlantic for 70km to the threshold of the high mountains, guarded by the Pic d'Anie (2504m), a few kilometres west of Vallée d'Aspe. The Hautes Pyrénées are a veritable maze of rugged ridges and long, spiny spurs, many summits rising above 2800m. Vignemale (3298m) is the highest, straddling the Franco-Spanish border. The supreme Pyrenean summits are in Spain: Pico d'Aneto (3404m) and Monte Perdido (3355m). To the east, the general elevation begins to decrease; Pic Carlit (2921m) and Pic Canigou (2784m) are the two most substantial peaks in the Pyrénées Orientales.

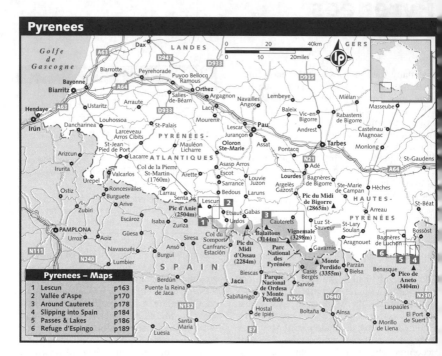

Pyrenees

Pyrenees – Maps

1	Lescun	p163
2	Vallée d'Aspe	p170
3	Around Cauterets	p178
4	Slipping into Spain	p184
5	Passes & Lakes	p186
6	Refuge d'Espingo	p189

Several long valleys – the Aspe, Ossau, Azun, Cauterets, Luz-Gavarnie and Aure – reach deep into the mountains. Some lead to high passes, only a handful of which carry roads across the border.

Above the large oak woodlands of the foothills, forests of beech and European silver fir clothe some of the lower mountain slopes of the Hautes Pyrénées. Between about 1500m and 2600m are hardy Scots pine, some birch and Norway spruce, with alpenrose and juniper scattered about the alpine meadows. At the limits of plant growth, dwarf willow creeps among the rocks.

The Parc National des Pyrénées is exceptionally rich in both flora and fauna: about 160 species of flora are endemic, including Pyrenean gentian, the yellow Turk's-cap lily, purple flowering ramonda and Pyrenean pheasant's-eye (of the buttercup family). This is one of the best places in Europe to see large birds of prey such as golden eagles,

griffon and bearded vultures (lammergeiers), booted eagles, buzzards and falcons. Plenty of smaller birds are also present in numbers: alpine accentors, alpine choughs, ptarmigan, rock buntings and alpine swifts.

The park is home to 42 of France's 110 species of mammal. Izards (close relatives of the chamois) are fairly common, marmots are well established, having been introduced from the Alps in the 1950s, and you may see badgers, red squirrels and perhaps pine martens in wooded areas. Brown bears, once numerous in the Pyrenees, are now very scarce indeed and confined to the foothill forests (see the boxed text opposite). Reptiles, including grass snakes and vipers, are quite common; their bite can cause an unpleasant reaction but isn't life-threatening.

CLIMATE

From the Atlantic coast east to the wild Ariège region on the edge of the Hautes Pyrénées, the Pyrenees are subject to the

The Brown Bear's Last Stand?

The brown bear (*l'ours brun*), widespread throughout Europe 3000 years ago, was mercilessly hunted and captured for public display. Although rigorously protected for nearly half a century, its very existence is threatened by loss of habitat, tourism and road-building, and not helped by its long, precarious two-year breeding cycle. Brown bears disappeared from the French Alps in 1937, while the Pyrenees sustain only a minute population – boosted by a trio from Slovenia who have successfully bred. However, it's quite possible that, as you read this, the last brown bear will have disappeared from the Hautes Pyrénées.

As we went to print, there were probably five at the most in the Aspe and Ossau Valleys: a couple of youngsters; venerable old Papillon who, experts fear, just can't manage it any more; Canelle, the only female; and Néré, imported from Slovenia and released amid great controversy.

In the Pyrenean valleys, you'll see slogans daubed on rocks: 'Non aux ours' (No to the bears), 'Pas d'ours' (No bears) and, our favourite, 'Bonne année et longue vie aux ours!' (Happy New Year and long life to the bears!).

Atlantic weather patterns. There, the climate is moist and relatively mild, except in the mountains, and prevailing winds southwesterly. East from the Ariège, the range is under the influence of the much drier and warmer Mediterranean climate. However, the dividing line between these two zones isn't clear-cut, and conditions in the central Pyrenees are also strongly influenced locally by altitude and aspect. Snowfalls are likely at any time of year over higher ground and guaranteed from early October until April. Snow may lie in high, north-facing valleys year-round and can linger on the highest passes (over 2500m) until early July.

During summer, and especially during August, conditions are especially volatile, with regular afternoon thunderstorms and heavy downpours. In the valleys of the central area temperatures reach 25°C or more and can exceed 30°C farther east.

September often brings more settled conditions with excellent visibility. Short-lived storms aren't unknown around the middle of the month, a prelude to the more tempestuous weather of late autumn and winter.

INFORMATION
What to Bring

In the early season, telescopic walking poles are very useful for negotiating snow banks.

Maps

For planning purposes, two maps in the IGN 1:100,000 series are useful: No 69 *Pau Bayonne* and No 70 *Pay Bagnères de Luchon*.

Books

Of the relatively few English titles devoted to the Pyrenees, Trailblazer's *Trekking in the Pyrenees* by Douglas Streatfield-James covers Spain as well; it describes the GR10 coast-to-coast trail on the French side and several shorter walks and is excellent value. Cicerone has two relevant guides: *The GR10 Trail* by Paul Lucia, gives a more detailed analysis of the route, while Kev Reynolds' *Walks & Climbs in the Pyrenees* gives a wealth of suggestions.

The list of French titles is huge. *Haute Randonnée Pyrénéenne* by Georges Véron, the originator of the high-level route through the range, provides a most informative and entertaining description of the journey. Four Fédération Française de la Randonnée Pédestre (FFRP) Topo-Guides cover the GR10 and some linked routes.

The national park publishes a series of walks leaflets, *Randonnées dans le Parc National des Pyrénées*, for each of the six valleys within the park. Each set has up to 15 leaflets, with clear contourless maps, somewhat generalised descriptions of the walks that vary in quality and often enlightening background information.

Of the plentiful natural-history books (in French) for the Pyrenees, two in particular are recommended. *Fleurs des Pyrénées Faciles à Reconnaître* by Philippe Mayoux is published by Rando Éditions, as is *Rochers et Paysages des Pyrénées Faciles à Reconnaître*, also by Mayoux.

PYRENEES

Vallée d'Aspe

The Vallée d'Aspe thrusts right into the heart of the Pyrénées Atlantiques to the broad Col du Somport on the Spanish border. Southwards to the pass for its final 16km, it's a deep, precipitous valley with forested slopes, embellished with some spectacular crags on either side. Villages huddle on small, more-or-less flat patches while the road and former railway snake round the mountainsides.

To find the best of the first-class walks in the area, you need to go into the smaller, although no less dramatic, tributary valleys east and west of the Aspe. Tiny Lescun, surrounded by a dramatic ring of cliffs, the Cirque de Lescun, is the base for three one-day walks described in this section: Lac de Lhurs, Around Ansabère and Les Orgues de Camplong. From the twin villages of Etsaut and Borce in the main valley, it's easy to reach the valleys and peaks to the east and west, as a further two one-day walks, Chemin de la Mâture and Pic de Labigouer, illustrate.

PLANNING
When to Walk
The walking season is from late May to mid-October, except for the highest summits; some snow may linger on more-elevated passes until well into July. The universal rule that July and August are busy and resources stretched applies here too. From mid-September onwards, bus services may be less frequent and some mountain *refuges* will be closed.

Maps & Books
The IGN 1:25,000 map No 1547OT *Ossau* covers the valley and is the best map for these walks. Rando Éditions 1:50,000 map No 3 *Béarn* is handy for an overview of the area.

Randonnées dans le Parc National des Pyrénées – Aspe, a set of 11 leaflets (in French), is worth reading for descriptions of other walks, although they're too vague to be used without the 1:25,000 map.

Camping in Parc National des Pyrénées

There's a difference in French between *le camping* and *le bivouac*. Camping, leaving your tent up as you head off for a day's walking, is forbidden within park boundaries. However, you're allowed to *faire le bivouac* – erect a lightweight tent between dusk and dawn (usually interpreted as 7pm to 9am) as long as you're more than an hour's walk from the nearest vehicle access.

There's a small library of excellent local guides (in French) to walks, climbs, flora, fauna and geology, at least some of which you'll find in newsagents and other outlets in the area. The walking guides include *Randonnées Choisies en Béarn: Aspe-Ossau* by Georges Véron and, offering more gentle recommendations, *Randonnees en Vallee d'Aspe* (a useful compendium) with explicit maps, of walks the length and breadth of the valley, varying from under two hours up to eight.

ACCESS TOWNS & FACILITIES
Bedous
Bedous, the valley's biggest village – with, despite this superlative, less than 600 inhabitants – is spread out along the main road (N134) that passes through the Vallée d'Aspe. It has a little more variety and choice than the hamlets that are closer to the trailheads.

The helpful **tourist office** (☎ 05 59 34 57 57; aspe.tourisme@wanadoo.fr; place Sarraillé; open Mon-Sat year-round), in the main square, covers the whole of the valley. The weather forecast is on display and it carries a few topographical maps, as does **Librairie d'Aspe** (rue de la Caserne).

Also in place Sarraillé is **Montagne Nature** (☎/fax 05 59 34 75 77; montagne. nature@libertysurf.fr; open daily Jul & Aug), a cooperative of outdoor-activity specialists that, among its many sporty activities, organises daily guided walks during the summer season.

The local branch of Crédit Agricole has an ATM.

Pont Valentré, Cahors, on the Chemin de St-Jacques pilgrimage trail

The Gavarnie Valley, Pyrenees, on the Cirque du Gavarnie walk

INGRID RODDIS

Lac de Lhurs, Pyrenees

INGRID RODDIS

Waterfall at Pont d'Espagne, Pyrenees

JEAN-BERNARD CARILLET

Monte Incudine seen from Refuge d'Usciolu, on the GR20 walk through Corsica

There's also a **mountain rescue contact** (☎ 05 59 39 86 22) for the area.

Places to Stay & Eat You're better off heading up the valley, where the really enticing walking lies.

Camping Municipal de Carole (☎ 05 59 34 59 19; camping per person/tent/car €2.70/1/1; open Mar-Oct) is 300m west of the N134, from where it's signposted.

Le Mandragot (☎ 05 59 34 59 33; place Sarraillé; dorm beds €8; open year-round) is a welcoming gîte d'étape with self-catering facilities, accommodation in rooms for two to eight and a cosy common room.

For self-caterers, the well-stocked **Petit Casino supermarket**, in the main street, sells camping gas, and a boulangerie (bakery) and boucherie (butcher shop) are nearby.

Among the few places to eat, **Chez Michel** (☎ 05 59 34 52 47; rue Gambetta; menus €10-16.50) is a neat little restaurant on the main street. Go for its menu saveur du pays ('flavours of the region' menu; €13).

Getting There & Away The TER Aquitaine region of **SNCF** (☎ 08 92 35 35 35) runs four buses daily through Vallée d'Aspe from the town of Oloron Ste-Marie to Canfranc in Spain. This service connects with regular trains on the branch line linking Oloron with Pau, on the Toulouse–Bayonne train line. From Pau you can make your way by rail to Paris.

Pau has a small **airport** (☎ 05 59 33 33 00) served by regular Air France flights from Paris and several provincial cities. Ryanair flies daily between Pau and London (Stansted).

By road, Bedous is 25km south of Oloron. Its petrol station **Garage & Taxi Lepetre** (☎ 05 59 34 70 06), on the main road at the southern end of the village, is the last one before the Spanish border. It charges €20 for a journey between Bedous and Lescun.

Lescun

The beautiful old slate-roofed village of Lescun (900m), neatly gathered around its large church, huddles below the cliffs of the Cirque de Lescun, to the west of and above

Vallée d'Aspe. It is within the periphery of the national park.

Places to Stay & Eat Spacious and walker-friendly **Gîte & Camping du Lauzart** (☎ 05 59 34 51 77; camping lauzart@wanadoo.fr; camping per person/tent/car €2.20/3.80/1; open 20 Apr-20 Sep) is on the GR10, 1.5km southwest of the village. The gîte charges €9.35. Its small grocery store stocks camping gas.

Maison de la Montagne (☎ 05 59 34 79 14; lescun.dom@clubinternet.fr; bed €10, half board €26; open year-round) is a cosy, rustic gîte, adapted from an old barn. The owner, a qualified guide, leads mountain walks and is a mine of information about walking opportunities.

In the centre of the village, **Hôtel du Pic d'Anie** (☎ 05 59 34 71 54; hotel.picdanie@club-internet; singles/doubles with bathroom €32/40; menus €15 & €23; open May–mid-Sep) does particularly hearty meals (including a vegetarian option) and has a good selection of local wines. A couple of doors away is its small **gîte** (dorm beds €10, half board €26; open year-round) with a kitchen for guest use.

There's a small **grocery store** in the town that has canned and dry foods, bread, meat and cheese. **Bar des Bergers**, in the lower part of the village, serves sandwiches and has a good selection of bottled beers.

Getting There & Away The daily Oloron–Canfranc bus stops on the main road 6km south of Bedous, at the junction with the steep D239 road to Lescun, a distance of 5km. However, there's no bus service to Lescun itself so you may need to call upon Garage Lepetre (see Bedous Getting There & Away, left).

Etsaut & Borce

The twin villages of Etsaut and Borce, the latter particularly proud of its medieval heritage, are set back on either side of the N134, 11km south of Bedous.

The **Maison du Parc National des Pyrenees** (park information centre; ☎ 05 59 34 88 30; open daily May-Oct) occupies the old

PYRENEES

train station in Etsaut. It organises guided walks and climbs (half/full day €9.15/15.25) during summer and also houses a good display (in French only) about the fauna of the Pyrenees.

If you crave the services of an ATM, the best options are dropping down to Bedous or slipping over the border to Candanchu, just in Spain.

Places to Stay & Eat In Etsaut, **La Garbure** (☎ 05 59 34 88 98; www.garbure.net - French only; Chemin de l'Église; beds in 2–8-person dorm €10; half board €21.50; open year-round) is down a lane beside the church. There's a kitchen for self-caterers – and donkeys for hire if you fancy a day or two's walking pack-free. The owners can offer a mountain of information about local walks and also run **Gîte Maison de l'Ours** (☎ 05 59 34 86 38), in the village square. Rates are the same as for La Garbure.

Hôtel des Pyrénées (☎ 05 59 34 88 62; basic room €24.50, with shower/bathroom €34/41; open year-round), full of character, also has a **restaurant** (menus €11.50-18.50) where the food's more appetising than the slipshod service.

Up in Borce the modern, cosy 18-bed **Gîte Communal** (☎ 05 59 34 86 40; dorm beds €10; open year-round) is beside the prominent church.

There's also the newly furbished **Gîte de St-Jacques de Compostelle** (☎ 06 81 32 58 32; dorm beds €10), a little gem of a place with one double and one quad. Priority is given to pilgrims heading for the Col du Somport and Santiago de Compostela.

For both placs in Borce, it's wise to ring ahead and reserve. Check in first at **Le Communal**, Borce's **bar-épicerie** (bar-grocery store) on the main street.

Le Randonneur, which doubles as grocery store and bar, opens daily and does sandwiches (€3) and a *charcuterie* (mixed cold meats) platter (€7). It also carries basic supplies, local maps and guides.

For what's probably the best-value meal in the whole valley, head for Urdos and the restaurant of **Hôtel des Voyageurs** (☎ 05 59 34 88 05; menus €16.50 & €23).

Getting There & Away The SNCF bus on the Oloron–Ste-Marie–Canfranc route passes by Bedous and stops in Etsaut; the journey from Oloron takes 40 minutes. A lovely grassy lane (no more than a five-minute downhill walk) runs between Borce and Etsaut. From the Etsaut bypass, look for twin white-tipped poles opposite the bridge at the southern end of the village. From Etsaut you can link up with the rail network to Paris.

Camping le Gave d'Aspe

The nearest camping ground to Etsaut and Borce, and well worth the short drive if you have your own transport, is **Camping le Gave d'Aspe** (☎ 05 59 34 88 26; legavedaspe@aol.com; camping per person & tent €5.50, extra person €2.75; open May–mid-Sep), right beside the river and just outside the village of Urdos, 4.5km south of Etsaut.

Lac de Lhurs

Duration	5–5½ hours
Distance	15km round trip
Difficulty	moderate
Start/Finish	Lescun (p161)
Transport	taxi
Summary	An ingenious and, in places, precarious path en route to a small, isolated lake, one of the very few near Lescun, surrounded almost entirely by towering peaks.

This lake is hidden in a high valley between the formidable ranks of cliffs on the western side of the Cirque de Lescun and the equally impressive crags along the Franco-Spanish border. The walk could conceivably be fitted into a half-day, but we recommend a full day as the going on forest tracks and narrow paths is quite rough, including a section across a relatively recent landslip.

From the Napia/Anapia parking area up through the forest, the route is waymarked – none too adequately in places – with single and double yellow stripes plus occasional

Lescun

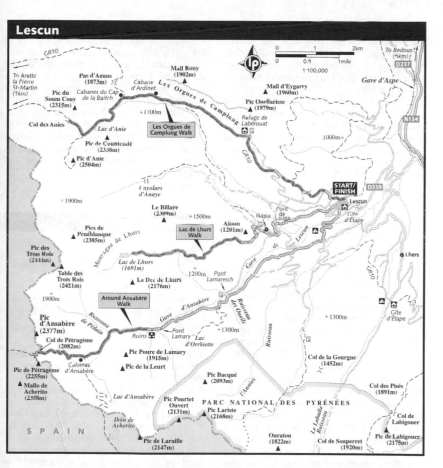

arrows, supplemented by cairns higher up. The statistics for the walk assume a start in Lescun; by driving to the parking area, you save about 100m of climbing, 5km and 1½ hours. Cattle and sheep graze the area through which you pass, so carry all the drinking water you'll need.

THE WALK

From the village post office, walk southwest to a crossroads and then follow the lightly trafficked road that is signposted 'Anapia–Lhurs (Lac)'. This leads downw, offering lovely views of the hayfields and farmsteads in the valley to the south. About 1.75km beyond the crossroads, pass over a small stream at Pont de Lauga. About 150m farther on, bear right at a sign for the parking area at Napia (Napia/Anapia – the two variants are used indiscriminately). Follow this road south and west, then take an earthen track to the right, signed 'Parking Napia 100m'.

Just beyond the car park – which is, in fact, a good 250m up the track – go left at a Y-junction following a pair of signs for Lac de Lhurs. Confusingly, and in conflict, one estimates two hours 25 minutes to the lake, the other three hours. Both, you'll probably find, are on the generous side (the tempting footpath heading up and southeast is too steep for comfort on the ascent – but it neatly cuts off a longish hairpin bend on the return leg).

The track winds around the steep-sided hill Aloun. Just before you reach a tiny stream, about 10 minutes beyond the car park, look out for a triangular boulder on the right, signed 'Lac de Lhurs' in very faded red paint. Turn right (north) to follow the stream through forest, cross at a ford two minutes later and continue upwards beside the stream, soon with a field on the left. At the top of the field, take a left bend away from the stream and go on up the track, bearing right at a fork, past a sign, 'Sauf Derogation', which forbids entry to all but official vehicles.

Waymarkers show the direction at two more junctions as the track leads generally southwest up the steep forested slope. In season, you can cut your thirst by culling bilberries and the odd wild strawberry from the borders of the track. Occasional openings in the trees give **dramatic views** of the cliffs on the peak of Le Dec de Lhurs (2176m) to the south.

At a bend, leave the track and go straight ahead to take a forest path (indicated by a wooden post with a yellow marker and not shown on the IGN map) that heads in a westerly direction. Where this meets a wider forest track, about an hour beyond the car park, turn left and pass between two boulders, positioned to impede vehicles from passing. The climbing continues a little farther to a rocky path that threads its way across a landslip. Then comes a section, short and quite safe, seemingly blasted or cut across the base of a towering, somewhat precarious-looking cliff. The rocky path then goes on up through beech forest and emerges out into the open to cross a steep slope. Follow cairns and the occasional waymarker across the stream bed and through yet more beech wood, the trees here are noticeably broader and more squat than their cousins at lower altitude that enjoy less-severe conditions.

Head up a spur covered with low scrubby vegetation and keep on, through a defile in the cliffs that leads to open rocky ground and, at last, the grassy surroundings of **Lac de Lhurs** (1691m), 2½ to 2¾ hours from Lescun and ideal for a lunchtime picnic. Here, the only habitation is a shepherd's hut. Beyond it, high above to the west, is the Table des Trois Rois (2421m; the Three Kings' Table). This is the meeting point, historically, of the three kingdoms of Aquitaine, in France, plus Navarre and Aragon in Spain. Return to Lescun by the same route.

Around Ansabère

Duration	6½–7½ hours
Distance	22km
Difficulty	demanding
Start/Finish	Lescun (p161)
Transport	taxi

Summary The awe-inspiring trio of Ansabère peaks is the objective of this outstandingly scenic walk.

The Grand and Petite Aiguilles d'Ansabère and the Pic d'Ansabère (2377m) stand on the Spanish border at the head of the Gave d'Ansabère ('gave' means mountain stream in the local patois), southwest of Lescun. The spectacular pinnacles of rock, the long Gave d'Ansabère valley and Col de Pétragème are the focus of this fairly demanding walk. If you have wheels, it can, however, be shortened (by 8km, 200m ascent and a good two hours) if you drive to the Masousa parking area beside Pont Lamareich, at the end of the sealed road. Alternatively, walk only as far as the Cabanes d'Ansabère, at the foot of the Aiguilles, rather than right up to the pass (saving 3km, 400m ascent and two hours). While the entire walk from Lescun definitely earns the demanding rating, both shorter versions qualify as easy to moderate.

The walk follows quiet country roads and forest and pastoral tracks before there is a final steep, lung-searing, well-cairned path up to the pass.

THE WALK (see map p163)

Follow GR10 red-and-white blazes down through Lescun past the Bar des Bergers and across the Gave de Lescun. Continue up past Camping du Lauzart to a cross-roads and turn right to leave the GR10 at a green sign marked 'Masousa–Ansabère'. Follow this quiet road through farmland to the Masousa parking area, just beside **Pont Lamareich** (980m; 1¼ to 1½ hours from Lescun). Cross the bridge over the Ruisseau des Oueils and walk up the forest track, gaining height gradually.

A little more than 30 minutes of forest walking, with the opportunity to shortcut a couple of broad bends and – in season, feast on ripe blackberries – and you're at the edge of open grassland. Soon you cross over **Pont Lamary** (1171m), with Pic Poure de Lamary (1915m) towering overhead. Here, beyond the point where even the most rugged vehicle can reach, is where the real fun begins.

The track climbs steeply through more shaded beechwood to another spacious, secluded meadow (which is reached about 30 minutes after leaving Pont Lamary), almost enclosed by rugged peaks. Here, the Gave d'Ansabère, tumbling down from the higher plateau, is replenished by the Ruisseau de Pédain (which may be dry in high summer). Cross the latter to head south and up into beech woodland.

Approximately a half-hour of steepish climbing, with the latter stages zigzagged, brings you to the magnificent valley of grassed, hummocky slopes below the Aiguilles d'Ansabère and the three stone-built **Cabanes d'Ansabère** (1580m), used by local shepherds. The most easterly one is unlocked year-round and can provide emergency shelter. The newest, engagingly called 'Villa des Prives d'Amour' (Villa of Those Denied Love), is a shepherd's summertime home, from where he sells his cheeses to passing walkers.

For the pass, head very briefly in a west-northwesterly direction, keeping just to the right of the giant boulders that threaten to tumble and crush the cabins, and join a clear path that rises towards the Petite

Aiguille. This bears away to the southwest, then it doubles back on itself, zigzagging steeply.

Here, you pick up the now-faded red and white flashes of what was once conceived of as a link route, joining France's Atlantic-to-Mediterranean GR10 and Spain's parallel equivalent, the GR11.

Leaving the grass and rock behind, follow the cairned route across a scree slope of small black boulders. From here, the narrow path crosses a stony slope then rises to cross the truncated grassy spur ahead. Beyond the spur there's a good 20 minutes or more of stiff, snaking ascent to the **Col de Pétragème** (2082m). Look upwards, towards the long finger of the Petite Aiguille. Here, you may well see climbers, stuck like flies to its sheer face. By comparison, your own puffing upward progress is like a high-street stroll...

At the pass, which makes a great lunch stop, a sign, 'Reserva de Caza' (No Hunting), planted by the regional government of Aragon, confirms that you've indeed just stepped into Spain.

The return to Lescun is simply a matter of retracing your steps.

Les Orgues de Camplong

Duration	6¼–6¾ hours
Distance	18.5km
Difficulty	moderate–demanding
Start/Finish	Lescun (p161)
Transport	taxi

Summary The massive cliffs of the Orgues de Camplong, frequented by golden eagles, form the spectacular backdrop to this walk towards prominent Pic d'Anie.

The main features of this flexible walk into the upper reaches of the Lauga Valley are the vast cliffs of Les Orgues de Camplong and the birds of prey, the resident *fromagerie* at Cabanes du Cap de la Baitch, and Col des Anie on the limestone plateau extending north from the massive Pic d'Anie (2504m). It's not difficult to climb to the peak itself, some 420m above

Col des Anie (although this is not described here), but you'd need to start from the parking area below Refuge de Labérouat (about 4km from Lescun) rather than from Lescun itself. The **refuge** (*☎/fax 05 59 34 50 43; beds €12; open Easter–mid-Sep*) is just above the car park.

An easy day's outing (around 2½ hours and only 630m ascent) could involve starting from the *refuge* and walking up to the Cabanes du Cap de la Baitch and back. Allow plenty of time for eagle and vulture watching near Les Orgues de Camplong – and for lunch with some freshly cut cheese from the *fromagerie*, perhaps packing a little robust red wine to accompany the cheese.

From Lescun to the *cabanes* (cabins), the walk follows the route of the GR10 and is well waymarked. Beyond the *cabanes* and up to the col, the path is fairly consistently cairned.

Wildflowers are another feature of this walk, and not only during spring. In early autumn, pink and purple heathers, purple and white crocuses, bright yellow gorse and the distinctive blue-stemmed and blue-flowering queen of the Alps (resembling a thistle) all adorn the rocky ground above and west of the *cabanes*.

THE WALK (see map p163)

In Lescun, pick up the GR10 just west of the church, beside a flowing tap where you can replenish your water bottles, walk up rue Henri Barrio to a T-junction and turn left up a track, signed 'Refuge de l'Abérouat' (this is an alternative spelling). Go right when you come to a road, then left again at a fork less than 150m farther on. Leave the road after 150m and turn right to follow a path between fields. This soon leads left and enters woodland. Climb steeply along a path that can be severely overgrown early in the season to meet a minor road and bear left. Continue for 75m, then turn right along a path that winds its way quite steeply up a partly wooded

Cheese-Making in the Mountains

At Cabanes du Cap de la Baitch, a pair of sturdy, weather-beaten shepherds, Messieurs Bouchoo, father and son, together with their young apprentice, Alain, a renegade from city life in Pau, are members of a dwindling breed of hardy people. The trio carry on the centuries-old tradition of spending summer in the high mountain pastures with their flocks of sheep, bred for the ewe's milk that goes to make distinctive cheeses, right at the source.

Every year in May the sheep are taken from their winter quarters in the valleys to nearby pastures. Then in late June or early July, once the snow has thawed, they patter on up into the mountains under the watchful eyes of the shepherds and their dogs. This is usually a major local event, with special traffic controls set up. Seeing rivers of sheep trotting through the villages, hurried along by barking dogs and whistling shepherds, is an unforgettable spectacle. In late September or early October, shepherds, flocks and dogs return to the valleys. Once threatened by the convenience of road transport, *transhumance* – this summer migration on foot – has revived in recent years, thanks to greater concern for animal welfare and an increased commitment to keeping traditional cultural practices alive.

The *cabanes* dotted about the mountainsides, always in sheltered sites, are simple stone structures, these days equipped with a slab of solar panels to provide electricity. Within the *cabane*, the shepherds heat the milk to 30°C and add rennet to make it coagulate. It's stirred, reheated and strained. Next it's put into moulds and drained then salted, ready to go into storage. The cheeses are put in a cool, damp place for two to three months and regularly turned around to settle properly.

Connoisseurs claim they can taste the mountain grasses in these cheeses – of subtle rather than sharp flavour. They're best at room temperature, with a baguette and a bottle of good local red. The Bouchoos, like many others, keep a pair of donkeys that regularly carry cheeses, loaded into a pair of wooden panniers, 5km down the steep path towards Lescun – while always holding some back to sell to passing walkers.

hillside. When you meet an old track along a grassed terrace, turn left (45 to 50 minutes from Lescun).

Here you can either faithfully follow the GR10 up to Refuge de Labérouat, along a somewhat circuitous route through meadows and woodlands, or head directly for the *refuge* up the road (about 30 minutes' walk), hugging the mainly grassy verge. Both options give magnificent **views** of the Lescun Valley and the distinctive Pic du Midi d'Ossau, its split peak clearly visible to the east. Here too, on a good day, you'll see vultures and perhaps golden eagles floating effortlessly above the crags.

From Refuge de Labérouat, reached about 1¼ hours from Lescun, the track leads into beech woodland; it's rocky in places and the wet limestone can be very slippery after rain. Less than an hour's walking takes you up and out of the woodland to an open valley, with the Cabane d'Ardinet just above you to the right. The *fromagerie* is barely 30 minutes farther on.

A stop at the **fromagerie** is a must, whether simply to replenish your water bottles at the pipe that spurts cold, clear and delightfully drinkable water from deep inside the mountain or to buy a hunk of couldn't-be-fresher ewes'-milk cheese.

To continue from the *fromagerie* towards Col des Anie, cross the bare ground where the sheep are gathered and pick up a clear path that leads generally southwest. After a few hundred metres, cross a stream, just above the point where the water spurts out of the rocks. The path climbs steadily over mainly rocky ground left of a large bluff to a tiny valley, then up on a rocky path to a grassy bowl. Cairns and faded orange and yellow flashes point the way on the southern side of the valley; fantastic views of Les Orgues de Camplong and of the plains far below will slow your progress.

Cross the bare limestone jumble of rocks and thread up towards the col as far as time and inclination permit. Allow about 1¼ hours from the *fromagerie* to the pass.

To return, simply retrace your steps. From the col back down to Lescun should take between 2½ and 2¾ hours.

Chemin de la Mâture

Duration	3¾–4 hours
Distance	10.5km
Difficulty	moderate
Start/Finish	Etsaut (p161)
Transport	bus
Summary	An exhilarating, spectacular walk centred on the historic Chemin de la Mâture, a path cut into vertical cliffs; superb views of the Vallée d'Aspe on the return.

The Chemin de la Mâture, although only about 1km long, is one of the best-known paths in the Pyrenees. Cut into a sheer rock face on a fairly steep gradient, it climbs through the deep gorge of Ruisseau Le Sescoué, a tributary of the Gave d'Aspe. At its narrowest the *chemin* (track) is an unnerving 1.8m wide, but most of it is closer to 3m across and all is perfectly safe and reassuring. The *chemin*, on the route of the GR10, is the centrepiece of a fine day walk from Etsaut, which returns from high above the valley via Col d'Arras and then down to the village. The walk can be part of a longer circuit around Pic du Midi d'Ossau (see Other Walks, p190).

HISTORY

The Chemin de la Mâture was built in 1772 to transport timber harvested from the forests on the southern side of the gorge. Built by convicts using primitive equipment, the path was, for its time, a miracle of surveying, engineering and construction. Timber was in great demand for beams, pulleys and *mâts* (masts) for constructing vessels of the French navy – hence the name Chemin de la Mâture. Each load of logs was hauled by a team of oxen: two in front and two pairs behind to act as brakes on the descent and stockpiled near Lées-Athas, southwest of Bedous, then shipped downriver to Bayonne, on France's Atlantic coast, and to the navy yards.

Of more recent date is the nearby Fort du Portalet, in the main valley, built in the 19th century then used as a customs post, and also as a prison during WWII (Marshal

Pétain, leader of the collaborationist Vichy government spent three months here during 1945).

PLANNING
Maps
The route of the GR10 southeastwards from Etsaut has changed from that shown on the IGN 1:25,000 map No 1547OT *Ossau*. It follows the old N134 main road, these days all but traffic-free now that it's superseded by the bypass, down which trucks from Spain thunder.

THE WALK (see map p170)
Walk southwards up the GR10 from Etsaut, following the old N134. At Pont de Cebers, pass a car park and keep straight ahead, up the main valley to reach a second, smaller parking area, 2.4km and about 35 minutes from Etsaut. Turn right to follow a good path, which leads onwards, overlooking the massive Fort du Portalet and one of the narrowest parts of the Vallée d'Aspe.

The path then abruptly turns into the gorge and the Chemin de la Mâture stretches improbably ahead under, or rather through, the overhanging cliff. The views all round are spectacular and several vantage points invite photo stops.

Eventually the path swings away from the gorge as the valley widens. About 45 minutes after starting on the *chemin*, you'll come to the stone buildings of **Grange de Perry**, where there's piped fresh water at a trough in the courtyard. From here, a comfortable path descends gently through a wonderful leafy tunnel to a junction, where a detour of merely 150m brings you to the **Pont des Trungas** and, beneath it, gentle waterfalls that make a great picnic and paddling spot.

Back at the junction, the path climbs steeply through woodland to another signposted meeting of the ways, 25 minutes from Grange de Perry. Here you leave the GR10 and head west, signed 'Col d'Arras-Etsaut'.

Continue uphill through forest, savouring the plunging views downwards into the valley of Ruisseau Le Sescoué, up which

you so recently trudged. Soon, you emerge into meadows on the steep hillside. After a few hundred metres the route, now blazed with intermittent yellow or red-and-yellow stripes, crosses the **Col d'Arras**, so inconspicuous that you'd never notice it unless it was signed.

The path leads into trees and continues to descend. At a junction (around 30 minutes from where you left the GR10), continue straight, leaving a path to drop, left, towards the Pont de Cebers. Shortly, you come round a corner and the Vallée d'Aspe in all its magnificence spreads before you with Borce in view far below.

The path drops steeply to meet a minor dirt road. Follow this across the steep hillside for about 2km to a tight bend. From it, another path, narrow unless the Strimmer man has been by and buzzed away the encroaching foliage, takes off and descends steadily through dense bracken to reach **Etsaut** (about 1¾ hours from the start of the yellow waymarked route; p161).

Pic de Labigouer

Duration	2 days
Distance	29km
Difficulty	demanding
Start/Finish	Etsaut or Borce (p161)
Transport	bus

Summary A superlatively scenic and challenging walk off the beaten track, across a ridge above Vallée d'Aspe.

Pic de Labigouer (2175m) caps a long ridge along the western side of the Vallée de Belonce, which parallels the Vallée d'Aspe above Borce and Etsaut. The peak also overlooks the Cirque de Lescun. Although not a particularly high summit by Pyrenean standards, its comparative isolation from the range along the Spanish border and from other nearby high ridges means that the views from the undulating ridge are truly panoramic in scope: from the lowlands to the north, to Pic d'Anie, the Ansabère peaks, Col du Somport, Balaïtous to the southeast, Pic du Midi d'Ossau and the deep trench of the Vallée d'Aspe.

Waymarking along the route is variable – from the familiar GR markers to none at all along a stretch of the main ridge.

If you're fit, you *could* belt round this circuit in 8½ to nine hours of walking. But that would be a pity; the views are superlative and well worth lingering over. Also, beyond Pic de Labigouer, with the day's hard work all over, the easy ambling along the crests and down the Vallée de Belonce is so agreeable that it seems wrong to rush it. An alternative, if time's a consideration, is to climb Pic de Labigouer and return to Borce by the same route; involving about the same amount of ascent, this saves at least 7km but you should still budget for around seven hours of walking.

We opt for overnighting at the Refuge d'Arlet, beside a splendid mountain lake. If you do the same, consider also doing the walk in reverse, as the climb up Vallée de Belonce is more gradual than the stiff ascent to Col de Barrancq, then up to the main ridge.

PLANNING

The route of the GR10 and the network of minor roads immediately west of Borce have changed slightly since the publication of the relevant maps for this walk: IGN 1: 25,000 No 1547OT *Ossau* and Rando Éditions 1:50,000 No 3 *Béarn*.

The route between the summit of Pic de Labigouer and Col de Souperret, marked on the Rando Éditions 1:50,000 map and indicated with dots on the IGN map, is too steep to be safely recommended.

Neither map shows all the tracks and paths in Vallée de Belonce.

THE WALK (see map p170)
Day 1: Etsaut to Refuge d'Arlet
15.5km, 6–6½ hours, 1360m ascent

Cross the Etsaut bypass by the footbridge and go straight ahead up a grassy lane to Borce. Turn left to pass the best of its well-preserved old buildings and narrow lanes. Pass the village church to your left and, now with the GR10, cross over the road ahead.

After 100m, bear left onto a steep, shady lane. At a second road, some 20 minutes beyond Borce, turn right. A little farther on at a crossroads signed 'Maison Sayerse-Nardet GR10', bear left. At a barred gate five minutes later, leave the bitumen road and turn right onto a narrow footpath.

There's little respite from climbing now, as the route ascends parallel to a deep ravine then crosses the stream and rises up the open hillside. A brief level stretch is succeeded by steep zigzags through shoulder-height bracken, soggy from the morning dew.

Then comes a stretch, heading generally southwards, on forest path, expanding to track through mixed woodland. You emerge onto expansive meadows with the **Cabane d'Udapet de Bas**, used by shepherds during summer, on the far side (1½ to 1¾ hours from Borce). Continue up, mainly across open ground, to the ruins of the Haute Udapet cabins. A faint path heads up across the grass and clumps of heather and bilberry towards the lowest point on the skyline. About halfway up this meadow the route veers to the right (north) and enters woodland to soon reach the Col de Barrancq (1601m), which is 30 minutes from Udapet de Bas.

At the pass, the route leaves the GR10 and continues southwards through closely spaced trees and along the narrow ridge – a path soon becomes clear, and in a few minutes you leave the trees behind. The route isn't waymarked and must be one of the few stretches in the French Pyrenees that isn't peppered with cairns. Even so, navigation up the usually evident path presents no problem. But it's a steep climb up to the broad and grassy ridge crest (1913m), reached a little under 45 minutes from the col and the ideal place for a break with the mountain panorama now spread out before you.

Follow the ridge down across Col des Pises (1891m), then steeply up along a fairly well-cairned path and down a narrow rocky spine to **Col de Labigouer** (2040m; about 45 minutes from the 1913m point). Here, you're at the boundary of the national park's heartland, identified by the national park logo (the red head of an izard on a white background) painted on rocks.

From the pass choose your approach to the top of **Pic de Labigouer**; on a very windy day, the western side was sheltered and not too steep. Whatever your route, 45 minutes should be adequate for the round trip, including a breather on the summit.

Return to Col de Labigouer. To continue south along the ridge, join a narrow path traversing the western flank of the peak; it starts strongly, fades for a few hundred metres on steep ground, then coalesces on the next prominent spur and descends to Col de Souperret (1920m). A thread-like path picked out with white-and-red waymarkers (faded or freshly painted, these will guide you all the way back to Borce) leads on, now on the eastern flank, maintaining a steady height across grassed slopes then along the base of some low cliffs. Two small crags, separated by a short open stretch, are easily negotiated, then it's down to Col de Saoubathou (1949m; around 1¼ hours from Col de Labigouer).

A well-trodden route crosses beneath the colourful Pic Rouge, its name coming from the deep-pink rock prevalent around here.

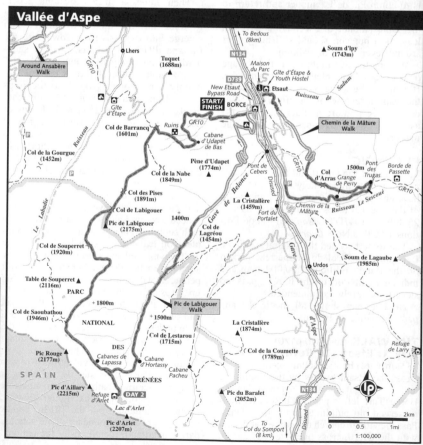

Vallée d'Aspe

There's also a great deal of very dense con-glomerate – multicoloured stones and peb-bles embedded in the pink matrix. The path contours around the southwestern slope of a small combe, clanging with cow and sheep bells, in which lies the **Cabane de Lapassa**, occupied in summer. About 200m farther on (and, bizarrely, 50m beyond the actual junction), you reach the signposted turn-off to Refuge d'Arlet. Take this minor track to ascend to the *refuge*, reached a little under 30 minutes later.

Refuge d'Arlet *(1986m; ☎ 05 59 36 00 99; dorm beds €9, half board €27; open mid-Jun–mid-Sep)*, run by the Parc National des Pyrénées, is right beside Lac d'Arlet, above the head of Vallée de Belonce.

Day 2: Refuge d'Arlet to Etsaut
13.5km, 3½-4 hours, 1395m descent

Retrace your steps from the *refuge* to meet up with the path below Cabane de Lapassa and rejoin the red-and-white markers. Continue down to the head of the Vallée de Belonce and on to **Cabane d'Hortassy**, the light-grey building halfway down the valley's eastern flank that's in your sights from the junction onwards. Pass below its outbuildings and enclosures and follow a narrow path towards, then into, the trees. The descent continues, back out into the open and sticking to the eastern side of the valley. Ignore a first concrete bridge over the Gave de Belonce and also a second one, parallel with a signposted path (about 1¼ hours beyond the junction) that leads up (right) to Col de Lagréou. Head once more into forest. Around 15 minutes from this sign, look out for a waymarked sharp left turn, where the route descends to cross the stream at a bridge just above a small dam. The path continues through open country, where you may need to be negotiate one or two electric fences across the route.

About 15 minutes from the bridge, you meet a dirt road, where there are signs to vari-ous destinations, including Refuge d'Arlet. From here it's just a matter of following the road down through the narrow gorge (where some landslips looked distinctly precarious) and on to the bitumen road. Turn right and,

beside a road sign announcing the village of Borce, turn right again, signed 'Village par Chemin de la Pouey,' to accomplish the final five minutes on soft grass. Borce is about 1¼ hours from the beginning of the dirt road, Etsaut around 10 minutes further.

Vallée de Cauterets

The Vallée de Cauterets, in the heart of the Hautes Pyrénées, isn't a name that appears on local maps. We use it here as a convenient general title for the area around the several streams that flow north through deep valleys from high in the mountains, feeding the Gave de Cauterets, which tumbles through the town of the same name. Thus the Vallée de Cauterets embraces the valleys of the Gave du Marcadau and the Gave de Gaube, which come together in spectacular fashion at Pont d'Espagne at the head of Val de Jéret. This in turn meets the Gave de Lutour at La Raillère, a cluster of bars and restaurants about 2km south of Cauterets. Here the cascading rivers unite to become the Gave de Cauterets.

Vignemale (3298m), the French Pyrenees' supreme summit, commands the head of Val-lée de Gaube and is at the crux of a complex pattern of extremely rugged ridges forming the mountainous chain along the Spanish border. The boundary of the Parc National des Pyrénées core area lies just south of Cauterets, so most of your walking will be within the park.

Walks in this area are in abundance: along wooded valleys, past beautiful lakes, up to high passes on or close to the border, and to a summit or two, although most require scram-bling or rock-climbing skills and equipment. The main walk described, In Vignemale's Shadow, focuses on Vignemale. It is accom-panied by two day walks (Lacs de Cambalès and Circuit des Lacs), described as side trips at the end of Day 1, which can be added to the longer walk or done independently.

With Cauterets as a base, two other day walks are described: Pic du Cabaliros and Vallée de Lutour. The Other Walks section gives suggestions for walks in the Gavarnie area to the east.

A Little Sweetener

Halitosis is rarely fun, especially among walkers who are in close proximity. Back in the 19th century, once the *curistes* of Cauterets had swallowed their daily dose of sulphurous spa water, they – and, even more, their nearest and dearest – would complain of vile dog's breath.

An enterprising villager, spotting a chance, set about making a boiled sweet or candy that would mask the odour. Shaped like a humbug and made in a rainbow of colours and flavours, *berlingots*, a speciality of Cauterets, are readily on sale in town. If you happen by a sweet shop at the right time, you can see them being made. For walkers, they beat stick-to-your-palate Power Bars hands down when you need that little extra boost...

PLANNING
When to Walk
Overall, the walking season in this area is fairly long; below about 2300m altitude snow shouldn't be an obstacle between early June and about mid-October. Above 2300m, and subject to local advice, you will probably be glad of an ice axe or walking poles in late spring or late October. July and August are very busy months, so you'd definitely need to book ahead to ensure a bed in the *refuges* and *gîtes d'étape* (essential for Refuge Wallon). Late September is particularly beautiful with the deciduous trees starting to change colour. Unfortunately, the useful local bus service has stopped by then.

Maps & Books
The best map for all the walks in this section is the IGN 1:25,000 map No 1647OT *Vignemale*. The Rando Éditions 1:50,000 map No 4 *Bigorre* also covers the area; it's useful for an overall view, but is less reliable for the waymarked walks and is more difficult to read than the IGN map.

The set of 15 leaflets, *Randonnées dans le Parc National des Pyrénées: Vallée de Cauterets*, describes a variety of walks and is the best local, French-language guide.

Several others are available, published by, for example, Rando Éditions.

ACCESS TOWN
Cauterets
At the foot of the river valleys, Cauterets is a fairly large and prosperous town with several fine late-19th-century and early-20th-century buildings. It caters generously for walkers (and in winter for skiers) and throughout the year for devotees of the thermal spas.

Information As well as posting the daily weather forecast, the **tourist office** (☎ *05 62 92 50 27; www.cauterets.com - French only; place Marechal Foch; open Mon-Sat & Sun morning year-round*) produces a detailed accommodation guide.

The **Maison du Parc National des Pyrenees** (☎ *05 62 92 52 56; www.parc-pyrenees.com; place de la Gare; open daily Jun–mid-Sep, Mon-Tue & Thu-Sat mid-Sep–Apr*), near the bus station, is the best place for maps, walking and natural history guides and general information about the park, including details of the guided walks programme during July and August (€9.15/15.25 per half-day/day). There's also an impressive display featuring the park's flora and fauna.

Maison de la Presse (*place Foch*) is also a good source of maps and guides.

For specialised information about the condition of routes over the high passes – particularly valuable in spring and early summer – and about weather in the mountains, contact the **Bureau des Guides** (☎ *05 62 92 62 02; place Clemenceau*). This is also the place to go if you're interested in climbing Vignemale with a guide.

Pizzeria Giovanni (see Places to Stay & Eat, opposite) has a couple of computers, where you can log on.

Places to Stay & Eat Of the camping grounds around Cauterets, **Le Mamelon-Vert** (☎/fax *05 62 92 51 56; mamvert@aol.com; 32 av du Mamelon-Vert; camping 2 people €9.90, car €1.10; open Dec-Sep*), overlooking the bus station, is the most central.

For those with a car, **Camping Le Peguère** (☎/fax 05 62 92 52 91; campingpeguere@ wanadoo.fr; camping 2 people & car €10.50; open Apr-Sep), 1.5km north of town on the D920, is grassy and shady with some choice sites right beside the Gave de Cauterets.

Cauterets has two particularly attractive gîtes, both run by keen outdoor folk.

Gîte Beau Soleil (☎ 05 62 92 53 52; gite .beau.soleil@wanadoo.fr; 25 Rue Maréchal Joffre; rooms for 1-5 people with bathroom per person €15.60; open year-round) has a small kitchen for self-caterers or you can enjoy half board for €32. The friendly, helpful owner can organise a tempting five-day circuit with accommodation prebooked and luggage carted ahead of you.

Le Pas de l'Ours (☎ 05 62 92 58 07; www.lepasdelours.com - French only; 21 rue de la Raillère; dorm beds €15, doubles with bathroom €42, half board €31, half board for 2 nights €40; open mid-May–Sep & Dec– mid Apr), another welcoming place, is both hotel and gîte. Dorm prices alos include use of the kitchen and all guests can use the sauna (€8).

Just inside the small **covered market** (av Leclerc), a stall does tasty takeaway regional dishes such as garbure and cassoulet - plus 30 kinds of pizza.

For a meal, the many hotel restaurants have menus in the €12 to €20 range, featuring local specialities. More informally, **Pizzeria Giovanni** (☎ 05 62 92 57 80; 5 rue de la Raillère; menu €14; open from 7pm)has superior pizzas (around €9; eat-in or takeaway). A generous steak is €13 and the irresistible homemade desserts are €4 to €5.50. A nice touch: diners can check their emails for free.

La Bodega (☎ 05 62 92 60 21; 11 rue de la Raillère; menu €13.50; open from 6pm), also known as Casa Manolo, is the place for genuine, tasty Spanish cooking, dished up in its menu or on filling mixed platters (€9 to €11.50).

Getting There & Away There's a daily bus service (€6.10; 50 minutes; five to seven daily) between Lourdes (from outside the train station) and Cauterets. In the handsome bus station there are some fascinating old photos of electric trains in the early years of the 20th century on the now-disused line. Lourdes station is on the busy Toulouse– Pau–Bayonne line, with good connections to Paris Montparnasse and Marseille.

In Vignemale's Shadow

Duration	3 days
Distance	30km
Difficulty	moderate–demanding
Start/Finish	Cauterets (opposite)
Transport	taxi, bus

Summary With Vignemale a constant, compelling presence, one of the finest circular walks in the Haute Pyrénées, overnighting at two refuges, one of which offers opportunities for day walks.

This flexible walk from Cauterets takes in a wealth of varied scenery: the cascades of the Gave de Cauterets, the beautiful Vallée du Marcadau, the granite formations and lakes high in the Vallée d'Arratille, two narrow cols on the Spanish border, Vignemale with its glaciers and moraines dominating the head of Vallée de Gaube, and the Gaube's own cascades and tranquil lake.

If your schedule allows, build in an extra couple of nights at Refuge Wallon and undertake a pair of splendid, highly recommended side trips. Both the Circuit des Lacs and Lacs de Cambale's routes (see the end of Day 1) give you a challenging workout and take in a cluster of the high Pyrenees' finest lakes.

The paths and tracks followed vary greatly from smooth and level to rough, steep and rocky but all are clearly defined. Yellow signposts at critical junctions give destinations and estimated times.

We take Cauterets as the starting and finishing point for this walk; it's also possible to start at Pont d'Espagne but this would mean missing the magnificent Chemin des Cascades beside the Gave de Cauterets. Transport (private or public) permitting, the ideal scenario is to start from Pont d'Espagne and finish at Cauterets, making

In Vignemale's Shadow

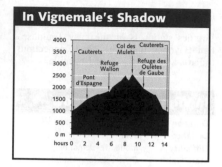

the first day less taxing by saving about 600m of climbing.

PLANNING

For overnight accommodation and meals there are two Club Alpin Français (CAF) *refuges*: Refuge Wallon and Refuge des Oulètes de Gaube. Bookings at both are essential at weekends and during July and August and strongly recommended at all times. *Refuge* telephones aren't connected to the standard France Telecom network and a conversation is carried on with disconcerting gaps between each statement – we give postal addresses for each in case you prefer to book by letter.

Near each *refuge* there's a hugely attractive, free, grassy area set aside for tents. Campers are welcome to take meals at the *refuge* (and therefore have access to the spartan toilets and washing facilities). National park regulations prescribe that tents can only be up between 7pm and 9pm.

GETTING TO/FROM THE WALK

The walk described starts and finishes in Cauterets. Pont d'Espagne, at the end of the D920 road, 8km south of and 600m higher than Cauterets, is usually an alternative, with the obvious advantage of saving time and energy.

In July and August, and also during the ski season, **Bordenave Frères** (☎ *05 62 92 53 68, mobile 06 71 01 46 86; place de la Mairie, Cauterets*), which also calls itself Allo Taxis, operates a useful *navette* (minibus) service between the centre of town and Pont

d'Espagne. The single/return fare is €3.50/5 and there are six departures from each end daily, starting at 8am from Cauterets and finishing with a 7pm departure from the large parking area at Pont d'Espagne. Year-round, a taxi to or from Pont d'Espagne costs €13, one way (irrespective of the number of passengers).

There's a small **information office**, plus telephone and toilets, at the Pont d'Espagne parking area.

THE WALK (see map p178-9)
Day 1: Cauterets to Refuge Wallon
5–5½ hours, 10km, 960m ascent

The walk starts at a cluster of yellow signs just above the northern entrance to the imposing cream building of the spa **Thermes César** on rue Maréchal Foch. Follow the red-and-white stripes of this variant of the GR10 as the path snakes up to a road. Cross over and continue along chemin des Pères. After a few more zigzags, this settles into a quite comfortable gradient through woodland. Shortly after crossing a section of mountain ripped apart by a recent avalanche, you reach the signposted junction above La Raillère (45 minutes from Cauterets). Turn right, descend to the footbridge just below Cascade de Lutour and continue to the road. Walk down 100m, cross the bridge over Gave de Cauterets and turn immediately left to join the signposted Chemin des Cascades.

The path climbs steadily, occasionally steeply, through woodland, with the thundering cascades rarely out of sight. The viewpoints at the named cascades – Escane Gat, Ceriset, Pouey Bacou, Pas de l'Ours and Boussès – provide good reasons for a breather or two en route. Although the D920 road follows the same tight valley on the opposite bank, it's never intrusive and the roar of the water drowns out that of the occasional vehicle.

About 1½ hours' climbing brings you to the short, paved section of path leading up to **Pont d'Espagne**. The bar and hotel beside the bridge advertises a wide range of snacks and drinks but the *café au lait*, at least, can't be recommended; better to hold your thirst until the quieter and altogether more appealing Chalet-Refuge du Clot.

If you're starting out from the Pont d'Espagne parking area, a 300m walk will bring you to the bridge. Follow the sign 'Télésiège du lac de Gaube' and, at the base of this chairlift, be guided by another reading 'Vallee du Marcadau par rive droite' (by the right bank).

Nearly 1km from the Pont d'Espagne you come to another bridge across Gave du Marcadau. For the next section up to Pont du Cayan, you have a choice between the old path on the northern side of the valley and the vehicle track on the opposite side. There's little difference between the two in time and distance. The path passes **Chalet-Refuge du Clot** (☎ 05 62 92 61 27; chalet ,du,clot@wanadoo.fr; dorm beds €14.50, half board €24; open Jun-Sep & Dec-Apr), a pleasant overnight venue whose shaded terrace makes a fine drinks stop. It then crosses wide water meadows beside the river below the steep mountainside, and is more open and attractive than the vehicle track, part of which goes through woodland. If you follow the path, cross Pont du Cayan at a sign, 'Refuge Wallon-Marcadau', and join the vehicle track near a national park information board (an hour from Pont d'Espagne).

About 150m beyond the bridge, you have another binary choice: the original path, steeper and cobbled in parts, which takes off to the right, or the wider 4WD track, whose bends ease the gradient. Both ascend through the forest, then meet to snake around the side of a tall crag.

In Memoriam

Nearly half a century ago, a local priest and lover of the mountains constructed, with the help of his walking mates, the small chapel beside Refuge Wallon. He's long since passed away but a tradition that he established lives on. Every 5 August, there's a pilgrimage from the chapel to the summit of Grande Fache, the peak to the west, in memory of all those who have died or disappeared in these mountains.

The track then descends slightly, back to river level. Pont d'Escalounque, a solid bridge that is reached about 30 minutes beyond Pont du Cayan, takes you across the stream, then a short, flat stretch leads to a steep winding climb. The gradient eventually slackens and the path emerges from the trees to swing round the foot of the ridge above.

Some 75m beyond a square stone sheepfold, bear right (west) as the path to Col d'Arratille, Day 2's challenge, heads away south. You soon come to a sign pointing the way to the camping area (400m to the left); Refuge Wallon (1865m) is only about 200m farther ahead (1¼ to 1½ hours from Pont du Cayan).

Refuge Wallon (☎ 05 62 92 64 28; dorm beds €13.50, half board €33.20; open Feb-Mar, Easter & Jun-Sep) is also called Refuge du Marcadau. It has a few small doubles, triples and quads, much coveted and available for an extra €2.30 per person.

For **postal bookings**, write to Le Gardien at Boîte Postale 41, 65111 Cauterets. Helpfully, the daily weather forecast is posted on a notice board beside the reception desk. Let the friendly wardens know in advance if you're a vegetarian (and be prepared for an omelette).

Side Trip: Lacs de Cambalès
5½ hours return, 10km
This not-too-taxing, out-and-back walk from Refuge Wallon takes in a cluster of colourful lakes ringed by soaring crags. The extra effort to reach Col de Cambalès, with its all-embracing view of the lakes and the prospect westwards to mighty Balaïtous (3144m), more than pays off on a fine day.

There are several unbridged stream crossings to negotiate, most with a line of stepping stones, and there's every chance you'll hear and see marmots and izards. Overhead, vultures, eagles and smaller raptors are a fairly common sight.

The route northwestwards is signposted from Refuge Wallon and again at a junction (25 to 30 minutes from the *refuge*) where you turn left (west); hop over the stream and continue across the meadows and up

PYRENEES

to a cascade whose waters tumble from the lakes that lie ahead of you.

A steep climb up and across the pronounced southern lip of the valley sheltering the lakes and navigation becomes, for the most part, easy as you follow the well-cairned route generally westwards past a succession of lakes, big and small.

Once you reach a vantage point above a tiny, anvil-shaped lake (just west of the point '2582m' on the recommended IGN 1:25,000 map), **Col de Cambalès** (2706m) is approximately 45 minutes away across a sea of shattered rock. Aim for the small stony gap in the otherwise unbroken line of cliffs.

For the return to the *refuge*, allow about 2½ hours from the col or two hours from the top lake. This is definitely the more scenic half of the walk, looking down the Vallée de Cambalès and across to the beautiful Vallée d'Arratille with majestic Vignemale towering above.

Side Trip: Circuit de Lacs
5–5½ hours return, 12km
This circular walk – strenuous one way, simplicity itself the other – takes you past a contrasting quartet of lakes and the rugged crags of the upper Vallée du Marcadau.

You can take the route clockwise or anticlockwise – by ascending towards the lakes or by descending the Vallée du Marcadau and beginning the climb from Pont du Cayan. Alternatively, the walk can serve as the second day of a two-day outing up to the *refuge* and back to Pont d'Espagne or Cauterets.

From the *refuge* to Lac du Pourtet, at 2420m, and down to Pont du Cayan, the path is well defined, though mostly rocky and slow going. You'll find that the spectacular views, especially of Vignemale, are more than adequate compensation. The route is cairned throughout and there are white waymarkers between Lac du Pourtet and the signposted turn-off to Col de la Haugarde (about 1.25km east of the lake).

From Refuge Wallon, take the Lacs de Cambalès side trip (see p175) as far as the junction some 30 minutes out, then follow the sign for Lac Nère (2310m). There's more

climbing beyond this lake, initially above the lake's eastern shore, then the path makes a safe crossing of a small cliff face and continues to gain height steadily to Lac du Pourtet (2420m; half an hour from Lac Nère).

Clamber over the moraine field at the lake's southern end, after which the path changes direction abruptly and turns east to start the often steep descent to Gave du Marcadau.

Once beyond the lower of the two Lacs de l'Embarrat, the path swings north, crosses a spur, wriggles through an extensive scree field, then turns sharp right (south) to snake down through pine forest to Pont du Cayan.

From this bridge, follow the end of the Day 1 walk description back up to Refuge Wallon.

Day 2: Refuge Wallon to Refuge des Oulètes de Gaube
4½–5 hours, 8km, 840m ascent
Up by the two passes, quite deep snow can linger on both north- and south-facing slopes until well into July. You might want to check conditions with the wardens of Refuge Wallon before setting out. An early start will let you bite off at least the first hour's walking in shade.

From the *refuge* walk back down the path towards Pont d'Espagne for 500m to a signed junction and head south towards Lac d'Arratille, across a pair of footbridges and onto the true right bank of Gave d'Arratille. The fairly rocky path pursues a not too steep route up through scattered pines and after about 30 minutes emerges into a delightfully scenic bowl, where waterfalls tumble between sprawling granite slabs, small clumps of grass, juniper and alpenrose.

The path then negotiates a dissected rocky bluff and climbs steadily to a footbridge across a small chasm that carries the offlow from beautiful **Lac d'Arratille** (1½ hours from the *refuge*), reached after less than five minutes striding over most welcome, flat upland meadow. Wander along the western shore, probably above, a gaggle of fisherfolk up bright and early, then continue generally south, across a small pond's outlet on the right (a difficult crossing only after heavy rain) and on, across two more fords, (both normally shallow). The climbing then resumes seriously; white-and-red flashes mark the way up through a succession of crags, boulders and large scree. Be sure to follow them westwards for some 200m, five minutes beyond the pond.

Then comes **Lac du Col d'Arratille**, seeming inordinately large just below the **Col d'Arratille** (2528m), on the Spanish border (an hour from the lower lake). On a fine day, the spectacle of Vignemale, at 3298m the highest point in the French Pyrenees, just across the wide valley below, is riveting and awe-inspiring.

To continue, follow the waymarked path into Spain as it keeps the height, curling around a bluff and contouring the steep scree slope northeastwards (this is a broken black line on the IGN map; don't be seduced into following the route indicated in red or you'll lose a frustrating amount of both height and time). The path is narrow but well built and sloping into the mountainside, so there's very rarely any feeling of exposure above the sharp drop on the right. Beyond a small stream, it climbs a rocky spur to the narrow Col des Mulets (2591m) with Pic des Oulettes towering directly overhead (an hour from Col d'Arratille).

The drop towards Vallée de Gaube (the signed route heads initially southeast from the pass, not northeast, as on the IGN map) is steep, down scree and rock. The path soon swings eastwards to cross the base of Pic des Oulettes, still on loose rock with hummocks of grass, and then the streamlet from Col des Oulettes. Zigzag down to the edge of the scree and fallen rock and pick you way down the edge of this unstable footing to the valley floor. The easiest approach to Refuge des Oulètes de Gaube, rather than weaving through the boulders littering the edge of the valley – and the camping area – is directly across the flat area at the foot of Vignemale's skirts of moraine and scree. A bridge just north of the *refuge* (an hour from Col des Mulets) lets you keep your feet dry to the last.

Refuge des Oulètes de Gaube *(2150m;* ☎ *05 62 92 62 97; dorm beds €13.50, half board €32; open Mar–mid-Oct, except for two variable weeks in May)* ranks as one of the Pyrenees' most attractively situated *refuges*; you'll never get a better view from your bedroom window than the sheer 900m wall of Vignemale (and its glacier in your face) and the wide flood plain below. It has a small, thought-provoking display of photos illustrating the dramatic retreat of Vignemale's glaciers over the last half century. For a **postal reservation**, write to La Gardienne at Boîte Postale 32, 65112 Cauterets. At the time of research, the *refuge* was due for a major makeover and upgrade in 2004.

Day 3: Refuge des Oulètes de Gaube to Cauterets
4– 4½ hours, 12km, 1250m descent
This is a pretty straightforward day, following the red-and-white flashes of a variant of the GR10. It starts with a sometimes steep (in places stepped) descent from the *refuge*, firstly through a broad rock barrier. After about 15 minutes, ignore a wooden bridge and hug the western side of a lovely high meadow. Around the half-hour mark, cross over a second footbridge onto the Gave des Oulètes de Gaube's true right bank – but not before taking one last glance back at Vignemale in all its morning splendour. Then it's on down past the impressive **Cascade Esplumouse**, through mixed woodland of pines and rowans. The well-graded path negotiates the steep, rock-encrusted mountainside and a solid bridge, bringing you back over the tumbling stream. The path loses more height, reaches serene **Lac de Gaube**, then settles down to cross the scree fringing the lake.

At the far end of the lake, reached after about 1½ hours' walking, there's a choice of routes. If you stick with the GR10 and the valley, from the end of Lac de Gaube turn right towards **Hôtellerie de Gaube** *(open daily Jun-Oct)*, which serves snacks and drinks. From the hotel, follow the path for a short distance then bear right to continue down the valley. Soon the path enters pine woodland and makes its way fairly steeply

Around Cauterets

Inset

Same scale as main map

Le Maliriat ▲ (2200m)

Soum d'Arrouyes ▲ (1997m)

Barrage du Tech

Pic de Sarret ▲ (2223m)

Lac d'Estaing

D103

To Argelès-Gazost (17km) Lourdes (28kr

Col de Sayette (2016m)

Pic du Cabaliros ▲ (2334m)

Lac d'Anapéou

Arriousec

CRIQ

Col de Contente (2134m)

Soum de Cot d'Omi (1740m)

To Lourdes (25km)

Pic de l'Arcoèche ▲ (2465m)

Soum de Lufusssou (2172m)

Tuc de Labasse (2201m)

Soum de Picarre ▲ (2307m)

Ruisseau d'Anapéou

Barbat

Ruisseau de Catarrabes

Soum de Bassia du Hoo (2571m)

Pourtet du Barbat ▲ (2353m)

Lac du Barbat

Pic du Cabaliros Walk

Conce

Bourdalats

D920

Canceru

Catarrabes

Gave de

Pic de Clot Bédout ▲ (2461m)

Pic Maleshores ▲ (2703m)

Grand Barbat ▲ (2813m) ▲

Ruisseau de Bourg Débat

Ferme Igau

D312

Les Matats

PARC NATIONAL DES

Cap des Blanques ▲ (1977m)

Lac du Plaa de Prat

Lac Nere

Lac du Pic Arrouy

Le Mamelon Vert

CAUTERETS

PYRÉNÉES

Lac de Liantran

Lac Long

Gîte d'Étape

START/FINISH

To Pont d'Espagne (5km)

Lacs de Bassia

Pic du Pourtet (2720m)

Pic Arrouy ▲ (2785m)

Palas ▲ (2974m)

Lacs de Batcrabère

Glacier du Pabat

Lacs de Remoulis

Lacs de Houns de Hèche

Lac du Pourtet

Glacier de las Neous

Pourtet Hèche ▲ (2476m)

Pic de Bernat Barrau ▲ (2793m)

Lac Nère

Lacs de l'Embarra

Mont Aigu ▲ (2558m)

Balaïtous ▲ (3144m)

Peyregnets de Costalade ▲ (2740m)

La Cardinquère (2509m)

Around Cauterets – Walks

1 In Vignemale's Shadow
2 Pic du Cabaliros
3 Vallée de Lutour

Gavizo-Cristail ▲ (2890m)

Peyregnets de Cambalès ▲

Lacs de Cambalès

Side Trip

Gave de Cambalès

Col de Cambalès (2706m)

Lacs d'Opale

Refuge Wallor

Pic de Cambalès ▲ (2965m)

Pic Arraillous ▲ (2704m)

DAY 2

Port de la Peyre-St-Martin (2295)

Petite Fache ▲ (2947m)

Refugio de Respumoso

Pène Aragon ▲ (2916m)

Col de la Fache (2664m)

Bridge

Gave d' Arrailli

Musales ▲ (2654m)

Embalse de Campoplano

Lacs de la Fache

Embalse de Respumoso

Grande Fache ▲ (3005m)

Pic Falisse ▲ (2765m)

Pic de l'Affron ▲ (2567m)

SPAIN

Port du Marcadau (2541m)

Grand Pic de Péterneille (2764m)

Le Chapeau d'Espagne

Pico Gaurier ▲ (2918m)

Punta Zarra ▲ (2947m)

Lagos de Bramatuero

Pic de la Badète d'Arratille ▲ (2805m)

Ibón Azul Superior

Embalse de Bachimaña

Embalse Inón Azul bajo

Pico del Infierno ▲ (3082m)

Pico de Arnales ▲ (3006m)

Embalse Bramatuero alto

0   1   2 km
0   0.5   1 mile
1:100,000

PYRENEES

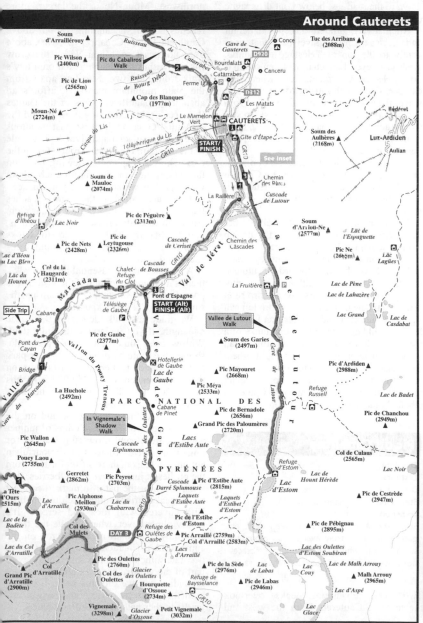

Around Cauterets

down to the road just below Pont d'Espagne (75 minutes from the lake).

Alternatively, turn left to keep both height and views, taking a gravel path that rises gently to the top of Télésiège de Gaube. Walk just beyond the chairlift to an orientation table and viewpoint, from where you can peer down with satisfaction at the point where the circuit began two days ago. From the lift, a broad track (a winter ski piste) winds down to the base of the *télésiège*, from where you retrace your Day 1 steps to Pont d'Espagne (see p178-9).

If you're returning to Cauterets on foot, make your way to the start of the Chemin des Cascades, in front of the bar-restaurant, and follow it down to La Raillère (1¼ hours from Pont d'Espagne).

One last choice now presents itself. Rather than having to retrace the outward route (up to the Chemin des Pères via Cascade de Lutour), you can avoid all this climbing by firstly walking down the road towards Cauterets, past the souvenir shops (although not immediately past one of the bars). At a sharp right bend 200m beyond the last shop, turn left at a sign for Cauterets beside the derelict La Raillère spa building with the holding tanks of a fish farm below you and cross the main road a couple of minutes later. Turn right where the track meets a bridge, which you cross and turn left almost immediately along a quiet road (rue Raillère) to continue into Cauterets (about 25 minutes from La Raillère).

Pic du Cabaliros

Duration	6¼–6¾ hours
Distance	14km
Difficulty	demanding
Start/Finish	Cauterets (p172)
Transport	bus

Summary A long but rarely steep climb on good paths to a truly exceptional mountain summit, from where the panorama embraces nearly all the peaks of the Haute Pyrénées.

Two very substantial peaks overlook the town of Cauterets from the west and northwest: Moun-Né is the larger, more rugged and more southerly of the two and reaches 2724m, a daunting 1800m above Cauterets. Pic du Cabaliros (2334m), about 5km northeast of Moun-Né, as the crow flies, is within reasonable reach on a day's walk from the town. Standing apart from the main mountain massif, it affords an absolutely magnificent view of the Hautes Pyrénées peaks, extending from around Pic du Midi d'Ossau in the west, past Balaïtous with its small glacier and pivotal Vignemale to the south, to the Pic de Troumouse in the east. There's a splendid viewing table on the summit, leaving you in no doubt about which peak is which as far as you can see.

There are cairns in the higher reaches but they're superfluous beside a clear path. Although the path crosses several streams, you should carry drinking water – the flanks of the mountain are grazing country for sheep and cattle.

A fine clear day is essential for this walk – there's no point in doing it if the visibility is poor. Beware of summer thunderstorms; the summit ridge is very exposed.

We grade this walk 'demanding' because of length, if you undertake its full extent. With wheels, you can, as most walkers do, shorten the route by driving to the car park at the entrance to Ferme Igau (shown on the recommended IGN 1:25,000 map), thus saving 200m of climbing, 2.5km horizontally and about 75 minutes.

Above the fine beech woodland on the lower slopes, you'll pass clumps of juniper and alpenrose; pink-flowering heather (or ling) and mauve crocuses are colourful in autumn. In season, there's fruit for free from the bushes of juicy *myrtilles* (bilberries) that flank much of the path. In marked contrast to the peaks farther south, Pic du Cabaliros isn't covered with rock and scree – it's grassy almost everywhere above the trees, with only one small rocky outcrop on the summit ridge. Characteristically spiky crags decorate some of the pic's spurs, but they're part of the view rather than obstacles to get around. When we did this walk, a pair of golden eagles were having fun, rising effortlessly on thermals into a brilliant blue sky.

THE WALK (see map p178-9)

From the Cauterets tourist office, head west for 200m to the Pont d'Espagne–Le Mamelon Vert road junction and turn right. Some 15 minutes later, on the edge of town, turn left up a minor road, signed 'La Ferme Igau'. After 75m, go left again (also signed for La Ferme Igau plus Cabaliros). On the second sharp bend, turn right up an unsigned but evident path. This soon becomes a pleasant, steepish lane that climbs to Ferme Igau, which is reached after about 45 minutes' walking.

Continue heading southwestwards from the farm, passing a tall aerial, as you follow a vehicle track. This climbs steadily, occasionally steeply, around a few bends and ends above a small stream at a sign, 'Zone Pastorale', a protected but accessible area for grazing sheep and cattle. A wide path leads on, gaining height quickly in and out of the woodland and past hay meadows, then becoming narrower as it turns sharply southwest to ascend more steeply in a series of switchbacks. Go through a gate, also signed 'Zone Pastorale'. The path contours the hillside and dips slightly to cross Ruisseau de Bourg Débat. The climbing continues through the last of the woodland, to Ruisseau de Catarrabes (1595m; 1¾ hours from Cauterets).

A steep path goes straight up from here, parallel to the stream, but it's easier (if that's the word) to stick to the older path, which copes with the rise in a series of short, gentle zigzags. Then, at an acute angled junction, continue up to the right.

Many zigzags farther on, you reach a narrow spur (point 1870m on the 1:25,000 map, 45 minutes from Ruisseau de Catarrabes). This is a fine place for a rest, especially as the view to the south now takes in Vignemale. A few hundred metres farther on, the path levels out on a fine traverse, providing a brief rest before the final rise to the broad summit ridge, which you reach a little east of Col de Contente (2149m). To the northeast, you can pick out the peak by the microwave aerial and three solar panels that jut from it. Continue past the substantial ruins of an elongated stone building to the start of the final, mainly steep, climb to the spacious **summit** (1¼ hours from the narrow spur).

Eventually – it's not easy to leave such a magnificent lookout – retrace your steps to return to Cauterets, allowing a minimum of 2½ hours.

Vallée de Lutour

Duration	5¾–6¼ hours
Distance	13km
Difficulty	easy–moderate
Start/Finish	Cauterets (p172)
Transport	taxi, bus

Summary By Haute Pyrénées standards, a moderately undemanding walk to a *refuge* beside a beautiful lake; refreshments are available en route at an excellent restaurant and bar.

Looking directly southwards from Cauterets, your eyes are drawn to the deep valley extending far into the mountains. This is the very scenic Vallée de Lutour, the venue for a fine day walk up to Lac d'Estom, high in the valley. It's a walk that feels much easier than the bare statistics suggest. The climbing – through deciduous forests, Scots pine and spruce woodland, and open valley – comes in stages, rather than one long haul. The route, on clearly defined paths, is not waymarked, but the standard yellow signposts point the way at each junction. For most of the walk, you're right on the edge of the national park heartland; the lake itself is within the park.

The walk can be shortened to an easy half-dayer, suitable for a family outing, by driving to La Fruitière (6km from Cauterets), thus saving three to 3½ hours and 470m ascent.

There's one change to the recommended IGN *Vignemale* map: the path to follow south from La Fruitière in Vallée de Lutour is on the eastern side of the stream.

THE WALK (see map p178-9)

Follow the beginning of the In Vignemale's Shadow walking route, Day 1 (p174), as far

as the signposted junction above La Raillère (45 minutes from Cauterets) where the
GR10 swings away right (southwest). Go
straight ahead as the path, now steeper, continues its zigzagging way up through beech
woodland. Just beyond a green metal gate,
it briefly emerges into meadow at Le Pradet
(15 minutes farther on), with its lone building just right of the track. It soon descends,
again in woodland, to the banks of the **Gave
de Lutour** stream, which will remain your
near-constant running mate all the way to
Lac d'Estom.

Around 1½ hours' walking from Cauterets
brings you to **La Fruitière** (☎ *05 62 92 52 04;
menus €13-31; open Easter-Oct)*, an excellent
small hotel with a restaurant that specialises
in serving up local dishes, including items
such as *garbure* (a thick soup of vegetables,
beans and ham). *Crêpes*, sandwiches and
drinks (including excellent hot chocolate)
are also available.

From here, the route on the eastern side
of the stream continues very pleasantly
for nearly an hour, past the tiny **Cabane
de Pouey-Caut** with its domed iron roof,
just off route to the left, past the turn-off
to 'Russell' (which is Refuge Russell) and
then across a footbridge (about an hour
beyond the hotel) to the western side of
the stream. The towering Pic de la Sède
(2976m), at the head of the valley, dominates the view before you.

A spell of fairly steep climbing through
pines and beside the cascading stream leads
into the open again and soon you come to
the **Refuge d'Estom** (1804m; ☎ *05 62 92
07 18; dorm beds €8.50, half board €26;
open Jun-Sep)*, perched most attractively
on a grassy apron at the northern end of
Lac d'Estom. The *refuge*, which is reached
about 45 minutes after crossing the stream,
makes a good base for treks deeper into
the Pyrenees and also does a great range
of snacks and dishes, including *garbure*
(€4.50), homemade *pâté* (€3) and omelettes
(€3-5). Give a greeting – and perhaps a car-
rot – to Tito, the handsome mule who hauls
up supplies twice a week.

Lac d'Estom is one of the most scenic of
the many lakes in the area, the steep slopes

rising from its eastern and western shores
wearing a blend of scree, grass and small
clumps of low pines, with soaring crags
in between.

Allow 2 to 2¼ hours' walking time back
to the signposted junction above La Raillère. From here, as a change from returning
to Cauterets along the Chemin des Pères,
you could descend to La Raillère past the
impressive cascades of the Gave de Lutour.
From La Raillère, walk down the road and
follow the route back to Cauterets (about
40 minutes from the junction), described
at the end of the In Vignemale's Shadow
walk (p180).

Around Bagnères de Luchon

Bagnères de Luchon makes a superb base
for a week or more of treks, exploring the
last high eastern Pyrenees peaks and passes
and with the opportunity to slip over into
Spain. Accommodation is plentiful in this
charming little spa town, in whose soothing
waters you can relax those weary limbs at
the end of the day.

PLANNING
When to Walk
Between June and October, you can usually
guarantee snow-free walking. This said,
deep – and usually circumnavigable – drifts
may linger in high places until early July.

Maps
All walks in this section are covered by
IGN 1:25,000 map No 1848OT *Bagnères-
de-Luchon*. They also feature on the Rando
Edition 1:50,000 map No 5 *Luchon*. You can
pick them up at the well-stocked **Librairie
des Thermes** (☎ *05 61 79 02 91; 54 allées
d'Etigny)* in Luchon.

ACCESS TOWN
Bagnères de Luchon
Bagnères de Luchon (or simply Luchon) is a
trim little 19th-century spa town that makes
a great base for exploring the surrounding

mountains, from which the reputedly health-restoring waters flow.

Information Check at the Luchon **tourist office** (☎ 05 61 79 21 21; 16 allées d'Etigny; www.luchon.com; open daily Jul-Aug, Mon-Sat Sep-Jun) for information about the area. You can log on at **A.J.C. Multimedia** (parking de l'Église; €8 per hour; open Mon-Fri), which also calls itself La Boutique du Web.

To relax those weary muscles, take a trip to the **Thermes** (Health Spa; ☎ 05 61 79 22 97) at the southern end of allées d'Etigny, which offers a whole range of relaxation and fitness activities. Loll in the scented steam of its 160m-long **vaporarium** (€13; open 3.30-7pm Apr-Oct).

If you're tempted to have a crack at some high mountain, off-piste walking, contact the excellent **Bureau des Guides de Luchon** (☎ 05 61 79 69 38; 18 allées d'Etigny). Beside the tourist office, it offers a whole range of outdoor activities.

Supplies & Equipment Also known as Intersport, **Freddy Sports** (☎ 05 61 79 35 27; 8 allées d'Etigny) carries a reasonable range of walking gear.

Self-caterers should pass by Luchon's daily **market**, established in 1897 and offering fine fresh fare ever since.

Places to Stay & Eat Of the two camping grounds in Luchon, **Camping Beauregard** (☎ 05 61 79 30 74, fax 05 61 79 04 35; 37 av de Vénasque; camping per person/site €3.50/4.50; open Apr–mid-Oct) is the larger and more welcoming

Hôtel des Sports (☎ 05 61 79 97 80; www.hotel-des-sports.net; 12 av Marechal Foch; singles/doubles/triples/quads €30/32/43/47; open year-round) is that rare institution in France: an entirely nonsmoking hotel. The friendly owner, himself a walker, happily dispenses local walking information and advice.

Allées d'Etigny is packed with bars and restaurants, some fine delicatessens and the usual pizza-and-pasta joints.

Two restaurants offer excellent value. **L'Arbesquens** (☎ 05 61 79 33 69; 47 allées d'Etigny; menus from €13) has fondue as its speciality (€14, minimum two people) – in 14 different varieties. Help it down with a jug of the fine Jurançon white wine.

Caprices d' Etigny (☎ 05 61 94 31 05; 30 bis allées d'Etigny; evening menus €14-20; open Fri-Wed), just across the road and staffed by a young friendly crew, does great grilled meats (three-course grill menu for €17) on its open fire.

Getting There & Away SNCF train and bus services operate regularly between Luchon and Montrejeau (€5.60, 50 minutes, five to seven daily), from where there are frequent connections to Toulouse (€16.80) and Pau (€17.70), from where you can travel on by rail to Paris.

Luchon's télécabine travels between the town and Superbagnères (see Getting To/From the Walk on p188).

For a taxi, contact **Farrus Voyages** (☎ 05 61 79 06 78; 28 allées d'Etigny) or **Deo-Taxis** (☎ 05 61 79 05 69; 13 av Marechal Foch).

Slipping into Spain

Duration	5½–6 hours
Distance	13.5km
Difficulty	moderate–demanding
Start/Finish	Hospice de France
Nearest Town	Bagnères de Luchon
Transport	taxi
Summary	Poke your head over the pass at Port de Vénasque for a sudden, heart-stopping view of the Maladeta glacier and Pic d'Aneto, the Pyrenees' highest point.

The walk, with a total height gain of 1120m, describes a wide circuit around Pic de la Pique. After a stiff climb up to the Franco-Spanish frontier at Port de Vénasque (2444m), it pokes its nose into Spain to take in a couple of cols, offering all the while a superb panorama of Pic d'Aneto and the Maladeta glacier. The great views continue as you walk the ridge of Crête de Crabidès before descending, gently for the most part, the flank of Vallée de la Frèche.

Slipping into Spain

GETTING TO/FROM THE WALK

A taxi between Hospice de France and Bagnères de Luchon costs about €27/50 one way/return.

THE WALK

The route is adequately signed by yellow waymarkers, sometimes supplemented by the number 23.

From the ruined buildings of Hospice de France (1385m), take the path leading southwest, signed 'Port de Vénasque.' After 10 minutes, cross the Pont de Penjat to the stream's true left bank.

The clearly defined path, its steepness eased by several zigzags, keeps always within sound and frequently within sight of the tumbling Rau du Port de Vénasque. Some 45 minutes after the bridge, it shifts to the right bank at a crossing that can mean wet feet after heavy rain or at a time of maximum snow melt. Three quarters of an hour later, an altogether easier, stepping-stoned ford brings you back over again.

About 1¾ hours out, a simple stone shelter can offer emergency cover. About 15 minutes later, the **Refuge de Vénasque** (2248m; ☎ 05 61 79 26 46; dorm beds €13.50; dinner €14.50; open mid-Jun–mid-Sep), with its friendly staff, makes a great lunch or drinks break (plat du jour and dessert €9). Should you wish to spend the night here, reservations are essential; the dorm – which remains open even when the refuge is unstaffed – sleeps only 15.

From the refuge, continue ascending the easily distinguished path, now running over shale and scree – and often bordered by névés until well into July – as it leaves the Boums du Port, a cluster of small, scenic tarns, increasingly far below.

Nothing can prepare you for the magnificent five-star vista as you pop your head over the col at **Port de Vénasque** (2444m), sitting snug between the twin masses of Pic de Sauveguarde (2738m) and Pic de la Mine (2707m). There on the horizon are Pic d'Aneto (Pico de Aneto in Italian), at 3404m the highest point in the Pyrenees, and at its feet, the Maladeta glacier. If you've staved off the hunger pangs so far, it's an inspirational spot for a picnic.

Should such a tale inspire you to greater heights, you can tack on an ascent of Pic de Sauveguarde from Port de Vénasque (see the Side Trip, opposite).

To continue, descend from the col and turn left after barely five minutes to follow a path that heads in a dead-straight line near the base of the cliff towards the notch of Port de la Picada, your next port of call,

Beyond Human Endurance

So you've taken something over two hours to reach Port de Vénasque – Pic d'Aneto's there before you and you've every right to feel quite proud of yourself. Just to put things in perspective, one Norbert Almendos, native of Luchon, has run – in only runners and T-shirt – from Luchon town to the summit of Aneto and back, covering 47km and around 3000m of height gain and loss in 6 hours 51 minutes. We bumped into him at Superbagnères. 'What do you do for the rest of the year,' I asked. 'I run', came the reply. Ask a silly question...

Miles Roddis

and clearly evident to the east. Walking over bare rock and scree, you stand a good chance of seeing majestic eagles wheeling overhead.

Once you've huffed and puffed your way up the steep last section to Port de la Picada (2470m), about an hour beyond Port de Vénasque, the day's really serious exertion is all but over.

You re-enter France about 15 minutes later at **Pas de l'Escalette** (2396m), called overdramatically in Spanish 'Collado del Infierno' (Hell's Pass). Bear away to the left (northeastwards) to pick up yellow and white stripes. Ten minutes later, after a short ascent, it's hands-in-pockets striding down a gentle, grassy descent, following the Crête de Crabidès with some great views westwards over and into the Vallée de la Frèche and the folds of its Spanish sisters to the east.

A short jinx eastwards brings you to the minor pass of Pas de la Mounjoye (2069m), from where the trail resumes its generally northwards progression. A little under 30 minutes later, stick to the main track (which is signposted 'Rouge, Hospice') to bear to the left as a fainter option keeps straight ahead.

A couple of minutes after a three-way junction, where you join route 22, there's a flowing spring.

The path skirts then enters a shady beech wood, broadening to become a 4WD track, most of whose curves you can avoid by pointing yourself directly downhill. As you emerge from the wood around 20 minutes later, the sad ruins of Hospice de France lie before you.

Side Trip: Port de Vénasque to Pic de Sauveguarde

1½ hours return, 3km

For really spectacular views in all directions, take the evident side trail from Port de Vénasque to the summit of **Pic de Sauveguarde** (2738m) to the west. It's much less daunting than the sight of spindly figures of other walkers, high against what appears to be a razor edge ridge, might make you think.

Passes & Lakes

Duration	2 days
Distance	19km
Difficulty	moderate–demanding
Start	Hospice de France
Finish	Vallée du Lis
Nearest Town	Bagnères de Luchon (p182)
Transport	taxi
Summary	Highlights are the deceptively gentle warm-up start along scenic Chemin de l'Impératrice and a bivouac beside a high mountain tarn. Day 2 brings more shimmering lakes and a wooded descent home.

This is a flexible walk. If you fancy taking an uncomplicated family stroll, follow the Chemin de l'Impératrice at the beginning of Day 1 as far as the Cirque de la Glère for a pleasant 2½ to three hours there and back.

It's also possible to squeeze the walk into one day (see the Alternative Route at the end of this walk description, p187), although if you do take this shorter route, you will miss out on some stirring high-mountain scenery.

Since the route we recommend posits an overnight camp, timings are for a walker carrying a heavyish pack. If you aren't planning for a night under canvas and are walking light, you may well find yourself making swifter time.

During the early season, the preceding winter's avalanches and landslides may have obscured upland sections of the trail. This is more a temporary navigating problem than a danger, though you will need to exercise extra care.

After leaving Lac Célinda on Day 2, the narrow path around Pic de Graves – with its vertiginous drops to the valley below – while quite safe, is not for those who suffer from vertigo.

GETTING TO/FROM THE WALK

A taxi between Luchon and Hospice de France costs around €27 and from the parking lot at the end of the sealed road in Vallée du Lis €21.

PYRENEES

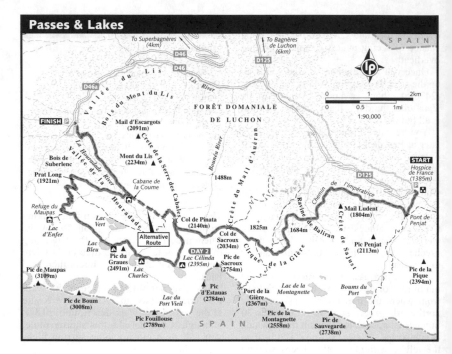

THE WALK
Day 1: Hospice de France to Lac Célinda

4¼–4¾ hours, 9.5km, 1030m ascent

From Hospice de France (1385m), follow the Slipping into Spain route as far as Pont de Penjat (p184) and turn right to take Chemin de l'Impératrice, a clear, well-maintained path that runs through mixed beech and pine forest, so named because Empress Eugénie (who came to take the waters of Luchon in 1867) and her cortège made their way along it. As it curls around the mountain, Luchon peeks through the nick of valley to the north with the gaunt buildings of Superbagnères above it.

Once you cross a brief stretch of open ground, the Ravine de Baliran (around the hour mark from the Hospice), you can pick out the V-shaped Col de Sacroux to the west. Around half an hour later, a short descent brings you to the bowl of **Cirque de la Glère**, its face streaked with snaking torrents.

Now begins the serious work of the day as the trail works its way steeply upwards. At a rock bearing (none too informatively) the numbers 31 and 33, take the right fork (No 31) to arrive at **Col de Sacroux** (2034m) – marked by a rusting metal post – after some 30 minutes.

From the pass, the path circles the wide Bouneu Valley with Luchon and Superbagnères once more in sight and Pic d'Aneto (see the Slipping into Spain walk, p184) prodding the eastern horizon.

More impressive views await you at the **Col de Pinata** (2140m), which is a generous 45 minutes from Col de Sacroux. Below and away to the west winks the aptly named Lac Vert (Green Lake), but it's other tarns you're after.

Now it's time to leave the main track as it snakes away, down into the valley. Instead, turn to the left (south) to follow the lesser-trodden path that stays west of the ridge. Climbing steadily, it features – not entirely accurately – as a line of small black dots on the recommended IGN map. Keep resolutely to the south, guided by the fairly frequent cairns and, in the latter stages, yellow blobs. During early summer after a severe winter, you may have to detour around a large, lingering névé, which will add up to half an hour to the day's walking time that we give here.

Lac Célinda (2395m), reached about an hour after setting off from Col de Pinata, the highest of the trio of high-mountain lakes and the last to melt, is bordered by several potential **camp sites**. From it, if you keep a low profile, you stand a very good chance of spotting izards and marmots. Hard though it is to believe, brown trout and other species survive the glacial winters and breed in such high-mountain tarns.

Day 2: Lac Célinda to Vallée du Lis

3¾–4¼ hours, 9.5km, 115m ascent

For most of the day the rocks are daubed with yellow, blue, red, green – and some-times even white – markers so there's little scope for going astray.

Head away northwest from the lake's tiny dam, following yellow circles and accom-panied by gurgles beneath your feet from the bore pipe that shoots water from Lac Célinda to Lac Charles. Your own, rather slower, time for the descent will be around 20 minutes.

From the lake, a narrow path with sheer drops on its northern side curls around the flanks of Pic de Graves, offering picture-postcard views of Lac Vert and – beyond in the valley bottom – the sparse houses of Vallée du Lis. It then descends by steep zig-zags to Lac Bleu (oh yes, it's indeed blue), 30 minutes from Lac Charles and another splendid **camp site**.

Cross over the dam head to pass by the foundations of its construction buildings, ascending northwards, then northwest. As you cross a ridge after some 30 minutes of steady ascent, your ears catch the steady thrum of a small hydro station while your eyes are assailed by the ugly black tube down which the water hurtles, sucked from

Lac d'Enfer up high, to drive the turbines. Visual pollution, undeniably, but it does save burning several tonnes of fossil fuel annually.

A succession of broad and gentle zig-zags mitigates the steep drop from the pumping station. Still cobbled and banked in places, this section was, like much of today's route, originally hewn from the hillside in order to transport materials for the construction of the high dams and their installations.

After passing Prat Long (1921m) and the briefest stretch of level ground (notice the large olive-green oval of reeds, occupying what was until quite recently a year-round tarn), the track turns in a southeasterly direction, and heads back up the valley. It then descends through alternating open meadow and beech wood (which offer the first shade of the day) and crosses a couple of footbridges.

When you reach the valley bottom, after about three hours of walking, cross a third footbridge onto the true right bank of the small Houradade stream to pass a couple of fine waterfalls.

About 30 minutes beyond the bridge, turn right at a T-junction at the end of a stretch of meadow to take the wider of the two options and re-enter woodland. Bear right at a fork, which is barely a couple of minutes later.

After around 20 minutes of agreeable, undemanding woodland descent, you reach the Vallée du Lis car park and, beyond it **Les Delices du Lys** *(open Jun-Oct)*, a bar/restaurant where a chilled draught beer awaits you.

Alternative Route: Home via the Vallée de la Houradade

2 hours, 2km

To squeeze the walk into one day, stay with the main trail at Col de Pinata as it zigzags steeply downhill to the Vallée de la Houradade. Drop down into the valley and rejoin the Day 2 route just below Cabane de la Coume.

Total walking time for the day is around 5½ hours.

Refuge d'Espingo

Duration	2 days
Distance	30km
Difficulty	moderate
Start/Finish	Bagnères de Luchon (p182)
Transport	bus, train

Summary Highlight of this popular two-dayer is the magnificent ridge walking along Chemin des Crêtes.

In July and August, you can shorten this out-and-back walk and compress it into one day of about six hours' walking by taking the *télécabine* in both directions between Bagnères de Luchon and Superbagnères (see Getting To/From the Walk below – and double-check with the tourist office). When the cabin lift is running, it's also possible, of course, to omit the initial haul up from Luchon to Superbagnères.

The day begins with a long, 2¼ to 2½ hour (sometimes steep, always shady) climb from Bagnères de Luchon to Superbagnères, representing some 1200m of height gain. The route follows the GR10 to above Lac d'Oô (no spelling mistake here!), embracing, from Superbagnères onwards, one of this long-distance trail's most spectacular sections.

GETTING TO/FROM THE WALK

Luchon's **télécabine** (cabin lift; one way €4.75, return €7.25; running 9.45am-12.15pm & 1.30-6pm daily Jul-Aug, 1.30-5.30pm 1st week of Sep, 1.30-5pm Sat-Sun Easter-Jun) operates between Bagnères de Luchon and Superbagnères.

THE WALK
Day 1: To the Refuge d'Espingo
5¾–6¼, hours, 15km

From Bagnères de Luchon's parish church, at the northern end of allées d'Etigny, walk westwards along rue Docteur Germès. Turn left into rue Laity, 100m beyond the market, then first right along chemin de Superbagnères. This bitumen road turns left and soon becomes a well-traced and well-maintained footpath.

Something over five minutes beyond the start of the footpath, turn right at a signed junction onto a lesser and steeper track. Beech leaves are underfoot, then as you progress higher, pine needles impart a spring to the step.

About 45 minutes out, the trail, in one of its few seriously steep patches, swings by a trio of huge, hydro bore pipes that pierce the forest.

Roughly half an hour beyond the pipes, turn briefly left (southeast) at a picnic table to take a forest 4WD track, only to leave it after 50m, continuing straight ahead. On rejoining this track around 10 minutes later, again turn left, then right after 100m to attack another steep, narrow footpath (the 1:25,000 map GR10 tracing is incorrect at this point).

Pass under the **Viaduc de Mailhtrincat**, a viaduct that used to bear the long-defunct rack-and-pinion railway linking Bagnères de Luchon and Superbagnères, and turn right to follow in its route (of which little trace remains, except for the occasional banking).

Around 15 minutes beyond the viaduct, turn right (southwest) at a four-way junction and leave it a couple of minutes later to take a footpath that heads up – inevitably! – and left. Once you emerge from the forest about 30 minutes later, briefly leave the GR10 (which bypasses Superbagnères) and scramble up a few metres to a small, distinctive pagoda. From here, a 4WD track leads up to the ski complex where, in season, you can grab a cool drink or snack.

Follow the sign 'Chemin des Crêtes' and, after a couple of minutes, make a brief detour to the orientation table at the station's highest point, where three ski lifts meet – the panorama is breathtaking.

After about 15 minutes, continue straight ahead at the last of the ski installations, following a sign, 'Lac d'Espingo 4 heures.'

It's a slow and steady, none-too-gruelling ascent with increasingly spectacular views over the Vallée du Lis and the high mountain chain to the south. At a flowing water pipe just below the unnamed col below La Coume de Bourg, an easy 45-minute round trip northeastwards allows you to bag **Pic de Cecire** (2403m).

PYRENEES

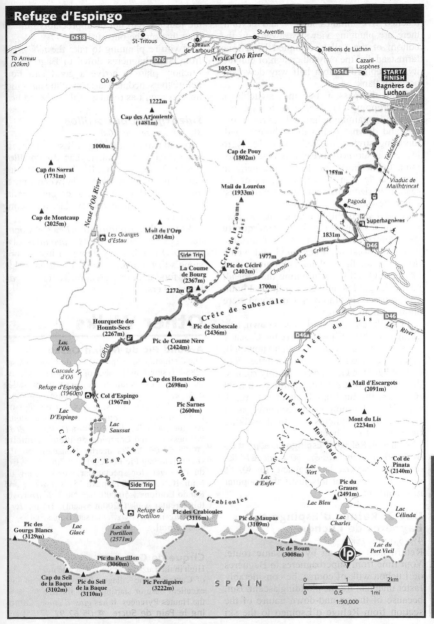

Refuge d'Espingo

To Arreau
(20km)

D618

St-Tritous

D76

Cazeaux
de Larboust

St-Aventin D51

Nest d'Oô River

Trébons de Luchon

D51a

Cazaril-
Laspènes

START/
FINISH
**Bagnères de
Luchon**

Oô

1053m

Télécabine

1222m

Cap des Arjouients
(1481m)

Cap de Pouy
(1802m)

1759m

Viaduc de
Mailhtrincat

1000m

Cap du Sarrat
(1731m)

Mail de Lourćus
(1933m)

Pagoda

Superbagnères

Cap de Montcaup
(2025m)

Neste d'Oô River

Les Granges
d'Estau

Mail de l'Orp
(2014m)

Crète de la Coume des Clais

Side Trip

1977m

des Crêtes

1831m

D46

Chemin

La Coume
de Bourg
(2367m)

Pic de Céciré
(2403m)

1700m

2272m

Crète de Subescale

Hourquette des
Hounts-Secs
(2267m)

Pic de Subescale
(2436m)

D46a

Vallée
du
Lis

Lis
River

D46

Pic de Coumé Nère
(2424m)

Lac
d'Oô

GR10

Cascade
d'Oô

Cap des Hounts-Secs
(2698m)

Mail d'Escargots
(2091m)

Vallée de la Houradade

Refuge d'Espingo
(1960m)

Col d'Espingo
(1967m)

Pic Sarnes
(2600m)

Mont du Lis
(2234m)

Lac
D'Espingo

Lac
Saussat

Cirque d'Espingo

Cirque des Crabioules

Lac
Vert

Lac
d'Enfer

Col de
Pinata
(2140m)

Pic du
Graues
(2491m)

Lac
Célinda

Side Trip

Lac Bleu

Lac
Charles

Refuge du
Portillon

Pic des
Gourgs Blancs
(3129m)

Lac
Glacé

Lac du
Portillon
(2571m)

Pic des Crabioules
(3116m)

Pic de Maupas
(3109m)

Lac du
Port Vieil

Pic de Boum
(3008m)

Pic du Portillon
(3060m)

Cap du Seil
de la Baque
(3102m)

Pic du Seil
de la Baque
(3110m)

Pic Perdiguère
(3222m)

SPAIN

0   1   2km

0   0.5   1mi

1:90,000

PYRENEES

From the anonymous **col** (2272m) – reached five minutes later – and beyond, there are plunging views westwards to the bottom of the valley, occupied by a lone farmstead and the only other sign of humanity, a shepherd's cabin half way down the northern flank.

From the pass, it becomes switchback time, dropping via a series of benign zigzags and regaining height only to ride more ups and downs. Along this whole varied, tumbling stretch, the only thing likely to leave you seriously breathless is the panorama to the north, altogether greener and more gentle than the rugged peaks of the eastern horizon that dominated those first super views after Superbagnères.

A final steep climb, taxing but less than five minutes long, brings you to **Hourquette des Hounts-Secs** (2267m), a notch through which the west wind can howl and which offers you the first, splendid plunging views of Lac d'Oô. It's worth noting that, for all the net height loss and gain of the last hour, you're precisely 5m up on where you were about an hour before!

From the pass, the trail snakes down, levelling out while still well above the Cascade d'Oô waterfall, spectacular after snowmelt, that gushes into Lac d'Oô at its southeastern end. Where the GR10 turns sharply right to drop down to the lake, continue straight ahead for the final uphill clamber to reach the Refuge d'Espingo some 3¼ hours after leaving Superbagnères – a total walking time of 5¾ to 6¼ hours.

Although **Refuge d'Espingo** (1960m; ☎ 05 61 79 20 01; dorm beds €13.50; dinner €14.50; open May–mid-Oct) has a capacity for 80, it's essential to book at this justifiably popular mountain hut.

Day 2: Refuge d'Espingo to Bagnères de Luchon
4½–5 hours, 15km

Return next morning by the same route. Your time from Superbagnères to Bagnères de Luchon will, of course, be considerably faster than that for the plodding ascent. But, because of the up-and-down nature of the section from Refuge d'Espingo to the ski

resort, your return time for the early part of the journey will not be appreciably quicker than that on the outward leg.

If you're planning to take the *télécabine* from Superbagnères down to Bagnères de Luchon, plan to arrive a good half hour before the scheduled last run of the day since timings aren't as regular as they should be.

Side Trip: Lac du Portillon
3½–4 hours return, 10km

A round trip from Refuge d'Espingo brings you, via Lac Saussat, to **Lac du Portillon** (2670m) and the really high stuff that cuts a formidable frontier between France and Spain. Here, it's wild, craggy terrain, with some of the Pyrenees' last remaining glaciers.

Refuge du Portillon (☎ 05 61 79 38 15; dorm beds €13.50, half board €33; open mid-May–mid-Oct) is relatively new and just a good stone's throw from Lac du Portillon, it has great food and, that great rarity for *refuges*, hot showers.

Other Walks

Around Pic du Midi d'Ossau

The distinctive split spire of Pic du Midi d'Ossau (2884m) stands at the head of the Vallée d'Ossau, the next north–south valley east from Vallée d'Aspe. The circuit around its base is another of the Pyrenees' finest walks, commonly undertaken as a day's outing from Lac de Bious-Artigues, with **Refuge Pyrénéa** (☎ 05 59 05 32 12) beside it and **Camping de Bious-Oumette** (☎ 05 59 05 38 76) nearby. Consider, too, the side trip to bag Pic Peyreget (2487m) above Col du Peyreget, for spectacular views of Pic du Midi. IGN 1:25,000 map No 1547OT *Ossau* and Rando Éditions 1:50,000 map No 3 *Béarn* cover this circular walk (1200m ascent). Trailblazer's *Trekking in the Pyrenees* (see Books, p159) is also helpful.

Cirque de Gavarnie

High in the Luz-Gavarnie Valley, the next one east of Cauterets, the village of Gavarnie is another excellent base or starting point for fine walks in the Hautes Pyrénées. It has *gîtes d'étape*, **Camping le Pain de Sucre** (☎ 05 62 92 47 55) and few hotels and shops. For information, contact the combined **tourist and national park office** (☎ 05 62 92 49 10).

The magnificent Cirque de Gavarnie, soaring 1500m into the sky about 6km to the south on the Spanish border, draws thousands of summer visitors who ride donkeys or walk to vantage points nearby. Fortunately it's possible to escape the crowds and walk up to the foot of the huge waterfall, an easy half-day walk.

Brèche de Roland

Also known as Refuge des Sarradets, **Refuge de a Brèche de Roland** (☎ 05 62 93 37 20) is a demanding climb from Gavarnie. Spectacularly located close to the western edge of the cirque, it's very popular both as a base for attacking some of the 3000m peaks along the rim of the cirque – such as Le Taillon (3144m) and Pic du Mabore (3248m) – and as a staging post for the Brèche de Roland (2807m).

This deep, geometric cleft in the border ridge is almost directly above the *refuge*. It's the gateway into Spain for a spectacular tour taking in Ordesa canyon and Mont Perdu (Monte Perdido; 3355m), the Pyrenees' second-highest summit – both are within Parque Nacional de Ordesa y Monte Perdido.

Two maps in the IGN 1:25,000 series cover the area: No 1748OT *Gavarnie* and No 1748ET *Néouvielle. Un Sentier Pour Deux Parcs – Cirque de Gavarnie, Ordesa, Mont Perdu* describes a three-to-five-day walk.

The Pyrenees End to End: the Lower-Level Route

Many walkers pick and mix from the couple of recognised routes (see Books, p159, for relevant titles in English). Best known as the GR10, this well-waymarked, well-used route is one of the longest of France's really long-distance trails. With about 860km between the end points at Hendaye on the Atlantic coast and Banyuls-sur-Mer on the Mediterranean, it's considerably longer than the Pyrenees themselves. This is because it avoids quite a lot of the highest ground and wanders up and down valleys. Nevertheless, the total ascent *and* descent is a respectable 47,000m.

Four Topo-Guides cover the route: No 1086 *Pyrénées Occidentales*, No 1091 *Pyrénées Centrales*, No 1090 *Pyrénées Ariégoises* and No 1089 *Pyrénées Orientales*.

Walkers are divided about this meandering route. Some enjoy the contrast between the mountains and the valleys and the experience of visiting the many villages. Others feel frustrated at being wrenched away from the mountains just when they're becoming addicted to the experience, and at the unnecessary height loss that needs to be regained the next morning.

Many walkers tend to spread their traverse over more than a single visit, since at least six weeks is needed and there are many unmissable side trips – like climbing some of the peaks or visiting the Cirque de Gavarnie (see opposite).

The Pyrenees End to End: the High-Level Route

The Haute Randonnée Pyrénéenne (HRP) is one of Europe's classic high-level walks. Measured in daily stages (a minimum of 43, with an average duration of around 6½ hours) rather than horizontal distance (about 800km), it involves 43,400m of ascent, much of it steep and over difficult ground. Sharing end points with the GR10, the HRP follows the watershed of the Pyrenees and quite often crosses the border into Spain. Relevant reference maps are as for the GR10 (see p170).

The route mostly stays above 1000m and crosses several passes over 2500m. It remains an undertaking for experienced walkers, used to crossing rough ground and exposed ridges and equipped for sudden changes in the weather. Although the route is not officially waymarked, it shares a few sections with the GR10 and the Spanish equivalent, the GR11. Elsewhere, you need a degree of navigational skill.

A tent is virtually essential and you often need to carry a few days' supplies. *Haute Randonnée Pyrénéenne* by Georges Véron, who pioneered the route in 1968, is indispensable.

Corsica

Corsica (Corse in French) is the most mountainous and geographically diverse of the Mediterranean islands, earning it the perfectly justified title of L'Île de Beauté (The Island of Beauty). Although it covers only 8720 sq km, Corsica in many ways resembles a miniature continent with 1000km of coastline lapped by azure seas, soaring granite mountains, desert, flatland marshes and a 'continental divide'.

Walking is one of the best ways to explore Corsica. An extensive network of paths criss-crosses the whole of the island, ensuring access to remote parts of the interior. Described in detail in this chapter, the GR20 is the most famous of the *grandes randonnées* (long-distance, waymarked walking routes), attracting 10,000 brave souls from all over Europe to take on its heights every year. It was created in 1972, linking Calenzana, in the Balagne, with Conca, north of Porto Vecchio, and has since become something of an institution.

NATURAL HISTORY

Corsica's main attraction is its beautiful and remarkably well-preserved natural environment. Its isolation from the mainland makes it home to many endemic species. In the mountains, nearly half of all known species are endemic.

In 1972, 3505 sq km of the mountainous interior, about 40% of the island, was set aside as a nature reserve. This is the Parc Naturel Régional de Corse (PNRC). With a charter to protect and encourage 'the survival of the natural, cultural and human heritage of the region for the future', the PNRC management has constructed 2000km of signposted footpaths and actively promotes environmental protection on the island.

In addition to the PNRC, there are four nature reserves on Corsica: the Îles Finocchiarola, Îles Lavezzi, Îles Cerbicale and the Réserve Naturelle de Scandola (a Unesco World Heritage-listed site).

Highlights

- Navigating the treacherous climb out of the glorious Cirque de la Solitude (p206)
- Walking along the carpet-like pozzines around Lac de Ninu (p208), and at the foot of Monte Incudine
- Crossing the Aiguilles de Bavella (p216) along the Alpine Route
- Passing through heavily scented maquis on the way to Conca (p217) on the last day

Flora

The rich Corsican flora is divided into three zones. The Mediterranean zone (up to about 1000m) is dominated by maquis, holm and cork oaks, and olive and chestnut trees. Olives, mass-planted by the Genoese centuries ago, have largely been left to grow wild.

The coastal fringe of the island is covered by the maquis, characterised by low, shrubby, mostly evergreen vegetation. It combines a variety of sweet-smelling species, including rock rose, myrtle (treasured for its blue-black berries, which are used in some excellent liqueurs) and tree heather, whose white flowers exude a honey scent.

Pine and beech forests occupy the mountainous zone between 1000m and 1800m. One of the dominant species in these superb forests is the *laricio*, or Corsican pine, which can grow to around 50m and up to 800 years old. Their long, straight trunks were much prized as boat masts and the trees have been extensively logged over the centuries.

In the alpine zone, above 1800m, vegetation is low and sparse, comprising grasses and small ground-hugging plants.

Fauna

Most of the fauna seen on Corsica today are domesticated animals – pigs, cows, goats, sheep and mules. However, a number of endemic species still exist on the island, several of which are endangered.

Corsica

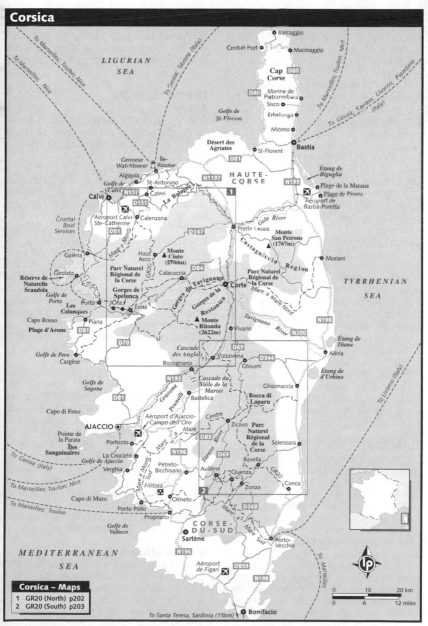

LIGURIAN
SEA

To Marseilles; Toulon; Nice

To Marseilles; Nice

To Savona (Italy)

To Marseilles; Toulon; Nice

To Genoa; Savona; Livorno; Piombino (Italy)

Barcaggio
Centuri Port
Macinaggio

Cap
Corse

D80

D80

Marine de
Pietracorbara
Sisco
Erbalunga
Mìomo

Golfe de
St-Florent

Désert des
Agriates

St-Florent

D81

Bastia

Étang de
Biguglia

N193

Plage de la Marana

Plage de Pineto

Aéroport de
Bastia-Poretta

Genoese
Watchtower
Île-
Rousse
Algajola
N197
St-Antonino

Calvi

Golfe de
Calvi

Cateri

D151

HAUTE-
CORSE

La Balagne

1

N1197

Aéroport Calvi
Ste-Catherine

Calenzana

Coastal
Boat
Services

D81

Golo River

Ponte Leccia

Monte
San Petrone
(1767m)

D147

Castagniccia

Region

Moriani

Galèria

Haut
Asco

Monte
Cinto
(2706m)

Parc Naturel
Régional de
la Corse

D84

Calacuccia

Réserve de
Naturelle
Scandola

Girolata

Gorges de
Spelunca

Gorges du Tavignano

Corte

Parc Naturel
Régional de
la Corse

Mare a Mare Nord

TYRRHENIAN

SEA

Golfe de
Porto

Porto

Ota
Evisa

Gorges de la
Restonica

Les
Calanques

Capo Rosso

Piana

Monte
Ritondu
(2622m)

Vivario

Tavignano River

N200

Étang de
Diane

Plage d'Arone

D81

D70

Cascade
des Anglais

D69

Vizzavona

Aléria

Golfe de Pero

Cargèse

Bocognano

Ghisoni

D344

Étang de
d'Urbino

Golfe de
Sagone

N193

D81

Cascade du
Voile de la
Mariée

Gravona

Bastelica

Ghisonaccia

Bocca di
Laparu

To Livorno (Italy)

Capo di Feno

Prunelli

Aéroport d'Ajaccio-
Campo dell'Oro

Centre

AJACCIO

Mare

Zicavo

Parc
Naturel
Régional
de la
Corse

Solenzara

Pointe de
la Parata

Îles
Sanguinaires

Porticcio

D83

Taravo River

D69

Bavella

To Genoa (Italy)

La Crociata

Verghia

Golfe de Ajaccio

N196

Aullène

Quenza

Conca

To Marseilles; Toulon; Nice

Capo di Muro

Filitosa

Petreto-
Bicchisano

Zonza

To Marseilles; Toulon

Porto Pollo

Olmeto

2

D368

Propriano

Golfe de
Valinco

CORSE-
DU-SUD

Mare e Sud

Porto-
Vecchio

MEDITERRANEAN

SEA

Sartène

N196

Aéroport
de Figari

D859

N198

To Marseilles

To Santa Teresa, Sardinia (15km)

Bonifacio

0   10   20 km

0   6   12 miles

Corsica – Maps
1 GR20 (North) p202
2 GR20 (South) p203

Once very common across Europe, Hermann's tortoise is now one of the rarest reptiles in France. Recognisable by its orange and black stripes, it is however relatively common in Corsica and can be found in the maquis.

The Corsican red deer was reintroduced to Corsica in 1985 from Sardinia at the instigation of the PNRC. The mouflon, a type of short-fleeced sheep, now a protected species, can be seen in south-facing valleys from December to February, but retreats to higher altitudes in summer. The males are easily recognisable by their huge horns. Along walking trails you're likely to come across some extensive damage caused by wild boars as they root for food. Hunting wild boar is a traditional activity in Corsica.

Bird species include the Audouin's gull, which is now only found on the shores of small Mediterranean islands; the bearded vulture, or lammergeier, which nests in rocky niches in the mountainous massifs; the Corsican nuthatch, one of the rare birds endemic to the island; and osprey and shag. With a wingspan of 1.6m, the fish-eating osprey can be seen in the Réserve Naturelle de Scandola. The island's population of osprey has grown from three couples in 1973 to around 20.

The common rorqual whale, a protected species, can sometimes be seen in the triangle of sea between Nice, the Île de Porquerolles and Corsica.

CLIMATE

The Mediterranean climate is characterised by summer droughts and sun. Average temperatures often exceed 25°C between June and September, while July and August can see temperatures of more than 35°C. Spring and autumn are both pleasant, with average temperatures of around 15°C. Temperatures between October and March reach a maximum of 20°C. The mountains are cooler, however, and the temperature drops significantly the higher you climb. Snow can be seen above 1600m from October to June and some of the island's peaks are snowcapped year-round. In contrast, sea temperatures rarely drop below 14°C and often rise above 25°C in summer.

Rainfall is highest during the last three months of the year, when there are often severe storms and flooding. July is usually a dry month.

INFORMATION
Maps

The Michelin 1:200,000 map No 90 *Corse* covers the entire island. For maps covering the GR20, see Maps, Planning (p199).

Books

Lonely Planet's *Corsica* is an excellent guide to the island beyond the walking trails, while *France* has a chapter devoted to Corsica.

The Corsican bible for visitors, Dorothy Carrington's revered 1971 *Granite Island: a Portrait of Corsica* is a travel book only in the sense that it is structured around the author's comings and goings around the island. Its learning and passion for Corsica is immense. Now out of print you may find it in a library, second-hand bookshop or on the Internet.

Paul Theroux describes a visit to Corsica during his circuit of the Mediterranean in *The Pillars of Hercules*.

There are two excellent Fédération Française de la Randonnée Pédestre (FFRP) Topo-Guide titles on Corsica: *À Travers la Montagne Corse* (No 67), which details the GR20 route, and *Corse: Entre Mer et Montagne* (No 65), describing walks both in the north and south of the island. Cicerone's *Corsican High Level Route: GR 20* is a handy English-language companion for the trail.

For walkers interested in exploring other trails and parts of the island, *Landscapes of Corsica* by Noel Rochford lists a number of short walking excursions as well as tours suitable for visitors with their own transport.

Information Sources
Maison d'Information Randonnée du PNRC
(PNRC Walking Information Office; ☎ *04 95 51 79 10; www.parc-naturel-corse.com - French only; 2 rue du Sergent Casalonga, Ajaccio; open 8am-3pm Sat summer, 8.30am-noon & 2-6pm*

Mon-Thu, 2-5pm Fri, 8am-6pm Mon-Fri rest of year) publishes a wealth of information about the park (including its *refuges*) along with a number of walking guides (mostly in French). It also provides sensible advice on walking routes across Corsica. Other information centres are listed under Gateways (this page) and Nearest Towns (p199).

Place Names

Two names exist for most places in Corsica: the original, Genoese-based *corsu* (Corsican) names, which often end in 'u', and the 'Frenchified' names, where the 'u' translates to 'o'. Some signs will carry both names; others just the Corsican.

GATEWAYS

The three towns most convenient to the GR20 – Bastia, Ajaccio and Calvi – have both air and sea links with the mainland. For information on travelling between these towns and the mainland, see Getting There & Away (p197).

Bastia

The second-largest town on the island, Bastia is Corsica's economic centre and is France's second most important port for passenger travel. Although it's not a tourist hub Bastia has a lively and busy town centre, a charming old port, long beaches and a rich cultural life.

Information Situated on the north side of place St-Nicolas is the small **tourist office** *(☎ 04 95 54 20 40; www.bastia-tourisme .com; open daily summer, closed Sun rest of year)*.

Warning

Take note of and observe PNRC rules and regulations; in particular, lighting fires at any point along a route in the park is strictly forbidden, as is camping outside the designated areas near *refuges*.

As far as water from streams is concerned, safety is not guaranteed: do not use it unless strictly necessary, and then purify it.

Maps and walking books are available in the **Librairie Jean-Patrice Marzocchi** *(☎ 04 95 34 02 95; 2 rue du Conventionnel Salicetti)*.

There are several banks along place St-Nicolas that have ATMs and offer exchange facilities. Exchange services are also available at the post office and, in summer, at the south ferry terminal.

Places to Stay Although few tourists stay in Bastia, it can still be difficult to find accommodation, especially in summer. It's best to book ahead.

Camping San Damiano *(☎ 04 95 33 68 02; www.campingsandamiano.com; lido de la Marana; camping per adult/site & car Aug €6.50/6.50, rest of year €5.50/5.50)* is about 5km south of Bastia next to the coastal road. A shuttle bus goes from the port in Bastia to the camping ground twice daily.

Hôtel Central *(☎ 04 95 31 71 12; www .centralhotel.fr; 3 rue Miot; singles €38-60, doubles €40-78)* offers the best value for money. It has some of the town's most comfortable rooms; some have a small balcony.

Hôtel de l'Univers *(☎ 04 95 31 03 38, fax 04 95 31 19 91; 3 av du Maréchal Sébastiani; singles/doubles/triples/quads €50/60/75/90)*, virtually opposite the post office, has clean, recently refurbished rooms.

Places to Eat Local traders and producers set up their stalls in the **market place** (place de l'Hôtel de Ville) each morning from around 8am.

Jo la Braise *(☎ 04 95 31 36 97; 7 blvd Hyacinthe de Montera; closed Sun; pizzas €5-6.50)*, close to the Palais de Justice, is small and nondescript but offers a warm welcome and good local fare at inexpensive prices.

La Voûte *(☎ 04 95 32 27 82, 04 95 32 47; 6 rue Luce de Casabianca; pizzas €7.35-9)* is just behind the harbour, but it is worth a detour for its rich and varied menu. For a meal that won't cost the earth, choose the excellent pizzas cooked over a wood fire.

Ajaccio

The busy port city of Ajaccio, birthplace of Napoleon Bonaparte (1769–1821), is a pleasant enough place, despite having some very busy roads and rather unattractive areas that rub shoulders with the old town.

Information There are heaps of brochures at the **tourist office** (☎ 04 95 51 53 03; www.tourisme.fr/ajaccio; 3 blvd du Roi Jérôme; open daily May-Oct, closed Sun Nov-Apr) and helpful multilingual staff.

The **kiosk** (cours Napoléon; open 6am-8pm) opposite the main post office has local, national and international newspapers.

There are plenty of ATMs; the one opposite the BNP, on Cours Napoléon, accepts Visa and MasterCard. You can change travellers cheques at the post office.

Places to Stay It is difficult to find cheap accommodation in Ajaccio, so book ahead in summer.

Camping de Barbicaja (☎ 04 95 52 01 17; route des Sanguinaires; camping per person/site/vehicle €5.85/2.30/2.30; open May-Sep), next to a beach about 4.5km from the town centre, is often full in summer. Its facilities are adequate. To get there catch the No 5 bus from blvd Lantivy.

Hôtel du Palais (☎ 04 95 22 73 68, 5 av Beverini Vico; singles/doubles/triples with shower & TV €50/65/75 Jul-Aug) is one of the best-value hotels in town. Rooms with toilet cost an extra €5.

Hôtel Kallisté (☎ 04 95 51 34 45, fax 04 95 21 79 00; 51 cours Napoléon; singles/doubles/triples €56/69/86) is a favourite haunt of independent travellers. It provides a wide range of facilities.

Places to Eat Ajaccio has plenty of supermarkets, including the well-stocked **Monoprix** (cours Napoléon; open 8.30am-7.15pm Mon-Sat). During summer it is open an extra half-hour.

With a few eat-in tables, **Fast-Food Asiatique** (☎ 04 95 21 23 31; 1 rue Maréchal Ornano; meals €4-6; open 11.30am-2pm & 6-10.30pm) offers fried noodles or stuffed crab for €4.

Avoid the touristy restaurants and pizzerias along rue des Anciens Fossés, a narrow street in the old town. **Pasta e Basta**

(☎ 04 95 50 18 92; 8 place Charles de Gaulle; pasta €6.10-12.20) has a great range of well-prepared pasta dishes and excellent *antipasti*. It also has a pleasant terrace overlooking the sea.

Calvi

Calvi, the capital of the Balagne, is a thriving little town stretched out along a bay under the watchful eye of two giants: the Citadelle and Monte Cinto (2706m).

Information In the marina, the **tourist office** (☎ 04 95 65 16 67; www.tourisme.fr/calvi; open 8.30am-1pm & 2.30-8pm Jun-Sep, 9am-noon & 2-6pm Mon-Fri Oct-May) is above the *capitainerie* (harbour master's office). There is plenty of information about Calvi as well as walks in the Balagne and around Calvi.

Places to Stay About 2.5km from the town centre and close to the beach, **Camping La Pinède** (☎ 04 95 65 17 80; www.la-pinede.net; Route de la Pinède; camping per person/vehicle/tent €7//2.50/2.50; open 1 Apr-15 Oct) is a quiet, pleasant choice. Sheltered by pine trees, the camping ground has a restaurant, bar, laundrette and grocery.

Auberge de Jeunesse BVJ Corsotel (☎ 04 95 65 14 15, fax 04 95 65 33 72; av de la République; dorm beds with/without breakfast €22/20; open Apr-Oct) is practically opposite the station; dorm rooms have a bathroom and two to eight beds.

Hôtel Belvédère (☎ 04 95 65 01 25; www.resa-hotels-calvi.com - French only; place Christophe Colomb; doubles €54-115, triples €70-130; open year-round) has comfortable but smallish doubles. The *chambres standing* (higher-priced rooms) are more spacious.

Places to Eat The **Super U supermarket** is on av Christophe Colomb.

Away from the restaurants, **Le Chalet du Port** (☎ 04 95 65 34 48 Quai des Ferries; meals €7-13) is a pleasant little bar near the harbour. The food is simple, good and affordable: pizzas (€7-9), lasagne (€8), chips (€2.50) or a plate of cooked meats (€8).

Tao (☎ *04 95 65 00 73; meals €12-22 desserts €9; open end May-Sep*) A real institution, Tao is perched at the top of the citadel. It was set up in the 1920s by Tao Kanbey de Kerekoff, who left his native Caucasus to accompany Prince Iousoupov (who took part in the assassination of Rasputin) into exile. To get there, take the little road off to the right when you get to place d'Armes.

GETTING THERE & AWAY

Corsica levies a 'regional tax' of €5 on all arrivals and departures, which will usually be included in your quoted air fare. Ferry passengers and vehicles are also charged an additional port tax, which varies between ports.

Air

Bastia-Poretta airport is 24km south of the town. A shuttle bus runs frequently (€8). The Campo dell'Oro airport is 8km southeast of Ajaccio and is well served by public transport, with an hourly airport bus (€4). Calvi's airport is 7km southwest of the city centre and is serviced by taxis. Figari serves southern Corsica and is north of Bonicafio.

The standard fare from Paris to Ajaccio, Bastia, Figari or Calvi is around €300 return. However, airlines offer various discounts. From April to October, and particularly during summer, charter flights meet the increase in passenger demand.

Air France (☎ *08 20 82 08 20*) offers daily direct flights from Paris. It also has flights from Lyon, Marseille, Nice and Montpellier. **Air Littoral** (☎ *08 25 83 48 34*) has regular flights between Corsica's airports and Paris, Bordeaux, Lille, Marseille, Nante, Nice, Toulouse, Strasbourg and Montpellier. The Corsican home-grown **CCM Airlines** (☎ *08 20 82 08 20*) connects French mainland cities, as well as Basel and Rome, with Corsica.

Charter flights start at around €170 from Paris, but don't always guarantee confirmed departure times or even days. For the high-season charter flights, try **Nouvelles Frontières** (☎ *08 25 00 07 47;* *www.nouvelles-frontieres.fr - French only*), who operates up to 10 flights per week to/ from Paris and other regional French cities.

Sea

Details on ferry services are available from many French travel agencies. During the summer (late June to September), reservations for vehicles and *couchettes* (sleeping berths) must be made well in advance.

For information on ferry transport between Corsica and Italy, see Getting There & Away in the Travel Facts chapter (p346).

Almost all ferry services between the French mainland (Nice, Marseille and Toulon) and Corsica (Ajaccio, Bastia, Calvi, Île Rousse, Porto Vecchio and Propriano) are handled by the state-owned **Société Nationale Maritime Corse-Méditerranée** (*SNCM; Marseille* ☎ *08 91 70 18 01; www.sncm.fr*). Schedules and fares are comprehensively listed in the free SNCM pocket timetable, distributed at tourist offices, some hotels and SNCM offices.

In the height of summer there are up to eight ferries a day. Single SNCM fares from Nice/Marseilles or Toulon to any Corsican port range from €30/35 (low season) to €41/53 (high season), plus from €5/8/28 for a *fauteuil* (reclining chair)/bed/cabin. Discounts are available for people aged under 25 and seniors. Children under 12 pay 50% less than the adult fare.

Transporting a small car one way costs between €40 and €100 depending on the season. Motorcycles cost from €23 to €59, and bicycles from €14.

The port tax (not included in these figures) is an additional €5 per passenger from the mainland French port, €3 to €6 for the Corsican port and around €5 to €10 per vehicle.

Daytime crossings take roughly 3¾ hours. Corsica Ferries and SNCM also run a 70km/h express NGV (Navire à Grande Vitesse; ☎ *08 36 64 00 95*) service from Nice to Calvi (2½ hours) and Bastia (3½ hours). Fares on these zippy NGVs are similar to those charged for passage on regular ferries, except that there is a €5 supplement on fast ferries from Nice and on summer weekends.

GETTING AROUND
Bus

Numerous bus companies offer services all over Corsica, but this does not mean it's easy to get around by bus. Working out which buses stop at any given place can be quite a challenge because many companies offer only a single service, and many services are infrequent (once or twice a day, often early in the morning) or seasonal. Except in July and August, only a handful of intercity buses operate on Sunday and holidays.

Although distances are short, fares are relatively high because the demand is so seasonal. You can buy your ticket from the bus driver.

Train

The **Chemins de Fer de la Corse** (CFC; ☎ 04 95 32 80 57, 04 95 32 80 61) network has four year-round services: Bastia–Ajaccio, Bastia–Corte, Ajaccio–Calvi and Calvi–Bastia. Prices are very reasonable. Services are slightly reduced in winter.

The CFC produces its own rail pass – La Carte Zoom – which is well worth buying if you intend making more than a couple of train journeys within Corsica (€47 for seven days).

Car Rental

Without a doubt, the best way to get around the island is by car or motorcycle. Some people bring their own cars to Corsica, but it is very easy to hire one on arrival. There are fewer motorcycle-hire companies, but you can hire a motorcycle in most of the big towns.

As well as the car-rental companies found in the regional towns, the international companies (Avis, Budget, Europcar and Hertz included) are represented at the airports and this is where you will get the widest choice. You need to have a credit card to hire a vehicle. Expect to pay between €230 and €260 for week's hire of a Category A vehicle (three doors, four seats). The daily rate is about €70, while the monthly rate is €680 to €750. It pays to shop around.

Bicycle

Cycling around Corsica can add an extra dimension to your holiday, and get you to many of the more remote trail heads without having to rely on infrequent public transport. However, Corsica is hilly on all but the east coast so you need to be reasonably fit. Some ferry companies transport bikes for free; others charge around €14; it costs €12.50 to take your bike on the train. Lonely Planet's *Cycling France* details two tours on the island, which pass several access points for the GR20 and the Mare e Monti routes.

The GR20

Duration	15 days
Distance	168km
Difficulty	demanding
Start	Calenzana (opposite)
Finish	Conca (p217)
Nearest Towns	Calenzana (opposite), Porto Vecchio (p200)
Transport	bus

Summary A legendary, if demanding, walk through the granite ranges of inland Corsica. Experience the isolation and grandeur of the mountains well away from the coastal crowds.

The GR20 stretches diagonally from northwest to southeast, following the island's continental divide (hence its Corsican name, Fra Li Monti, which means 'Between the Mountains'). The diversity of landscapes makes this an exceptional walk, with forests, granite moonscapes, windswept craters, glacial lakes, torrents, peat bogs, maquis, snow-capped peaks, plains and névés (stretches of ice formed from snow).

Consider using the resources available close to the route. Villages linked to the GR20, where you can stop off and stock up, are detailed in the walk description. The paths connecting the GR20 to the villages are marked with yellow painted lines (these can sometimes be confusing or inadequate on some of the less frequently used paths). For a discussion of points where you can join or leave the GR20, see the boxed text on p201.

PLANNING
When to Walk

The GR20 can be comfortably walked any time between May and October, but some parts of the route remain snow-covered until June, making them tricky to negotiate. The peak-season months of July and August are best avoided if you have an aversion to crowds. From mid-August to the end of September, there are frequent afternoon storms.

What to Bring

The GR20 is a long and challenging walk, and requires some preparation. You will need to carry food with you for at least part of the trail as some of the *refuges* (refuges or mountain huts) only provide light snacks. Depending on the amount of time at your disposal, plan on making detours to local villages for further supplies. Don't forget to carry a good supply of cash, as there are no ATMS on the GR20 and credit cards are only accepted in a few places. As a general rule, you'll need between €10 and €25 per day.

Water and thirst can also be real problems on the GR20. You will be able to find water at every *refuge*, but between stops there are very few sources of drinking water. These have been detailed in the text.

Camping gear is also essential, as there is only a limited number of places available in *refuges* along the way. Note that reservations cannot be made at the PNRC-run *refuges*. When camping you do not have access to equipment inside the huts and fires are prohibited, so bring your own stove and fuel.

Weather in the mountains can fluctuate quickly between extremes, so come prepared for all conditions. You can call ☎ 08 92 68 02 20 for the latest weather reports in French. A length of rope is a handy addition, as it will allow you to lower your backpack down particularly steep sections of the trail, leaving you free to descend without extra bulk.

Maps

Choose the IGN 1:25,000 maps or Didier Richard's 1:50,000 No 20 *Corse du Nord*

> ## Warning
>
> The GR20 is a genuine mountain route that requires physical commitment, and should not be taken lightly. The changes in altitude are unrelenting, the path is rocky and sometimes steep, the weather conditions can be difficult and you have to carry enough equipment to be self-sufficient for several days. Good physical condition and advance training are essential.
>
> Some stretches of the traverse, in particular navigating rickety bridges, snow-covered ground, granite slabs and slippery rock faces, require sure-footedness and a reasonable head for heights.

and No 23 *Corse du Sud*. While the 1:25,000 maps are more detailed, you'll need six (Nos 4149OT, 4250OT, 4251OT 4252OT, 4253OT, 4253ET) of them to cover the GR20, whereas you'll only need two of the 1:50,000 maps.

NEAREST TOWNS
Calenzana

Thirteen kilometres from Calvi, Calenzana is the northern starting point for the GR20 and is also on the route of the Mare e Monti Nord (Sea to Northern Mountains; p218) walk, making it very popular with walkers.

Places to Stay & Eat A few hundred metres on the road to Calvi, **Gîte d'étape municipal** (☎ 04 95 62 77 13; camping per person & tent €9.60, dorm beds €14; open Apr-Oct) is on the right-hand side, with hostel-style walkers' accommodation. You can also pitch a tent close by. It has four-bed dormitories that are comfortable and recently renovated. There's a kitchen, and the showers are hot.

Hôtel Bel Horizon (☎ 04 95 62 71 72/70 08; singles/doubles/triples €45/55/60; open Apr-Oct), opposite the church, is popular with weary walkers. It offers clean rooms with en suite shower and shared toilet.

L'Auberge A Flatta (☎ 04 95 62 80 38; www .aflatta.com - French only; doubles €69-100; pasta & pizza €7-9.50; open end Mar-mid-Nov,

CORSICA

reservations recommended) has spectacular sea views and fine food. Try the Corsican veal in a parsley sauce (€15.50). The evening *menu* offers good value for money. There are also a few well-kept rooms and a swimming pool. To get there, turn right into the first street off blvd François Marini behind the church and follow the sign to the auberge.

Stock up on supplies at the small **grocery** near the post office.

The popular **Le Calenzana – Chez Michel** (☎ 04 95 62 70 25; cours St-Blaise; Corsican *menu* €15, pizzas €6-6.90; open Apr-Oct), on the main road behind the church, serves wood-fire pizzas and a Corsican *menu* that includes wild boar during the hunting season. Another option for pizzas is **Pizzeria Prince Pierre** (☎ 04 95 62 81 97; pasta & pizza €7-9.50), in front of the church.

Getting There & Away During July and August **Les Beaux Voyages bus company** (☎ 04 95 65 11 35) has a service from Calvi to Calenzana (€4.60 and €0.70 per piece of luggage, 20 minutes) twice daily except Sunday and public holidays. Buses leave from Calvi, opposite the agency's offices in place de la Porteuse d'Eau. In winter they run once daily on Monday, Tuesday, Thursday, Friday and Saturday.

Porto Vecchio

Porto Vecchio is the nearest town of a reasonable size to Conca, at the end of the walk. It makes a good base for exploring the

---

Starting Out

From which direction should you tackle the GR20? Nearly two-thirds of walkers opt for the north–south route, as does this guide. There are various reasons for this: access to Calenzana is easier; the main guide to the route is in this direction; habit...but logic would dictate going from south to north. The southern section between Conca and Vizzavona is easier, giving your body a chance to get used to the effort. Going in this direction also means that you don't have to walk with the sun in your eyes.

---

surrounding areas, especially the Alta Rocca region, Bocca di Bavella and the spectacular coast north and south of the town.

The **tourist office** (☎ 04 95 70 09 58, rue du Député Camille de Rocca Serra; open 9am-8pm Mon-Sat & 9am-1pm Sun May-Sep, 9am-12.30pm & 2-6.30pm Mon-Fri, 9am-noon Sat Oct-Apr) has information on *gîtes* and *chambres d'hôtes*.

The **Société Générale** (rue du Général Leclerc; open 8.15am-noon & 1.45-4.50pm Mon-Fri) will change money, and **Crédit Lyonnais** (cnr rue du Général Leclerc & rue Scaramoni), near the post office, has an ATM. There is also an ATM at the **post office** (rue du Général Leclerc; open 8.30am-6pm & Sat morning Mon-Fri), where you can change travellers cheques at a better rate than the banks offer.

Places to Stay Four kilometres southeast of Porto Vecchio, **Camping Les Jardins du Golfe** (☎ 04 95 70 46 92, fax 04 95 72 10 28, route de Palombaggia; camping per person/site/car €4.95/2.15/2.15; open year-round) has all facilities, a grocery store, a pizzeria and a pool.

Hôtel Holzer (☎ 04 95 70 05 93, fax 04 95 70 47 82, 12 rue Jean Jaurès; singles/doubles/triples €61/91/118, with half board per person €75/59.50/53.40), with comfortable rooms and all the mod cons, is a good choice near the Ville Haute (upper town). Half board is obligatory in August.

The family-run **Hôtel Le Goéland** (☎ 04 95 70 14 15; hotel-goeland@wanadoo.fr; av Georges-Pompidou; doubles €59-143; open Easter-Nov), between the harbour and the roundabout before the carrefour des Quatre Chemins, is on the waterside. A good choice, it's quiet and has a lovely garden. The owners are planning to renovate the rooms and add a pool, so prices are likely to rise. In July and August, the rates include breakfast.

Places to Eat North of the Ville Haute, the **Hyper U supermarket** (carrefour des Quatre Chemins), and the **Géant supermarket**, on the next roundabout out, are a boon to self-caterers.

In the Ville Haute, **Les 40e** *(rue Borgo; crepes €4-7.9; 5pm-midnight Jun-Sep)* is a *crêperie* offering a great range of savoury and sweet crepes.

Le Bistrot *(☎ 04 95 70 22 96; av Georges Pompidou; lunch/dinner menus €17/30)* has a good reputation for its fish offerings (from €18). The atmosphere is nautical and the setting is very pleasant, with prices to match.

In the upper town, **rue Borgo** is home to a number of **restaurants** that backing onto the ramparts and with attractive terraces facing over the sea.

Getting There & Away Between Bastia and Porto Vecchio **Les Rapides Bleus-Corsicatours** *(☎ 04 95 31 03 79; 7 rue Jean Jaurès)* operates a twice-daily bus service (daily except Sunday and public holidays in winter) via Ste-Lucie de Porto Vecchio, Solenzara and Ghisonaccia (€18.50). There's also a shuttle bus to Santa Giulia in summer.

Île de Beauté Voyages *(☎ 04 95 70 12 31; 13 rue du Général de Gaulle)* has a service to Ajaccio (€19.90) via the mountains (daily except Sunday and public holidays in July and August, and Monday and Friday only in winter).

GETTING TO/FROM THE WALK

Start walking at Calenzana (p199). There is no public transport from Conca, at the end of the walk, to Porto Vecchio. However, staff at La Tonnelle (p217) in Conca can arrange a shuttle-bus service to Porto Vecchio on request (€6). However, you will have to wait until there is a minimum number of people ready to leave – this is no problem in the high season.

Some of the alternative access points to the GR20 are served by public transport.

Haut Asco (Day 3) is accessible on the D147, which meets the N197 2km north of Ponte Leccia.

Castel di Verghio (Day 5) is served by a daily bus between Corte and Porto via the D84. It passes by the Hôtel Castel di Verghio.

Tattone (reached via a side trip on Day 8) is on the Bastia–Vizzavona–Ajaccio train line. It takes just seven minutes and €2.40 to get from Tattone to Vizzavona by train or by phoning for a taxi (see the side trip, p209).

Vizzavona (Day 9) is on the train route between Ajaccio (€8.40) and Bastia (€23.50). Trains stop four times a day in each direction. Two of the services continue beyond Bastia to Île Rousse (€14.90) and Calvi (€17.60).

Cozzano (reached on a side trip on Day 12) is linked to Ajaccio daily except Sunday by

Alternative Access Points

Completing the GR20 will give you a sense of pride and achievement, and rightly so. It is a demanding course that requires commitment. But while the goal of many is to walk it end to end, there is no shame in biting off just a small section. Even a couple of days on the traverse will allow you to experience the beauty of Corsica's mountain wilderness and sample the physical challenges of the trail.

The obvious way to divide the GR20 is into two sections: from Calenzana to Vizzavona (over nine days), and south from Vizzavona to Conca (in six days). Vizzavona is the most convenient midway point, with train and road links to Ajaccio and Bastia.

Between Calenzana and Vizzavona, it's possible to join the trail at several villages along the way: Haut Asco (at the end of Day 3), Castel di Verghio (at the end of Day 5) and Tattone, a short side trip from the main trail (on Day 8). For just a small taste of the GR20, Days 4 and 5 take in some of the most spectacular scenery of the whole walk, across the Cirque de la Solitude.

In the southern section of the GR20, Cozzano (Day 12), Zicavo (Day 13), and Quenza and Bavella (Day 14) are all popular access points for walkers. Reaching Cozzano, Zicavo and Quenza involves a detour from the GR20, but these traditional villages, tucked away in remote valleys, are the very soul of Corsica and well worth exploring in their own right.

For details of transport links to places along the GR20, see Getting To/From the Walk, this page.

CORSICA

GR20 (North)

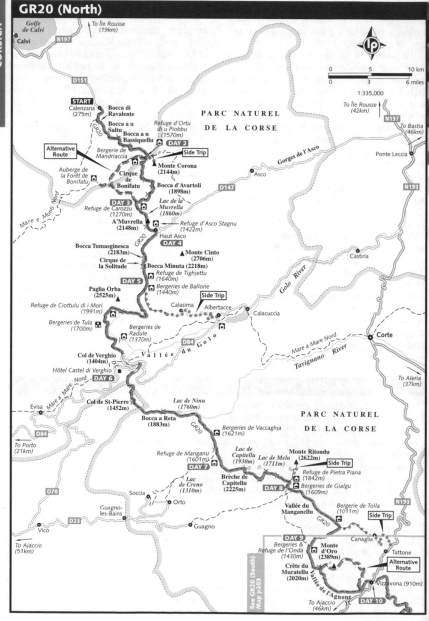

Golfe de Calvi

Calvi

N197

To Île Rousse (19km)

D151

START
Calenzana (275m)

Bocca di Ravalente

Refuge d'Ortu di u Piobbu (1570m)

Bocca a u Saltu

Bocca a u Bassiquellu

DAY 2

Alternative Route

Bergerie de Mandriaccia

Side Trip

Auberge de la Forêt de Bonifatu

Cirque de Bonifatu

Monte Corona (2144m)

Bocca d'Avartoli (1898m)

D147

Asco

DAY 3

Refuge de Carozzu (1270m)

Lac de la Muvrella (1860m)

A'Muvrella (2148m)

Refuge d'Asco Stagnu (1422m)

Haut Asco

DAY 4

Bocca Tumasginesca (2183m)

Monte Cinto (2706m)

Cirque de la Solitude

Bocca Minuta (2218m)

Refuge de Tighjettu (1640m)

DAY 5

Paglia Orba (2525m)

Bergeries de Ballone (1440m)

Side Trip

Refuge de Ciottulu di i Mori (1991m)

Calasima

Albertacce

Calacuccia

Bergeries de Tula (1700m)

Bergeries de Radule (1370m)

D84

Vallée du Golo

Golo River

Castirla

Corte

Mare a Mare Nord

Tavignano River

Col de Verghio (1404m)

Hôtel Castel di Verghio

DAY 6

Col de St-Pierre (1452m)

Lac de Ninu (1760m)

Bocca a Reta (1883m)

Bergeries de Vaccaghja (1621m)

To Aleria (37km)

Evisa

To Porto (21km)

D84

Refuge de Manganu (1601m)

DAY 7

Lac de Capitellu (1930m)

Lac de Melu (1711m)

Monte Ritondu (2622m)

Side Trip

Refuge de Pietra Piana (1842m)

D70

Lac de Creno (1310m)

Brèche de Capitellu (2225m)

DAY 8

Bergeries de Gialgu (1609m)

Soccia

Orto

D23

Guagno-les-Bains

Guagno

Vallée du Manganellu

Bergerie de Tolla (1011m)

Side Trip

N193

Vico

To Ajaccio (51km)

DAY 9

Bergeries & Refuge de l'Onda (1430m)

Monte d'Oro (2389m)

Canaglia

Tattone

Alternative Route

Crête du Muratellu (2020m)

Vallée de l'Agnone

Vizzavona (910m)

To Ajaccio (46km)

DAY 10

See GR20 (South) Map p203

PARC NATUREL DE LA CORSE

Ponte Leccia

N193

To Île Rousse (42km)

N197

To Bastia (46km)

Gorges de l'Asco

To Île Rousse (42km)

0   5   10 km
0   3   6 miles

1:335,000

Mare e Moni Nord

Mare a Mare Nord

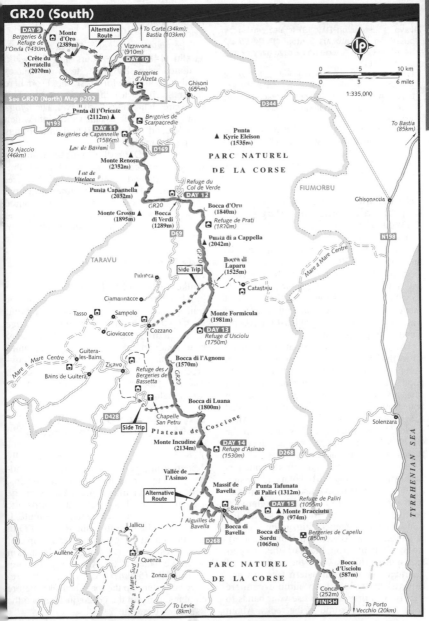

GR20 (South)

DAY 9
Bergeries &
Refuge de
l'Onda (1430m)
Monte
d'Oro
(2389m)
Alternative
Route
To Corte (34km);
Bastia (103km)
Vizzavona
(910m)
DAY 10
Crête du
Muratellu
(2020m)
GR20
Bergeries
d'Alzeta
Ghisoni
(655m)
See GR20 (North) Map p202
D344
Punta di l'Oriente
(2112m)
N193
Bergeries de
Scarpaccedie
Punta
Kyrie Eleison
(1535m)
To Bastia
(85km)
DAY 11
Bergeries de Capannelle (1586m)
Lac de Bastani
D169
PARC NATUREL
DE LA CORSE
FIUMORBU
To Ajaccio
(46km)
Monte Renosu
(2352m)
Ghisonaccia
Lac de
Vitelaca
Refuge du
Col de Verde
DAY 12
Punta Capannella
(2032m)
GR20
Bocca d'Oru
(1840m)
Monte Grossu
(1895m)
Bocca
di Verdi
(1289m)
Refuge de Prati
(1820m)
D69
Punta di a Cappella
(2042m)
TARAVU
Palneca
Side Trip
Bocca di
Laparu
(1525m)
Mare a Mare Centre
Ciamannacce
Catastaju
Tasso
Sampolo
Monte Formicula
(1981m)
Giovicacce
Cozzano
DAY 13
Refuge d'Usciolu
(1750m)
Mare a Mare Centre
Guitera-
les-Bains
Zicavo
Bocca di l'Agnonu
(1570m)
GR20
Bains de Guitera
Refuge des
Bergeries de
Bassetta
D428
Bocca di Luana
(1800m)
Solenzara
Chapelle
San Petru
Plateau de Coscione
Side Trip
Monte Incudine
(2134m)
DAY 14
Refuge d'Asinao
(1530m)
D268
Vallée de
l'Asinao
Massif de
Bavella
Punta Tafunata
di Paliri (1312m)
Refuge de Paliri
(1055m)
Alternative
Route
Bavella
DAY 15
Monte Bracciutu
(974m)
Jallicu
Aiguilles de
Bavella
Bocca di
Bavella
Bocca di
Sordu
(1065m)
Bergeries de Capellu
(850m)
Aullène
D268
GR20
Bocca
d'Usciolu
(587m)
I Quenza
PARC NATUREL
Zonza
DE LA CORSE
Conca
(252m)
FINISH
To Levie
(8km)
Mare a Mare Sud
To Porto
Vecchio (20km)

TYRRHENIAN SEA

0   5   10 km
0   3   6 miles
1:335,000

buses that are operated by **Autocars Santoni** (☎ *04 95 22 64 44).*

Zicavo (a detour on Day 13) is also served by buses run by **Autocars Santoni** *(☎ 04 95 22 64 44)* between Ajaccio and Zicavo daily except Sunday *(€13).*

Bavella (Day 14) can be reached daily except Sunday in the peak season by an **Autocars Balesi** *(☎ 04 95 70 15 55)* on the Ajaccio–Porto Vecchio line (only Monday and Friday in the low season).

Quenza (on Day 14) can be a departure point from the GR20. **Autocars Balesi** *(☎ 04 95 70 15 55)* buses stop daily except Sunday (only Monday and Friday in the low season) on the Ajaccio–Porto Vecchio service.

THE WALK (See maps pp202-3)
Day 1: Calenzana to Refuge d'Ortu di u Piobbu
7 hours, 10km

You are confronted with the tough conditions of the GR20 from the very outset or the walk. This first day is one long ascent, crossing a series of ridges, with hardly a downhill break and long stretches without shade. There's no guaranteed source of water, so be sure to bring at least the recommended 2L per person.

The walk starts in Calenzana by winding up to the top of the village. The path then starts to climb steadily through ferns, with good views back to Calenzana and Moncale, another hillside village. Less than an hour from Calenzana, at the well-signposted 'Carrefour de Sentiers' (550m), the Mare e Monti Nord route (p218) splits from the GR20. Soon after, the trail reaches the rocky Bocca di Ravalente at 616m.

From the pass, the trail skirts a wide terraced valley, staying fairly level and passing a few small streams that usually dry up later in the season, before climbing relatively gently to 820m. After this easy stretch the trail becomes steeper, zigzagging uphill to another pass, Bocca a u Saltu (1250m). About 3½ hours from the start, this is a perfect spot for lunch. Over the other side of the ridge, on the northeastern face of Capu Ghiovu, the trail starts to climb even more steeply; you may have to use your hands to hoist yourself up some of the rocks. About

halfway up this stretch is a stream that is a good source of drinking water if it hasn't dried up.

The wide grassy col at **Bocca a u Bassiguellu** (1486m), 5½ hours into the walk, is dotted with shady pine trees and makes another good place for a rest stop. From here the trail crosses a rather rocky and unsheltered stretch but stays fairly level. The *refuge* comes into view across the valley, into which you descend before a final short climb brings the day to an end.

Refuge d'Ortu di u Piobbu *(camping €3.50, dorm beds €9; meals €7),* at 1570m, has 30 beds and plenty of camping space. However, it has just one rather primitive toilet and shower; there is a water source about 200m beyond the *refuge* along the GR20. There are a few meals and drinks on offer as well as snacks.

Side Trip: Monte Corona
2½–3 hours

Walkers who still feel strong may want to climb nearby Monte Corona (2144m). A trail, marked by cairns and flashes of paint, goes up the slope directly behind the *refuge* to Bocca di Tartagine (1852m). From there head south and climb the rocky ridge until you see the rounded summit, which is covered in loose stones and marked by a cairn. The spectacular view stretches from the *refuge* below to the north coast.

Day 2: Refuge d'Ortu di u Piobbu to Refuge de Carozzu
6½ hours, 8km

Two routes exist for this day. The one fully described in this section is graded demanding. It cuts across a range of mountains, with rocky and often spectacular scenery. The alternative low-level route skirts the mountain range crossed by the main route. It leads off to the west from the Refuge d'Ortu di u Piobbu, meeting a road after a couple of kilometres, which it follows for about 5km down the valley to the Auberge de la Forêt de Bonifatu (540m). From the auberge retrace your steps up the road for 1.5km before climbing to rejoin the GR20, just beyond the R uge de Carozzu.

The day's walk starts with a gentle ascent through pine forest to a ridge (1630m). In front of you is a sharp drop to the valley bottom and then a long, steep ascent (500m) to an even higher ridge on the other side.

The trail descends quickly to the valley floor, passing the ruined **Bergerie de Mandriaccia** (1500m) shepherd's hut and the Mandriaccia stream, then starts the long climb up the other side. About halfway up this unrelenting ascent there's a good source of drinking water, probably the only one you'll come across all day.

Eventually, about three hours from the start, you'll come to Bocca Piccaia (1950m). There's very little shade.

The trail does not cross the ridge immediately but stays on the northern side, remaining at a fairly high altitude until it crosses to the other side and gently descends to Bocca d'Avartoli (1898m). Traversing the southern and western faces of the next ridge, the trail drops steeply before climbing sharply to cross the next pass. It then goes to the eastern side of the ridge, crossing back again to the western side at **Bocca Carozzu** (Inuminata; 1865m), about five hours into the walk.

From here the route begins the long and somewhat tedious descent to the *refuge*. At the start of the descent it's worth looking back at the wonderful views enjoyed in the last couple of hours of the walk. It's only towards the end of this descent that you'll find some shady trees. A short distance before the *refuge* the trail crosses a stream.

Refuge de Carozzu (*camping €3.50, dorm beds €9; meals €4-7*), at 1270m, is in a magnificent setting, hedged in by sheer rock faces on three sides, but with an open terrace looking down the valley. It sleeps 26 and there are plenty of **camp sites** in the surrounding woods. Corsican cheese omelettes, soup and other **foodstuffs** are on offer. Beer, wine, soft drinks, sausage, cheese and other supplies are also sold.

If you follow the path from the *refuge* towards Lac de la Muvrella for 10 minutes, past a passage of rocks with cables, you'll come to a stream with a series of delightful (albeit chilly) swimming pools. You might also spot some mouflon here.

Day 3: Refuge de Carozzu to Haut Asco
6 hours, 6km

This part is graded moderate. Note that there is little water once you've left the Spasimata River behind.

The day starts with a short, rocky zigzagging path up through the forest to a ridge, then a slightly longer drop to the Spasimata River at 1220m. This is crossed on a rickety suspension bridge that is not for the fainthearted. At first the trail edges along above the river, crossing long sloping slabs of rock At some points plastic-coated cables offer handholds, which are reassuring, but note that these rocks can be dangerously slippery when it rains.

Leaving the river with its tempting rock pools, the trail then starts a long, rocky ascent to **Lac de la Muvrella** (1860m), which is reached after three to 3½ hours. The lake water is not safe to drink. If you look back during the final stages of the ascent, you'll see Calvi on the north coast. From the lake it's only a short scramble to the knife-edged ridge. After a short drop on the other side, the trail soon starts to climb again, skirting around the side of A'Muvrella to Bocca a i Stagni (2010m). The total time of ascent from the river is roughly four hours. You can make a one-hour detour from Bocca a i Stagni to the summit of A'Muvrella (2148m).

The day is less taxing than the previous two, ending with a long, 600m descent to Haut Asco, visible far below. **Haut Asco** looks like any ski resort in the off season – bare, dusty and forlorn – but it's a haven for walkers after the spartan conditions of the last couple of days. Changes are in store, however, as there are plans to demolish some of the buildings in coming years.

Refuge d'Asco Stagnu (*camping €3.50, dorm beds €9; menu €13*), at 1422m, has 30 beds in rooms for two, four or six people. It also has hot showers, a huge kitchen and a dining area as well as a terrace. There's plenty of **camping** space on the grassy ski slopes and campers can use the showers at the *refuge*. The welcoming wardens offer a choice of Corsican soup, spaghetti bolognaise, Corsican cheese and desserts.

You can also stay at the **chalet** (☎ 04 95 47 81 08; doubles with shower & toilet €39-46; gîte with/without half board €26/6.50; menu €15, meals €7-11; open 15 May–end Sep) at Haut Asco.

A small **shop** (open 11am-8pm) sells trekking essentials, including freeze-dried food, sausage, cheese, bread, energy bars, chocolate, cereals, fresh fruit and even hiking shoes.

Day 4: Refuge d'Asco Stagnu to Bergeries de Ballone
7 hours, 8km

This is generally held to be the most spectacular day on the GR20, crossing the Cirque de la Solitude, which requires some technical climbing. There is water at the Refuge d'Altore, and from there to the Bergeries de Ballone the trail follows a mountain stream.

From Haut Asco the trail starts on the left (south) side of the ski run. It's easy to lose the trail at the start when it heads away from the ski slope into the trees. If you do wander off the trail, it's not a problem: you can rejoin the route when it climbs above the valley and the ski slopes to cross the glacial moraines. The views over the valley and Haut Asco are stunning.

Allow about two hours to reach the site of the old Refuge d'Altore at 2000m. From the small lake at the site, a steep 45-minute climb leads to Bocca Tumasginesca, or Col Perdu (Lost Pass), at 2183m. From the pass the **Cirque de la Solitude** falls dramatically away beneath your feet. For most walkers this is the highlight of the entire GR20, and one's first reaction is probably sheer amazement that its navigation is possible.

The descent and ascent of the Cirque de la Solitude is more of a rock climb than a walk. However, there are chains bolted into the rock face to make the climb easier. Since other walkers are often almost vertically below you, it's important to take great care not to dislodge rocks or stones as you climb. Typically it takes about 2½ hours to cross the cirque (a steep-sided basin formed by the erosive action of ice).

From Bocca Tumasginesca it is 200m down to the scree-covered valley floor, where many walkers stop for lunch. On the other side the route crosses rock slabs, often guided by fixed cables, and makes a series of steep, rocky, chain-assisted ascents before emerging into an equally steep gully (or couloir) filled with loose rocks and stones. Towards the top the climb becomes a little gentler, before emerging 240m above the valley floor at **Bocca Minuta** (2218m), the second-highest point on the GR20.

Past the ridge the scenery is dramatically different: much wider and more open. The trail makes a long and at times steep descent down the Ravin de Stranciacone before reaching the Refuge de Tighjettu about 1¼ hours after leaving Bocca Minuta.

Refuge de Tighjettu (camping €3.50, dorm beds €9), at 1640m, has limited camping space, so many campers prefer to pitch their tents lower down, by the river. Note that the river rises rapidly when there are storms. The warden sells **food**, such as Corsican cheese and sausage, but doesn't prepare meals.

It's only another 30 minutes' walk down the valley to the **Bergeries de Ballone** (camping €3.50; menu €14; open Jun-Oct), at 1440m. There are lots of good spots at which to pitch your tent around the bergeries and **camping** or bivouacking is free. Beds are also available in a large tent for €5.

The bergeries has a popular **restaurant** and **bar**, with beer, wine, snacks and breakfast, and three-course Corsican meals.

Day 5: Bergeries de Ballone to Castel di Verghio
7 hours, 13km

Day 5 contains a half-day option, with the possibility of breaking the journey at the Refuge de Ciottulu di i Mori, with access to the villages of Calasima and Albertacce – from Bergeries de Ballone (for details, see the Side Trip: Calasima & Albertacce, opposite). It has been graded moderate.

The day begins with a gently undulating ascent through pine forests where streams tumble down from the hills to the west to join the Viru River at the valley floor. Across the valley to the east you can see the road leading up from Albertacce to Calasima, at

1100m the highest village in Corsica. The trail turns west round the eastern slope of Paglia Orba and then emerges from the forest for the steep and rocky slog up to Bocca di Foghieghiallu (Col de Fogghiale; 1962m) after about three hours.

On the other side of the pass a wide valley opens out to the south, but the route continues west crossing the slopes of Paglia Orba and climbing slightly to reach the *refuge*.

Refuge de Ciottulu di i Mori *(camping €3.50, dorm beds €9; meals €5-7)*, at 1991m, is the highest *refuge* in the entire GR20; it has 26 beds. Along one side of the building there's a terrace looking out over the valley below. Directly behind the *refuge* is Paglia Orba (2525m), the third-highest peak in Corsica. Climbers may want to attempt the three-hour round trip to the summit of the mountain via the Col des Maures, but the final stretch includes some reasonably challenging rock climbing. This is not an ascent for beginners.

The route continues round to the western side of the Vallée du Golo, descending slightly to 1907m before dropping steeply down to the river at 1700m, just below the ruins of the Bergeries de Tula. For the next couple of hours the walk follows the impressively rocky ravine of the **Golo River**, passing a series of appealing rock pools. The **path** tracing the lower part of the valley was, for many centuries, a traditional route along which farmers took their livestock when migrating to summer pastures.

The valley narrows before the trail reaches the Cascade de Radule (1370m) and the **Bergeries de Radule**, after five to six hours. Cheese is sometimes sold at the *bergeries*. For the final hour you walk through the beech forests of the Valdu Niellu, passing the signposted turn-off to the Fer à Cheval bend (many walkers choose to join the GR20 at this point) and crossing the Mare a Mare Nord trail (p218) before finally emerging on the D84 just 100m west of the ski station of Castel di Verghio (1404m). The ski slopes are on the other side of the road.

Hôtel Castel di Verghio *(☎ 04 95 48 00 01; camping €5; gîte with/without half board*

A Taste of Corsica

Corsican food is essentially Mediterranean food embellished with local produce. Some of its more characteristic dishes are best eaten in the winter: game, stews, soup with green beans, potatoes and ham bones, and sumptuous casseroles *(stufati)*. Pigs are allowed to range freely through the inland forests, feeding on acorns and chestnuts, and their meat is turned into excellent *lonzu* (preserved pork fillet), *prisuttu* (cured ham) and sausages. Local preserved meats *(charcuterie)* are rarely supplied commercially, but can be sampled in the B&B farmhouses around the island.

Brocciu, a Corsican version of fromage frais, is an indispensable ingredient in many Corsican dishes. Best tasted when very fresh (within three days of making), it features in omelettes, lasagnes, sweet and savoury fritters, or is served simply with a sprinkling of maquis herbs.

No discussion of Corsican gastronomy is complete without mention of its superb seafood. Sea urchins, grilled moray eels, sardines stuffed with *brocciu* and bouillabaisse are some of the fresh local delicacies available.

€29/12, singles/doubles/triples €40/43/61 with shower & basin; menu €15; open Apr-Oct) is about 2km from Col di Verghio on the main D84 road between Porto and Corte. The hotel also has washing machines and dryers, though they don't always work.

The hotel's **restaurant** attracts hordes of hungry walkers every evening. The hotel **bar** sells a good range of basic foodstuffs. Credit cards are not accepted.

For information on transport from Castel di Verghio, see p201.

Side Trip: Calasima & Albertacce
3 or 5 hours return

You can get to Calasima (1100m) in 1½ hours from the Bergeries de Ballone. The only facility in Calasima is the **Bar d' Centre**, but it's only another 6km downh' to Albertacce which is on the D84.

Albertacce has shops, cafés and resta ants. There's a small **grocery** oppo the *gîte d'étape*. Restaurants include the very popular **Auberge U Cintu** *(Chez Jojo;* ☎ *04 95 95 48 06 87; menus €13 & €17)* and the **Brasserie du Golo**, where you can get *panini* and sandwiches.

Day 6: Castel di Verghio to Refuge de Manganu
5½ hours, 14km

This day of the GR20 follows a particularly shady route and is of moderate difficulty. Water is available at a spring in a shrine just above Lac de Ninu and at a stream flowing from the lake close to the night's stop.

The GR20 runs gently through pine and beech forests, dropping gently to 1330m before making a sharp turn to the right (west) and climbing to the small shrine at Bocca San Pedru (Col de Saint Pierre; 1452m), reached after about 1½ hours.

From the pass the route continues to climb, following the carefully laid stones of an ancient mule path and offering superb views to the east. The trail climbs to a ridge, drops off it, climbs back on to it and eventually reaches Bocca a Reta (1883m). It then descends to **Lac de Ninu** (1760m), 3½ hours from the start. Surrounded by grassy meadows and *pozzines* (interlinked waterholes – see the boxed text on p210), the lake makes a wonderfully tranquil stop for lunch.

The trail continues to the east, following the course of the Tavignano stream, which drains the lake, across meadows and then through patches of beech forest past the remains of an abandoned *refuge* to the **Bergeries de Vaccaghja** (1621m), one to 1½ hours from the lake. The *bergeries* usually sells wine, cheese and bread. From here you can see the Refuge de Manganu, less than an hour's walk across the valley. The trail drops gently from the *bergeries* to Bocca d'Acqua Ciarnente (1568m) and finally makes a short, sharp ascent, crossing a bridge over the Manganu stream to the Refuge de Manganu.

The pleasant **Refuge de Manganu** *(camping €3.05, dorm beds €8.40)*, at 1601m, has 5 beds and plenty of grassy **camping space** around the building, good showers and toilets and a selection of tempting swimming spots

in the Manganu stream. Cheese, cooked meats and drinks should be available.

Day 7: Refuge de Manganu to Refuge de Pietra Piana
6 hours, 10km

This is a hard day, as the route climbs to the highest point on the GR20 before teetering round a spectacular mountain face that drops down to glacial lakes. Water is available from streams during the first ascent and from another stream on the final descent to the Refuge de Pietra Piana.

After crossing the bridge from the Refuge de Manganu, the GR20 immediately begins to climb, emerging onto a small meadow after 30 minutes, climbing again to another brief, horizontal break at around 1970m and then ascending even more steeply up a rocky gully. This finally becomes a scramble to the **Brèche de Capitellu** (2225m), a spectacular small slot through the spiky ridge line of peaks. Around 2½ hours from the *refuge*, this crossing is the highest point on the GR20 and the view to the east is breathtaking.

The trail bends to the southeast and edges around the eastern face of the ridge, high above the lake. There's often snow on the path well into the walking season, so take great care; it's a long way down. Just before another small pass at 2000m, where the trail crosses to the southern side of the ridge, another trail diverges off to the east and drops down to Lac de Capitellu. It's possible to continue down from there to Lac de Melu (1711m) and then climb back up to the GR20 at Bocca a Soglia.

The main route climbs slightly to reach Bocca a Soglia (2050m), about an hour's walk from the Brèche de Capitellu. Lots of day-trippers drive into the valley from Corte to walk up to the lakes.

The trail then bends to the northeast, high above Lac de Melu, climbing to the soft-edged little Bocca Rinosa (2150m) and passing Lac de Rinosa before reaching Bocca Muzzella (Col de la Haute Route; 2206m), about five hours from the start of the day. From here it's less than an hour, downhill all the way, to the Refuge de Pietra Piana.

The small, 28-bed **Refuge de Pietra Piana** (camping €3.50, dorm beds €9; meals €5-7), at 1842m, is nicely situated right on the edge of the ridge, looking south down the Vallée du Manganellu. There's plenty of grassy camping space and good facilities. There are two toilets and two solar-heated showers that sometimes have hot water. Various hot dishes, home-made cakes, snacks and bread are also sold.

Side Trip: Monte Ritondu
3 hours return
The keen walkers may consider climbing Monte Ritondu (2622m), the second-highest mountain in Corsica. It's not a technically demanding climb, although the 800m ascent may be a little tiring at the end of the day.

Cairns mark the route to a meadow and dried-up lake just above the *refuge*. The trail then zigzags uphill before crossing the ridge at 2260m, south of the peak. Don't descend from the ridge towards the small lakes below – continue north along the eastern side of the ridge, crossing patches of snow until the large Lavu Bellebone lake comes into view. The trail drops down to the lake's southern end and edges round the southeastern side before starting the steep climb up the slope of the rocky gully that leads to the spiky rock marking the Col du Fer de Lance. From here the trail turns west and climbs to a small metal-roofed shelter, huddled just below the summit. There are superb views in all directions from the summit.

Day 8: Refuge de Pietra Piana to Refuge de l'Onda
5 hours, 10km
An easy, mostly shady day's walk, the trail follows streams almost all day so water is no problem.

After the dramatic ascents and descents of the previous day, this section of the walk is gentle and predominantly downhill. As soon as the trail leaves the *refuge* there's a choice between following the main GR20 through the Vallée du Manganellu or taking an alternative high-altitude route (with double-yellow markings), which follows ridges to the Refuge de l'Onda. The high-altitude route is quicker but less interesting. It takes four hours, includes some technical and exposed stretches and has superb views over Ajaccio.

The main GR20 starts to drop almost immediately and soon reaches the Bergeries de Gialgu (1609m). The trail continues to drop, following an ancient mule track of neatly laid stones that winds down the hill to the Manganellu stream at 1440m. It then plunges through often dense forest to the **Bergerie de Tolla** (1011m), about three hours from the start. This pleasant little haven sells the usual supplies, and also serves snacks and meals.

Just below the *bergerie* a bridge crosses the Manganellu stream (940m). From here you can detour off the GR20 to the villages of Canaglia and Tattone (see the side trip on this page).

The GR20 then turns upstream from the bridge and almost immediately passes over the Goltaccia, which flows into the Manganellu. Do not cross over this bridge; instead continue upstream and uphill beside the Goltaccia. Eventually the trail crosses the river and climbs away to the north side, soon reaching the **Bergeries de l'Onda** (camping €3.50; meals €5-7), a summer hive of activity next to the Refuge de l'Onda's grassy camping site. The *bergeries* sells wine, bread, cheese, sausages and prepared meals. It is surrounded by fences to keep the many pigs and sheep from poking around the site.

Refuge de l'Onda (dorm beds €9) itself is higher up the hill, overlooking the *bergeries* and camp site from 1430m. It has 16 beds, one shower and one toilet, but is not as appealing as the *bergeries*.

Side Trip: Canaglia & Tattone
2 or 4 hours return
The walk is between a half and one hour from the Manganellu bridge on the GR20 to the pretty village of Canaglia. The wide track running alongside the river and the string of little pools make this a popular route with walkers. At Canaglia's small **restaurant**, the **Osteria u Capitan Moru**, trout and Corsican dishes are a speciality. There's a phone in the restaurant.

Lakes & Pozzines

Corsica's 40-odd high-altitude lakes, formed from the glaciers that used to cover the mountains, were unknown to scientists until the 1980s but are now actively monitored by PNRC personnel. A number of different analyses have shown that some are endangered by the digging of pigs and the pollution caused by tourist overpopulation in the summer. The PNRC has implemented a protection programme for the most popular lakes – Melu, Ninu and Creno – in the summer. Seasonal workers collect the rubbish left by walkers and ensure that the camping bans are upheld. The GR20 has even been diverted so that it does not contribute to the destruction of the grassy areas around Lac de Ninu. Respect the rules: no fires, no rubbish and no walking at inappropriate times.

The *pozzines* (from the Corsican *pozzi*, meaning pits) are also a fragile environment, threatened by intensive farming. *Pozzines* are little water holes that are linked together by small streams and are on an impermeable substratum – they're like peat bogs. They feel like a carpet of cool moss to walkers. They are found near Lac de Ninu and on the Plateau de Coscione, between the GR20 and the Refuge des Bergeries de Bassetta.

From Canaglia it's 4km by road to Tattone. For a taxi call Alain (☎ 04 95 47 20 06, 06 07 89 16 10) in Vivario.

In Tattone, the **Bar Camping du Soleil** (☎ 04 95 47 21 16; camping €6; pizzas €5-8), near the train station, has a **pizzeria** and a **bar** that also sells snacks.

Refuge Chez Pierrot (☎ 04 95 47 20 65, 06 14 66 42 20, gîte with/without half board €26/11, bookings essential) has 18 beds in three dorms and two bathrooms with hot showers. Pierrot is a real character and offers local specialities as well as snacks.

From Tattone, Pierrot (of the eponymous *refuge* on the N193) will come and pick you up in Canaglia or Vizzavona and will take you to your preferred departure point the following day. This is a good way to short-circuit the GR20 route between Pietra Piana and Vizzavona.

Day 9: Refuge de l'Onda to Vizzavona

5½ hours, 10km

This is traditionally the mid-stage of the GR20, and ends in Vizzavona (opposite), the best-equipped stop along the GR20. Water is plentiful along the trail.

This moderately graded route sets off north, following the high-altitude alternative route to the Refuge de Pietra Piana, but soon doubles back to head south up the long climb to the **Crête du Muratellu** (2020m), reached after 2½ hours. From this windswept height the rest of the day's walk is a long descent.

An alternative route, marked only by stone cairns, continues up the Crête du Muratellu and turns slightly northeast to Bocca di u Porcu (2159m), from where it turns southeast to climb to the summit of Monte d'Oro (2389m), the fifth-highest mountain in Corsica. There are stretches of difficult rock climbing on this route, which should not be attempted by inexperienced climbers. It rejoins the main GR20 route just before Vizzavona and adds about three hours to the day's walk.

The main GR20 makes a steep and rocky descent (which can be slippery in the rain) from the Muratellu ridge into the upper heights of the Vallée de l'Agnone. The descent becomes less steep and the surroundings greener as the route drops below 1600m and passes the remains of an abandoned *refuge* at 1500m. The trail passes a high waterfall, the **Cascades des Anglais** (1150m), roughly four hours from the start and continues through pine forests, sometimes high above the tumbling stream. Monte d'Oro broods over this scene from the northeast.

A **snack bar** and a bridge over the Agnone hint at the proximity of civilisation, and from here into Vizzavona the route makes the transition from walking path to a track quite suitable for cars. There are several turns, several bridges and what seems like an interminable trudge before the trail finally emerges onto the road right in the middle of the village of Vizzavona, only a short distance from the train station.

Vizzavona

Vizzavona (910m) is a tiny health spa at the foot of the massive Monte d'Oro. Those who tackle the whole of the GR20 consider it a welcome return to civilisation and generally make the most of the opportunity to restock with provisions and have a decent meal and a good night's sleep in a **hotel**. Vizzavona traditionally marks the division between the north and south sections of the GR20.

Vizzavona is situated at the heart of one of the prettiest forests in Corsica, an excellent setting for a number of well-marked shady walks.

Places to Stay & Eat Campers should be able to pitch their **tents** on a new site opposite the station, which is often full to bursting in summer. There are no toilets or washing facilities. You can have a hot shower (€1) at the station; ask the station master. The PNRC plans to set up an official camping ground with bathrooms and toilets.

Hôtel I Laricci (☎ 04 95 47 21 12; www.ilaricci.com - French only; dorm beds/singles/doubles €25/54/70, with half board €29/58/75; menu €15; open Apr-end Oct), looking like a big Swiss chalet, has 12 spacious and pleasant, though somewhat noisy, double rooms. Several rooms have views over Monte d'Oro. You'll need to book ahead as it's very popular. You can do your washing for €8. Credit cards are accepted.

Just opposite the station is the friendly, family-run **Resto Refuge de la Gare** (☎/fax 04 95 47 22 20; dorm beds with/without half board €23/12; menu €12; open Jun-Sep), home to a restaurant and clean, renovated dormitories that accommodate 25 people. Meals are optional, but there are no self-catering facilities. There are also two rooms with half board at €50.

You can do some serious stocking up at the grocery store, **Épicerie Rosy** (open from 7.30am daily), which is in the station. It sells just about everything walkers could want at quite reasonable prices.

Just opposite is the **Restaurant-Bar l'Altagna** (menus €12-15). Local specialities and tasty snacks are also served all day.

Getting There & Away For information on public transport services between Vizzavona and the coastal towns of Ajaccio and Bastia, see p201.

Day 10: Vizzavona to Bergeries de Capannelle

5½ hours, 13.5km

This section of the walk, graded moderate, is punctuated by magnificent views as you approach Monte Renosu against a background of laricio pine and beech trees.

From the station in Vizzavona, follow the marked route for the GR20 Sud, which passes in front of Hôtel I Laricci. It first crosses the access path to the GR20 Nord on the right and then crosses a little bridge before climbing to rejoin the N193 and the ONF (Office National des Forêts; National Forestry Office) house, which you'll reach after 15 minutes. The trail then joins a wide path leading to a sign that tells you that Bergeries de Capannelle is five hours away. Shortly after, the GR20 leaves this path and ascends to the left. You'll then come to a fork (the right fork leads to a spring 450m away).

The route quickly leaves the dirt track behind and makes a twisting ascent to a high-voltage power cable (about an hour from the start) that marks the start of a long, flat trek through the undergrowth. A steep little path leads straight ahead until it intersects with a path with yellow markings. Here the GR20 goes off to your left, but make a detour 100m down the right fork for a wonderful **view** of Monte d'Oro and Vizzavona below.

Back on the GR20, the path emerges from the undergrowth into a bare, almost lunar landscape from where you can see Bocca Palmente (1647m) ahead. Pay attention to the markings and the junction where the GR20 turns right to the pass, just over 15 minutes' climb away.

The path goes back down towards the Bergeries d'Alzeta before continuing level. After about 30 minutes a hairpin bend marks the left turn-off that leads to Ghisoni. This **turn-off**, with a stunning view over the Monte Renosu massif, is an ideal spot for a picnic.

The GR20 continues along the hillside and goes through a forest of laricio pines, some of which are an impressive size. About 1¼ hours later it reaches the charming Bergeries de Scarpaccedie.

A short distance on, the route bears to the right before a steep uphill stretch (a good 20 minutes of solid effort) to a wonderful view of Monte Renosu (2352m). You'll then see a sign extolling the virtues of the beer on tap at the Gîte U Fugone at Capannelle. It's a 20-minute walk from the sign to the **Bergeries de Capannelle**, which are at the foot of the ski lifts in the resort area of Ghisoni (not the village). Although there is only one remaining shepherd, all the *bergeries* kept by local families now serve as cottages for holidaymakers and hunters.

Straight ahead, the **Gîte U Fugone** (☎ 04 95 57 01 81, 04 95 56 39 34; *dorm beds with half board €28; menus €9.20-18.50; open May-Sep*) offers good value for money. The dorms have four or five beds, and showers and toilets are in a big building that resembles a high-altitude restaurant. There are 70 beds all up and half board is preferred. A little **grocery** sells basic foodstuffs; the **restaurant** has *menus* based on Corsican specialities and generous meals for those who opt for half board.

The **Gîte U Renosu**, 300m away, is only open in winter.

Just before the Gîte U Fugone is the **PNRC refuge** (*dorm beds €4.50*). Although in a charming house made entirely of stone, the *refuge* is somewhat dubious in terms of comfort. The fee is collected by the warden of the Gîte U Fugone, where you can have a hot shower (€2.50). Information about the rest of the GR20 is sometimes displayed here.

You can also **camp** for free near the Gîte U Fugone. Cold showers are available and also free but you can have a hot shower at the *gîte*.

Day 11: Bergeries de Capannelle to Bocca di Verdi
5 hours, 11.5km

This day is relatively short and easy, keeping largely to a plain at around 1500m. If you wish to extend the day, a two-hour detour to the *pozzi* plain is an attractive option. The route begins at the foot of the ski lifts (follow the white-and-red markings to Bocca di Verdi and not the path leading to Lac Bastani) and rapidly heads into a forest of beech trees that hint at the once idyllic setting of the Bergeries de Capannelle before the construction of the ski resort.

It will take less than 30 minutes to reach the Bergeries de Traggette (1520m). You then follow a fast-flowing stream down to the D169, which you should reach within an hour. Fifty metres farther on the route heads uphill again. There are views over the Fiumorbu region and the Kyrie Eleïson range before the path enters a thick forest of pine and beech.

After 45 minutes, the GR20 rounds a hairpin bend to the right. When the snow is melting you will have to cross a string of streams here, some of which may require acrobatic skills. Another 45 minutes later there's a second hairpin bend, this time in the open.

You are now halfway through the day's walk and right next to **Punta Capannella** (2032m); above you, the Lischetto stream, which flows from the little Lacs de Rina (1882m), cascades down in a profusion of small waterfalls.

Once you have crossed the Lischetto, it will not take more than 30 minutes to get to the **Plateau de Gialgone** (1591m), with an invigorating view over Bocca di Verdi. In front of you is **Monte Grossu** (1895m) and, at the edge of the plain, a wooden sign directs you to the *pozzi*, a magnificent grassy plain that may be worth the detour (allow two hours to get there and back).

The GR20 itself carries straight on towards Bocca di Verdi and begins an impressive zigzagging descent that culminates some 30 minutes later in a little wooden bridge straddling the Marmanu stream.

A few metres on you'll see the remains of a giant fir tree that once rose to the amazing height of 53.2m. The path then continues level until it reaches a big group of rocks. The trail then widens out and after about 15 minutes reaches a large picnic area.

To the right is a path through the forest that goes to the village of Palneca, while a path to the left leads to Bocca di Verdi (Col de Verde) after about 300m.

Relais San Pedru di Verde (☎ 04 95 24 46 82; *camping per person/tent €4/5; dorm beds with/without half board €27/10; daily special €12; open May-15 Oct),* better known as the Refuge du Col de Verde, is in a lush green setting on the edge of the D69. The main, wooden cottage has a dorm for 20 people and is equipped with a stove. The sanitation facilities are in good order and the two showers (included in the price) are hot.

One of the best things about this *refuge* is its lovely terrace, where you can enjoy salads and grilled and cooked meats. The place is sometimes overrun by walkers wanting to **lunch** there.

Day 12: Bocca di Verdi to Refuge d'Usciolu

7–7½ hours, 14km

This is one of the longer and more difficult days of the GR20, including some very steep sections and occasional high winds on the exposed ridges.

After crossing a minor road, the trail ascends gently through a pine forest to a turn-off (10 minutes). Once it turns left, the real climbing begins. It takes 20 minutes of sustained effort to reach an intermediate plateau – the end of the first section.

A stream marks the start of the second steep section (which is at least shaded by beech trees). After another hour of tough, unshaded climbing, you will reach **Bocca d'Oru** (1840m), with excellent views over the eastern plain.

A very pleasant walk then leads, after about 15 minutes, to **Refuge de Prati** *(camping €3.50, dorm beds €9; meals €8)* at 1820m. It has been totally rebuilt after being destroyed by lightning. This PNRC *refuge*, which has 28 beds and one (cold) shower, attracts many walkers who prefer to add two hours to Day 11 in order to make Day 12 easier. The *refuge* also has other attractions: it's in a beautiful setting with a lawn that's ideal for camping and has a friendly warden who has good hot and cold **food** on offer.

You should fill your flask at the *refuge*'s **water fountain**, as there are no other water sources for the rest of the day. The GR20 follows the path to the right (a path to the left marked in yellow goes down to the village of Isolacciu di Fiumorbu) and leads straight on to the ridge.

This very steep stretch only lasts about 20 minutes, but the rest of the path remains steep and rocky. Make the most of the view (over the villages of Palneca, Ciamannacce and Cozzano) because you will need all your strength to negotiate the next 30-minute section up through large rocks (this can be dangerous in bad weather conditions – so take great care). For the next 1¼ hours the path along the ridge is rocky and difficult, coming very close to some frightening precipices at times. However, you do get some spectacular views.

Once past Punta di a Cappella (2042m), the trail skirts round the Rocher de la Penta before moving off the ridge and into a little forest that is an ideal spot for a picnic. From here it's less than 30 minutes to **Bocca di Laparu** (1525m), where the route crosses the Mare a Mare Centre walk (p218). There's a sign to a spring here. Count on three hours to go from the Refuge de Prati to Bocca di Laparu. The trail to Cozzano leaves the GR20 from here (see the side trip, p214).

After the pass, the trail continues along the ridge, climbing steadily up to **Monte Formicula** (1981m), the highest point of the day and a little less than 500m above Laparu. Allow between 1¾ and two hours for the climb. You'll walk along the east side of the ridge before shifting to the windier western side.

Once past Monte Formicula, it is not much farther to the Refuge d'Usciolu (roughly 30 to 45 minutes) and, rather like a Sunday afternoon walk, it's downhill all the way.

Leaning against the mountain, **Refuge d'Usciolu** *(camping €3.50, dorm beds €9; meals €7)* has a bird's-eye view over the whole valley. The *refuge* (the only accommodation on this day) has 32 beds and is clean and well kept. The **camp site** is just below the *refuge*. The warden there will prepare pasta and meat dishes on request and has a range of supplies fit for a grocery, including cooked meats, cheese, bread, chocolate, sweets and drinks.

Side Trip: Cozzano
5 hours return
The route to Cozzano forms part of the Mare a Mare Centre walk (p218). It descends from Bocca di Laparu for about 25 minutes before crossing two streams and entering a splendid forest of laricio pine. It then leads to a forest track. Turn left and before long you'll pass a fast-flowing stream. There's a natural spring next to the path 200m farther on. Follow the path for half an hour until you see a sign for Cozzano pointing towards a little path heading down into the forest.

Forty minutes later the trail joins a recently made forest road that continues down. After 10 minutes you'll come to a small stream on the left; at a bend a few hundred metres farther on, the path goes back into the forest. Be careful as it's easy to miss the orange markings (don't follow the red markers). The path is lined with oak trees and majestic *châtaigniers* (chestnut trees) and crosses the forest road, before following a dry river bed, which starts at a pigsty on the left.

After three hours of downhill walking, you'll come to a large **stream**, where you can bathe, and finally to a sealed road. Turn left and the road will take you into the centre of Cozzano; turn right and you'll reach the *gîte rural*.

On the other side of the village, towards Palneca (to the north), a large building houses the **Gîte Rural Bella Vista** (*☎ 04 95 24 41 59; camping per person €5, dorm beds/ doubles €10/28, half board per person €28; breakfast €5*), which has six dormitories for six people each. You can **camp** in the garden and there is a self-catering kitchen. For those who don't feel like cooking, an evening meal is offered.

There are two **snack bars** in Cozzano, one at either end of the village: **U Mezzanu** (*☎ 04 95 24 40 82; meals €5.35-9.20, sandwiches €3.80; open May-Sep*) and **Snack Bar Terminus**.

Cozzano is the only village in the area with a **pharmacy** (*☎ 04 95 24 40 40; open 9am-12.30pm & 3-7.30pm Mon-Sat*); it's in the main square. The main square also contains a well-stocked **grocery** (*open 9am-noon & 3-7pm Mon-Sat & Sun morning*). For information on public transport links to Cozzano, see p201.

Day 13: Refuge d'Usciolu to Refuge d'Asinao
7½–8 hours, 14.5km
It's possible to do this section over two days, with a detour to the village of Zicavo (not described here) or a stop-off at the Bergeries de Bassetta, climbing Monte Incudine on the second day.

From the Refuge d'Usciolu, a short, steep path leads back up to the ridge. There's a sign to Cozzano, where it is possible, but not very practical, to stop off. From here it's a tightrope walk along the **ridge**, which is particularly steep at this stage, for a good two hours.

The altitude is an almost constant 1800m, but the trail goes up and down in a continual series of tiny ascents and descents, making the going very hard, particularly across large slabs of rock. There's no shade and the signs are not always easy to find, but the views are sublime.

Two hours from the start the trail passes a distinctive U-shaped gap, then drops down towards a grove of beeches on the western side of the ridge.

After about three hours you'll reach a wonderful, shady clearing – an ideal place for lunch. The pastoral setting, with streams and majestic beech trees, is in stark contrast to the barren austerity of the route along the top of the ridge. There's also a spring, which is signposted. About 10 minutes from here the trail reaches the crossroads at Bocca di l'Agnonu, about 3¼ hours from the start of the day.

The route continues among the beech trees for about 20 minutes, leading to an overhang with wonderful views. The trail then moves out of the beeches and onto the hilly plain. The route is easy until it reaches the foot of Monte Incudine, which you summit later in the day. After about an hour the trail reaches the southern junction with the alternative route via Zicavo and the Refuge des Bergeries de Bassetta to the west.

Another option, if you would rather complete this section over two days, is the impeccably run **Refuge des Bergeries de Bassetta** (☎ *04 95 25 74 20, 06 87 44 04 08; dorm beds €11, half board in chalet per person €30.50; menu €17, daily special €8)*, roughly 1½ hours' walk off the GR20 (with only a slight change in altitude). This private *refuge* is a converted old *bergerie* and is well worth the detour as this is a very picturesque area. It is 1.5km from the Chapelle San Petru and is also accessible by road from Zicavo, about 14km away along the D428 and D69. The refuge has 17 beds, some in the former *bergerie*, others in small, recently built chalets. Excellent Corsican meals are served in a big communal room with a fireplace.

Shortly after the junction for the Bergeries de Bassetta, the trail crosses a rickety wooden footbridge over the Casamintellu and the ascent of Monte Incudine begins. After about 30 minutes, you reach **Aire de Bivouac i Pedinieddi**. This little plateau used to be home to the Refuge de Pedinieddi, until it was destroyed by lightning. It's possible to **bivouac** here and there is a water supply.

About one hour's walk from the footbridge, you reach Bocca di Luana (1800m), which is on a ridge. The route turns to the right and begins the difficult climb to the ridge leading to the summit. A strenuous 1¼ hours from Bocca di Luana, you'll reach the cross on the summit of **Monte Incudine** (2134m). It is not uncommon for there to be snow here until June.

All that's left now is the descent to the *refuge*. The first 15 minutes is an easy walk along the ridge. The trail reaches a junction and you can see what lies ahead: the path plummets down to the *refuge* 500m below. The slope really is impressive, and your joints will certainly feel it. Allow 1¼ to 1½ hours to descend from the summit to the Refuge d'Asinao.

Refuge d'Asinao *(camping €3.50, dorm beds €9)*, at 1530m, only has room for 20 people. Basic **refreshments** (cooked meats, honey, cheese, beer and wine) are sold and the warden sometimes prepares soup (€3 to €4). From the *refuge* you can see the Bergeries d'Asinao below.

Day 14: Refuge d'Asinao to Refuge de Paliri via the Alpine Route
6¼ hours, 13km

This day offers a spectacular alpine alternative to the main trail not long after starting out. From the Refuge d'Asinao, the GR20 path heads west before gradually turning south to reach the valley, where you ford the Asinao River at about 30 minutes' walk. On the way you will pass a sign indicating a turn-off to Quenza, a jewel among villages on the Mare a Mare Sud trail (p218). It is three to four hours from the GR20 and boasts a *gîte d'étape*, several hotels, as well as two grocery stores, a post office and telephone boxes.

On the other side of the Asinao River the path climbs gently and then evens out along the side of the mountain at an average altitude of 1300m. The route is easy and pleasant, following a ledge above the Asinao for about one hour. In places you can just about see through the foliage to the towering foothills of the Massif de Bavella.

After about 1½ hours of walking you reach a crossroads. Straight ahead is the main GR20 route, which skirts the Bavella mountainside to the southwest of the massif. Taking off at 90° to the left of the normal path, the **Alpine Route** (described here) takes you to the heart of the massif and is marked out in yellow – it is, without doubt, one of the highlights of the GR20. The two paths converge shortly before Bocca di Bavella.

Deviating from the official trail to follow the Alpine Route, this section of the GR20 is one of the most beautiful. However, it is also demanding technically, passing through fallen rocks and stones and requiring you to use your hands across a chained slab of rock in one section. If you get vertigo or feel uneasy about heights, it is advisable to take the main route. It is also worth avoiding this option in the wet, as there is a real risk of slipping.

The climb up the mountainside is very steep. There is a short respite for about 10 minutes, then the path leaves the wooded section and continues to climb towards **Bocca di u Pargulu** (1662m), reaching it after an hour. Towards the end, the rock faces, with their knife-edge points, can feel overwhelming. When you get to the top and see the panoramic views, however, it will all seem unimportant. In the jagged landscape you can make out peaks that look like huge sharp teeth – these are the **Aiguilles de Bavella** (Bavella Needles).

From here the path descends steeply through a stony gully for about 30 minutes until it reaches the famous chain across a smooth, steep slab, about 10m in width. This should pose no problems in dry weather. After another 30 minutes of tricky progress along rocky slopes you'll reach a pass, where you have a wonderful view of the peaks and the village of Bavella close by to the east. The path to Bavella plunges through a deep gully of pink granite. The markings are sometimes less than adequate during this difficult descent.

Roughly four hours after you set out, the path rejoins the normal route of the GR20. It is then only a short stroll through a pine forest to Bocca di Bavella car park.

Go past the Madone des Neiges (a statue of the Virgin Mary) and take the sealed road (one of the few concessions to civilisation on the GR20) to the left for about 300m. This leads into the village of **Bavella**.

It may be worth stopping off in Bavella, as the Refuge de Paliri, at the end of the day, does not provide refreshments. Some walkers choose to leave the GR20 here, although this is a shame as the last stage of the traverse is quite picturesque.

Les Aiguilles de Bavella (☎ *04 95 72 01 88; beds in 2–4-bed rooms €12.50, half board €27.50; open Apr-15 Oct*), near the Madone des Neiges, provides food and shelter. There is a kitchenette and the **restaurant** provides Corsican meals.

About 300m farther towards the village, on a hairpin bend, is the **Auberge du Col de Bavella** (☎ *04 95 72 09 87; dorm beds with/ without half board €28/12.50; menus €14.50 & €20; open mid-Mar–mid-Nov*), which has dorms with six beds and an excellent reputation, especially for its food. You can choose from three Corsican *menus* or a range of salads, omelettes, pasta dishes and desserts. Credit cards are accepted.

Next door is **Le Refuge** (☎ *04 95 72 08 84; rooms €23; open May-Sep*), another *refuge-restaurant-bar*. Rooms accommodate up to four people, and simple meals are available.

There's a **grocery** opposite the Auberge du Col de Bavella, but it's not particularly well stocked.

For information on public transport services to Bavella, see p201.

If you wish to continue to the Refuge de Paliri, allow another 2¼ hours. The only difficult section is around Bocca di Foce Finosa. When you reach the Auberge du Col de Bavella on the road into Bavella, take the turn-off to the right, which changes into a forest track 50m farther on.

The walk is pleasant and easy, and follows a level route through a forest of pine trees and ferns for 15 minutes. The path then narrows before forking to the left and descending to a small stream. About 10 minutes later you come to a forest track – follow it to the right for 50m. Turn left at the fork and cross the Volpajola stream on the small concrete bridge.

Opposite, to the east, is a long range of mountains, which you will cross via Bocca di Foce Finosa. Five minutes from the stream, the path forks to the right to begin the ascent. It takes a strenuous 45 minutes to climb 200m in altitude to Bocca di Foce Finosa (1214m).

The last section of the route is the hour's walk to the Refuge de Paliri (1055m), down the east face of the range. The descent starts sharply, then turns northeast and levels out. A small peak just before you reach the *refuge* marks the end of this long section.

Built on the site and with the stones of a former *bergerie*, the little **Refuge de Paliri** (*dorm camping €3.50, dorm beds €9*) has 20 beds and is not lacking in style. It is also in a magnificent setting. On a clear day you can see as far as Sardinia to the south. The warden has looked after the *refuge* since 1981, and it is clean and well maintained. There are toilets and a kitchenette area with equipment but the *refuge* does not sell any food. The only source of drinking **water** is a stream 200m below the *refuge*.

Day 15: Refuge de Paliri to Conca

5 hours, 12km

From the *refuge* the path descends briefly before coming to the heart of a superb forest of maritime pines and ferns. On the left is the imposing spectre of the Anima Danata (Damned Soul) at 1091m, with its distinctive sugar-loaf shape. After a short walk along a ledge, you can easily make out the Monte Bracciutu massif to the east and Monte Sordu to the southeast (25 minutes away). The path then follows a ridge that curves northeast round a cirque, in the middle of which are the peaks of the Massif du Bracciutu.

Looking back you can see the hole in the Punta Tafunata di i Paliri, which almost looks like a bull's-eye in the line of mountains extending from northeast to southwest. Follow this ledge for about 30 minutes (there's no shade), until you reach Foce di u Bracciu (917m). At this point the trail turns to head due south.

The trail follows the contour line for about 10 minutes before tackling the ascent of **Bocca di Sordu** (1065m). It takes 30 minutes of difficult climbing to reach the pass, with its distinctive masses of fallen rock. The view from here stretches as far as the sea.

Just after the pass you climb 50m down across a relatively steep granite slab (it could easily become a natural slide in the wet). This leads to a sandy path that slices through a pine forest (about two hours from the start). Five to 10 minutes later the trail emerges at a little plateau dotted with granite domes and strangely shaped piles of rocks. In the background are maquis and a few maritime pines. After about 15 minutes in this setting the path starts to descend. About 2½ hours after setting out you will reach the ruins of **Bergeries de Capellu** (850m). A signpost leads to a spring about 300m to the left of the main path, a good spot for a picnic.

The path leads steadily down to the Punta Pinzuta stream, which you can hear running through the valley.

After three to 3½ hours from the start, the trail fords the stream, then follows its course for a while before crossing back at a large bend. There are big **rock pools** here where you can cool off. A good 20-minute climb takes you out of this steep-sided valley and up to a pass. The path continues along the mountainside, almost level, for 45 minutes until it reaches **Bocca d'Usciolu** (587m), a narrow U-shaped passage through a wall of granite.

The descent into **Conca** in the valley below (20 to 30 minutes) passes through thick undergrowth, emerging at a sealed road (about five hours from the Refuge de Paliri). Turn left, follow the road to a crossroads and then take the road leading down. You will soon be able to see the main road.

On the way into Conca, just opposite the cemetery, is the *gîte d'étape* **La Tonnelle** (*☎ 04 95 71 46 55; camping per person €5, doubles/triples/quads per person €17/14/13, half board €17; breakfast €4; open year-round*). The *gîte* is clean and functional and each room has an en suite. There is also a big common room and a kitchenette. It's also possible to camp (in a shady site). Half board is obligatory in July and August. Foreign currency can be changed here. The *gîte* can also organise shuttle buses to Porto Vecchio (€6) or Sainte Lucie de Porto Vecchio (€3), with a connecting bus to Porto Vecchio.

There's a choice of **snack bars** and **restaurants** in the centre of the village. Conca also has a post office and a well-stocked **grocery**, open daily in summer.

Other Walks

Walking in Corsica is by no means limited to the GR20. Other well-known and much enjoyed walks across the island include the Mare e Monti and Mare a Mare trails, outlined briefly here. Although less publicised than the GR20, these routes take in some spectacular mountain and coastal scenery, with the added bonus of ending each day comfortably in a village. For those who doubt their ability to cope with the GR20, they also offer a shorter and less daunting physical challenge.

THE MARE E MONTI ROUTES

As the name suggests, these are paths between the *mare* (the sea) and the *monti* (the mountains).

Mare e Monti Nord

The Sea to the Northern Mountains route is a superb (and not very demanding) walk from Calenzana (p199) in the Haute-Balagne region to Cargèse, south of Golfe de Porto. It's divided into 10 days of four to seven hours each. Its highest point is 1153m. It passes through several exceptional natural sites, such as the Forêt de Bonifatu, the Réserve Naturelle de Scandola and the Gorges de Spelunca, and stops in some charming villages, notably Galeria, Ota and Évisa.

The route is passable year-round, but the periods before and after the main season (May to June and September to October) are preferable to avoid the worst of the heat. The path crosses the Mare a Mare Nord in two places: Évisa and nearby Marignana.

Mare e Monti Sud

This path runs between the bays of two well-known resorts in the southwest – Porticcio and Propriano. It's divided into five days of five to six hours and ascends to a maximum height of 870m, with stops in Bisinao, Coti-Chiavari (above the two bays), Porto Pollo and Olmeto. The walk ends in Burgo (7km north of Propriano).

There are only two **gîtes d'étape** on the route: in **Bisinao** (☎ *04 95 24 21 66*) and **Burgo** (☎ *04 95 76 15 05*). In the other villages you can stay in a **hotel** or at a **camping ground** or at the **Baracci equestrian farm** (☎ *04 95 76 19 48*).

The highlights are the views over the bays, the historic Genoese towers and the beaches (the Baie de Cupabia and Porto Pollo). Like its northern counterpart, this path is passable year-round and is not particularly difficult. Spring and autumn are the best times. The path meets the Mare a Mare Sud in Burgo.

THE MARE A MARE ROUTES

(see map p193)

Three Mare a Mare (Sea to Sea) paths link the west and east coasts via the mountains in the centre of the island.

Mare a Mare Centre

The Mare a Mare Centre provides an excellent opportunity to explore the more traditional, inland areas of Corsica. The walk can be completed in seven days of three to seven hours each. Starting in Ghisonaccia, on the east coast, and finishing in Porticcio, on the west coast, it passes through the little-known districts of Fiumorbu and Taravu before crossing the hinterland of Ajaccio.

Unlike the GR20, which stays high in the mountains away from settlements, the Mare a Mare Centre passes through some of the prettiest villages on the island. The route is generally less taxing and less crowded than the GR20. It offers considerable comfort with **gîtes** (with restaurants) and **hotels** every night.

The maximum altitude is 1525m at Bocca di Laparu, so the best time to undertake the walk is between April and November. Take a detailed map as the markings are not very regular. There are no ATMs on the trail and the *gîtes* don't take credit cards.

Mare a Mare Nord

From Moriani on the east coast to Cargèse in the west, this path passes through vastly contrasting areas and is split into 10 days, each lasting from four to six hours and reaching altitudes of up to 1600m. For the final section of the walk, between Évisa and Cargèse, the route merges with that of the Mare e Monti Nord.

It is better to avoid the period between November and April, when parts of the route may still be under snow.

Mare a Mare Sud

This route is passable year-round. It is a famous, easy walk that links Porto Vecchio in the southeast to Propriano in the southwest. The walk is divided into five days, each of which lasts an average of five hours, and reaches a maximum altitude of 1171m. With fine views to the Aiguilles de Bavella and Monte Incudine, it crosses through the magnificent region of Alta Rocca and many of the island's most beautiful villages. The third day of the trail offers three options: a short version that skips the Plateau de Jallicu, a detour through the village of Aullène or a long version that goes via Zonza, which adds a day to the itinerary.

Provence

Provence occupies the southeastern corner of mainland France. It is the country's most varied area. Cosmopolitan coastal centres like Marseille contrast with inland areas where tiny villages are linked by deserted mountain roads. Many of the region's towns date from at least Roman times and offer a wonderful array of cultural treasures, from Roman theatres and medieval fortifications to outstanding art museums.

For walkers, rural Provence is a delight of colour, light and scent. The same light that fired the palette of the Impressionists enhances the greenness of the Luberon's gentle hills, the turquoise and cobalt blue of the Mediterranean and the dusty beige of the dry, sun-drenched plains and plateaus.

The typical vegetation is garrigue, a potpourri of kermes oak and holm oak, gorse, thistle, cistus, broom – and headily scented rosemary, lavender and thyme.

Once the walking's over, consider lingering for a few more days to explore Provence's rich Roman legacy; the watery Camargue, one of Europe's most fruitful areas for bird watching; or the brassy Côte d'Azur, its bloom nowadays a little faded.

For other walks in the Alpine regions of Provence, see the Southern Alps chapter (p237).

CLIMATE

Over 2500 hours of sunshine, an average of some seven hours a day, bathe Provence each year. Most of the region enjoys hot, dry summers, with midday maximums up in the high 30s, compensated for by mild winters. Rainfall is low and, while intense showers in spring and autumn can drench, they're usually brief. If you're walking at the height of summer, watch out for late afternoon thunderstorms which, though usually brief, can be violent.

The infamous *mistral* is a biting northwesterly wind that howls southwards down the Rhône Valley and can reach more than 100km/h – 'a wind strong enough to pull the

tail off a donkey' is the way that the Provençals describe it. A dry wind that chills and chaps the skin, it blows in spring and winter, although summer gusts are not unknown. But let's think positive: when the mistral rampages, skies are cloudless and blue.

INFORMATION
When to Walk

It's three-season walking in Provence, avoiding the torrid times between July and mid-September, when many trails are closed by law anyway because of the risk of fire. These dates may be extended if the danger is deemed to be high. Inquire at the nearest tourist office – and remember the fines for transgressors can be savage.

Maps

The IGN 1:250,000 map No 115 *Provence et Côte d'Azur* and Michelin's 1:200,000 map No 245 of the same title are both good overview maps.

Books

Lonely Planet's *Provence & the Côte d'Azur* is rich in detailed, practical information and local background; it's compact enough to slip into a pocket and includes a guide to Provençal wine. The enormously successful *A Year in Provence* and its sequels, written by Peter Mayle, local resident and very Brit, offer a fairly arch vision of the Luberon area.

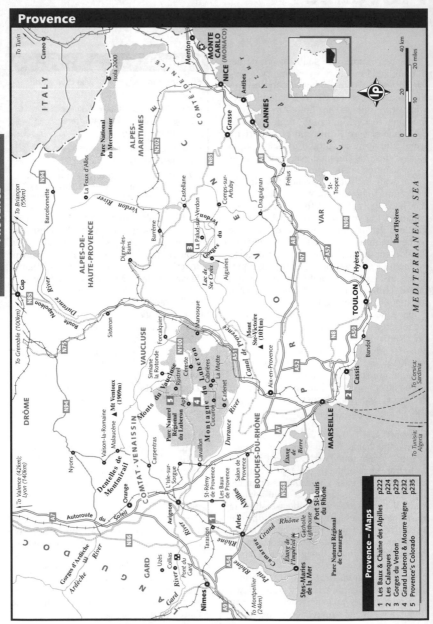

Provence

Provence – Maps

1 Les Baux & Chaîne des Alpilles   p222
2 Les Calanques   p224
3 Gorges du Verdon   p229
4 Grand Luberon & Mourre Nègre   p232
5 Provence's Colorado   p235

Les Baux & Chaîne des Alpilles

Duration	5–6 hours
Distance	26km
Difficulty	moderate
Start	St Gabriel
Finish	St-Rémy de Provence
Nearest Town	Tarascon
Transport	taxi, bus

Summary A great day's walking through rich pastures to the limestone jumble of Les Baux and a brush with Roman history.

From St-Gabriel, it's level walking to Les Baux de Provence (usually called simply Les Baux), which swarms with day visitors. But along the GR6 route, you'll be almost alone to savour the splendid ridge-top views along the Chaîne des Alpilles, backbone of the route. Follow the Gaudre du Rougadou Valley to pass the remains of Roman Glanum to St-Rémy. The walk, mostly through pine forest, is generally undemanding – we grade it as moderate because of its length and because of the steep clamber from the Barrage des Peïroou towards the end of the day.

PLANNING
When to Walk
The route is closed between 1 July and 15 September, when it's disagreeably hot and fire danger is high.

Maps
IGN's 1:25,000 map No 3042OT *Tarascon, St-Rémy-de-Provence & Chaîne des Alpilles* covers the whole route. You can pick it up at **Librairie Mireille** *(29 rue des Halles)* in Tarascon.

NEAREST TOWN
Tarascon
Built beside the murky grey waters of the Rhône River, Tarascon is dominated by the gaunt mass of the Château du Roi René. Across the river is Beaucaire, with its own mighty chateau.

Tarascon's **tourist office** *(☎ 04 90 91 03 52; www.tarascon.org; 59 rue des Halles;*

open Mon-Sat Jan-Jun & Sep-Dec plus Sun morning Jul-Aug) can provide information about the castle.

Places to Stay & Eat The rather scruffy **Camping Tarascon** *(☎ 04 90 91 01 46; camping per person/tent/car €3.40/3/1.70; open Apr-Oct)* is just north of the castle.

Camping St-Gabriel *(☎ 04 90 91 19 83; camping per person/site €3.25/3.50; open May-Sep)*, at the start of the walk and in the village of St-Gabriel, is a more pleasant option and has a swimming pool.

The HI-affiliated **youth hostel** *(☎ 04 90 91 04 08; tarascon@fuaj.org; 31 blvd Gambetta; dorm beds €8.40; open Mar-Nov)* is in the heart of Tarascon.

Hôtel Le Provençal *(☎ 04 90 91 11 41, fax 04 90 43 57 56; 12 cours Aristide Briand; doubles with bathroom €37-43)* is comfortable and welcoming.

If you draw a blank in Tarascon, walk over the bridge to Beaucaire on the Rhône's west bank. Its **tourist office** *(☎ 04 66 59 26 57; 24 cours Gambetta)* can provide accommodation information.

Getting There & Away Around 10 trains daily link Tarascon with both Avignon (€3.60, 15 minutes) and Marseille (€13.10, one hour). From Avignon, there are good rail connections north to Lyon (€27.50) and Paris (€113).

GETTING TO/FROM THE WALK
A taxi costs about €10 one way from Tarascon to St-Gabriel and, between Tarascon and St-Rémy, €27. Ring **Taxi Tarasconnais** *(☎ 06 11 55 90 00, 04 90 91 06 16)*.

From St-Rémy-de-Provence, a bus leaves for Tarascon from Bar du Marché late afternoon weekdays (plus Saturday during the school year). Two afternoon buses (not Sunday) leave for Avignon daily. From there regular trains and buses head for Paris. For confirmation of timetables, ring **Rapides du Sud-Est** *(☎ 04 90 14 59 00)*.

THE WALK
Ascend a set of steps on the left of the D33 about 50m beyond Camping St-Gabriel to

PROVENCE

PROVENCE

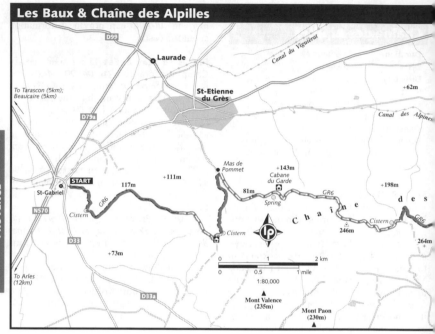

Les Baux & Chaîne des Alpilles

pass beside Chapelle St-Gabriel and, five minutes later, a ruined keep. After a further five minutes, turn left beside a cistern at a GR6 sign for Les Baux and St-Remy.

At about the hour mark, fork left at a cabin with a red-tiled roof and in a few minutes turn left (north) beside a cistern. After about 20 minutes of gentle descent, turn right along a lane serving Mas de Pommet. Follow the valley bottom beside rich pasture where bulls are wont to graze, taking on board a lamentably (and ironically) small sign, *'Danger: Taureaux Sauvages'* (Danger: Bulls at Large).

The track passes above **Cabane du Garde** with its flowing water pipe and small picnic area. Within a fenced enclosure on the right, reached after about two hours' walking, strut pheasant chicks reared for the hunter's gun. Hereabouts in spring, you also stand a reasonable chance of spotting wild boar. Soon after comes the first glimpse of the jagged peaks of Les Baux piercing the southeastern horizon and, far below to the northeast,

St-Remy, your destination, distinguished by its tall church spire.

Turn briefly north to curl around a small hillock, then right at a T-junction 300m later to head southeast, the general direction to Les Baux. Soon after meeting a sealed road, leave the GR6 as it swings away east (an alternative route if you want to avoid Les Baux, passing a series of caves cut deep into the rock. Just off route is the Cave de Sarragan wine cellar, a deep cave and sometime quarry. A glass of its chilled Rose Spec ial from the wine-tasting booth at its deepest, coolest recess works wonders.

Just before the village, the **Cathedrale d'Images** (☎ 04 90 54 38 65; *adult/child €7/4.10; open daily mid-Feb–Dec*) punches up 3000 images onto 4000 sq metres of one-time quarry walls in a hugely impressive, 30-minute continuous spectacle.

Les Baux, reached after 3¼ to 3½ hours of walking, is pandemonium. Visitors, disgorged from coaches and cars, throng the

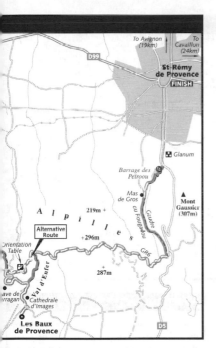

PROVENCE

narrow streets. But the detour (for which we've factored both time and distance into the walk statistics) is still worthwhile for the plunging views of the limestone anarchy of Val d'Enfer (Hell's Valley) and perhaps lunch or a drink, albeit at premium tourist prices, in one of its **restaurants** and **cafés**.

Les Baux has given its name to bauxite, the clay-like white, brown – even red – ore from which aluminium is extracted. First identified in 1821 at a site about 1.5km from what was then a sleepy pastoral village, its commercial potential remained unfulfilled for decades. Mining, ripping away swathes of the hillside, began at the end of the 19th century and the last digger fell silent as recently as 1990.

Retrace your steps to the Cathedrale d'Images. About 150m beyond, turn right and pass beyond a metal barrier to follow a stony and well-defined path. After about 15 minutes of ascent, turn right again as the trail rejoins the GR6 at a T-junction. Navigation

is easy beyond a chain barrier as you head towards and skirt beneath a fire watchtower.

Ignore all tempting left turns until you reach a sign, 'St-Remy de Provence 1 hour', about 45 minutes after rejoining the GR6. Take this secondary track to the left and descend to join the Gaudre du Rougadou Valley. Barely 100m beyond the forbidding walls of Mas de Gros, a substantial farmhouse, turn right down a tarred road that drops to Barrage des Peïroou. Follow the path hugging the lake's eastern shore then turn right to climb – really climb, using all four limbs in places – up the limestone crags. At the steepest point, steps have been hacked into the rock, plus metal rungs and a cable handhold to help. It isn't nearly as daunting as it sounds and the final brief clamber through a natural tunnel in the rock makes a dramatic conclusion to the last of the day's off-road walking.

Soon after turning left along the D5, the extensive remains of the Roman settlement of **Glanum** (☎ 04 90 92 23 79; admission €6.10; open daily) merit a short detour. Right beside the road and there for free are **Les Antiques**, an impressive triumphal arch and mausoleum.

Continue along the D5 for another 1.25km to St-Rémy. If you plan to overnight here, the **tourist office** (☎ 04 90 92 05 22; place Jean Jaurès; open daily Easter-Oct, Mon-Sat Nov-Easter), on the way into town, can supply details of accommodation, including camping grounds.

Les Calanques

Duration	5½–6½ hours
Distance	15.3km
Difficulty	demanding
Start	Cassis (p225)
Finish	Morgiou
Transport	train, bus

Summary Unrivalled seascapes clambering in and out of the dramatic *calanques* of the coast around Cassis.

In Provençal, a *calanque* is a steep-sided rocky inlet. This coastal walk, embracing

Les Calanques

To Les Baumettes (4km); Marseille (11km)

Falaise des Toits

Col de la Candelle

La Cheminée du Diable

FINISH Morgiou

La Grande Candelle (454m)

Calanque de Morgiou

Calanque de Sugiton

Falaises du Devenson

Puits de l'Oule

Col de l'Oule

Alternative Route

Belvédère d'En Vau

Vallon d'En Vau

GR98

Aiguille de l'Eissadon

Calanque de l'Oule

Cap de Morgiou

Warning: Very steep descent

Calanque d'En Vau

Calanque de Port-Pin

MEDITERRANEAN SEA

PROVENCE

the main six calanques, comes in three tones – green pine, bright white limestone and, beneath all, the cobalt-blue, sometimes turquoise Mediterranean. It's a classic walk, challenging and with some scrambling from Cassis to the tiny harbour of Morgiou, ascending and descending the intervening *calanques*. We grade the walk as demanding because of the very steep descent to Calanque d'En Vau and one or two other briefer passages that will stretch you.

NATURAL HISTORY

Europe's biggest snake and lizard slither and clamber around the Calanques but you'll be very lucky – or unlucky, depending upon how comfortable you are in the company of large reptiles – to see either. The ocellar lizard, a giant of its genre, can exceed 60cm. But it's way outstripped by the harmless Montpellier grass snake, which can grow to over 2m.

PLANNING
When to Walk

A year-round walk, it's at its very best during spring and autumn. With their own micro-

Warning

This is no walk for those who suffer from vertigo. Several steep ascents and descents challenge even the most level-headed of walkers. Also, the predominantly limestone surface, worn smooth by tens of thousands of boots, can be very slippery both after rain and until the morning dew has evaporated.

climate, temperatures along the *calanques* can be up to 10°C warmer than elsewhere along the coast – caressing in winter but seriously energy-sapping during summer.

On the positive side, Les Calanques trail, unlike most wooded areas of southern Provence, normally remains open to walkers throughout the summer months of maximum fire risk. This said, check with the Cassis tourist office between July and September, just to be sure.

What to Bring

Pack plenty of water since there's not a dribble en route. A telescopic pole makes a useful third leg on the longish scree descent towards the end of the walk.

Maps

The route is well blazed and, once beyond the first bay, the only way is forward or back so a map is not essential. The IGN 1:15,000 map No 82011 *Les Calanques* shows every coastal dimple. You can pick it up at **Astrée** *(4 av Victor Hugo)* or **Librairie Preambule** *(8 rue Pierre Eydin)*, both in Cassis.

NEAREST TOWN
Cassis

Cassis, a dinky little port, comes complete with a 14th-century chateau and France's highest coastal cliff. It's noted for its white wine – and as the starting point for boat trips to view the *calanques*.

The **tourist office** *(☎ 04 42 01 71 17; www.cassis.fr - French only; quai des Moulins; open Mon-Sat & Sun morning)* is beside the port. **Côte Cassis** *(9 rue Authemann; €1.60 per 15 min)* is an Internet joint.

Places to Stay & Eat Near route de Marseille **Camping Cigales** *(☎ 04 42 01 07 34; av de la Marne; camping per person/site €5/4.60; open mid-Mar–mid-Nov)* is 1km from the port.

The spartan, ecofriendly **youth hostel** *(☎ 04 42 01 02 72; dorm beds €8.70; open*

mid-Mar–Dec) is a 2km walk from Port-Miou (see p226). Bring your own food and don't expect to shower.

Hôtel du Commerce *(☎ 04 42 01 09 10, fax 04 42 01 14 17; 1 rue St-Clair; basic doubles €33, with shower €43, with bathroom €48-61; open mid-Jan–mid-Nov)*, at the northern limit of the port, is a welcoming one-star option with a good **restaurant**.

Cassis' quayside restaurants serve fine fish and seafood. Among several pizza places-cum-restaurants, **Le Romarin** *(☎ 5 rue Docteur Icard; pizzas €7-8.50; menus €15 & €18)* has the most agreeable atmosphere and also does takeaways (€1 extra).

In town, you'll eat like an emperor at **Le Bonaparte** *(☎ 04 42 01 80 84; 14 rue General Bonaparte; menus €13-20; open Tue-Sun)*. Reserve or arrive early; Le Bonaparte's superb value for money is an open secret.

Getting There & Away Regular trains link Marseille's St-Charles train station with Cassis (€3.90, 22 minutes), whose own train station is 3km east of town. Buses (to confirm schedules, ring ☎ 04 42 08 41 05) leave for Cassis from both Marseille's place Castellane (hourly) and Rond Point du Prado (five to seven daily) bus stations.

From Marseille, you can link up with multiple transport options to Paris.

GETTING TO/FROM THE WALK

The walk begins in Cassis. At the end, cars cannot descend beyond the small parking area 2.5km above Morgiou between 15 June and late August. It's a 4km walk from Morgiou to Les Baumettes, from where buses leave about every half hour for Marseille's Rond Point du Prado bus station. There, you can pick up the 6.20pm (Monday to Friday) or 7.30pm (daily) run to Cassis.

Another option is to take the 10.30am boat (€15, one hour) from Cassis to Morgiou and do the walk in reverse. Tell the crew in advance that you want to land at Morgiou.

THE WALK

In Cassis, at the port's northern limit, go up the steps of Rompe Cuou and turn left, then left again into av de l'Amiral Ganteaume, guided by signs for Plage du Bestouan. At this pebbly beach, follow the twists of av des Calanques to the end of the sealed road at **Calanque de Port-Miou**. Deepest of the inlets, its quarries were exploited until 1981 and prized Cassis limestone was used on projects as distant as the Suez Canal.

Turn left, paying no attention to the illicitly erected *'Acces Interdit'* (No Access) sign, to follow the inlet's northern shore, hugging the path nearest to the cliff base. As you cross the neck of land separating Calanque de Port-Miou from Calanque de Port-Pin, you pick up the GR98, whose at times sparse red-and-white blazes will accompany you all the way to Morgiou.

A steep climb is followed by a dizzying, four-limbed descent to **Calanque d'En Vau**, reached after about 1½ hours of walking. (If you prefer to avoid this clamber, follow the route, waymarked in green, that heads off northwest, then rejoins the GR98 in Vallon d'En Vau.) With its jagged limestone pinnacles and near-vertical cliffs, Calanque d'En Vau is a mecca for climbers. Its sandy beach and emerald water are an equally strong pull for day visitors who disembark in droves from pleasure boats.

Head north up Vallon d'En Vau along what's about the only flat track of the day. Some 20 to 25 minutes beyond the bay, turn west towards Col de l'Oule, distinguished by a cistern (No 243) and a rusting Club Alpin Français (CAF) sign. Here, ignore the seductive path leading straight ahead to the Belvédère d'En Vau viewpoint. Instead, turn back on yourself to descend to the well at Puits de l'Oule. From this minuscule, shady oasis, its waters inaccessible, the route runs southwards down a tight, winding valley.

Before reaching the *calanque*, veer right to climb the valley's steep western flank. The reward for 10 minutes of lung-searing ascent is the first of many plunging views of the Mediterranean and the Aiguille de l'Eissadon, through whose twin holes sea and sky wink. Shortly after, the boot-shaped Cap de Morgiou and the offshore islands – Île de Riou with its smaller sisters, Plane and Jarre – appear to the west and the distinctive slim dome of la Grande Candelle beckons.

After 15 tough minutes of half-walking, half-scrambling beyond the first viewpoint, the payoff is to stride the flat clifftop of **Falaises du Devenson** with magnificent seascapes and views back to the Baie de Cassis and the pinkish sandstone Cap Canaille.

After 30 to 40 minutes of thrilling, cliff-edge walking, descend north to curl round the great bowl of La Cheminée du Diable (the Devil's Chimney). At the insignificant rusting pole that marks Col de la Candelle, take your last view of Cap Canaille before tacking briefly northwest. About 20 minutes later, painted arrows on a rock indicate *éboulis* (scree) to the right and *rocher* (rock) to the left. If your boots have a sound tread, you'll probably find the scree alternative easier.

Some 20 minutes after making this choice, a four-limbed clamber down a steep chimney is followed by easy walking at the base of Falaise des Toits, where the only potential danger is from an unhitched climber falling on your head.

Work your way around **Calanque de Sugiton**, at whose western side an iron ladder and chains help you up the steepest part of the very last of the day's promontories. Negotiate one last chimney to enjoy a final and fairly gentle descent to the tiny port of Morgiou, where you can enjoy a thoroughly deserved drink or snack at **Restaurant Le Nautic**.

Gorges du Verdon

Duration	2 days
Distance	26.8km
Difficulty	moderate–demanding
Start	La Palud-sur-Verdon
Finish	Point Sublime
Nearest Towns	La Palud-sur-Verdon (p227), Castellane (p227)
Transport	bus, taxi
Summary Descend into France's deepest canyon, where sunlight rarely penetrates.	

Starting with a steep ascent over open hillside, you then descend though woods to Belvédère de Maireste viewpoint. Many walkers only undertake the classic Sentier Martel to

Point Sublime (see Day 2) following the bed of Europe's largest canyon, the Gorges du Verdon, first explored less than a century ago. At the height of summer, walkers are almost as dense as ants on the march. Day 1, by contrast, affords some fine plunging views while the Sentier du Bastidon, much less trodden, is in places just as breathtaking.

Strangely for such a wonder, the Gorges du Verdon were only given statutory protection as recently as 1997 when the Parc Naturel Régional du Verdon was established.

PLANNING
When to Walk
Any time is possible. The canyon's steep walls and its cladding of woolly oak, maple, boxwood and ash give shade in summer, although the early part of Day 1 can make the sweat trickle. Many camping grounds and hotels are open only between April/May and September/October.

What to Bring
Take water for each day. Unless you drop purifying tablets into Verdon River water, there's no natural supply. Pack a torch (flashlight) to negotiate the tunnels on Day 2.

Maps
The trail is so well blazed that a map is far from essential. Indeed, once down in the canyon, there's only one way out apart from retracing your steps. Should you want the fine detail, pick up Top 25 map No 3442OT *Gorges du Verdon*. Produced in several different languages, including English, *Canyon du Verdon – The Most Beautiful Hikes* describes 28 walks in the region.

NEAREST TOWNS
Castellane
Castellane, fairly unexciting in itself, is a gateway to the gorges and has a **tourist office** (☎ 04 92 83 61 14; www.castellane.org - French only; rue Nationale; open Mon-Sat).

Places to Stay & Eat Take your pick from the **camping grounds** – around 15 of them – which line the nearby river. **Le Frederic Mistral** (☎ 04 92 83 62 27; camping per person/site €4/4), conveniently central, is the only one open year-round.

L'Oustaou (☎ 04 92 83 77 27, fax 04 92 83 78 02; chemin des Listes; dorm beds with breakfast €19; open Tue-Sun Easter-Sep) is a budget hostel.

Hôtel du Levant (☎ 04 92 83 60 05; place Marcel Sauvaire; doubles/triples/quads €53/74/78; menus from €14.50; open mid-Apr–Oct) is an excellent choice with a good **restaurant**.

Getting There & Away From 1 July to mid-September, **Voyages Sumian** (☎ 04 42 54 72 82) runs between Marseille and Bar L'Étape in Castellane on Monday, Wednesday and Saturday (3½ hours). Outside this period, there's only a Saturday service. From Marseille you can get connections to Paris.

La Palud-sur-Verdon
Tiny La Palud-sur-Verdon (or, more simply, just La Palud), dead as a doornail out of season, is a popular centre for walkers from late spring to autumn. The **Maison des Gorges du Verdon** (☎ 04 92 77 32 02; www.lapaludsurverdon.com – French only; open daily) is in Château de Demandocx. It has a stimulating exhibition (adult/child €4/2) – in French but highly visual – on the gorges and local life and also acts as La Palud's tourist office.

Places to Stay & Eat There are five camping grounds in and around La Palud, including **Camping Municipal Le Grand Canyon** (☎ 04 92 77 38 13; camping per person/tent/car €2.65/2/1.70; open mid-Apr–Sep) on the D952, just east of town.

La Palud's **youth hostel**, 500m southwest on La Maline road, was closed for renovations at the time of writing.

Gîte le Wapiti (☎ 04 92 77 30 02; B&B €20, half board €30; open Easter-11 Nov) is a friendly place with a relaxing garden.

Auberge des Crêtes (☎ 04 92 77 38 47; aubergedescretes@wanadoo.fr; doubles €46.50-53, triples €54-58, half board €48.50; menus €14-23.50; open Easter-Sep), which is 1km east of the village, also manages a good **restaurant**.

Lou Cafetie (☎ 04 92 77 38 41), popular with outdoor folk, does filling sandwiches, pizzas and other dishes.

Bar Restaurant de la Place (☎ 04 92 77 38 03) is a friendly, informal place, also favoured by walkers and climbers (see the harnesses, carabinas and assorted climbing gear dangling from the ceiling).

Getting There & Away During summer, **Transports Guichard** (☎ 04 92 83 64 47) runs two convenient buses (daily July and August, weekends June and September) between Castellane and La Maline. There is one in the morning and one in the afternoon each way. They stop at Port Sublime and La Palud en route.

GETTING TO/FROM THE WALK

You can pre-arrange a taxi pick-up by calling ☎ 06 76 30 97 06 or ☎ 06 08 05 67 78 from the public phone (phonecards only) at Point Sublime. From La Palud-sur-Verdon, a taxi to Point Sublime or La Maline costs €15, between Point Sublime and La Maline it is €25 and La Palud to Castellane is €36.

THE WALK (Map p229)
Day 1: La Palud-sur-Verdon to Chalet La Maline
5–5½ hours, 16.3km

From the village fountain with its four fine, brass-headed spouts, head up the D123. After 150m, bear left at a fork beside a small wayside cross, on it the first of the day's red and white GR4 stripes. Some 75m later, turn left up a steep footpath gouged into the hillside.

After 15 to 20 minutes of steady climbing, cross a gravel track and go up the wooded flanks of a steep valley before joining more open terrain. As you ascend, La Palud and its fertile plain fall away while the thin line of the D952 with its toy vehicles snakes to the south.

At something over the hour mark, the path curls around a large bare limestone bluff to reach its highest point, then re-enters pine wood. Shortly after the gradual descent starts, fork left (northwest) down a grassy trail, which soon joins a logging track. Subsequent forks are clearly signed 'Moustiers'.

At a T-junction, turn right beside a log picnic table and almost immediately left onto a footpath, signed 'Maireste', to leave the GR4. From here until the end of Sentier du Bastidon, you're guided by red – almost fluorescent red – dots and less frequent yellow stripes. What starts as a pleasant, grassy path lined with boxwood soon drops vertiginously southwest down the Ravin du Grinhan.

At a hairpin bend of the D952, take the right-hand prong to reach the car park for the Belvédère de Maireste after 2¼ to 2½ hours' walking. This viewpoint, a worthwhile 15-minute detour over spiky karst, gives a great first view of the Gorges du Verdon. Just east of the car park is the farm of La Graou with a simple **camping ground**.

The Sentier du Bastidon leads away, initially southeast. Starting as an easy, fairly level clifftop path, it provides magnificent views of the canyon below. After around 15 minutes, it begins a steep, zigzagging descent to Ravin de Ferné, the first of several steep valleys cutting in from the north.

About 40 minutes beyond the car park, reject the path ahead in favour of the second of two cable-assisted clambers, which takes you up and left.

Between 1¼ and 1½ hours beyond the Maireste car park, the scooped bowl of **Ravin de Mainmorte** comes into view with, high on its eastern flank, the winding D23 corniche road. The path switchbacks steeply up to meet the road – where it's possible to cut out, turn left and return to La Palud (3.5km). To continue, go right to reach **La Maline** after about an hour of roadwork, offering more plunging views of the gorge.

The friendly CAF **Chalet La Maline** (☎/fax 04 92 77 38 05; la.maline@wanadoo.fr; camping per person €3.80, dorm beds €11.65, half board €28; open Easter-11 Nov), also known as Refuge des Malines, has limited provision for camping. Advance reservation is advisable at any time and essential for campers.

Day 2: Chalet La Maline to Point Sublime
4½–5½ hours, 10.5km

It's still far from being 'Gorges for Softies' but recent 'improvements' at the eastern,

Gorges du Verdon

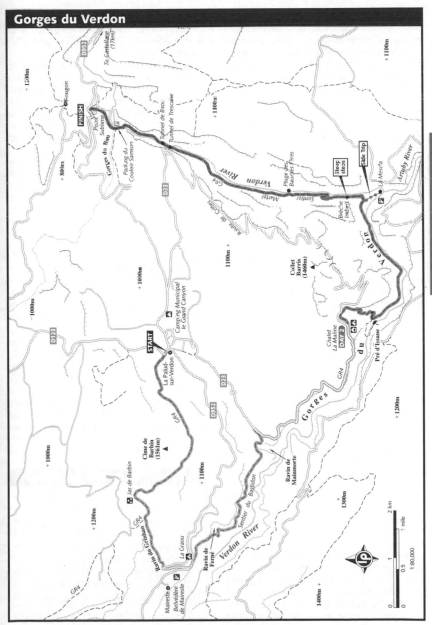

Couloir Samson end – which have been vehemently contested on both environmental and aesthetic grounds – have made the canyon more accessible to more people.

Leave by the path which heads initially northeast from the flowing fountain at the *refuge*. Curl around the *combe* (shallow valley) dropping gently towards the canyon floor down a banked, well-maintained trail. About 20 minutes out, take the first of the day's metal ladders positioned along the route, together with hawsers and rope, to help you over the most difficult stretches.

Around 45 minutes' walking brings you to river level and **Pré d'Issane**, a small pebble beach where the milky eau-de-nil waters of the Verdon River race by.

A little over 30 minutes later, just about every device possible (a metal stairway, iron railings, cable and rope) help the brief downward passage over a steep scree field. After about 15 minutes, a signed path to the right leads to La Mescla. For a great view of the confluence of the Verdon and Artuby Rivers, take the easy 45-minute diversion to the lone rock at La Mescla.

A brief, steep ascent leads to the narrow defile of **Brèche Imbert**, approximately halfway through the day's walk in terms of distance, but considerably more, in terms of energy spent. From here, steep flights of steps lead down a tight chimney. If you find the drop unnerving, simply turn around and take them backwards, facing into the rungs.

About 20 minutes beyond Brèche Imbert, the path begins a series of bends, even doubling back on itself briefly. Ten minutes later, the briefest of detours leads to Plage des Baumes Fères, a minuscule pebble beach that makes an agreeable lunch stop.

Once beyond a small promontory with plunging views both to the north and south – another potential lunch spot – it's almost level walking through sun-dappled woodland for the next 45 minutes all the way to two tunnels. (Don't be tempted into the gloom of the first tunnel the route passes; with a pair of narrow-gauge tracks leading in, it's blocked after some distance.)

Enter **Tunnel de Trescaire** (110m) and, after the briefest interlude of sunlight

(pause to look at the swirling waters beneath), plunge into **Tunnel de Baou**, whch is considerably longer (670m) and often flooded in places.

As you emerge, steps lead down to river level. Cross a footbridge over the minor Gorges du Bau and ascend the recently laid steps to Parking du Couloir Samson. Leave at its northwestern corner, still following the GR4 flashes. Less than a minute later, turn right beneath an overhang to reach **Point Sublime** about 30 minutes later.

A roadside *buvette* (refreshment kiosk) serves drinks, at a price; a fountain just across the road gushes cool water for free.

Auberge du Point Sublime (☎ *04 92 83 60 35; point.sublime@wanadoo.fr; half board with bathroom per person €50; open Easter–mid-Oct*) is an end-of-walk inn.

The Luberon

The deep bowl of Combe de Lourmarin divides the Luberon range into the Petit Luberon to the west and the Grand Luberon to the east. The Grand Luberon, of softer limestone and culminating in the Mourre Nègre (1125m), has been eroded into gentle, rounded contours. The Petit Luberon, lower and more brittle, has weathered into crags, ravines and sharp, spiky angles. There's a similar contrast between north- and south-facing slopes. Woolly oak, needing a cooler, more humid climate, clads the former. Holm oak and garrigue populate the more sparsely vegetated south-facing slopes.

A Small Yet Acute Problem

Seldom can a tiny speck on the page have aroused such – albeit mild – controversy. In defiance of local custom and preference, this part of Provence was usually spelt *Lubéron* (note that acute accent) in maps and texts, more often than not emanating from distant Paris.

As always, we run with the locals – and also in the good company of the IGN, FFRP and Parc Naturel Régional. Welcome to free, unaccented Luberon!

PROVENCE

PLANNING
When to Walk

Unlike the more desiccated areas of southern Provence, the Luberon's trails remain open even during high summer, the period of maximum fire risk. It can, however, be decidedly hot and sticky between June and August.

Maps & Books

IGN, 1:25,000 map No 3243OT *Pertuis/Loumarin* covers the Grand Luberon & Mourre Nègre walk. Its 1:25,000 map No 3242OT *Apt* covers the Provence's Colorado walk (p234).

The excellent Fédération Française de la Randonnée Pédestre (FFRP) Topo-Guide in English, *Walks in Provence: Luberon Regional Nature Park* describes 24 walks in and around the area. Its *Tour du Luberon et du Ventoux* (No 905, in French) describes the GR trails that crisscross the two massifs – the main GR9 and its offshoots.

ACCESS TOWN
Apt

The **tourist office** (☎ *04 90 74 03 18; www.ot-apt.fr - French only; 20 av Philippe de Girard; open Mon-Sat year-round plus Sun morning May-Sep*) has walking information.

The small Parc Naturel Régional exhibition at the **Maison du Parc** (☎ *04 90 04 42 00; place Jean Jaurès; open Mon-Sat Easter-Sep, closed Sat afternoon Oct-Easter*), the park information office, is very visual and has a stunning selection of fossils downstairs.

Infotelec (*88 rue de la Sous Prefecture; €5/hr*) provides Web access.

The tourist office, the Maison du Parc and **Librairie Dumas** (*16 rue de Marchands*) all carry maps and guidebooks.

Places to Stay & Eat For those with a tent, **Camping Municipal Les Cèdres** (*☎/fax 04 90 74 14 61; campinglescedres@free.fr; av de Viton; camping €9.60; open mid-Feb–mid-Nov*) is conveniently central.

The **Youth Hostel** (☎ *04 90 74 39 34, fax 04 90 74 50 90; dorm beds €16; open mid-Feb–mid-Jan*) is 7km from Apt, near the village of Saignon.

Relais de Roquefure (☎ *04 90 04 88 88, fax 04 90 74 14 86; dorm beds €13; open Feb-Nov*), the nearest *gîte d'étape*, is at Le Chêne, 4km west on the Avignon road.

Hôtel du Palais (☎ *04 90 04 89 32, fax 04 90 04 71 61; 24 place Gabriel Péri; singles/doubles/triples from €35/48/56; open Apr–mid-Nov*), under new ownership, is a pleasant, welcoming option.

The Saturday morning **market** and Tuesday's **farmers' market** are perfect for self-caterers.

Brasserie Le Gregoire (☎ *04 90 74 10 26; place de la Bouquerie 19; plat du jour €7.50, menus €11.50 & €15*) is in the Hôtel du Palais and is popular.

Getting There & Away There are at least five daily buses between Apt and Avignon (€6.90), most of which continue to the TGV station. For information ring **Autocars Barlatier** (☎ *04 90 74 20 21*) in Apt or Avignon's bus station (☎ *04 90 82 07 35*).

From Avignon, there are good road and rail connections northwards to Lyon and Paris and south to Marseille.

For a taxi ring **Taxis Aptesiens** (☎ *04 90 04 70 70*) or call by the rank in place de la Bouquerie, near the tourist office.

Grand Luberon & Mourre Nègre

Duration	5–5½ hours
Distance	21.5km
Difficulty	moderate
Start/Finish	Cucuron
Nearest Town	Apt (p231)
Transport	bus, taxi
Summary	It's a long, steady haul up to the ridge of the Grand Luberon but, wow, it's worth it for the panoramas and easy ridge walking that follows.

This walk is a steady haul up Vallon de la Fayette to the Grand Luberon ridge and Mourre Nègre. There's more open ridge-walking before descending Vallon de Vaunière to Vaugines and on to Cucuron.

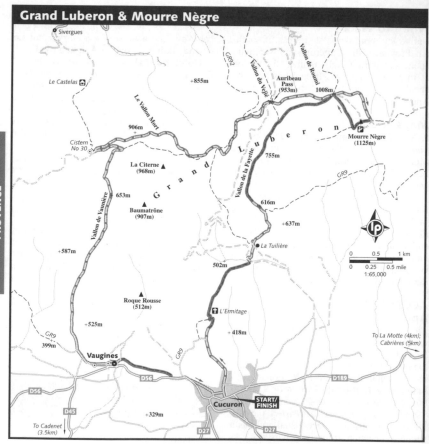

Grand Luberon & Mourre Nègre

The walk's only potential difficulty is the long, steadily uphill walk for over two hours to the summit of Mourre Nègre, the day's highest point. This accomplished, the rest of the day is all flat or downhill.

GETTING TO/FROM THE WALK

If you're prepared to rise early, it's possible to get to Cucuron and back without your own wheels. The morning bus for Marseille leaves Apt at 6.35am daily, calling by Cadenet at 7.30am. From there, you can take a taxi to Cucuron for around €14. Ring **Taxi Arcole** (☎ 04 90 08 58 58) in Cadenet or **Mme Morra**

(☎ 04 90 77 20 69) in Cucuron and ask them to meet you at the bus stop. When you're dropped off, agree upon a time to be collected for the return journey to Cadenet, from where the evening bus for Apt departs at 6.20pm. A taxi all the way to or from Apt will set you back a hefty €20-25.

THE WALK

From the pool in Cucuron's place de l'Étang, head north up rue de Berard du Roure, pass beside the village school, then fork left onto chemin de l'Ermitage. At a second Hermitage sign, continue straight and weave through

Pine Processionary Caterpillar

Even the birds turn up their bills at the pine processionary moth, whose hairy caterpillars devour pine needles, threatening whole forests. Between October and March you can see their large silvery nests on the sunnier side of trees.

Come spring, they're on the march in single file, as fat as your little finger and 5cm long. Along the branch, down the trunk, into the roots: they bury themselves underground and enter the chrysalis stage. In July, the cycle begins again as the female moths fight their way loose and lay their eggs in another tree victim. Bristling with irritating hairs, the caterpillars can provoke a nasty allergic reaction if you touch them. Applying vinegar is said to provide relief.

orchards, guided by a 'Chemin Comunal' sign, indicating a public footpath. Turn right as the route joins the GR9 and hairpins up to **L'Ermitage** and the **chapel of Notre Dame de Beauvoir**, reached after about 30 minutes of walking. From here, a wide, stony track heads north up a spur then descends and contours round a fruit orchard.

Where it meets another, jinx left and almost immediately right onto a narrow linking footpath. This soon merges into a wide, sunken 4WD track that ascends north, bypassing the farm of La Tuilière. Continue up the Vallon de la Fayette when the GR9 heads away northeast. As the route climbs, woolly oak gives way to holm oak, fighting its corner with beech above 800m, where the first pines put in an appearance.

About two hours from Cucuron, the path emerges onto the high ridge beside a sign warning of the perils of the *chenille processionaire* (pine processionary caterpillar); turn right onto the unpaved service road for the TV relay station at the summit of **Mourre Nègre** (1125m). The looming structure, looking like a giant space station, leaves you feeling dwarfed. But if the air's clear, nothing can diminish the panorama as far as the Alps on the eastern horizon and the Massif Central to the west.

Follow a path dropping southwest from the summit. Turn north after 200m onto a track that takes you back to the caterpillar warning board (don't be tempted by the broad, seductive alternative that heads west, following the crest; it soon peters out). From the board, continue west along the service road, which gives fine vistas of the Vallon de la Fayette, up which you earlier toiled.

At the Auribeau Pass and cistern No 28, a circular underground water reservoir, there's scope for confusion at a seven-way junction. Go straight ahead (west) along Piste des Cavaliers and follow it for a generous 45 minutes as you walk the spine of the Grand Luberon as far as cistern No 30. Here the route turns sharply east then south to descend Vallon de Vaunière as far as the hamlet of **Vaugines**, a blessed spot with a **cafe** and several fountains.

Just before Vaugines, you pick up the blazes of the GR9 again. Follow them as the route wiggles through the village and east onto a farm track that runs parallel to the D56 as far as the outskirts of Cucuron. Leave the GR9 as it heads north, take Chemin des Vaugines, the next left turn, and follow a spattering of orange blobs back to place de l'Étang.

Should you wish to overnight in Cucuron, **Hôtel Restaurant de l'Etang** (☎ 04 90 77 21 25, fax 04 90 77 10 98; singles €58, doubles €58-74, triples €90), right beside the finishing post, is a friendly option with a great **restaurant**.

Provence's Colorado

Duration	5¾–6¼ hours
Distance	20.5km
Difficulty	moderate
Start/Finish	Rustrel
Nearest Town	Apt (p231)
Transport	taxi

Summary Le Colorado's one-time ochre quarries and an ancient packhorse track. A steep, zigzagging descent into Rustrel.

The walk is essentially two circles that intersect in the village of Rustrel. The southern one, easier and more scenic, takes you through and around the now-abandoned ochre quarries of Le Colorado. On the more challenging, less-frequented northern loop via Marinier, the vegetation gradually changes from Mediterranean to mountain as you ascend, and is mainly through forest. The walk is easily divided into two halves and can be spread over a couple of days.

GETTING TO/FROM THE WALK

A taxi between Apt and Rustrel costs €15. If you're game for some supplementary exercise, you could hire a bicycle for the easy 19km round trip.

In Apt, **Cycles Agnel** (☎ 04 90 74 17 16; 27 quai Général Leclerc) and **Gassou Shop** (☎ 04 90 74 61 66; 422 av Victor Hugo) rent bikes.

THE WALK

Head eastwards from a notice board, just opposite the village war memorial, illustrating walking routes around Rustrel. Where

---

Ochre

Ochre, essentially a blend of sand and clay modified by iron oxides, was mined until quite recently in the low hills to the north of the Luberon.

About 100 million years ago, not far from today's village of Rustrel, a thick layer of green sand was deposited, grain by grain, over a bed of grey marl. The harsh atmosphere and raging rainstorms high in acid content turned the sands white, yellow and red, metamorphosising the mixture into ochre. Millennia later, these primal colours inspired the name 'Provence's Colorado'.

On the first part of the walk, look out for the former sediment settling beds just before recrossing the Doa. Shortly after, between Istrane and Bouvène, you can see an old ochre processing plant.

The industry was decimated by the introduction of chemical dyes in the 1920s. You can visit the small exhibition at Europe's last surviving ochre enterprise, **Les Ochres de Gargas** (☎ 04 90 74 53 76; admission €1.50; open Mon-Wed & Sat afternoon) in the village of Gargas, 5km northwest of Apt.

---

the red-and-white flashes of the GR6 lead right down chemin de St Joseph, continue straight along the D30a. Pass over a crossroads and along a lane beside La Maison du Colorado, a souvenir shack, and on beside an extensive car park. Continue straight as the blacktop gives out and descend towards an easily forded stream, the Doa. After passing through lavender fields, the route curls around the **Cirque de Barriès**, a bowl of contorted yellow whorls and pinnacles, the first ochre outcrop of the day.

Stay on this compacted 4WD route, following yellow flashes once a major track bears away to the left after about 45 minutes' walking. As you ascend, there are increasingly fine views of Rustrel and the yellow gash of the ochre *combe* now far below.

Turn left at a junction with a bitumen road then right at the next intersection beside a post indicating 'Pradenques 541m'. At a left-hand bend, take a cart track to the right and follow the edge of the plateau with great vistas both to the north and, to the southwest, with Grand Luberon and Mourre Nègre, topped by its TV relay station.

After a brief descent, turn right at a T-junction along a sandy path, which eventually runs beside a long, narrow cultivated field and curls round the rim of the ravine of Les Gourgues.

Turn right at a sign for Istrane to descend through juniper and maritime pine, both hardy varieties that thrive in this inhospitable soil. Another sheer ochre cliff comes into view across the cirque to the west as pine gradually gives way to woolly oak. Cross a bed of rich burnt ochre and re-cross the muddy Doa. Take the sealed road as far as the hamlet of Istrane, no more than a couple of dwellings and an old wash house, long since dry.

Turn right here along a sparsely trafficked road. Shortly after the side track for Bouvène leads away south, opposite a pipe gushing fresh water, turn left to follow the GR6 blazes back to **Rustrel** and the notice board that marked your departure point.

Just west of this board, take rue de l'Église northwards to pass Rustrel's tiny church and cemetery. Scramble up a short

Provence's Colorado

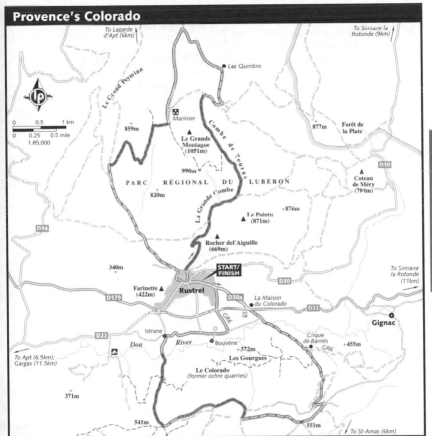

To Lagarde
d'Apt (6km)

To Simiane la
Rotonde (9km)

Les Quintins

Le Grand Peyman

Marinier

859m

Le Grande
Montagne
(1051m)

990m

Combe de Touras

877m

Forêt de
la Plate

D30

Coteau
de Méry
(794m)

PARC   RÉGIONAL   DU   LUBERON

820m

La Grande Combe

Le Pointu
(871m)

+876m

Rocher del'Aiguille
(669m)

D34

340m

START/
FINISH

D30

To Simiane
la Rotonde
(11km)

Farinette ▲
(422m)

Rustrel

D179

D30a

La Maison
du Colorado

D22

Gignac

Istrane

GR6

Doa   River   Bouvène

To Apt (6.5km);
Gargas (11.5km)

D22

Cirque
de Barriès

GR6

+455m

+372m

Les Gourgues

371m

Le Colorado
(former ochre quarries)

541m

551m

To St-Amas (6km)

PROVENCE

0   0.5   1 km
0   0.25   0.5 mile
1:65,000

bank, cross a road and continue straight along a bitumen lane into the mouth of **La Grande Combe**. Behind a forbidding fence on the left is what's signed as an underground laboratory, sunk deep into the hillside, and a helipad – a pair of structures that smack of a James Bond film.

At a fork just beyond, take the left-hand option, which soon leads into an ancient packhorse track that linked the communities of Rustrel and Lagarde d'Apt and also served to transport charcoal from the wooded hills to the valley below. Note the sturdy stone banking on the steeper bends as the track

climbs the western flank of the steep valley, densely and impenetrably clad with holm oak. The jagged spike to the northeast is Rocher de l'Aiguille (Needle Rock). The rounded hilltop above it – called paradoxically Le Pointu (The Pointed One) – was once occupied by a Gallo-Roman fort.

Turn right at a sign reading 'La Grande Montagne' and left at another, some 15 to 20 minutes later. The main track ascends the flank of Combe de Touras through a shady tunnel of trees, levelling out as the woodland becomes sparser. Follow open meadow, initially to your left, then on your right (be-

Provençal Bories

It's estimated that there are about 3000 *bories* in the Luberon. Dry stone huts, they come in a variety of sizes and shapes – round, square, rectangular, even ovoid.

Evidence suggests they may go back as far as the Iron Age, when they were used as dwellings. Permanent? Refuge in times of strife? Seasonal? Historians still quibble over their function. Many are of much more recent provenance and even today function as temporary sheepfolds, tool sheds or repositories for general junk.

In their construction, natural or shaped flakes of limestone called *lauzes* were skilfully interleaved without a single wooden roof beam and not a trace of mortar or cement to create a natural, roofed, dry stone structure.

Great shelter if you're caught unawares in a Provençal downpour.

ware the bee hives!) and once beyond a trio of wrecked vehicles, turn left onto a tarred track at the farm of Les Quintins. After 1km, turn left at a T-junction to pass by the ruined buildings of **Marinier** after something over two hours of walking.

About 250m beyond the ruins, turn right at a couple of plain metal posts onto an indistinct track and follow it west across flat, relatively open ground. Soon after passing an enigmatic hump across the path, the trail widens into a well-defined, stony cart track that plunges southwest, once more in woodland. At the first of several zigzags, an area of open forest, cleared for parapenting, gives splendid views of the Grand and Petit Luberons.

Where the trail meets a wider track, just beside a large underground cistern, turn left for the final uncomplicated 2km descent to Rustrel, keeping straight ahead on a lesser but still substantial track where the main one bends right.

Other Walks

Cap Canaille

This 21km, four- to five-hour circular walk circumnavigates the spectacular pink sandstone promontory of Cap Canaille. A coloured pamphlet *Balade au Cap Canaille*, available from Cassis' tourist office, has a good map of the cliff walk from Cassis to La Ciotat.

Leave Cassis following signs for Route des Crêtes and take a footpath, waymarked in yellow, at Pas de la Colle. If you only want to do the more spectacular outward cliff-top leg, a daily bus leaves La Ciotat for Cassis at 4.35pm in summer (at weekends year-round). During the school year, there's also a weekday service at 6.15pm.

The Camargue

A 22km out-and-back walk, including a 7.5km walkway along the *digue de la mer* (sea dike), takes you from Stes-Maries de la Mer to the Gacholle lighthouse. En route there are magnificent views of the Réserve Naturelle de l'Étang de l'Impérial and its rich birdlife. IGN 1:25,000 maps No 2944O *Stes-Maries-de-la-Mer* and No 2944E *Salin-de-Giraud* cover this watery area.

For information about this and other walking trails in the Camargue, consult the **tourist office** (☎ 04 90 18 41 20; ot.arles@visitprovence.com; blvd des Lices) in Arles.

Mont Ventoux

You probably won't be alone on top of Mont Ventoux (1909m), accessible by car and a popular destination for the tougher kind of cyclist. Satisfaction comes as much from the quieter contemplation of equally splendid views from its 25km windy ridge as from reaching the peak, which stays snowcapped from December to April. Possible routes feature on the IGN 1:25,000 map No 3140ET *Mont Ventoux*. For further information, contact the **Malaucène tourist office** (☎/fax 04 90 65 22 59), 10km south of Vaison-la-Romaine.

Southern Alps

The Southern Alps extend in a vast arc from the central Isère valley south to the Alpes Maritimes within sight of the Mediterranean coast. Four major conservation reserves protect a large part of these ranges: Parc National des Écrins, Parc National du Mercantour, Parc Naturel Régional du Vercors and Parc Naturel Régional du Queyras. Less well known and less frequented than the Northern Alps' Vanoise and Mont Blanc areas, they contain just as much variety: alpine meadows and plateaus, high passes, lakes, valleys broad and narrow – and summits that don't demand mountaineering skills and equipment. There are also many unspoiled, traditional villages and some of the wildest country in France in the remote reaches of all four reserves.

Networks of waymarked routes, making use of traditional paths and byways, provide an almost inexhaustible array of walks, from day-long outings to extended treks of several weeks. This chapter describes three-day walks in the Vercors and the Écrins-Oisans, a four-day tour through the Queyras and a collection of day walks in the Mercantour.

CLIMATE

Atlantic and Continental (eastern European) weather systems and, in the far south, the Mediterranean bring dry, warm summers and wet, mild winters with a wide seasonal range of temperatures. The weather is changeable with occasional high-pressure systems ensuring extended settled periods.

Fine summer mornings are often followed by cloudy afternoons over high ground around noon, while the valleys stay sunny and very warm. It's almost guaranteed that a spell of fine weather will bring an afternoon or evening *orage* (thunderstorm preceded by massed cumulus – billowing – cloud and rising humidity). However, the vivid lightning, loud thunderclaps, heavy rain and, sometimes, hail usually clear to another fine day.

During summer the average daily maximum temperature at 850m is about 24°C

while at 2500m it's 7°C. The wettest months in the valleys are between September and November, and from June to August in the mountains, except in the far south.

When the weather's settled, winds tend to blow up the valleys during the day and back down at night, while winds may come from quite different directions higher up. Overall, colder more settled weather is accompanied by northerly and easterly winds, and wetter, less settled conditions arrive with westerlies.

Snowfalls can be expected above 1200m from October until May; snow may lie above 2300m until late July.

INFORMATION
Maps & Books

IGN's Top 1:100,000 maps No 52 *Valence*, No 54 *Grenoble and Nice* and No 61 *Barcelonnette* are useful for planning your visit to the area. Lonely Planet's *Walking in the Alps* also describes the walks of Alpine France in the context of the surrounding countries. Four chapters of Cicerone's *Walking in the Alps* by Kev Reynolds are wholly or partly devoted to France. The brief descriptions give a feel for each area and outline some of the extended walks available. Also published

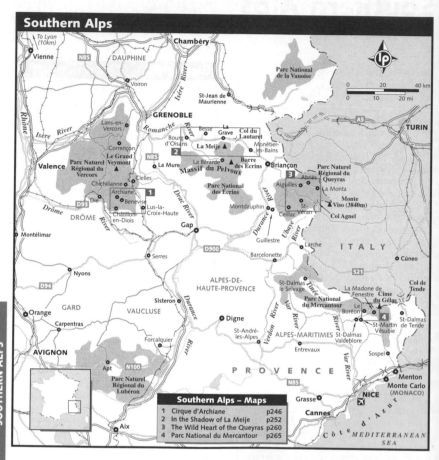

Southern Alps

To Lyon (10km)
Vienne
Chambéry
DAUPHINE
N85
Voiron
Parc National de la Vanoise
St-Jean de Maurienne
A5
TURIN
GRENOBLE
Lans-en-Vercors
Romanche River
Besse
La Grave
Col du Lautaret
Monêtier-les-Bains
Correncon
Bourg d'Oisans
2
La Meije
Le Grand Veymont
N85
La Mure
La Bérarde
Barre des Écrins
Briançon
Parc Naturel Régional du Queyras
Valence
Parc Naturel Régional du Vercors
Massif du Pelvoux
Abriès
3
La Monta
Chichilianne
Clelles
Drac River
Parc National des Écrins
Aiguilles
St-Véran
Monte Viso (3840m)
Archiane
1
Benevise
Die
Châtillon-en-Diois
Lus-la-Croix-Haute
Montdauphin
Ceillac
Col Agnel
Drôme
DRÔME
Drôme River
Gap
Guillestre
Larche
ITALY
Cúneo
Montélimar
D93
D900
Serres
Barcelonette
Nyons
D94
ALPES-DE-HAUTE-PROVENCE
Ubaye River
Tinée River
St-Dalmas le Selvage
La Madone de Fenestre
Cime du Gélas
Col de Tende
GARD
Sisteron
Durance River
VAUCLUSE
Digne
St-André-les-Alpes
Parc National du Mercantour
Le Boréon
St-Martin Vésubie
St-Dalmas de Tende
Orange
Carpentras
Forcalquier
Verdon River
ALPES-MARITIMES
St-Dalmas Valdeblore
AVIGNON
N100
Entrevaux
Var River
Sospel
Apt
Parc Naturel Régional du Lubéron
PROVENCE
N85
Menton
Monte Carlo (MONACO)
Grasse
NICE
Southern Alps – Maps
1 Cirque d'Archiane   p246
2 In the Shadow of La Meije p252
3 The Wild Heart of the Queyras p260
4 Parc National du Mercantour p265
Aix
Cannes
Côte d'Azur
MEDITERRANEAN SEA

0   20   40 km
0   10   20 mi

by Cicerone, *Walking the French Alps: GR5* by Martin Collins covers the long-distance route from north of the Queyras through to Nice.

Emergency
The **mountain rescue contact** for the Vercors, Écrins and Queyras is ☎ 04 92 22 22 22; for the Mercantour it's ☎ 04 97 22 22 22.

GATEWAYS
Grenoble
Grenoble, spectacularly dominated by the northern cliffs of the Vercors Plateau and

the self-styled 'Gateway to the Alps', is inevitably on your itinerary if you're travelling by public transport to the Vercors, Oisans and, quite likely, the Queyras.

Information With a multilingual staff, the **tourist office** (☎ 04 76 42 41 41; www .grenoble-isere-tourisme.com; 14 rue de la République; open daily) includes an SNCF agency; accommodation contact information is posted outside the main entrance.

The **Bureau Info Montagne** (☎ 04 76 42 45 90; infos.montagne@grande-traversee -alpes.com; 3 rue Raoul Blanchard), near the tourist office, sells maps and guides and can provide advice on access to mountain areas; the daily forecast is displayed outside.

The best place to go for maps, guide-books (but not Topo-Guides) and general references is **Glénat Librairie** (☎ 04 76 46 34 60; www.glenatpresse.com - French only; 19 av Alsace Lorraine).

Of the several outdoor equipment shops, the most useful is **Clavel Sports** (☎ 04 76 87 19 11; 54 cours Jean-Jaurès; open Tue-Sat).

Le New Age Cyber Cafe (☎ 04 76 51 94 43; 1 rue Barnave; €2/3/5 for 15/30/60min; open daily) is near place Notre Dame .

Places to Stay & Eat In the western suburb of Seyssins, **Camping Les Trois Pucelles** (☎ 04 76 96 45 73, fax 04 76 21 43 73; 58 rue des Allobroges; camping 2 people & tent €11.50; open year-round) is a neatly laid-out site, complete with pool. From the train station take No 1 tram towards Fontaine and alight at the Maisonnat stop. Then catch bus No 51 to Mas des Îles and walk 400m east along rue du Dauphiné.

The new **Grenoble-Echirolles Youth Hostel** (☎ 04 76 09 33 52; www.fuaj.fr; 3 av Victor Hugo, 38130 Echirolles) had not yet opened at the time of publication. Check the website for details.

Hôtel Alizé (☎ 04 76 43 12 91, fax 04 76 47 62 79; 1 rue Amiral Courbet; singles/doubles with bathroom €28/40; breakfast €4) near the train and bus stations, has clean, modern rooms.

Hôtel Lux (☎ 04 76 46 41 89; www.hotel-lux.com - French only; 6 rue Crépu; rooms €28, singles/doubles with bathroom €39/41; breakfast €5), on a quiet street, has compact, nicely decorated rooms and is also conven-ient for the station.

Hôtel Victoria (☎ 04 76 46 06 36; 17 rue Thiers; singles/doubles with bathroom €34/40; breakfast €5.50) is pleasantly located in a courtyard, quiet and comfortable.

Hôtel de l'Europe (☎ 04 86 46 16 94; www.hoteleurope.fr; 22 place Grenette; singles/doubles €26/28, with bathroom €45/54) is the oldest hotel in Grenoble; most of the rooms have splendid, old-style wrought-iron balconies.

Warning

Snow can linger in the higher passes well into spring and may not disappear above 2500m until July. If you plan to walk high in the South-ern Alps during May, an ice axe is essential and crampons highly desirable.

Always be aware of the wind-chill factor, the dramatic cooling effect of wind at low temperatures. In calm conditions at 0°C you will feel cool, but bitterly cold if even only a moderate breeze is riffling past. Pack that windproof jacket!

There's a **Casino supermarket** (28 cours Bernal, open Mon-Sat) for self-caterers.

Restaurant des Montagnes (☎ 04 76 15 20 72; 5 rue Brocherie; open daily) lives up to its name with a menu focussed on the sustaining alpine specialities, including raclette (€22) and fondue with wild mushrooms (€18).

Chez La Mère Ticket (☎ 04 76 44 45 40; rue Jean-Jacques Rousseau; menus €17-23; open daily) is a small, homely place offer-ing traditional fare such as snails, frogs' legs and kidneys in red wine.

Restaurant de l'Arche (☎ 04 76 44 22 62; 4 rue Pierre Duclot; menus €22-38; open Mon-Sat) prepares a range of more unusual dishes, including pigeon with mixed green salad and roast rabbit with mustard sauce.

Getting There & Away Forty-five kilometres north of the city, **Grenoble-St-Geoirs airport** (☎ 04 76 65 48 48; www.grenoble.aeroport.fr - French only) handles internal Air France flights and some from neighbouring coun-tries. **Autocars Monnet** (☎ 04 76 87 90 31) operates a bus service from the airport to the bus station (about €15, 35 minutes).

Intercars (☎ 04 76 46 19 77; www.intercars.fr - French only) has long-distance bus services to several European cities, including London (€85, 15 hours, three per week), Munich (€72, 13½ hours, three per week) and Amster-dam (€63, 15 hours, three per week).

Grenoble is connected to Paris' Gare de Lyon by both TGV and conventional train services (€73.20/53.50, 3½/four hours, sev-eral daily). Other services link Grenoble via

Lyon with destinations in the north and south of France. For information about schedules phone ☎ 08 92 35 35 35.

Nice

This colourful, crowded city on the Mediterranean Côte d'Azur might seem utterly unconnected with walking, but it's crucial for public transport access and a night there en route to the Mercantour may be unavoidable – and not without enjoyment.

Information The main and very busy **tourist office** (☎ 08 92 70 74 07; www.guideriviera.com; av Thiers; open daily) is next to the main train station. There's another, quieter **office** (☎ 08 92 70 74 07; 5 promenade des Anglais; open Mon-Sat) at the eastern end of the lively promenade.

For maps and guides, head for the **Maison de la Presse** (place Masséna).

Places to Stay & Eat Just a shortish walk from the station, in a quiet street, **Hôtel du Petit Louvre** (☎ 04 93 80 15 54; www.hotelgoodprice.com; 10 rue Emma Tiranty; singles/doubles with bathroom €36/44; breakfast €5) has compact rooms enlivened by reproduction paintings.

Hôtel Notre-Dame (☎ 04 93 88 70 44; www.hotelgoodprice.com; 22 rue de Russie; singles/doubles with bathroom €39/44; breakfast €5) occupies a splendid old building and has very good rooms for the price.

Hôtel du Centre (☎ 04 93 88 83 85; www.webstore.fr/hotel-centre; 2 rue du Suisse; doubles with bathroom €55; breakfast €5) is close to the station; rooms are refreshingly uncluttered and tastefully decorated.

There's a **Casino supermarket** (27 blvd Gambetta; open Mon-Sat) southwest of the train station.

Le Toscan (☎ 04 93 88 40 54; 1 rue de Belgique; menus €13-20; open Tue-Sat) is a good-value Italian restaurant with lots of traditional dishes; its pasta is excellent.

L'Allegria (☎ 04 93 87 42 00; rue d'Italie; menus from €13; open Tue-Sat) offers the chance to try something quite different – Corsican specialities; the soupe Corse is especially recommended.

Le Faubourg Montmartre (☎ 04 93 62 55 03; 32 rue Pertinax; menu €13; open daily) offers no-frills, good-value meals. The house speciality is bouillabaisse (€22 for two).

Getting There & Away About 6km west of the city centre, **Aéroport International Nice-Côte d'Azur** (☎ 04 93 21 30 30; www.nice.aeroport.fr) is on the St-Martin bus route. It handles internal Air France flights and international flights to several UK cities, Amsterdam, Frankfurt, New York and many more, with British Airways, Lufthansa and American Airlines among numerous carriers.

Intercars (☎ 04 93 80 08 70; www.intercars.fr - French only) operates bus services from the bus station on blvd Jean Jaurès to several European cities, including London (€100, 19¾ hours, two per week), Munich (€98, 13½ hours, three per week) and Amsterdam (€80, 21½ hours, two per week).

Nice is linked by regular and fairly frequent **SNCF** (☎ 08 92 35 35 35) TGV services to Paris' Gare de Lyon via Marseille (€82, 5½ hours) and many other towns and cities.

Cirque d'Archiane

Duration	3 days
Distance	62km
Difficulty	moderate–demanding
Start	Lus-la-Croix-Haute (p242)
Finish	Châtillon-en-Diois (p242)
Transport	train, bus

Summary Explore the truly magnificent Cirque d'Archiane from above and below; discover the secret delights of the Jardin du Roi and the expansive Glandasse meadows.

The towering cliffs of the Vercors Plateau are stunningly impressive, whichever way you approach the area. Bounded in the north and east by the Drac River, in the west by the Isère and in the south by the Drôme, this triangular plateau extends for 63km

Ecological Diversity & Traditional Culture

The Réserve Naturelle des Hauts Plateaux du Vercors, within the regional park, is France's largest such reserve, protecting 17 sq km of the plateau. It extends south from near the village of Corrençon to the plateau rim overlooking Châtillon-en-Diois (p244); the rim also forms the eastern and southern boundaries and it includes the extraordinary pinnacle Mont Aiguille.

Set aside in 1985 the reserve, lying at the intersection of Mediterranean, Continental and Atlantic climatic influences, is of outstanding importance for its ecological diversity and the evolution of its landscape is a result of forestry and summer grazing; up to 20,000 sheep still spend high summer up there. No less important are the karstic limestone features – the intricate mosaic of channels dissecting the flat rock beds – and the absence of surface water.

Walkers are very welcome in the reserve, though several regulations, much the same as those for national parks, must be heeded (see Responsible Walking, p41). Notably, camping is allowed only close to the designated waymarked routes, including the GR91 and the GR93.

from north to south, but nowhere more than 40km from east to west. It is rimmed with spectacular limestone cliffs, pierced with deep gorges in the west. The massive Grand Veymont (2341m) in the southeast is the highest point; nearby is the extraordinary isolated rock of Mont Aiguille. The southern reaches of the plateau are more dissected with the huge Cirque d'Archiane taking a great bite out of the otherwise smooth profile. Almost the entire plateau is within the 180-sq-km Parc Naturel Régional du Vercors, which is home to 30,000 people. The park includes the 17-sq-km Réserve Naturelle des Hauts Plateaux du Vercors (see boxed text above).

The long-standing tradition of taking sheep up to the plateau for summer grazing continues; the annual *Fête de Transhumance* at the town of Die in the Drôme Valley marks the beginning of the season, usually in late June.

Around 2850km of waymarked paths crisscross the park making a wealth of walks possible, from multiday treks to day outings, from the several villages and small towns on the plateau and scattered around its foothills.

The walk described here follows part of two waymarked long-distance routes (GR91 and GR93); the second day's walk includes an exploration of the beautiful and much less frequented Jardin du Roi. If for whatever reason, this is impracticable, you can go direct from Benevise to Archiane, following the GR93 (one hour, 3.5km).

NATURAL HISTORY

In the wetter parts of the foothills, up to around 900m, woodlands of downy and sessile oak, ash and Scots pine shelter box and laburnum. The drier southeastern slopes support oak, beech, fir and Scots pine, with lavender and wild thyme emphasising the Mediterranean character of the area.

Forests dominate the undulating plateau between 900m and 1500m, beech, fir and Norway spruce being the main species. They provide shelter for squirrels and mice, and some of the several species of mammals introduced to the Vercors: red deer, roe deer and mouflons (wild sheep). The park's emblem bird, the black capercaillie, is also found here.

The subalpine areas, above 1700m, merge with the very small extent of alpine habitat above 2200m. Spruce and silver fir survive, though not on the highest ground. The

Cirque d'Archiane

abundant and colourful wildflowers include yellow wild tulips, buttercups, narcissus (daffodils), brilliant deep blue gentians, white St Bruno's lilies and purple alpine asters. You're likely to see chamois, which have survived thanks to stringent controls on hunting; marmots are relatively common, though the ibex (another introduction) is less so.

PLANNING
What to Bring
Don't forget a compass for the second day across the plateau – it is *not* the place to be in poor visibility, or indeed in bad weather of any kind.

Maps & Books
The walk is covered by the IGN 1:25,000 map No 3237OT *Glandasse*. The FFRP's Topo-Guide No 904 *Tours et Traversées dans le Vercors, le Diois et les Baronnies* is a weighty tome but invaluable for extended visits to the area. However, don't rely on the information under the 'Revitaillement' (food shops) heading – the current edition has at least two errors (Benevise and Les Nonnières).

Information Sources
The headquarters of the park is located at **Maison du Parc** (☎ 04 76 94 38 26; www .parc-du-vercors.fr; 255 chemin des Fusillés, 38250 Lans-en-Vercors).

For regionwide tourist information contact **CDT de l'Isère** (☎ 04 76 54 34 36; www.isere-tourisme.com; 14 rue de la République, 38019 Grenoble) and **CDT de la Drôme** (☎ 04 75 82 19 26; www.drometourisme.com; 8 rue Baudin, 26000 Valence).

The weather forecast is available from ☎ 3250, followed by 4 (Montagne) and the *département* number – 26 for Drôme or 30 for Isère.

NEAREST TOWNS
Lus-la-Croix-Haute
A large village in the Buech Valley, its eyes are firmly fixed on the southeastern escarpment of the Vercors Plateau.

You wil find a **tourist office** (☎ 04 92 58 51 85; otlus@free.fr; rue Principal, 26620 Lus-la-Croix-Haute; open Tue, Fri & weekend mornings) in the village, but no ATM.

Places to Stay & Eat Between the train station and the village, **Camping de la Condamine** (☎ 04 92 58 50 86, fax 04 92 58 55 92; Le Grand Logis; camping per adult & tent €4.70, free hot showers; menu €10.50) has grassed, shady sites and superb views as well as a **bar** and **restaurant**.

Gîte d'étape Point-Virgule (☎ 04 92 58 52 79; gite.point.virgule@wanadoo.fr; dorm beds €13.30, half board €25.70; open year-round) occupies a 300-year-old farmhouse. The very friendly and helpful owner will meet guests at the station by arrangement.

Hôtel de la Poste (☎ 04 92 58 50 05, fax 04 92 58 52 22; place de la Mairie; singles/doubles with shower only €25/31, doubles with bathroom €35; menu €13; dishes €8.50) is a simple, homely place in the centre of the village with a **bar-brasserie**.

Hôtel le Chamousset (☎ 04 92 58 51 12; chr.garcia@wanadoo.fr; doubles with bathroom €35, half board €33; menu €11), close to the village centre, extends a friendly welcome and has comfortable, neatly furnished rooms. The **restaurant** offers salads (€7 to €8), omelettes (€5 to €7) or pizzas cooked in a wood-fired oven (€6 to €8).

There's a **8 à Huit supermarket** (closed Mon & Sun afternoon) and a **boulangerie** (place de la Mairie).

Getting There & Away Lus is located on the Grenoble–Veynes–Gap **SNCF** (☎ 08 92 35 35 35) train line (Grenoble: €10.80, 1¼ hours, at least two Monday to Saturday and four on Sunday).

Châtillon-en-Diois
This large, yet compact village with many centuries-old buildings is scenically located at the foot of the southwestern corner of the Vercors Plateau. The **tourist office** (☎ 04 75 21 10 07; square Jean Giono, 26410 Châtillon-en-Diois; open most afternoons) is a very helpful source of local information.

Places to Stay & Eat With a sheltered, shady site beside the river, **Camping Les**

Chaussières (☎ *04 75 21 10 30, fax 04 75 21 26 63; camping 2 people & tent €9.10)* is 200m west of the tourist office.

Gîte d'étape du Suel *(☎/fax 04 75 21 13 49; Montée du Tricot; dorm beds €12, half board €27)* is the first place you hit on reaching the village. It has various-sized bunk rooms, none too cramped, and a large kitchen-dining room.

Hotel du Dauphiné (☎ *04 75 21 13 13; hoteldudauphine@wanadoo.fr; place Pierre Dévoluy; doubles with washbasin/bathroom €34/48)* is a large rambling old building in the village centre. Its **Le Bistroquet** *(entrees €4.50-9, mains €11-19.50; menu €22)* restaurant has a rustic *carte*, including pan-fried snails to start followed by roast pigeon with chestnuts.

Café de La Mairie (☎ *04 75 21 19 31; place du Reviron; doubles with washbasin/ bathroom €40/45; menu €13)* is a homely B&B above the eponymous **bar-restaurant** where you can try the local lamb.

Libre Service *(place du Reviron, open daily except Thu & Sun afternoon)* is much smaller than the **8 à Huit supermarket** *(rue du Reclus; closed Mon & Sun afternoon)*. There's also a good **boulangerie** *(rue du Reclus)*.

Getting There & Away From Châtillon (rue de Reclus, beside the tourist office), **Regie Voyages** (☎ *04 75 81 72 62; www.cg26.fr)* operates a bus service to Die train station (€2.60, 30 minutes, at least two Monday to Saturday). From Die, trains (☎ 08 92 35 35 35) go to Valence-Ville and to Valence TGV station (€7.80, two hours, several daily) with connections to Grenoble for Lyon and Paris, and to Briançon (€20.30, 2¾ hours, at least two daily) for Marseille.

THE WALK
Day 1: Lus-la-Croix-Haute to Benevise
7–7½ hours, 24.5km, 960m ascent

Facing the *mairie* in place de la Mairie, cross place de la République to the right and turn left down a lane from the corner of that place and rue Daniel Pavier. Continue along the D505, past the camping ground, and bear right to the N75. Cross diagonally right to a vehicle track, which goes under a rail bridge. The track, then a road, takes you through the hamlet of Les Villageois. Just around a left bend, go right along a track and on to the next hamlet, Les Fauries. From here a vehicle track leads into a dramatic, narrow, steep-sided valley. At the locality of **Les Chaumets** leave the track on the south side of a small stream (the map in the Topo-Guide is incorrect here) and follow a path, faint at first, northwestwards and parallel to the stream. Kept left after a few hundred metres; next, bear right across the stream then shortly after cross another and ascend steeply to Col de Grimone (1½ hours from the start).

Walk northwest down the D538 for 1km; on a bend go right to a path leading up a fairly broad spur. Turn left along the second track you come to; 200m further on continue left along a grassed track. After about 600m maintain direction downhill on a forest road for 200m. Take the first track to the right and regain height; a few hundred metres further on, turn right up a path, soon emerging into the open. On the crest of a spur the path turns into a spectacular, wide valley. It then follows a superb rising contour across scree and over grass – richly carpeted with wildflowers in spring – across two small gullies and up to **Col de Seysse** (two hours from Col de Grimone). The massive peak Le Jocou (2051m) broods over the col to the southeast and, below, the wide valley on the eastern side of the Vercors Plateau stretches to the horizon.

Cross the steep flank then gain the top of **Crête de Jiboui**. About 1.2km from the col and just beyond a small pinnacle, turn sharp left to leave the ridge. The sparsely waymarked route makes a tight zigzag, heads south then northwest, soon following a clear track past a clump of conifers and a small cabin. Leave the track beside a small pond and descend a grassy spur briefly, then leave it to cross a stream and enter woodland where the path is clear. Beyond the belt of trees, maintain direction down the shallow valley to pass the derelict **Ferme du Désert** (1½ hours from Col de Seysse). Follow a wide track down through some woodland;

10 minutes from the farm, turn right along a vehicle track and continue to the D120 road. Walk left down it for 500m, leaving it along a path to the left (just past a small concrete building on the right) which drops into a precipitous wooded valley. After about 20 minutes, follow a vehicle track down the valley for about 1km. Turn left off it down a path signed *'Cascade'* and go down to another vehicle track, straight on into the hamlet of **Les Nonnières** (1¼ hours from Ferme du Désert). Here you'll find just one hotel – worth a detour for a drink at the bar before the last ascent of the day. To reach the hotel, turn right at a T-junction.

Le Mont Barral (☎ *04 75 21 12 21; mtbarral@aol.com; doubles with bathroom €48, half board €49; entrées €8.50-11, mains €10.50-16.50, menus €18.50 & 27)* is, contrary to first impressions, an unpretentious place with comfortable rooms and an enticing swimming pool. In the **restaurant** you can choose from the *carte* with salads, frogs' legs or roast guinea fowl.

To continue to Benevise, walk left down the road from the T-junction for 600m to a track on the right beside a cemetery; 500m along it crosses a stream from where a path rises fairly steeply to the D515. Turn left and on the edge of the hamlet of **Benevise** branch right along a minor road; bear right uphill just before a small church to a road. Turn left then right and go on for 50m to another junction where accommodation is 150m to the left (45 minutes from Les Nonnières).

Gîte de Benevise (☎/*fax 04 75 21 16 14; dorm beds €12.50, half board €29; breakfast €4)* is definitely a walkers' haven, a well-run place with comfortable bunk rooms. Booking is absolutely essential. Benevise does not have a shop.

Day 2: Benevise to Archiane
6–6¼ hours, 15km, 820m ascent
Follow the D515 east from Benevise for about 15 minutes; leave it opposite road warning signs, up a wide gravel track. This track relentlessly eats up the long ascent, through woodland and finally, a gap in the cliffs, to **Tussac** (1¼ hours from Benevise).

Here, six cabins – scattered about the green pastures – enjoy a superb outlook across the spires of Vallée de Combau to Mont Barral and rows of higher peaks further east.

From here follow paths and tracks generally north across the plateau, route finding being simplified most of the way by regularly spaced cairns. From Tussac continue to the right of the largest cabin to follow a vehicle track up a shallow grassy valley; about 20 minutes from Tussac pass a timber cabin on the right. Here the track fades – head northwards up a slope and through conifers, keeping east of La Grande Pigne, distinguished by many dead trees. Then, the wide valley of Combe du Coureau opens out on the right and you pass a tiny stone cabin in a shallow valley on your left. Here, pick up a track that traverses the *combe* and follow it northwest between the Têtes d'Agnelet and Rancou, the hill to the east. Along the way you may notice an engraved cairn sitting on a stone – which certainly isn't the local altitude. The way onward leads through a gracefully hummocky valley west of Rancou and its northern ridge. Eventually the track starts to bend northwestwards and you reach the large cabin and an adjacent ruin at **Bergerie du Jardin du Roi** (1733m; 1½ hours from Tussac).

Take care to turn west along a cairned route (another leads north) – a well-worn path soon materialises among some trees. It arcs north for a few hundred metres then resumes a westward course. Approximately 30 minutes from the Bergerie pass the remains of a stone hut surrounded by the ruins of a stone wall. About 500m further on through more dissected terrain, you come to a path intersection. Continue westwards, soon crossing a grassy glade pockmarked with sinkholes. Further on, the path bends slightly south and the vast depths of the **Cirque d'Archiane** materialise before you. Head northwest with steep wooded ground close on the right and descend the rocky path, through crags, across scree and down to a clearer path in the narrow valley. The next extraordinary kilometre takes you down a scree-filled canyon; in the later stages the path keeps to the western side through trees to Les Quatre Chemins path junction and a huge cairn (two hours from the *bergerie*).

The awesome route down through the cirque crosses small scree fields and follows narrow paths below soaring cliffs – take care here, the path is not what you'd call stable. It then veers away from the cliffs to descend steadily through dense woodland. At L'Aubaise (an hour from the junction) there's a turnoff for an alternative route to Archiane via Le Belvédère. From there, via the direct route it's another 25 minutes down to the hamlet of **Archiane** where the refuge is on the far side.

Refuge d'Archiane (☎ 04 75 21 24 47; *www.archiane.net - French only; dorm beds €8.50, half board €28)* is a traditional refuge with a sleeping platform in one dorm and double bunks in another. The friendly, enthusiastic host is an excellent chef and evening meals are bound to be lively and enjoyable.

Otherwise, in this home for just a dozen permanent residents, there's **Buvette Ferme Tosato** across the road where you can buy local honey, nuts and goats' cheese.

Day 3: Archiane to Châtillon-en-Diois

8–8½ hours, 22.5km, 1180m ascent, 1250m descent

Retrace your steps of yesterday afternoon to Les Quatre Chemins junction. If you've arrived at Archiane by a different route, walk up past the *buvette* and soon start ascending, up past L'Aubaise path junction, through dense woodland, to the base of the cliffs. The path, very narrow in three places, snakes along beside the rock wall then crosses huge masses of scree filling the valley, across which you might see chamois bounding effortlessly and with sublime disregard for dislodged stones. Continue on through woodland to **Les Quatre Chemins** path junction (1¾ hours from Archiane).

Go left up the scree on a zigzagging path, interspersed with easier sections through trees and head up to the lowermost ramparts of the Montagne du Glandasse Plateau

Alpine Menus Explained

Several staple items appear on many restaurant menus in the Alps, all of which are worth trying at least once, though come prepared with a ravenous appetite to tackle their combinations of rich ingredients, especially the generous use of cheese.

Crozet marries raw ham, hand-made pasta, meat and vegetables.

Farci (literally 'stuffed') combines raw ham, vegetable croquettes with lightly salted ham, and steamed potatoes, and is served with a green salad.

Fondue comes in at least two guises: **bourguignonne** – small chunks of beef cooked in oil and dipped in a selection of sauces – and, most likely **savoyarde** – bread dipped in hot melted cheese flavoured with white wine, garlic and cherry brandy.

Pierrade appears at the table on a heated stone and may comprise a selection of meats (beef, turkey, duck) with appropriate sauces, vegetables and *gratin dauphinois* – oven-cooked sliced potatoes with eggs, cream, garlic and cheese.

Poêlee queyrassine could presumably be found in other areas beyond the Queyras, and is a mixture of pan-fried potatoes, bacon and onions laced with local cheese and served with salad.

Raclette (literally 'scraper') indicating that cheese is scraped – grated – from a large block, strewn across potatoes and pork (or perhaps gherkins) and melted under a grill.

Tartiflette brings together potatoes, bacon, onions and a soft, mild cheese, which oozes through the dish as it cooks in the oven.

(30 minutes from the junction). Then it's delightful walking generally northwards, initially past lowish cliffs on the left, across limestone pavement, grassland rich with wildflowers in spring, and through scattered conifers. As the terrain opens out, the fantastical column of Mont Aiguille comes into view to the northeast. Descend slightly to a path junction (40 minutes from the edge of the plateau). Here you leave the waymarked route No 93 and join No 91, with a major change in direction to the southwest. Follow

Cirque d'Archiane

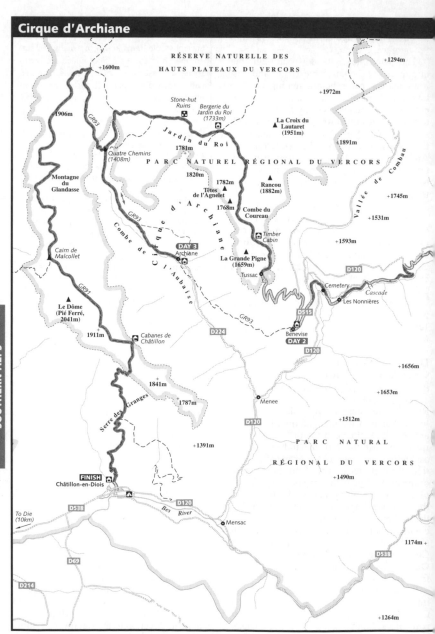

RÉSERVE NATURELLE DES
HAUTS PLATEAUX DU VERCORS

+1294m

+1600m

+1972m

Stone-hut
Ruins

Bergerie du
Jardin du Roi
(1733m)

La Croix du
Lautaret
(1951m)

1906m

GR93

Jardin du Roi

+1891m

Quatre Chemins
(1408m)

1781m

PARC NATUREL RÉGIONAL DU VERCORS

Vallée de Combau

Montagne
du Glandasse

1820m

1782m

Têtes
de l'Agnelet

Rancou
(1882m)

+1745m

GR93

1768m

Combe du
Coureau

+1531m

Combe de l'Aubaise

Cirque d'Archiane

+1593m

Cairn de
Malcollet

Timber
Cabin

DAY 3

Archiane

La Grande Pigne
(1659m)

D120

GR91

Le Dôme
(Pié Ferré,
2041m)

Tussac

Cemetery

Cascade

1911m

Les Nonnières

Cabanes de
Châtillon

GR93

D515

D224

Benevise

DAY 2

D120

+1656m

1841m

+1653m

1787m

Menee

+1512m

Serre des Granges

D120

+1391m

PARC NATURAL

RÉGIONAL DU VERCORS

+1490m

FINISH

Châtillon-en-Diois

To Die
(10km)

D538

D120

Bes River

1174m +

Mensac

D69

D538

D214

+1264m

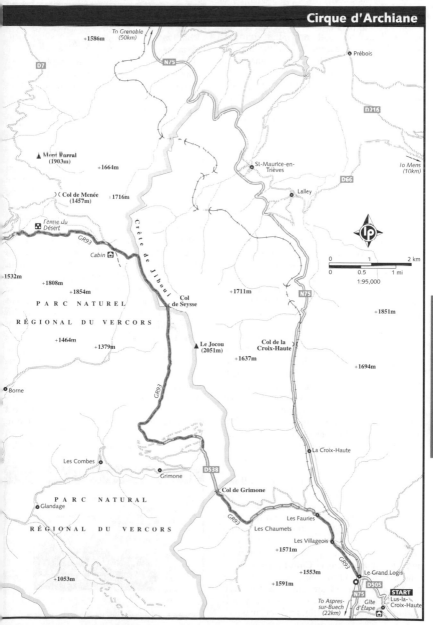

a well-defined path in that direction; after about 10 minutes bear left along a slightly less well defined path and start gaining height. It's a steep ascent most of the way to the crest of the ridge (1906m; 1¼ hours from the GR93-GR91 junction).

From there the well-cairned route leads generally south along the plateau, past innumerable sink holes – cavernous and cup-sized – across shallow basins, steering a fairly level course between higher ground to the east and west, with wide views a constant distraction. For a while, you're close to the western rim, with quite a different outlook to the wide settled valley of the Drôme River below. At length a shortish ascent brings you to the 3m-high **Cairn de Malcollet** perched on the western rim (1½ hours from 1906m). From here the path trends southeastwards and descends slightly across a lovely grassy valley with the massive Le Dôme above on the right. Then, Cirque d'Archiane appears below, with the Jardin du Roi Plateau to the north and, beyond, the top of Mont Aiguille and Grand Veymont, the wedge-shaped peak towering above all else.

The route then contours a steep slope and descends to the vast plain where the two **Cabanes de Châtillon** sit close to the eastern edge (an hour from the cairn). The smaller of the two is always open to walkers: it has a small wood-fired stove for heating, table and sleeping platforms for about eight people. Water is available from a point on the western rim, east of the waymarked route. For magnificent views of the cirque, go up to the eastern edge, just above the *cabanes*.

To continue, cross the meadow, following a line of stones southwards to a large sprawling cairn and the start of a wide track. It deals with the very steep descent in a long series of comfortable zigzags down through woodland. About an hour from the top, cross a vehicle track at Serre des Granges and continue down to **Châtillon-en-Diois** (another hour). From the *gîte* on the edge of the village, follow the road down through the village to the main road where you'll find other accommodation and services.

In the Shadow of La Meije

Duration	3 days
Distance	54km
Difficulty	moderate–demanding
Start	Bourg d'Oisans (p249)
Finish	Le Monêtier-les-Bains (p250)
Transport	bus

Summary A truly scenic traverse of the northern valleys and passes of the Écrins massif and a crossing of the glorious Plateau de Paris.

The Écrins massif is a gathering of rugged peaks and the southernmost glaciers in all the Alps, within the larger area of the Oisans, sprawling across the triangle linking Grenoble, Briançon and Gap. The Parc National des Écrins, greatly extended from its 1913 origin in the Vénéon Valley, comprises a central zone of 91 sq km and a peripheral zone around twice that size, home to about 27,000 people. The three highest peaks in France outside the Mont Blanc massif lie within the park, all in the northern Massif de Pelvoux: Barre des Écrins (4102m), La Meije (3983m) and Mont Pelvoux (3932m); altogether more than 100 summits top the 3000m mark. These peaks cluster at the heads of a complex array of ridges separating several deep valleys thrusting into the icy heartland from all directions: the Romanche in the north; Guisane in the northeast; Durance in the west; then Vallouise (the most developed and settled), followed by Drac in the south; Valjouffrey and Valgaudemar in the west; and the Vénéon in the northwest.

In the Shadow of La Meije

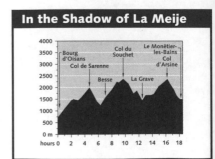

The highest peaks and ridges are strictly for mountaineers and rock climbers, while walkers can easily reach relatively high passes within sight of the central massif. The walk described here, part of the Tour de l'Oisans (or the GR54) takes you across the northern flank of the massif, dominated by the magnificent peak La Meije (see also Other Walks, p272).

NATURAL HISTORY

It's certain you'll see marmots and chamois, and possibly mountain hares too. Of the 110 species of birds, you might just spot a golden eagle soaring above the cliffs or come upon a black capercaillie in the forests. Jackdaws are more common and you'll probably hear a black woodpecker before you see one.

PLANNING
When to Walk

The highest pass on this walk, Col du Souchet, at 2365m, should normally be accessible from late May.

Maps & Books

The IGN 1:25,000 maps No 3335ET *Le Bourg d'Oisans* and No 3436ET *Meije, Pelvoux* cover the walk. The IGN 1:60,000 map No 5 *Écrins* is useful for planning.

Écrins & Oisans

The earliest name on record for the massif appears to be Massif de Pelvoux, after the peak long believed to be the highest in the area. It's thought that Écrins, the name now used and meaning 'casket', derives from early mapping surveyors' interpretations of the local dialect and in particular the name for the highest summit, now known as La Barre des Écrins. In conversations with prospectors in the mineral-rich hills northeast of Mont Pelvoux, mention was made of *écrins*, wooden casks placed in streams below small cascades to trap fine, water-borne mineral deposits.

The name Oisans goes back much further, to the occupation of the Romanche Valley by the Ucenii, a Gallic tribe overwhelmed by Roman forces around AD 52.

The FFRP's Topo-Guide No 508 *Tour de l'Oisans* and Cicerone's *Walking in the Écrins National Park* by Kev Reynolds are both recommended. The national park's own publications include guides to geology, flora and walks in the park, available online or from park offices.

Information Sources

The national park has an office in Briançon at **Maison du Parc à Briançon** (☎ 04 92 21 08 49; www.les-ecrins-parc-national.fr; place Médécin Général; open daily Jul-Aug, Tue-Sat rest of year). The website is worth a look for a detailed list of *gîtes d'étape* and *refuges*, transport information and environmental topics.

Regional tourist information is available from **CDT de l'Isère** (☎ 04 76 54 34 36; www.isere-tourisme.com; 14 rue de la République, 38019 Grenoble) and **CDT des Hautes-Alpes** (☎ 04 92 53 62 00; www.hautes-alpes.net; rue Capitaine de Bresson, 05000 Gap).

Local weather forecasts are available from ☎ 3250, followed by 4 (Montagne) and the *département* number – 26 for Drôme or 30 for Isère.

NEAREST TOWNS
Bourg d'Oisans

A town that lives for and on cycling – traditionally on the route of the famous Tour de France, it's spread out along the busy N91, deep in the Romanche Valley.

There's a list of hotels posted on a board near the **TIC** (☎ 04 76 80 03 25; www.bourgdoisans.com; quai Girard, 38250 Bourg d'Oisans; open daily Jul-Aug, Mon-Sat rest of year) in the centre of town. The daily forecast is posted on the front door.

There's a small **national park office** (rue Général de Gaulle; open daily Jul-Aug) in town.

There are ATMs in rue de la République, and in the nearby **post office** (open Mon-Fri & Sat morning), where Internet access is available via Cyberposte (see Post & Communications, p342).

Maison de la Presse (19 rue de la République; closed Sun afternoon) has all the maps, guides and books you'll need.

La Montagne Sports (*quai Professeur Berlioux*) is well stocked with walking and camping equipment.

Places to Stay & Eat Just south of the town centre, **Camping le Colporteur** (☎ *04 76 79 11 44; info@camping-colporteur.com; Le Mas du Plan; camping 1/2 people & tent €8.25/ 10.50; open mid-May–mid-Sep*) is quiet and very well set up.

Camping la Cascade (☎ *04 76 80 02 42; lacascade@wanadoo.fr; Sarenne; camping 2 people & tent €16, 2-person chalet €37-57*) is beside the route, well away from the main road. During July and August, chalets cannot be hired by the day.

La Val de la Meije (☎ *04 76 80 03 62; valdemeije@libertysurf.fr; Le Vert; dorm beds/ B&B doubles €18/42*), a *gîte d'étape*, is 2km southeast of the town via a road branching from the N91 near the supermarket.

Hôtel la Cascade (☎ *04 76 79 16 39; www.la-cascade.com - French only; Pont de la Romanche; singles/doubles with bathroom €28/35; breakfast €5.50*) is in an old building beside the river, about seven minutes' walk from the centre of the town, and is good value.

Hôtel le Terminus (☎ *04 76 80 00 26, fax 04 76 11 05 02; av de la Gare; singles/ doubles €27/30, doubles with bathroom €45; breakfast €6*) is on the main road opposite the bus station; ask for a quiet room at the back. The hotel is superbly maintained by the friendly and attentive hosts.

Hôtel des Alpes (☎ *04 76 80 00 16, fax 04 76 79 15 13; av Général de Gaulle; doubles with shower/bathroom €30/40; breakfast €5*) is in an intriguing old building between the town's colourful shopping street and the busy central place.

Three supermarkets vie for patronage: **Casino** (*N91; open Mon-Sat*) near Pont Romanche, **Petit Casino** (*11 rue du Général de Gaulle; open Tue-Sun noon*) and **Proxi** (*34 rue de la République; open Mon-Sun noon*). **Market** day is Saturday morning.

La Rive Gauche (☎ *04 76 80 13 14; quai Professeur Berlioux; menu €13*) is a popular restaurant with several tables right beside the river; specialities include fondues (to

€25 per person), local trout and better-than-average pizzas (€6 to €10).

La Crepizza (☎ *04 76 80 20 73; place lo Barruel; menus €15.10 & 14.50*) is intriguingly hidden away in a back street but not quite buried among old houses. Try the cross-cultural *savoyarde breton galette* – and the pasta's not bad either.

Le Moulin des Truîtes Bleues (☎ *04 76 80 00 26; av de la Gare; menus €12.50-22*) prepares trout and grilled *andouilette* (tripe sausage), plus *raclette* and a hefty Norwegian omelette.

Getting There & Away Grenoble–Briançon bus (No 306), run by **VFD** (☎ *08 20 83 38 33; www.vfd.fr*) stops here (to/from Grenoble: €4.80, one hour five minutes, one daily; fo/from Briançon: €3.70, one hour 55 minutes, one daily).

Le Monêtier-les-Bains
At the foot of the northeastern corner of the Écrins massif, Mônetier's centuries-old heart is almost completely surrounded by not-too-unsightly, low-rise modern apartments.

The **TIC** (☎ *04 92 24 98 99; www.monetier .com - French only; route du Grenoble; open daily*) has accommodation information.

There's an ATM at the post office on the main street at the eastern end of the village. **Parenthese** is a we-sell-everything shop, including maps, on the main road near the prominent church.

Places to Stay & Eat With a very friendly and knowledgeable host, **Gîte le Flourou** (☎ *04 92 24 41 13; flourou@chez.com; 31 rue Bonbouget; half board €29.50*) has slightly cramped two-, four- or six-bunk rooms. The homemade four-course evening meal is superb.

Hôtel de l'Europe et des Bains (☎ *04 92 24 40 03; www.grandski.com; 1 rue St-Eldrade; singles/doubles with bathroom €53/61, half board €58/70; breakfast €7.60; menus €16-30*) is a long-established, family-run hotel in the older part of the village, though lacking an outlook. It has its own **restaurant**.

Hôtel Alliey (☎ *04 92 24 44 20; www .alliey.com; B&B doubles with bathroom €68,*

La Meije

Although not the highest peak in the national park, La Meije (3982m) reigns supreme: for its spectacular beauty, as a respected mountaineering challenge and for the saga of attempts to conquer its summit – conquest rather than communion was the hallmark of 19th-century philosophy. It comprises three summits: the Grand Pic de la Meije in the west (the highest), the central Doigt de Dieu and the eastern Meije Orientale. The name derives from a local-dialect word meaning 'midday'.

By 1870 most of the major Alpine summits had been climbed, including La Barre des Écrins (4102m) in 1864 by a party containing Edward Whymper of Matterhorn fame. However, La Meije remained inviolate, despite attempts by various notable mountaineers. In 1877 young Baron Emmanuel Boileau de Castelneau seized the challenge and hired locals Pierre Gaspard and his 20-year-old son to accompany him; they set out from la Bérade near the head of the Vénéon Valley. The Gaspards were determined to win the summit rather than surrender it to their Chamonix rivals. The glacier guarding the southern face was easily surmounted but the party hesitated just below the summit. Boileau retreated but the Gaspards, not to be beaten so close to victory, found a route around the northern face and up to the top. Other ascents soon followed; the first all-woman party to climb la Meije was led by British mountaineer Nea Morin in 1933. Nowadays ascents are almost daily events, weather permitting.

half board €63; menus €24-31.50) is another long-standing establishment, located opposite the church with crisply modern decor in the rooms and an innovative restaurant. Meals might feature fondue with wild mushrooms and smoked ham, local trout and lamb.

A **Sherpa** minimarket, two **boulangeries** and a handful of **bars** are strung out along the main street; **market** day is Friday.

Restaurant de la Mangeoire (☎ 04 92 24 41 15; route du Grenoble; menu €21) is a small, homely place near the tourist office,

which features fondues (€18 to €19) among standard meat and fish dishes.

Getting There & Away The Grenoble–Briançon bus (No 306) run by **VFD** (☎ 08 20 83 38 33; www.vfd.fr) stops here (to/from Grenoble: €7, 2¼ hours, one daily; to/from Briançon: €2.60, 35 minutes, one daily).

THE WALK
Day 1: Bourg d'Oisans to Besse
7–7¼ hours, 18km, 1600m ascent

Walk out of Bourg d'Oisans northeastwards (towards Briançon) beside the main road, bear left at a T-junction along the D211 towards Huez for 600m. Turn right on the far side of the entrance to Camping la Cascade beside the river and along a wide path. Very soon the fun starts, with natural steps rising across the jagged cliff. Then comes the first of five cable-protected sections, across the cliff and up wide chimneys, separated by interludes through trees or in the open. In places you look straight down, vertiginously perhaps, to the camping ground, so you need to move carefully. The cables, threaded through bolts are, rest assured, very firmly driven into the rock. With that behind you, follow the path through trees to a vehicle track and turn left and soon reach the hamlet of La Garde (an hour from the start). Turn right by the *mairie* to gain height along a path. About 1.5km from La Garde, turn left along a road, which takes you to the hamlet of **Le Châtelard** and a drinking water fountain. Nearby is a hotel-bar-restaurant **La Forêt de Maronne** (☎ 04 76 80 00 06; fax 04 76 79 14 61; single/double with bathroom €40/50; breakfast €6.50).

With the serried ranks of apartments in L'Alpe d'Huez high above, continue along the road, rising gradually through the hamlet of **Maronne** and on to **Le Rosay**, at the entrance to which bear left (1¼ hours from La Garde). Through the hamlet's well-maintained stone houses, bear right past a tiny chapel along a path. From a sharp bend, the path then drops steeply into the deep gorge of the Sarenne River. Cross an old stone bridge, go up a few metres and right

In the Shadow of La Meije

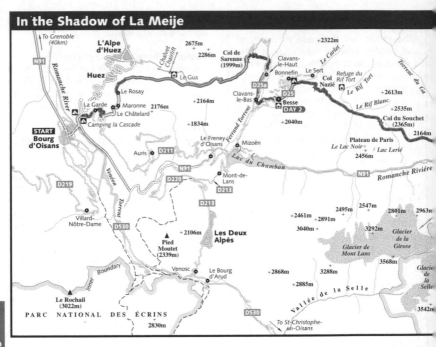

along a wide path. After about 10 minutes, keep right along a vehicle track which, at length, brings you to one end of the Chalvet chairlift (an hour from Le Rosay). Here, **Auberge de Combe Haute** (☎ 04 76 80 61 38; half board €32; open from mid-Jun) has a bar and **restaurant**.

The vehicle track leads on across the open expanses of Le Gua and up through the Sarenne Valley. About 3km from the auberge, bear right at a road junction; then 50m along turn left up an old track to bypass some of the gravel road. When you return to the road it has, amazingly, acquired a bitumen surface to waft you up to **Col de Sarenne** (1¼ hours from the auberge), where new vistas of the grey-green peaks and ridges around the Vallée du Ferrand present themselves. Continue down the road, around a couple of bends, and the elegant spire of La Meije (3982m) and its attendant peaks and glaciers come into view to the southeast.

Then, leave the road via a signposted path to descend the steep, often rocky slope. Eventually the path straightens becoming rather vague (with sparse waymarkers) as it leads over a flat-topped knoll to a vehicle track. Bear left for no more than 50m to a wide rocky gully and follow a narrow path, obscure at first, down to a road. Cross straight over and continue down an old track between low walls to a U-bend in a road. Follow the road down into the village of **Clavans-le-Haut**. At a T-junction turn right and continue along a narrow street between traditional stone and timber houses. Pass a drinking fountain to reach a U-bend on the edge of the village and bear right. A couple of hundred metres along, continue straight ahead from a bend down a wide woodland track that leads back to the road (D25a) at the entrance to the village of Clavans-le-Bas (1½ hours from Col de Sarenne). In about 200m you come to a T-junction and nearby on the right is **Auberge du Saval** (☎ 04 76

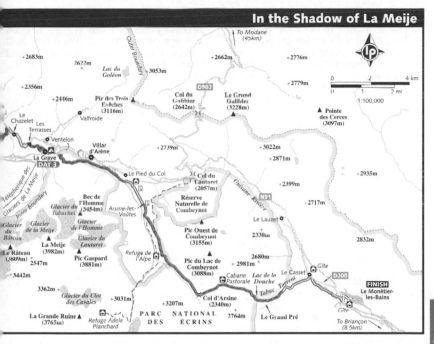

In the Shadow of La Meije

DAY 3

FINISH
Le Monêtier-
les-Bains

80 25 28; *doubles with bathroom, half board
€43; closed Thu*). The menu features fondue,
raclette and *tartiflette* and it sells local
cheese, honey and much else.

Go left at the junction nearby and down a
path to a vehicle track. Follow it down to a
road and turn left. Cross the Ferrand River
and go up past the old Besse communal mill
to the *Chemin des Voûtes*. It zigzags up the
steep spur to the road; cross and follow a
track up the road again. Continue uphill for
about 50m then bear left along a track and
back to the road for 60m to a path on the left.
Go up the road, on the edge of the village
of **Besse**, cross straight over then take the
first left, a cobbled lane, which lands you on
Besse's main road (an hour from Clavans-
le-Bas). The hotel is to the left, the *gîte* to
the right.

Besse

A compact, traditional village of narrow
streets and alleys, stone houses with timber

verandas, Besse is light years removed from
the angular modern ski towns dominating
the scene earlier in the day. Its name comes
from *bès* the local term for *bouleaux* meaning birch trees.

The nearest tourist office and ATM are in
Bourg d'Oisans.

La Maison des Alpages (☎ *04 76 80 19
09; open daily Jul-Aug, Tue-Thu afternoon
rest of year; admission €3*) houses an exhibition featuring the traditions and practices of
summer grazing on the high pastures.

Le Gay Aire du bivouac (☎ *04 76 80 29 63;
camping €2.80*) is 10 minutes' walk from the
village along the route starting Day 2. Toilets,
drinking water and terraced sites are beside
the river; pick up a €1 token for a hot shower
from the *épicerie* or the *gîte* in the village.

Le Sarret Gîte d'étape (☎ *04 76 80 06 22,
fax 04 76 80 14 01; dorm beds €13-15, half
board €28-30; menus €10-20*) is popular with
walkers, and villagers gravitate to the **bar**
from an early hour. There's a small kitchen

and a **restaurant**. The traditional menu offers several substantial dishes such as fondue, raclette, *crozet* and *farci* (see the boxed text on p245), steak and chips (€12) or pizzas baked in a wood-fired oven (€7 to €12)

Hôtel Alpin (☎ *04 76 80 06 55, fax 04 76 80 12 45; singles/doubles with bathroom €37/43, half board €41)* has comfortable rooms in a beautifully restored old stone building. Its restaurant presents two menus (€13, 16) and specialises in *farcis* and *crozets* (€19.50; see the boxed text on p245).

Bar des Touristes *(open daily)* has a small grocery shop attached. **La Tourte de Besse** *(open Mon, Tue & Fri)* is a unique bakery at the far end of the village. All bread is handmade using only organic flour and baked in a wood-fired oven; it's delicious and very sustaining. Other days the bakery has a stall at Bourg d'Oisans and La Grave **markets**.

There's no public transport to Besse.

Day 2: Besse to La Grave

5¼–5½ hours, 14km, 970m ascent

Set out on the road leading northeast out of the village; at the camping ground, bear right across a stream then go up a track beside it, but after 50m continue straight ahead along a path. This takes you very abruptly up the side of the dramatic valley carved by Le Carlet stream, soon looking down on the tiny clusters of stone buildings that are the traditional, and surviving, hamlets of Bonnefin and Le Sert. A series of zigzags lands you at Col Nazié (one hour from Besse); then it's steeply up the broad spur to an unnamed col at 2244m (45 minutes from Col Nazié). Spectacular views span La Meije, the rugged Pic de l'Etendarde range to the northwest and the Plateau de Paris rolling away eastwards.

From the prominent crucifix, go southeast along the col then down into the wide valley. Here you could diverge just 1km to **Refuge du Rif Tort** (☎ *04 76 80 24 11, 04 76 80 04 91; dorm beds €11.50, half board €28.50, shower €2; open mid-Jun–early Sep)*, where drinks and snacks are always available.

To continue, follow a delightful grassy path with waymarker posts through veritable carpets of buttercups, violets and gentians in early summer, straight towards La Meije,

which becomes an almost overpowering presence the further east you go. Cross a vehicle track and descend to ford two small streams – there's a large information board nearby. Then, it's up the grassy slope (no waymarker posts) to Col du Souchet (an hour from 2244m). From there you have a long steady descent to the '2164m' point where you look straight down to the village of Le Chazelet. Pass beneath an old ski tow, go through a gate (in a seasonal sheep enclosure) and follow knee-friendly zigzags down through another gate, to the bridge over Torrent du Ga. From here you're confronted with a most unkind, steep pull up to **Le Chazelet** (1¾ hours from Col du Souchet). The route leads straight through the village though you could stop here – there are two *gîtes*. **Chez Baptiste** (☎ *04 76 79 92 09, fax 04 76 79 91 21; dorm beds €14, half board €34)* and **Jacquier** (☎ *04 76 79 92 62; bed/B&B €9/13.50)* both offer accommodation in rooms or dorms. There's a kitchen at Jacquier.

Continue along the main road; about 500m from the edge of Le Chazelet and on a bend, go down a track on the right, cross the road and continue down a rough track back to the road. Shortly after, leave it at a U-bend and follow a concreted lane into the village of Les Terrasses. Bear right at a junction and drop down to the road in front of a large church. Go down a ramp, past a drinking fountain, then follow a steep track between stone buildings to a minor road; bend left and down to a wider road. Then turn right to a path that soon crosses the slope for the final descent into **La Grave**. You hit the small town (one hour from Le Chazelet) beside a small chapel; turn right and go down to a junction – the *refuge* is on the left here. For the lower town head right and descend steep wide paths to the main road.

La Grave

Spectacularly located deep in the Romanche Valley and dominated by the La Meije massif, La Grave is a small town of two parts: the old, upper quarter and the lower, more recent and noisy quarter.

The well-organised **tourist office** (☎ 04 76 79 90 05; www.lagrave-lameije.com; open daily) is on the main road at the eastern end of town; an accommodation list with contacts and the local forecast are displayed outside. There's an ATM diagonally opposite.

For maps and guides, try the **Tabac-Presse** (place Victor Chaud) or **Matériel de Montagne** on the main road; the latter also stocks a wide range of outdoor clothing and equipment.

Places to Stay & Eat Well below the busy main road, **Camping de la Meije** (☎ 04 76 79 93 94; www.camping-delameije.com; camping 2 people & tent €9.30; hot shower €1; open May-Sep) is a shady site with good facilities right beside the route of the walk.

Le Refuge (☎ 04 76 79 91 89; place de l'Église; dorm beds €10) is a traditional, alpine-style refuge with fairly basic facilities, including a kitchen.

Le Vieux Guide (☎/fax 04 76 79 90 75; dorm beds €14, half board €29; entrées €7-13, mains €12-14, menus €16-26) has dorm and room accommodation. The **restaurant** emphasises traditional cuisine and the carte features snails with garlic cream and cod with smoked bacon.

Hôtel l'Edelweiss (☎ 04 76 79 90 93, fax 04 76 79 92 64; singles/doubles with bathroom €42/54, with half board €49/62) offers a warm welcome; most of the timber-panelled rooms have a view of La Meije. Don't be deterred by the approach to the hotel up a forbidding flight of concrete steps from the main road.

Hôtel le Serac (☎ 04 76 79 91 53; www .hotel-le-serac.com; singles/doubles with bathroom €62/63, half board €55-70; menus €13-24) probably has the best views of the mountain from its largish rooms, most with a small balcony. The **restaurant** offers venison terrine, trout and traditional tripe sausage.

Hôtel le Castillan (☎ 04 76 79 90 04; ca stillan.hotel@wanadoo.fr; doubles with bathroom €38-54, half board €40-50; menus €14-29) is a chalet-style building that overlooks place Victor Chaud. The **restaurant** goes in for hearty traditional dishes, including a fondue savoyarde (€15).

Sherpa Alimentation (closed Mon) is a small supermarket on the main road. Thursday is **market** day.

Getting There & Away The Grenoble to Briançon (No 306) bus **VFD** (☎ 08 20 83 38 33) stops here (to/from Grenoble: €3.70, 1½ hours, one daily; to/from Briançon: €2.60, one hour 10 minutes, one daily).

Day 3: La Grave to Le Monêtier-les-Bains

6¼-6½ hours, 22km, 1020m ascent

From the tourist office, walk down a minor road towards the camping ground. Cross a bridge and bear left then right and you soon come to a signposted path junction, where you take the right path towards Villar d'Arène 'par forêt'. Keep to the right through the trees to reach meadow land. Follow a vehicle track up through a series of bends; cross a stream and you should find the first waymarker since La Grave; bear left towards a nearby stone building. From here follow a clear path to the right steeply up to reach a gate bearing a 'Troupeau' (flocks/herds) sign then promptly descend to the Romanche River opposite Villar d'Arène (one hour from the start). Head uphill towards L'Alpe de Villar d'Arène; the path soon levels, and descends gradually back to the river. Follow a path along the bank – with the rugged Combeynot massif filling the outlook upriver – to a road (40 minutes from near Villar d'Arène). Turn left to cross the bridge then turn right and continue, past **Refuge du Pas de l'Âne** (☎/fax 04 76 79 94 28; dorm beds €15, half board €35), which also offers refreshments during the day. Cross a bridge to a car park and bear right along a wide vehicle track to reach **Arsine-les-Voûtes**, where you'll find large national park information boards (30 minutes from the first bridge).

The way onward is along the path across scree towards the steep slope seeming to block the valley ahead; traverse a small cliff, scree and a narrow bridge. A steep zigzagging path surmounts the slope, swinging away from the thunderous canyon on the Romanche River. Pass the turn-off to Refuge Adele Planchard and, further on, the path to Col du Lauteret to

Brewed in Briançon

A beer at the end of a long, hot day's walk can do much to restore spirits and slake your thirst. Several well-known (and mass-produced) varieties are readily available in bars and some supermarkets. However, if your tastes veer in the direction of distinctive products from small breweries, look out for the Brasserie Artisanale des Grands Cols label. Expect to pay around €3.20 for a 500mL bottle.

La Tourmente is a 'blond' style, not dissimilar to a lager – effervescent and full of tangy hops. *La Tau Genepi* combines the best of two worlds – a light but not insipid beer, which has been combined superbly with the delicious liqueur *genepi*, which has a distinctive herbal-flowery bouquet. The Brasserie also produces a full-bodied *'brun'* style, better perhaps with or after a meal than before.

the left. An hour from Arsine-les-Voûtes you reach a path to the right to nearby **Refuge de l'Alpe** (☎ 04 76 79 94 66; *dorm beds €13.50; open early Jun-late Sep*) serving lunch, or drinks and snacks during the day. Continue up the path across grassed mountainside – good marmot territory – through the long, wide valley dominated by the multitudinous crags, spires and snowfields of Montagne des Agneaux to the south. Then a final steep section lands you on Col d'Arsine (one hour from the refuge).

The first part of the descent is through a classic glaciated valley – a steep drop into the wide, flat-bottomed valley of Tabuc Torrent, dotted with moraine humps. Pass close to the ruins of Les Châlets d'Arsine, then nearer the path **Cabane pastorale d'Arsine**, overnight accommodation if you're completely self-contained. You soon start to lose height seriously and come to a path junction; go left for a direct descent on slippery gravel or right for more sedate progress. Then, on more-level ground, pass **Lac de la Douche**, though with water only a few degrees above freezing the thought of a swim isn't exactly inviting. Soon you're in larch woodland on a wide path; just past Le Grand Pré, turn right along a vehicle track, then watch for waymarked shortcuts to

take you down to a small car park. Continue down the road, across a bridge and right into the old village of Le Casset (1¾ hours from Col d'Arsine).

About 200m on is a *gîte d'étape* **Le Reb-anchon** (☎/fax 04 92 24 45 74; *rue de Lauzet; dorm beds €12*). Continue down to a bridge over the Guisane, opposite an old church and **Chez Finette** snack bar; cross the bridge and turn left. Follow the vehicle track downstream to a bridge; cross and turn right along a river-bank path. Soon, veer left on a track; a few hundred metres later you come to a road on the edge of **Le Monêtier-les-Bains**, 30 minutes from Le Casset. To reach the town centre, go left up the road for about 400m and right towards St-Pierre along a wide street to a T-junction; turn left up to the main road. For the *gîte*, turn right to the square in front of the *Salle Communale* on the left; bear right down rue de la Turière for about 250m – the *gîte* is signposted to the left.

The Wild Heart of the Queyras

Duration	4 days
Distance	47km
Difficulty	moderate
Start	Ceillac (p258)
Finish	Abriès (p259)
Transport	bus

Summary Magnificent panoramic views from high passes, superlatively beautiful remote lakes, and traditional hamlets and villages.

The Parc Naturel Régional du Queyras has over a dozen summits above 3000m, though the terrain is neither seriously rugged nor completely inaccessible. With no glaciers and snowfields, there's generous scope for walking along narrow ridges, through valleys and to many lakes and waterfalls. The 60-sq-km park was reserved in 1977 to support traditional agriculture and crafts in harmony with tourism and winter sports. Depopulation had blighted the Queyras, down to fewer than 2000 people in the 1960s from 8000 in the mid-19th century but up to 2300 near the end

MICHELLE LEWIS

The Verdon River snakes through Provence's Gorges du Verdon, the largest canyon in Europe

INGRID RODDIS

Calanque d'En Vau, Provence, great for a dip after a exhilarating descent down the limestone cliff

INGRID RODDIS

Calanque de Port-Miou, Provence, a gentle beginning to the demanding Les Calanques walk

Tranquil Lac Egorgéou on The Wild Heart of Queyras walk, Southern Alps

Jagged cliffs above Bourg d'Oisans, Romanche Valley, are negotiated with the help of cables

The Wild Heart of the Queyras

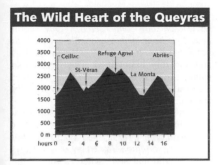

of the 20th century. Typically, the villages are clusters of traditional timber houses around an old church. The origin of the unusual name 'Queyras' remains a mystery, though it has been in use since the 13th century.

The park is essentially the naturally secluded basin of the Guil River. There is only one way in and out year-round – up the Guil Valley from Guillestre. The main waymarked walking routes are the GR58, the Tour du Queyras and a section of the GR5; these core routes, with several variants, and many other paths, offer weeks of first-class walking and the weather is ideal – 300 sunny days annually.

The walk described here follows a section of the GR58, with one variation (between La Monta and Abriès). Each day is of relatively short duration, but combining any two would make a heroic marathon. With a car or carefully planned use of public transport, it's possible to do the last day as a day walk; the first day and first part of the second day can be also adapted as day walks.

NATURAL HISTORY

In the lower reaches of the valleys, up to around 1500m, the Queyras forests consist of beeches and firs in wetter areas and pines on drier ground; above that level, arolla pines and larches thrive. Here you'll find the greatest concentration of wildflowers, making a stunning display during June. Of the 2000 species of flowering plants in the park, 40 are protected, including edelweiss and arnica. Above 2000m, grasses and stunted juniper bushes predominate.

Marmots are the most common mammal. Chamois are more elusive, though there are around 12,000 of them throughout the Queyras; there are also a few mouflon, introduced from Corsica. Birds include royal and golden eagles, falcons, ptarmigan on the rocky open ground, black capercaillies (aggressive woodland birds) and numerous smaller species, including woodpeckers.

Geologically, the Guil and Aigue Blanche Valleys are dominated by schist, a rather friable rock resembling slate. Limestone is the main rock type in the southwestern Queyras. The rocks around St-Véran are rich in minerals – copper has been mined high in the valley in times past.

Sundials

One of the Queyras' distinctive traditions, both artistic and practical, is gnomics – the creation of sundials (*cadrans solaires*). From at least the 18th century, artists – mainly Italian – painted or carved sundials on the walls of houses and other buildings, decorating them with eye-catching motifs and a proverb, so that no two are alike. Popular inscriptions, in French or Latin, reflect religious beliefs or concern with the passage of time: *Il est plus tard que vous ne croyez* – It's later than you think, and *Vita fugit* – Life flies past. Only natural dyes were used: yellow ochre, red iron oxide, sienna earth, mixed with melted wax to ward off the ravages of sun, wind and snow. There are more than 400 sundials in the area, some of the best being in St-Véran, blessed as it is with 300 days of sunshine annually.

Ancient Greek astronomers perfected the calculations necessary for the accurate design of the sundial and the Crusaders brought home from the Middle East the practice of placing the pointer at an angle. The form of *cadrans solaires* has changed very little since. It's easy to read the time accurately: in summer add about 30 minutes, or 1½ hours in winter, to the time shown by the pointer.

Despite the prevalence of electronic counting of the passing moments, sundials are being restored and maintained, thus preserving traditional skills.

PLANNING
When to Walk
Refuge Agnel (the highest accommodation on the walk) opens in mid-June by which time Cols de Chamoussière and Vieux should normally be passable.

Maps & Books
The IGN 1:25,000 maps No 3537ET *Guillestre* and No 3637OT *Mont Viso* cover the walk. The FFRP Topo-Guide Ref 505 *Tour du Queyras* has lots of background information. The park's several publications include guides to its geology and architecture, and a report on the introduction of the ibex, available online or from park offices.

Information Sources
The park's headquarters is at **Maison du Parc** (☎ 04 92 45 06 23; www.parcduqueyras.com; *route de la Gare, 05600 Guillestre*). For general information, the first port of call is **Office de Promotion du Queyras** (☎ 04 92 46 76 18; www.queyras.com - *French only; Maison du Queyras, Aiguilles*).

For local weather forecasts, ring ☎ 3250 followed by 4 (for Montagne) and 05 (for Hautes Alpes *département*).

NEAREST TOWNS
Ceillac
A village of two parts sitting in a wide reach of the Mélezet Valley: the original 'Le Village' with its many and varied stone buildings and the modern outlying L'Ochette, its apartments and houses free of gruesome concrete blocks of flats.

The **tourist office** (☎ 02 92 68 02 05; www.ceillac.com - *French only; place Philippe Lamour; open daily Jul-Aug, Mon-Fri rest of year*) is in the *mairie*. The weather forecast is posted outside. There's an ATM in the same building. **Nevé Sports** stocks stove fuel, maps and guides; the last are also available from **Lou Bouqui'n** in the Centre Commercial (near the *gîte*).

Places to Stay & Eat Set in larch woodland, **Camping les Mélèzes** (☎ 04 92 45 21 93, fax 04 92 45 01 83; *camping 2 people & tent €14.50*) is 2km east of the village.

Gîte les Baladins (☎ 04 92 45 00 23; www.lesbaladins.com - *French only; dorm beds €11, beds in dorms/double rooms with bathroom & half board €27/35*) is spotless and superbly maintained. The five-course evening meal is magnificent (wine and beer are available) and the hosts are very friendly and knowledgeable.

Le Matefaim (☎ 04 92 45 15 90; www.matefaim.com - *French only; singles/doubles with bathroom €18/32, half board €29.50; specialties montagnards €11-22*) is a B&B in the traditional style where some of the timber-panelled rooms are blessed with a balcony. You can discover its namesake in the **restaurant**: a traditional dish of a thick *galette* (pancake) with a savoury or sweet filling (€6.50). Other specialities include fondues, *raclette* (using local cheese) and *clocherade* (veal, pork and kangaroo with various sauces).

Hôtel les Veyres (☎ 04 92 45 01 91, fax 04 92 45 41 16; *doubles with washbasin/bathroom €37/60, half board per person €38/51; meals €20*), in L'Ochette, is a modern building where most of the compact rooms have a pleasant view. The **restaurant** has a better than average *carte*, including salmon with dill and steak with a Queyras blue-cheese sauce.

There are two **boulangeries** in the village; **Proxi** supermarket (*closed Wed afternoon & Sun*). **Market** day is Thursday during July and August.

L'Escale Bar-Restaurant (☎ 04 92 45 21 71; *specialties montagnards €11.50-19*), in the lower part of the village, is possibly the best bet apart from the *gîte*. It (too) offers *tartiflette*, *raclette* and fondue, or more conventional meat dishes (€10 to €13).

Getting There & Away From Montdauphin train station (near Guillestre) to Ceillac there's a **Favier Minibus** (☎ 04 92 45 07 71) service (€7.60, 35 minutes, two daily Monday to Friday year-round; one on weekends, school holidays only). Montdauphin is on the Briançon–Marseille train line (☎ 08 92 35 35 35; to/from Briançon: €4.70, 35 minutes, to from Marseille: €30.30, three hours 50 minutes; at least two daily to each).

Ceillac is also a stop on the **SCAL** (☎ 04 92 51 06 055) Briançon–Marseille bus route (to/from Briançon: about €3, 40 minutes; to/from Marseille: €25.75, 4½ hours; two daily Monday to Saturday, one on Sunday to both).

There are trains (€24.20, 4½ hours, six daily) between Briançon and Grenoble, as well as regular buses.

Abriès

This small, largely traditional village sits at the confluence of the Guil and Bouchet Rivers. The **tourist office** (☎ 04 92 46 72 26; www.abries.ristolas.queyras.com; open Mon-Sat) is very helpful; the forecast is posted on the door; Internet access via France Telecom (by card) is available inside. The nearest ATM is in Ville-Vieille, 10km to the southwest. Maps, guides, local background books and much else are to be had in **Le Bric Bazar** (open daily).

Places to Stay & Eat A sheltered site on the northern edge of the village, **Queyras Caravaneige** (☎ 04 92 46 71 22; caravaneig@aol.com; camping €7.80; menu €13) is quite large with a **restaurant**.

Le Villard di Marco (☎ 04 92 46 71 14; www.abries.fr.st - French only; dorm beds €12, half board €28) is a welcoming gîte d'étape close to the walk. The evening meal is not up to usual gîte standards – there's plenty of it, but too much originates in packets and lacks the homemade touch.

Auberge l'Edelweiss (☎ 04 92 46 71 09; www.edelweiss.queyras.com - French only; doubles with bathroom €48, half board €45; menu €13) has timber-panelled rooms. The **restaurant** makes a feature of typical Alpine dishes – fondue and raclette (€13), and a similar concoction poêlee queyrassine (€9).

There are two supermarkets in the village centre, **Spar** (closed Wed & Sun afternoon) and **Proxi** (closed Thu & Sun afternoon).

La Marmotte (☎ 04 92 46 74 71; meals €10-13.50) opposite the tourist office is a popular place with tables inside and out. Apart from standard mountain fare, it offers an assiette montagnarde (green salad with potatoes and raw ham), followed by fruit and crème fraiche.

La Fenière (☎ 04 92 46 78 24) an unobtrusive restaurant at the northern end of the village offers relief from raclette and so on with pasta (€5.50 to €6.30), trout and lamb (€6.70 to €7.60).

Getting There & Away The bus to Montdauphin (€9.30, 55 minutes, two daily Monday to Friday late March to late June, two every day late June to the end of August) is operated by **Autocars Imbert** (☎ 04 92 45 18 11; www.autocars-imbert.com - French only).

Navette de Haut Guil (☎ 04 92 46 72 26) is a useful summer-only shuttle service between Château Queyras and L'Echalp, stopping at villages in between (€2 village-to-village, 15 minutes Abriès to L'Echalp, four daily late June to the end of September). The service is free to bearers of a carte d'hôte (available from most accommodation hosts). From Château Queyras, there are connections with to and Montdauphin and, from Ville-Vieille, to St-Véran.

From Montdauphin trains and buses go to Briançon then Grenoble (for details see Getting There & Away for Ceillac).

THE WALK
Day 1: Ceillac to St-Véran

4½–4¾ hours, 10km, 1010m ascent

The starting point is place Philippe Lamour in the village. With the old church and its 1732 sundial and curious campanile on your left, walk straight ahead (northeast) out of the village and into Vallée du Cristallan. After about 400m bear left up a path; it zigzags comfortably up to a vehicle track, which you then follow up to the hamlet of **Le Villard**, all six buildings of it (40 minutes from the start). The now little-if-ever used pastures become multicoloured patchworks of wildflowers in early summer; another obvious sign of the decline of grazing is the gradual spread of larches across the terraced mountainsides.

Continue along the upper track to some crumbling ruins and two standing buildings at **Le Tioure** then turn left up a path passing a single house at Le Rabinoux. The path winds up through scattered trees then tackles the long, steep open slopes in an extended flight of bends. Pass a path junction

SOUTHERN ALPS

The Wild Heart of the Queyras

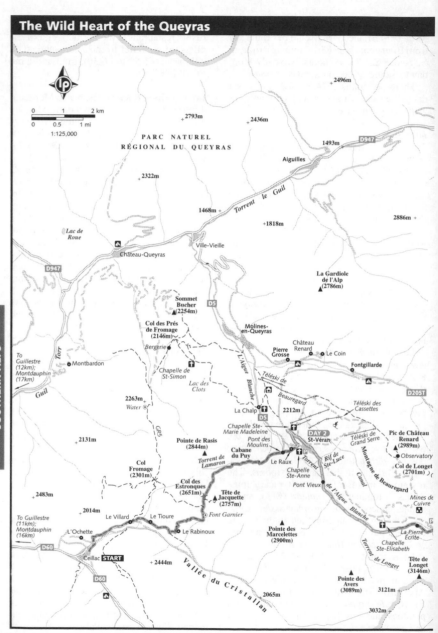

SOUTHERN ALPS

and go up beside a small stream for a short way to **Font Garnier**, a pretty reliable source of fresh water. Further up, a path to Col Fromage leads away west and up one more sustained burst of energy you reach **Col des Estronques** (1½ hours from Le Villard). From here you can see not St-Véran but the villages of Pierre Grosse and Château Renard in the next valley north.

You have to descend the steep head of the valley for about 10 minutes before St-Véran comes into view, with the sharp blade of Pic du Château Renard (2989m) and the white-domed observatory above to the east. Further down you may be able to see Mont Viso on the eastern skyline, poking far above a long ridge. The path winds down, through larch woodland and on to cross the stream near Cabane du Puy (45 minutes from the col). About 30 minutes further, cross the bridge over Torrent de Lamaron, then descend a path to a vehicle track. Follow it for about 300m; bear right along a path that soon takes you back to the road; then drop down to Pont des Moulins across Torrent de l'Aigue Blanche (1¼ hours from the cabane).

Walk up the road for about 50m then bear right along a path; be prepared to crawl under several electrified enclosures if cows are about; beyond a chook pen you reach a road in the hamlet of **Le Raux**. There are two accommodation places to the left (see Places to Stay & Eat, p262); the way to St-Véran is to the right. Continue past early-18th-century Chapelle Ste-Anne and on the bend there, go right up a path to the main road (D5) and up to a T-junction. From here it's left for the *gîte* and B&B at the western end of the village, right for other accommodation options in St-Véran (20 minutes from the bridge).

St-Véran

Proud of its verifiable claim to the highest inhabited commune in Europe, at 2040m, the village (home for 250 souls) is a veritable Alpine architectural museum and has a good range of services.

The **tourist office** (☎ *04 92 45 82 21; www.saintveran.com; open Mon-Sat*) is near the prominent church. The staff are very helpful and knowledgable.

SOUTHERN ALPS

There's an ATM at the post office at the southeastern end of the village, where you'll also find **L'Arbiot**, the best source of maps and books.

Musée le Soum *(admission €3.80; open Tue-Sun afternoons only, closed Nov)*, in the oldest house in the village (1641), features displays about local history and traditions.

Places to Stay & Eat The nearest camping ground, **Camping de Chanterane** *(☎ 04 92 45 83 70)* is at least 6km northwest along the D5 to Molines-en-Queyras, then east along the D205 to Pierre Grosse.

Le Chante de l'Alpe *(☎ 04 92 45 86 59; beds in dorms/private rooms €11.50/13.50; breakfast/evening meal €5.50/11.50)*, at the northwestern end of the village, has a small, well-equipped kitchen and a great view towards Col des Estronques.

At **Les Fontettes** *(☎ 04 92 45 81 77; www.altitude2040.com - French only; singles/ doubles with bathroom & breakfast €32/38)* each room has a south-facing balcony. The hostess is boundlessly knowledgeable about local walks.

Auberge Coste Belle *(☎ 04 92 45 82 17, fax 04 92 45 86 62; singles/doubles €20/39, half board €39; menus €13 & 15)*, at the south-eastern end of the village, is a deservedly popular, informal establishment. Its **restaurant** offers simple, unpretentious dishes including tripe, plus fondues and *pierrades*.

Châlet Rochebrune *(☎ 04 92 45 89 43; rochebrune@free.fr; singles/doubles with bathroom & breakfast €37/42; evening meal €13)* is in Le Raux below St-Véran, and is highly recommended. The large, very comfortable rooms are perfectly maintained by the attentive hosts.

Auberge les Estoilies *(☎ 04 92 45 82 65; www.estoilies.com - French only; singles/ doubles with bathroom €33/36, with half board per person €45/38)*, also in the hamlet of Le Raux, incorporates many centuries-old features with very pleasant rooms. The **restaurant** menu includes staples like *raclette* and fondue (€13 to €15), traditional tripe sausage (€8.50) and crêpes (€2.20 to €3.90).

Libre Service minimarket *(closed Wed & & Sun)* is towards the southeast. **Le Carotto**,

at the T-junction between Le Raux and St-Véran, is the best place for local products. There's a good **boulangerie** *(open daily Jul & Aug, Tue-Thu & Sat morning rest of year)* at the bottom of the village.

La Fougagno *(☎ 04 92 45 86 39; entrees €2.60-8.70, mains €8.70-16.10, menus €11.50-18.50)*, in the centre of the village, has a superb south-facing terrace. The *carte* includes lamb sausage, tripe sausage and fondues.

Getting There & Away The bus to Montdauphin (€9.30, one hour 10 minutes, two daily Monday to Friday late March to late June, two daily late June to end of August) is run by **Petit-Mathieu** *(☎ 04 92 46 71 56; www.autocars-imbert.com - French only)*. From Montdauphin trains and buses go to Briançon then Grenoble (for details see Getting There & Away, p258). See Getting There & Away for Abriès (p259) for details of the Haut Guil summer bus service between Ville-Vieille and L'Echalp.

Day 2: St-Véran to Refuge Agnel
4½–4¾ hours, 12km, 990m ascent

Walk southeast through the village to reach the bridge over Rif de Ste-Luce, about 200m past the last building. Bear right along a signposted vehicle track and drop down to the bridge over Torrent de l'Aigue Blanche. The track soon starts eating into the ascent through the deep, wooded, precipitous-sided valley. After about 40 minutes, cross Torrent de Longet, from where you can spot Chapelle Ste-Elisabeth perched on the mountainside. Another 30 minutes brings you to **La Pierre Écrite**, a small flat area, with a derelict copper-mine building above and opposite. From here a path soon leads on and, in a few hundred metres, rises very sharply to a junction. Either bear right to have a look at Chapelle de Clausis or left to continue the walk, and on to a vehicle track. Cross the bridge nearby to a path junction (1¾ hours from the start of the day).

It's a fairly steep pull at first, up to a path junction (Col de St-Véran is to the right). The route (with red and white marker posts up to Col de Chamouossière) then crosses a shallow boggy valley beyond which the path rises to another valley, which you contour on the northern side. In early summer the flowers are superb: gentians, globe flowers, violets; and the whistles of tame marmots echo around the cliffs above. Go up beside a small stream and soon cross it, from where there are a dramatic **views** of the massive rock spire of Tête des Toillies (3177m) to the south. The route crosses a string of shallow basins and finally reaches the broad Col de Chamoussière (1½ hours from the road). To the east, the huge soaring spikes and pinnacles of Mont Viso in Italy (3841m) dominate the outlook across Col Agnel.

The descent starts very steeply through a gully then the well waymarked path makes a long traverse, steadily losing height across scree and mud. Even if the col were snow-free, it's quite likely that in early summer you'll have to cross several snow drifts on this south-facing slope. After about an hour, bear left at a path junction; another 15 minutes of much easier going brings you to the refuge.

Refuge Agnel (☎ 04 92 45 83 90; info@ refugeagnel.com; *dorm beds €15, half board €33; open mid-Jun–mid-Sep)* has accommodation in traditional dorms with sleeping platforms as well as some less-crowded bunk rooms. Even though it's beside a road, this is very much a walkers' refuge with hot showers and a small kitchen. The four-course evening meal is only average; beer and wine are available. You can camp for free on a flat site about 300m to the east and use the showers and toilets but not the kitchen.

Day 3: Refuge Agnel to La Monta
3¾–4 hours, 11km, 230m ascent, 1590m descent

Head up the road from the refuge for 50m then turn left along a path leading up the wide shallow valley of Rios de l'Eychassier. After about 600m the well-used path crosses the stream, rounds a bluff and leads up to **Col Vieux** (an hour from the *refuge*). It takes a while to absorb the magnificent view: the vast sloping slabs of Crête de la Taillante forming the eastern wall of the long deep valley of Torrent de Bouchouse below, with the huge bulk of Le Pain de Sucre at its head.

The descent is surprisingly straightforward following cairns down the western side of the valley to the shore of placid Lac Foréant (30 minutes from the col). The path then drops down to pass beside Lac Egorgéou; then, as the valley steepens and narrows, grassland, patches of red alpenrose and stunted larch start to take over from boulders and scree. About 1¼ hours from Lac Foréant, cross two streams close together, then a low col, beyond which is a memorable view of Mont Viso to the southeast. Continue down to a gravel track on the bank of Torrent de Guil; in a few minutes pass the bridge to the hamlet of **L'Echalp** – there are some revelatory early-20th-century photos of the hamlet and of neighbouring La Monta on a notice board in the nearby car park.

Continue along the river bank to Pont de la Monta; cross and turn left along the road for about 150m to **La Monta** (one hour from the Viso view).

La Monta
Now only the *gîte* and a large disused church, La Monta comprised around 40 homes and farm buildings until they were almost all destroyed late in WWII.

About 1km further down the valley from the *gîte*, **Camping Municipal du Chardonnet** (☎ 04 92 46 76 32; *camping per person & tent €3.95; open Jun-Sep)* is a pleasant riverside site. Hot showers are free and there's a small shop.

Gîte La Monta (☎ 04 92 46 71 35; fhecq@ libertysurf.fr; *dorm beds €12, half board €28)* is a friendly, welcoming place with most of the accommodation in traditional dorms. The four-course evening meals, served in a homely dining room, are outstanding; wine (€10 to €15) and beer are available. The weather forecast is provided daily.

Autocars Imbert (☎ 02 92 45 18 11; www .autocars-imbert.com - French only) extends its service from Montdauphin to La Monta (via Abriès) during school holidays (€10.50, one hour 10 minutes, two daily late June to the end of August). See Getting There & Away for Abriès (p259) for details of a summer shuttle-bus service.

Day 4: La Monta to Abriès

4½–4¾ hours, 14km, 920m ascent

On the road in front of the *gîte* turn right beside a fountain to a signposted path that goes up, past a small cemetery, for about 300m then swings left to cross Torrent de Chapelle. Continue up for about 100m then bear left along a path leading northwest, steadily up through long-disused terraces, past a wooden crucifix. A few hundred metres further on, the path trends northeast into woodland where it's much easier to follow. At length the direction changes as the route traverses below a boulder field, then zigzags tightly beneath impressive crags and the jagged spire of Tête du Pelvas. Soon the path dips to pass below the extremity of the *tête* then rises fairly steeply (follow the waymarker poles) to **Crête de Peyra Plata** (two hours from the day's start). The awesome view takes in long ridges, and deep valleys punctuated by dramatic peaks almost encircling the entire area in view. The *crête* has an airy, up-in-the-sky feel, but certainly isn't exposed.

Continue along the path, bypassing a knob topped with two prominent cairns. Cross the highest point on the ridge then descend Crête de Gilly to Col de Gilly (40 minutes from Crête de Peyra Plata). Drop into a beautiful green valley above which the scree and shattered rock of Tête du Pelvas broods in stark contrast. Soon, bear left at a junction and continue downhill. About 20 minutes from the col go straight on (towards Abriès) at a path junction. Descending through woodland, you need to watch the waymarkers closely through the web of paths; 10 minutes from the junction, bear left down a wide track. In another 15 minutes, leave the track at a signposted junction to follow a path that bypasses the track briefly. With the village of Le Roux below, the track swings markedly west then southwest. About 75m round the bend, bear right down a signposted path. Beyond a clearing from where Le Roux is directly below, cross a forest road and continue down. The route then turns north briefly; at a junction go left along a level track. At the point where it becomes overgrown, bear right down to meet a track and continue in the same direction. In grassland, you soon pass below the ruins of **Le Cros**; beyond here the path may be partly overgrown in places. A little further on, bear right at a fork and descend, soon crossing Torrent de la Combe. Go on down to a lane between houses in **Abriès**, which leads to a road beside Torrent du Bouchet. Turn right for the *gîte*, left for everything else (one hour from the road bend).

Parc National du Mercantour

Protecting the heart of the Maritime Alps, the park is dominated by spectacularly rugged rocky peaks and deep sinuous valleys. The long narrow park, created in 1979, extends for 80km southeast from the town of Barcelonette to the road across Col du Tende into Italy; part of its northern boundary touches the Italian border where, in the east, it adjoins Italy's Parco Naturale delle Alpi Marittime. No one lives in this central area (685 sq km), though the park's more extensive outer area, embracing the Verdon, Ubaye, Var, Tinée, Vésubie and Roya Valleys is home to about 18,000 people. Here you'll find almost Provençal-style villages with prominent churches often built on extraordinarily isolated promontories high above the valleys. The traditional practice of taking large flocks of sheep up to Alpine pastures from the lowlands survives, on a very small scale. The area has a long, rather sad history of depopulation during the 20th century, reversed – or at least attenuated – in recent years by the influx of retired people and second-home owners, especially from Nice.

The glacially sculpted granite peaks, separated or linked by sharply angled ridges, may not be high by alpine standards, with only four over 3000m (topped by Cime du Gélas, 3143m), but they lack nothing in scenic splendour.

Two long-distance routes cross the park: the GR5 threads through the northwestern half then heads south to Nice, and the GR52

Parc National du Mercantour

Parc National du Mercantour – Walks
1 Col de Cerise
2 Lac de Trécolpas
3 La Madone de Fenestre
4 Vallon de Prals Lakes & Peaks

SOUTHERN ALPS

more or less continues east then south and out of the park to the Mediterranean coast near Menton (see Other Walks, p272). There are many other linked routes to lakes, passes and peaks. The four walks in this section focus on the Vésubie and Boréon Valleys in the centre of the park.

NATURAL HISTORY

In excess of 2000 species of flowering plants are found in the park, among which orchids are particularly numerous – 64 of France's 150 species. Forests of holm oak, groves of olives and fields of fragrant lavender

clothe the southernmost slopes giving way to firs, larch, juniper, alpenrose and bilberry. Brilliant displays of wildflowers carpet the Alpine meadows during springtime, heralded by vivid blue gentians, followed by primroses, lilies and, later, colourful thistles, including the unusual ground-hugging carline thistle.

The lammergeier, or bearded vulture, has been reintroduced to the park and royal eagles are also present. There are now more than 400 ibex (another reintroduction) in the park. Infinitely more controversially, the wolf returned to the area in the early 1990s (see the boxed text on p271). You're certain to see plenty of chamois and marmots and perhaps red squirrels, roe deer and hares. Cicadas in the forests and grass snakes near lakes are reminders of the Mediterranean character of part of the park.

PLANNING
When to Walk
Passes should normally be snow-free by early June though *refuges* generally don't open until mid-June.

Maps & Books
The IGN Top 1:100,000 map No 61 *Nice, Barcelonette* is useful for trip planning.

All walks are shown on the IGN 1:25,000 map No 3741OT *Vallée de la Vésubie*.

The FFRP's Topo-Guide Ref 507 *Tinée-Vésubie: Vallée des Merveilles* covers the area. The park's publications include local walks pamphlets, a guide to the park's orchids and a booklet about the controversial wolf.

Information Sources
The **national park head office** (☎ 04 93 16 78 88; www.parc-mercantour.fr; 23 rue d'Italie, 06006 Nice) can provide information and advice.

Weather forecasts are available by calling ☎ 3250 followed by 4 (Montagne) and 06 (Alpes Maritimes *département*).

ACCESS TOWNS
St-Martin-Vésubie
A large traditional village high in the precipitous Vésubie Valley, its old quarter – a maze of narrow cobbled streets – contrasts with the rather elegant *mairie* and central place.

The **tourist office** (☎ 04 93 03 21 28; o-t-hautevesubie@wanadoo.fr; place Félix Faure; open daily) has plenty of useful information; an accommodation list and the weather forecast are posted on a notice board outside. The **Maison du Parc** (☎ 04 93 03 23 15; av Kellermann Sérurier; open daily Jul-Aug) is the place to go for specialised information about the national park.

There's an ATM on place Félix Faure. **Aux Mille Articles** (50 rue Cagnoli; open Tue-Sun)

stocks local maps and guides. **Technicien du Sport** (38 rue Cagnoli) is the best outdoor equipment shop.

Places to Stay & Eat Five hundred metres from the village centre, **La Ferme St-Joseph** (☎ 06 70 51 90 14; camping 2 people & tent €6.40; hot shower €1.50) is in a shady one-time orchard beside the main road.

Hôtel les Alpes (☎ 04 93 03 21 06; singles/doubles €23/26; breakfast €4) is an old-style, slightly dilapidated place overlooking place Félix Faure.

Hôtel la Trappa (☎ 04 93 03 29 23; www.latrappa.com - French only; doubles with bathroom €40, half board €38) marks itself out from other hotels here by providing a small kitchen in the simply furnished rooms.

La Bonne Auberge (☎ 04 93 03 20 49, fax 04 93 03 20 69; singles/doubles with bathroom €44/47, with half board per person €68/44) is a well-maintained hotel where some rooms have their own balcony.

There are two supermarkets: **Petit Casino** (place Félix Faure; open Tue-Sun morning) and **Proxi** (allés de Verdun; open Mon-Sat, closed Thu afternoon). Three **boulangeries** can be found on and near place Félix Faure.

La Trappa (☎ 04 93 03 29 23; menus €15 & 20, entrées €6-11, mains €9-18) has a rather enclosed terrace where you can discover regional/Niçoise specialities such as wild boar in wine with polenta, and homemade ravioli with wild mushrooms.

La Bonne Auberge (☎ 04 93 03 20 49; menus €16 & 23, entrées €6-15, mains €12-22) is definitely not a place for vegetarians – the totally carnivorous menu includes rabbit, and veal with morel mushrooms.

La Treille (☎ 04 93 03 30 85; 70 rue Cagnoli; entrées €5.50-16, mains €7-20) has tables inside and, preferable on a nice day, on a terrace with valley views. The menu steers away from the conventional with hare terrine *au chablis*, sea bass with leeks, plus excellent pasta and pizzas.

Getting There & Away Bus No 730, which is operated by **TAM** (☎ 08 00 06 01 06; www.cg06.fr - French only), links Nice and St-Martin-Vésubie (€9.80, 1¾ hours, two daily Monday to Saturday, one Sunday September to July, three daily July to August).

Le Boréon

Not even a village, this scattered collection of houses and accommodation feels more remote than the few kilometres from St-Martin-Vésubie might suggest.

Gîte du Boréon (☎ 04 93 03 27 27; giteduboreon@free.fr; dorm beds €12.50, half board €30; open year-round) is a congenial place to stay. You can anticipate a substantial, wholesome evening meal (wine and beer are available). The hosts are knowledgable and helpful.

Hôtel du Boréon (☎ 04 93 03 20 35; www .hotelboreon.com - French only; doubles with bathroom €45, half board €44; menus €16.50-26), beside Lac du Boréon, has nicely furnished rooms. The rustic **restaurant** offers several unusual dishes such as saddle of young rabbit.

Hôtel du Cavalet (☎ 04 93 03 21 46; www.lecavalet.com - French only; doubles with bathroom & breakfast €70, half board €60; menus €21 & 26) also overlooks Lac du Boréon. The **restaurant** meals don't rise to exotic heights but do make a feature of local trout and lamb.

There's no public transport to Le Boréon, but from St-Martin-Vésubie, **Taxi Altitude** (☎ 06 08 26 59 58; rank on place Félix Faure) will take you there for €20 or try **Taxi Ciais** (☎ 04 93 03 20 19).

Col de Cerise

Duration	4–4¼ hours
Distance	9km
Difficulty	moderate
Start/Finish	Le Boréon
Transport	taxi

Summary Larch woodland and a rocky valley, cradling a small lake – inviting on a hot day – to a col guarded by dramatic peaks.

This walk is a fine introduction to the park, starting with a steep ascent through Vallon du Cavalet to a scree-encrusted valley framed by towering cliffs, hiding tiny Lac de Cerise. From the narrow Col de Cerise (2543m) you look across some of the rugged peaks of Italy's Parco Naturale delle Alpi Marittime. The path, marked with cairns, is easy to follow. The ascent totals 1050m. A side trip to secluded Lac du Mercantour, filling a small hanging valley, is well worth the modest extra effort.

THE WALK (see map p265)

From Gîte du Boréon walk a short distance up the road, past national park information boards to follow a path up to a concrete road; turn right for 150m. Then bear right along a path almost on a right bend and go up to a path junction – turn left. The long ascent is mostly well graded, through woodland interspersed with grassy glades, a few ruinous small buildings and stone-walled enclosures. About 30 minutes from the last junction bear left at an intersection, then a few minutes further on go right for the col. Next (500m along) comes a stream crossing from where the path zigzags up scree to a dry rocky valley and on to tiny Lac de Cerise (about 50 minutes from the stream crossing). The path continues up to the base of a cliff then veers left to the western side of the valley – where, incongruously, coils of barbed wire recall less-peaceful times. It's not much further up to **Col de Cerise** on the Italian border, just below which a derelict barracks building is another haunting reminder of wartime (40 minutes from the lake).

The return is simply a matter of retracing your steps; soon after you start descending, a well-concealed old guard house is visible above. Allow about 30 minutes to the lake and another 1¼ hours to the *gîte*.

Side Trip: Lac du Mercantour
40 minutes, 750m, 200m ascent

Descend from Col de Cerise; just beyond the end of a traverse at the base of cliffs on the eastern side of the valley, continue straight on and down across scree. Close to the stream on the left and on a right bend in the main path, diverge to cross the stream, then bear left and ascend to the shore of Lac du Mercantour. Retrace your steps to the main path.

SOUTHERN ALPS

Lac de Trécolpas

Duration	5¼–5½ hours
Distance	12km
Difficulty	moderate
Start/Finish	Le Boréon (p267)
Transport	taxi
Summary	Through conifer woodlands to spectacular rocky valleys and a tranquil lake overlooked by towering crags; drop in to an isolated refuge high in the Boréon Valley

The upper reaches of the Boréon Valley are magnificently rugged, with towering rocky peaks, scree-strewn slopes and tumbling streams. Near the head of the valley, beautiful Lac de Trécolpas is an alluring objective for a day out from Le Boréon. (The lake is also on the route of the La Madone de Fenestre walk) Rather than retracing your steps from the lake, a detour via Refuge de la Cougourde is highly recommended. The walk involves 720m ascent.

Although the walk along the northern side of the Vallée du Boréon is very pleasant it can be left for another day if you have a car. Drive east from Le Boréon along a minor road to the car park near Vacherie du Boréon (where you can buy locally made cheese) and follow the signposted and waymarked path from there. It joins the main route via Pont de Peïrastrèche, upstream from the cascades.

THE WALK (See map p265)

Follow the Col de Cerise walk (see p267) out of the village, but at the path junction turn right. About 15 minutes from the start, mostly uphill, turn right at a T-junction to cross a small stream then, shortly, another larger one. A 1km-long traverse of the steep wooded mountainside leads to another junction – continue straight on, descending slightly. Bear right down to the river bank, then promptly head uphill again on a wide track, passing the private Refuge A Saladin (50 minutes from the start). Bear left along a stony path into the upper reaches of the Boréon Valley. Gaining height with little respite, you come to a fine **view** of Cascade de Peïrastrèche (20 minutes from Refuge Saladin).

Pass a path junction on the right (where you'd join the walk if starting from Vacherie du Boréon); the path leads into more open country and the rugged ridges and peaks to the north come into view. Cross a footbridge over the Vallon Sangué stream (see Les Lacs Bessons, p272) then a few minutes further on, pass the path to Refuge de la Cougourde (40 minutes from the cascade).

Cross the nearby bridge over Torrent du Boréon; the path leads to the right for about 200m then bends left and rises steeply across the northern side of a small valley. Continue past another path junction to **Lac de Trécolpas** (50 minutes from the lower junction).

Return to the first junction and go straight on (the right fork) to reach the *refuge*, following cairns across scree, in and out of woodland, over a footbridge to **Refuge de la Cougourde** (☎ 04 93 03 26 00; dorm beds €13.50). Accommodation is in smallish bunk rooms; the *refuge* (opened in 2003), somewhat incongruously, sprouts a satellite dish and solar-heating panels. The site of its humble predecessor nearby is marked with a simple wooden cross.

To continue, go back to the footbridge from where the croded path descends steeply at first to the junction with the path through the valley (25 minutes from the *refuge*). Then, it's only 1¾ hours to retrace your steps to Le Boréon.

La Madone de Fenestre

Duration	2 days
Distance	21km
Difficulty	moderate
Start/Finish	Le Boréon (p267)
Transport	taxi
Summary	Over a high pass separating the upper Boréon and Vésubie Valleys; take in Col de Fenestre on an ancient Roman road en route to the historic sanctuary of La Madone de Fenestre.

From Pas des Ladres (2448m) high above Lac de Trécolpas, there are superb vistas of many of the rugged peaks further east in the

La Madone de Fenestre

Contemplating the view from Col de Fenestre, try to imagine what it would have been like here more than 500 years ago, en route from the Mediterranean coast to Italy, lugging valuable cargoes of salt. The route was pioneered by the Romans who built a temple dedicated to Jupiter where the Madone de Fenestre chapel now stands. In 867 Benedictine monks established a chapel and wayside inn there but it was later ransacked. A vision of the Virgin Mary then appeared nearby prompting the monks to start again. Notre Dame de Fenestre was built and a wooden statue, attributed to St Luke and made of oriental cedar, was placed inside. Burnt during the French Revolution, the chapel (or *sanctuaire*) came into the care of the parish of St-Martin at the beginning of the 19th century. Miraculously the statue had survived; then began the tradition of removing it to the church in St-Martin during autumn and returning it to Madone for the summer. For many years during the 20th century the statue made the journey by vehicle but in recent years the parish priest persuaded his flock to reject this untraditional practice. Each May the statue is now carried to Madone on the shoulders of local people and brought back in late September.

The *sanctuaire* is a place of pilgrimage – inside are many grateful tributes by people miraculously cured of ailments and disabilities. Certainly, there is something special about this lovely, dimly lit chapel with its richly decorated altar, graceful stone arches and pillars.

A souvenir shop next door might seem out of place – but this is the 21st century! For more information, see http://madonedefenestre.free.fr – French only

Mercantour, including the highest, Cime du Gélas (3143m). What's more, a grassy spur a few hundred metres east of the pass is a favourite haunt of young chamois and their mothers in early summer – the author saw about 30 frisking insouciantly on the rocks, oblivious to several passing walkers nearby. From the pass you can descend directly to the CAF *refuge* at La Madone de Fenestre (Madone) or, more scenically, go via Col de Fenestre and Lac de Fenestre.

Madone is accessible by road but there is no public transport, so the walk is necessarily an out-and-back expedition if you don't have your own transport. You can vary the first part of the return by going directly up to Pas des Ladres, rather than via Col de Fenestre. Madone is an interesting destination in its own right (see the boxed text) and a base for the marvellous Vallon de Prals Lakes & Peaks walk (see p270).

THE WALK (See map p265)
Day 1: Le Boréon to La Madone de Fenestre
5–5½ hours, 10km, 1160m ascent
Follow the directions for the Lac de Tré-colpas walk up to the lake (see opposite; 2½ hours from Le Boréon). A rocky path

leads on slightly above the northern shore to another shallow valley. As you continue to climb, a wide valley opens out to the north, partly enclosed by an arc of massive peaks and flat-topped pinnacles. Then the serious stuff starts as the path zigzags up a steep spur and then through steep scree to Pas des Ladres (one hour from the lake).

To continue to Col de Fenestre, head east (left) across indeterminate spurs and into the valley above Lac de Fenestre. The path descends, crosses scree, passes a junction then winds up to the col (30 minutes from the pass). A derelict wartime barracks building sits just below on the Italian side, peaks and walls of rock soar skywards on both sides.

Go back to the path junction and follow the long, loping zigzags down past Lac de Fenestre. Further on is the junction with the direct route for Pas des Ladres. Continue on to Refuge de la Madone de Fenestre (1¼ hours from Col de Fenestre).

The **Refuge de la Madone de Fenestre** (☎ 04 93 02 83 19, 04 93 03 91 02; *dorm beds €10; breakfast €4.90, evening meal €12.20*) is very popular at weekends, because it is directly accessible by car. It has compact bunk rooms, hot showers and a kitchen for guests' use. Satisfying meals

La Madone de Fenestre

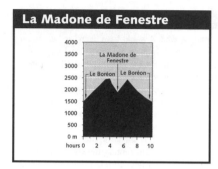

are dished up in generous quantities (wine and beer are available) and the staff are friendly and helpful.

Day 2: La Madone de Fenestre to Le Boréon

5¼-5¾ hours, 11km, 800m ascent

Follow the direct path up from behind the *refuge* towards Pas des Ladres. It rises steeply most of the way to the pass (1¾ hours from the *refuge*). Descend to Lac de Trécolpas and continue down to a path junction (one hour from the pass). Go straight on, following cairns across scree, in and out of woodland, over a footbridge to **Refuge de la Cougourde** (see p268; 35 minutes from the path junction).

Return to Le Boréon along the same route as the Lac de Trécolpas walk (p268).

Vallon de Prals Lakes & Peaks

Duration	5¼–5½ hours
Distance	11km
Difficulty	moderate
Start/Finish	La Madone de Fenestre (p269)
Transport	private

Summary Five small, serene lakes guarded by rugged peaks; magnificent views of the Mercantour's highest peak and its satellites from a superb ridge walk.

It isn't necessary to follow the main route through the park to enjoy outstanding, if not incomparable views of the myriad peaks and deep valleys and, as a bonus, some of the loveliest lakes are well away from the beaten track. This walk takes you to the delightful cluster of ponds, the five Lacs de Prals, deep in the mountains southeast of Madone, then traverses a beautiful undulating ridge, crowned by Cime de la Valette de Prals (2496m). Standing slightly aloof from the main range, it gives a grandstand view of the peaks along the border, including Cime du Gélas and the awesomely jagged ridge extending generally south from its precipitous slopes.

The walk is described clockwise so that you ascend via the steep rocky path through Vallon du Ponset and return down the gentler Vallon de Prals. It involves 810m of ascent. The main path junctions are signposted and the route is marked by cairns and yellow waymarkers.

GETTING TO/FROM THE WALK

La Modone de Fenestre is accessible by car from St-Martin-Vésubie along the D94 road (11km).

THE WALK (see map p265)

With the *refuge* behind you, walk down the path between the souvenir shop and the private hotel, and on to the bridge over Torrent de la Vésubie. Cross and turn left, then shortly right in the direction of Baisse des Cinq Lacs. The well-used path gets stuck into the ascent straightaway, up the timbered Vallon du Ponset. About 45 minutes from the start you reach a beautiful hanging valley, the grass dotted with alpenrose and small larches, the slopes streaked with scree and boulders. Cross the main stream here; then comes a rising traverse of the western side of the valley leading to a spur that rises to **Baisse des Cinq Lacs** a col on the northwestern side of the valley cradling the five lakes (45 minutes from the hanging valley).

To continue, descend between the westernmost and the nearby largest of the five lakes, then follow a rather faint path southeast to pass the western shore of a teardrop-shaped pond. The path, which is clear from here, leaves the lakes' valley and descends

Le Loup

Almost inevitably when a group of French walkers settles down to some serious discussions, as is the custom before, during and after dinner at *refuges* and *gîtes*, the subject of 'Le Loup' prowls in.

'Has anyone seen one?' 'Are there many of them in the Mercantour especially, and in other mountain areas?' 'Have they spread naturally north and northwest from Italy, or have they – dare it be said – been (secretly) introduced?'

While all the discussions I heard were polite, even-handed though usually sceptical, it's very clear indeed that the issue has dramatically polarised mountain people – whose attitudes towards the wolf are variously fear/hate/opposition/total scepticism – and the 'pro-loups', who regard the animal as a valuable addition to France's relatively small number of resident fauna species.

The wolf, the stuff of folklore and legend, is a predator and many mountain dwellers, though in dwindling numbers, still keep sheep flocks, so the potential for serious conflict undoubtedly exists. However, the number of sheep and goats killed vary enormously, with up to 7000 since 1993 being claimed by farming organisations. This number sits rather awkwardly beside the estimated French population of wolves – less than 100.

This is an issue that will undoubtedly be around for some time, though the Groupe Loup France was trying to reconcile opposing sides during 2003. The website www.loup.org contains a huge amount of information, including several anti-wolf sites and is strongly recommended – if you can read French!

south and southwest across steep scree and rock below cliffs. Beyond the scree, bear right at a minor path junction and soon start to ascend; long zigzags take you up to a path junction just below the ridge crest. Bear right and, in another five minutes, reach a col, revealing views of peaks and valleys to the east and southeast. A well-defined path leads up to the summit of **Cime de la Valette de Prals** topped by a crucifix (1½ hours from the lakes). As well as the multifarious peaks, prominent in the view are Col de Fenestre and Pas des Ladres – central features of the La Madone de Fenestre walk (see p268) – Madone itself, and the five lakes.

Continue along the ridge northwestwards, over a nameless bump, from where the vast depths of Cirque de Férisson appear below to the northwest. Walk down to a small col where the crest path ends. Veer left for a short distance to pick up a clear path that leads generally north, making a superb traverse of the broad western flank of Cime du Pertus before descending to a path junction (30 minutes from Cime de la Valette). Go on in the same direction and in about 100m cross a rocky spur and bear right across the slope of Tête de la Lave. A few hundred metres further on the path winds down into the Vallon de Prals to cross a stream. Follow yellow waymarkers

across the meadow for about 250m to meet the main path through the valley at Plan de Prals (30 minutes from Tête de la Lave).

The rather worn path loses height steadily through the valley, crossing the main stream twice via log bridges. From the second of these, it veers north away from the valley across the lowermost slopes of Mont Caval and on to a road. Walk uphill for no more than 200m and, immediately before a bridge, turn right along a vehicle track. This leads past a car park, then to the **Vacherie de la Madone** (where you may be able to buy cheese), to reach the Torrent de la Vésubie bridge. From here it's one more short ascent to the *refuge* (one hour from Plan de Prals).

Other Walks

PARC NATUREL RÉGIONAL DU VERCORS
Circumnavigating the Vercors

A scenic eight- to 10-day circuit of around 140km, starting and finishing in Grenoble links the GRs 9, 91, 93, and 95, passing through only a few small towns, including Corrençon-en-Vercors, Vassieux-en-Vercors and Pont-en-Royans. Linked routes offer access to alternative finishing points, including Châtillon-en-Diois and Die (see the Cirque d'Archiane walk, p240). You'd need at least a sleeping bag, cooking equipment and food to use the small *cabanes* in more isolated areas.

Contact the **park headquarters** (☎ *04 76 94 38 26; www.parc-du-vercors.fr; 255 chemin des Fusillés, 38250 Lans-en-Vercors)* for more information.

From Grenoble, VFD buses serve Correncon (No 510). Details of services to other towns (including Pont en Royans and Vassieux, are available from the bus station (☎ 04 76 87 90 31).

PARC NATIONAL DES ÉCRINS
Tour de l'Oisans
This is a challenging, outstandingly scenic and varied circuit of the core of the national park, starting and finishing at the town of Bourg d'Oisans in the Romanche Valley. Part of the tour is featured in the walk In the Shadow of La Meije (see p248). The full distance is around 200km with over 6000m ascent. Once you leave Bourg d'Oisans (717m) the route stays above 1000m most of the way, crossing eight passes above 2300m. Allow 11 to 14 days.

The Tour – the GR54 – is the subject of the FFRP's Topo-Guide *Tour de l'Oisans* No 508. Six IGN 1: 25,000 sheets are needed. A useful first point of contact is the **Parc National des Écrins** (☎ *04 92 40 20 10; www.les-ecrins-parc-national.fr)*.

VFD buses from Grenoble pass through Bourg d'Oisans, La Grave, Le Monêtier-les-Bains (No 306); Valjouffrey (No 412); and Venosc (No 304). **Courriers Transalpins** (☎ *04 92 23 33 54; www.lavallouise.com)* buses link Vallouise, L'Argentière la Besse and Briançon.

PARC NATUREL RÉGIONAL DU QUEYRAS
Tour du Viso (39km, 3080m ascent)
From La Monta in the upper Guil Valley (see The Wild Heart of the Queyras walk, p256) you can join the hugely scenic and rewarding Tour du Viso (or, in Italian, the Giro del Viso), a magnificent three- to five-day circuit of the entire massif. A popular walk, it follows waymarked paths all the way. The route from La Monta goes up the Guil Valley via Belvédère du Viso, or direct to Lac Lestio and Colle del Viso. From here the not particularly scenic conventional route, crosses Col Traversette (2999m) into France. The alternative is less likely to be snow-bound and somewhat less hazardous: via Colle Armoine, Col Manzol and Col Sallière to the Guil Valley. Generally, the *refuges* aren't open until mid- or late June and you can expect snow on, or more likely below, the passes until mid-July.

The IGN 1:25,000 No 8 *Monviso* in the *Alpes sans Frontières* series covers the route but isn't 100% reliable. Preferably, use Italian Istituto Geografico Centrale's 1:25,000 No 6 map *Monviso*.

You'll also find a full description of the walk in Lonely Planet's *Walking in the Alps*.

PARC NATIONAL DU MERCANTOUR
Les Lacs Bessons
At 2540m this beautiful pair of remote lakes lie much higher than most, if not all other accessible lakes in the central Mercantour. Just below the Italian border and separated by a slender rock bar, they're almost enclosed by steep, smooth walls and slabs of pink-grey granite, at the head of the Vallon Sangué, a tributary of the upper Boréon River. A clear path branches from the main route (the GR52) through the Boréon Valley, about 15 minutes northeast of the path junction near Pont Peïrastrèche. It leads steeply and unremittingly northwest then northeast and north up the valley to the southern shore of the more southerly lake.

Allow 6½ to 6¾ hours for this 14km walk, involving 1040m ascent. Take the IGN 1:25,000 map No 3741OT *Vallée de la Vésubie* .

Vallée des Merveilles
Near the eastern edge of the park, the Vallée des Merveilles and the nearby Cirque de Fontanalbe is a unique, internationally important site where, about 3500 years ago, early Bronze Age people created about 40,000 rock engravings, the largest such open-air site in Europe. Access to the most vulnerable area is very strictly regulated and visits are permitted only with approved guides, or on a guided walk from the nearby Refuge des Merveilles. Part of the area can be explored independently on defined paths with interpretive signs. The GR52 (see the La Madone de Fenestre walk, p268) crosses the area en route from La Madone de Fenestre to Sospel and Menton on the Mediterranean coast.

Check www.parc-mercantour.fr or contact the **Maison du Parc** (☎ *04 93 03 23 15; open Jul & Aug only)* in St-Martin-Vésubie. The **Musée des Merveilles** (☎ *04 93 04 32 50; av du 16 Septembre 1947, Tende; admission €4.55; open Wed-Mon May–mid-Sep)* has archaeological, ethnological and natural history displays and a shop.

The area is covered by IGN 1:25,000 map No 3741OT *Vallée e de la Vésubie* and features in the FFRP's Topo-Guide No 507 *Tinée-Vésubie: Vallée des Merveilles*.

Northern Alps

Boasting the highest and most spectacular mountains in Western Europe, the Northern Alps is one of the classic walking areas in France, if not the world. Several thousand kilometres of well-maintained and well-signed paths give access to virtually every valley, meadow and glacier in the region. Most walkers will find there to suit their level of fitness, whether it's enjoying low-level valley trails with views of the high mountains or strenuous outings above the tree line.

This chapter is divided into two sections. In the northern half of the region (Haute-Savoie), the Chamonix Valley gives a wide range of convenient one-day walks dominated by impressive views of the Mont Blanc massif. *Téléfériques* (cable cars or funiculars) can often be used here to access high-altitude trails with minimal effort. To the south, in the *département* of Savoie, the Parc National de la Vanoise offers the multiday Tour of the Vanoise Glaciers, with good mountain scenery and excellent opportunities for enjoying abundant alpine flora and fauna in less developed surroundings. Public transport is excellent in both areas and a liberal scattering of *refuges* (refuges or mountain huts) means that most overnight trips can be made with little more than a day pack.

CLIMATE

The mountains of the Northern Alps have a huge influence on the climate of the area. In some instances the region enjoys better weather than the rest of France, with the Pre-Alps taking the sting out of the Atlantic weather systems that bring rain to the rest of the country. However, with strong summer sun, evaporation of snowmelt and localised winds created by deep valleys, the summer weather can also be markedly poor. It is not uncommon during summer to experience a fine morning followed by heavy rain and electrical storms in the afternoon, while just 100km away on the plains west of Grenoble, the skies remain clear all day. At an even

> ## Highlights
>
> - Taking in a classic view of Mont Blanc from Lac Blanc (p277)
> - Looking out across the Mer de Glace from Signal Forbes on the Grand Balcon Nord (p279)
> - Getting up close and personal with the Bossons Glacier on the Montagne de la Côte walk (p282)
> - Watching a herd of ibex moving beneath the glaciers of the Parc National de la Vanoise (p284)

more localised level, a bad storm can generate over the Mont Blanc massif while the sun may still be shining in the Chamonix Valley.

Summer daytime temperatures in the valleys commonly reach 25°C and sometimes rise as high as 30°C. At 2000m, summer daytime temperatures rarely exceed 20°C (although the strong sun will make it feel hotter), with night-time temperatures falling close to freezing. Typically, June and July are unsettled months – you might experience two days of fine weather followed by three or four days of cloudy skies and evening storms. By August, the weather has generally settled down, and September, although cooler, can give long spells of fine weather.

INFORMATION
When to Walk

The walking season in the Northern Alps is all too brief. Typically, people begin to venture onto the trails in early June when the spring thaw is over, the avalanche risk has fallen and the snow has largely melted from the paths. June is the best time for wildflowers, but late-lying snow and poor weather can still make walking difficult (see the Warning on p275). The mountains are at their busiest during July and August, when the popular trails attract tremendous numbers of walkers. September is quieter and often sees more settled weather than the other summer months.

Northern Alps

Lake Geneva

N1

Thonon-les-Bains

Évian-les-Bains

GR5

Yvoire

Lajoux

Mijoux

Gex

Lélex

Abondance

Châtel

Ferney Voltaire

N5

HAUTE-SAVOIE

GENEVA

Annemasse

Morzine

Avoriaz

Les Gets

Martigny

Cluses

SWITZERLAND

N201

N205

Vallorcine

To Lyon

Col des Montets

Argentière

N508

Sallanches

Le Grand Bornand

La Clusaz

St-Gervais

Chamonix

Mt Dolent (3823m)

Annecy

Lac d'Annecy

Megève

GR5

Mont Blanc Tunnel

A41

Duingt

Le Semnoz

Mont Blanc (4809m)

Courmayeur

N212

To Aosta (12km)

Parc Régional du Massif des Bauges

SAVOY

Le Châtelard

Aix-les-Bains

Albertville

Col du Petit St-Bernard

Chambéry

Bourg St-Maurice

Seez

ITALY

Tarentaise Valley

N90

Les Arcs

GR5

La Plagne

Tignes

Moûtiers

Parc Régional de Chartreuse

Brides-les-Bains

Val d'Isère

Col de l'Iseran

ISÈRE

DAUPHINE

SAVOIE

D915

N6

Courchevel

Parc National de la Vanoise

Bonneval-sur-Arc

Pralognan-la-Vanoise

Maurienne

Les Menuires

GR5

Bessans

La Dent Parrachée (3639m)

Val Thorens

Lanslebourg

Valley

Col du Mont Cénis

A
L
P
S

Modane

To Turin (40km)

To Grenoble (5km)

Susa

Isère River

Northern Alps – Maps

1	Lac Blanc	p278
2	Grand Balcon Nord	p280
3	Montagne de la Côte	p284
4	Tour of the Vanoise Glaciers	p288

TMB

A40

0 10 20 km

0 5 10 miles

Early October sees the walking season drawing to an end, with snow falling and accumulating below 2000m.

What to Bring

Although all the routes in this chapter follow paths, many of the trails are rough and boulder-strewn in places. Walking boots with ankle support are recommended. Given the unpredictability of mountain weather, warm clothing (even gloves) should also be carried at all times. Walking poles are recommended for support if there is a possibility of encountering snow, especially early in the season.

All of the walks described cross streams formed from snowmelt, which means there are opportunities to refill water bottles along the way. Most walkers seem to drink the water without purification, though you may prefer to treat it anyway for peace of mind.

Maps

The IGN has two overview maps of the area covered by this chapter. The 1:250,000 map No 112 *Savoie/Dauphiné* gives a good

---

Warning

Trails at elevations of 2000m or more can be covered by banks of snow well into the summer. Following exceptional winters, paths above 2300m may remain difficult throughout July. Typical problems with snow banks include navigation: if the trail is covered with snow and the cloud is down, staying on course can be tricky without an obvious path or frequent cairns to guide you. If the snow is icy (first thing in the morning) and/or the slope is steep then a slip can also be disastrous.

If you expect to encounter icy snow early in the season, before steps have been kicked in it, then an ice axe and crampons might be appropriate. On most walking routes however, summer daytime temperatures rapidly soften the snow, passing feet cut a secure trail and a walking pole is sufficient for balance. If you are uncertain about trail conditions, be sure to check local information sources before heading out.

---

general overview of the French Alps, while 1:100,000 map No 53 *Grenoble/Mont Blanc* is a great reference for more detailed trip planning.

Chamonix Valley

Bound to the south by the glaciers and soaring rock spires of the Mont Blanc massif and to the north by the Aiguilles Rouges, the Chamonix Valley is one of the most popular walking destinations in Europe. More than 300km of trails provide opportunities for walks of all difficulties. Several *téléfériques* further enhance the potential for walkers of modest fitness, allowing access to high-level trails without the effort of ascent and descent. The down-side to such convenience is that these mountains can feel rather developed; walkers seeking a greater sense of wilderness may prefer to explore the Parc National de la Vanoise (p284) to the south.

The extremely rugged Aiguilles Rouges provide some of the classic routes in the valley, and some of the best views of the Mont Blanc range. Lac Blanc is the jewel of the area, with waters that might reflect the spectacular vista or might still be frozen depending on the time of your visit. On the other side of the valley, the Grand Balcon Nord and the walk on Montagne de la Côte bring the walker as high into the mountains as they can go without becoming mountaineers.

The 10-day Tour du Mont Blanc (TMB) also passes along the northern side of the Chamonix Valley. There are opportunities for various one- to two-day routes that sample this famed long-distance path. The two-day Grand Balcon Sud is one such route; see the boxed text on p295 for more details.

PLANNING
When to Walk

The Chamonix Valley attracts a tremendous number of walkers during July and August and solitude can be hard to find. Yet even in peak season it is possible to avoid the crowds by walking in the early morning or evening, when the light is also at its best. The only drawback is that you will have to ascend and descend the slopes on your own steam if you walk outside the operating hours of the *téléfériques*.

Maps & Books

Rando Editions, 1:50,000 *Pays du Mont Blanc* is a sensible yet detailed map that covers all of the walks in the Chamonix Valley. While this is sufficient for walking, details of relevant 1:25,000 maps are also provided for each walk. Keep an eye out for the new IGN 1:25,000 series *Alpes sans frontières*.

Chamonix Mont Blanc – A Walking Guide by Martin Collins gives in-depth coverage of the popular and less popular walks in the valley. *Mont Blanc Trails* by René Bozon is also a detailed guide compiled from local knowledge and is widely available in Chamonix in both French and English.

Information Sources

The **Agence Touristique Départementale Haute-Savoie Mont Blanc** (☎ *04 50 51 32 31; www.hautesavoie-tourism.com; BP 348-74012, Annecy Cedex)* provides general tourist information on the Haute-Savoie.

Agence Touristique Départmentale de la Savoie (☎ *04 79 85 12 45; www.savoie -tourisme.com; 24 blvd de la Colonne, 73000 Chambéry)* provides similar information for the Savoie.

Permits & Regulations

Wild camping is forbidden in the Chamonix Valley, although discreet camping is permitted between 7pm and 7am. In practice this means you can camp overnight, but you can't leave your tent up during the day. Although many people appear to flout this rule without any trouble, you do run the risk of having your tent confiscated.

In the Réserve Naturelle des Aiguilles Rouges, wild camping and picnicking are forbidden in order to protect the delicate alpine habitat.

GETTING AROUND

Chamonix Bus (☎ *04 50 53 05 55)* operate frequent local bus services up and down the Chamonix Valley, running from Servoz in the south to the Col des Montets and Le Tour in the north. There are departures from all stops between these points at least every hour from 7am to 11.30pm. All journeys cost €1.50 before 8pm and €2 thereafter.

A narrow-gauge railway also runs up the valley, linking St-Gervais-les-Bains to Martigny in Switzerland. All the villages in the valley have their own SNCF stations and services run at least seven times daily. Prices vary depending on the length of your journey, but tickets are generally significantly more expensive than the bus.

ACCESS TOWN
Chamonix

Chamonix is a hub of Alpine activity and is one of the most popular destinations for visitors to the Alps. It is packed every summer with walkers and mountaineers from around the world, as well as with general tourists who come to gaze at the mountains and take a ride on the highest *téléférique* in Europe (the Aiguille du Midi; 3842m). It's hard to escape the sense of purpose when every second person you pass sports a walking pole or a pack laden with ropes and ice tools.

The town centre contains a concentration of banks, shops, restaurants and cafés and there's plenty of accommodation nearby. Note, however, that even camping grounds fill up in the peak season of July and August. With this in mind, and given the convenience of public transport in the valley, it may be easier to seek accommodation in smaller neighbouring towns such as Les Praz (see p278).

Information Chamonix's efficient and helpful **tourist office** (☎ *04 50 53 00 24; www.chamonix.com; 85 place du Triangle de l'Amitié)* provides advice and listings on accommodation, public transport, local events, walking routes, *refuges* and *téléfériques* for the entire Chamonix Valley.

For more informed advice about local trail conditions, go to the nearby **Office de Haute-Montagne** (☎ *04 50 53 22 08; www .ohm-chamonix.com; 190 place de l'Église)*, on the 2nd floor of the Maison de la Montagne. A notice board at the entrance displays the long-term weather forecast in English.

Three-day weather forecasts for the Mont Blanc massif are also available in English at http://meteo.chamonix.com. Alternatively, recorded English forecasts can be heard at ☎ 08 92 70 03 30, with calls charged at €0.34 per minute.

Every third shop in Chamonix is an **outdoor shop** so you shouldn't have any trouble buying equipment. The town also has a wide selection of internet cafés; one of the cheapest is **Cybar** (rue des Moulins).

Places to Stay & Eat Camping grounds close to Chamonix centre include the small and simple **Camping Les Arolles** (☎ 04 50 53 14 30; 181 chemin du Cry; camping per person/tent/car €4.15/2.80/0.90; open mid-Jun–Sep), and the more formal **L'Île des Barrats** (☎ 04 50 53 51 44; 185 chemin de L'Île des Barrats; camping per person/tent/car €5.20/4.80/2.20; open May-Sep).

The **Auberge de Jeunesse** (☎ 04 50 53 14 52; 127 montée Jacques Balmat; dorm beds €12.70), 2km south of the centre in Les Pélerins, is on the bus route to Les Houches but has no kitchen. **Gîte La Montagne** (☎ 04 50 53 11 60; 789 promenade des Crémeries; dorm beds/half board €11/26.55) has self-catering facilities and is situated in an attractive location 1km north of the town centre.

Chamonix has a wide selection of hotels. **El Paso** (☎ 04 50 53 64 20; 37 impasse des Rhododendrons; singles/doubles €35/42) is just one option; it has a lively atmosphere and is centrally located.

There are several **supermarkets** around the centre of Chamonix. If you prefer to eat out, **Le Bumbelbee Bistrot** (☎ 04 50 53 50 03; rue des Moulins; (menus from €7), is an attractive little place with vegetarian dishes and international snacks. **Brasserie L'M** (☎ 04 50 53 00 11; rue du Docteur Paccard; menus from €19) is a stylish restaurant at the north end. Nearby, **La Taverne de Chamouny** (menus from €11) serves food until midnight. Crêpes, pizzas, fondues and plenty of fish are available.

Getting There & Away At the end of av Michael Croz, Chamonix **SNCF station** (☎ 04 50 53 00 44) is a five-minute walk

from the town centre. The narrow-gauge line that serves Chamonix joins the main French railway network at St-Gervais-les-Bains, from where there are connections to all major destinations, including Grenoble, Paris, Geneva airport and Moûtiers for Parc National de la Vanoise.

Chamonix bus station shares the train station building and buses depart from just outside. **SATOBUS** (☎ 04 72 35 94 96) has services to Lyon-Satolas airport (€69, 3¼ hours, two to three daily Monday to Friday and once daily at the weekend). **SAT Autocar** (☎ 04 50 53 01 15) has regular links to Geneva airport (€32, two hours, two to three daily) and Annecy (€15.30, 2½ hours, once daily except weekends). Services through the Mont-Blanc tunnel to Italy also link Chamonix to Courmayeur (€9.50, 45 minutes, six daily), where connecting services continue to Aoste, Milan and Turin (see Courmayeur Getting There & Away, p308 for details).

The closest international airports to Chamonix are Geneva, Lyon-Satolas and Turin.

Lac Blanc

Duration	4 hours
Distance	7.5km
Difficulty	easy–moderate
Start/Finish	La Flégère
Nearest Town	Les Praz (p278)
Transport	cable car, bus

Summary A visit to a beautiful high alpine lake. Views are excellent and in still weather the lake gives a classic reflection of the Mont Blanc massif.

The main focus of this trip is Lac Blanc, a dramatic alpine tarn held within the rock walls of the Aiguille du Belvédère. These northern slopes of the Chamonix Valley also offer spectacular views of the Mont Blanc range, and many walkers visit Lac Blanc seeking the famed reflection of the mountains when the water is still (your best chance of catching these conditions is in the early morning). The lake is likely to be completely frozen until mid-June,

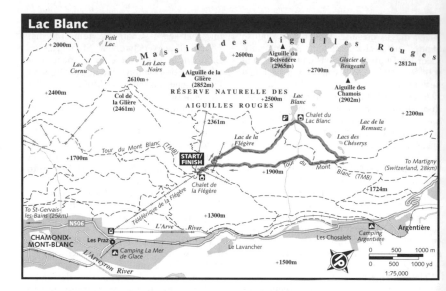

Lac Blanc

but by August it should be largely free of ice and snow. The beauty of the lake and its surrounds means that this is one of the most popular outings in the Chamonix Valley – you are unlikely to have the trail to yourself!

The walk described here assumes that you will use the *téléférique* to reach La Flégère, saving yourself around 800m of ascent and descent. Even with this mechanical assistance, the route still involves 475m of ascent. Paths are signed throughout and although the terrain is rough and rocky in the vicinity of Lac Blanc, the obstacles are not sufficient to deter most walkers.

For those who prefer to avoid the section by *téléférique*, several signed paths climb from both Les Praz and Chamonix, ascending through pleasant pine forest and arriving at La Flégère – just above the tree line – in about two hours. There are *refuges* at La Flégère and Lac Blanc, providing the opportunity to stay up high overnight if you like. It is also possible to access Lac Blanc from the Col des Montets to the north, or to it visit it as a sidetrip from the Tour du Mont Blanc – for more details see p318.

PLANNING
Maps

The IGN 1:25,000 map No 3630OT *Massif du Mont Blanc* covers this route.

NEAREST TOWN
Les Praz

The small village of Les Praz is 30 to 40 minutes' walk north of Chamonix. There is an outdoor gear shop in the main street if you need to pick up last-minute supplies, but the nearest bank and ATM are in Chamonix.

Places to Stay & Eat The well-organised **Camping La Mer de Glace** (☎ 04 50 53 08 63; *camping per person/site €5/4.30; open mid-Jun–mid-Sep*) has excellent facilities, and although slightly more expensive than some of the Chamonix camping grounds, small tents can sometimes be pitched without a site charge, reducing the price and making it excellent value.

Auberge Gîte La Bagna (☎ 04 50 53 62 90; *337 rue des Gaudenays; dorm beds/ singles/doubles €22/24/56; half board per person €12 extra*) is a friendly place with its own bar, **restaurant** and outside terrace. There are also several hotels in Les Praz;

Les Lanchers (☎ 04 50 53 47 19; *1459 route des Praz; doubles/half board €65/55*) is very central. For further accommodation options, see nearby Chamonix (see p277).

For self-caterers, there is a **shop** in the main street. Alternatively, try **La Cabane** (☎ 04 50 53 23 27), an attractive chalet-style restaurant on the main road with a terrace and good views of Mont Blanc.

Getting There & Away There is a bus stop opposite the *téléférique* in the centre of Les Praz and the **SNCF station** (☎ 08 36 35 35 35) is at the eastern end of the village. See p277 for details of services to/from Chamonix.

GETTING TO/FROM THE WALK

The **Téléférique de la Flégère** (☎ 04 50 53 18 58), in the centre of Les Praz, runs cable cars to La Flégère and the higher station of L'Index. The route starts and finishes at La Flégère (one way/return €8.20/10.20; 8.40am to 4.30pm June to September, 7.40am to 5.30pm July and August).

THE WALK

La Flégère is marked by a small collection of buildings. Beside the cable-car station is a small café, and slightly lower down, the **Chalet de la Flégère** (☎ 04 50 55 85 88; *dorm beds/half board €15/32; open late Jun–late Sep*) also serves refreshments on its terrace.

From La Flégère, follow signs to the right. Descend slightly to pass beneath a chairlift and then turn left onto a path signed to Lac Blanc. Climb steep switchbacks alongside another chairlift before passing underneath it and continuing more gently to Lac de la Flégère. Shortly after the lake a large cairn is reached, marking the boundary of the Réserve Naturelle des Aiguilles Rouges. The path now begins to ascend steeply again on rocky ground, and early in the season you may encounter patches of snow near the top. Pass a stone hut and arrive at **Lac Blanc**, 1½ to two hours from La Flégère.

The **Chalet du Lac Blanc** (☎ 04 50 53 49 14; *half board €44.50; open mid-Jun–late Sep*) is set above the eastern shore of the lake

and was recently rebuilt after being partially destroyed by an avalanche. Lac Blanc itself is actually two lakes; many people miss this point entirely. Beside the *refuge* is a small lake, around 30m wide, where you can sometimes see the famed reflection of the Mont Blanc range. It is fed by a small stream which, if followed, leads to a much larger lake set behind the first, but not visible from the *refuge*.

From Lac Blanc, take the path heading east and descend over rocky ground. A short ladder must be negotiated before the gradient eases and wider switchbacks lead to the shore of the first of the **Lacs des Chéserys**. Continue to descend along a ridge from where, if you want to see the other lakes, you'll need to detour off the path to the left.

Around 45 minutes from Lac Blanc you come to a prominent stone cairn marking the junction with the Grand Balcon Sud. Turn right here (following the sign to La Flégère), and contour easily across slopes covered with alpenrose and crossed by several tumbling streams. At the end of this delightful section you will pass a wooden cabin and join a track that takes you back up to La Flégère (45 minutes from the cairn).

Grand Balcon Nord

Duration	6–7 hours
Distance	13km
Difficulty	moderate–demanding
Start/Finish	Chamonix (p276)
Transport	train, bus

Summary A challenging walk with superb scenery, including a classic view over the Mer de Glace, Europe's second longest glacier.

The Chamonix Aiguilles (Needles) form what is probably the most celebrated mountain ridge in Europe. Stretching northeast from Mont Blanc, the 4km-long fin of rock is broken into a series of tremendous pinnacles and spires. The Grand Balcon Nord contours across the base of these mountains at a height just above the tree line and just below the level where you need to be a climber to go

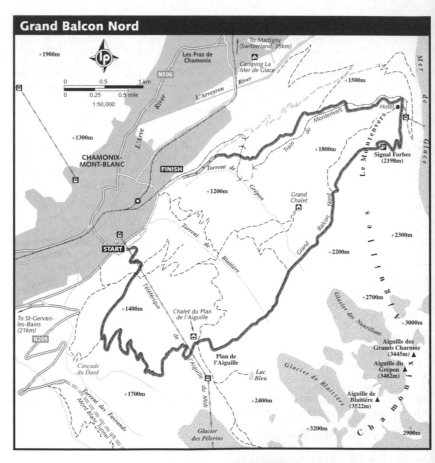

much farther. The path gives a great impression of the high alpine environment, and includes a superlative lookout across the Mer de Glace glacier (see the boxed text on p281 for more about this glacier).

The walk described here has a total ascent and descent of 1330m, and makes for a strenuous but rewarding day out. Note that the accessibility and scenic splendour of the route also means that it is very popular, and the *balcon* section of the trail can be busy at peak times. The walk can be made easier by using a *téléférique* and/or a mountain railway.

PLANNING
Maps
The IGN 1:25,000 map No 3630OT *Massif du Mont Blanc* covers this route.

GETTING TO/FROM THE WALK
While the described route starts and finishes in Chamonix, the level of difficulty of this route can be greatly reduced with the use of mechanical transport. To avoid the initial climb from Chamonix, use the **Téléférique de l'Aiguille du Midi** (☎ 04 50 53 30 80) to ascend 1200m to the mid-way station of Plan de l'Aiguille (one way/return

Living Glaciers: The Mer de Glace & Bossons

The Mer de Glace (visited on the Grand Balcon Nord walk, p279) and Bossons Glacier (see the walk Montagne de la Côte, p282) are two spectacular examples of very different types of glacier.

The Mer de Glace is a classic example of a *valley glacier*, a slow-moving tongue of ice descending to low elevations from a meeting place of several smaller glaciers. It is probably the best-known glacier in Europe, and at 14km long it is the second longest in the Alps. It is 1800m across at its widest point, and up to 400m deep. The movement of the ice varies from year to year but recent flow has been measured at 45m a year at the edges and 90m a year in the middle. Although it does contain crevasses, the moderate gradient of the valley floor means that the Mer de Glace is not as heavily crevassed as some other glaciers. It often serves therefore as a route of ascent and descent for mountaineers climbing the Grandes Jorasses.

By contrast, the Bossons Glacier is an *icefall*, extremely steep and heavily crevassed, with a gradient of 45° in many places. It is in fact the largest icefall in Europe, driven downwards by the weight of snow accumulating in the extensive névés on Mont Blanc. Huge séracs collapse continuously under the pressures of a fast descent: the glacier currently moves at a rate of some 250m to 300m a year.

A branch of the Bossons Glacier, the Taconnaz Glacier (also seen on the Montagne de la Côte route) is a typical *hanging glacier* with its terminal face resting on very steep ground. Violent avalanches from these glaciers are not uncommon, as large sections of sérac break away and thunder towards the valley. You'll also see many hanging glaciers on the Tour of the Vanoise Glaciers walk (see p285).

For a description of landform features left behind by melted glaciers, see the boxed text on p33. Other glacier terminology includes:

ablation zone – where the annual rate of melt exceeds snowfall
accumulation zone – where the annual snowfall exceeds the rate of snowmelt
bergschrund – crevasse at the head of a glacier
blue ice – ice compacted and metamorphosised into an airtight mass
crevasse – deep crack or fissure in the ice
firn line – the line between the accumulation and ablation zones
icefall – the frozen equivalent to a waterfall as the glacier descends over steep ground
lateral moraine – mounds of debris deposited along the flanks of a glacier
névé – masses of porous ice not yet transformed into blue (glacier) ice; also called firn
sérac – pinnacle of ice among crevasses on a glacier
sink hole – depression in the glacial surface where a stream disappears underground
terminal moraine – mound of debris at the end of a glacier

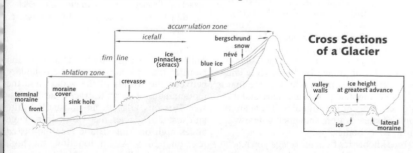

Cross Sections of a Glacier

€12.30/14.40, services from 8.10am to 5pm June to September and from 6.10am to 5pm July and August). From here, turn left and follow a signed trail for 600m to the Chalet du Plan de l'Aiguille, where you will join the described route.

At the northern end of the *balcon* trail, the **Train du Montenvers** *(☎ 04 50 53 12 54)* can also transport you from Montenvers back to Chamonix (one way/return €10.30/ 13.40, services from 8.30am to 5pm June to September and from 7am to 6pm July and August). Using both these forms of transport means that you will be left with a generally flat, 5km-long *balcon* walk that merits a grade of easy.

THE WALK

The walk starts from a large car park across the main road from the Aiguille du Midi *téléférique* station. A path enters the forest from the far right-hand corner of the car park, marked by a sign for the Plan de l'Aiguille. The path climbs immediately into the forest, with switchbacks leading steadily upwards. Within the first 30 minutes there are two trail junctions; keep right at both.

The trail continues to climb steadily, passing a long straight section and then weaving back and forth on wide switchbacks. The slope opens out as you gain height and there are good views across the Glacier des Bossons and Montagne de la Côte. Pass some large granite boulders and climb through tighter switchbacks to **Chalet du Plan de l'Aiguille** *(☎ 06 65 64 27 53; dorm beds/half board €10/30; open mid-Jun–mid-Sep)*, a small *refuge* that marks the top of the climb (2½ hours from the start).

Follow signs behind the *refuge* for Montenvers, ignoring a trail dropping off towards Chamonix. The *balcon* path to Montenvers is a joy, winding across wild slopes strewn with jumbles of granite boulders. Here and there a few stunted pines flout the tree line. Just above, moraine precedes glacier and the high rock walls of the Aiguilles. There are a couple of streams from snowmelt where you can fill water bottles.

Three kilometres from the *refuge* you reach a trail junction. The main path continues to contour directly to Montenvers. This route follows the right-hand trail towards 'La Signal', climbing over a shoulder and leading to the superlative viewpoint at **Signal Forbes** (2198m). The view of the Mer de Glace from here is one of the classic sights of the Chamonix Valley (1½ to two hours from the *refuge*).

Descend steeply to the buildings and the train station at Montenvers (20 minutes from Signal Forbes). The **Grand Hotel du Montenvers** *(☎ 04 50 53 87 70; doubles/half board €47/55)* serves refreshments on a terrace overlooking the glacier. A footpath and *téléférique* (return €3.50) give access to the glacier itself, where there's a crystal gallery and an **ice cave** (admission €3.60).

From Montenvers, follow the path to the **Museum of Alpine Fauna** (free entry). The descent path leaves from the back of this building and winds steadily through pine forest back to Chamonix, following roughly along the same course as the railway (1½ hours). Halfway through the descent is a small **cabin** selling cold drinks.

Montagne de la Côte

Duration	5–6 hours
Distance	8km
Difficulty	moderate–demanding
Start	Chalet du Glacier des Bossons
Finish	Les Bossons (p283)
Transport	chairlift, train, bus

Summary A tremendous walk with magnificent views of the Bossons Glacier and the upper reaches of Mont Blanc. The route was originally used by Balmat and Paccard on the first ascent of Mont Blanc.

This walk is similar to the Grand Balcon Nord in that it brings you to the boundary between the worlds of the walker and the mountaineer. The route traces the impressive Bossons Glacier, an unusually white and tortured glacier that flows from huge névés high on Mont Blanc (see the boxed text on p281). At La Jonction, the high point of the walk, you can look out across an ocean of crevassed ice to the summit of Mont Blanc, only 4km away. Even for walkers used to glacier scenery, it is difficult not to be impressed.

This is a straight up and down route involving some 1200m of ascent. The path is well benched in its lower reaches but crosses rocky terrain near the top. Though it necessitates some (very easy) scrambling manoeuvres, it should be suitable for all walkers who can cope with the climb. The variation followed on the return is less frequented and rather eroded in places; return by reversing the outward route if you prefer the security of a well-made trail. The walk is described assuming that the *télésiège* (chairlift) is used to reach the Chalet du Glacier des Bossons, thus avoiding 400m of ascent from Les Bossons.

PLANNING
Maps
The IGN 1:25,000 map No 3531ET *St-Gervais* covers this route.

NEAREST TOWN
Les Bossons
Les Bossons is an elongated village that is really a southern continuation of Chamonix. For supermarkets, outdoor gear shops and banking facilities you'll have to visit the larger town. Most tourist activity in the village centres around the *télésiège*.

Following in the Footsteps of History

The route up Montagne de la Côte was first forged during early attempts to climb Mont Blanc, and is now a landmark in Alpine history. On 7 August 1786, Jacques Balmat and Dr Michel Paccard climbed the ridge as far as the area now known as the Gîte à Balmat. They bivouacked here and the following day became the first people to summit Mont Blanc. The first female ascent, made by Marie Paradis in 1808, traced the same route. Today, the trail has been superseded as a way to Mont Blanc by other routes accessible by *téléférique* and cog railway.

Places to Stay & Eat Three camping grounds lie side by side just below the *télésiège* and all offer flat, grassy tent sites. **Les Deux Glaciers** (☎ 04 50 53 15 84; *per person/tent & car €4.50/3; open year-round*) has a **restaurant**, while **Les Cimes** (*04 50 53 58 93; per person/ tent & car €1.50/3; open Jun-Sep*) has a **snack bar** serving pizza and chips. Alternatively, **Chalet Glacier du Mont Blanc** (☎ 04 50 53 35 84; *224 route des Tissières; dorms/singles/ doubles €19/25/45*) is a *gîte d'étape* situated next to the *télésiège*.

There are also several places to eat around the *télésiège*. **Le Tremplin** (*snacks from €6*) is 40m uphill from the chair-lift station and offers warm snacks and main courses. At **Restaurant du Télésiège** (*mains €10*) also has meals.

Getting There & Away The 'Glacier des Bossons' bus stop is conveniently situated adjacent to the *télésiège*, while the **SNCF station** is in the centre of the village. See p277 for details of services to/from Chamonix.

GETTING TO/FROM THE WALK
The **Télésiège du Glacier du Mont Blanc** (☎ 04 50 53 08 97) takes you to the start of the route at the Chalet du Glacier des Bossons (one way/return €6/9; 1pm to 6pm mid-June to September, 8am to 6pm July and August).

If you prefer to negotiate the 400 vertical metres on foot, follow the trail that begins by ascending the ski slope from the right of the *télésiège*. The trail is signed to Le Mont and then Chalet du Glacier des Bossons (45 minutes).

THE WALK
From the **Chalet du Glacier des Bossons** (☎ 04 50 53 03 89), which serves meals and drinks on its terrace, there is already a good view of the Bossons icefall and its huge, deeply crevassed terminal face. An optional side trip climbs to a lookout over the glacier. Well-benched switchbacks then lead through the forest to **Chalet des Pyramides**, a smaller, more basic rest-point also serving refreshments; it's reached one to 1¼ hours from the start. At this point the Bossons Glacier is left behind; the trail climbs

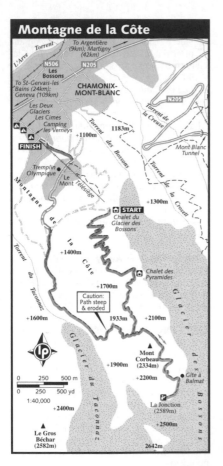

Montagne de la Côte

To Argentière (9km); Martigny (42km)

L'Arve Torrent

N506
N205
Les Bossons

To St-Gervais-les-Bains (24km); Geneva (109km)

CHAMONIX-MONT-BLANC

N205

Les Deux Glaciers
Les Cimes
Camping les Verneys

+1100m
1183m

FINISH

Torrent des Bossons

Torrent de la Creuse

Mont Blanc Tunnel

Tremplin Olympique
Le Mont télésiège

Torrent de la Creuse

START
Chalet du Glacier des Bossons
+1300m

Montagne de la Côte
+1400m

Chalet des Pyramides

+1700m

Caution: Path steep & eroded

Torrent du Taconnaz

+1600m   1933m   +2100m

0   250   500 m
0   250   500 yd
1:40,000

Mont Corbeau (2334m)
+1900m

+2200m

Gîte à Balmat

Glacier du Taconnaz

+2400m

La Jonction (2589m)

+2500m

Le Gros Béchar (2582m)

Glacier des Bossons

2642m

ground. The trail contours beside the glacier and offers a short respite from the ascent, before it veers right and begins to climb again over rocky ground. Yellow splashes of paint on the boulders mark the line of least resistance. The climb from here to La Jonction is rough but generally straightforward, though there are two or three rocky steps where you'll need to use your hands for support.

The rock scramble leads you to a group of house-sized granite boulders, the historic bivouac site known as **Gîte à Balmat** (see the boxed text on p283). **La Jonction**, the point where the rock of Montagne de la Côte is finally subsumed by the icy fortress protecting Mont Blanc, is a short climb beyond the boulders (one to 1½ hours from the trail junction).

Return along the same trail to the junction with the path descending to the Taconnaz Glacier. For the easiest descent, keep right and retrace your outward path. The left-hand path offers a slightly more challenging descent. Though the trail is rough and awkward in several places, it gives excellent views of Taconnaz. Once past the terminal face of this glacier, the path descends along a grassy moraine ridge. Note the avalanche deflectors far below – this whole valley sees large and violent avalanches in the spring.

Re-enter the pine forest and follow the trail to the right, soon joining the 4WD track to the Chalet du Glacier des Bossons. The top of the *télésiège* is a 500m climb up this track. To descend on foot, follow the 4WD track downhill and join a lane. Continue past the ski jump and turn left along a signed path down the ski slope to reach the finish (two to 2½ hours from La Jonction).

Parc National de la Vanoise

Created in 1963, the Parc National de la Vanoise was France's first national park. Its fully protected central zone covers almost 530 sq km of 3000m-high peaks, attendant glaciers and high alpine meadows.

steeply and crosses to the western slopes of Montagne de la Côte to gain views of the Glacier du Taconnaz.

Thirty minutes from the chalet you come to a trail junction, presided over by the bulk of Mont Blanc. To the right a path descends towards the terminal face of the Taconnaz Glacier (the return route). For the moment, keep left and climb on steep switchbacks to a notch in the ridge, where you cross back to the eastern side of the spur. The Aiguille du Midi now sits on the skyline while the twisted spires and convoluted pinnacles of the upper Bossons icefall dominate the fore-

For the walker, the Vanoise offers a mark-edly different experience from the Chamonix Valley, where the construction of ski pistes and *téléfériques* have detracted from the inherent wildness of the Alpine environment. With lower mountains (the highest summit in the park, La Grand Casse, is only 3855m), the Vanoise attracts fewer walkers and the trails tend to be quieter. Everything is relative, however, and the area will still seem busy to walkers accustomed to true isolation. An average of around 7000 walkers used the principal trails of the Tour of the Vanoise Glaciers compared with around 10,000 for the world-famous Tour du Mont Blanc.

The Tour of the Vanoise Glaciers is the only walk we describe in detail. The views on this circuit are excellent throughout and the trails are generally well benched and signed. However the area offers a great deal more walking opportunities in terms of both one-day and multi-day walks. See p292 for other suggestions.

NATURAL HISTORY
Alpine flora and fauna are found in abundance in the Parc National de la Vanoise, and are one of the area's primary attractions. More than 1000 species of plant can be found above the 1500m contour comprising alpine, oriental, southern and arctic species. Nationally protected species include alpine columbine, bicoloured sedge, cortusa, dwarf scorpion grass, alpine eryngo and the only French colonies of linnaea.

The fauna of the park is perhaps even more spectacular, with 1200 ibex and 4700 chamois roaming the central area (see the boxed text on p287). Rodents such as marmot, mountain hare and snow vole are preyed upon by fox. Other carnivorous mammals include badgers, pine martens, beech martens and stoats. With an eye to the sky you might be lucky enough to spot one of the 16 pairs of golden eagles resident in the park. Other notable bird species include black grouse, ptarmigans, rock partridges, eagle owls, Tengalm's owls and black woodpeckers. Look out too for bearded vultures, or lammergeiers, recently reintroduced into the Haute-Savoie/Mont

Blanc region and now spreading south into the Vanoise.

PLANNING
Maps & Books
The Libris 1:60,000 map No 4 *Vanoise Parc National, Beaufortain* is a good overview map of the area. In addition, a useful booklet, *Itinéraires Remarquables*, is produced by the Agence Touristique Départementale de la Savoie (see p276). It describes a variety of walks in the Parc National de la Vanoise and in the Savoie region as a whole.

Information Sources
For general information on Parc National de la Vanoise, contact **La Direction du Parc National de la Vanoise** (☎ 04 79 62 30 54; *www.vanoise.com; 135 rue du Docteur Julliand, BP 705, F 73007, Chambéry Cedex*).

Permits & Regulations
No permits are required to walk in the park, although you will be subject to the usual restrictions governing protected areas (see the boxed text on p42).

Wild camping is prohibited throughout the park. However, camping is permitted in designated areas beside most of the *refuges* in July and August; the *refuges* charge €4.20 for campers, who are then allowed to use the facilities. Tents can be erected between 7pm and 7am only.

Tour of the Vanoise Glaciers

Duration	5 days
Distance	61km
Difficulty	moderate–demanding
Start/Finish	Pralognan-la-Vanoise
Transport	bus

Summary A memorable circuit in a national park created to protect the ibex. It has all the flavour of alpine walking: good mountain scenery, abundant wildlife and several tough climbs.

This varied route circumnavigates a mountain massif with glaciated, dome-like summits reaching heights of 3500m. The *refuges*

Tour of the Vanoise Glaciers

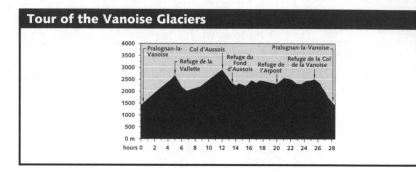

are set amid spectacular alpine surrounds and frequent lakes and streams provide daily opportunities for refreshing swims. Coupled with an almost guaranteed sighting of ibex at some point, this walk is a classic alpine outing.

Some walkers complete the circuit in four days, but five is a much better schedule, and almost mandatory if you are carrying camping gear. Even six would not seem unduly leisurely given the abundant opportunities to watch the wildlife, appreciate the wildflowers and take in the views. Each day ends at a *refuge*, although in July and August it is necessary to book a bed in advance. All of the *refuges* except the Refuge de la Col de la Vanoise have adjacent camping areas and two (Refuge de l'Arpont and Refuge de la Col de la Vanoise) also have kitchens. All *refuges* are wardened and offer meals from mid-June to mid-September, but remain open on a self-catering basis outside this period. Water is never in too short supply and it is easy to refill water bottles along the trail.

NATURAL HISTORY

The Vanoise glaciers descend from a broad mountain backbone ranging in height from 3000m to 3500m. The extensive area of high ground has allowed deep and substantial névé (masses of porous ice not yet frozen into glacier ice) to form, pushing tongues of ice down across the steeper ground below. This has resulted in some beautiful hanging glaciers. See the boxed text on p281 for more information on the way various types of glacier form.

You'll be unlucky if you don't see ibex (see the boxed text, opposite) on the circuit and you'll find it impossible not to see marmot scampering away across the grass and rocks, especially at the Col de la Vanoise where feeding has left them virtually tame. The best place to see ibex is probably between Refuge de l'Arpont and the Col de la Vanoise (Day 4). For more information on ibex in the Vanoise see the boxed text (opposite).

PLANNING
Maps & Books

For this route you will need two IGN maps: No 3534OT 1:25,000 *Les Trois Vallées*, covering the western half of the park, and No 3633ET 1:25,000 *Tignes Val d'Isère*, covering the eastern extent of the walk.

Tour of the Vanoise by Kev Reynolds gives a day-by-day account of a 10- to 12-day circuit of the entire park, half of which emulates the general direction of this route.

NEAREST TOWN
Pralognan-la-Vanoise

The small but beautiful mountain town of Pralognan-la-Vanoise is an excellent base for walking in the national park. At the head of the steep-sided Pralognan Valley, the approach to the area gives the impression of penetrating the heart of the mountains. The setting is spectacular: the 1000m-high rock faces of Le Petit Marchet and Aiguilles de l'Arcelin tower over the town; to the north-west serrated peaks and hanging glaciers peer over the grassy dome of Le Moriond.

The Ibex

During five weeks' walking in the Northern Alps my most impressive experience was following a herd of male ibex (Capra ibex), known in France as bouquetin, in the Parc National de la Vanoise. In the high Alpine setting, against a backdrop of snow and ice, these powerful animals with their huge curved horns seemed like true lords of their world. They regarded us with a casual indifference, moving together over banks of snow and pausing to graze wherever they found patches of vegetation. Later I also spotted a pair of ibex calves standing atop a cliff, separated from the rest of the herd by a group of walkers. Unsure of themselves for a few moments, instinct kicked in and they launched themselves down the cliff face in what seemed like a controlled fall. They landed upright and at a full run, already true masters of the mountain environment.

It is hard to believe that these animals were actually extinct in France by 1800. From the 16th century they were a prime game animal and supposed medicinal properties found in their flesh and horns exacerbated hunting pressure throughout the Alps. Fortunately, 50km from the Vanoise across the border in Italy, a small population of around 100 ibex managed to hold on in the fastness of Gran Paradiso. This herd was later to form the nucleus for reintroduction programmes.

The Parc National de la Vanoise was primarily created to provide a protected environment for the new herds of French ibex. From the 50 individuals originally placed in the park, there are now some 1200, representing 50% of the French, and 5% of the European populations. The park has also benefited the chamois, with which female ibex are often confused, increasing their population from 500 animals in 1963 to about 4300 in 1986.

Gareth McCormack

Information Despite its relative remoteness, Pralognan-la-Vanoise has all the facilities you are likely to need. There are several outdoor-gear shops and banks with ATMs on the main street. There is also a local medical centre.

The **tourist office** (☎ 04 79 08 79 08; www.pralognan.com) is in the main street and also serves as the **national park office** (☎ 04 79 08 71 49; www.vanoise.com). Together they can provide a host of information on the town and park, including a copy of the free park magazine, L'Estive. The building also houses a display on the history and natural history of the park.

Park wardens organise regular half-day and full-day walks during the summer months – you'll need to reserve in advance at the park office. For other guided walks, contact the **Bureau des Guides et Accompagnateurs** (☎ 04 79 08 71 21), just opposite the tourist office.

Places to Stay & Eat Pralognan has two camping grounds to choose from. **Camping Municipal le Chamois** (☎ 04 79 08 71 54; camping per person/tent & car €3.30/2.35; open Jun–mid-Sep) and **Camping Isertan** (☎ 04 79 08 75 24; camping per person/tent/ car €5/3/2; open Jun–mid-Sep) are situated side by side at the eastern edge of the town. Neither camping ground has particularly good shade, but they're perfectly located for walks heading into the national park.

Le Petit Mont Blanc (☎ 04 79 08 72 73; Côte du Barioz; half board €32) is an attractive gîte at the top of the main street. For something more up-market, try the nearby **Hotel de la Vanoise** (☎ 04 79 08 70 34; chemin du Dou des Ponts; singles/doubles/half board €43/78/62).

There are two **supermarkets** and a host of restaurants and cafés on the main street. Good restaurants include **Le Chardon Bleu** (☎ 04 79 08 73 07), but the best advice is to peruse the many menus for whatever suits your taste.

Getting There & Away A regular bus service run by **Transavoie** (☎ 04 79 24 21 58) links Pralognan to the town of Moûtiers, 27km away (€11.20, 1¼ hours, two to three daily). Moûtiers is on mainline bus and railway networks.

Tour of the Vanoise Glaciers

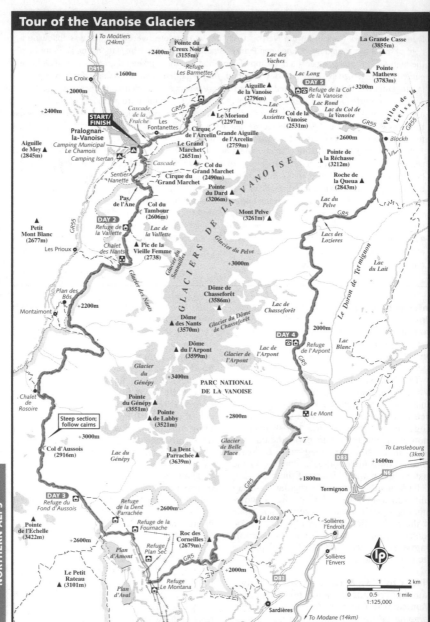

To Moûtiers (24km)

D915

La Croix

+1600m

+2000m

+2400m

Aiguille de Mey ▲ (2845m)

START/ FINISH
Pralognan-la-Vanoise
Camping Municipal Le Chamois
Camping Isertan

Cascade de la Fraîche
Les Fontanettes

Sentier Nanette

Pas de l'Âne

DAY 2
Refuge de la Vallette

Petit Mont Blanc (2677m)

Les Prioux

Chalet des Nants

Pic de la Vieille Femme (2738)

Plan des Bôs

Montaimont

+2200m

Chalet de Rosoire

Steep section; follow cairns

+3000m

Col d'Aussois (2916m)

DAY 3
Refuge du Fond d'Aussois

Pointe de l'Echelle (3422m)

+2600m

Le Petit Rateau ▲ (3101m)

Plan d'Amont

Refuge Plan Sec

Plan d'Aval

Refuge Le Montana

Pointe du Creux Noir ▲ (3155m)

Refuge Les Barmettes

GR55

Le Moriond ▲ (2297m)

Cirque de l'Arcelin

Le Grand Marchet (2651m)

Col du Grand Marchet (2490m)

Cirque du Grand Marchet

Grande Aiguille de l'Arcelin (2759m)

Pointe du Dard (3206m)

Col du Tambour (2606m)

Lac de la Vallette

Glacier du Pelve

Glacier des Nants

Glacier du Génépy

Dôme ▲ des Nants (3570m)

Dôme du l'Arpont (3599m)

+3400m

Pointe du Génépy ▲ (3551m)

Pointe ▲ de Labby (3521m)

Lac du Génépy

La Dent Parrachée ▲ (3639m)

Refuge de la Dent Parrachée

Refuge de la Fournache

+2600m

Roc des Corneilles (2679m)

GR5

Lac des Vaches

Lac Long

DAY 5
Refuge de la Col de la Vanoise

Aiguille de la Vanoise (2796m)

Lac des Assiettes

Col de la Vanoise (2531m)

Lac Rond

Lac du Col de la Vanoise

La Grande Casse (3855m)

Pointe Mathews (3783m)

+3200m

GR55

Vallon de la Leisse

+2600m

Blockh

Pointe de la Réchasse (3212m)

Roche de la Queua ▲ (2843m)

Lac du Pelve

Lacs des Lozières

Mont Pelve (3261m) ▲

GLACIERS DE LA VANOISE

Glacier des Sonnailles

Dôme de Chasseforêt (3586m)

+3000m

Glacier du Dôme de Chasseforêt

Lac de Chasseforêt

DAY 4
Refuge de l'Arpont

Glacier de l'Arpont

Lac de l'Arpont

+2000m

GR5

Le Doron de Termignon

Lac du Lait

Lac Blanc

PARC NATIONAL DE LA VANOISE

Le Mont

+2800m

Glacier de Belle Place

To Lanslebourg (3km)

D83

+1600m

N6

+1800m

Termignon

La Loza

Sollières l'Endroit

Sollières l'Envers

La Dent Parrachée ▲ (3639m)

GR5

To Modane (14km)

+2000m

D83

Sardières

0   1   2 km
0 0.5   1 mile
1:125,000

NORTHERN ALPS

Alpenrose on the Grand Balcon Sud, overlooking Glacier d'Argentière, Tour du Mont Blanc walk

On the Tour of the Vanoise Glaciers walk

Near the Col de la Vanoise, Northern Alps

INGRID RODDIS

Vineyards on the Crête des Vosges walk

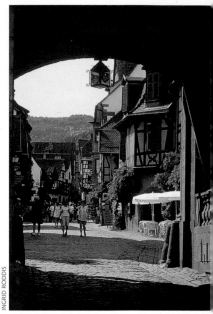

INGRID RODDIS

Riquewihr at the end of the Crête des Vosges walk

GARETH McCORMACK

Sunset on Mont Blanc, Tour du Mont Blanc walk, Chamonix Valley

THE WALK
Day 1: Pralognan-la-Vanoise to Refuge de la Vallette
5 hours, 6km, 1200m ascent

There are two options for beginning the long, steep ascent to Refuge de la Vallette. The more direct route is signed from the end of the road between Pralognan's two camping grounds. The option described here is slightly less direct but more interesting, taking in a thundering waterfall.

From the northeastern end of Camping Municipal le Chamois, follow signposts for the waterfall and the Sentier Nanette. The gradient is immediately steep, setting the tone for the rest of the day. Switchbacks lead up through pine forest, passing a couple of junctions where you should follow signs for the Sentier Nanette. In a few places, the route crosses wooden gangways built into rock faces. There are fastened chains to lend security here. After one hour, pine gives way to birch and, shortly after, you reach a viewpoint at the edge of a ravine. On the far wall of the ravine are a number of powerful **cascades**, one of which pours out of a cave in the cliff face.

The route now climbs above the tree line and then flattens out as it contours beneath rock faces. A brief descent brings you to a junction, one to 1½ hours from the top of the pine trees. Here you should follow the sign for Refuge de la Vallette, and turn left onto a path known as the **Pas de l'Âne** (Donkey Steps). Climb steeply on a rough staircase through a rocky gully, and at the top look carefully for a couple of cairns above and to the right, which lead back to a more defined trail.

Continue through switchbacks to reach a junction amid a boulder field (one hour from the start of the Pas de l'Âne). From here, you can make out the path climbing up to the **Col du Tambour**, 20 minutes away. There may be patches of snow to cross before the top. From the col, the view to the northeast is dominated by the snowy peaks of Le Grand Bec and Le Grand Casse. To the south the *refuge* is visible, now just 1km away. Descend slightly and then climb above Lac de la Vallette to reach the *refuge*.

Refuge de la Vallette (☎ 04 79 22 96 38; *dorm beds/half board €11.60/30.60*) consists of several small and attractive chalets, and is surrounded by wonderful alpine scenery. There is plenty of scope for exploration if you have the energy. A path to the southwest leads onto Pic de la Vieille Femme (2738m), a rocky peak with expansive views (one hour return from the *refuge*).

Day 2: Refuge de la Vallette to Refuge du Fond d'Aussois
8–9 hours, 17km, 1200m ascent/descent

This is the most challenging day of the circuit. From Refuge de la Vallette, the trail drops steeply in switchbacks to the Chalet des Nants, a ruined herding shelter. Follow the sign for the Col d'Aussois and ford several streams before curving round a spur onto a trail that runs along the boundary of the park. The recommended IGN 1:25,000 map now shows a significant detour down towards Plan des Bôs. In reality a trail continues over the grass all the way along the park boundary, though it is not signed and you will need to look out for the left turn. A ruined stone shelter marks the junction with the main path at the end of this shortcut, 1½ to two hours from the start.

Turn left onto the main path and climb into the **Cirque du Giverny**, at first along a ridge and then contouring across steep slopes. The valley opens out at a bridge across the powerful torrent draining the Glacier du Génépy. On the right, a few hundred metres ahead, is a moraine ridge. Trace the switchbacks up this stony slope and then loop back to the west. The trail now undulates around the 2400m contour before descending steeply to reach two trail junctions just above the Chalet de Rosoire (two hours from the ruined shelter). This chalet marks the beginning of the climb to the Col d'Aussois. Keep left at the junctions – one signpost indicates the top of the col to be 2½ hours. Most walkers will need at least two hours for the steep and unrelenting ascent.

After a large switchback the trail crosses the thundering Ruisseau de Rosoire on a plank bridge, and then steepens as it climbs through rocky outcrops. The terrain then settles into a steep, stony slope. The trail becomes confused by the rocky ground, and even dissipates entirely as you gain height. Though cairns are in place to help out, route finding can be tricky in poor visibility. Early in the season there may also be large snow banks near the top. Continue uphill, climbing almost directly south to reach the col.

The **Col d'Aussois** (2916m) is marked by a small wooden signpost. Keep an eye out for animals – you stand a good chance of seeing chamois and ibex in this area. Follow cairns to within sight of a wooden cross, which marks the beginning of the descent route. The cairns lead east and then south, weaving between rock slabs and descending steeply but easily into a large and impressive glacial bowl. The **Refuge du Fond d'Aussois** (☎ *04 79 20 39 83; dorm beds/half board €13.50/30*) is reached around 1½ hours from the col, and is situated beside a stream where the valley widens and begins to flatten out. At the time of writing this once-lovely *refuge* was overshadowed somewhat by a new building under construction nearby.

Day 3: Refuge du Fond d'Aussois to Refuge de l'Arpont
6–7 hours, 18km, 700m ascent/descent
Though easier than the previous day, this section still manages to cover significant ground. Leave the *refuge* and follow a vehicle track across the flat, grassy valley floor. After 1km you reach a ruined stone building, where there are good views down across the Plan d'Amont. Turn left here along a path signed to the Refuge de la Fournache and climb through boulders and stunted pines. Pass the *refuge* and continue right, dropping to join another vehicle track. Turn right and follow the track to ski lifts, where a footpath is signed towards the Refuge de l'Arpont.

The path contours easily across steep grassy meadows for 2km; early in the season the wildflowers are particularly impressive in this area. Two hours from the start of the day, you cross a stream and re-enter the national park. On the opposite bank of the stream a trail junction lies beneath a series of limestone escarpments. Turn left and trace the switchbacks through the crags, climbing for 1km to a flat, grassy *balcon* path leading to the spur of La Loza, a popular lunch spot.

The trail continues to contour northwards from La Loza but the nature of the route soon begins to change, growing more rugged in character. Shattered cliffs and pinnacles throw down sheets of scree across the path and early in the season there may be a large snow bank to cross. The trail rounds a ridge and descends steeply across several streams, around 2½ hours beyond the escarpments. It then climbs over another spur and drops down to several stone ruins and a trail junction above Le Mont.

Keep left at the junction and begin the final, 2km climb to the *refuge*. The ascent begins though scrub but sweeps round onto slopes cut by several torrents draining the glaciers that are visible not far above. **Refuge de l'Arpont** (☎ *04 79 20 51 51; dorm beds/half board €11.60/30*) sits on a spur and commands a fine view over the scene.

Day 4: Refuge de l'Arpont to Refuge de la Col de la Vanoise
5–6 hours, 12km, 500m ascent, 300m descent
A beautiful day's walking with probably the best mountain scenery of the route, and a very good chance of seeing ibex. The trail climbs immediately from Refuge de l'Arpont, zigzagging up steep and broken slopes and gaining almost 300m in 1.5km. It then flattens out and rounds a broad spur to enter a vast **cirque** of moraine, streams and lakes, which it crosses for the next 3km. Given good weather, views of the Dôme de Chasseforêt (3586m) and Mont Pelve (3261m) are superb. North of the moraine the trail passes three beautiful lakes among meadows and boulder fields. Though only two to 2½ hours from the *refuge*, this is a tempting place for a break.

The route climbs slightly above the lakes and rounds a broad spur before descending to a trail junction (30 to 45 minutes from the lakes). Walkers heading for the eastern half of the park would turn right here. The trail for the Col de la Vanoise keeps left and stays around the 2300m level, heading north across steep scree slopes and then climbing over a boulder field to reach another trail junction overlooking the Vallon de la Leisse. There are good views here of the ridge between La Grande Casse (3855m) and La Grande Motte (3605m). The trail to the Col de la Vanoise climbs to the left past two block shelters and enters the valley of the Ruisseau de la Vanoise.

Three lakes are passed on the gradual, 2km ascent to the col, with buttresses, scree slopes and glaciers towering over the trail on either side. The **Refuge de la Col de la Vanoise** (☎ 04 79 08 25 23; dorm beds/half board €13.50/30) is a large refuge that feels rather impersonal after the small, homely places already visited on the route. Camping is not permitted and there is a gas surcharge for self-caterers.

Day 5: Refuge de la Col de la Vanoise to Pralognan-la-Vanoise

3 hours, 8km, 1400m descent

A long but beautiful descent. Walk west on a path that skirts around the base of Aiguille de la Vanoise and then descend steeply towards the **Lac des Vaches**. At most times this lake will be shallow enough to allow use of the stepping stones across the middle, and late in the season the waters may have dried up altogether. Continue to descend from the lake, with a wild vista of La Grande Casse opening up behind.

Cross a vigorous stream and descend steeply to **Refuge Les Barmettes**, where refreshments are available (around 1½ hours from the col). Just after the refuge take a left turn signed for the Cirque de l'Arcelin, and descend on this small path into pine forest. In 30 minutes you reach a vehicle track coming up from the hamlet of Les Fontanettes. Above and to your left is the Cirque de l'Arcelin with its glacially carved rock walls and impressive cascade. Descend along the vehicle track, keeping to the left of the Torrent de la Glière. The track passes through pine forest on its way back to Camping Municipal Le Chamois, offering a good view of the Cascade de la Fraîche on the way.

Other Walks

CHAMONIX VALLEY
Desert de Platé

The limestone plateau of the Desert de Platé is a wonderful contrast to the granite and glacier of the Mont Blanc massif. This six-hour, 13km, moderate-grade route begins with a steep and exciting climb of 850m to a high plateau of limestone pavement and wildflowers. For some, reaching **Refuge de Platé** (☎ 04 50 93 11 07) will be enough, but others will want to climb to the Col du Colonney and return via a circuit across the rocky Tête des Lindars. Complete the walk by retracing the outward ascent route.

The walk starts and finishes at Praz Coutant, 3km east of Plateau d'Assy. Praz Coutant is served by regular **SAT** (☎ 04 50 53 01 15) buses from Sallanches. If you are driving, follow the D43 east from Plateau d'Assy for 3km to a very sharp right-hand hairpin bend, with a parking area on the right and a wooden cross on the left. The walk starts and finishes here. Use the IGN 1:25,000 map No 3530ET Samoëns Haut-Giffre.

For more information get in touch with the tourist office and Office de Haute Montagne in Chamonix (see p276).

Vallorcine & Alpages de Loriaz

Starting and finishing at the train station in Vallorcine, 30 minutes north of Chamonix, this circuit is a great way to escape the crowds of the Chamonix Valley. The five-hour, 11km route passes through lovely Alpine meadows on the way to a reservoir on the Swiss/French border, and offers excellent views of the Mont Blanc massif. From Vallorcine, follow signs for the **Refuge de Loriaz** (☎ 04 50 54 06 45), climbing through pine forest before reaching open flower meadows and the refuge itself. From here a balcon trail is signed to Lac d'Émosson. From the impressive dam at the end of this lake, return via a steep path signed to Vallorcine. The IGN 1:25,000 map No 3630OT Massif du Mont Blanc covers the route.

For more information about the walk contact the tourist office and Office de Haute Montagne in Chamonix (see p276).

GR5

Although it actually begins in the Netherlands, most people get interested in the long-distance GR5 when it reaches the French Alps. From Lake Geneva the route climbs through the forests and pastures of the Pre-Alps around Morzine, before crossing to the Aiguilles Rouges and the Chamonix Valley. It then passes Aiguille du Grand Fond and Bourg St-Maurice before climbing back into the mountains of the Parc National de la Vanoise and reaching Modane. The distance from Lake Geneva to Modane is approximately 250km. The path is well marked and maintained throughout, and accommodation is provided by *refuges* and *gîtes d'étape*.

For more information, see *Walking the French Alps: GR5* by Martin Collins.

PARC NATIONAL DE LA VANOISE
Cirque du Grand Marchet

This is a demanding and dramatic seven-hour walk across the Col du Grand Marchet (2490m). The route, which starts and finishes in Pralognan-la-Vanoise, follows the same route as Day 1 of the Tour of the Vanoise Glaciers (see p289) until a trail junction just above the Pas de l'Âne. Turn left here and cross rugged ground into the Cirque du Grand Marchet, where numerous waterfalls cascade down the rock walls from the glaciers above. A steep climb leads to the top of Col du Grand Marchet and an equally steep, difficult descent is made into the Cirque du Dard. The route then passes through a narrow gap between soaring rock walls and descends into the Cirque de l'Arcelin. The descent to Pralognan is straightforward from here. Use IGN 1:25,000 map No 3534OT *Les Trois Vallées-Modane*.

For more information see the Tour of the Vanoise Glaciers walk, p286.

Cirque de l'Arcelin

This four-hour walk, which starts and finishes in Pralognan-la-Vanoise (p286), features some beautiful waterfalls and impressive views of the mountain scenery around the town itself. From the northeastern end of Camping Municipal Le Chamois, climb through forest to the junction of the Torrent du Dard and the Nant de la Crépéna. After views of waterfalls the trail climbs round the back of Le Moriond (2297m) and then joins the GR55 descending from the Col de la Vanoise. This trail is followed back to Pralognan. Use the IGN 1:25,000 map No 3534OT Les Trois Vallées-Modane.

For more information see the Tour of the Vanoise Glaciers walk, p286.

TOUR DU MONT BLANC

The Tour du Mont Blanc (TMB) is one of the world's classic walks – a truly international route with sections in France, Italy and Switzerland. Circumnavigating the highest and most spectacular mountain massif in Western Europe, the TMB takes walkers right to the foot of the towering rock faces and glaciers where alpinism was born. The views in good weather are unsurpassed in the Alps and compare favourably to the mountain scenery of higher ranges such as the Himalaya. On lower sections the route wanders amidst the gentle sights and sounds of the Alps: traditional wooden chalets with their window boxes of geraniums, the rushing of clear meltwater streams and the ever-present tinkling of cowbells.

It's perhaps fitting that the first tour of Mont Blanc is credited to Horace-Benedict de Sassure, the man who put up the reward that inspired the first ascent of the mountain. From a starting point in Chamonix he crossed the Col du Bonhomme and Col de la Seigne to reach Courmayeur, before entering Switzerland via the Col du Grand St-Bernard. The route became popular in the Victorian era as the English flocked to the Alps. Those that could climb enjoyed the fruits of the 'Golden Age' of mountaineering while those with lesser ambition crossed passes, using donkeys to carry food, clothing and equipment. In the 20th century, with the construction and development of paths used purely for recreation, the TMB evolved into a more compact circuit with *variante* (variant) routings tackling the higher passes and allowing the TMB walker to get even closer to the world of permanent snow.

Day 11 – the Chamonix Aiguilles, after leaving La Flégère

GARETH MCCORMACK

Tour du Mont Blanc

Duration	11 days
Distance	167km
Difficulty	moderate–demanding
Start/Finish	Les Houches
Nearest Towns	Les Houches (p298), Chamonix (p276)
Transport	bus, train

Summary The classic long-distance Alpine route, crossing the borders of three countries and affording ever-changing views of the highest mountain in the Alps.

The TMB is a challenging route, even for walkers who are fit and well prepared. At the very least you're facing over 8000m of ascent and descent, and perhaps as much as 11,000m if you take the most strenuous route. To put that in perspective, the vertical ascent from Base Camp to the summit of Mt Everest is less than 4000m. The level of difficulty varies depending on your choice of route and accommodation. If you want to make it as easy as possible then avoid the more difficult *variante* options, stay in huts or hotels, and use mechanised transport in selected areas. The toughest way to walk the TMB is to carry a tent across all of the highest passes.

Most people will need 10 to 12 walk days to complete the circuit, but after factoring in a day or two for resting and/or bad weather, the

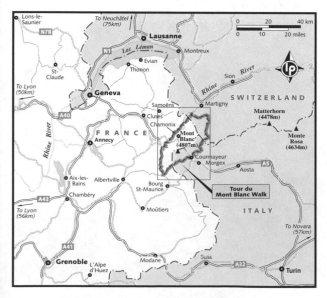

Route Highlights

If you want to get a taste of the TMB without attempting the entire route, one of the best sections is along the Grand Balcon Sud starting at Tré le Champ and finishing at Le Brévent, perhaps taking in Lac Blanc along the way (see Days 10 and 11, pp317-19). In good weather the views of the Mont Blanc massif are unsurpassed. Very fit walkers carrying only a daypack might expect to complete this section in a single day of perhaps eight hours, arriving at Le Brévent in time to catch the last descent on the *téléférique*. Otherwise expect to spend a night at La Flègère. Public transport along the route makes getting between the start and finish very convenient (see Chamonix Getting There & Away, p277).

Other highlights of the route can be found on the Italian side near Courmayeur (see p308). The *balcon* section between upper Val Veni and the Col Chécroui boasts views of the entire south face of Mont Blanc (see Day 4, p307). You can either catch a cable car from Courmayeur to the Col Chécroui and walk out and back along the path (three to four hours return) or take a bus up Val Veni and walk back around to the Col Chécroui and perhaps back down into Courmayeur (four to five hours).

Alternatively the stretch of walking between Rifugio Bertone and the Col Sapin across Mont de la Saxe offers a feeling of being on top of the world that is unmatched by any other section of the TMB (see Day 5, p309). Try walking from Courmayeur to the Rifugio Bertone, staying there overnight, and then continuing across Mont de la Saxe to Col Sapin and back to Courmayeur via Val Sapin or Rifugio Bonatti on the second day.

actual time needed could be more like 12 to 14 days. We describe a walk that takes 11 days, with some alternative routes that you may like to choose. Of course it can be completed more quickly by squeezing days together and using *téléférique* (cable cars) and buses to whiz through less-interesting stages, and this is worth considering if you don't have two weeks available. Alternatively there are some excellent options for sampling the best and most spectacular sections of the TMB – see the Route Highlights above.

Given good weather most walkers seem to opt for the more difficult *variante* routings, which are unquestionably more scenic than the traditional alternatives. This special section covers most of the possibilities, describing the traditional route and then giving a detailed description of the alternative *variante*. However, in the case of Day 8 between Champex and Trient, the suggested route is the *variante* via the Fenêtre d'Arpette with the easier and more traditional route via Bovine described as an alternative. The starting and finishing points for each day are only a guide and can be adjusted to suit your own schedule and the prescriptions of the weather. It is also traditional to walk in an anticlockwise direction from a starting point in Les Houches or Chamonix, but in reality you can start anywhere on the circuit and walk in either direction.

As you might expect, the route is generally well marked with distinctive splashes of red and white paint (France) and yellow diamonds (Italy and Switzerland). The variations to the classic routing are normally marked on maps as *TMB Variante*. Don't, however, confuse the TMB with the Tour de Pays du Mont Blanc (TPMB), with which it shares routings close to Chamonix and Les Contamines. The day-by-day statistics for the route described here are:

Day	From	To	Distance	Ascent/Descent
1	Les Houches	Les Contamines	16km	890m/730m
2	Les Contamines	Les Chapieux	19km	1300m/930m
3	Les Chapieux	Rifugio Elisabetta	14km	1000m/400m
4	Rifugio Elisabetta	Courmayeur	16km	490m/1400m
5	Courmayeur	Rifugio Bonatti	14km	1600m/680m
6	Rifugio Bonatti	La Fouly	20km	880m/1420m
7	La Fouly	Champex	15km	430m/575m
8	Champex	Trient	15km	1185m/1385m
9	Trient	Tré le Champ	13km	960m/830m
10	Tré le Champ	La Flégère	9km	790m/330m
11	La Flégère	Les Houches	16km	770m/1615m

PLANNING
When to Walk

The popularity of the TMB can be a serious drawback. Every year as many as 10,000 people walk the route and it is a major destination for organised walking groups, which can sometimes dominate *refuges* (mountain huts – *rifugio*s in Italy). July and August are the busiest months but the real peak comes in the last two weeks of July and the first half of August when the weather can also be very hot. Expect *refuges* to be busy at this time; booking in advance is almost mandatory. June is relatively quiet but you may have to contend with snow on the passes, and some of the *refuges* and camping grounds may be closed. September is perhaps an ideal month when temperatures have moderated and there are fewer walkers but, again, some of the *refuges* close in the middle of September, limiting your options at this time of year.

What to Bring

If you're staying in the *refuges* you should carry a sheet sleeping bag (silk models are lightest), although not all *refuges* require them. You should also carry a valid passport and enough cash to pay for accommodation and meals (there are ATMs in Chamonix, Les Houches, Les Contamines, Courmayeur, Champex and Argentière). Fortunately you don't need to carry Swiss Francs as the Euro is accepted just about everywhere. During the early season you may need galters, and perhaps even an ice axe depending on the conditions, to deal with snow on the higher sections. See the Warning on p275.

Accommodation

The TMB is well provided for by *refuges* at strategic points. Many *refuges* offer meals à la carte so you don't always need to pay for half board, and most can prepare a packed lunch of cheese, bread, ham and fruit if you order in advance. Expect to pay around €7 for this. Some *refuges* also have showers. Most are happy to let you fill your water bottle, but not always! Expect to buy a coffee or something small if you want to use the toilets.

If your budget allows you to use the *refuges* then you don't have to carry too much weight. Furthermore, opportunities to buy food are never more than two days apart, so even campers don't need to carry excessive weight. *Refuges* are generally busy during peak season (see When to Walk, opposite), and therefore noisy and stressful places to stay.

Although wild camping is officially forbidden in most valleys on the TMB, the discreet pitching of a tent for a single night is generally not a problem, as long as you're not too close to a village or official camping ground. Several *refuges* permit camping close by, often for no charge, but you should always check with the warden who will tell you where to pitch and if there is a charge.

Maps & Books

Many of the maps covering the Mont Blanc area are unsuitable for the TMB because they either miss out a significant section of the route or else they are simply inaccurate. However the Rando Editions 1:50,000 *Pays du Mont Blanc* is a detailed map covering the entire route. At a slightly larger scale the Libris 1:60,000 map *Mont Blanc* also covers the whole route but marks the route of the TMB incorrectly between Rifugio Bertone and Rifugio Bonatti. Alternatively you could use maps on a 1:25,000 scale combining IGN map Nos 3530ET, 3531ET and 3630OT with IGC (Istituto Geografico Centrale) map No 107 *Monte Bianco*. Look out for a new series of 1:25,000 maps *Alpes sans frontières*, published by the IGN. Map Nos 16 and 17 will cover the TMB with the exception of areas west of Chamonix.

The main English-language guidebook to the route is *Tour of Mont Blanc* by Kev Reynolds, which describes the walk in both directions. For background reading on Mont Blanc try *Mont Blanc: Discovery and Conquest of the Giant of the Alps* by Stefano Ardito or *Savage Snows: The Story of Mont Blanc* by Walt Unsworth.

Information Sources

A list of accommodation for the route, including prices and phone numbers, is available free from the **Office de Haute Montagne** (☎ 04 50 53 22 08; www.ohm-chamonix.com - French only; Maison de la Montagne, 190 place de l'Église, Chamonix). Three-day weather forecasts for the Mont Blanc massif are available in English at http://meteo.chamonix.com. You can also get a recorded forecast in English by phoning ☎ 08 92 70 03 30, with calls charged at €0.34 per minute. For accommodation and trip planning, www.chamonix.com has plenty of valuable information.

Guided Walks

The Tour du Mont Blanc appears on the brochures and websites of almost any reputable adventure travel company and the Web is a good place to search for a guided trip to suit your needs. Most operators will transport bags between overnight stops and some offer 'best of' trips as well. Among the prominent operators:

Great Walks of the World (☎ *01935-810 820; www.greatwalks.net)* UK-based company offering 14-day excursions from Les Houches for £1095.
Distant Journeys (☎ *888-845-5781; www.distantjourneys.com)* Highly respected US-based company offering 12-day drips starting from $2250.
Wilderness Travel (☎ *1-800-368-2794; www.wildernesstravel.com)* Long-established US company offering a 13-day itinerary for $3595.
La Compagnie des Guides de Chamonix Mont Blanc (☎ *04 50 53 00 88; www.chamonix-guides.com)* Historic guiding company, offering six-day trips and longer excursions on request. It would be hard to ignore the services of these local experts.

See Organised Walks on p40 for details of more French operators.

NEAREST TOWNS
See Chamonix (p276).

Les Houches

The strung-out village of Les Houches, just 7km down the Arve Valley from Chamonix, is the traditional start and finish point for the TMB and has lots of accommodation and services.

The **tourist office** (☎ *04 50 55 50 62; www.leshouches.com)* is on the main road through the village and is open daily. The staff can help with accommodation bookings and transport information, and you'll also find a weather forecast posted outside. There are several outdoor-equipment shops nearby that sell a range of topo maps and supplies for the walk.

Places to Stay & Eat A basic camping ground, **Bellevue** (☎ *04 50 54 42 30; camping per person/tent/car €3.60/1.20/0.80; open Jun-Sep)* is close to the village – follow signs for 'Salle d'Escalade'.

You'll find some of the village's cheapest beds at **Gîte Michel Fagot** (☎ *04 50 54 42 28; http://gite-fagot.ifrance.com - French only; allée de Sorbiers; dorm beds €13; open year-round)*, close to the church.

Les Melèzes (☎ *04 50 54 40 09; 333 rue de L'Essert; doubles €41; breakfast €5.50, menus from €11; open year-round)* is a cheap, one-star hotel conveniently located on the main road. The **restaurant** serves good-value meals.

Beau Site (☎ *04 50 55 51 16; www.hotel-beausite.com; rue de l'Église; doubles €96; meals from €20; open year-round)* has a beautiful back garden with a **restaurant**.

There is a good **supermarket** and **bakery** in the village and most of the hotels have restaurants open to non-residents.

Climbing Mont Blanc

When Jacques Balmat and Dr Michel Paccard became the first people to stand on the summit of Mont Blanc they would never have foreseen the modern summer scene of maybe 100 people or more summiting on a fine day. But Mont Blanc is not a technically demanding mountain if climbed by the popular Gôuter route, and is within the reach of fit walkers with a good head for heights who are prepared to hire a guide. Walkers with mountaineering experience could easily go it alone, as long as they are extremely careful in choosing the correct weather conditions.

My own ascent followed a period of poor weather and there were maybe 200 climbers setting off from the Refuge de l'Aiguille du Gôuter at 2am, forming a surreal procession of head torches that snaked up the mountain. By sunrise, we had reached the Bosses Ridge, a knife-edge of snow not far from the summit. Strong winds had already turned many people back and we were lashed with painful icy spindrift. The altitude was also beginning to tell – walking seemed to involve a few paces at a time, all the while intently studying the gaiters of the climber in front and trying to ignore the tremendous drops on either side. We summited at 7am, dazed by the altitude and thinking more about the descent than the view. What took five hours to ascend took an hour to descend, seeing us back at the *refuge* in time for breakfast!

The world-famous **La Compagnie des Guides de Chamonix Mont Blanc** (☎ *04 50 53 00 88; www.chamonix-guides.com)* guide the mountain every summer. A two-day guided ascent costs €640, with a maximum of two people per guide. You can find out more about the route at the **Office de Haute-Montagne** (☎ *04 50 53 22 08; 190 place de l'Église)* in Chamonix.

Gareth McCormack

Refuge de l'Aiguille du Gôuter (3786m), on the Mont Blanc ascent

If you're looking for a special dining experience try **La Ferme des Agapes** (☎ *04 50 54 50 69)*, opposite the cable car with main-course *savoyard* specialities starting at €12.

For something more informal, **Brasserie Christiania** (☎ *04 50 54 46 76)*, just opposite, serves snacks and light meals starting from €5.

Getting There & Away Les Houches is served by Chamonix's train and bus services (see p277).

Argentière

The village of Argentière is a popular alternative base to Chamonix. See p317 for details of facilities and transport.

THE WALK
Day 1: Les Houches to Les Contamines Montjoie
5–6 hours, 16km, 890m ascent, 730m descent

The traditional starting point in Les Houches is beside the **Téléférique Bellevue** (☎ *04 50 54 40 32)*. The TMB is signed to the left about 30m west of the *téléférique*. Although it might seem sacrilegious to purists, there is considerable merit in taking this cable car (€9.40) and skipping the first ascent, which is largely on uninteresting lanes and tracks. From the top of the lift it's a 10-minute walk downhill to the Col de Voza where you can rejoin the TMB. By taking the lift you save yourself over 600m of ascent and two hours of walking. This could make the alternative route via the Col de Tricot an option for those who would otherwise have considered it too tough for the first day.

If you decide to walk, however, the route follows a steep sealed road out of Les Houches. This quickly becomes a gravel track that winds past several houses. The route then returns to sealed road for a while before following a wide track (a winter ski piste) all the way to the broad, grassy **Col de Voza** (1653m), two hours from the start. There are fine views from the col north to the limestone cliffs guarding the Plateau D'Assy. If you are taking the high route to Les Contamines, see the Alternative Route: Les Houches to Les Contamines Montjoie via Col de Tricot (opposite).

Cross the tracks of the Tramway du Mont Blanc and descend on a vehicle track past **Refuge du Fioux** (☎ *04 50 93 52 43; camping/dorm beds/half board €3/17/30; open late May-Sep)* and then on down to a sealed road. Follow this into the hamlet of Bionnassay, where you'll find **Auberge de Bionnassay** (☎ *04 50 93 45 23; dorm beds/half board €10.50/26.50; open Jun-late Sep)*. Now follow a track through forest to **Le Champel** with its tiny, quaint church, and continue along a tarmac road past **Gîte d'étape Le Champel** (☎ *04 50 47 77 55; dorm beds/half board €16/32; open Jun-Sep)*. The road soon leads around into the Val Montjoie and then a combination of road and track takes you through La Villette and La Gruvaz. Now cut down through the forest on a path through Tresse continuing to the D902 St Gervais–Les Contamines road. Cross over this and, using tracks and sections of road, walk up the valley to reach a pleasant path running along the banks of the Bon Nant River. Follow this the rest of the way into Les Contamines.

Alternative Day: Les Houches to Les Contamines Montjoie via Col de Tricot
7–8 hours, 17km, 1480m ascent, 1340m descent

Follow the description for Day 1 from Les Houches to the Col de Voza. Walk southeast from the col, climbing gently along a broad ridge and across the tracks of the Tramway du Mont Blanc. A pleasant path now contours through forest high above the Bionnassay Valley. One hour from the Col de Voza the path descends along the fringes of a moraine field and crosses the Torrent de Bionnassay on a swinging bridge. On the other side climb steeply at first and then more steadily across vege-tated slopes to reach the **Col de Tricot** (2120m) in 30 to 45 minutes. Views back across the Glacier de Bionnassay are superb.

The south side of the col is much steeper and switchbacks take you down to a little hamlet in another 30 minutes. Centre-stage is the attrac-tive **Refuge de Miage** *(☎ 04 50 93 22 91; dorm beds/half board €15/32; open late May–mid-Sep)*. Ask the *refuge* wardens if you want to camp. The TMB crosses the Torrent de Miage on a footbridge and climbs steeply for 30 to 45 minutes to a broad plateau. Descend gently past the appealing **Refuge du Truc** *(☎ 04 50 93 12 48; dorm beds/half board €9/27; open mid-Jun–mid-Sep)* and on to a vehicle track that leads you down into the forest with glimpses of Les Contamines far below.

Look out for a path leaving the track on the left. Follow this steeply down through the trees, turning right at an unsigned junction and returning to the vehicle track. Descend on this all the way to Les Con-tamines, where signed sections of path lead down past pretty chalets. If you're heading to the camping ground (see the walk description for Day 2), follow the Chemin Loyer down to the main road. For the village centre go straight ahead on Chemin du P'tou.

Les Contamines Montjoie
Les Contamines has a **tourist office** *(☎ 04 50 47 01 58; www.lescontamines .com)*, bank and outdoor shop in its small main street.

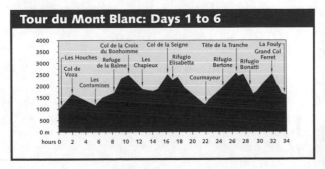

Tour du Mont Blanc: Days 1 to 6

Tour du Mont Blanc

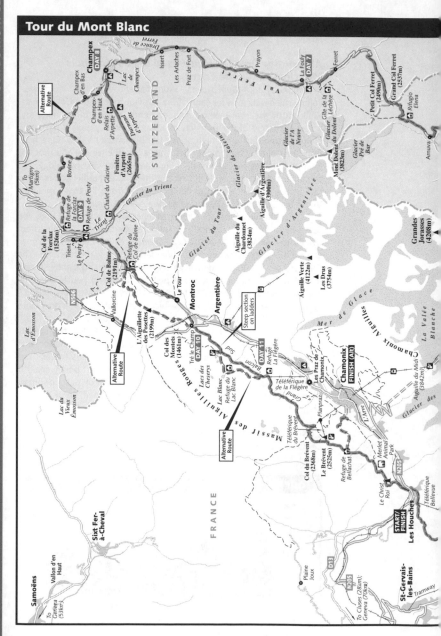

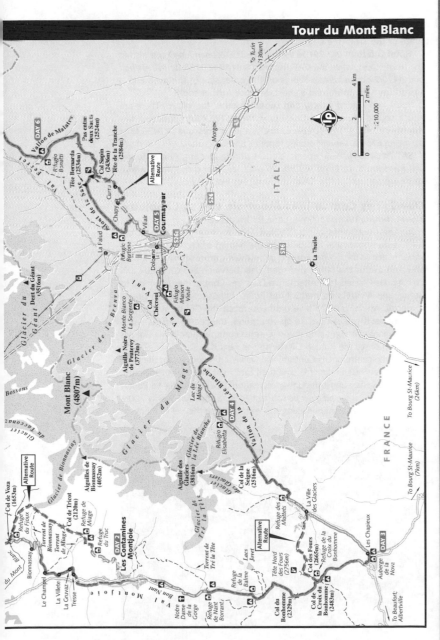

Tour du Mont Blanc

The **camping ground** is 30 minutes' walk south of the village on the route of the TMB (see Day 2).

Hôtel Grizzli (☎ 04 50 91 56 55; dorm beds €16; open Jun-Oct) is also in the main street, while the **CAF Refuge** (☎ 04 50 47 00 88; dorm beds/half board €10/29; open Jul–mid-Sep) is on the other side of the river, and is signed from the main road a short distance further south.

You'll find a good **bakery** and **supermarket** in the village. There are also a couple of decent restaurants in the village centre including **Les Airelles** (☎ 04 50 47 10 49; crêpes €5 to €7), and **La Cressoua** (☎ 04 50 47 03 31; menus €16-20), serving pizzas, fondues and other meals.

SAT (☎ 04 50 78 05 33) operates buses during July and August to the SNCF station at Le Fayet (€3.90, 25 minutes, four daily), from where there are connections to Chamonix and Les Houches.

Day 2: Les Contamines Montjoie to Les Chapieux
6½–7½ hours, 19km, 1300m ascent, 930m descent

From Les Contamines the traditional TMB routing takes you across the Col du Bonhomme and down to the hamlet of Les Chapieux. The variante across the Col des Fours is undoubtedly more scenic and enjoyable and avoids the rather dull road walk between Les Chapieux and La Ville des Glaciers (see Alternative Day: Les Contamines Montjoie to Refuge des Mottets via the Col des Fours, opposite). You don't need to decide which route to take until you reach the Col de la Croix du Bonhomme. If you can't make up your mind, the nearby refuge makes a convenient overnight stop if you want to continue across the Col des Fours and on to the Rifugio Elisabetta the next day.

From the centre of Les Contamines, walk southwards along the main road for a few hundred metres and then turn right onto a riverside path. Follow this gently uphill through a recreation area. **Camping Le Pontet** (☎ 04 50 47 04 04; camping per person/tent €4/3.30; open Jun-Sep) is 200m away on the right. Continue along the wide path up the Val Montjoie to

GARETH McCORMACK

Day 1 – suspension bridge over the Torrent de Bionnassay

a junction. The church of Notre Dame de la Gorge is on the right while a wide track of rocky slabs – an old Roman road – climbs abruptly straight ahead with the Col du Bonhomme signed as three hours.

This track winds steeply through pines beside a narrow gorge, where the blue-tinged waters of the Torrent de Tré la Tête boil and thunder between smooth rock walls. Cross a bridge and climb past a quaint restaurant and the **Refuge de Nant Borant** (☎ 04 50 47 03 57; dorm beds/half board €10/28; open Jun-Sep) to reach a wide, gently inclined upper valley. There is a free TMB overnight **camping ground** on the left, with water and toilets. Just visible at the head of the valley is the **Refuge de la Balme** (☎ 04 50 47 03 54; dorm beds/half board €10/26; open mid-Jun–mid-Sep), 30 to 40 minutes' walk away. Just before the refuge are toilets, a water fountain and another free **camping ground**.

Above the refuge the TMB climbs southeast on a steep, braided path into another flat valley. There is a signed side trip here to the **Lacs Jovet**, a pair of beautiful alpine lakes tucked away in a cirque at almost 2200m; allow 1½ hours for the return trip.

Meanwhile the TMB climbs steadily for the next 45 minutes to one hour towards the discernible outline of the **Col du Bonhomme** (2329m). Early in the season there may be a large bank of snow to cross just beneath the top. The best views from the pass are back to the northeast. The path doesn't descend from the col, but instead climbs gently across the steep slopes and rounds a broad spur to reach the **Col de la Croix du Bonhomme** (2483m), with long-reaching views to the southeast towards the summits of the Vanoise. To the northeast, a signposted path climbs from the col towards the Col des Fours (see the Alternative Day: Les Contamines Montjoie to Refuge des Mottets via the Col des Fours). The **Refuge de la Croix du Bonhomme** (☎ 04 79 07 05 28; dorm beds/half board €13.50/33.50; open mid-Jun–mid-Sep) is visible immediately beneath the col along the path descending to Les Chapieux. A short distance beyond the refuge you'll find several **camp sites**.

The descent to **Les Chapieux** continues from here, cutting diagonally across broad slopes and then more steeply down to a track. A signed path on the left takes you away from the track and directly to the **Auberge de la Nova** (☎ 04 79 89 04 15; dorm beds/half board €12/27; open May-Nov). **Camping** is permitted near the refuge; ask the warden where to pitch your tent. There is also a small **shop** in Les Chapieux, but otherwise this is a very isolated settlement, the nearest town being some 18km away.

Alternative Day: Les Contamines Montjoie to Refuge des Mottets via Col des Fours

7–8 hours, 20km, 1550m ascent, 880m descent

Follow the normal routing as far as the Col de la Croix du Bonhomme. From here a faint path is signed to the northeast and a steady ascent of 30 minutes leads to the **Col des Fours** (2665m). Snow patches may complicate this section of the route early in the season. From the col there is a dramatic view of the Aiguille des Glaciers and the heavily crevassed Glacier des Glaciers. An optional side trip from the col follows a cairned route north to the pillar on the Tête Nord des Fours (2756m), from where there are extensive views back to the north and west across Val Montjoie and the limestone pre-Alps. This side trip should take 30 to 45 minutes return and is the highest point you can reach on the TMB.

The descent from the col begins steeply across bare slopes of shale and gravel, which may be snow-covered early in the season. The path then crosses a small flat area before dropping steeply once more past curious slabs of water-carved rock. At an unsigned trail junction turn right and drop into a valley to a junction with a vehicle track. The stone buildings and car park at La Ville des Glaciers are now visible below. Look out for the continuation of the path, which descends directly to the buildings; if you miss the path simply follow the vehicle track.

Beaufort cheese (see the boxed text below) is still made at **La Ville des Glaciers** and is available for purchase along with milk and eggs, but there are no other facilities for walkers. The *variante* now rejoins the main TMB routing. Cross the bridge and another 30 minutes of gentle ascent on a vehicle track will bring you to the **Refuge des Mottets** (*☎ 04 79 07 01 70; dorm beds/half board €11.50/30; open mid-Jun–early Sep*), a small and cosy place with good views of the Aiguille des Glaciers.

Day 3: Les Chapieux to Rifugio Elisabetta
4–5 hours, 14km, 1000m ascent, 400m descent

It's a fairly dull walk along a narrow bitumen road from Les Chapieux to La Ville des Glaciers (1½ hours). The main stone building here is still

Beaufort Cheese

What could be better than packing a slice of cheese with all of the flavours of the Alpine pastures you've been walking through. Beaufort is the traditional cows' milk cheese of the Savoy region, and has been made since Roman times. A good beaufort cheese will carry a subtle hint of herbs and flowers behind an otherwise rich and creamy flavour. Beaufort is a big regional speciality and most restaurants advertising *savoyard* dishes will probably serve *fondues* and *raclettes* made with beaufort cheeses.

Roughly 10L of milk are used to produce a single kilo of beaufort. The cheese matures for four to six months in a cool cellar, where it is turned regularly to encourage the formation of an even rind. The name to look out for is the traditionally made Beaufort d'Alpage, a label given only to beauforts derived from the milk of Tarine cows grazing in pastures above 1500m.

Apart from the issue of weight, cheese makes a great walking food, packed with plenty of protein, fat and calcium. It tastes great with just a lump of bread and dried sausage. If you happen to have it, a glass of Chablis is also recommended, but you might have to make do with a draught of nature's finest instead.

used to make beaufort cheese (see the boxed text opposite), which is available for purchase along with milk and eggs.

At La Ville des Glaciers the TMB turns right across a bridge and climbs steadily, first on a vehicle track and then on a path to the rustic and cosy **Refuge des Mottets** (see opposite), reached in 40 to 50 minutes. Now climb steeply through switchbacks with Glacier des Glaciers a constant companion across the valley. A steadier ascent leads north and then northwest, crossing open pastures towards the **Col de la Seigne** (2516m), which you should reach in 1¼ to 1¾ hours. The col, with its ruined customs hut, presents the first view of the southern side of the Mont Blanc massif as you cross into Italy.

The descent is quite gentle and you soon reach a vehicle track that leads down to the northwestern side of the Vallon de la Lée Blanche. The floor of this valley is a pan-flat bed of gravel and stone. As you reach the lip of the valley, where it drops steeply into Val Veni, **Rifugio Elisabetta** (☎ 01 65 84 40 34; dorm beds/half board €14/34; open mid-Jun–mid-Sep) comes into view on the right, framed by the icefalls of the Glacier de la Lée Blanche. A steep track winds up to the *refuge*; about a five-minute walk. The views from here extend all the way to the head of Val Ferret, with the snow and rock pyramid of the Grand Combin (4314m) prominent on the skyline to the east. The owners of the *refuge* may permit **camping** on the flatter ground beneath the building.

Day 4: Rifugio Elisabetta to Courmayeur
4½–5½ hours, 16km, 490m ascent, 1400m descent

The few hours of walking from the *refuge* to the ski area around Col Chécroui are among the best on the TMB, with views across Val Veni to the immense rock walls and icefalls on the south face of Mont Blanc.

Descend from the *refuge* on sections of steep, rocky path that shortcut the hairpins of the vehicle track. Now strike out along 2km of straight dirt road (the low retaining walls on each side provide easier walking). The flat valley floor contrasts starkly with the immense Aiguille Noire de Peuterey (3773m), soaring skyward for some 2000 vertical metres. It's hard to believe this pinnacle has been climbed solo in winter, yet it's only part of one of several serrated rock ridges rising towards the Fréney Pillar, the summit buttress of Mont Blanc's southern face.

Walk to the left of some long pools where the river has backed up behind the huge lateral moraine of the Glacier du Miage. Look out for the signs to Rifugio Maison Vielle on the right (one hour from Rifugio Elisabetta). These mark the start of the path climbing up onto the southern side of Val Veni. The climb is steep, taking you past some ruined stone buildings, and then alongside a stream. The path then swings northwest past a shepherd's hut before climbing more gently onto a steep spur high above the valley at approximately 2400m. The sense of space and grandeur at this point is hardly matched at any other point along the TMB, and on a calm day the regular thunder of collapsing seracs and rockfalls carries across Val Veni to remind you that this is a landscape of constant drama and change.

The path descends gently to a stream and then climbs slightly to reach a jumble of boulders housing a marmot colony. There is a small, Mont Blanc-reflecting tarn on the right. The route now descends steadily to **Rifugio Maison Vielle** (☎ *03 37 23 09 79; dorm beds/half board €15/35; open mid-Jun–mid-Sep)* on the rather charmless Col Chécroui. **Camping** is permitted near the *refuge*. The unrelenting descent to Courmayeur is signed to the right past the top of a **chairlift** (☎ *0165 8 99 25; one way €8; last descent 5.30pm)*. Most walkers don't particularly enjoy this piece of walking on an ugly track and the chairlift will whisk you down to Courmayeur in 20 minutes. One benefit of walking down, however, is the opportunity to wander through the pretty hamlet of **Dolonne** with its traditional chalets and flagstone roofs (one hour from the Col Chécroui and 15 minutes from Courmayeur).

Courmayeur

The 'Italian Chamonix', Courmayeur is a pleasant town on the southern side of Mont Blanc and linked to Chamonix by the infamous Mont Blanc road tunnel. It is an important staging post on the TMB, providing an opportunity to stock up on food, rest for a day or two, or perhaps escape back to Chamonix if you feel you've taken on too much. The **tourist office** (☎ *0165 84 20 60; www.courmayeur.com; Piazzale Monte Bianco 13)* is beside the bus station and post office next to the main road junction. It is open daily but closes between noon and 3pm. There is an **outdoor shop** *(Via Roma)*, the main pedestrianised street.

Places to Stay & Eat One of the best camping grounds is **Monte Bianco La Sorgente** (☎ *01 65 86 90 89; www.campinglasorgente.net; camping per person/tent/car €4.80/3.60/3.50; open mid-Jun–mid-Sep)* in Val Veni, 5km outside Courmayeur. There are also **camping grounds** in Val Ferret. There are frequent local buses to both valleys – ask at the tourist office for a timetable.

Hotels in Courmayeur are expensive and heavily booked, but **Hotel Venezia** (☎ *01 65 84 46 12; dorm beds with breakfast €21.50; open year-round)* caters specifically for TMB walkers. Otherwise the best-value accommodation is to be found in the villages surrounding Courmayeur like La Palud (3km) where you'll find **Hotel Funivia** (☎ *01 65 899 24; dorm beds/singles/doubles €16/21/42; open Jun-Sep)*. The tourist office can help with reservations and times of local buses.

There is a **supermarket** above and to the right of the tourist office – ask for directions as it can be hard to find. There is also one on the road heading south out of town. There are many good places to eat along Via Roma.

At the southern end of the street **Pizza Sprint** *(pizza slices €2.30)*; has very satisfying fare after a morning's walk.

A good sit-down lunch option is the **Petit Bistrot** *(crêpes €4-6)*, just off Via Roma is a *crêpes* specialist.

For an evening meal try **Caldran Solaire** *(menus €13-20)*, also at the southern end of Via Roma, which serves interesting and varied fare.

Getting There & Away Buses are run by **SAVDA** *(☎ 0165 84 20 31)* to Chamonix (€9.50, 45 minutes, six daily), Milan (€14.50, 4½ hours, four daily) and Turin (€7.50, 3¼ hours, four daily). Reservations are necessary for the Chamonix bus.

Day 5: Courmayeur to Rifugio Bonatti
6–7 hours, 14km, 1600m ascent, 680m descent

The route across Mont de la Saxe from Courmayeur features one of the toughest climbs on the TMB if it is walked in one day. It would perhaps be better to spend the night at the charming and spectacularly situated Rifugio Bertone and split the climb, letting you walk up the Mont de la Saxe ridge to the Tête de la Tranche in the cool of the morning. If the weather is fine the views from this section of the TMB are quite sublime. In poor weather or if there is a risk of thunderstorms, the *variante* via the Col Sapin is easier and less exposed (see Alternative Day: Courmayeur to Rifugio Bonatti via the Col Sapin, p310). If the weather is truly awful you can take a bus up Val Ferret and then walk up to either the Rifugio Bonatti or the Rifugio Elena.

The TMB leaves Courmayeur on the Strada del Villair just to the left of the church. The road climbs steadily past increasingly pretty chalets and through the hamlet of Villair, where the sealed road becomes a vehicle track. About 15 to 20 minutes above Villair, the track crosses a bridge and the TMB is signed to the right, up a steep path through stands of birch. The path rejoins the track higher up but soon turns off to the left and climbs steeply all the way to the tree line and the

Day 5 – the Grandes Jorasses, from the TMB route over Mont de la Saxe

Rifugio Bertone (☎ *01 65 84 46 12; dorm beds/half board €16/35; open mid-Jun–Sep)*, two to 2½ hours from Courmayeur. Free **camping** is permitted on the flat ground above the *refuge*.

The path climbs very steeply onto the broad shoulder of **Mont de la Saxe**, where there are great views of the Grandes Jorasses across Val Ferret. The path continues more gently past some avalanche fences and then descends slightly before climbing steeply again to the right (south) of the Tête Bernarda to arrive at a col just five minutes below the summit of the **Tête de la Tranche** (2584m). The final section to this summit climbs along a superb ridge with tremendous views all around (1½ to two hours from the Rifugio Bertone).

The descent to Col Sapin is short (15 to 20 minutes) but quite steep and slightly exposed. However, with a modicum of care most walkers will find it quite straightforward. At the col turn left (east) and descend gently at first and then more steeply into the Vallon d'Armina. The path flattens out for a short distance, crosses a stream and then begins to climb steadily once again to reach the **Pas entre deux Sauts** (2524m), one to 1½ hours from the Col Sapin.

Now descend gently into the Malatra Valley past jumbles of partly grassed-over boulders and then along the left (southwest) side of the valley where it is broad and quite flat. The prominent white buildings over to the right are not part of the *refuge*. A further 20 minutes' descent across steeper ground brings you to the excellent **Rifugio Bonatti** (☎ *01 65 86 90 55; dorm beds/half board €15/38; open Jun-Sep)*. The food here is great and the modern facilities, although somewhat clinical, provide great comfort. You'll find **camp sites** among the old buildings above the *refuge*.

For the story of Walter Bonatti, see the boxed text opposite.

Alternative Day: Courmayeur to Rifugio Bonatti via the Col Sapin
5½–6½ hours, 12km, 1460m ascent, 460m descent
Follow the normal routing along the vehicle track above Villair, turn right at the first signpost for Rifugio Bertone and rejoin the vehicle track a little higher up. Now continue along the vehicle track ignoring a signed left turn where the main route climbs steeply to the Rifugio Bertone. Stay on the vehicle track, which climbs steadily into Val Sapin and as far as Chapy (two hours). A path climbs south and then north-east, passing the shepherds huts at Curru, before climbing very steeply to reach the Col Sapin (2436m), one to 1½ hours from Curru, where you rejoin the normal route.

Day 6: Rifugio Bonatti to La Fouly
5½–6½ hours, 20km, 880m ascent, 1420m descent
Be wary of choosing to shortcut this stage by climbing the slightly lower Petit Col Ferret, which takes you to La Fouly by a more direct route. The climb is extremely steep and savings in time will be offset by the exertion.

From the Rifugio Bonatti the path into Val Ferret descends steeply through the trees to reach a sealed road in 30 to 40 minutes. Turn right (northeast) and follow the road gently uphill for another 30 minutes to a bridge at Arnuva. On the other side of the bridge the road becomes a vehicle track and off to the right is a restaurant-café. The track soon steepens and the roof of Rifugio Elena becomes visible on a bluff up to the right. Look out for a couple of unsigned paths on the right that climb quite directly to the *refuge*, shortcutting the track and saving 10 or 15 minutes' walking. **Rifugio Elena** *(☎ 01 65 84 46 88; dorm beds €15, half board €33; open mid Jun–Sep)* has great views of the Glacier Pré de Bar (45 minutes from Arnuva).

Walter Bonatti

Much of the climbing history of the Mont Blanc massif is tied up with the name of Walter Bonatti, the Italian climbing legend whose *refuge* is a recommended stop on the TMB. Born in Bergamo in 1930, Bonatti was arguably the finest Alpinist of his generation and pioneered several of the Alps' classic mountaineering routes, like the Bonatti Pillar on the Dru, which Bonatti climbed solo over a six-day period in 1955. The tenacity and courage he displayed on this route were a hallmark of his career.

He also made difficult first ascents on the Grand Capucin, the Red Pillar of Mont Blanc, the Piz Badile and the Pilier d'Angle – all in the Mont Blanc area. His penchant for solo climbing continued in the winter months as he made audacious winter solo ascents of the north faces of both the Matterhorn and Grandes Jorasses. In 1961, while attempting the first ascent of Mont Blanc's Central Freney Pillar, Bonatti and his party of seven were trapped high on the face for several days by an unusually severe storm. Four of the party perished and Bonatti received the French Legion d'Honneur for his efforts in keeping himself and the two other climbers alive.

In 1958 Bonatti made the first ascent of Gasherbrum IV in the Karakorum Himalaya, and he was also a member of the Italian team that made the first ascent of K2 in 1954. An incident during this expedition clouded his reputation for some 40 years until the Italian Alpine Club cleared his name in 1994. Among other things he was accused of attempting a summit bid of his own using oxygen destined for use by the two climbers who had been officially nominated for the summit push. Bonatti won a libel action against a journalist who printed the allegations. In actual fact, Bonatti had spent a night in the open at 8000m in order to stash the oxygen within reach of the other climbers. This act, which almost cost him his life, ensured that the summit attempt on the following day would be successful.

Bonatti also pioneered new routes on the granite pillars of Patagonia and travelled extensively in Africa. The walls of the *refuge* are graced by many of his travel photos. Several of Bonatti's books have become classics of mountaineering literature and have been translated into English, including: *The Mountains of My Life*, *Great Days* and *On the Heights*. The small library in the *refuge* has an English edition of *Great Days*.

The route to the Grand Col Ferret is signed from the rear of the *refuge* and the climb is initially quite steep, following switchbacks along the side of a small gorge. The path then swings to the north, still climbing steeply, and then suddenly flattens out to cruise the final few hundred metres to the **Grand Col Ferret** (2537m), 1¼ to 1¾ hours from Rifugio Elena. The col is on the border between Italy and Switzerland and there is a fine view back down the Italian Val Ferret, with patches of pine forest dwarfed by the 2000m rock walls plunging down from the Grandes Jorasses. You can't see into the Swiss Val Ferret from the col but you do have a fine view of the Grand Combin off to the east.

The descent begins gently on a very wide and well-built path. Short detours to the left afford views directly down the Swiss Val Ferret. After 45 minutes to one hour you reach a café and join a vehicle track winding steeply down to the valley floor. During the descent, look out for unsigned paths that shortcut the hairpins on the track. At the bottom the track crosses a bridge and there are some damned pools in the stream for bathing. On the other side a sealed road begins, leading to the first Swiss village on the TMB after another 20 to 30 minutes.

Ferret has one accommodation option, **Pension du Col Fenêtre** (☎ *027-783 30 64; dorm beds/half board Sfr27/76; open Jun-Sep)*, which also has a **restaurant** open for lunches and evening meals. Ferret is the last stop on the Val Ferret bus route (see La Fouly below).

The path swings out to the left (northwest) from Ferret, passes beneath **Gîte de la Léchère** (☎ *027-783 30 64; half board €35; open Jun-Sep)* and approaches the village of La Fouly via **Camping des Glaciers** (☎ *027-783 17 35; person & tent Sfr18; open mid-May–Sep)*, 20 minutes from Ferret. The centre of the village is now five minutes away along a sealed road.

La Fouly

The mountain views from this village are the best you will see for the next couple of days, especially looking up to the Glacier du Dolent and Glacier de l'A Neuve with their meltwater torrents plunging down ice-scoured cliffs.

Hôtel Edelweiss (☎ *027-783 26 21; dorm beds/half board Sfr23/54; open Jun-Oct)* and **Hôtel des Glaciers** (☎ *027-783 11 71; dorm beds/half board Sfr27/54; open Jun–mid-Oct)* are both on the main street.

There is a small **supermarket** and an **outdoor shop** in the centre of the village. There are also several places to eat and the **restaurant** in the Hôtel Edelweiss has some interesting photographs illustrating the retreat of the glaciers.

Regular buses are run by **St-Bernard Express** (☎ *027-783 11 05)* between Ferret, La Fouly and Orsières (Sfr7, 30 minutes, eight daily). From Orsières there are connecting buses to Champex (Sfr7, 30 minutes, four daily). A special TMB ticket will get you from Ferret/La Fouly to Champex for Sfr11. Orsières is also on the train line between Martigny (Switzerland) and Aosta (Italy). From Martigny there are connections to Chamonix (see p276).

Day 7: La Fouly to Champex
4–5 hours, 15km, 430m ascent, 575m descent

The walk down Val Ferret is arguably the least interesting stage of the TMB and many walkers choose to take the bus (see La Fouly, opposite), especially if the weather is particularly hot or simply inclement. Otherwise the route is pleasant if undramatic, with plenty of glimpses of Swiss mountain life.

The TMB stays on the western side of the valley for the first two to 2½ hours, descending through patches of pine forest. In the village of Praz de Fort the route crosses to the eastern side of the valley and then passes through the hamlet of Les Arlaches before reaching the village of **Issert**, 30 minutes from Praz de Fort. At 1055m, this is the lowest point you've reached on the TMB since leaving Les Houches several days ago.

The route now crosses the road, turns left onto a track and follows good, signed paths on the steady ascent to the resort town of Champex (1466m), 1½ hours from Issert.

Champex
Famous for its lake and distant views of the Grand Combin, Champex is a pleasant if somewhat pricey place to stay.

Camping Rocailles *(☎ 027-783 19 79; camping per person Sfr13; open year-round)* is on the main road at the northern end of the town.

Chalet Bon Abri *(☎ 027-783 14 23; dorm beds/half board Sfr26/60; open year-round)*, **Gîte en Plein Air** *(☎ 027-783 23 50; dorm beds/half board Sfr24/62; open May-Nov)* and **Chalet du Club Alpin Suisse** *(☎ 027-783 11 61; half board Sfr68; open Jun-Oct)* cater specifically for TMB walkers.

There are a **supermarket** and **bakery** in Champex. It also has a wide selection of places to eat including the excellent **Restaurant Pain de Seigle** *(pizzas Sfr16)*.

Day 8: Champex to Trient via the Fenêtre d'Arpette
6–7 hours, 15km, 1185m ascent, 1385m descent

Although this is a *variante* of the TMB, it carries far more traffic than the easier Bovine routing (see the Alternative Day: Champex to Col de

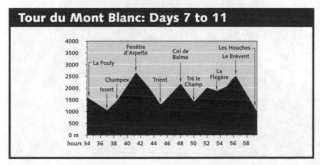

Tour du Mont Blanc: Days 7 to 11

la Forclaz/Trient via Bovine, opposite). The reputation of the Fenêtre d'Arpette as a challenging pass obviously has something to do with this, although some walkers struggling up the final boulder field look as though they are deeply regretting their choice. The climb is tough simply because the path is much rougher than those you've been used to. Early season walkers should be wary of steep snow slopes on both sides of the pass.

Follow the main road north out of Champex and turn left onto a narrow road beside a chairlift. Turn right on a signed path that passes under the chairlift and heads off through pine forest beside an irrigation channel. In 20 to 30 minutes the path joins a vehicle track. Turn left on this and walk up past **Relais d'Arpette** (☎ *027-783 12 21; camping/half board Sfr9/57; open Jun-Sep)*, climbing gently across open pastures. As the ground steepens the track becomes a rough path bearing towards the right-hand side of the valley.

Once you clear the tree line, the path climbs alongside a stream. Late in the summer this may be the last water until well down the other side of the pass. The path turns away from the stream and climbs quite steeply across open slopes. Keep to the right at a junction of paths that is not marked on some maps. There is now a bit of respite before the path enters a huge boulder field with the top of the pass now visible as a notch in the rock ridge high above. After negotiating the boulder field the path splits into several strands, all zigzagging their way very steeply up the narrowing slope to the **Fenêtre d'Arpette** (2665m), 2½ to 3½ hours from Champex. From the top there is a great view to the northwest across the heavily crevassed Glacier du Trient.

The path heading down into the Trient Valley is initially very steep but the gradient soon eases. In 45 minutes to one hour you come to the ruins of several buildings. Continue to descend steadily across

GRANT DIXON

Day 8 – jagged peaks from the Fenêtre d'Arpette

steep vegetated slopes to reach the shade of pine forest and the banks of the Trient torrent some 45 minutes to one hour from the ruined buildings. A stony track leads in five minutes to the **Chalet du Glacier**, which serves meals and cold drinks.

The route now splits in two. The right-hand route leads along a level path to the Col de la Forclaz (40 minutes), but there's no great reason to stay here. The *refuge* and camping ground at the col are more commonly used by walkers on the Bovine route (see Alternative Day: Champex to Col de la Forclaz via Bovine, below).

Turn left across the river onto a bitumen road, which winds down to the hamlet of **Le Peuty** (30 minutes). There is a basic **camping ground** *(camping per person Sfr3)* with toilets, water and a sheltered cooking area. A warden collects the fee in the evening. Adjacent to the camping ground is the cramped **Refuge du Peuty** *(☎ 027-722 09 38; dorm beds Sfr12; open mid-Jun–mid-Sep)*, which does not serve meals but has a self-catering kitchen. Rather conveniently, Le Peuty is also where the climb to the Col de la Balme begins (see Day 9).

If you walk 10 minutes further along the road you'll come to the village of **Trient**, which has three accommodation options: **Relais du Mont-Blanc** *(☎ 027-722 46 23; dorm beds/half board Sfr23/53; open Jun-Oct)*, **Café Moret** *(☎ 027-722 27 07; dorm beds/half board Sfr31/62; open Jun–mid-Oct)* and **La Gardienne** *(☎ 027-722 12 40; dorm beds/half board Sfr22/49; open year-round)*.

At least two of these have **restaurants** open to nonresidents and there is also a small **shop** along the main road.

Alternative Day: Champex to Col de la Forclaz via Bovine
4–5 hours, 14km, 780m ascent, 730m descent
The route follows the road as far as Champex d'en Bas (45 minutes to one hour), and then turns left onto a track signed for Bovine. The track soon gives way to a path that climbs gently around a forested spur before ascending more steeply above the tree line and round another spur to the buildings of **Bovine** alp, where you may be able to buy refreshments (1¾ to 2¼ hours from Champex d'en Bas). There are great views from here over the town of Martigny and down to the Rhône Valley and the distant mountains of the Bernese Alps.

The path continues to climb for a short distance to reach the high point of the day at 2049m and then begins the long sidling descent to the Col de la Forclaz. Here you'll find **Camping Arpille** *(☎ 027-722 26 88; camping per person/tent Sfr7/6; open May-Oct)* and **Refuge Hôtel de la Forclaz** *(☎ 027-722 46 23; dorm beds/half board Sfr20/54; open year-round)*.

Day 9: Trient/Col de la Forclaz to Tré le Champ
4½–5½ hours, 13km, 960m ascent, 830m descent
For walkers who have just come over the Fenêtre d'Arpette, the stage over the Col de la Balme into the Chamonix Valley will seem relatively easy. There is also a seldom-walked *variante* of the TMB that avoids

the Col de Balme and instead climbs over a steep ridge to the village of Vallorcine (four to five hours), where there is accommodation. You'd need to spend the night here before continuing via the Col des Montets onto the Grand Balcon Sud, where you rejoin the main TMB route after a further four to five hours of walking.

For the Col de Balme route, walkers starting at the Col de la Forclaz need to make their way down to Le Peuty using a path that cuts across the main road (25 minutes). Walkers starting in Trient have a gentle 10-minute walk back to Le Peuty.

From Le Peuty the TMB is signed to the right (north) of the camping ground, following a track that climbs steadily into the forest (20 to 30 minutes). For the next 1¼ to 1½ hours you climb up switchbacks through the trees, emerging onto open slopes above a deep valley. A wide path climbs steadily to reach the Col de Balme (2191m) in another one to 1½ hours. You can't miss **Refuge du Col de Balme** (☎ 04 50 54 02 33; dorm beds/half board €15/35; open Jun-Sep). Here you cross back into France and are rewarded with a tremendous view down the Chamonix Valley to Mont Blanc, the Aiguilles Rouges and the final days of the TMB.

For the descent you have a choice of two routes. The standard route cuts straight down across the ski slopes under a chairlift to Le Tour. It then follows the road as far as Montroc before climbing to Tré le Champ on a path (two to 2½ hours). Along the way you'll pass close to **Gîte d'alpage de Charamillon** (☎ 04 50 54 17 07; dorm beds/half board €16/29; open Jul-Sep) and **Chalet Alpin du Tour** (☎ 04 50 54 04 16; dorm beds/half board €18/38; open Jun–mid-Sep).

GRANT DIXON

Day 8 – looking down the Chamonix Valley from the slopes near Le Tour. Mont Blanc dominates the background

A *variante* route climbs from the Col de Balme on to l'Aiguillette des Posettes (2199m) and then descends directly to Tré le Champ (two to 2½ hours). The views from this airy ridge are far superior to the normal route. A third option is to take the **Téléférique Le Tour** (☎ 04 50 54 00 58) from the Col de la Balme to Le Tour (€9.20).

Tré le Champ has limited accommodation options. The attractive **Gîte La Boerne** (☎ 04 50 54 05 14; dorm beds/half board €13/29; open Jun–mid Nov) has only around 40 places. Many walkers therefore choose to stay in Argentière (see below), where there is a good range of accommodation and places to eat. The quickest route to Argentière is via the normal route, following signs from Montroc downhill for 20 minutes. Otherwise Argentière is a 30-minute signed walk down the valley from Tré le Champ.

Argentière

The village of Argentière is a popular alternative to Tré le Champ as a place to stay at the end of Day 9. There is a good range of accommodation and services, and the public transport connections are excellent. The village has a **tourist office** (☎ 04 50 54 02 33) and several outdoor shops.

Ten minutes' walk south of the village, the two-star **Camping Glacier d'Argentière** (☎ 04 50 54 17 36; camping per person/tent €4.20/2.10; open mid-Jun–Sep) is 200m off the N506.

Le Belvédère (☎ 04 50 54 02 59; dorm beds/half board €12/27; open year round) is a friendly and comfortable *gîte d'étape* just downhill from the centre of the village. **Hôtel des Randonneurs** (☎ 04 50 54 02 80; half board €38; open year-round) is five minutes' walk downhill from the centre.

The **sandwich bar** in the Galerie Commerciale south of the village centre serves cheap sandwiches and pizzas from €8. There are several restaurants in Argentière. Worth mentioning is **Le Dahu** (menus from €13.50), which serves local specialities.

Argentière is served by Chamonix's train and bus services (for details, see Getting There & Away, 277).

Day 10: Tré le Champ to La Flégère
3–4 hours, 9km, 790m ascent, 330m descent

The day starts with a long and steep ascent enlivened by a section of iron ladders used to negotiate a band of cliffs. Vertigo sufferers will probably want to avoid this and use the *variante* via the Col des Montets. Both routes take you onto the classic Grand Balcon Sud, one of the most popular and famed sections of path in the Alps, with views of Glacier d'Argentière. This *balcon* route forms the last two days of the TMB and is a fitting end to the walk with tremendous ever-changing views of the Mont Blanc massif. Note that camping is not officially permitted along this section of the route, although bivouacs between the hours of sunset and sunrise are permitted and in practice you'll find many people do pitch tents discreetly.

The path from Tré le Champ climbs across mostly forested slopes to the base of steep granite cliffs. Before you reach this point you'll notice a signed junction with a path that climbs up from Argentière. Walkers who have spent the night there can rejoin the route by using this path, which is signed from the northwestern side of the main street in Argentière.

A section of ladders and handrails are in situ to help walkers over the cliffs and, once above these, a final steep climb brings you to a large cairn and junction of paths 1¾ to 2¼ hours from Tré le Champ. The Grand Balcon Sud and La Flégère (1¼ to 1½ hours) are signed straight ahead, while the wonderful Lac Blanc is signed to the west (see the Alternative Day: Tré le Champ to La Flégère via Lac Blanc, below).

A short descent is made past some ruined buildings to reach a stream and footbridge. Keep an eye out in this area for ibex and chamois. The path climbs around a rocky spur and then descends onto a track just beneath the obvious cable car station. A steep 10-minute climb along the track takes you up to the station. **Refuge de la Flégère** (☎ 04 50 53 06 13; dorm beds/half board €15/35; open mid-Jun–Sep) is a short distance downhill from here. If the *refuge* is full you may need to use the **Téléférique de la Flégère** (☎ 04 50 53 18 58; one way/return €8.20/10.20; services 8.40am-4.30pm Jun-Sep, 7.40am-5.30pm Jul & Aug) to descend to the valley where you'll find more accommodation options (see Les Praz, p278).

Alternative Day: Tré le Champ to La Flégère via Lac Blanc
4½–5½ hours, 10km, 990m ascent, 675m descent
Follow the route for Day 10 as far as the cairn and path junction. The path to Lac Blanc climbs steeply along a broad spur and then makes a short descent to the shores of a beautiful lake (one of the Lacs des Cheserys). The path then climbs steeply again, using a ladder over one section, to reach **Refuge du Lac Blanc** (☎ 04 50 53 49 14; half board €44.50; open mid-Jun–Sep). The *refuge* is set above the eastern shore of a small lake and reservations are recommended. Lac Blanc itself is set into the rocky hollow above this small lake. See the Lac Blanc walk (p277) for more information.

The descent from Lac Blanc to La Flégère is steep and requires a little care in places. You will rejoin the main TMB route on the track beneath the cable-car station.

Day 11: La Flégère to Les Houches
5½–6½ hours, 16km, 770m ascent, 1615m descent
The first section of this route continues in the same vein as the previous day, contouring across the slopes and affording relatively easy walking. Take the path that leads from the front of Refuge de la Flégère, signed to Planpraz. Pass beneath the cables of the *téléférique* and start onto the *balcon* trail, which is interrupted by a short flight of rock steps near the start. The views across the valley to Mont Blanc and the Chamonix Aiguilles continue to draw the eye. After 45 minutes to one hour you

meet a vehicle track; cross this and then continue straight ahead at a signed junction to walk beneath the cables of another chairlift. The path rounds a rocky spur and crosses another vehicle track before you begin the climb to the ridgetop *téléférique* station at Planpraz. The final ascent follows a steep, stony track – you should reach the top around 1½ hours from La Flégère.

Turn right off the main track at the top of the ridge and follow a path signed to the **Col du Brévent**. This climbs steadily north over rocky ground before making a few steep switchbacks and reaching the large cairn marking the col around 45 minutes from Planpraz. The col is situated along a rugged, rock-strewn ridge and is a dramatic spot. The route to the summit of Le Brévent veers left at the cairn and climbs a little farther up the ridge before dropping behind it and crossing a basin of boulders and shattered rock slabs. You then climb around a shoulder, where handrails are in place to aid your passage up a series of rock steps. At the top you meet the rough vehicle track from Planpraz. Turn right onto this and ascend steadily for a further 10 minutes to reach the summit restaurant and *téléférique* station of **Le Brévent** (2525m; 30 to 40 minutes from the col).The views from the 360° viewing terrace are excellent, but you will probably have to share them with many tourists who have ascended this far on the cable car.

If you want to avoid the long descent to either Chamonix or Les Houches, you can finish the TMB at Le Brévent and descend to Chamonix on the **Téléférique du Brévent** (*☎ 04 50 53 13 18; one way €12.20; last descent 5pm)*. Those who continue are rewarded with at least another hour of very fine walking. Retrace your steps down the track from Le Brévent and turn left after 100m along a path signed to Bellachat. Descend over a steep rock stairway before the gradient eases and the path winds between several tarns and small pools. You reach the small **Refuge de Bellachat** (*☎ 04 50 53 43 23; dorm beds/half board €12/32; open late Jun–mid-Sep)* around one hour from Le Brévent.

The route now splits in two. The left-hand path descends past the *refuge* and weaves through countless switchbacks on its way to the centre of Chamonix (1½ to two hours). The right-hand path closes the TMB circuit by continuing to Les Houches (1¾ to 2¼ hours). Though this descent also starts along steep switchbacks, it then continues more steadily through pine forest. You then trace the northern boundary of the Merlet Animal Park to reach the statue of Le Christ Roi just above Les Houches. A short descent then leads to a road that takes you past Les Houches SNCF station. Either finish here or continue for another few hundred metres into the centre of Les Houches to celebrate the end of one of the world's classic walks.

Wine & Mountains

The Jura range overlooks Switzerland. To the north, the Vosges mountains look out over the Rhine plain to the dark stain of Germany's Black Forest beyond. Green, rolling and temperate, they offer stimulating walking which, while challenging, is considerably more gentle than in the rugged Alps to their south.

Both sustain forest, conifer and broad-leaf, and in summer sheep and cattle graze the grasses of their open, upper slopes. The eastern flanks of the Vosges mountains, in Alsace, produce some of France's finest white wines, fruity and aromatic.

As a counterpoint to all that elevation – and exchanging white wines for full-bodied red Burgundy wines in all their glory – we describe a two-day walk in Bourgogne (Burgundy) that takes in Vézelay, one of the four French departure points for the Chemins de St-Jacques, medieval pilgrim routes leading to Santiago de Compostela in Spain.

Combine the three walks (and regions) into one holiday and it's as much a gastro-nomic as a walking tour. In Alsace, tuck into a platter of *choucroute alsacienne*, sauer-kraut with thick hanks of sausage and boiled ham. More subtly, nibble at a *tarte flambée*, a thin-crusted Alsatian pizza. In the Jura, spear your bread and dip your fork into a *fondue comtoise*, where local Comté cheese and white wine bubble in the pan. Then again, there's no better region in all France than Burgundy to replenish energy for the next day's trek. Specialities include *escargots de bourgogne*, snails plump and sizzling in their sauce of butter and garlic, and *bœuf bour-guignon*, a happy synthesis of world-famous local Charolais beef and red wine.

Massif des Vosges

Thousands of millennia ago, the Massif des Vosges and the Black Forest were part of the same mountain mass. Then, in the same violent movement of the earth's crust that created the Alps and the Jura,

---

Highlights

- Striding the springy turf of the Ballons des Vosges (this page) under a clear sky.
- From up high, catching the first glimpse of the Rhine Valley (p325) and Germany's Black Forest beyond
- Emerging at the end of the day's walk into the square before Vézelay's magnificent basilica (p334)
- Taking in the panorama of Lake Geneva and the Alps beyond, seen from Colomby de Gex (p338)

---

the central part of the formation collapsed, creating the wide Rhine Valley.

The granite massif stretches north-south for about 100km. To the east, the steep Alsatian side with its scree and glacial cirques dominates the vineyards of the Rhine plain. The western slopes of Lorraine and Franche-Comté descend more gently and are more densely populated.

Crête des Vosges

Duration	4 days
Distance	84km
Difficulty	moderate
Start	St-Amarin (p322)
Finish	Riquewihr (p322)
Transport	bus, train

Summary From Le Grand Ballon, exhilarat-ing ridge walking along the border between Alsace and Lorraine – the one-time Franco-German frontier – ending at the walled town of Riquewihr with its fine wines.

The walk mostly follows the GR5 as it winds across the rounded summits of the Ballons des Vosges. It's moderate mountain walking, rarely taxing, with fabulous views of the gentler green slopes to the west and, to the east, the wide Rhine Valley, then the

Wine & Mountains

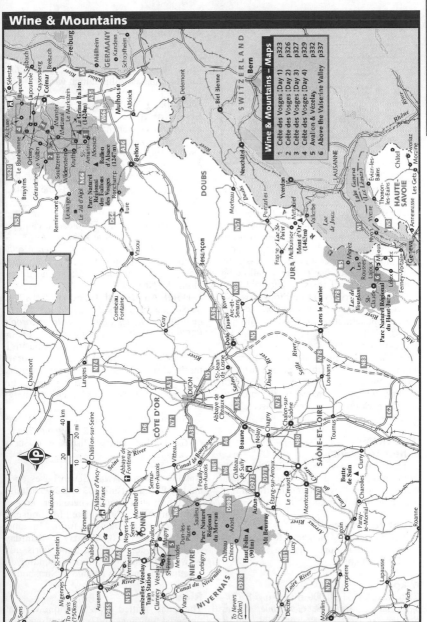

Wine & Mountains – Maps

1 Crête des Vosges (Day 1)	p323
2 Crête des Vosges (Day 2)	p326
3 Crête des Vosges (Day 3)	p327
4 Crête des Vosges (Day 4)	p329
5 Avallon & Vézelay	p332
6 Above the Valserine Valley	p337

Crête des Vosges

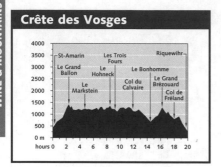

Black Forest (Schwarzwald), over the frontier in Germany.

The open grasslands above the tree line are known locally as *hautes chaumes*, where for centuries farmers brought their cows to graze the high pasture in summer. These days, however, fewer and fewer make the journey so the grass isn't cropped, allowing shrubs and stunted trees to encroach and reclaim their territory. The hilltops now risk reverting to their natural condition – dense, scarcely penetrable woodland – with the loss of all those sweeping vistas that are the prime joy of this stirring walk.

The lakes that you look down on are no more 'natural' than the *hautes chaumes*. Most were created at the end of the 19th century, when streams were dammed to provide back-up power for small-scale textile mills.

PLANNING
When to Walk
Normally it's possible to walk the crests from mid-May to mid-November. Summer is a delight, with temperatures rarely becoming uncomfortably hot.

What to Bring
Self-caterers need to pack food for three days as there are no shops between St-Amarin and Le Bonhomme.

Maps
Club Vosgien's 1:50,000 map No 6/8 *Colmar, Munster, Hohneck, Gerardmer & Les Ballons des Vosges*, based on IGN data, is superior to the IGN's own 1:100,000 *Parc Naturel des Ballons des Vosges*, as it includes more walking routes and information. Reliable and covering the whole route, its only disadvantage is that, being so vast, it handles like a spinnaker sail in a high wind.

NEAREST TOWNS
St-Amarin
St-Amarin's efficient **tourist office** (☎ *03 89 82 13 90; www.ot-saint-amarin.com - French only; 81 rue Charles de Gaulle; open Mon-Fri & Sat morning year-round, Mon-Sat & Sun morning Jul & Aug*) carries a small stock of maps and guidebooks and posts the weather forecast.

Places to Stay & Eat The nearest camping ground is **Les Bouleaux** (☎ *03 89 82 64 70; www.alsace-camping.com - French only; camping per person/site €3.60/3.60; open Apr-Oct*), in Ransbach, 1.5km northwest along the N66.

Hôtel Au Cheval Blanc (☎ *03 89 82 64 80, fax 03 89 38 77 72; 88 rue Charles de Gaulle; singles/doubles with bathroom €35.50/42, half board €45; salads, €5.25-6.50, menus €12.65-19*) in St-Amarin is a friendly family hotel with a **restaurant** that's ideal for hikers; a buffet breakfast fires you up in the morning while the gargantuan salads and grills replace energy burnt on the hills.

For something simpler, **Mega Doner Kebap** (☎ *03 89 38 24 27; 69 rue Charles de Gaulle*) does Turkish dishes, to eat in or takeaway.

Getting There & Away Seven buses operated by **Prêt à Partir** (☎ *03 29 23 95 88*) link St-Amarin with Thann, where there are bus and train connections to/from Mulhouse.

There are 15 trains to/from Mulhouse (€5.20, 40 minutes), Monday to Saturday. Trains between Mulhouse and Paris take between 4¾ and 6½ hours, depending on whether you need to change in Strasbourg.

Riquewihr
The small walled town of Riquewihr, all timbered buildings and bright with window

boxes of geraniums, is like a transplant from a Germanic fairy story. It fairly seethes with tourists during the high season.

The **tourist office** (☎ 03 89 49 08 40, 08 20 36 09 22; www.ribeauville-riquewihr.com; open Mon-Sat & Sun morning) is at the junction of rue du Général de Gaulle (the main street) and rue de la Première Armée.

Places to Stay & Eat The facilities creak a little at **Camping Intercommunal** (☎ 03 89 47 90 08; camping per person/site €3.70/4; open mid-Apr–mid-Dec), a 15-minute walk east of Riquewihr, but it does have the distinction – rare among French camping grounds – of providing toilet paper.

There's no shortage of places to stay and eat in this tourist-oriented town. Ask at the tourist office for a copy of its *Liste des Chambres d'Hôte*.

Hôtel-Restaurant Au Dolder (☎ 03 89 47 92 56; 52 rue Général de Gaulle; doubles €36-56) is Riquewihr's cheapest hotel and runs a decent **restaurant**.

For something snacky, try the street terrace of **Le Bistrot** (☎ 03 89 49 00 74; 17 rue Général de Gaulle; pizzas €8.50-9), where you can watch the world stroll by. It does

tarte flambée (€7 to €8.50), a tasty local version of the ubiquitous pizza that you really ought to try in preference.

Au Tire Buchon (☎ 03 89 47 91 61; rue Général de Gaulle; menus €12-26) also does a mean *tarte flambée* and regional à la carte dishes. The cosy traditional interior and flower-bedecked external terrace (with a drunk, decidedly confused waiter when we dined) have equal charm.

Getting There & Away Seven to nine Autocar Pauli (☎ 03 89 78 11 78) buses travel between Riquewihr and Colmar daily except Sunday. The last buses leave Riquewihr and Colmar train station in the early evening. From Colmar, there are trains to Paris, with a change at Mulhouse or Strasbourg.

THE WALK
Day 1: St-Amarin to Le Markstein

4½–5 hours, 18km, 1140m ascent

It's work all morning, play all afternoon: a constant, rarely steep but not very varied ascent to the peak of Le Grand Ballon then, once back at Col du Haag, easy striding with great views and little change in elevation all the way to Le Markstein. From St-Amarin to Col du Haag, you're following yellow rectangles and the GR532. From the col onwards, it's the single red stripe of the GR5.

From rue Charles de Gaulle in St-Amarin (420m), go north up rue Georges Clemenceau. Walk round the southern side of the church and, 50m later, head southeast up Kattenbach, a steep lane where bright flowers trail from hanging baskets. Cross straight over a wider road and turn left to take a steep bitumen lane. After only 20m be careful not to miss a narrow footpath taking off to the right and into a wood, signed 'Grand Ballon par Col du Haag'.

About half an hour out, turn left (north) at a T-junction onto a wide grassy forest track, leaving it after five minutes to fork right onto a footpath.

Fontaine des Mulhousiens, or Milhuser Brennala, is a spring just below the track, overlooked by a small, rather tacky shrine and sprays of plastic flowers nailed to a

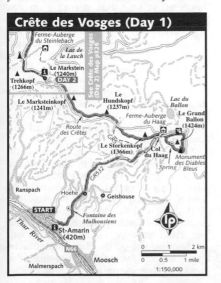

Crête des Vosges (Day 1)

tree. The flowing water, by contrast, is delightfully cool and natural.

Fifteen minutes beyond the spring, leave the houses of Hoehe (763m) on your right, cross a sealed road and take the middle tine of a three-pronged fork. Some 10 minutes later, a recently swathed forest track cuts across the path; go left, then right after 20m to continue upwards. After a further 30 minutes, go left where the footpath meets a stony track, then right (southeast) at a four-way junction 75m later. Just as this grassy track begins to descend, fork left onto a narrow footpath that continues to rise gently as Le Grand Ballon, topped

The Ferme-Auberge

There are over 70 *fermes-auberges* (farm-inns) in the Vosges. Farms that are usually still worked, they offer meals and often accommodation too.

Known locally as *marcairies*, they were for centuries the summer home and workplace for *marcaires* (derived from the Alsatian *malker* – literally 'the one who milks'), or cowherds. You could tell when a *marcaire* was in residence by the flag flying from a tall flagpole.

Walking in the Vosges is a long-established tradition, and it was back in the 19th century that the *fermes-auberges* first began opening their doors to hikers. Nowadays, some are accessible by car but travellers on foot are still the main clientele.

The degree of comfort can vary from simple bunks to double rooms with more mod cons than a walker needs. Some allow you to camp for a modest fee or for free if you take dinner with them. Most, especially in the high season, expect you to take half board, which normally costs between €31 and €38.

Regulars salivate at the thought of the *repas marcaire* (around €15) which in some *fermes-auberges* may be the only dish on offer. Expect to receive in gargantuan portions: a hunk of pie, smoked pork and *roïgabrabeldi* (sliced potato with onions, slow cooked in butter), a slab of Munster cheese and a local dessert.

by what looks like a giant golf ball, looms solid against the sky.

Turn left onto a track that intersects with the GR5 that comes in from the west just a few metres later. Go straight ahead at a bitumen road to reach, after a couple of minutes, **Ferme-Auberge du Haag** (*☎/fax 03 89 48 95 85; menu €13; open Thu-Tue year-round*), which prepares snacks, a great four-course menu and also has a couple of dormitories.

From the farm and Col du Haag (1280m), strike southeast along a clearly defined path that runs beside a brimming water trough as it climbs towards the peak. A couple of minutes before the orientation table that marks the summit, it passes the **Monument des Diables Bleus**, erected in memory of the 'Blue Devils', a crack WWI Alpine regiment from Savoy that fought and suffered massive losses in these same hills.

Le Grand Ballon (1424m) is both the highest and farthest east of the peaks along the crest of the Vosges. From its summit there's a fine panorama of the Rhine Valley and the hills of the Black Forest, beyond the river in Germany.

At the summit, reached after 2¼ to 2½ hours of walking, that strange giant golf ball – humming in the high winds that regularly sweep the peak – is revealed as an aircraft tracking station. Look backwards as you descend its flight of steps and it could be some displaced Inca temple.

Turn left to follow the sign 'Circuit Versant Ouest' and drop to **Chalet Hôtel du Grand Ballon**, which does a three-course *menu marcheur* (walkers' menu; €9) and also welcomes picnickers, provided that you buy a drink.

Follow a footpath running parallel to the bitumen road. This is the first of several encounters with the **Route des Crêtes**, originally a military road constructed by the French to supply and control the ridge.

Back at Col du Haag, you can briefly abandon the GR5, which builds in some needless road work. Go along the left side of Ferme-Auberge du Haag beside a recently erected fence to join a footpath that heads westwards, up into the woods. This

The Killing Fields

From Day 2 onwards, there are constant reminders of man's inhumanity to man. You're walking a small part of the vast WWI and WWII killing fields near the Franco-German border. The slaughter in WWI was infinitely greater as hilltop after hilltop, vantage point after vantage point, was fought over, lost and regained only to be recaptured. In WWII by contrast, the German forces ripped through Belgium and rolled south to attack from the rear the French Maginot Line, which ran the length of Alsace, and was believed to be impregnable.

Over half a century since the last shot was fired, nature is stealthily effacing the evidence of trenches, bunkers and gun emplacements.

From Le Rainkopf, you pass the boundary stones that demarcated the frontier from 1871, when Alsace was occupied by Germany, until the treaty of Versailles in 1919. With 'F' for France chiselled on one side and with an often defaced 'D' for Deutschland on the other, these days the stones mark the boundary between the French *départements* (departments) of Haut-Rhin on the eastern side and Vosges on the west, and between the regions of Alsace and Lorraine.

makes a shorter if steeper alternative to the more frequented GR5 route.

Once over the crest, pass through a revolving stile and descend to rejoin the Route des Crêtes and GR5, then head northwest along the latter. From here to Le Markstein, navigation is simplicity itself, aided by the twin clues of the GR's waymarkers and the winding course of the Route des Crêtes, never long out of sight. There are continuously stirring views to the west – less so to the eastern, Alsatian side, as much of the route runs just below the crest.

Le Markstein

Outside the busy ski season, Le Markstein (1240m) is a mournful dump whose accommodation options aren't great. More attractive choices lie ahead if you're prepared to push on a little into Day 2.

Chalet St-Antoine (☎ *03 89 82 72 66, reservations after 8pm* ☎ *03 89 38 71 39; dorm B&B €15; open Jul & Aug)*, beside Ferme Le Markstein, belongs to the local ski club and, when open, is your best option.

Hôtel Restaurant Wolf (☎ *03 89 82 64 36; www.hotelwolf.info; doubles €28, doubles/triples with bathroom €50/61, half board €54; menus €11.50-22.50)* is a rambling, none too congenial old place whose **restaurant** offers a veggie *menu* option at €11.50. **Maison d'Accueil** (☎ *03 89 82 74 98; dorm beds €9)* doubles up in a desultory way as the **tourist office**. It's cosier than the down-at-heel exterior would suggest. The small **bar** does snacks and breakfast and can supply meals, if warned in advance. Despite the decidedly limited charms of these two places, it's advisable to reserve on summer weekends and in July and August.

Two kilometres beyond the ski station and into Day 2 is the comfortable **Ferme-Auberge du Steinlebach** (☎ *03 89 82 61 87; half board in dorm/room €31/37)*, where you're guaranteed to eat well and copiously.

Day 2: Le Markstein to Les Trois Fours

4¼–4¾ hours, 19km, 520m ascent

From the base of a summer sledging run, follow the GR route as it curves westwards around a small hill. After around 20 minutes, cross the Route des Crêtes and continue along the clearly defined path (a short detour northeast from the crossing brings you to Ferme-Auberge du Steinlebach, a pleasant overnight option (see above).

A small stone **monument** just to the left of the route commemorates the spot where, in 1940, a company of beleaguered French soldiers burnt their regimental flag rather than surrender it to the German invaders. Here too you see the first of many **slit trenches** from both WWI and WWII. Nowadays they're banked by bilberries and are being colonised by shrubs and small trees. Violence is difficult to imagine amid such splendid views – back to Le Grand Ballon and eastwards to the wide plain of the Rhine Valley with the dark stain of the Black Forest beyond.

Crête des Vosges (Day 2)

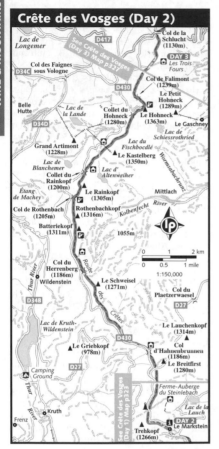

verted 'V' of the hotel-restaurant that crowns its summit.

Leave the road after 200m to take a wide track beneath beech and a sprinkling of plane trees as you advance in parallel with the clear traces of slit trenches. A small cairn at ankle level marks the highest point of Le Schweisel (1271m).

From the Col du Herrenberg (1186m), about an hour beyond Col d'Hahnenbrunnen, the GR5 descends to the village of Mittlach with an altitude loss of over 650m. Our route by contrast sticks to the tops, continuing resolutely northwards. Some 300m beyond the col, there's a small Club Vosgien unstaffed **refuge** – essentially a hut with a fireplace and space to stretch a sleeping bag.

Along a clear, unambiguous trail, tick off the summits: Batteriekopf (1311m) and, 10 minutes later, Rothenbachkopf (1316m), topped by a stone cairn. Just beneath the peak is a small **wooden cross** in memory of two young Germans who, one night in December 1965, perished in a blizzard.

Having dropped to Col de Rothenbach (1205m), instead of the waymarked trail choose the minor right-hand footpath, which hugs the lip of the Mittlach Valley, thus retaining the magnificent plunging vista as long as possible. This curves west for the final 200m to the summit of Le Rainkopf (1305m) and the first of the one-time **frontier markers** (see the boxed text on p325).

Just beyond Collet du Rainkopf (1200m) is the Club Vosgien's **Refuge du Rainkopf** (reservations ☎ 03 89 74 25 25; dorm beds €8; open mid-May–mid-Oct), with a trough and flowing water. It has self-catering facilities but doesn't do meals or drinks. By contrast, 150m away, **Ferme-Auberge Firstmiss** (also called Ferschmuss) provides both, but not accommodation. Perfect symbiosis!

At a four-way junction, go left then right (northeast) after 50m to stay in woodland. Beside the flat, sandy track bordered by meadows of wildflowers are a couple of strange phenomena. Giant granite boulders, for all the world like tumbled megaliths, are in fact the work of farmers long ago who, without mechanical assistance, cleared the land for cultivation. The line of large orange

Recross the Route des Crêtes just below Le Breitfirst (1280m). The recommended **Refuge du Hahnenbrunnen** (reservations ☎ 03 89 59 55 56; dorm beds €8; open daily Jul & Aug, Sat & Sun year-round) is at Col d'Hahnenbrunnen (1186m), where the trail briefly follows the bitumen road. The refuge is run by volunteers from the Touring Club de Mulhouse, has self-catering facilities and hot showers. Even if it's closed, its picnic tables, perched over the upper reaches of the wooded Mittlach Valley, make a great rest stop. From here you can clearly see Le Hohneck to the north, recognisable by the in-

lollipops marching parallel to the ridge are to guide travellers when snow conceals other landmarks. All the same, they're an ugly stain on the summer landscape and could surely be either removed until snow returns or replaced by something less intrusive.

At the summit of Le Hohneck (1363m) are an orientation table and **Hôtel Restaurant du Sommet du Hohneck** (☎/fax 03 29 63 11 17; doubles with/without bathroom €55/43, half board €45; lunch menus €7.50-14.50; open year-round, accommodation Jul & Aug only). Its **bar-restaurant**, although often crowded with motorists, makes a welcome rest stop. Open until 7pm, it serves snacks and lunch – or you can eat your own picnic inside provided you buy a drink.

Having rejoined the GR5, head initially northwest from the summit – still following those old stones – to drop to Col de Falimont (1239m). The three buildings of Les Trois Fours stand out clearly to the northeast. Follow the trail as it veers around the rim of the steep valley that drops eastwards.

At a sign reading 'Champ des Trois Fours', turn right onto a bitumen lane. Where the GR5 forks left onto a dirt track after 100m, continue straight as far as the three houses – a farm that makes and sells fresh dairy produce, including the local Munster cheese, a *refuge* and a *ferme-auberge* (see the boxed on p324) – which constitute Les Trois Fours, barely five minutes off the GR.

Ferme-Auberge des Trois Fours (☎ 03 89 77 31 14, fax 03 89 77 97 33; half board €31.50; open Tue-Sun May-Oct), more an auberge than *ferme*, has a bar and vast dining room that can cater to 80. Just beyond is the friendly, spick and span **chalet-refuge** (☎/fax 03 89 77 32 59; dorm beds €26.35, with half board €39.65, of the Club Alpin Français (CAF). Its self-catering facilities, including a microwave. If you prefer to stay in a hotel, push on for less than half an hour into Day 3 as far as Col de la Schlucht.

Day 3: Les Trois Fours to Le Bonhomme

5–5½ hours, 20.5km, 280m ascent
Return to the point where you left the GR5 and turn right onto a dirt track, which drops

down through beech wood to **Col de la Schlucht** (1130m).

At the pass, there are a couple of hotels that cater mainly to the transit trade.

Hôtel-Restaurant du Chalet (☎ 03 89 77 04 06, fax 03 89 77 06 11; doubles/triples/quads €48/65/72, half board €45) is instantly recognisable by the replica of Brussels' famous Manekin Pis, spurting potable water from its diminutive dong.

Hôtel-Restaurant Le Tetras (☎ 03 29 63 11 37; www.laschlucht-remy.com - French only; rooms €29, with shower €32, with bathroom €41; mains €5.20-9.50), also called Hôtel de

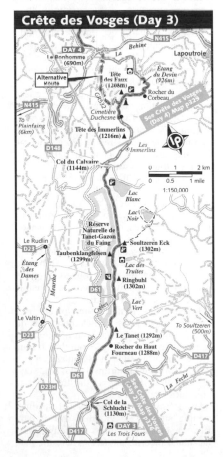

Crête des Vosges (Day 3)

la Schlucht, has a speedy self-service section and also offers à la carte meals.

Turn right on the D417 and take a path to the left just beyond Hôtel Le Tetras. A little over 10 minutes of steep, bouldery ascent brings you to a four-way junction, where the GR531 heads off right towards Munster.

Pass Rocher du Haut Fourneau (1288m), also called Le Wurzelstein – and on occasion Le Wourzelstein – a rocky outcrop popular with climbers. A brief scramble over boulders leads to Le Tanet (1292m), reached about an hour beyond Col de la Schlucht and recognisable by the rusting iron and concrete of a wartime pillbox lookout post.

Re-entering the forest, the trail fleetingly converges with the Route des Crêtes. Emerge to ascend gradually and scarcely noticeably, now on grass, then on dry peat that's bouncy underfoot and jet black.

Once beyond Ringbuhl (1302m), pause at an orientation table planted at the heart of the **Gazon du Faing**, a flat upland grassy plateau. It's a popular spot with motorists who make the short stroll up from Auberge du Faing and its adjacent car park, a 10-minute detour westwards.

In season, you'll find the bilberries of Gazon du Faing especially juicy. But, as you tuck in, be careful not to unwittingly transgress local law: an official ordinance decrees a maximum culling of 3L per person per day!

There are gorgeous views of the valley to the east and back towards Le Hohneck, with Le Grand Ballon – topped by what now appears as a tiny pimple – still visible on the southeastern horizon.

Taubenklangfelsen (1299m) towers over Lac des Truites with Ferme-Auberge Lac du Forlet at its western end, both of them too far below to be tempting. From this granite outcrop, bear briefly east to Soultzeren Eck (1302m) then turn northwards again, staying with the GR route as the trail to Lac Noir goes straight ahead.

From here it's yet more level striding, heading straight as an arrow for 2.5km, between stunted pine forest on the right and marsh and moor to the left. Where the path

re-enters woodland about 30 minutes beyond Soultzeren Eck, it's worth making the briefest of detours east to look down over Lac Blanc (White Lake – in fact a mournful grey), glittering at the base of its glacial cirque.

As you descend through spruce wood, notice how the trees are taller and more mature than their more exposed and stunted cousins on the upland plateau.

Just before **Auberge du Lac Blanc**, which does drinks and pancakes, take a path to the left for Col du Calvaire (1144m). To vary the pace and terrain a little, ignore the GR5 flashes and instead take a wide, level 4WD track, signed 'Cimetière Duchesne', along which you can really stride out. This passes beside Source Rosalie, an icy-cold spring beside the farm of Les Immerlins.

At a four-way junction around 30 minutes beyond the col, fork left and head uphill. A couple of minutes later, you reach the sobering French WWI military cemetery **Cimetière Duchesne**. Its simple stone crosses are now dwarfed by tall conifers.

Picking up the GR5 again, continue northeast up a track paved with blocks of granite, now much eroded, originally laid to ease the provisioning of the military post on top of Tête des Faux.

About 10 minutes later, you have a choice: to turn left and take the alternative GR532, shortening the day's walk by 2km and avoiding some stiff altitude gain; or to continue on the main route to the peak, scene of a fierce battle in December 1914. Continuing, pass a **monument** to the Chasseurs Alpins (see the boxed text on p325). At the summit of **Tête des Faux** (1208m), a simple white cross seems to grow from the debris of the fortification that once dominated the hilltop.

Descending to the northeast, note the rusting coils of barbed wire, slit trenches, craters and bunkers on both sides of the track. Perhaps pause at an orientation table that looks east over the Rhine and the frontier to the hills of the Black Forest, and hope that in today's and tomorrow's Europe, such carnage may never happen again.

At a T-junction 15 minutes beyond Tête des Faux, turn left onto a track to reach Rocher du Corbeau, a megahunk of granite. At a bend two minutes later, take a steep footpath to the left (northeast). Pass a huge concrete cavern, once a store at the top of a *téléférique* (cable car or funicular) constructed by the Germans to transport supplies. From here, the descent through mixed beech and conifer is easy and pleasant after the sombre debris of the mountain's upper reaches.

The path meets a wide 4WD track beside the pool of Étang du Devin (926m), reverting to bog as grasses and sedges inexorably occupy the site. Here, an old bunker in the hillside offers spartan shelter. Turn left for the superior comfort of **Hôtel Résidences Étang du Devin** (☎ 03 89 47 20 29; *www.etangdevin.com; dorm beds €8, room per person €13.50, with bathroom €24, half board €24-39*), a little over five minutes away, just beyond a former German military cemetery.

Continue along the bitumen lane as far as **Les Myrtilles** (☎ 06 68 67 92 06; *camping per person €3.50, doubles/triples/quads with bathroom €42/52/62; open year-round*), a charming *gîte d'étape*. Just beyond, turn right down an easily missed footpath to reach **Le Bonhomme**.

Hôtel de la Poste (☎ 03 89 47 51 10; *www.hotel-la-poste.com - French only; singles/*doubles with bathroom & buffet breakfast €44/ 64, half board €61; menus €10-20), where the owner himself is a keen walker, is an excellent option with a sauna and pool for weary hikers and tasty food.

There are three to five **STAHV** (☎ 03 29 34 20 34) buses running daily except Sunday to/from Colmar (45 minutes) between early morning and early evening. From Colmar, trains run to Paris regularly.

Day 4: Le Bonhomme to Riquewihr
5½–6¼ hours, 26.5km, 700m ascent

From the church in Le Bonhomme (690m), head north along route des Bagenelles (D48). Fork right after less than five minutes onto a lane, which soon narrows to overgrown footpath.

Continue straight where this path merges with a wide cart track and cross the D48 a couple of times (here, as so often in France's hills and mountains, the walkers' way follows a long-established track while the modern road has to wind and snake to gain the same height).

Turn left down a bitumen lane that descends towards Les Bagenelles. Just before

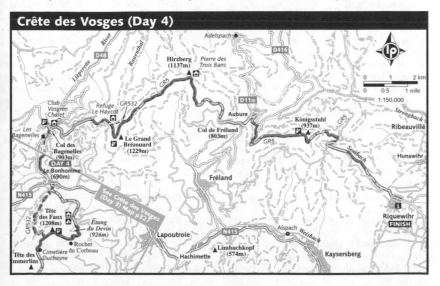

Crête des Vosges (Day 4)

this farm, the trail follows a 'Z' (not as on the Club Vosgien reference map) to reach Col des Bagenelles (903m) about 45 minutes from Le Bonhomme. From the pass there's a magnificent view northwards of the valley of La Lièpvrette and the succeeding ripples of hills beyond. A Club Vosgien **chalet** (reservations ☎ 03 88 68 81 67; dorm beds €12; open Sat-Sun year-round, daily Jul & Aug), with self-catering facilities and hot showers, makes an agreeable alternative to overnighting in Le Bonhomme.

Go up chemin du Haycot, a wide dirt track, then, as it levels out, fork left to stay in woodland. About 30 minutes beyond the col, cross a major track and take a narrow footpath signed 'Ski Club'. Pass a chalet belonging to the eponymous club and, five minutes or so later, emerge into a vast forest clearing (1075m) where tracks scatter in all directions.

Just off the clearing and off-route is the stone-carved crest of an infantry battalion from Bonn, another relic of WWI. Barely 50m beyond is **Refuge Le Haycot** (reservations ☎ 03 89 58 59 79; dorm beds €7). It's worth dropping by for a drink while savouring the magnificent view of the Rauenthal Valley to the north.

From the clearing, it's a steep, unrelieved ascent for 10 to 15 minutes before the trail levels out and passes the summit of Le Grand Brézouard (1229m), the last peak of any consequence on the walk. (If you prefer to bypass it, simply take the alternative GR532 eastwards and rejoin the trail 1.2km later.)

From the peak, the northward descent, much more gentle, follows the ridge. At a four-way junction beside an unstaffed Club Vosgien chalet, continue straight (northeast) then, 20 minutes from Le Grand Brézouard, turn left at a junction with a broader path. After a further 20 minutes, the route forks left and uphill, leaving the main track.

At the five-way junction of Pierre des Trois Bans, a tiny, trim wayside chalet provides shade and emergency accommodation. Of the two tracks signed 'Aubure', take the one heading south towards Col de Fréland.

It's the lesser travelled and, once you're beyond the dead zone of factory forestry, the more scenic.

About 15 minutes beyond the chalet, turn left at an intersection to enjoy some easy, agreeable walking along a wide forest track. Some 25 minutes later, turn left onto a bitumen road then, just after an ugly stone belvédère (viewpoint), turn left again at Col de Fréland (803m) to descend to the village of **Aubure**.

Turn right down chemin du Combattant. At the post office, hairpin right along chemin du Kalblin, then turn sharp left beside the last house in the village. At a bench 15 minutes later, stay with the main track (ignoring the sign 'Kœnigsstuhl Variante'), then fork right after 100m onto a pleasant footpath bordered by ferns. A further 20 minutes brings you to a jumble of giant granite boulders from where there are the first fine views of wooded hills rolling to the southern horizon, the broad plain to the east and the town of Colmar to the southeast.

At **Kœnigsstuhl** (937m; 'the seat of the king'), about an hour beyond Aubure, you can take a breather on its giant throne before beginning the descent. Continue straight at the end of a long dogleg as the narrow path merges with a broad logging track.

Say a last farewell to the GR5 as it veers left beside a small crucifix, marking the spot where one Johan Floderer had the misfortune to be terminated by lightning back in 1887. At a four-way junction 100m later, where three of the four options are signed 'Riquewihr', go straight ahead (southeast) then right after 150m to follow red-and-white waymarkers all the way to Riquewihr. Ten minutes from the crucifix, turn right and soon go over a track to continue heading southwest (from here until the path meets a sealed road around 10 minutes later, the route may be thick with undergrowth early in the season).

At the road, turn left and, after a further 10 minutes, fork left onto chemin de la Grande Vallée, a dirt track that descends gently to **Riquewihr** (283m; p322), following the stream of Le Sembach.

Burgundy

Burgundy, with its lazy, brown rivers and gently rolling hills where vineyards and cereal fields sweep broad brushstrokes of colour, offers many splendid, gentle walks. The walk below remains one of our favourites.

Avallon & Vézelay

Duration	2 days
Distance	37.5km
Difficulty	easy–moderate
Start/Finish	Avallon
Transport	bus
Summary	Play the pilgrim – through woods, fields, dozing hamlets and vineyards – on a walk that links a pair of Burgundy's most historically rich small towns.

Tread in the footsteps of medieval pilgrims who, after attending mass in Vézelay's magnificent basilica (see the boxed text on p334), set out on the long journey to Santiago de Compostela in Spain. For more about Chemin de St-Jacques, see p134).

PLANNING
When to Walk
Any season is walking season in Burgundy, although you need to wrap up warmly between November and March. From June to October, when the weather's warm but rarely uncomfortable, is the optimum period.

Maps
The route features on IGN 1:25,000 maps No 2722E *Vézelay* and No 2722O *Avallon*. You'll find them at **Maison de la Presse** (cnr rue de Lyon & rue du Maréchal Foch) in Avallon and, in Vézelay, at **Librairie L'Or des Étoiles** (rue St-Étienne). The tourist offices in each town also stock them.

NEAREST TOWN
Avallon
From a hilltop site, the walled town of Avallon looks over the Cousin River, which snakes around its base. The **tourist office** (☎ 03 86 34 14 19; www.avallonnais-tourisme.com; 6 rue Bocquillot; open daily Jul–mid-Sep, Mon-Sat mid-Sep–Jun), in the old town, has an Internet point (€3 for 15 minutes – and thus is a serious contender for France's most expensive log-on).

Places to Stay & Eat Southeast of the old town and a 20-minute downhill walk from the tourist office, shady and grassy **Camping Municipal Sous Roche** (☎/fax 03 86 34 10 39; camping per person/tent/car €3/2/2) occupies a delightful, roomy site beside the Cousin River.

Jump out of bed at **Hôtel du Rocher** (☎ 03 86 34 19 03; doubles €19, with shower €26, hall shower €1), beside Cousin-le-Pont, and set off walking the route. Its wood-panelled rooms are nothing fancy but great value.

The ebullient young team at **Restaurant de la Tour** (☎ 03 86 34 24 84; 84 rue Aristide Briand; pizzas €6-8.50, mains €7.50-9.50), near the tourist office, offers eat-in or takeaway pizza, and a variety of well-prepared meaty dishes. Check the blackboard for the specials of the season.

Le Gourmillon (☎/fax 03 86 31 62 01; 8 rue de Lyon; menus €14-28; open lunch Mon-Sun) does a particularly lip-smacking *menu gastronomique*.

Getting There & Away Between Avallon and Dijon **Transco** (☎ 03 80 42 11 00) operates two to three bus services daily (€15.25, two hours).

Four buses daily (two only on Sunday) link Avallon's train station and the TGV hub at Montbard, from where there are frequent trains to/from Paris' Gare de Lyon (€35.50).

Between June and August, one **Rapide de Bourgogne** (☎ 03 86 34 00 00) bus a day from Montbard continues to Vézelay town (€3.50, 25 minutes) – not its train station, which is 10 inconvenient kilometres away – passing by Avallon train station in the morning daily. The return bus (very useful if you prefer to come back to Avallon at the end of Day 1) leaves Vézelay in the early evening.

For a cab in Avallon, telephone **Taxi Hannequin** (☎ 03 86 34 04 52) or **Taxi Quincy**

(☎ 03 86 34 15 15). In Vézelay, call **Laurie et Sylvain** (☎ 03 86 33 19 06) or **Taxi Vézelay** (☎ 03 86 32 31 88). The fare between the two towns is around €22 per vehicle.

THE WALK
Day 1: Avallon to Vézelay
4¼–4½ hours, 18.5km

From the tourist office, take rue Bocquillot to the town ramparts. Turn left, then left again after the first bend to follow a pedestrian lane downhill. Descend to the bridge over the river at Cousin-le-Pont. Here, you pick up the red-and-white waymarkers cut by an oblique white stripe that indicate an alternative GR13 route.

Go under the road bridge and cross a small footbridge to the river's true left bank. As you follow the trail downstream, notice on the opposite bank the weirs and raceways channelling water to small water-powered flour mills, a couple of them now converted to hotels. It's gentle, shaded woodland walk-

ing beside the gurgling river, punctuated by the occasional stretch of easy scrabbling over rocks and tree roots.

An hour from the bridge, walk beside a mossy wall to enter Pontaubert. Go straight across the D957 and take chemin de Ronde, a narrow lane that curves around the village.

At a T-junction, turn right onto the D142 towards Vault de Lugny. The road runs beside the boundary wall of **Château de Vault de Lugny** (☎ 03 86 34 07 86), these days a luxury four-star hotel where the grounds and gourmet restaurant are the preserve of hotel guests only; it's not every walker's choice.

At Vault de Lugny, the route finally leaves the Cousin River, which has been a constant companion since Avallon. Before turning left along chemin de Borland, make a slight detour to visit the village's 16th-century **parish church of St-Germain**, with its frescoes and finely carved pulpit.

Back on route, go straight ahead at the first bend onto a dirt track. After a brief rise,

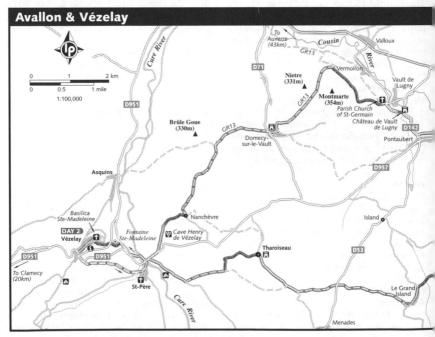

it levels out to give great views of the patchwork plain to the east before curling round the wooded hill of Montmarte. At a T-junction with the true GR13, coming in from the northeast and reached about 50 minutes beyond Pontaubert, turn left to follow its stripes, which from here onwards lose their oblique white bar.

After 25 minutes, go right at a T-junction and drop down a gravel lane to the red-roofed village of **Domecy-sur-le-Vault**. Turn right down rue de l'Église, beside which are a couple of water troughs and a handsome chateau. Fork right beside the church, cross the main village street and head straight up a narrow footpath, adjoinng a wide 4WD track just beyond a stone cross.

After running through woodland and beside hay and cereal fields, the track passes the first of the Côte de Vézelay vineyards. A sunken lane leads to the hamlet of **Nanchèvre** 25 to 30 minutes later. Go down rue du Lavoir, turn left onto route de Fontette, then almost immediately right to mount a grassy footpath, with the basilica of Vézelay soon prominent on the hilltop to the west.

Where the trail rejoins the road from Nanchèvre, turn left towards St-Père and its prominent church spire, perhaps calling by the **caves of Henry de Vézelay** (wine cellars; www.henrydevezelay) for a little nip and to pack away a bottle in your rucksack.

Thus fortified, press on to St-Père, briefly joining the D957. Cross the bridge over the Cure River to leave the GR13 as it heads southwest. The route returns through St-Père on Day 2. If you've time and prefer to visit its magnificent **church** now, go down the main street and turn left into rue de la Mairie.

Otherwise, turn right (northwest) just over the bridge to take tranquil rue du Colombier around the rear of the village. Turn right again on rejoining the D957 at a fork, taking the lower option, signed 'Asquins'.

Go left onto a cart track then left again after 50m beside the murky Fontaine Ste-Madeleine (note the traces of a large stone building that would once have enclosed it).

Five minutes beyond, turn left along a sealed road then right after 25m to attack an overgrown footpath that rises towards Vézelay's ramparts. After a further five minutes, go right up a flight of stairs penetrating the ramparts (if you come to a small grey metal gate on the right, you've overshot the turning). Wriggle through narrow lanes to emerge into the square in front of the **basilica's** magnificent façade (see the boxed text on p334).

Vézelay

Vézelay's **tourist office** (☎ *03 86 33 23 69; www.vezelaytourisme.com - French only; rue St-Pierre; open daily Jun-Oct, Fri-Wed Nov-May*), on the main street, is destined to move to place du Champ-de-Foire, just outside the town gates at the western end of town.

Centre Ste Madeleine (☎ *03 86 33 22 14; rue St-Pierre; dorm beds €7, doubles per person €13.50*) is run by Franciscan sisters. It has self-catering facilities.

Of the cluster of hotels located in place du Champ de Foire, the most reasonable is the **Hôtel-Restaurant Le Cheval Blanc**

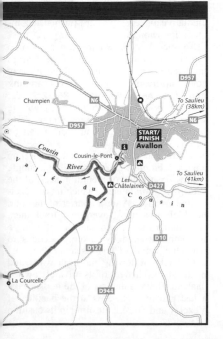

Champien — N6 — D957 — D957 — To Saulieu (38km) — N6
START/FINISH Avallon
Cousin-le-Pont
Cousin River
Vallée du Cousin
Les Châtelaines — D427 — To Saulieu (41km)
La Courcelle
D127 — D10
D944

The Basilica at Vézelay

The Basilique Ste-Madeleine is a Unesco World Heritage List site. Now assailed daily by throngs of tourists, it has known more exciting times and more exotic visitors.

In 1146 St Bernard preached the Second Crusade from a nearby hillside. Half a century later, King Philippe-Auguste of France and Richard the Lionheart arranged to meet in its shadow before setting out on the Third Crusade.

More peacably, as the repository of relics of Ste-Madeleine (Mary Magdalene) and a reputed place of miracles, it drew pilgrims by the thousand and became one of the main French departure points for the Chemin de St-Jacques pilgrimage to Santiago de Compostela in northwestern Spain (see the special section, p134).

Vézelay and its basilica began to decline in the 13th century when word spread (miraculously, one might say) that other parts of Mary Magdalene had turned up at St-Maximin in Provence.

Ransacked by Huguenots during the 16th-century Wars of Religion, desecrated and deconsecrated during the French Revolution, neglected and on the point of collapse, it was restored in the 1840s by Viollet-le-Duc, the famous and, for many, controversial 19th-century restoration architect.

(☎ 03 86 33 22 12, fax 03 86 33 34 29; rooms €25-40; open Feb-Nov).

The municipal **Camping de l'Ermitage** (☎/fax 03 86 33 24 18; camping per person/tent/car €3/2/1) and **youth hostel** (dorm beds €7) share a common telephone. Both are 500m along the road towards the hamlet of L'Étang and open April to October. The youth hostel has self-catering facilities.

It's essential to reserve accommodation in July and August and at weekends throughout the year. Alternatively, abridge or extend Day 1 by staying at St-Père (see the Day 2 route description for accommodation details). Vézelay's train station is 10km north of the town. From Vézelay, buses go to Avallon (p331) from where there are trains connections to Paris. Taxis are also available in Avallon and Vézelay.

Day 2: Vézelay to Avallon

4¼–4¾ hours, 19km

From Basilique Ste-Madeleine's western façade, take rue St-Pierre, which becomes rue St-Étienne.

Once through the town gates, turn left onto the D957. At the first left-hand bend go straight ahead to take a cart track, signed with the stylised scallop shell on a yellow background of the Chemin de St-Jacques. Then the second turning on the left, which gives impressive views of Vézelay and its basilica as it heads southeast towards St-Père.

Reaching **St-Père** about 30 minutes out, turn left along rue des Marguerites. Before turning left again at a T-junction with rue de la Mairie, make a 100m diversion to the right to visit the village's superb 12th- to 14th-century Gothic church of **Notre Dame**, the inspiration for Vézelay's basilica.

Continuing, a left turn at the end of rue de la Mairie brings you to **Hôtel-Bar à la Renommee** (☎ 03 86 33 21 34, fax 03 86 33 34 17; doubles from €30, with bathroom from €37; open Mar–mid-Dec), an attractive alternative to Vézelay's hard-pushed accommodation choices.

To stay with the route, turn right onto rue du Pont, cross the Cure River, then go immediately right again to follow its lazy course upstream, passing St-Père's **camping municipal** (reservations ☎ 03 86 32 26 62; camping/site €1.75/1.45). A favourite with canoeists, it's a pleasant alternative to Vézelay's camping ground, which can be very crowded.

A little under 10 minutes later, turn left up a narrow bitumen lane to pick up the single yellow flashes, intermittent in places, of the PR2 (petite randonnée), which links Vézelay and Avallon. After a quarter of an hour, head left up a stony, overgrown track then, five minutes later, turn sharp right along a footpath bordered by unkempt hedges to reach the hamlet of Tharoiseau (290m).

Go right, following the high walls and neatly shaped hedges of its privately owned chateau. Beyond the last of the houses take a last glance backwards at the basilica of Vézelay and St-Père, nestling in its cushion of trees.

Around 15 minutes beyond Tharoiseau, fork left onto a dirt track. Cross over the D53 as the trail continues to follow the fringe of a wood. Bear left onto a sealed minor road, then left again a couple of minutes later to pass through the pretty hamlet of **Le Grand Island**.

Just beyond the last house, turn right (northeast) down a track that crosses a tiny stream then mounts the opposite eastern flank of the shallow valley.

Go left along a minor road to bypass La Courcelle, no more than a cluster of houses. At a junction with another bitumen road five minutes later, go straight ahead along a cart track.

Now comes some tricky navigation, unaided by waymarkers, just when they're most needed. A little over five minutes from the junction, go straight ahead at a yellow flash to take a path that meanders through the debris of a devastating storm. Hug the northern side of the clearing and, after five minutes, turn left at a T-junction, then right after three minutes to rejoin the main track at a yellow blaze and continue resolutely northeast, now in oak forest.

Just after fording a narrow stream, turn left, then immediately right to stay on the same bearing, guided by the wooden posts of a VTT (mountain bike) route. Ten minutes later, leave the VTT trail and turn right at a grassy track, then almost immediately left. At a T-junction with a meadow before you and Avallon in sight, turn right, then left a minute later to leave the PR2 and in defiance of a yellow cross painted on a tree.

Turn left at a small bitumen road to reach the friendly **Les Châtelaines** (☎ 03 86 34 16 37, fax 03 86 34 55 95; camping per person/ site €2/2), a working farm with a simple camping ground.

Continue northwest along the track, which becomes less defined as it heads towards the edge of a wood. Here a signpost and blue dots direct you east along the field boundary then left and down towards the Cousin River and the intersection with the alternative GR13. Turn right to retrace the early steps of Day 1, back to the bridge at Cousin-le-Pont and up the hill to Avallon (p331).

The Jura

Unlike more popular walking areas such as the Alps, Pyrenees and Provence, visitors to the Jura remain predominantly French, as this medium-mountain region of dense forest and grassy crests is relatively undiscovered by walkers from other nations.

Above the Valserine Valley

Duration	2 days
Distance	37.5km
Difficulty	moderate
Start/Finish	Lajoux (p336)
Transport	train, bus

Summary High above the Valserine Valley, a day in the forest and another of open ridge walking with magnificent views of Lake Geneva and, if it's clear, the Alps and Mont Blanc.

This is a walk of opposites, following the western and eastern flanks of the Valserine Valley. The forest trails of Day 1 are succeeded by Day 2's breathtaking vistas from the long spine running parallel to Lake Geneva (Lac Léman). At each end of the slim rectangle are a couple of more gentle interludes as the trail cuts across the tranquil Valserine Valley.

PLANNING
When to Walk
The route is usually free of snow from mid-May to mid-November. Rain, while rarely long-lasting in summer, can fall in any season.

Maps
The IGN 1:25,000 map No 3328OT *Crêt de la Neige* covers 90% of the route, the remainder featuring on its No 3327OT *St-Claude*. The IGN 1:50,000 map No 3615 *Parc Naturel Régional du Haut-Jura* has the walk in its entirety. The local map *Les Chemins de Randonnée du Jura Gessien* is a useful supplement, but has no contours and is inadequate on its own for navigation.

NEAREST TOWN
Lajoux
The small **tourist office** (☎ 03 84 41 24 10, fax 03 84 41 25 15; open Mon-Sat & Sun morning Jul & Aug, Dec-Mar) shares its premises with the village post office.

Places to Stay & Eat With hot showers and attractive bedrooms, **Gîte d'Étape La Trace** (☎ 03 84 41 27 27; B&B €16, half board €27; open Jul & Aug, mid-Dec–mid-Mar), is about 1km into the walk, along the D292.

Hôtel Restaurant de la Haute Montagne (☎ 03 84 41 20 47; www.hotel-de-la-montagne.com;singles/doubles/triples/quads €31/44/54/69.50, half board €43; menus €15.30-27.30; open May-Sep plus ski season), a cosy Logis de France, has a **restaurant** that's strong on regional dishes.

Getting There & Away Public transport is lamentable. For Lajoux, take the train from Dole or Mouchard (both on the TGV line to Paris) to St-Claude. From St-Claude, **Jura Bus** (☎ 03 84 24 33 07) runs services to Lajoux (50 minutes) and on to Mijoux (one hour), leaving twice on Wednesday and three times on Saturday. The most convenient return bus calls by Lajoux in the early evening.

THE WALK
Day 1: Lajoux to Lélex
4–4½ hours, 18.5km
Leave Lajoux by the D292 towards La Trace, 100m east of the tourist office. Take a cart track on the near side of Gîte d'Étape La Trace and head southeast over open meadow.

About 30 minutes out, veer right as the track joins the GR9B, goes under an electricity pylon and heads southwest. Crosses a recently felled area to plunge into forest. Excellent waymarking will guide you to Lélex. After an hour, a large **grassy glade**, speckled in spring with wild narcissuses, makes a pleasant rest stop. After a brief, steep ascent and at the end of a second meadow are the foundations of a two dilapidated stone houses and, implausibly, the carcass of an old Panhard, a classic 1950s saloon car.

A couple of minutes later, turn left along a narrow footpath. Yet another open patch offers the first clear views over to Colomby de Gex and the bare crests of the valley's eastern flank, to be savoured on Day 2.

In spring and early summer, clearings are bright with wildflowers: yellow primroses, buttercups, gentians, trolles and narcissus. In many such meadows, the remains of an old stone building are a reminder that the days of pasturage on these slopes are not so distant. Up until WWII, grass grew in profusion and the slopes were as free of trees as those on the opposite, eastern flank. But once cattle were no longer grazed, the forest rapidly reasserted itself on the more sheltered western face.

Notice too the old, crumbling boundary walls, built perpendicular to the valley. Unlike many areas in the Jura, where the forest is literally communal (belonging to the *commune*), the wooded slopes of the Valserine are divided into private holdings. Cutting property lines across the valley meant that each landowner had a share of the river and a right to its fishing, a slice of fertile river bank, a tranche of forest for firewood and building materials, and upland pasture for summer grazing.

Half an hour beyond the ruined pair of houses, go straight where the track meets a wide dirt road beside a green metal cabin, ignoring a sign for Lélex that points downhill. Turn left 200m later at a sign, 'Les Trois Cheminées', to cross a grassy knoll and head away southwest up a cart track. Around 25 minutes later, fork left along a delightful grassy path at a battered wooden sign for Lélex – which you also ignore. After 30 minutes, turn left at a T-junction, signed Lélex and Le Truchet, to begin the long descent to the valley floor. After a further 15 minutes, turn left again to pick up the main GR9.

From here on, every junction, major or minor, tempting or unremarkable, has its wooden signpost. As you lose elevation, ash, maple and hazel trees, abundant on lower, more protected slopes, begin to assert themselves among the beech and spruce.

At the brow of a short, sharp rise, make a 50m diversion to the viewpoint of Le Truchet (1188m) with its plunging views of the Valserine and Lélex, dominated by the chain of bald crests to the east.

Above the Valserine Valley

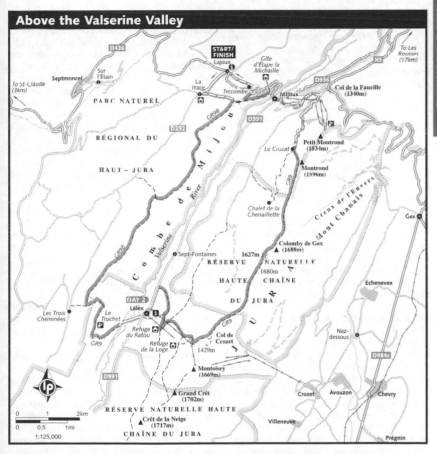

The route soon turns sharp left (east) to continue descending along a well-banked path. Just before another signed (abrupt) left turn for Lélex, a circular cistern is another reminder that the days of cattle grazing in thick wood are not all that distant. Five minutes later, turn left along a wide, stony track and left again after about 20 minutes onto a bitumen road to cross the Valserine River and reach Lélex.

Lélex

The **tourist office** (☎ 04 50 20 91 43) is at the base of the *téléférique*.

Mme Vacher's excellent **Gîte d'étape** (☎ 04 50 20 90 98; giteartisanatvacher@free .fr; open year-round; dorm beds €10) is a bargain and has a self-catering kitchen.

Hôtel Crêt de la Neige (☎ 04 50 20 90 15; maryline.grospiron@wanadoo.fr; doubles €32, with shower or toilet €42, with bathroom €48, half board €35.50-45.50; menus €14.50-21; open 20 Jun–mid-Sep) – a trim and walker-friendly Logis de France – also runs a fine **restaurant**.

Crêperie le Dahu (☎ 04 50 20 95 72; open Jul & Aug plus ski season), near the *téléférique*, is something of a misnomer – it does more

Small-Time Smugglers

Until the 1950s the Valserine Valley, its north–south axis parallel to and west of the Franco–Swiss frontier, was a recognised customs-free zone. In the days before winter skiers and summer walkers brought greater wealth, local farmers and woodcutters supplemented a meagre income from the land by a little small-time smuggling. Walking minor trails through dense woodland, they bore goods into France from Switzerland, where the duty levied was low or negligible. Their packs were stashed with items such as tobacco, playing cards, matches, chocolate, sugar, coffee and watches, all of which brought a higher price in France.

than the humble pancake. The staff whips up sandwiches (€2.50 to €3.50), salads (€7), *diots au vin blanc* (sausage, potato, onion and salad; €11) and other simple mains.

A further 45 minutes' uphill walking or a *téléférique* ride brings you to **Refuge de la Loge** (see Day 2).

Day 2: Lélex to Lajoux

5¼–5¾ hours, 19km

If you want to omit the first strenuous hour, you *might* be lucky enough to find the *téléférique* running from Lélex (900m) to 1450m, just below the Col de Crozet, though its operation recently has been limited to weekends in July and August.

Before leaving Lélex notice how, typically for a Jura village, the north façade of many of the older houses – the side that bears the force of the dominant winter winds and lashing rain – is faced with hundreds of *tavaillons* (small protective shingles) usually in wood, sometimes in beaten tin. These days, they're rarely maintained or repaired so many look as though they're moulting or peeling away.

From the tourist office, walk north up the D991 for 400m. Just beyond a shop, L'Etabli, go right up a narrow lane (look out for a sign, 'Crêt de la Neige par l'Armion', placed – unhelpfully – on the left-hand side of the D991) and, at the farm of Les Cornes, head up a steep grassy path into the forest.

After around 30 minutes of unremitting uphill climbing, the route, brightly blazed

in red and yellow, emerges from the trees and turns right at a T-junction. Passing under the cables of the *téléférique* and a drag lift, it picks up the GR9 again. Just beyond the private Refuge du Ratou (more often closed than open and not a realistic overnight option) leave the Crêt de la Neige route and keep following the wide dirt track around to the left (northeast), staying with it as it wriggles under the *téléférique* cables and back again. Alternatively and more pleasurably, just head straight up the grassy slope. (The GR9 follows a sizable dogleg to the east to pass by **Refuge de la Loge** (☎ 04 50 20 90 46; dorm beds €7.50, half board €22.50; open mid-Dec–Oct).

Allow 1¼ to 1½ hours for the slog from Lélex to the top of the *téléférique* and the welcome and welcoming **Bar-Restaurant La Catheline** (open Jul & Aug, Dec-Mar) for a well-merited drink. Continue along the dirt track, being sure not to omit a signed 100m detour to **Col de Crozet** (1429m) for a first, fine view of Lake Geneva. Back on the track, you enter the Réserve Naturelle de la Haute Chaîne du Jura, a nature reserve of 107.8 sq km, where walkers are asked to stick to designated trails.

The rich upland pasture – dimpled, rolling and treeless – is a delight all the forest. As you progress, each gap in the skyline to the east gives glimpses of Lake Geneva, the long gash of Geneva airport, the city beyond and the high Alps on the far side of the lake.

The footpath is faint in places but the GR waymarking, by means of calf-height wooden posts, is excellent – except where cows and their calves have bowled them over!

Once around the rim of a small hollow, there's an abrupt but brief ascent to the rounded summit of an unnamed hill. From this peak, follow a crumbling limestone wall that drops without a kink to the intervening saddle (1627m), then rises up to **Colomby de Gex** (1688m), topped by a rusting metal pylon commemorating some long-forgotten congress, reached after around 2½ hours.

The wraparound **view** is breathtaking. To the southeast is Geneva with its fountain. Looking north, the telecommunications tower at the peak of Petit Montrond tests the air like a giant thermometer, while the bulbous dome on the top of La Dôle awaits some celestial golfer. Far to the south is Crêt de la Neige, undistinguished in appearance yet the highest point in the massif, while to its southwest rises the pointed peak of Crêt de Chalam. You don't have to take all this in at once; from here until Montrond, the path follows the cliff's edge, from which the vistas are consistently magnificent.

The small cave near Chalet de la Chenaillette, a working farm left of the route, was once used as an ice house and, in summer, storage for fresh milk and cheeses.

Just after the first of two unnamed hills, recognisable by its cairn and trig point, the route leaves the nature reserve. Ten minutes later, it passes over the second hill and continues to **Montrond** (1596m). From here, you can see Lajoux to the northwest, sitting in a swathe of pasture surrounded by forest.

Descend northwest to pass **Le Crozat**, a farm selling fresh cheese. Pick up the stony track leading northeast from it. Just after passing under the cables of a drag lift, turn left on a grassy footpath. Five minutes later, go straight over a bitumen road and, on meeting it for a second time, turn right along it.

At the first buildings of the ski station of **Col de la Faucille**, turn left down route Royale, a wide stony track. After 25 minutes of easy descent, go right down a narrow, rocky footpath, cutting off a significant bend in the track and rejoining it a few minutes later. Turn right and, a couple of minutes later, left to pass through **Mijoux** along rue Royale.

Mijoux has several **bars** and **cafés** where you can refresh yourself before the final ascent to Lajoux. Cross the Valserine River, take a small lane beside the church and turn left at a T-junction just beyond. Should you be tempted to postpone the last leg to Lajoux until the next day, **Gîte d'Étape la Michaille** (☎ 04 50 41 32 45; dorm beds €15, doubles with bathroom €44, half board €31) lies temptingly alongside the route – and, should you so wish, they'll even hire you a donkey to get you and your pack up to Lajoux!

Beside the gîte, follow a footpath that ascends steadily west below a meadow then into deep woodland.

About 15 minutes later, turn sharp right up a minor trail. Where this meets the D436 from Mijoux, follow the road for 100m then veer left onto a track, which re-crosses the highway a couple of minutes later. Pass by the farm of Trecombe and head along a level track to reach Lajoux 15 minutes later.

Other Walks

MASSIF DES VOSGES
Around Alsatian Vineyards
Riquewihr (p322), the end of the four-day Crête des Vosges walk in Alsace, is also the main stop on a 14km, 3½- to 4-hour circular stroll that takes in six of Alsace's premier wine-producing villages, plus a memorial to a major WWII battle. Ask at Riquewihr's tourist office for the brochure *Le Sentier Viticole des Grands Crus*, a plan of the route that includes information, in French, about the various *crus*, or named wines – white, fruity and full of subtle flavours – through whose vineyards the walk passes. It's a walk you can undertake at any time; September and October, when the grape harvest is under way, are the optimum months.

BURGUNDY
Canal du Nivernais
Running through the *département* of Nièvre, in Burgundy, this 107km circuit from Clamecy to Vézelay (p333), is usually divided into five or six days. Mostly easy walking, it follows the canal and returns via a tranche of the GR13. Ask for the pamphlet *Sentier du Flottage du Bois* at Nièvre tourist offices or contact **Randonièvre** (☎ 03 86 36 92 98; www.nievre-sur-mesure.com).

THE JURA
Métabief & Le Mont d'Or
From the small winter ski and summer sports resort of Métabief in the Jura, you can make a magnificent 16.5km, 4½- to five-hour circuit that dips into Switzerland, then takes in some splendid ridge walking up to Le Mont d'Or, on to Le Morond and back down to the village. The route's covered in full on the IGN 1:25,000 map No 3426OT *Mouthe Métabief*. The locally produced pamphlet in French, *Guide de Randonnées Pédestres au Départ de Métabief Mont d'Or*, describes the route in full – and also enough alternatives for a fulfilling week and more of walking in the area.

Travel Facts

TOURIST OFFICES
Local Tourist Offices

Every city, town and village has either an *office de tourisme* (a local government-run tourist office) or a *syndicat d'initiative* (a tourist office run by local business people). Both have an avalanche of information about places to stay and eat and a local map; you'll probably need to ask for specialised walking information. Some will exchange foreign currency, especially when banks are closed, though rarely at a favourable rate. Many will make hotel reservations for a small fee.

Tourist Offices Abroad

French government tourist offices (usually called Maisons de la France) have a vast array of printed information about France; or for a full listing check the Net: www.franceguide .com. The offices abroad include:

Australia (☎ 02-9231 5244; *france@bigpond.net.au; 25 Bligh St, 20th floor, Sydney, NSW 2000*)
Ireland (☎ 01560 235 235; *frenchtouristoffice@eircom.net; 30 Merrion St Upper, Dublin 2*)
UK (☎ 09068 244 123 0.60p/min; *info.uk@franceguide.com 178 Piccadilly, London W1J 9AL*)
USA (☎ 410-286 8310; *www.info-france-usa.org 444 Madison Ave, 16th floor, New York, NY 10022-6903*)

VISAS & DOCUMENTS
Visas

EU nationals are free of entry requirements, and citizens of Australia, the USA, Canada and New Zealand do not need a visa to visit France as tourists for up to three months.

Travel Insurance

Buy a policy that generously covers you for medical expenses, theft or loss of luggage and tickets, and cancellation of and delays in your travel arrangements. It may be worth taking out cover for mountaineering activities and the cost of rescue. Check your policy doesn't *exclude* walking as a dangerous activity.

Buy travel insurance as early as possible to ensure you'll be compensated for unforseen accidents or delays. If items are lost or stolen get a police report immediately – otherwise your insurer might not pay up.

For information about medical cover see p57 in the Health & Safety chapter.

Driving Licence

Many non-European driving licences are valid in France, but it's still a good idea to carry your International Driving Permit (IDP) with you. It can make life much simpler if you want to hire cars and motorbikes. It is invalid unless accompanied by your original licence. An IDP can be obtained for a small fee from your local automobile association.

Travel Discounts

A Hostelling International (HI) card is necessary only at official *auberges de jeunesse* (youth hostels); see Accommodation (p42). HI members are entitled to a range of discounts on travel, visits to museums, car hire and much else.

An International Student Identity Card (ISIC; www.istc.org) is available to full-time students and is issued by Student & Youth Travel Offices around the world. In Paris contact **OTU Voyages** (☎ 0805 11 37 21; *www.otu.fr - French only; 30 av Georges Bernanos; metro St-Michel, line 4*); the cost is €12. The card paves the way for discounted air and ferry travel, among other things.

The International Youth Travel Card (IYTC) is for people under 26 who are not students; the International Teacher Identity Card (ITIC) is for teachers at recognised institutions (working at least 18 hours per week). Both may be obtained from Student and Youth Travel Offices.

Copies

All important documents (passport, credit cards, travel-insurance policy, driving licence, etc) should be photocopied before you leave home. Leave one copy at home and keep another with you, separate from the originals.

EMBASSIES
French Embassies

Australia (☎ 02-6216 0100; www.ambafrance-au .org; 6 Perth Ave, Yarralumla, ACT 2600)

Ireland (☎ 01-260 1666; www.ambafrance-ie .org; 36 Ailesbury Rd, Ballsbridge, Dublin 4)

UK (☎ 020-7201 1000; www.frenchembassy.org .uk; 58 Knightsbridge, London SW1X 7JT)

USA (☎ 202-944 6000; visas-washington@ amb-wash .fr; 4101 Reservoir Rd NW, Washington DC 20007)

Embassies in France

Australia (☎ 01 40 59 33 00; www.austgov.fr; 4 rue Jean Rey, 75015 Paris)

Ireland (☎ 01 44 17 67 00, fax 44 17 67 60; 16 rue Rude, 75116 Paris)

UK (☎ 01 44 51 31 00; www.amb-grande bretagne.fr; 35 rue de Faubourg St-Honoré, 75383 Paris)

USA (☎ 01 43 12 22 22; www.amb-usa.fr; 2 av Gabriel, 75008 Paris)

CUSTOMS

The usual allowances apply to duty-free goods purchased at airports or on ferries outside the EU: tobacco (200 cigarettes or 250g of loose tobacco); alcohol (1L of strong spirits or 2L of less than 22% alcohol by volume and 2L of wine); 500g of coffee; 100g of tea; 50g of perfume.

Do not confuse these with duty-paid items, including alcohol and tobacco, that is bought at normal shops in another EU country and brought into France, where certain goods are more expensive. The allowances are particularly generous: you are allowed to bring with you 800 cigarettes, 90L of wine or 110L of beer (but can you fit it all in one backpack?).

Duty-free shopping within the EU was abolished in mid-1999 so that you can't buy duty-free goods in France and take them straight to the UK.

MONEY
Currency

France's official currency is the euro. One euro is divided into 100 cents or centimes. Coins come in denominations of one, 25, 10, 20 and 50 centimes; notes in five, 10, 20, 50, 100, 200 and 500 euros.

Exchange Rates

A good currency converter is www.oanda .com. At the time of going to print, exchange rates were:

country	unit	euro (€)
Australia	A$1	0.61
Canada	C$1	0.61
New Zealand	NZ$1	0.53
UK	UK£1	1.44
USA	US$1	0.78

Exchanging Money

Cash Banks and exchange bureaus (bureaux de change) often give a better rate for travellers cheques than they offer for cash. Post offices that exchange travellers cheques give a good rate, but rates at the exchange offices on major train stations are generally poor.

In big cities, exchange bureaus are faster and easier, are open longer hours and give better rates than banks.

Travellers cheques The most flexible variety are issued by AmEx (in US dollars or euros) and Visa (in euros) – they can be changed at many post offices, commercial banks and exchange bureaus. Remember that you won't be able to pay most bills with travellers cheques directly, even if they're denominated in euros.

ATMs The cheapest and most convenient way of changing money is via Automated Teller Machines (ATMs) – known most commonly in French as points d'argent. These days you'll find at least one ATM even in quite small towns, sometimes hidden away in the post office.

Credit Cards The most widely accepted card in France is Visa (Carte Bleue) followed by

MasterCard (Access or Eurocard). AmEx cards are useful at more upmarket establishments and allow you to withdraw cash at certain ATMs, and at AmEx offices. Don't assume that you can pay for a meal or a budget hotel with a credit card – ask first.

On the Walk
You'll definitely need cash to pay your way at *refuges* and at many *gîtes d'étape*, so our advice is to always carry enough cash to cover such costs during multiday walks.

Costs
Transport costs can wreak havoc with your budget, but needn't be ruinous if you use public transport when possible. Two people travelling together can keep accommodation costs low as single-room rates are not much lower than doubles (see also Accommodation, p42). Apart from transport, you can live comfortably on €25 to €45 per day.

Typical daily expenses might include:

item/service	cost (€)
camping ground (tent & person)	10
night at hostel/*gîte d'étape*	12-18
B&B (per person sharing)	25
two-course dinner at modest restaurant	18
baguette and filling	3.70
espresso coffee	1.70
glass of wine	4
glass of beer	3

Tipping
French law requires that restaurant, café and hotel bills include the service charge (usually 10% to 15%), so a *pourboire* (tip) is neither necessary nor, usually, expected. Most people do leave a few euros in restaurants unless the service was abysmal. It's rare to tip in cafés or bars after just a coffee or beer.

Taxes & Refunds
France's VAT is 19.6% on most goods sold except food, medicine and books, for which it's 5.5%, though up to 33% for watches and cameras. If you're not an EU resident, you can obtain a refund of most of the VAT (TVA in French) provided that you're over 15; you'll be spending less than six months

in France; you purchase goods (not more than 10 of the same item) worth at least €175 (tax included) at a single shop; and the shop offers *vente en détaxe* (duty-free sales). The procedure is tediously bureaucratic and the refund may take its time in reaching your bank account.

POST & COMMUNICATIONS
Post
Even villages in relatively remote areas have a post office *(La Poste)*, though opening hours may shorter than those in towns and cities (see Business Hours, opposite).

It costs €0.41 to send a letter or postcard within France, €0.46 to European destinations (including the UK), €0.67 to North America and €0.79 to Australia and New Zealand. A packet of 10 prepaid envelopes for local use will set you back €5.60, or €6.40 for the same to international destinations.

A €0.46 charge is levied on each item of *poste-restante* mail (up to 20g) you collect. You'll need to present your passport or national ID card when picking up mail.

Telephone
All public telephones in France are card-operated; France Telecom phone boxes are in all but the tiniest hamlets in remote areas.

Phonecards The simplest option is France Telecom's widely available *télécarte*. They cost €7.40 for 50 units and €14.60 for 100 units; one unit represents three minutes (€0.18 worth) for a local call or 39 seconds for a call beyond the local area. Calls to international numbers are much more expensive (eg, €0.34 per minute to the UK).

Alternatively for international calls, buy France Telecom's *Le Ticket de téléphone*

Useful Numbers
The following telephone numbers are toll-free.

EU-wide emergency services	☏ 112
SAMU medical treatment/ambulance	☏ 15
Police	☏ 17
Fire brigade	☏ 18
Directory assistance within France (operator may not speak English)	☏ 12

international (€7.50). This gives you 50 minutes for calls to Europe (including the UK) and North America, or 25 minutes to Australia and New Zealand.

Mobile Phones France uses GSM 900/1800 which is compatible with the rest of Europe, Australia and New Zealand, but not with North American GSM 1900. If you have a GSM phone check with your service provider about using it in France and beware of calls being routed internationally, which are very expensive for a 'local' call. Mobile phone numbers in France begin with 06.

As a visitor you could consider buying a phone kit with a mobile phone number and rechargeable card. The major providers are **Bouygues** (☎ 0 810 63 01 00; www.bouygtel .com), France Telecom's **Orange** (☎ 0 800 83 08 00; www.orange.fr) and **SFR** (www.sfr.fr). All three websites include a map showing their coverage of the country – excellent in lowland areas, patchy in the mountainous areas of the Alps and the Pyrenees

Email
At 800 post offices across France, a Cyberposte – a card-operated Internet terminal – is provided for public use. Use is restricted to post office *(La Poste)* hours; buy a rechargeable card at the counter. €7 gives you an hour's connection time. Additional hours cost €4. For a list of post offices with a Cyberposte, check www.illiclic.com (French only).

Internet cafés, found in almost all towns and many villages, will probably have a wider range of opening hours than the post office; rates vary but are competitive with Cyberposte – around €3 for 30 minutes.

TIME
France uses the 24-hour clock – 15.30 is 3.30pm, 21.50 is 9.50pm, 00.30 is 12.30am and so on. The country is on Central European Time, GMT/UTC plus one hour. During daylight-saving time, from the last Sunday in March to the last Sunday in October, France is GMT/UTC plus two hours. Without taking daylight-saving time into account, when it's noon in Paris it's 6am in New York, 11am in London and 9pm in Sydney.

ELECTRICITY
France, like the rest of continental Europe, runs on 220V at 50Hz AC. In the USA and Canada, the 110V supply is at 60Hz. Your 220V appliance may be plugged into a French outlet with a plug adapter but its 110V cousin needs a transformer. While it's easy enough to buy transformers in electrical supply shops, you may run into problems when you try to plug it in.

BUSINESS HOURS
Business hours are regulated by the limit of 35 hours on the working week. French law requires that most businesses close on Sunday. Exceptions include grocery shops, *boulangeries*, *patisseries* and tourist enterprises. Other businesses open daily except Sunday and often Monday; some close Saturday afternoon too. Lunch breaks commonly last an hour between noon and 3pm.

Banks usually open Monday to Friday or Tuesday to Saturday; lunch breaks are the norm. Post offices generally open on weekdays, with perhaps a lunch break, and on Saturday morning. National museums close on Tuesday, local museums on Monday, and often also at lunchtime.

There are both permanent and seasonal tourist offices and national park offices. The permanent ones are usually open daily during summer and for 5½ or six days the rest of the year. The seasonal offices are usually in small towns or near the edge of national parks and are only open in summer.

Many businesses shut up shop during July and August when owners and employees head for the hills or the beaches on holiday.

PUBLIC HOLIDAYS
The following *jours fériés* (public holidays) are observed in France:

New Year's Day *Jour de l'An* 1 January – parties in larger cities
Easter Sunday & Monday *Pâques & lundi de Pâques* Late March/April
May Day *Fête du Travail* 1 May – traditional parades
Victoire 1945 8 May – the Allied victory in Europe that ended WWII

Ascension Thursday *L'Ascension* May – celebrated on the 40th day after Easter
Pentecost/Whit Sunday & Whit Monday *Pentecôte & Lundi de Pentecôte* Mid-May to mid-June – seventh Sunday after Easter
Bastille Day/National Day *Fête National* 14 July – *the* national holiday
Assumption Day *L'Assomption* 15 August
All Saints' Day *La Toussaint* 1 November
Remembrance Day *Le onze novembre* 11 November – WWI armistice
Christmas *Noël* 25 December

Most shops and museums (but not restaurants or *boulangeries*) are closed on public holidays. When a holiday falls on a Tuesday or Thursday, many French people take the Monday or Friday off as well, making a four-day weekend. Almost all cities and larger towns, and many villages and small towns, host at least one annual *fête* (festival) to honour anything from the local saint to the year's garlic crop. These are universally popular, placing a high premium on accommodation; contact the local tourist office well in advance if you're operating a tight timetable.

Getting There & Away

AIR

Many airlines link Paris with every corner of the globe; international flights also operate to and from several regional airports.

It's likely that you'll arrive in France at one of Paris' airports: Aéroport d'Orly, 18km south of central Paris or, more likely, Aéroport Roissy Charles de Gaulle, 30km northeast of the city centre. A third airport at Beauvais, 81km to the north, is used by charter flights and by Ryanair. For details of connections into the city from the airports, see p65 in the Paris Region chapter.

The UK & Ireland

Direct flights to Paris operate from most British regional airports. French provincial airports served include Lyon, Bordeaux, Marseille and Nice. From Dublin you can fly direct to Paris and a few regional cities.

Fare deals offered by the budget airlines can be very attractive.

The main carriers are:

Air France (☎ 0845 359 1000; www.airfrance.co.uk)
British Airways (☎ 0870 850 9850; www.britishairways.com)
British Midland (☎ 0870 6070 555; www.flybmi.com)
easyJet (☎ 0871 7500 100; www.easyjet.co.uk)
Ryanair (☎ 1570 22 44 99; www.ryanair.ie)

Continental Europe

Air France is the major operator, though all other national carriers (Alitalia, Lufthansa, KLM and so on) fly to Paris and regional airports.

North America

The range of flights across the North Atlantic is vast. Among the major carriers are:

Air France (☎ 800-237 2747; www.airfrance.com/us)
American Airlines (☎ 1-800-433-7300; www.aa.com)
Continental Airlines (☎ 1-800-523-FARE; www.continental.com)
Delta Airlines (☎ 800-241-4141; www.delta.com)

Best-Value Air Tickets

For short-term travel, it's usually cheaper to travel mid-week and to take advantage of short-lived promotional offers. Return tickets usually work out cheaper than two one-way tickets.

Booking through a travel agent or via airlines' websites is generally the cheapest way to get tickets. However, while online ticket sales are fine for a simple one-way or return trip on specified dates, they're no substitute for a travel agent who is familiar with special deals and can offer all kinds of advice.

Buying tickets with a credit card should mean you get a refund if you don't get what you paid for. Go through a licensed travel agent, who should be covered by an industry guarantee scheme.

Whatever your choice, make sure you take out travel insurance (see p340).

Australia & New Zealand

A small number of companies operate flights to Paris. From New Zealand the best route will usually be via Asia.

The major carriers include:

Qantas (☎ 13 13 13; www.qantas.com.au)
Singapore Airlines (☎ 02 93 500 100; www.singaporeair.com)
Thai Airways (☎ 02 9251 1922; www.thaiair.com)

Baggage Restrictions

Airlines impose tight restrictions on carry-on baggage. No sharp implements of any kind are allowed onto the plane, so pack items such as pocket knives, camping cutlery and first-aid kits into your checked luggage.

If you carry a camping stove, remember that airlines also ban liquid fuels and gas cartridges from *all* baggage, both check-in and carry-on. Empty all fuel bottles; buy what you need at your destination. Some airlines have further regulations about carrying stoves and fuel bottles – even empty ones. Check before flying.

LAND
Bus

Buses are slower and less comfortable than trains, but they are cheaper, especially if you qualify for a discount by being under 26 or over 60, or pick up one of the periodic discount fares. Return tickets cost about 20% less than two one-ways; 30-day advance return fares are particularly attractive. During July and August make reservations at least two working days in advance.

Eurolines (☎ 08705 8080 80; www.gobycoach.com), a consortium of 31 coach companies, runs coach services from London's Victoria coach station to its base in the Paris suburb of Bagnolet (Metro Galliéni, line 3); the journey takes eight hours 45 minutes.

Eurolines (Paris ☎ 01 43 54 11 99; www.eurolines.fr) links Paris and numerous other French cities and towns with Western and central Europe and Scandinavia.

Intercars' Paris office (☎ 01 42 19 99 35; www.intercars.fr - French only) handles services between Paris and Berlin. **Intercars' Nice office** (☎ 04 93 80 08 70) looks after Nice to London, Berlin and Amsterdam (and other) services.

Train

Rail services link France with every country in Europe; timetables are available from major train stations in France and abroad.

Eurostar UK (☎ 08705 186 186; www.eurostar.com) takes only two hours 35 minutes (excluding the one-hour time difference to go from London to Paris via Ashford, the Channel Tunnel and Calais-Frethun). There are several departures daily throughout the year. Book ahead to take advantage of attractive discount fares.

Eurotunnel (☎ 08705 35 35 35; www.eurotunnel.com) shuttle trains carry cars, motorcycles, bicycles and coaches from Folkestone through the Tunnel to Coquelles, 5km southwest of Calais. Frequent daily services operate year-round. Prices vary with market demand and are most expensive during July and August. Reservations are mandatory.

Thalys (bookings Mon-Fri ☎ 0825 84 25 97; www.thalys.com) is a daily international TGV (high-speed) service linking Paris' Gare du

Nord with Amsterdam, Brussels and Cologne. Contact **Rail Europe** (www.raileurope.com) for information and tickets. In France ticketing is handled by Thalys and **SNCF** (French ☎ 08 92 35 35 35, English ☎ 08 92 35 35 39).

Artesia (www.raileurope.com) is a service operated jointly by SNCF and Ferrovie dello Stato, the Italian state railways. Daylight services link Paris' Gare de Lyon, Turin and Milan (six hours 40 minutes) and you can travel overnight from Paris' Gare de Bercy to Florence, Venice and Rome.

SEA
UK & Ireland
Reservations and tickets for ferry travel from the UK and Ireland are available from most local travel agents. Children aged four to somewhere between 12 and 15 travel for half to two-thirds of the adult fare.

Fares vary widely according to seasonal demand; tickets can cost far more in July and August than at other times. To take advantage of promotional fares, you may have to reserve 24 hours or more in advance. Discounts may be available to holders of some or all of the rail passes (see p348).

The following ferry companies operate those services most likely to tie in with the walks described in this guide.

Brittany Ferries (UK reservations ☎ 08703 665 333; www.brittany-ferries.com) Plymouth to Roscoff, Portsmouth to St-Malo (Brittany), Cork to Roscoff

Irish Ferries (Ireland reservations ☎ 1890 31 31 31; www.irish-ferries.ie) Rosslare to Cherbourg (Normandy) and Roscoff (Brittany)

P&O Portsmouth (☎ 08705 20 20 20; www .poports mouth.com) Portsmouth to Le Havre

Italy
Between April and October, scheduled ferry boats link Corsica with the Italian mainland ports of Genoa, Livorno and Savona, and Porto Terres on neighbouring Sardinia. The season is a tad shorter for smaller boats that yo-yo between Bonifacio and Santa Teresa di Gallura on Sardinia.

Several companies have services over these routes, with Corsica Ferries and Moby Lines the main operators.

Corsica Ferries (France ☎ 08 25 09 50 95; Italy - Livorno ☎ 0586 88 13 80, Savona, 019 215 62 47; www.corsicaferries.com) Ferries to/from Livorno (from Bastia, April to early November) and Savona (from Bastia, Calvi & Île Rousse, April to September) in Italy

La Méridionale (CMN; France ☎ 08 10 20 13 20; www.cmn.fr) Ferries (April to October) to/from Propriano and Ajaccio to Porto Terres (Sardinia)

Moby Lines (Corsica ☎ 04 95 34 84 94; Italy ☎ 010 254 15 13, 0565 93 61; www.mobylines .it) Ferries (May to September) to/from Bastia to Genoa and Livorno (mainland Italy) and boats (April to September) to/from Bonifacio and Santa Teresa di Gallura (Sardinia)

Saremar (Corsica ☎ 04 95 73 00 96; Sardinia ☎ 0565 90 89 33; www.traghettiservice.com /saremar) Sardinia's public ferry line; daily sailings to/from Bonifacio and Santa Teresa di Gallura (April to September)

From Livorno (near Pisa and Florence) it's a two-hour voyage to Bastia; a Propriano–Porto Terres trip takes 3½ hours; Genoa–Bastia is a 6½-hour crossing; and Savona to Bastia/Calvi takes six/eight hours.

Fares from mainland Italy are lower than from mainland France. Corsica Ferries charge €40 to €110 to transport a small car one way and upwards of €16/23 per person (up to €33/33 in high season) on a day/night crossing from Savona to Bastia, Calvi or Île Rousse. Passengers sailing with La Méridionale to Ajaccio or Propriano from Porto Terres pay €19, plus €35 for a car.

Port taxes are approximately another €6 per passenger and €5 per car on each of the above-mentioned one-way fares.

Getting Around

Much of France's domestic transport network is owned or subsidised by the government. SNCF operates most of the land transport between *départements*; short-haul bus companies are run by *départements* or local private companies.

AIR
Paris and France's numerous regional airports are linked by the services of a few carriers including:

Air France (☎ 08 20 82 08 20; www
.airfrance.com)
Air Littoral (☎ 08 25 83 48 34; www
.airlittoral.com)

However, travel by high-speed TGV trains
is in many cases faster and easier than by
air, when you allow for the time and trouble of getting to and from airports, often
far from the city centre. Air fares can be
competitive however, especially if you
can take advantage of special last-minute
offers. Any French travel agent can make
bookings for domestic flights and explain
the complicated fare structure. By way of
an example, a Paris–Marseille flight could
set you back at least €70.

BUS

Although inter-regional bus services are
limited, there are plenty of short-distance
services within most départements, especially in rural areas with relatively few train
lines (eg, Brittany). Bus travel is generally
inexpensive and services to even quite remote areas are regular, if not frequent. Many
are more plentiful during school term time
than during holidays, though you'll also find
special high season (July and August) shuttle services in popular areas. Many services
are provided by SNCF where uneconomical
train lines have been terminated; tickets are
available at the guichets (ticket windows)
in the train station. The train timetables
include such bus services, designated by
the word car.

TRAIN

France's excellent rail network, operated
by SNCF, reaches most parts of the country. Although the grandes lignes (main
lines) radiate from Paris like the spokes of
a wheel, journeys between provincial towns
on different spokes need not involve routing
through Paris. However, stringing together
several connections can be a fraught experience and it may ultimately be easier to
travel via the capital.

TGV

The TGV train à grande vitesse (pronounced
'teh-zheh-veh'; meaning 'high-speed train')

is still one of Europe's transport wonders.
Its maximum speed is 300km/h and three
regional routes provide fast, frequent travel
to main junction stations (see also Eurostar
and Thalys, p345). The routes are:

TGV Sud-Est & TGV Midi-Méditerranée link
Paris' Gare de Lyon with the southeast including
the Alps, Avignon, Marseille and Nice
**TGV Atlantique Sud-Ouest & TGV Atlantique
Ouest** link Paris' Gare Montparnasse with
western and southwestern France, including
Brittany, Bordeaux and Toulouse
TGV Nord links Paris' Gare du Nord with Calais
and the Eurostar and Thalys services

Information
Larger train stations have information/
reservation counters where you can obtain
details of travel throughout France.

SNCF's small, free horaires (timetables)
for individual services are readily available
at stations. Two sets are issued annually: for
summer (end of May to end of October) and
winter (November to end of May).

Information about schedules and fares is
available on ☎ 08 90 35 35 35 (in French)
and ☎ 08 90 35 35 39 (in English). Check
www.ter-sncf.com for full timetable information, region by region.

Classes & Sleepers
Most French trains, including TGVs, have
1st- and 2nd-class sections. Overnight trains
(eg, to the Alps) usually have couchettes
(sleeping berths) and, in some cases, 2nd-
class sièges inclinables (reclining seats);
reservations are necessary for both.

Costs & Reservations
For 2nd-class travel, expect to pay at least €6
per 100km for cross-country trips and around
€12 for short hops. Regular return journeys
cost twice the one-way fare. First-class travel
is 50% more expensive than in 2nd class.

Reservation is essential for TGVs and
for a couchette, and highly desirable during
peak holiday periods, especially if you want
a seat on a popular train.

Make reservations at any SNCF ticket
office, by telephone or over the Web at
www.voyages.sncf.com.

Buying a Ticket

At the largest stations there are separate ticket windows for *international*, *grandes-lignes* (long-haul) and *banlieue* (suburban) lines.

You can usually use any one of the major credit cards to pay for train tickets, in person or via the SNCF's website. On almost every station you'll find at least one easy-to-use *billetterie automatique* (ticket machine) that accepts credit cards.

Validating Your Ticket

Before boarding, you *must* validate your ticket in a *composteur*, an orange pillar standing between the ticket windows and the platform. Insert the ticket printed side up and the machine will take a nick out of the side and print the time and date on the back.

Rail Passes

The raft of passes on offer cannot be purchased or used by residents of the country (countries) in which the pass is valid.

The price does not include SNCF reservation fees or *couchette* charges, but they may entitle you to discounts on Eurostar and/or ferry services. They can be purchased in your home country and in Europe, most usefully from **Rail Europe** (*www.raileurope.com*).

Eurail This pass is available in several varieties and offers reasonable value if you'll be doing a lot of train travel. The Eurail Youth Flexipass, for people under 26 on the first day of travel, provides travel on any 10/15 days over a period of two months in 2nd class. People over 26 can only purchase the expensive 1st-class version. The Eurail Selectpass lets you travel in any combination of three to five contiguous countries for between five and 15 days within a two-month period.

France Railpass Sold at major train stations in France (and available from Rail Europe), this pass gives you four days of travel over a period of one month. Additional days, up to a maximum of six, are charged at pro rata.

If you're under 26, the France Youthpass is for you; the France Seniorpass is for travellers over 60.

SNCF Discount Tickets

SNCF offers a range of discount tickets, unencumbered by residency requirements. These tickets give reductions of up to 50%. Full details are available in leaflets at all SNCF stations. The Découverte series is for people aged 12 to 25, for people over 60, and for couples. Découverte J8 and J30 require reservation of tickets eight or 30 days in advance to attract reductions of up to 60%.

CAR & MOTORCYCLE

The advantages of having access to a vehicle – ease of travel where there is no public transport and savings for a couple or group – need to be weighed against the inconvenience of making arrangements to access through-walks, and the fact that the rate of fatalities on French roads is terrifyingly high.

Riders of any type of two-wheel vehicle with a motor must wear a helmet. During the day, headlights on bikes of more than 125cc must be illuminated.

Documents

All drivers must always carry:

- a national ID card or passport
- a valid driver's licence
- car ownership papers, known as a *carte grise* (grey card)
- proof of third-party (liability) insurance, known as *carte verte* (green card; see http://europa.eu.int/abc/travel). This is available from your insurer.

Road Rules

French law requires all passengers, including those in the back seat, wear seat belts.

Any car entering an intersection, including a T-junction, from a road on your right has *priorité à droite* (right of way). If you're turning left you have to wait for cars coming from your right.

Priorité à droite is suspended at *ronds-points* (roundabouts or traffic circles) where vehicles already in the roundabout have right of way, and on priority roads marked by a yellow diamond with a black diamond in the middle.

North American drivers should remember that turning right on a red light is illegal in France.

French law is very tough on drunk drivers. The police conduct regularly random breathalyser tests in search of drivers with a blood-alcohol concentration above 0.05%. Fines range from €135 to €4500. You can be arrested on the spot.

Speed Limits Unless otherwise indicated a limit of 50km/h applies in all designated built-up areas. Elsewhere the limits are:

- 90km/h (80km/h on wet roads) on undivided N and D motorways/highways
- 110km/h (100km/h on wet roads) on dual carriageways (divided highways)
- 130km/h (110km/h on wet roads; 50 km/h in fog) on *autoroutes* (multilane divided highways)

Costs

Fuel The price very much depends on where you buy it. Supermarket service stations are cheapest, those at rest stops along the autoroutes the most expensive. At the time of writing, *sans plomb* (unleaded) petrol cost around €0.95 per litre and *gazole* (diesel) €0.85 per litre.

Tolls These are charged on almost all autoroutes and many bridges. Some autoroutes have toll plazas every few dozen kilometres; on others a machine issues a ticket to be handed over at a *péage* (toll booth) at the exit, where payment by credit card is possible. Rates per 100km vary according to size of vehicle and between the different autoroute operators; as a rough guide expect to pay around €8 per 100km. Tolls can mount up – as much as €35 for the run from Paris to Grenoble, or €59 from Paris to Nice. Check www.autoroutes.fr, the site of the Association des Sociétés Françaises d'Autoroutes (ASFA) for full details.

BICYCLE

France is a very cycle-friendly country, which is thanks in part to the extensive network of secondary and tertiary roads, many with only light traffic. A combined walking and cycling holiday offers the advantage of a potentially wider range of accessible countryside; for a predominantly walking holiday, a bike can be useful for reaching the start of some walks, beyond the limit of vehicle access.

Indispensable for planning such a visit is Lonely Planet's *Cycling in France* which contains all the practical advice you'll need.

There's usually at least one shop in most towns that rents *vélos tout-terrains* (mountain bikes), popularly known at VTTs for up to €18 per day; a substantial deposit (up to €300) may be required, which you forfeit if the bike is damaged or stolen.

All bicycles must have two functioning brakes, a bell, a red rear reflector and yellow reflectors on the pedals. After sunset and in poor visibility cyclists must turn on a front white light and a rear red one. Cyclists must ride single file when being overtaken.

HITCHING

Hitching is never safe in any country and we don't recommend it. Women travelling alone should be extremely cautious about hitching anywhere.

Of the organisations that can put people looking for rides in touch with drivers heading in the same direction, the best-known and longest-established is **Allostop Provoya** (☎ *01 53 20 42 42 for long-distance rides; 8 rue Rochambeau, Paris; metro Cadet, line 7; open Mon-Sat*).

LOCAL TRANSPORT

France's larger cities and towns are served by excellent public-transport systems: buses universally; metros in Paris, Marseille and Toulouse; and trams in Paris, Strasbourg and Grenoble. Information about routes and fares is usually available at tourist offices and local bus-company information counters.

Taxis are generally expensive but in a few areas you'll have to depend on them to reach the start of a walk if you don't have a car. Taxi ranks are found near the train or bus station in most towns. Expect to pay between €1.30 and €2 per kilometre, depending on the time of day, day of the week and distance travelled. An extra charge may be levied for each piece of baggage.

Language

While the French rightly or wrongly have a reputation for assuming that all human beings should speak French – until WWI it was the international language of culture and diplomacy – you'll find that any attempt to communicate in French will be appreciated. Probably your best bet is to always approach people politely in French, even if the only sentence you know is *Pardon, madame/monsieur/mademoiselle, parlez-vous anglais?* (excuse me, madam/sir/miss, do you speak English?).

An important distinction is made in French between *tu* and *vous*, which both mean 'you'. *Tu* is only used when addressing people you know well, children or animals. When addressing an adult who is not a personal friend, *vous* should be used unless the person invites you to use *tu*. In general, younger people are less likely to insist on this distinction, and they may use *tu* right from the start of a contact. In this guide the polite form is used in most cases; where both forms are given they are noted by the abbreviations 'pol' and 'inf' respectively.

All nouns in French are either masculine or feminine and adjectives reflect the gender of the noun they modify. The feminine form of many nouns and adjectives is indicated by a silent **e** added to the masculine form, as in *ami* and *amie*, the masculine and feminine for 'friend'. In the following phrases we have indicated both the masculine and feminine forms where necessary, separated by a slash, with the masculine form first. The gender of a noun is often indicated by a preceding article: 'the/a/some' *le/un/du* (m), *la/une/de la* (f); or a possessive adjective, 'my/your/his/her', *mon/ton/son* (m), *ma/ta/sa* (f). Unlike English, the possessive adjective in French agrees in number and gender with the thing possessed, eg, *sa mère* (his/her mother).

For a more comprehensive guide to the language, pick up a copy of Lonely Planet's *French phrasebook*. It has pronunciation guides for all the French words and phrases

throughout the book, and covers most of the situations you're likely to encounter while travelling.

Pronunciation

Most letters in French are pronounced more or less the same as their English equivalents. The few examples that may cause confusion are:

j	as the 's' in 'leisure', eg, *jour* (day)
c	before **e** and **i**, as the 's' in 'sit'; before **a**, **o** and **u**, as English 'k'. When underscored with a 'cedilla' (**ç**), it's always pronounced as the 's' in 'sit'.

French has a number of sounds that are difficult for Anglophones to produce. These include:

The distinction between the 'u' sound (as in *tu*) and 'oo' sound (as in *tout*). For both sounds, the lips are rounded and projected forward, but for the 'u' the tongue is towards the front of the mouth, its tip against the lower front teeth, whereas for the 'oo' the tongue is towards the back of the mouth, its tip behind the gums of the lower front teeth.

The nasal vowels. With these the breath escapes partly through the nose and partly through the mouth. There are no nasal vowels in English; in French there are three, as in *bon vin blanc* (good white wine). These sounds occur where a syllable ends in a single **n** or **m**; the **n** or **m** is silent but indicates the nasalisation of the preceding vowel.

The letter **r**. The standard **r** of Parisian French is produced by moving the bulk of the tongue backwards to constrict the air flow in the back of the throat while the tip of the tongue rests behind the lower front teeth. It's similar to the noise some people make before spitting, but with much less friction.

Greetings & Civilities

Good morning.	*Bonjour.* (pol)
Hello.	*Salut.* (inf)
Good evening.	*Bonsoir.*

Good night.	*Bonne nuit.*
Goodbye.	*Au revoir.* (pol)
	À bientôt/À plus tard. (inf)
Please.	*S'il vous plaît.*
Thank you (very much).	*Merci (beaucoup).*
That's fine/You're welcome.	*De rien/Je vous en prie.*
Excuse me.	*Excusez-moi.*
Sorry/Forgive me.	*Pardon.*
Yes.	*Oui.*
No.	*Non.*
OK.	*D'accord.*
How are you?	*Comment allez-vous?* (pol)
	Comment vas-tu/ Comment ça va? (inf)
Fine, thanks.	*Bien/ça va, merci.*
I'm tired.	*Je suis fatigué/e.* (m/f)
And you?	*Et vous?*
What's your name?	*Comment vous appellez-vous?* (pol)
	Comment tu t'appele? (inf)
My name is ...	*Je m'appelle ...*
I'm pleased to meet you.	*Enchanté* (m)/ *Enchantée.* (f)
Where are you from?	*De quel pays êtes-vous?*

Language Difficulties

Do you speak English?	*Parlez-vous anglais?*
I speak a little French.	*Je parle un peu de français.*
I understand.	*Je comprends.*
I don't understand.	*Je ne comprends pas.*

Getting Around

I want to go to ...
Je voudrais aller à ...
I'd like to book a seat to ...
Je voudrais réserver une place pour ...

What time does the ... leave/arrive?	*À quelle heure part/arrive ...?*
bus (city)	*l'autobus*
bus (intercity)	*l'autocar*
plane	*l'avion*
train	*le train*

Signs

Entrée	**Entrance**
Sortie	**Exit**
Chambres Libres	**Rooms Available**
Complet	**No Vacancies**
Renseignements	**Information**
Ouvert/Fermé	**Open/Closed**
Interdit	**Prohibited**
(Commissariat de) Police	**Police Station**
Toilettes, WC	**Toilets**
Hommes	**Men**
Femmes	**Women**

Where is (the) ...?	*Où est ...?*
bus station	*la gare routière*
bus stop	*l'arrêt d'autobus*
train station	*la gare*
ticket office	*le guichet*

I'd like a ... ticket.	*Je voudrais un billet ...*
one-way	*aller simple*
return	*aller-retour*
1st class	*première classe*
2nd class	*deuxième classe*

How long does the trip take?
Combien de temps dure le trajet?
Please let me know when we get to ...
Voulez-vous me dire quand nous arrivons à ...
I'd like to get off at ...
Je veux descendre à ...

left-luggage locker	*consigne automatique*
platform	*le quai*
timetable	*l'horaire*

I'd like to hire ...	*Je voudrais louer ...*
a car	*une voiture*
a bicycle	*un vélo*

Around Town

I'm looking for ...	*Je cherche ...*
an ATM	*un distributeur (de billets)*
a bank	*une banque*
an exchange office	*un bureau de change*
the market	*le marché*

the police	la police
the post office	le bureau de poste/ la poste
a public phone	une cabine télé- phonique
a public toilet	les toilettes
the tourist office	l'office de tourisme/ le syndicat d'initiative

What time does it open/close?
Quelle est l'heure d'ouverture/de fermeture?
I'd like to make a phone call.
Je voudrais téléphoner.

Shopping

bookshop	une librairie
chemist/pharmacy	une pharmacie
laundrette	une laverie
newsagency	une agence de presse
outdoor equipment shop	un magasin de sports et loisirs
supermarket	un supermarché

Accommodation

I'm looking for ...	Je cherche ...
Where is ...?	Ou est-ce qu'il y a ...?
a camping ground	un camping
a gite	une gîte d'étape
the youth hostel	l'auberge de jeunesse
a B&B	une chambre d'hôte
a hotel	un hôtel

What's the address?
Quelle est l'adresse?
Could you write it down, please?
Est ce que vous pourriez l'écrire s'il vous plaît?
Do you have any rooms available?
Est-ce que vous avez des chambres libres?
Do you have any beds available?
Est-ce que vous avez des lits libres?

How much is it ...?	Quel est le prix ...?
per night	par nuit
per person	par personne

| May I see the room? | Est-ce que je peux voir la chambre? |

I'd like to book ...	Je voudrais réserver ...
a bed	un lit
a single room	une chambre pour une personne
a double room	une chambre double
a room with a shower and toilet	une chambre avec douche et WC

I'd like to stay in a dormitory.
Je voudrais coucher dans un dortoir.

I'm going to stay for ...	Je resterai ...
one night	une nuit
three nights	trois nuits

kitchen	la cuisine
sheet	le drap
inner sheet/sleeping bag liner	le sac à viande
blanket	la couverture (f)
pillow	l'oreiller (m)
shower	la douche
tent pitch/site	l'emplacement (m)
token	le jeton (m)

Time & Dates

What time is it?	Quelle heure est-il?
It's 10 am.	Il est dix heures.
It's 10 pm.	Il est vingt-deux heures. ('22 hours')
It's five past six.	Il est six heures cinq.
It's five to six.	Il est six heures moins cinq.
When?	Quand?
today	aujourd'hui
tonight	ce soir
tomorrow	demain
yesterday	hier
all day	toute la journée
in the morning	du matin
in the afternoon	de l'après-midi
in the evening	du soir
public holiday	jour férié

Monday	lundi
Tuesday	mardi
Wednesday	mercredi
Thursday	jeudi
Friday	vendredi
Saturday	samedi
Sunday	dimanche

January	*janvier*
February	*février*
March	*mars*
April	*avril*
May	*mai*
June	*juin*
July	*juillet*
August	*août*
September	*septembre*
October	*octobre*
November	*novembre*
December	*décembre*

Numbers

0	*zéro*
1	*un*
2	*deux*
3	*trois*
4	*quatre*
5	*cinq*
6	*six*
7	*sept*
8	*huit*
9	*neuf*
10	*dix*
11	*onze*
12	*douze*
13	*treize*
14	*quatorze*
15	*quinze*
16	*seize*
17	*dix-sept*
18	*dix-huit*
19	*dix-neuf*
20	*vingt*
21	*vingt et un*
22	*vingt-deux*
30	*trente*
40	*quarante*
50	*cinquante*
60	*soixante*
70	*soixante-dix*
75	*soixante-quinze*
80	*quatre-vingts*
90	*quatre-vingt-dix*
95	*quatre-vingt-quinze*
100	*cent*
1000	*mille*
2000	*deux mille*
one million	*un million*

Emergencies

Help!	*Au secours!*
Call a doctor!	*Appelez un médecin!*
Call the police!	*Appelez la police!*
Careful!	*Attention!*
I'm lost.	*Je me suis égaré/ égarée.* (m/f)
Leave me alone!	*Fichez-moi la paix!*

quarter	*quart*
half	*demi/e* (m/f)
dozen	*douzaine*

Health

I'm sick.
  Je suis malade.
I need a doctor.
  Il me faut un médecin.
Where is the hospital?
  Où est l'hôpital?
It hurts here.
  J'ai une douleur ici.
I've been bitten by a dog.
  J'ai été mordu par un chien.
I have a sprain.
  Je me suis fait une entorse.

antiseptic	*l'antiseptique* (f)
aspirin	*l'aspirine*
blister	*l'ampoule* (f)
diarrhoea	*la diarrhée*
medicine	*le médicament*
nausea	*la nausée*

FOOD & DRINK

breakfast	*le petit déjeuner*
lunch	*le déjeuner*
dinner	*le dîner*
snack	*le casse-croûte*

I'm a vegetarian.	*Je suis végétarien/ végétarienne.* (m/f)
I don't eat meat.	*Je ne mange pas de viande.*
I'd like the set menu.	*Je prends le menu (à prix fixe).*
menu (free choice)	*la carte*
bill	*l'addition*
service charge included	*service compris*

bottle	*bouteille* (f)
cup	*tasse* (f)
fork	*fourchette* (f)
glass	*verre* (m)
knife	*couteau* (m)
plate	*assiette* (f)

bread	*pain* (m)
butter	*beurre* (m)
cheese	*fromage* (m)
chips (french fries)	*frites* (f/pl)
eggs	*oeufs* (m)
jam	*confiture* (f)
oil	*huile* (f)
(thin) pancake	*crêpe* (f)
pasta	*pâtes* (f/pl)
pepper	*poivre* (m)
rice	*riz* (m)
salt	*sel* (m)
sugar	*sucre* (m)

water	*eau* (m)
mineral water	*eau mineral* (m)
orange juice	*jus d'orange* (m)
milk	*lait* (m)
coffee	*café* (m)
decaffeinated	*décaféiné*
tea	*thé* (m)
herbal tea	*tisane* (f)
hot chocolate	*chocolat chaud* (m)

baker	*boulangerie* (f)
butcher	*boucherie* (f)
cheese shop	*fromagerie* (f)
delicatessen	*charcuterie* (f)
grocery store	*épicerie* (f)/ *alimentation* (f)
market	*marché* (m)
supermarket	*supermarché* (m)

a carton of ...	*une barquette de ...*
a slice of ...	*une tranche de ...*
a small piece of ...	*un morceau de ...*

Fruit & Nuts

apple	*pomme*
apricot	*abricot*
blackcurrant	*cassis*
cherries	*cerises*
grapefruit	*pamplemousse*
grapes	*raisins*

peach	*pêche*
pineapple	*ananas*
plum	*prune/mirabelle*
raspberries	*framboises*
strawberries	*fraises*

almonds	*amandes*
chestnuts	*châtaignes/marrons*
hazelnuts	*noisettes*
peanuts	*cacahuètes*
walnuts	*noix*

Meat & Poultry

bacon	*lard*
beef	*boeuf*
chicken	*poulet*
duck	*canard*
ham	*jambon*
kidneys	*rognons*
lamb	*agneau*
meat	*viande*
poultry	*volaille*
rabbit	*lapin*
turkey	*dinde/dindon*
veal	*veau*
venison	*chevreuil*

Fish & Seafood

crayfish	*écrevisses*
fish stew	*bourride*
fish	*poisson*
lobster	*homard*
mussels	*moules*
oysters	*huîtres*
prawns	*crevettes roses*
scallops	*coquilles Saint-Jacques*
seafood	*fruits de mer*
trout	*truite*
tuna	*thon*

Vegetables & Grains

artichoke	*artichaut*
asparagus	*asperges*
beetroot	*betterave*
buckwheat	*sarrasin*
cabbage	*chou*
capsicum (pepper)	*poivron*
cauliflower	*chou-fleur*
celery	*céleri*
chickpeas	*pois chiches*

corn	maïs
cucumber	concombre
french/string beans	haricots verts
garlic	ail
leek	poireau
lettuce	laitue
mushrooms	champignons
onion	oignon
parsley	persil
peas	petits pois
potato	pomme de terre
rye	seigle
vegetables	légumes

Cooking Methods

baked	au four
cooked in a wood-burning oven	au feu de bois
fruit or vegetable purée	coulis
poached	poché
roast	roti
steamed	à la vapeur
stuffed	farci

WALKING
Preparations

Where can we buy food?
Où est-ce qu'on peut acheter de la nourriture?
We'll return in one week.
Nous serons de retour dans une semaine.
Can I leave some things here for a while?
Puis-je laisser des affaires ici pendant quelques temps?
Can you repair this for me?
Pourriez-vous me le/la réparer?

Clothing & Equipment

backpack	sac à dos (m)
battery	pile (f)
(walking) boots	chassures (de montagne) (f)
camera	appareil photo (m)
camp stove	réchaud (m)
cooking fuel (gas)	cartouche de gaz (f)/ camping gaz (m)
cooking pot	marmite (f)/ casserole (f)
compass	boussole (f)

film	film (m)/pellicule (f)
fleece jacket	veste polaire (f)
gloves	gants (m)
map	carte (f)
matches	alumettes (f)
pocket knife	canif (m)
rainjacket	cape de pluie (f)
sleeping bag	sac de couchage or duvet (m)
sleeping mat	tapis de sol (m)
socks	chausettes (f)
sunglasses	lunettes de soleil/ lunettes solaires (f)
tent	tente (f)
toilet paper	papier hygiénique (m)
torch	lampe de poche (f)
walking pole	bâton (m)
warm hat	bonnet (m)
water bottle	gourde (f)

On the Walk

How many kilometres/hours are we from ...?
Nous sommes à combien (de kilometres/ d'heures) de ...?
Does this path go to ...?
Est-ce que ce chemin/sentier mène à ...?
Is there a short cut?
Est-ce qu'il y a un raccourci?
Can you show me on the map?
Pouvez-vous me le montrer sur la carte?
What is this place called?
Comment s'appele ce lieu?
Where have you come from?
D'où arrivez-vous?
How long did it take you?
Ça vous a pris combien de temps?
We're walking from ... to ...
Nous allons de ... à ...
Is there much snow on the pass?
Le col est-il fortement enneigé?
Can the river be crossed?
Est-il possible de franchir la rivière?

Directions

Go straight ahead.	Conduisez tout droit.
Turn left.	Tournez à gauche.
Turn right.	Tournez à droite.
Take the first left.	Empruntez la première à gauche.
one way	aller-descente/ascente

round trip	*aller-retour*	forest	*forêt/bois* (m)
turn-off	*bifurcation* (m)	glacial snowfield	*névé* (m)
ahead	*devant*	glacier	*glacier* (m)
behind	*derrière*	gorge	*gorge* (f)
above	*au-dessus*	highway	*route* (f)
below	*au-dessous*	house/building	*maison* (f)/
before	*avant*		*bâtiment* (m)
after	*après*	hut/chalet	*refuge* (m)
beside	*à côté de*	island	*île* (m)
between	*entre*	lake	*lac* (m)
downstream (from)	*en aval (de)*	landslide	*éboulement* (m)
upstream (from)	*en amont (de)*	lighthouse	*phare* (m)
flat	*plat*	lookout	*belvédère* (f)
steep	*raide*	loop	*boucle* (f)
high	*haut*	moor	*lande* (f)
low	*bas*	moraine	*moraine* (f)
near	*proche/voisin*	mountain	*mont/pic* (m)/
far	*éloigné/loin*		*montagne/tête* (f)
level with	*au niveau de*	mud	*boue* (f)
opposite	*en face de*	pass	*col* (m)
		path	*sentier* (m)
north	*nord*	peninsula	*presqu'île* (m)
south	*sud*	plain	*plaine* (f)/*plan* (m)
east	*est*	plateau	*plateau* (m)
west	*oeust*	pond, pool	*étang* (m)
		ridge	*arête/crête* (f)

Features & Weather

avalanche	*avalanche* (f)	river	*fleuve* (m)/*rivière* (f)
bay/cove	*anse/baie/golfe* (f)	river bank	*rive* (f)
beach	*plage* (f)	rock	*roche* (f)
bend (road, track)	*lacet/virage* (m)	quarry	*carrière* (f)
bog/marsh/swamp	*marais* (f)	road	*chemin* (m)/*rue/voie* (f)
bridge	*pont* (m)	sand	*sable* (m)
cairn	*cairn* (f)	scoria	*scorie* (f)
canal lock	*écluse* (f)	scree	*éboulis* (m)
cape/headland	*cap* (m)/	signpost	*poteau indicateur* (m)
	promontoire (m)	slope	*pente* (f)/*vente* (m)
cave	*caverne/grotte* (f)	snowfield	*champ de neige* (m)
chapel	*chapelle* (f)	spring	*fontaine* (f)
chasm	*gouffre* (m)	spur	*épaulement* (m)
cliff	*falaise* (f)	stream	*courant/ruisseau* (m)
coast	*côte* (f)/*littoral* (m)	stream junction	*confluent* (m)
crag	*rocher* (m)	summit	*cime* (f)/*sommet* (m)
crater	*cratère* (m)	town	*ville* (f)
dam	*barrage* (f)	tree	*arbre* (m)
estuary	*estuaire* (m)	valley	*val* (m)/*vallée/combe/*
farm	*ferme* (f)		*cuvette* (f)
fence	*burrière* (f)	village	*village/hameau* (m)
footbridge	*passerelle* (f)	volcano	*volcan* (f)
ford	*gué* (m)	waterfall	*cascade/chute d'eau* (f)
		waymarker	*balise* (f)

What's the forecast?
Quel est le météo/le prevision de temps?

Tomorrow it will be ...
Demain il fera ...

good weather	*beau temps*
bad weather	*mauvais temps*
clear/fine	*beau*
cloudy	*nuageux/couvert*
cold	*froid/frais*

flood	*inondation* (f)
fog	*brouillard* (m)/ *brume* (f)
hot	*chaud*
ice (icy)	*glâce* (f) *(glâcial)*

lightning	*éclairs* (m)/*foudre* (f)
mist	*brume* (f)
overcast	*couvert*
rain	*pluie* (f)
(It's raining.)	*(Il pleut.)*
snow	*neige* (f)
(It's snowing.)	*(Il neige.)*
storm, gale	*tempête*
sunny	*du soleil, ensoleillé*
thunder	*tonnerre* (f)
thunderstorm	*orage* (f)
wind	*vent* (m)
(It's windy.)	*(Il y a du vent.)*

high tide	*haute marée* (f)
low tide	*basse marée* (f)

Glossary

Here you'll find English terms (denoted by 'Eng') and some of the more commonly encountered French words, including those used in place names on maps. The (m) indicates masculine gender and (f) feminine gender. Words that appear in italics within definitions have their own entries.

abbaye (f) – abbey
aber (m) – estuary
aiguille (f) – needle; sharp rocky peak
alimentation (f) – grocery, food shop
anse (f) – natural harbour or cove; handle
aqueduc (m) – aqueduct
arête (f) – narrow ridge separating two glacial valleys
arribet, arriou (m) – small stream in the Pyrenees
ATM – (Eng) automated teller machine, in French *point d'argent*
auberge (f) – inn, hotel
auberge de jeunesse (f) – youth hostel

baie (f) – bay
balcon (m) – mountain path contouring above a valley floor, normnally above the tree line
balise (f) – waymarker
barrage (m) – dam
bastide (f) – fortified town or village in southwestern France
belvédère (f) – lookout, viewpoint
bergerie (f) – shepherd's hut
bivouac (m) – site for spending the night in the open, without tent or facilities
bocca (f) – mountain pass in Corsica
bois (m) – wood
borie (f) – small stone building; farmhouse in southern France
boulangerie (f) – bakery, bread shop
brasserie (f) – restaurant usually serving food all day; brewery
breton (m) – Breton language; a native of Brittany
buron (m) – shepherd's summertime cabin
butte – (Eng) isolated, steep-sided, flat-topped hill

buvette (f) – refreshment kiosk, serving drinks and snacks

CAF – Club Alpin Français; French Alpine Club
cairn (Eng) – pile of stones, often used to mark a path and/or path junction
calanque (f) – rocky inlet
calvaire (m) – large crucifix, cross
camping (m) – organised camping ground with facilities
camping municipal (m) – municipal camping ground
cap (m) – cape or headland; summit in the Pyrenees
carrefour (m) – crossroads
carte (f) – menu (from which a choice of dishes can be made); map
cascade (f) – waterfall
causse (m) – limestone plateau with low, dense vegetation, in southwestern France
cave (f) – wine cellar
CDT – Comité Départemental du Tourisme; tourism committee of a *département*
chambre d'hôte (f) – bed and breakfast accommodation
charcuterie (f) – delicatessen; the prepared meat it sells
chemin (m) – path
chemin forestier (m) – forest track, track through forested area
cime (f) – mountain summit or peak
cirque (m) – small, high, cup-shaped valley often of glacial origin
cistern – (Eng) underground water reservoir
col (m) – pass; lowest point on a ridge between two peaks
combe (f) – shallow valley
commune (f) – the basic unit of local government in France
corniche (f) – coastal, cliff road; cornice or rock ledge
corrie – (Eng) *cirque*
côte (f) – coast
couderc (m) – enclosed field in southern France
cour (f) – courtyard, square

courbe de niveau (f) – contour interval, the vertical distance between contour lines on a topographical map
crête (f) – narrow rocky ridge

demi-pension (f) – half board; B&B and dinner
département (m) – one of 96 administrative units in France
doline (f) – sheltered dip or bowl in the landscape
dolmen – (Eng) prehistoric burial tomb

eau potable (f) – drinking water
éboulis (m) – scree, large areas of small stones or boulders on mountain slope
église (f) – church
emplacement (m) – tent site
épaulement (m) – spur, subsidiary ridge branching from main ridge
épicerie (f) – small grocery shop
étang (m) – pond or pool

falaise (f) – cliff
ferme-auberge (f) – farm-inns
FFRP – Fédération Française de la Randonnée Pédestre; French Walking Federation
fontaine (f) – fountain or spring
forêt (f) – forest

garrigue (f) – ground cover of aromatic plants; Mediterranean heathland
gare (f) – train station
gare routière (f) – bus station
gave (m) – mountain stream in the Pyrenees
gîte d'étape (f) – hostel-style walkers' accommodation
GR – *grande randonnée*, a trademark of the *FFRP*
grande randonnée (f) – long-distance waymarked walking route
grotte (f) – cave
gué (m) – ford

half board – see *demi-pension*
hôtel de ville (m) – city or town hall
hourquette – steep pass in the Pyrenees

IGN – Institut Géographique National; national mapping authority

île (f) – island
itinéraire (m) – route followed by a path, not necessarily waymarked

jeton (m) – token
jlac (m) – lake

mairie (f) – city or town hall
maison du littoral (f) – coastal information centre
maison du parc (f) – information centre in national or regional natural park
maquis (m) – scrubland vegetation, mainly broad-leaved evergreen shrubs or small trees
marché (m) – market
mas (m) – farmhouse, small hamlet in southern France
menhir – (Eng) a single standing stone, often carved
menu (m) – fixed-price meal of two or more courses
mistral (m) – persistent north wind in southern France
moraine – (Eng) debris left behind by retreating glaciers
moulin à vent (m) – windmill

névé (m) – frozen snow; glacial snowfield

office du Tourisme (m) – tourist information office
ONF – Office National des Forêts; National Forestry Office
oratoire (m) – tiny chapel, often found beside paths or tracks

palud (m) – marsh
parc national (m) – national park
parc naturel régional (m) – regional natural park
pech (m) – hill, mountain (southern France)
petite randonnée (f) – short-distance, waymarked route
phare (m) – lighthouse
pic (m) – mountain peak
piste (f) – trail or slope for skiing
pla (m) – area of flat ground in the Pyrenees; also spelt 'plan'
plage (f) – beach
plat du jour (m) – restaurant's daily special

pont (m) – bridge
portillon (m) – gate
pouy (m) – hill or rise in the Pyrenees; also spelt 'pouey'
PR – *petite randonnée*, a trademark of the FFRP
presque'île (f) – peninsula
puits (m) – (water) well
puy (m) – plug or dome of an extinct volcano

randonneur (m/f) – walker
ravin (m) – ravine or gully
refuge (m) – mountain hostel providing accommodation and usually meals
réserve naturelle (f) – nature reserve
rivière (f) – river
rue (f) – street
ruelle (f) – alley or lane
ruisseau (m) – stream

scorie (f) – scoria; volcanic rock material
sentier (m) – *chemin*
sentier côtier (m) – coastal path
sentier littoral (m) – *sentier côtier*
sentier des douaniers (m) – customs officers' path

serrat or **serre** (f) – long crest or ridge in the Pyrenees
site naturel classé (m) – classified natural site
SNCF – Société Nationale des Chemins de Fer; state-owned railway company
supermarché (m) – supermarket
syndicat d'initiative (m) – small tourist information office, often seasonal

tabac (m) – tobacconist selling newspapers, phonecards and possibly bus tickets
téléférique (m) – cable car or funicular
télésiège (m) – chairlift
tête (f) – literally head but also used for a mountain peak
TGV (m) – train 'à grande vitesse'; high-speed train
torrent (m) – river
trez (m) – (Breton) beach, strand
tree line – (Eng) altitude above which trees cannot survive
true left/right bank – (Eng) side of the river as you look downstream

vallée (f) – valley
vallon (m) – small valley

Index

Text

For a full list of walks and maps see the Table of Walks (pp4–7) and Table of Maps (p8).
For individual mountains and peaks, see under the entry 'mountains & peaks'.

A

Abbaye St-Pierre 148
Abriès 256, 259
accidents 60, *see also*
    emergencies
accommodation 42-4, 324
adder 28
Aiguille des Glaciers 305
Aiguille Noire de Peuterey 307
Aiguilles d'Ansabère 164
Aiguilles de Bavella 216
Aiguilles Rouges 275, 316
air travel
    to/from France 344-5
    within France 346-7
Ajaccio 195-6
Alagnon Valley 120
Albertacce 207-8
Aleppo pine 30
Allanche 121
Alpages de Loriaz 291
alpenrose 29
alpine accentor 25
alpine chough 25
alpine ibex 26
alpine pasqueflower 29
Alpine Route (GR20) 215
alpine snowbell 29
Alps 32
    Northern 273-92, **274**
    Southern 237-72, **238**
Alsace 32
altimeters 55
animals, *see* fauna
Ansabère Valley 164-5, **163**
Apt 231, 233
Archiane 245
Ardennes Plateau 22
Arènes de Lutèce 67
Argentière 300, 317
Association for the Protection
    of Wild Animals 35
Aubure 330
Audouin's gull 194
Auvergne 107-33, **108**
Avallon 331-2, **332-3**
Avranches 101-2
Azinières 129

B

Bagnères de Luchon 182-3,
    185, 188
Bagnères de Luchon region
    182-90
Baie du Mont St-Michel 102,
    104
Baisse des Cinq Lacs 270
Ballons des Vosges 320
Balmat, Jacques 283
Barrage des Peïroou 223
Barre des Écrins 248
Basilique Ste-Madeleine 334
Bastia 195
Bavella 201, 204, 216
Bay of Biscay 22
bearded vulture 158, 194,
    265, 285
Beaucaire 221
Beaufort cheese 306
Bédouès 127
Bedous 160-1
beer 256
Beg ar Gador Site Naturel
    Protégé 92
bell heather 29
Benevise 244
Bercy Village 69
Bergerie de
    Mandriaccia 205
Bergeries de Ballone 206
Bergeries de Capannelle 212
berlingots 172
Besse 253-4
Bionnassay 300
bird-watching 23, 35, 158,
    167, 236
birds, *see* fauna
bluebell 29
boat travel
    to/from Corsica 197
    to/from France 346
Bocca di Laparu 213
Bocca di Sordu 217
Bocca di Verdi 212
Bocca Minuta 206
Bois des Sablons 96
Bonal 153
Bonatti, Walter 311

books 49
    Alps 237-8
    Auvergne 109
    Chemin de St-Jacques
        136-7, 156
    Corsica 194
    health 57
    natural history 49
    Pyrenees 159
    Tour du Mont Blanc 297
Borce 161-2, 168
Boréon Valley 268
bories 236
Bossons Glacier 281
Bourg d'Oisans 248, 249-50
Bovine 315
Brèche de Capitellu 208
Brèche de Roland 121, 191
Brèche Imbert 230
Briançon 256
Brittany 32, 80-93, **82-3**
broom 29
brown bear 23, 158, 159
brown hare 26
Burgundy 331-5, **321**
business hours 343
bus travel
    to/from France 345
    within France 347
buzzard 25

C

Cabanes du Cap de la
    Baitch 166
Cahors 147-9
Cajarc 142-4
Calanque de Port-Miou 226
Calanque de Sugiton 226
Calanque d'En Vau 226
Calasima 207-8
Calenzana 198, 199-200
Calvi 196-7
Camaret-sur-Mer 88, 89-90
Camargue, the 22, 236
camping 42-3
Camping le Gave d'Aspe 162
Canaglia 209-10
Canal du Nivernais 339
Cap Canaille 226, 236

Bold indicates maps.

Cap de la Chèvre 92
Cap de Morgiou 226
car travel 348-9
    driving licence 340
Cascade de Lutour 174
Cascade de Peïrastrèche 268
Cascade Esplumouse 177
Cascades des Anglais 210
Cassis 223, 225
Castel di Verghio 201, 207
Castellane 226, 227
Cathédrale St-Étienne 148, 150
Causse Méjan 129-31
Causses, the 126, 135
Cauterets 172-3, 180, **178**
Ceillac 256, 258-9
Célé Valley 135
Cévennes 107, 126-33
Ceyrat Robinson 110
Chaîne des Alpilles 221-3, **222-3**
chambres d'hôtes 44
chamois 26, 285, 318
Chamonix 276-7, 279, 294
Chamonix Aiguilles 279, 293
Chamonix Valley 275-84,
    291-2, 316
Champex 313
Chapelle de St-Sernin 155
Château de Fontainebleau 76
Châtillon-en-Diois 240, 242-3
cheese-making 107, 166, 306
Chemin de la Mâture 167-8,
    170
Chemin de l'Impératrice 185,
    186, **186**
Chemin de St-Jacques 134-56,
    134, **137**, **142-3**, **146-7**, **152**
Chemin des Cascades 174-5
Chemin du Littoral 85
chestnut 129
children, walking with 47-8
Cime de la Valette de Prals 271
Cime du Gélas 269
Circuit de Lacs 176
Cirque d'Archiane 240-8, **246-7**
Cirque de Barriès 234
Cirque de Gavarnie 157, 190-1
Cirque de la Solitude 206
Cirque de l'Arcelin 292
Cirque de Lescun 162, 168
Cirque de Troumouse 157
Cirque du Giverny 289
Cirque du Grand Marchet 292
Cité des Sciences 70
Clermont Ferrand 109-10
climate 32, 34, 39, 49-50
clothing 51-2, 53

Club Alpin Français (CAF) 21
Col Chécroui 295, 307
Col d'Aussois 290
Col de Balme 316
Col de Barrancq 169
Col de Cambalès 175-6
Col de Cerise 267, **265**
Col de Ceyssat 113
Col de Guéry 118-19, **116**
Col de la Croix du Bonhomme
    305
Col de la Croix Morand 115
Col de la Forclaz 315
Col de la Schlucht 327
Col de la Seigne 307
Col de Pétragème 165
Col de Pinata 186
Col de Prat de Bouc 125
Col de Rombière 120
Col de Sarenne 252
Col de Seysse 243
Col de Voza 300
Col des Laupies 133
Col des Montets 317
Col des Mulets 177
Col du Brévent 319
Col du Gliziou 123
Col Sapin 295, 309, 310
Col Vieux 263
Colomby de Gex 338
Combe de Lourmarin 230
Combe du Coureau 244
Comité National des Sentiers
    de Grande Randonnée
    (CNSGR) 21
Commission National de
    Protection de la Montagne
    (CNPM) 22, 35
common alder 30
common beech 30
common hazel 31
common juniper 29
common rorqual whale 194
compasses 54
Conca 217
Confraternity of Saint James
    137, 139
conservation 23, 34-5, 81, 89,
    see also environment
    organisations 35
Corsica 22, 32, 192-218, **193**
    food 207
    travel to/from 197
    travel within 198
Corsican nuthatch 194
Corsican pine 31, 192

Corsican red deer 194
costs 342
Cotentin Peninsula 105-6
Côte d'Albâtre 97-101, **98-9**
Côte de Granit Rose 80-8, **86-7**
Courmayeur 295, 308-9
Cozzano 201, 204, 214
Crête de Peyra Plata 264
Crête des Vosges 320-30, **323**,
    326, **327**, **329**
Criquebeuf-en-Caux 100
cuckoo 25
Cucuron 231, 233
cultural considerations 37
customs regulations 341
cycling 198, 349

D

Dampierre-en-Yvelines 79
Desert de Platé 291
diarrhoea 59-60
dipper 24
discount cards 340
documents 340-1
dolmen, see prehistoric sites
Dolmen du Joncas 145
Domecy-sur-le-Vault 333
Dordogne River 118
drinks 45-6, see also water,
    wine, beer
driving, see car travel
Durfort-Lacapelette 155

E

Écrins massif 248
Eiffel Tower 66
elder 31
elder flower 28
electricity 343
email services 343
embassies 341
emergencies 62
    telephone numbers 342
endangered species 23, 123,
    158, 159, 194, 265-6
English oak 31
environment 23, 34-5, 103,
    109, 210, see also conser-
    vation, responsible walking
Epte River 94
equipment 52-5
Ermenonville 79
Étretat 97, 99
Etsaut 161-2, 168
European larch 31
evacuation services 62

F

Falaises du Devenson 226
fauna 23-31, 35, see also
  individual species
  Auvergne 123, 126
  Brittany 81, 89
  Corsica 192-4
  Provence 224, 233, 236
  Pyrenees 158, 159
  Northern Alps 285, 286, 287
  Southern Alps 241-2, 249,
    257, 265-6, 271
Faycelles 141
Fécamp 97-9
Fédération des Clubs Alpins
  Français (CAF) 49
Fédération des Parcs Naturels
  Régionaux de France
  (FPNRF) 35
Fédération Française de Camp-
  ing et de Caravanning
  (FFCC) 42, 49
Fédération Française de la
  Randonnée Pédestre
  (FFRP) 21-2, 49
Fédération Unie des Auberges
  de Jeunesse (FUAJ) 49
Fenêtre d'Arpette 314
ferme-auberge 324
Ferret 312
Figeac 135, 137-9
Finistère 88
fires 42
flora 28-31, see also individual
  species
  Auvergne 129
  Brittany 89
  Corsica 192
  Crête de Vosges 322
  Northern Alps 285
  Pyrenees 158, 166, 180
  Southern Alps 241-2, 257,
    265
Florac 126-7, 129
Fontainebleau 75, 76-7, **77**
food 44-4, 57
  Alpine 245, 306
  Auvergne 107
  Corsica 207
  Pyrenees 166
footwear 51, 52, 53
Forêt de Bonifatu 204, 218
Forêt de Fontainebleau 75-9
Forêt d'Ermenonville 79

forêts domaniales, see national
  parks & reserves
Fort du Kador 92
Fort du Portalet 167
fulmar 24

G

Gacholle lighthouse 236
Gally 130-1
gannet 24
Garonne River 22
garrigue 29
Gaudre du Rougadou
  Valley 221
Gavarnie 190
Gazon du Faing 328
geography 22
geology 32, 33
Gîte à Balmat 283
Gîtes de France 49
gîtes d'étape 21, 43
Giverny 94-6, **96**
glaciers 22, 33, 157, 281
  Bossons Glacier 281
  Glacier d'Argentière 317
  Glacier de Bionnassay 301
  Glacier de l'A Neuve 312
  Glacier de la Lée Blanche 307
  Glacier des Bossons 284
  Glacier des Glaciers 305
  Glacier d'Ossoue 157
  Glacier du Dolent 312
  Glacier du Miage 307
  Glacier du Trient 314
  Taconnaz Glacier 281, 284
  Vanoise glaciers 285-91, **288**
Glanum 223
Global Positioning Systems
  (GPS) 55
globeflower 29
glossary 358-60
golden eagle 26, 158, 167, 285
golden oriole 25
Golo River 207
Gorges de Spelunca 218
Gorges du Tarn 133
Gorges du Verdon 226-30
gorse 29
Grand Balcon Nord 275,
  279-82, **280**
Grand Balcon Sud 295, 316,
  317
Grand Col Ferret 312
Grand Luberon 231-3, **232**
Grand Veymont 241
grande randonnée, see GR
  trails

Grandes Jorasses 281, 309, 312
Grands Causses 129
grass snake 28
greater flamingo 24
green lizard 28
Grenoble 238-40
grey heron 25
grey seal 27
griffon 158
GR trails 21, 48, see also indi-
  vidual trail names
  GR1 21, 75
  GR2 21, 94
  GR3 21
  GR4 109, 110, 112-13,
    115, 120, 124-5, 133,
    228-9
  GR5 230, 257, 264, 291-2,
    320, 323, 324-30
  GR6 221, 222-3, 234-6
  GR7/GR67 131, 132-3
  GR9 231, 233, 271, 336-9
  GR9B 336
  GR10 159, 165, 166-7,
    167-8, 169, 174-80,
    182, 191
  GR11 72, 75
  GR11 (Spain) 191
  GR13 332-3, 339
  GR20 41, 192, 198-217,
    202, **203**
  GR21 97
  GR22 101
  GR30 117, 118
  GR34 81, 88
  GR52 264-5, 272
  GR54 249, 272
  GR55 292
  GR58 257
  GR60 130-1
  GR65 135, 136
  GR70 131, 133
  GR72 131
  GR91 241, 245-8, 271
  GR93 241, 245, 271
  GR95 271
  GR98 226
  GR223 105
  GR400 121-3, 126
  GR441 109
  GR531 328
  GR532 323, 330
  GR653 156
  GR654 156
  GRP2 66, 70
Guil Valley 257
guillemot 24

Bold indicates maps.

H

halitosis 172
Haut Asco 201, 205-6
Haute Randonnée Pyrénéenne
191
health 39, 46, 56-62
    emergencies 62
    insurance 56
    planning 56-7
Hermann's tortoise 194
herring gull 24
history 19-22
    walking 20-2, 121, 293, 311
hitching 349
holm oak 31
Hôpital La Pitié-Salpêtrière 68
Hospice de France 183, 185
hostels 43-4
Hôtel des Invalides 66

I

ibex 23, 26, 265, 285, 287, 318
Île de Jarre 226
Île de l'Aber 93
Île de Plane 226
Île de Riou 226
Île d'Ouessant 105
Île St-Louis 72
Impressionism 95
Institut Géographique National
    (IGN) 21, 48, 63
insurance
    health 56
    travel 340
Internet
    access 343
    resources 49, 57
Issert 313
itineraries 38-9
izard 27

J

Jardin des Plantes 67
Jardin du Roi 244
Jardins du Luxembourg 67
Jaudy estuary 81
Jordanne Valley 120-4, **122**
Jura, the 22, 32, 335-9, **321**

K

kermes oak 31

L

La Banne d'Ordanche 119
La Bourboule 114-15, 118

La Butte St-Louis 78
La Cheminée du Diable 226
La Flégère 277, 279, 318
La Fouly 312
La Fruitière 181, 182
La Grande Cascade 117
La Grande Combe 235
La Grand Roche 92
La Grave 254-5
La Jonction 284
La Ligue Française pour la
    Protection des Oiseaux 35
La Madone de Fenestre
    268-70, **265**
La Maline 228
La Meije 248-56, **252-3**
La Monta 263
La Palud-sur-Verdon 226, 227-8
La Pierre Écrite 262
La Roche Jaune 88
La Ville des Glaciers 306
Labastide-Marnhac 151
Lac Blanc 275, 277-9, 295,
    318, 328, **278**
Lac Célinda 187
Lac Charles 187
Lac Creno 210
Lac d'Arratille 176
Lac de Capitellu 208
Lac de Gaube 177
Lac de Guéry 118
Lac de la Douche 256
Lac de la Muvrella 205
Lac de Lhurs 162-4, **163**
Lac de Melu 208
Lac de Ninu 208
Lac de Trécolpas 268, **265**
Lac des Truites 328
Lac des Vaches 291
Lac d'Estom 181, 182
Lac d'Oô 190
Lac du Col d'Arratille 177
Lac du Mercantour 267
Lac du Portillon 190
Lac du Pourtet 176
Lac Melu 210
Lac Ninu 210
Lac Vert 187
Lacs de Cambalès 175-6
Lacs de l'Embarrat 176
Lacs de Prals 270
Lacs des Chéserys 279
Lacs Jovet 305
Lajoux 335, 336
lammergeier, see bearded
    vulture
language 250-7, 358-60

Laschamp 112
Lauzerte 153-4
Le Bonhomme 329
Le Boréon 267, 268
Le Brévent 295, 319
Le Casset 256
Le Chaos de
    Nîmes-le-Vieux 129-31, **130**
Le Chazelet 254
Le Colorado 233-6, **235**
Le Lioran 120, 124
Le Markstein 325
Le Monêtier-les-Bains 248,
    250-1
Le Mont-Dore 114, 115
Le Peuty 315
Le Rainkopf 325
Le Raux 261
Le Relais Stevenson 131
Le Rosay 251
Le Souc 131
Le Tour 316
Le Touring-Club de France
    (TCF) 21
Le Veygalier 129, 130
Le Villard 259
L'Echalp 263
Lélex 337-8
Les Baux de Provence 221-3,
    222-3
Les Bossons 282, 283
Les Calanques 223-5, **224-5**
Les Chapieux 305
Les Combettes 128
Les Contamines Montjoie 301,
    304
Les Herbus 103-4
Les Houches 294, 298-300
Les Lacs Bessons 268, 272
Les Nonnières 244
Les Orgues de Camplong
    165-7, **163**
Les Praz 277, 278-9
Les Puechs 128
Les Tas de Pois 89
Les Trois Fours 327
Lescun 161, 162, **163**
L'Hom 130
Ligue Française pour les
    Auberges de la Jeunesse
    (LFAJ) 49
lily of the valley 23, 29, 30
Limogne-en-Quercy 144-5
Loire River 22
Lombardy poplar 31
Longueville 72
Lot Valley 135

Luberon, the 230-6
Lus-la-Croix-Haute 240, 242

M

magazines 49
Maladeta glacier 183, 184
Malatra Valley 310
Malbosc 128
mammals 23, 26-8
Mandailles 122-3
maps 48, 54-5
  maps in this book 14-15
maquis 29
Mare a Mare Centre 214, 218
Mare a Mare Nord 207, 218
Mare a Mare Sud 215, 218
Mare e Monti Nord 204, 218
Mare e Monti Sud 218
marmot 27, 256, 257, 285, 308
Massif Armoricain 22, 32
Massif Central 22, 32,
  107-33, **108**
Massif de Bavella 215
Massif des Vosges 22, 32,
  320-30, 339, **321**
medical treatment, see health
medicinal plants 28
menhirs, see prehistoric sites
Mer de Glace 281
Métabief 339
Mijoux 339
Moissac 135, 139-40, 148
Monet, Claude 94, 95
money 341-2
Mont Blanc 22, 282-3, 293,
  299, 311, 316, **294**, **302-3**
Mont Blanc massif 275, 295,
  307
Mont de la Saxe 295, 309-10
Mont Dôme 133
Mont Lozère range 126, 127
Mont St-Michel 101-5, **104**
Mont St-Michel (landward)
  101, 105
Mont Ventoux 236
Mont Viso 261
Montagne de la Côte 282-4,
  284
Montcuq 151-3
Monte Corona 204
Monte Ritondu 209
Montenvers 282
Montpellier grass snake 224
Montrodeix 113

Bold indicates maps.

Monts d'Arrée 22
Monts Dômes 107, 110-13
Monts Dore 107, 113-19
Monts du Cantal 107, 119-26
Monts du Cézallier 121
Monument des Diables
  Bleus 324
Morgat 92-3
Morgiou 223
motorcycle travel, see car travel
mouflon 27, 194
mountain hare 27
mountain pansy 29
mountain thrift 30
mountains & peaks
  Balaïtous 180
  Barre des Écrins 248
  Bataillouse 125
  Batteriekopf 326
  Brèche de Roland 191
  Chavaroche 125
  Cime du Gélas 269
  Doigt de Dieu 251
  Grand Pic de la Meije 251
  Grand Veymont 241
  Kœnigsstuhl 330
  La Banne d'Ordanche 119
  La Barre des Écrins 251
  La Grand Casse 285
  La Meije 248-56, **252-3**
  Le Dec de Lhurs 164
  Le Grand Ballon 324
  Le Grand Brézouard 330
  Le Griounou 123, 125
  Le Hohneck 327
  Le Mont d'Or 339
  Le Rainkopf 326
  Le Tanet 328
  Meije Orientale 251
  Mont Aigoual 132
  Mont Aiguille 241
  Mont Blanc 293, 294, **302-3**
  Mont de la Saxe 309-10
  Mont Dôme 133
  Mont Lozère 133
  Mont Pelvoux 248
  Mont Ventoux 236
  Mont Viso 261
  Montagne de la Côte 282
  Monte Corona 204
  Monte d'Oro 210, 211
  Monte Formicula 213
  Monte Grossu 212
  Monte Incudine 215
  Monte Perdido 157
  Monte Renosu 211-12
  Monte Ritondu 209

Moun-Né 180
Mourre Nègre 230, 231-3,
  232
Pic Canigou 157
Pic Carlit 157
Pic d'Aneto 157, 183, 184
Pic d'Anie 157, 165
Pic d'Ansabère 164-5, **163**
Pic de Cecire 188
Pic de Graves 187
Pic de la Mine 184
Pic de la Sède 182
Pic de la Vieille Femme 289
Pic de Labigouer 168-71,
  170
Pic de Sauveguarde 184, 185
Pic de Troumouse 180
Pic des Oulettes 177
Pic du Cabaliros 180-1,
  178-9
Pic du Château Renard 261
Pic du Midi d'Ossau 180, 190
Pic l'Ourč de Larrary 165
Plomb du Cantal 124-6,
  125
Punta Capannella 212
Puy Chavaroche 121
Puy de Barbier 117
Puy de Dôme 110-13
Puy de la Tache 115
Puy de la Vache 112
Puy de l'Angle 117
Puy de Lassolas 112
Puy de Monne 117
Puy de Peyre Arse 120-1, 125
Puy de Sancy 115-18, **116**
Puy des Crebasses 117
Puy Griou 123, 125
Puy Gros 118, 126
Puy Loup 119
Puy Mary 120-4, 125, **122**
Rothenbachkopf 326
Taubenklangfelsen 328
Tête des Faux 328
Vignemale 22, 157, 171,
  173-80, **178-9**
Mourre Nègre 230, 231-3,
  232
muguet, see lily of the valley
Murat 119-20, 124
museums
  International Museum to the
    Battle of the Atlantic 90
  Musée d'Art Americaine 95
  Musée de Provins 75
  Musée des Merveilles 272
  Musée le Soum 262

Museums *continued*
  Musée National Picasso 72
  Museum of Alpine Fauna 282
  opening hours 343

N
Nanchèvre 333
national parks & reserves 35-7
  Castel Meur reserve 81
  Fôret Domaniale de
    Fontmont 131-3, **132**
  Îles Cerbicale 192
  Îles Finocchiarola 192
  Îles Lavezzi 192
  Landes et Rochers de
    Ploumanac'h 81
  Parc des Volcans 133
  Parc National de la Vanoise
    284-91, 292, **288**
  Parc National des Écrins
    237, 248, 272
  Parc National des Pyrénées
    157, 158, 171
  Parc National du Mercantour
    237, 264-71, 272, **265**
  Parc Naturel Régional
    d'Armorique 88-9
  Parc Naturel Régional de
    Corse 192, 195, 210
  Parc Naturel Régional
    de la Haute Vallée de
    Chevreuse 79
  Parc Naturel Régional des
    Volcans 107
  Parc Naturel Régional du
    Queyras 237, 256-64,
    272, **260-1**
  Parc Naturel Régional du
    Vercors 227, 237, 241,
    271-2
  Parc Naturel Régional du
    Verdon 227
  regulations 42, 195, 276, 285
  Réserve Naturelle de la
    Haute Chaîne du Jura 338
  Réserve Naturelle de l'Étang
    de l'Impérial 236
  Réserve Naturelle de
    Scandola 192, 194, 218
  Réserve Naturelle des
    Aiguilles Rouges 276
  Réserve Naturelle des Hauts
    Plateaux du Vercors 241
Nez de Jobourg 106
Nice 240
Nid de la Poule 113
Normandy 94-106, **82-3**
Notre Dame 72

O
ocellar lizard 224
ochre 234
olive 31
organisations 48-9, *see also*
    individual entries,
    conservation
organised walks 40-1
  Tour du Mont Blanc 298
osprey 194
otter 27
oystercatcher 24

P
Paccard, Michel 283
Panthéon 67
Paradis, Marie 283
Parc des Buttes Chaumont 70
parcs naturels regionaux, see
    national parks & reserves
Paris 63-73
  accommodation 64-5
  city walks 66-9, 70-3, **68-
    9, 71**
  travel to/from 65
  travel within 65-6
Paris region 63-79, **64**
Pas de l'Escalette 185
Pas de Peyrol 121
Pech Favard 141
people 37
Perros-Guirec 85
Phare d'Antifer 101
photography 50
Pic d'Ansabère 164-5, **163**
Pic de Labigouer 168-71, **170**
Pic de Sauveguarde 184,
    185, **184**
Pic du Cabaliros 180-1, **178-9**
Pic du Château Renard 261
Pic du Midi d'Ossau 190
Picasso, Pablo 72
pilgrimage routes 134-5, 139,
    156, **134**
pine 28
pine processionary
    caterpillar 233
place des Vosges 72
Plage de Trestraou 85
Plage de Trestrignel 85
planning 39-40
  itineraries 38-9
plants, *see* flora
Plateau de Coscione 210
Plateau de Gialgone 212
Plomb du Cantal 124-6, **125**
Plougrescant 81

Point Sublime 226, 230
Pointe de Pen-Hir 89
Pointe du Château 81, 87
Pointe du Menhir 93
Pont des Trungas 168
Pont d'Espagne 174-5
Pont Valentré 148, 149
Pontaubault 103-5
Pontorson 101, 102-3
population 37
Port Blanc 81, 86
Port de Vénasque 183, 184
Port l'Epine 85-6
Porte d'Amont 100
Porto Vecchio 198, 200-1
Porz Hir 88
Porz Scaff 87
postal services 342
pozzines 210
Pralognan-la-Vanoise 286-7
Pré d'Issane 230
prehistoric sites 127-9, 132,
    142, 145
Presqu'île de Crozon 88-93, **91**
Provence 219-36, **220**
Provins 72, 73-5, **74**
ptarmigan 26
public holidays 343-4
public transport 349
puffin 24
Puy de Dôme 110-13, **111**
Puy de Sancy 115-18, **116**
Puy Griou 124
Puy Gros 126
Puy Loup 119
Puy Mary 120-4, **122**
Pyrenees 22, 32, 157-91, **158**
  food 166

Q
Quenza 201, 204, 215
Queyras, the 256-64, **260-1**

R
rail passes 348
Ravin de Mainmorte 228
red deer 27
red fox 28
red squirrel 28
Refuge de Ciottulu di i Mori 207
Refuge d'Espingo 188-90, **189**
Refuge d'Usciolu 213
Refuge Wallon 175
refuges 43
Relais Stevenson 131
reptiles 28

rescue services 62
réserves naturelles, see
    national parks & reserves
responsible walking 41-2, 109
Rhine River 22, 32, 320
Rhône River 22, 32
Riquewihr 320, 322-3, 339
Robert Louis Stevenson Trail
    (GR70) 131, 133
Roc de Cuzeau 117
Roche Éponge 77
Roche Sanadoire 119
Roche Tuilière 118
Rocher de l'Aiguille 235
Rocher du Bec de L'Aigle 124
Rocher St-Germain 78
rockrose 29
roe deer 28
Roman sites 67, 223, 268
Romanche Valley 255-6
rosemary 28, 29
Route des Crêtes 324, 328
Route des Menhirs 127
Royat 110, 113
rubbish disposal 41
Rustrel 233, 234

S

safety 42, 61-2, 239, 275
St-Amarin 320, 322
St-Gabriel 221
St-Germain 332
St-Hernot 92
St-Jacques 136
St-Martin-Vésubie 266-7
St-Rémy de Provence 221,
    223
St-Véran 261-2
Sassure, Horace-Benedict de
    293
sea campion 30
Sée River 101
Seine River 22
Sélune River 101, 103
Sentier des Douaniers 84
Sentier des Muletiers 113
Sentier du Bastidon 228
Sentier Nanette 289
shag 24
sites naturels classés, see
    national parks & reserves
smuggling 338
snakes 28, 61, 158
snow finch 26

Bold indicates maps.

society 37
sparrowhawk 25
special events 343-4
spring gentian 30
Station du Mont-Dore 115, 117
Stevenson, Robert Louis
    131, 133
strikes 47
sundials 257
Super Lioran 124
Superbagnères 188
sweet chestnut 31

T

Table des Trois Rois 164
Taconnaz Glacier 281, 284
Tal ar Groaz 88, 90
Tarascon 221
Tarn River 133
Tattone 201, 209-10
taxes 342
taxis 349
Téléférique Bellevue 300
telephone services 342-3
    emergency numbers 62, 342
Telgruc-sur-Mer 93
Tête de la Tranche 310
Tête Nord des Fours 306
TGV 347
thrift 30
ticks 60, 61
time 343
tipping 342
Torrent de Bionnassay 304
Torrent de Bouchouse 263
Torrent de Tré la 305
Torrent du Boréon 268
Tour de l'Oisans (GR54) 249,
    272
Tour de Queyras (GR58) 257
Tour du Mont Blanc (TMB)
    293-319, **302-3**
    accommodation 297
    planning 296-8
Tour du Mont Lozère 127, 128
Tour du Viso 272
Tour of the Vanoise Glaciers
    286-91
tourist offices 340
train travel
    to/from France 345-6
    within France 347-8
transhumance 121, 241
Tré le Champ 295, 317
Trégastel 80, 82-4
Tréguier 80, 84
trekking, *see* walking

Trient 315
trumpet gentian 30
Tussac 244

U

Unesco Biosphere Reserves 126
Unesco World Heritage Sites
    72, 101, 135, 192, 334

V

Val Ferret 311-13
Val Veni 295, 307-8
Vallée d'Aspe 160-71, **170**
Vallée de Belonce 168, 171
Vallée de Cauterets 171-82,
    178-9
Vallée de la Houradade 187
Vallée de Lutour 181-2, **178-9**
Vallée des Merveilles 272
Vallée du Lis 185, 187, **186**
Vallée du Marcadau 176
Vallon d'Armina 310
Vallon de la Lée Blanche 307
Vallon de Prals 270-1, **265**
Vallon d'En Vau 226
Vallorcine 291, 316
Valserine Valley 335-9, **337**
Vanoise glaciers 285-91, **288**
Vaugines 233
Vaux de Cernay 79
Vénéon Valley 251
Vercors 271-2
Veryac'h Plage 90
Vésubie Valley 266
Vézelay 331, 333-4, **332-3**
Viaduc de Mailhtrincat 188
Vignemale 22, 157, 171,
    173-80, **178-9**
visas 340
Vizzavona 201, 211

W

walking
    children 47-8
    etiquette 41-2
    history 20-2, 121, 293, 311
    safety 275
    standards 13
    terminology 13
    tour operators 40-1
    when to walk 39
    women 47
wartime sites 325-30
water 46, 57, 195
Way of St James, *see* Chemin
    de St-Jacques

weather information 49-50
white (or downy) oak 31
wildlife, see fauna
wild olive 31
wine 46, 320-39
wolves 23, 123, 265-6, 271
women walkers 47

wood anemone 30
woodpigeon 25

yellow anemone 30
yellow gentian 28

yellow iris 30
Yport 100

Zicavo 201, 204

Boxed Texts

Alpine Menus Explained 245
Alternative Access Points 201
Auvergnat Cheeses 107
Basilica at Vézelay, The 334
Beaufort Cheese 306
Beyond Human Endurance 184
Brewed in Briançon 256
Brittany is Different 81
Brown Bear's Last
  Stand, The? 159
Buying Tips 53
Cahors & Moissac 148
Camping in Parc National des
  Pyrénées 160
Château de Fontainebleau 76
Cheese-Making in the Moun-
  tains 166
Chestnut: All-Purpose Tree 129
Climbing Mont Blanc 299
Ecological Diversity &
  Traditional Culture 241
Écrins & Oisans 249

Ferme-Auberge, The 324
Following in the Footsteps of
  History 283
Friend & Foes 30
Giverny, Monet &
  Impressionism 95
Ibex, The 287
In Memoriam 175
Killing Fields, The 325
La Madone de Fenestre 269
La Meije 251
Lakes & Pozzines 210
Le Loup 271
Little Sweetener, A 172
Living Glaciers: The Mer de
  Glace & Bossons 281
Maps & Compass 54
Maquis & Garrigue 29
Medicinal Trees & Plants 28
Mont St-Michel & the
  Future 103
National Park Regulations 42

Ochre 234
Pilgrim's Passport, The? 139
Pine Processionary
  Caterpillar 233
Provençal Bories 236
Signs of a Glacial Past 33
Small Yet Acute Problem, A 230
Small-Time Smugglers 338
Starting Out 200
Strikes 47
Sundials 257
Surviving Summer 39
Taking Photos Outdoors 50
Taste of Corsica, A 207
Tide Watch 102
Useful Numbers 342
Walk Safety – Basic Rules 62
Walking a Little History 121
Walter Bonatti 311
Who was St-Jacques?
Wines of France 46
Wolf Trap, The 123

LONELY PLANET OFFICES

Australia
Locked Bag 1, Footscray, Victoria 3011
☎ 03 8379 8000 fax 03 8379 8111
email: talk2us@lonelyplanet.com.au

USA
150 Linden St, Oakland, CA 94607
☎ 510 893 8555 TOLL FREE: 800 275 8555
fax 510 893 8572
email: info@lonelyplanet.com

UK
72-82 Rosebery Ave, London, EC1R 4RW
☎ 020 7841 9000 fax 020 7841 9001
email: go@lonelyplanet.co.uk

France
1 rue du Dahomey, 75011 Paris
☎ 01 55 25 33 00 fax 01 55 25 33 01
email: bip@lonelyplanet.fr
www.lonelyplanet.fr

World Wide Web: www.lonelyplanet.com or AOL keyword: lp
Lonely Planet Images: www.lonelyplanetimages.com